HISPANICS AND THE FUTURE OF AMERICA

Marta Tienda and Faith Mitchell, *Editors*
Panel on Hispanics in the United States

Committee on Population

Division of Behavioral and Social Sciences and Education

NATIONAL RESEARCH COUNCIL
OF THE NATIONAL ACADEMIES

THE NATIONAL ACADEMIES PRESS
Washington, D.C.
www.nap.edu

THE NATIONAL ACADEMIES PRESS • 500 Fifth Street, N.W. • Washington, D.C. 20001

NOTICE: The project that is the subject of this report was approved by the Governing Board of the National Research Council, whose members are drawn from the councils of the National Academy of Sciences, the National Academy of Engineering, and the Institute of Medicine. The members of the committee responsible for the report were chosen for their special competences and with regard for appropriate balance.

This study was supported by Contract No. N01-OD-4-2139, TO #123 between the National Academy of Sciences and the National Institute of Child Health and Human Development, the National Cancer Institute, the Office of Behavioral and Social Sciences Research, the National Institute of Mental Health, and the National Institute on Aging of the National Institutes of Health; the U.S. Census Bureau; the National Center for Health Statistics; the National Institute for Occupational Safety and Health; the Andrew W. Mellon Foundation, the Robert Wood Johnson Foundation, the California HealthCare Foundations, and the California Endowment.

Library of Congress Cataloging-in-Publication Data

Hispanics and the future of America / Marta Tienda and Faith Mitchell, editors ; Panel on Hispanics in the United States [and] Committee on Population, Division of Behavioral and Social Sciences and Education.
p. cm.
ISBN 0-309-10051-8 (pbk.) — ISBN 0-309-65478-5 (PDFs) 1. Hispanic Americans—Social conditions. 2. Hispanic Americans—Economic conditions. 3. United States—Ethnic relations. 4. Hispanic Americans—Statistics. 5. United States—Population. I. Tienda, Marta. II. Mitchell, Faith. III. National Research Council (U.S.). Panel on Hispanics in the United States. IV. National Research Council (U.S.). Committee on Population.
E184.S75H593 2006
305.868'073—dc22

2005034173

Additional copies of this report are available from the National Academies Press, 500 Fifth Street, N.W., Lockbox 285, Washington, D.C. 20055; (800) 624-6242 or (202) 334-3313 (in the Washington metropolitan area); http://www.nap.edu.

Printed in the United States of America

Suggested citation: National Research Council (2006). *Hispanics and the Future of America.* Panel on Hispanics in the United States. Marta Tienda and Faith Mitchell, eds. Committee on Population, Division of Behavioral and Social Sciences and Education. Washington, DC: The National Academies Press.

THE NATIONAL ACADEMIES

Advisers to the Nation on Science, Engineering, and Medicine

The **National Academy of Sciences** is a private, nonprofit, self-perpetuating society of distinguished scholars engaged in scientific and engineering research, dedicated to the furtherance of science and technology and to their use for the general welfare. Upon the authority of the charter granted to it by the Congress in 1863, the Academy has a mandate that requires it to advise the federal government on scientific and technical matters. Dr. Ralph J. Cicerone is president of the National Academy of Sciences.

The **National Academy of Engineering** was established in 1964, under the charter of the National Academy of Sciences, as a parallel organization of outstanding engineers. It is autonomous in its administration and in the selection of its members, sharing with the National Academy of Sciences the responsibility for advising the federal government. The National Academy of Engineering also sponsors engineering programs aimed at meeting national needs, encourages education and research, and recognizes the superior achievements of engineers. Dr. Wm. A. Wulf is president of the National Academy of Engineering.

The **Institute of Medicine** was established in 1970 by the National Academy of Sciences to secure the services of eminent members of appropriate professions in the examination of policy matters pertaining to the health of the public. The Institute acts under the responsibility given to the National Academy of Sciences by its congressional charter to be an adviser to the federal government and, upon its own initiative, to identify issues of medical care, research, and education. Dr. Harvey V. Fineberg is president of the Institute of Medicine.

The **National Research Council** was organized by the National Academy of Sciences in 1916 to associate the broad community of science and technology with the Academy's purposes of furthering knowledge and advising the federal government. Functioning in accordance with general policies determined by the Academy, the Council has become the principal operating agency of both the National Academy of Sciences and the National Academy of Engineering in providing services to the government, the public, and the scientific and engineering communities. The Council is administered jointly by both Academies and the Institute of Medicine. Dr. Ralph J. Cicerone and Dr. Wm. A. Wulf are chair and vice chair, respectively, of the National Research Council.

www.national-academies.org

PANEL ON HISPANICS IN THE UNITED STATES

MARTA TIENDA (*Chair*), Department of Sociology, Woodrow Wilson School of Public and International Affairs and Office of Population Research, Princeton University
LOUIS DeSIPIO, Department of Political Science and Chicano/Latino Studies Program, University of California, Irvine
JORGE DURAND, Social Anthropology, University of Guadalajara, Mexico
JOSÉ J. ESCARCE, David Geffen School of Medicine, UCLA and RAND, California
V. JOSEPH HOTZ, Department of Economics, University of California, Los Angeles
NANCY S. LANDALE, Department of Sociology, Pennsylvania State University
CORDELIA W. REIMERS, Department of Economics, Hunter College and the Graduate School, City University of New York
RUBÉN G. RUMBAUT, Department of Sociology and Center for Research on Immigration, Population, and Public Policy, University of California, Irvine
BARBARA SCHNEIDER, Department of Sociology, University of Chicago
EDWARD TELLES, Department of Sociology, University of California, Los Angeles
STEVEN J. TREJO, Department of Economics, University of Texas at Austin
PETER WARD, Department of Sociology, University of Texas at Austin*

National Research Council Staff

BARNEY COHEN, *Director, Committee on Population*
FAITH MITCHELL, *Senior Program Officer*
ANA-MARIA IGNAT, *Senior Program Assistant***
ANTHONY S. MANN, *Senior Program Assistant*
AMY GAWAD, *Research Associate****

*Until January 2004
**Until November 2004
***Until December 2004

COMMITTEE ON POPULATION

Acknowledgments

The sponsors of this project recognized the timeliness of a study on Hispanics and in doing so made possible a far-reaching and provoking look at the nation's fastest-growing minority population. We gratefully acknowledge support of the National Institute of Child Health and Human Development, the National Cancer Institute, the Office of Behavioral and Social Sciences Research, the National Institute of Mental Health, and the National Institute on Aging of the National Institutes of Health; the U.S. Census Bureau; the National Center for Health Statistics; the National Institute for Occupational Safety and Health; the Andrew W. Mellon Foundation, the Robert Wood Johnson Foundation, the California HealthCare Foundations, and the California Endowment. Along with this volume, their support resulted in a committee report, *Multiple Origins, Uncertain Destinies: Hispanics and the American Future*, for which this is a companion volume.

We also acknowledge the following individuals for their workshop presentations and other contributions to the material in this volume: Jorge Del Pinal, Patricia Fernández-Kelly, Claudia Galindo, John Gallegos, Eugene Garcia, Roberto Gonzalez, John Iceland, J. Gerardo Lopez, Maria Lopez-Freeman, Elizabeth Martin, Jeff Morenoff, Charles V. Morgan, Chandra Muller, Jeff Passel, Yasmin Ramirez, Sean Reardon, Catherine Riegle-Crumb, Jerry Valadez, William A. Vega, Bruce Western, and Marilyn Winkleby.

The papers in this volume have been reviewed in draft form by individuals chosen for their diverse perspectives and technical expertise, in accordance with procedures approved by the NRC's Report Review Committee. The purpose of this independent review is to provide candid and critical comments that will assist the institution in making its published report as sound as possible and to ensure that the report meets institutional standards for objectivity, evidence, and responsiveness to the study charge. The review comments and draft manuscript remain confidential to protect the integrity of the deliberative process.

We thank the following individuals for their review of one or more papers in this volume: Frank D. Bean, Center for Research on Immigration, Population, and Public Policy, University of California, Irvine; Bruce E. Cain, Institute of Governmental Studies, University of California, Berkeley; Janet Currie, Department of Economics, University of California, Los Angeles; Rodolfo de la Garza, Tomas Rivera Policy Institute, Columbia University; Nancy A. Denton, Center for Social and Demographic Analysis, University at Albany, SUNY; Reynolds Farley, Population Studies Center, University of Michigan; Eugene E. Garcia, College of Education, Arizona State University; James S. House, Institute for Social Research, University of Michigan; Wendy D. Manning, Center for Family and Demographic Research, Bowling Green State University; Eliseo Perez-Stable, General Internal Medicine, University of California, San Francisco; Richard Santos, Department of Economics, University of New Mexico; William A. Vega, Behavioral and Research Training Institute, UMDNJ-Robert Wood Johnson Medical School; John R. Weeks, International Population Center, San Diego State University; and David R. Williams, Institute for Social Research, University of Michigan.

Although the reviewers listed have provided many constructive comments and suggestions, they were not asked to endorse the content of any of the papers nor did they see the final version of any paper before this publication. The review of this volume was overseen by Charles Hirschman, Department of Sociology, University of Washington. Appointed by the NRC, he was responsible for making certain that an independent examination of the papers was carried out in accordance with institutional procedures and that all review comments were carefully considered. Responsibility for the final content of this report rests entirely with the authors and the institution.

Contents

HISPANICS AND THE FUTURE OF AMERICA

1

Introduction: *E Pluribus Plures* or *E Pluribus Unum?*

Marta Tienda and Faith Mitchell

Although the U.S. Hispanic population predates the founding of the United States, the recent emergence of Hispanics as the largest minority group is one of the most important demographic changes of the 20th century. Officially coined in the 1970s by congressional action and government regulation, "Hispanic" in fact refers to a population that differs enormously by history, nationality, social class, legal status, and generation.[1] It encompasses both the descendants of early Spanish settlers in what is now the United States and immigrants and their offspring from Spanish-speaking countries in the Caribbean, Central America, and South America.[2] Altogether, the category subsumes 20 nationalities, of which the most numerous are Mexicans (about two-thirds of Hispanics), Puerto Ricans, Cubans, Central and South Americans, and Spaniards.[3]

---

[1]In the papers, the terms Hispanic and Latino are used interchangeably.

[2]Excluded from the Hispanic label are Latin Americans who are not Spanish speaking, from the French-speaking Haitians (although they share the island of Hispaniola with the Spanish-speaking Dominicans) in the Caribbean to the English- and French-speaking Guyanese and Dutch-speaking Surinamese in South America. Brazilians are not Hispanic either—and do not consider themselves as such—although they are Latin Americans. In general, Portuguese-speaking people originating in Portugal and Brazil are excluded from the Hispanic category, which evolved from the Spanish-origin and Spanish-language population constructs used in 1970 and thereafter by the U.S. government.

[3]Since the Jones Act in 1917, all island-born Puerto Ricans are U.S. citizens by birth. However, those who are island-born are considered to have an immigration-like experience coming to the mainland that is comparable to that of other Hispanic immigrant groups.

The rapid growth and increasing diversity of today's Hispanic population is primarily a result of major waves of migration from Puerto Rico after World War II, the exodus from Cuba after the 1959 revolution, and especially the surge of immigration from Mexico and Latin America since 1970. In 1960, approximately 4 percent of U.S. residents were Hispanic; today, they are close to 14 percent. Almost two-thirds of the foreign-born Hispanics have arrived since 1980, but fertility will overtake immigration as the driver of Hispanic population growth in the current decade. Continuing the fertility and immigration trends now under way, by 2030 Hispanics are projected to comprise about one-fourth of the U.S. population.

Behind the numbers resides a complex story of diversity along many dimensions that will shape Hispanics' social and economic narratives in the decades ahead. This volume, which serves as a companion to *Multiple Origins, Uncertain Destinies: Hispanics and the American Future* (National Research Council, 2006), provides detailed analyses using multiple sources to characterize this dynamic, eclectic population from multiple perspectives; to evaluate whether and in what ways Hispanics are distinctive from other immigrant and minority groups; and to assess the social integration prospects of recent arrivals and their descendants.[4] Collectively, the volume documents how the growing Hispanic presence is being felt in schools, in workplaces, at the ballot box, and in health care systems throughout the nation.

Two overarching themes unify the papers. One theme is whether apparent differences between Hispanics and other race and ethnic groups are real—that is, whether there is something distinctive about "Hispanicity" not shared by other groups. The second theme is whether Hispanics, particularly immigrants and their native-born offspring, are assimilating into the U.S. mainstream and along what dimensions. Because changes in the composition of the Hispanic population by national origin, immigrant status, and generation bear decisively on both themes, the authors have considered, where data permitted, both temporal and intergenerational changes in their analyses and inferences.

Hispanics differ from non-Hispanics in several ways that set them apart from other race and ethnic groups in the United States: a youthful age structure; low average education levels; disproportionate concentration in unskilled jobs; a common ancestral language; and, among the foreign-born, a significant share who are legally undocumented. Each of these differences

---

[4]Many of the authors used a common file of the March Current Population Survey for the years 1998, 1999, 2000, 2001, and 2002, including specially constructed variables for data about Hispanic ethnicities and generational cohorts defined by age at arrival and nativity of self and parents. Nonetheless, care should be used in comparisons across chapters.

has important implications for integration prospects, but collectively they appear to distinguish Hispanics from non-Hispanics. Yet the chapters in this volume also document significant temporal improvements in educational attainment, earnings, household income, homeownership, and political participation, which indicate that Hispanics are replicating the integration path of prior immigrant groups.

Most comparisons between native- and foreign-born Hispanics reveal how much the growing representation of recent immigrants among their ranks masks the cultural assimilation and socioeconomic progress of later generations. Spanish-language maintenance is a telling example: the proliferation of Spanish in immigrant communities belies the rapid language shift that is under way. The vast majority—93 percent—of foreign-born Hispanics speak some Spanish at home, compared with only 63 percent of the native born. However, the preponderance of evidence shows that proficiency in and preference for Spanish decline over time and across generations. According to Rubén Rumbaut (Chapter 2), the grandchildren of the present wave of immigrants will for the most part be monolingual English speakers.

Evidence that cultural expressions of ethnicity are rendered largely symbolic by the third generation notwithstanding, there are several reasons to expect that Hispanics' integration experiences will deviate from those of earlier groups: success in the U.S. labor market now requires higher skill levels than was true in the past; there is a rising share of undocumented people among the foreign born; whether or not the Hispanic geographic dispersal now under way will promote or retard acceptance is still unclear; and the burgeoning second generation is coming of age as the majority society ages. Individually and collectively, these circumstances have profound implications for Hispanics' terms of belonging and how their growing numbers will imprint the nation as a whole.

The chapters in this volume use a variety of data sources to describe the changing contours and future prospects of the Hispanic population, focusing on several key social and institutional domains—the family, the labor market, educational institutions, health care systems, and the polity. Each provides nuance and detail that was used in crafting the companion volume, while providing a comprehensive treatment of specific topics. In the rest of this chapter we provide a brief synopsis of their main findings and offer concluding thoughts about risks and challenges facing the Hispanic second generation.

THE HISPANIC POPULATION IN NUMBERS

In "The Making of a People," Rubén G. Rumbaut examines three aspects of the evolution of the Hispanic population: their historical origins, contemporary diversity, and the social construction of the catchall "Hispanic" category. Hispanics are at once a new and an old population, made up both of recent immigrants and groups who claim a history that precedes the establishment of the nation. The ethnic groups now labeled as Hispanics—the 20 nationalities from Latin America and Spain itself—were not "Hispanics" or "Latinos" in their countries of origin; they only became so in the United States, where the use and meaning of the label itself continues to evolve.

Rumbaut's chapter highlights the differences that most clearly distinguish the Hispanic population from non-Hispanics, while at the same time illustrating and emphasizing the group's vast heterogeneity. Reviewing the historical record and drawing on data from the decennial census, the Children of Immigrants Longitudinal Study, and other published sources, he addresses several fundamental questions, among them: In what way can this diverse group be considered a unique population? Does Hispanic represent a cohesive and self-conscious ethnic group, sharing a sense of peoplehood akin to that of African Americans, or is the label Hispanic merely an administrative convenience? And by designating themselves "some other race," are Hispanics revamping the U.S. racial classification?

In answering these questions, Rumbaut identifies a confluence of circumstances that shapes a distinctive profile for Hispanics as a whole and for particular Hispanic ethnic groups. These include the history of the incorporation of particular groups (with detailed attention to those from Mexico, Puerto Rico, and Cuba, who account for more than three-fourths of the Hispanic population on the U.S. mainland); the different national origins that are subsumed by the label (focusing on the characteristics of the nine largest groups); racial categorization (including the increasing use of Hispanic or Latino as *racial* rather than *ethnic* identities); immigration and naturalization patterns; and intergroup and intergenerational differences in linguistic acculturation and social status.

Rumbaut claims that Hispanics, who collectively comprise half of all immigration to the United States, differ collectively and decisively from non-Hispanic immigrants in two key respects—a common language and the social class disadvantages of the immigrant generation. Unlike most immigrants from Europe and Asia, who speak various languages, Hispanics speak Spanish. More than 28 million people in the United States in 2000 reported speaking Spanish at home—some 10 million more than spoke all other languages combined. Second, among foreign-born adults, non-Hispanics are four times as likely to have college degrees as Hispanics, while Hispanics are three times as likely as non-Hispanics to lack a high school diploma. This comparative human capital disadvantage of Latin American immigrants, which relegates them to the lower rungs of the occupational structure, is reduced significantly but not eliminated by the

U.S.-born generations. As other chapters elaborate, that central fact has profound long-term implications for the social and economic prospects of their children's generation and is also the basis for common stereotypes that disparage and stigmatize the population as a whole.

"The Demographic Foundations of the Latino Population," by Jorge Durand, Edward Telles, and Jennifer Flashman, uses data from multiple sources to characterize the dimensions and components of Hispanic population change. They trace Hispanics' youthful age structure to high rates of immigration and fertility and discuss how changing immigration policies, social networks, and other factors contribute to the changing volume, composition, and settlement patterns of legal and illegal labor flows from Latin America. These demographic foundations—the components of growth, the changing age structure, and new settlement patterns—are fundamental to understanding how the growing Hispanic presence will affect schools, labor markets, and social institutions.

Durand, Telles, and Flashman also show how historical settlement patterns that concentrated Mexicans in the Southwest, Puerto Ricans in the Northeast, and Cubans in South Florida have evolved in recent years. Although traditional settlement areas, such as California, Texas, and New York, still house the largest Hispanic communities, the most rapid growth is occurring in states that had tiny Hispanic populations just 15 years ago. Significantly, the Hispanic geographic dispersal predominantly involves recent immigrants. In Nevada, for example, the Hispanic population more than tripled between 1990 and 2000, while Hispanics quadrupled their presence in Georgia and nearly quintupled their numbers in North Carolina. It is too early to tell whether the new settlement patterns will promote or retard integration prospects of new immigrants.

On the subject of identity, Durand, Telles, and Flashman observe, like Rumbaut, that despite class, race, and national differences, Hispanics have found ways to coalesce on the basis of a shared language and, above all, a common identity forged by a panethnic label. Their chapter concludes with the projection that, despite uncertainty about the size of future immigration flows, the Hispanic population is likely to continue its growth trend for at least two decades because of its youthful age structure and fertility rates above the national average.

Residential location is a powerful predictor of well-being because of the myriad social amenities that are unequally distributed across space, such as affordable housing, quality schools, public safety, and transportation. Location also influences access to jobs that pay family wages, as well as the likelihood of mingling with nonminority groups. Therefore, in "Redrawing Spatial Color Lines: Hispanic Metropolitan Dispersal, Segregation, and Economic Opportunity," Mary J. Fischer and Marta Tienda examine trends in spatial segregation, school segregation, homeownership, and employment outcomes for native- and foreign-born Hispanics since 1980. Focusing on the 100 largest metropolitan areas, which they sort into three strata—traditional metros, new Hispanic destinations, and other large metros—they consider whether, where, and how Hispanics' new settlement patterns alter the racial and ethnic landscape.

Fischer and Tienda conclude that the Hispanic geographic scattering, which began during the 1970s and gained momentum during the 1990s, is a significant agent of urban social transformation, both because of the pace of change and because of the large number of places involved. Widespread declines in racial residential segregation during the 1990s, especially in areas where Hispanics have recently emerged on the scene, suggest that the newcomers may serve as a buffer between blacks and whites, but it is too early for definitive conclusions. The movement of Hispanics into non-Hispanic communities, as well as the varying levels of segregation and integration they experience in those settings, has broad implications for intergroup relations and for the contours of ethnic and racial stratification more generally.

The implications for school segregation and homeownership of the Hispanic geographic scattering are mixed. What is the most clear is that changes in labor demand are the major force attracting Hispanics to new destinations throughout the nation. The rapid expansion of immigrant job niches in the new destinations—notably, construction, domestic maintenance and repair services, nondurable manufacturing, and personal and household services—largely explain why the Hispanic dispersal disproportionately involves immigrants, among whom recent arrivals predominate.

FAMILY, SCHOOL, AND WORK

In large part, Hispanics' current economic and social status reflects their youthful age structure, their low average education levels, and the large shares of recent immigrants with limited English skills. Owing to the dominance of Mexicans, who are the least educated of all Hispanic groups, the foreign-born Hispanic population is disproportionately concentrated at the bottom rungs of the occupational and wage structure. Hispanic immigrants with less than a high school education are relegated to unstable, low-wage jobs that offer few or no social benefits and poor working conditions. Chapters 5-8 examine connections among family, school, and work and their implications for Hispanic's economic well-being.

Family

"Hispanic Families in the United States: Family Structure and Process in an Era of Family Change," by Nancy S. Landale, R. Salvador Oropesa, and Cristina Bradatan, situates trends in Hispanic families in the context of significant changes in U.S. family life. These trends include the rising age of marriage, an increase in cohabitation, a dramatic shift in the proportion of children born outside marriage, high divorce rates, high rates of female family headship, and a growing share of children with restricted access to their fathers' resources. Using data from the census, the National Center for Health Statistics, and published sources, the authors document trends in several indicators of family change, systematically comparing Hispanic national subgroups with non-Hispanic whites and non-Hispanic blacks. They also examine generational variation in family patterns within Hispanic subgroups, paying particular attention to whether the strong family orientation—sometimes termed "familism"—that is part of Hispanic immigrant culture is retained over time and across generations or whether Hispanics are also experiencing what has been termed "family decline."

Landale, Oropesa, and Bradatan identify several patterns that are consistent with claims that Hispanics are more familistic than non-Hispanics, such as higher fertility (with the exception of Cubans), larger households, and greater prevalence of extended living arrangements in comparison with non-Hispanic whites and blacks. Also, with the exception of Puerto Ricans and Cubans, Hispanic women are more likely to be married at a young age (20-24) than are non-Hispanics. Their analysis also notes signs of declining familism, especially for Mexican-origin Hispanics. On every indicator used, they found that the second and third (or later) generations exhibited less traditional family behavior than the first generation. Most worrisome, say the authors, is the rise of nonmarital fertility for all Hispanic groups and the rising percentage of children living in mother-only families across generations.

Intermarriage is a crucial indicator of assimilation because, by blurring racial and ethnic boundaries or reducing the numbers who self-identify as Hispanic, it has direct implications for the future size and shape of ethnic populations, as well as for the persistence of Hispanic as an ethnic category. Examining racial and ethnic mixing in sexual partnerships of various types, including marriage, cohabitation, and parenthood, Landale, Oropesa, and Bradatan find evidence that as the number of children of mixed ethnic backgrounds grows, boundaries among Hispanic subgroups and between Hispanics and non-Hispanics are weakened. That Hispanics of Mexican origin are less likely to intermarry than other Hispanic subgroups implies fewer exits from the Mexican American population due to mixed racial-ethnic backgrounds of offspring (and consequent identity shifts) compared with other nationalities.

Education

Youth reared in families with only one parent or by parents with low education levels face formidable challenges as they enter a monolingual U.S. school system. Over one-fourth of Hispanic adults have less than a ninth-grade education, with Mexican Americans averaging the lowest educational levels and Cuban Americans and other Hispanics the highest. "Barriers to Educational Opportunities for Hispanics in the United States," by Barbara Schneider, Sylvia Martinez, and Ann Owens, uses data from the Census Bureau, the College Board, and the Department of Education to examine the institutional and student-level factors behind the poor scholastic achievement and low educational attainment levels of Hispanic youth.

By examining the entire educational trajectory, from preschool to college, the authors illustrate the lasting consequences of suboptimal early school experiences of Hispanic students for their final attainment, emphasizing how transitions between levels affect the likelihood of school persistence. The high school dropout rate for Hispanic students (28 percent in 2000) is more than double that of non-Hispanic whites and blacks. However, very high dropout rates for foreign-born Hispanics—43 percent in 2001—inflate the average figures because many adolescent immigrants never enter the U.S. system.

Among the issues that increase Hispanic students' vulnerability to failure are lower levels of exposure to preschool literacy activities; biased teacher assessments of non-English speakers during the early school years; the quality of relationships between Hispanic students and non-Hispanic teachers; the concentration of Hispanic students in large, urban schools that, more often than not, represent suboptimal instructional environments; and failures of the academic guidance programs directing Hispanic students toward college preparatory courses. The authors also examine various objective indicators of academic success, including cognitive test performance, high school completion, and college enrollment. They show that Hispanic students trail non-Hispanic whites on most outcomes, including school readiness, elementary school math and reading scores, and the share of students who take SAT or advanced placement exams.

Schneider, Martinez, and Owens claim that different factors influence scholastic success throughout the school process. Before Hispanic students begin formalized schooling, family resources are critically important: at this stage, the confluence of low parental English proficiency and educational attainment combined with limited educational resources at home hinders Hispanic parents from engaging their children in early literacy activities that contribute to academic success. In elementary school, teacher stereotyping and low expectations for Hispanic students further undermine their academic achievement. And, in high school, Hispanic students receive limited guidance about college-oriented coursework and are among the least likely either to take high-level mathematics and science courses or to enroll in four-year colleges.

After high school, the cost of higher education and immigrant parents' unfamiliarity with the complex policies and practices of the U.S. education system foment low rates of Hispanic college attendance, particularly at four-year institutions. As discussed by the authors, students who enter the labor force immediately after high graduation embark on a course that virtually ensures a lifetime of low wages. Although rising numbers of Hispanic high school graduates are enrolling in college—about one in three in 2000—their degree completion rate four years later trails that of non-Hispanic whites. In part this is because Hispanic students are more likely than other groups to enroll in two-year colleges and less likely to transfer to a four-year institution.

Despite this discouraging picture, Schneider, Martinez, and Owens are optimistic that further improvements are possible with strategic interventions, provided that academic interventions for Hispanic youth become a national priority. The authors also identify strategic interventions to overcome the barriers Hispanic parents face in connecting with monolingual public schools. Moreover, they argue that Hispanic-serving institutions can play a pivotal role in promoting educational achievement at the college level.

Work and Well-Being

Based on analyses of public-use census data and the Current Population Survey, in "Hispanics in the U.S. Labor Market" Brian Duncan, V. Joseph Hotz, and Stephen J. Trejo chart trends and differentials in employment and earnings and compare the life-cycle patterns of schooling and work between Hispanics and both non-Hispanic blacks and non-Hispanic whites. To address whether Hispanics experience economic mobility, they also evaluate changes in Hispanics' earnings over time and across generations. The authors conclude that the large gaps in human capital—both educational attainment and proficiency in English—between native- and foreign-born Hispanics and relative to non-Hispanics—both whites and blacks—decisively influence their labor market outcomes.[5] For immigrants, the effect of these disadvantages is multiplied by the imperfect transferability of

[5]Only about one-third of Hispanic immigrants speak English "very well," compared with 90 percent of the U.S. born (and 99 percent of U.S.-born whites and blacks); Mexicans have the lowest levels of proficiency and Cubans and Puerto Ricans have the highest.

schooling and work experience obtained in foreign countries. Although undocumented workers may experience higher levels of market discrimination than legal residents, the authors claim that legal status plays a smaller role in their labor market standing than their relative lack of human capital.

To make their case, Duncan, Hotz, and Trejo standardize employment and earnings rates for differences in educational attainment and English language proficiency and show that Hispanics fare almost as well as whites with respect to both employment and labor market earnings. This is in stark contrast to blacks, for whom similar adjustments do not significantly reduce racial disparities in labor market outcomes. Finally, the authors show how increased educational attainment between first- and second-generation Hispanics translates into appreciable improvements in their employment and earnings both in absolute terms and relative to whites, noting that socioeconomic progress between the second and later generations is less clear. Although a scenario of downward mobility is possible, more likely this reflects a higher tendency for the more successful among later generations to "opt out" of Hispanic ethnicity, thereby introducing a downward bias in their measured economic status. The large heterogeneity of the "third plus" generation is an additional source of potential bias.

In "Economic Well-Being" Cordelia Reimers paints a detailed portrait of Hispanic household incomes, illustrating a close correspondence with labor market experiences. Her chapter uses the various social arrangements described in preceding chapters—national origin, family structure, education, and earnings—to analyze total household income, which is a measure of economic well-being that includes the earnings of all household members, plus unearned income from public benefits and other sources. She uses Current Population Survey data for 1998-2002 to depict variation in income packaging among working-age Hispanics, including contributions from earnings, public benefits, and the incomes of extended household members. Reimers also compares poverty rates and household income sources for elderly Hispanics, who are more likely than non-Hispanic whites and blacks to have worked in jobs that do not offer pensions.

Paralleling the variation in education levels and household structure among Hispanic groups, she documents wide dispersion in median household incomes and poverty rates, with large disparities across nationalities and generations. First-generation Puerto Ricans and Dominicans are at the bottom on most measures of economic well-being and Mexicans near the bottom, while U.S.-born South Americans and Cubans rank close to non-Hispanic whites. Later generations of every national origin are better off than immigrants, and, like Duncan and his colleagues, she notes that most of the improvement occurs between the first and second generations. Reimers cautions that cross-sectional differences among generations do not necessarily reflect future intergenerational change because the parents and grandparents of today's second- and third-generation Hispanics are not necessarily comparable to contemporary immigrants from the same country. Overall, her findings support claims in other chapters that the future economic well-being of Hispanics in the United States hinges crucially on education and family structure of new immigrants and their U.S.-born children and grandchildren.

HEALTH STATUS AND HEALTH CARE

Although less frequently considered in analyses of employment and earnings, health status is an important dimension of human capital that influences productivity and economic well-being. "The Health Status and Health Behaviors of Hispanics," by José J. Escarce, Leo S. Morales, and Rubén G. Rumbaut, provides a comprehensive overview of Hispanics' physical and mental well-being, comparing Hispanic nationalities and generations to the extent that available data permit. The authors review existing literature and use data from the National Center for Health Statistics, the National Health Interview Survey, and other sources.

Many findings reported by Escarce, Morales, and Rumbaut encourage optimism about Hispanics' health status. For example, with the exception of Puerto Ricans, Hispanics have lower age-adjusted mortality than non-Hispanic whites despite their lower socioeconomic status, which is usually associated with higher mortality. Research on this "epidemiological paradox" suggests that Hispanics' mortality advantage is concentrated among the foreign born, and that selective migration (i.e., the tendency for immigrants to be healthier than the people who stay behind) is partly responsible. For most U.S.-born Hispanics, in whom selective migration is not a competing explanation, mortality rates are at least as favorable as those for non-Hispanic whites. Birth outcomes present a similar paradox in that Hispanic women have a comparable or lower incidence of low birthweight babies and infant mortality rates than non-Hispanic white women, again with the exception of Puerto Ricans. As with mortality, the advantage is greater for foreign-born Hispanics; why it obtains also for U.S.-born Hispanic women remains poorly understood.

That acculturation appears to worsen the health status of Hispanics is cause for concern. Deleterious effects of acculturation are especially evident among second-generation youths and in birth outcomes. In fact, recent trends in overweight and obesity among Hispanic youth suggest that the Hispanic population will be increasingly burdened by the complications of obesity, including diabetes, hypertension, and cardiovascular disease, in the decades to come. As a result, the U.S. health care system may be faced with much larger numbers of Hispanic patients suffering from chronic conditions and their consequences.

However, in "Access to and Quality of Health Care," José J. Escarce and Kanika Kapur warn that Hispanics already face numerous barriers to receiving timely, appropriate, and high-quality health care—some because they are poor and others because of features specific to the population. This chapter, which reviews evidence on Hispanics' access to and quality of health care, also presents new data from recent national surveys to show how national origin, English fluency, and citizenship status are associated with access to, and quality of, health care. The authors use data from the National Heath Interview Survey, the Medical Expenditure Panel Survey, and other sources to document barriers to access, with particular attention to the role of health insurance coverage and sources of care, patterns of health care utilization, and the quality of health care received.

Escarce and Kapur find that, in comparison with non-Hispanic whites, Hispanics' lower access to health care and lack of a usual source of care largely reflects their lower levels of insurance coverage. Hispanics use prenatal care and many preventive services less than non-Hispanic whites, make fewer visits to physicians and other medical providers, and have lower total medical care expenditures, including expenditures for prescription drugs. Foreign-born Hispanics, except for Puerto Ricans, consistently have much worse access indicators than U.S.-born Hispanics. Nationality breakdowns reveal that Puerto Ricans and Cubans are more likely than Hispanics of Mexican origin to have health insurance coverage and a usual source of health care; as such, they register more physician visits and higher expenditures for medical care. Studies on the quality of health care for Hispanics are even more limited than those about access to care, but available data suggest that the quality of the medical treatment for Hispanics is similar or slightly worse than that for non-Hispanic whites. For Spanish speakers, however, language not only poses an important barrier to access but also has a negative influence on patients' experiences with care.

The chapter raises several issues for policy makers by drawing attention to the large (and rising) disparities in health insurance coverage by economic status. It calls attention to inadequacy of current approaches for providing health insurance coverage and health care to populations of low socioeconomic status. In particular, given recent trends in the provision of employer-sponsored health insurance, Escarce and Kapur project that the number of uninsured Hispanics will grow rapidly over the next few years, even if immigration drops. If this does occur, the number of uninsured Hispanics will further strain health care delivery systems, especially the so-called health care safety net, particularly in the new communities in which Hispanics are settling.

CIVIC AND POLITICAL ENGAGEMENT

Hispanics participate in social transformation through their political participation and civic engagement. However, a major characteristic of Hispanics' political behavior is their low civic engagement, clearly evident across a range of electoral, civic, and organizational activities. Most notable, among registered voters Hispanics' voter turnout rates trail those of non-Hispanic whites and blacks. There is widespread consensus that lower participation levels largely reflect differences in population composition between Hispanic and non-Hispanic populations—especially differences in the share of noncitizens. Yet, with each election, claims of Hispanics' political influence grow, and increasing efforts are made to capture "the Hispanic vote." In "Latino Civic and Political Participation," Louis DeSipio questions assumption that Hispanics represent a singular voice at the ballot box. Major sources for his analysis include census data and various published analyses.

On the issue of an identifiable Hispanic political community, DeSipio argues that perceptions are more apparent than real. He notes that mass and elite interests diverge considerably, although this division is narrowing. Over the past 20 years, Hispanic elites, particularly non-Cuban Hispanic elites, have organized primarily as Hispanics and not around their national origin identities. The boards of directors of major Hispanic organizations—including the Mexican American Legal Defense and Education Fund (MALDEF), the League of United Latin American Citizens (LULAC), the National Council of La Raza (NCLR), the National Association of Hispanic Elected and Appointed Officials (NALEO), the Tomás Rivera Policy Institute (TRPI), and the Congressional Hispanic Caucus—reflect both the Hispanic community's diversity and shared issues. In contrast, at the mass level, national identities remain salient in defining the contours of Hispanic civic engagement.

Although many Hispanics do not identify with panethnic labels or understand what they share in common with people of other national origins, DeSipio claims that a set of issues that bridge national origin groups and generations loosely cohere into a common political agenda. These issues, which include public education, social services, health issues, and the enhancement of government capacity in domestic politics, are neither outside the American mainstream nor particularly controversial, although they can potentially shift national debates by matters of degree. Still, the extent to which Hispanics have successfully organized around shared political agendas is limited by institutional and demographic barriers that are not unique to Hispanics, but that have a disproportionate effect because of their demographic composition, notably two large population segments that are ineligible to vote—foreign-born adults who have not become naturalized citizens and school-aged youth.

DeSipio argues that for Hispanics to use politics effectively, democratic institutions must be more responsive to their demands. Casting an eye to the future, he anticipates that the Hispanic electorate will grow incrementally over successive election cycles, gradually raising the chances that Hispanics will become the swing vote in electoral outcomes. However, the tensions between the low levels of political engagement across Hispanic subgroups and the reality of diverse political interests may undermine the likelihood of this outcome. He suggests that an increase in the number of elected national Hispanic leaders is needed to fortify a Latino politics that has been unfolding over the past 30 years.

RETROSPECT AND PROSPECT

Because of their large numbers, rapid growth, and unprecedented geographic dispersal, Hispanics will affect American society in profound ways even as they experience considerable transformation as a people. Numbering about 10 million today, children of Hispanic immigrants—both legal and undocumented—are projected to grow to 26 million over the next 25 years. With a median age below 13 years in 2000, most second-generation Hispanics are now enrolled in school; by 2030 the majority will be in the labor force. Because college attainment is increasingly mandatory for labor market success and English proficiency is vitally important for navigating health care systems and meaningful civic engagement, Hispanics' economic prospects may hinge crucially on their mastery of English and their success in closing postsecondary education gaps with non-Hispanics.

With time, most immigrant communities become ethnic groups, and within three generations, most expressions of ethnicity are rendered largely symbolic as cultural, structural, spatial, and marital assimilation blurs ethnic distinctions. Hispanic communities are undergoing these processes. The key question, as yet unanswered, is whether "Hispanic" will eventually prove to be a symbolic identity for people of Latin American descent or whether it will become an enduring marker signaling membership in a disadvantaged minority group.

Assuming that Hispanic is rendered a largely symbolic identity in the future, two alternative scenarios are conceivable. One is *e pluribus unum*: Will Hispanicity become a real panethnic identity defined by a collective sense of peoplehood? The alternative is *e pluribus plures*: Will expression of nationalities persist and possibly reassert themselves in order to preserve the cultural foundation of group identity? If Hispanicity becomes synonymous with minority group status in the future, would this, in turn, redefine racial boundaries into black, white, and brown, thereby undermining "*unum?*" Although this extreme scenario seems highly unlikely, it is unclear how the burgeoning second generation will resolve Hispanics' longstanding quest for recognition and empowerment.

As several chapters document, there are many signs that Hispanicity will become a symbolic identity rather than that of a disadvantaged minority. Since 1980, U.S.-born Hispanic adults have closed the educational attainment gap with non-Hispanic whites by more than half a year. Furthermore, there is ample evidence of intergenerational economic mobility, particularly between the first and second generations, which shows in annual earnings, median household income, and homeownership rates. Following the pathways of prior immigrant groups, the language shift from Spanish to English is virtually complete by the third generation. Whether these trends will continue, and at what pace, depend on several factors that are currently in flux. The factors include the level and composition of future immigration flows; whether Hispanic immigrant's geographic dispersal accelerates spatial and social assimilation; whether growing numbers of foreign-born Hispanics become citizens and vote; the future vitality of the U.S. economy; and, especially, significant gains in educational attainment.

In sum, the momentous generational transition now under way is a pivotal, yet unwritten, chapter of the Hispanic integration narrative.

REFERENCE

National Research Council. (2006). *Multiple origins, uncertain destinies: Hispanics and the American future.* Panel on Hispanics in the United States, Marta Tienda and Faith Mitchell, editors. Committee on Population, Division of Behavioral and Social Sciences and Education. Washington, DC: The National Academies Press.

2

The Making of a People

Rubén G. Rumbaut

Americans have their leveling ways: La Ciudad de Nuestra Señora la Reina de Los Angeles de Porciúncula has become, in one hundred years, L.A.

—Richard Rodríguez (1993)

In 2003 the Hispanic population of the United States reached 40 million—or 44 million if the inhabitants of the Commonwealth of Puerto Rico are included (U.S. Census Bureau, 2004b). Only Mexico (with a population above 100 million) is larger among Spanish-speaking countries today. The rapid growth of the Hispanic population—which had been estimated at only 4 million in 1950—has been stunning (Table 2-1).[1] Its current growth rate is four times that of the total population. The U.S. Census Bureau (2004a) has projected that, given continuing immigration and moderate levels of natural increase, Hispanics will grow by 2050 to an estimated 103 million people and account for 25 percent of the national total, significantly exceeding the proportions of other ethnic or racial minorities. And while Hispanic Americans now account for one of every seven persons in the United States, their impact—social, cultural, political, and economic—is much more profound because of their concentration in particular states and localities. The origins, present status, and complex trajectories of this population thus merit careful analysis.

[1]The Hispanic population (as variously defined over the years and estimated by the U.S. Census Bureau) grew from 6.9 million in 1960 to 9.1 million in 1970, 14.6 million in 1980, 22.4 million in 1990, and 35.2 million in 2000. In 1960, Hispanics accounted for only 3.9 percent of the total U.S. population; that proportion tripled to 12.5 percent in 2000. For a detailed analysis of the growth of the U.S. Hispanic population between 1960 and 1980 and of the problems of measuring it (and of adjusting for census undercounts and intercensal comparability), see Bean and Tienda (1987). For its growth from 1980 to 2000, see Table 2-1.

TABLE 2-1 Size (1000s) and Growth of the Hispanic Foreign-Born Population of the United States, by Spanish-Speaking Country of Birth, 1980–2000

	Year of Census			% Population Growth	
Country of Birth	1980	1990	2000	1980–1990	1990–2000
North America and Caribbean					
Mexico	2,194	4,263	9,177	94	115
Puerto Rico[a]	1,011	1,180	1,437	17	22
Cuba	617	738	873	20	18
Dominican Republic	166	344	688	107	100
Central America					
El Salvador	95	465	817	392	76
Guatemala	64	221	481	246	118
Honduras	37	106	283	185	166
Nicaragua	44	168	220	282	31
Panama	60	83	105	38	26
Costa Rica	29	31	72	3	134
South America					
Colombia	147	287	510	95	78
Ecuador	88	139	299	57	116
Peru	57	144	278	155	93
Argentina	68	95	125	40	32
Venezuela	32	42	107	29	157
Chile	37	56	81	54	43
Bolivia	14	30	53	119	79
Uruguay	14	22	24	58	10
Paraguay	3	6	12	90	101
Spain	54	78	87	44	12
Total	4,831	8,498	15,786	76	86

[a]Puerto Ricans born in Puerto Rico are included here as foreign-born.

SOURCE: U.S. Census Bureau, Census 2000 Summary File 3; 1980, 1990, and 2000 Integrated Public Use Microdata Series, at http://www.ipums.org.

The making of this population needs to be understood from three vantage points. Hispanics are at once a new and an old population made up both of recently arrived newcomers and of old timers with deeper roots in American soil than any other ethnic groups except for the indigenous peoples of the continent.[2] They comprise a population that can claim both

[2]Many Latin Americans mix indigenous pre-Columbian ancestries with European, African, and even Asian roots. In the islands of the Caribbean, the aboriginal populations were virtually extinguished after the coming of the Europeans, as were Amerindian languages and

a history and a territory in what is now the United States that precede the establishment of the nation.

At the same time, it is a population that seems to have emerged suddenly, its growth driven both by accelerating immigration from the Spanish-speaking countries of Latin America—above all from Mexico, which shares a 2,000 mile border with the United States—and by high rates of natural increase. Indeed, 45 percent of the total Hispanic population of the United States today is foreign-born, and another 31 percent consists of a rapidly growing second generation of U.S.-born children of immigrant parents. Table 2-1 shows the growth of the foreign-born Hispanic population from 1980 to 2000 by country of birth. Already by 1990, for the first time in U.S. history, Spanish-speaking Latin Americans formed the largest immigrant population in the country—larger than the flows from Asia and Europe combined. By 2000, Mexican immigrants alone were more numerous than all European and Canadian immigrants combined, and more than all Asian, African, and Middle Eastern immigrants combined.

And the label itself—"Hispanic"—is new, an instance of a pan-ethnic category that was created by official edict three decades ago. The ethnic groups subsumed under this label—the Mexicans, Puerto Ricans, Cubans, Dominicans, Salvadorans, Guatemalans, Colombians, Peruvians, Ecuadorians, and the other dozen nationalities from Latin America and from Spain itself—were not "Hispanics" or "Latinos" in their countries of origin; rather, they became so only in the United States. That catchall label has a particular meaning only in the U.S. context in which it was constructed and is applied, and where its meaning continues to evolve.

This chapter reviews each of these three aspects—the classificatory, the historical, and the contemporary. The chapter highlights differences that most clearly distinguish the Hispanic population from non-Hispanics—especially in history and language, as well as place, race, national origins, immigration, generation, citizenship, and social status.[3] Moreover, the chap-

---

cultures, above all in Cuba; for three centuries, African slave labor was brought in successive waves. In the continent, native American populations were concentrated especially around two agrarian empires in what are now Mexico and Perú; their physical and cultural continuities have been preserved by their descendants in the mainly Nahuatl and Maya speakers of Mexico and Guatemala, and the mainly Quechua and Aymara speakers of Perú, Ecuador, and Bolivia. For a population history and an analysis of current ethnic profiles and Amerindian survivals in each of the countries of the region, see Collier, Blakemore, and Skidmore (1985, pp. 127–160).

[3]To sketch those contemporary profiles, the chapter relies on data from the 5 percent Public Use Microdata Sample (PUMS) of the 2000 census, focusing on demographic factors, ethnic and racial self-identification, immigration and citizenship, generation and language, and socioeconomic status. The analysis of linguistic acculturation and social mobility will compare the foreign-born first generation of Hispanic and non-Hispanic populations against

ter takes account of the differences between the largest Hispanic ethnic groups, emphasizing that Hispanics as a whole are not a homogeneous entity and should not be presumed to be so. However, despite those group differences, the tens of millions of persons so classified do share a common label that symbolizes a minority group status in the United States, a label developed and legitimized by the state, diffused in daily and institutional practice, and finally internalized (and racialized) as a prominent part of the American mosaic. That this outcome is, to a considerable extent, a self-fulfilling prophecy does not make it any less real.

I raise and address a number of questions about Hispanic Americans: Who are they, where did they come from, and when? In what ways can their diverse peoples be considered a unique population? How do they differ from non-Hispanics in the United States? Do a common language and cultural tradition, as well as a shared history once in the United States, make the essential difference in the maintenance of a pan–Latin American ethnicity? Is there a Hispanic or Latino ethnic group, cohesive and self-conscious, sharing a sense of peoplehood in the same way that there is an African American people in the United States?[4] Or is it merely an administrative aggregate devised for statistical purposes, a one-size-fits-all label that subsumes diverse peoples and identities? Is the focus on Hispanics or Latinos as a catchall category misleading, since it conceals not only the enormous diversity of contemporary immigrants from Spanish-speaking Latin America but also the substantial generational differences among groups so labeled? How do the labeled label themselves? How do the

---

the U.S.-born second-and-beyond generations. Since 1980, the decennial censuses have been constrained by the deletion of the parental nativity question that had been asked from 1870 to 1970—making it impossible to distinguish the first and second (foreign parentage) generations from each other and from the third-and-beyond (native parentage) generations. Fortunately, since 1994 the annual Current Population Survey (CPS) has included items on maternal and paternal country of birth, permitting such intergenerational analysis. For this reason, several of the chapters in this volume make use of the CPS as a primary data source. However, the CPS has its own limitations—including the fact that, unlike the decennial census, it does not collect data on languages spoken, level of English proficiency, or linguistic isolation. Given the central importance of language in the study of Hispanic Americans, in this chapter the 2000 census is used as the primary data source.

[4]Douglas Massey (1993) has argued that "There is . . . no Hispanic population in the sense that there is a Black population . . . . The only thing reasonably certain is that the person in question or some progenitor once lived in an area colonized by Spain." But in fact not even that is the case. The Philippines, named after Philip II, were colonized by Spain for three centuries (until the United States replaced it as the colonial power in 1898), its population of more than 80 million people today are largely Spanish-surnamed Catholics (though not Spanish speakers), and Filipinos are the second largest immigrant group in the United States (after Mexicans), yet they are not considered Hispanics but classified racially as Asian under Directive 15 of the Office of Management and Budget.

quintessential markers of group difference in the American experience (phenotype, language, religion, nationality, citizenship, ancestry) differentiate Hispanics or Latinos as a whole from other pan-ethnic or racial aggregates (the non-Hispanic white, black, Asian, and American Indian populations)?

I begin with a discussion of the origin of the category itself and its use in official ethnic and racial classification. I then examine the historical origins of the Hispanic presence in the United States, tracing the roots of its three oldest and largest groups (Mexicans, Puerto Ricans, and Cubans). Finally, I highlight a set of salient characteristics and contexts that distinguish the contemporary Hispanic population as a whole from non-Hispanics and the major Hispanic ethnic groups from each other—issues elaborated in greater detail in the chapters that follow.

THE MAKING OF A CATEGORY

Beginning in 1850, the U.S. Census Bureau relied on objective indicators, such as country of birth (or decades later, parent's birthplace, mother tongue, or Spanish surname), to identify persons of Mexican origin in its decennial counts.[5] A century later, in the 1950s, the Census Bureau first published information on persons of Puerto Rican birth or parentage; tabulations on people of Cuban birth or parentage were first published in 1970. Efforts to demarcate and enumerate the Hispanic population as a whole, using subjective indicators of Spanish origin or descent, date back to the late 1960s (Bean and Tienda, 1987). At that time—in the context of surging civil rights activism, new federal legislation that required accurate statistical documentation of minority group disadvantages, and growing concerns over differential census undercounts—Mexican American organizations in particular pressed for better data about their group (Choldin, 1986). The Nixon White House ordered the addition of a Spanish-origin self-identifier on the 1970 census (it was included only in the "long form" sent to a 5 percent sample, since 109 million copies of the "short form" had already gone to press); to test it, the same question was inserted in the November 1969 CPS (the first time that subjective item was used).[6]

In 1976, the 94th Congress of the United States passed a remarkable

[5]Mexicans were classified as a "race" in the 1930 U.S. census, but Mexican Americans, with the support of the Mexican government, demanded not to be so designated. That usage was eliminated in subsequent censuses.

[6]Later analyses by the Census Bureau, comparing the results nationally of the (subjective) Hispanic self-identification in the CPS versus the (objective) use of Spanish surnames, found wide-ranging differences between the two measures, raising questions of validity and reliability. For example, in the Southwest, only 74 percent of those who identified themselves as Hispanic had Spanish surnames, while 81 percent of those with Spanish surnames identified

bill—Public Law 94-311 (see Box 2-1), a joint resolution "relating to the publication of economic and social statistics for Americans of Spanish origin or descent." It remains the only law in the country's history that mandates the collection, analysis, and publication of data for a specific ethnic group, and it goes on to define the population to be enumerated. The law, building on information gathered from the 1970 census, asserted that "more than 12 million Americans identify themselves as being of Spanish-speaking background and trace their origin or descent from Mexico, Puerto Rico, Cuba, Central and South America, and other Spanish-speaking countries"; that a "large number" of them "suffer from racial, social, economic, and political discrimination and are denied the basic opportunities that they deserve as American citizens"; and that an "accurate determination of the urgent and special needs of Americans of Spanish origin and descent" was needed to improve their economic and social status. Accordingly, the law mandated a series of data collection initiatives in the federal departments of Commerce, Labor, Agriculture, and Health, Education, and Welfare, specifying among other things that the Spanish-origin population be given "full recognition" by the Census Bureau's data collection activities through the use of Spanish language questionnaires and bilingual enumerators, as needed; and that the Office of Management and Budget (OMB) "develop a Government-wide program for the collection, analysis, and publication of data with respect to Americans of Spanish origin or descent."

In May 1977, as required by Congress, OMB's Statistical Policy Division, Office of Information and Regulatory Affairs, issued Directive 15: Race and Ethnic Standards for Federal Statistics and Administrative Reporting to standardize the collection and reporting of "racial" and "ethnic" statistics and to include data on persons of "Hispanic origin." Directive 15 specified a minimal classification of four "races" (American Indian or Alaskan Native, Asian or Pacific Islander, black, and white) and two "ethnic" backgrounds (of Hispanic origin and not of Hispanic origin) and allowed the collection of more detailed information as long as it could be aggregated within those categories. Since that time, in keeping with the logic of this classification, census data on Hispanics have typically been officially reported with a footnote indicating that "Hispanics may be of any race."

Tellingly, however, the term led to the development of another category, "non-Hispanic white" (a catchall for persons who identify as white but whose ancestry does not include a Spanish-speaking nation), which has

---

themselves as Hispanic; in the rest of the United States, only 61 percent of those who identified as Hispanic had Spanish surnames, and a mere 46 percent of those with Spanish surnames identified as Hispanic (U.S. Census Bureau, 1975).

BOX 2-1
Americans of Spanish Origin—Social Statistics
Public Law 94-311 [H.J.Res. 92]; June 18, 1976

Joint Resolution relating to the publication of economic and social statistics for Americans of Spanish origin or descent.

Whereas more than twelve million Americans identify themselves as being of Spanish-speaking background and trace their origin or descent from Mexico, Puerto Rico, Cuba, Central and South America, and other Spanish-speaking countries; and

Whereas these Americans of Spanish origin or descent have made significant contributions to enrich American society and have served their Nation well in time of war and peace; and

Whereas a large number of Americans of Spanish origin or descent suffer from racial, social, economic, and political discrimination and are denied the basic opportunities they deserve as American citizens and which would enable them to begin to lift themselves out of the poverty they now endure; and

Whereas improved evaluation of the economic and social status of Americans of Spanish origin or descent will assist State and Federal Governments and private organizations in the accurate determination of the urgent and special needs of Americans of Spanish origin or descent; and

Whereas the provision and commitment of State, Federal, and private resources can only occur when there is an accurate and precise assessment of need:

Now, therefore, be it

Resolved by the Senate and House of Representatives of the United States of America in Congress assembled, that the Department of Labor, in cooperation

been typically set against the term "Hispanics" and the other racial minority categories, conflating the distinction. In the news media, academic studies, government reports, and popular usage the "ethnic" constructs "Hispanic" or "Latino"[7] have already come to be used routinely and equivalently alongside "racial" categories such as Asian, black, and non-

[7]The terms themselves are contested and there is no consensus on usage, although neither "Hispanic" nor "Latino" is a term of preference used by Latin American migrants in the United States to label themselves; rather, *the research literature shows that they self-identify preponderantly by their national origin*. To what extent their U.S.-born children or grandchildren adopt such made-in-the-USA pan-ethnic labels as their own remains to be ascertained definitively, but longitudinal studies of the second generation suggest that only a small minority (about one in four) tends to adopt a pan-ethnic identity, although they are much more likely than their parents to accept "Hispanic" or "Latino" as a *racial* self-identifier (see Castillo, 2003; Fears, 2003a; Pew Hispanic Center/Kaiser Family Foundation, 2002; Portes and Rumbaut, 2001; Sachs, 2001).

with the Department of Commerce, shall develop methods for improving and expanding the collection, analysis, and publication of unemployment data relating to Americans of Spanish origin or descent.

SEC. 2. The Department of Commerce, the Department of Labor, the Department of Health, Education, and Welfare, and the Department of Agriculture shall each collect, and publish regularly, statistics which indicate the social, health, and economic condition of Americans of Spanish origin or descent.

SEC. 3. The Director of the Office of Management and Budget, in cooperation with the Secretary of Commerce and with the heads of other data-gathering Federal agencies, shall develop a Government-wide program for the collection, analysis, and publication of data with respect to Americans of Spanish origin or descent.

SEC. 4. The Department of Commerce, in cooperation with appropriate Federal, State, and local agencies and various population study groups and experts, shall immediately undertake a study to determine what steps would be necessary for developing creditable estimates of undercounts of Americans of Spanish origin or descent in future censuses.

SEC. 5. The Secretary of Commerce shall ensure that, in the Bureau of the Census data-collection activities, the needs and concerns of the Spanish-origin population are given full recognition through the use of Spanish language questionnaires, bilingual enumerators, and other such methods as deemed appropriate by the Secretary.

SEC. 6. The Department of Commerce shall implement an affirmative action program within the Bureau of the Census for the employment of personnel of Spanish origin or descent and shall submit a report to Congress within one year of the enactment of this Act on the progress of such program.

Approved June 16, 1976.

Hispanic white, effecting a de facto racialization of the former. It is now also commonplace to find newspaper articles that report matter-of-factly that the country's first Hispanic astronaut was Franklin Chang-Díaz, a Chinese Costa Rican, or that the first Latina chancellor of a University of California campus (Silverstein, 2003) is France A. Córdova, a French-born physicist who majored in English at Stanford, whose mother is an Irish American native New Yorker and whose father came to the United States as an 8-year-old from Tampico.[8]

[8]For those so classified, the subjective meaning of such labels, and whether they are situationally asserted as an ethnic self-identity, remain open empirical questions. Contexts shape the meanings of identity assignments and assertions, and the present historical context—of civil rights, affirmative action, and ethnic revivals—stands in sharp contrast to the way immigrants were treated during the heyday of hegemonic Americanization in the early 20th century, and in particular to the opprobrium meted out to assertions of a Mexican ancestry. An instructive example involves Ted Williams, universally known as one of baseball's

Later criticism of the categories led to a formal review of Directive 15, beginning in 1993 with congressional hearings and culminating in revised standards that were adopted in 1997 (U.S. Bureau of the Census, 1997; see also Fears, 2003b; Snipp, 2003; Wallman, Evinger, and Schechter, 2000; Wright, 1994). The changes now stipulated five minimum categories for data on "race" (American Indian or Alaskan Native, Native Hawaiian or Other Pacific Islander, Asian, black or African American, and white); offered respondents the option of selecting one or more racial designations (an option used for the first time in the 2000 census); and reworded the two "ethnic" categories into "Hispanic or Latino" and "not Hispanic or Latino." "Hispanic or Latino" was defined as "a person of Cuban, Mexican, Puerto Rican, South or Central American, or other Spanish culture or origin, regardless of race. The term, 'Spanish origin,' can be used in addition to 'Hispanic or Latino.'" The notice in the *Federal Register* of these revisions to OMB Directive 15 (as adopted on October 30, 1997) pointedly added that "The categories in this classification are social-political constructs and should not be interpreted as being scientific or anthropological in nature . . . . The standards have been developed to provide a common language for uniformity and comparability in the collection and use of data on race and ethnicity by Federal agencies." Nonetheless, Directive 15's definitions of "racial" and "ethnic" populations are used not only by federal agencies, but also by researchers, schools, hospitals, business and industry, and state and local governments—and are conflated, abridged, and diffused through the mass media, entering thereby into the popular culture and shaping the national self-image.

THE MAKING OF A PAST

The Hispanic Prologue

Despite the seemingly sudden emergence of Hispanics or Latinos as a new, prominent—and official—part of the American mosaic, it is also the case that, with the sole exception of the indigenous inhabitants of the Americas, the country's Spanish roots are much older than those of any other groups. They antedate by a century the creation of an English colony

greatest hitters but not as a Latino player: his mother, May Venzer, was a Mexican American Baptist who married a soldier named Samuel Williams and moved to San Diego, where Ted grew up and May came to be known as "the Angel of Tijuana" for her Salvation Army work there. In his autobiography, Ted Williams (2001) wrote that "if I had had my mother's name, there is no doubt I would have run into problems in those days, [with] the prejudices people had in Southern California."

in North America and have left an indelible if ignored Spanish imprint, especially across the southern rim of the United States, from the Atlantic to the Pacific (Fernández-Shaw, 1972; Fuentes, 1992; Jiménez, 1994; Sánchez, 1991; Weber, 1992). In U.S. popular culture and in official narrative and ritual the American past has been portrayed as the story of the expansion of English America, suppressing if not silencing the Hispanic presence from the nation's collective memory (see Walton, 2001). But past is prologue, and no understanding of the Hispanic peoples in the United States today or of the category under which they are now grouped can ignore the historical and geographic contexts of their incorporation.

The Spanish origins of what is now the United States date to 1513, when Juan Ponce de León first came to La Florida, as he named it. Spanish explorers drew the first maps of the Texas coast and of the northern Atlantic coast through Georgia and the Carolinas (where a colony was established in 1526) and up to the mouths of what would later be named the Hudson, the Connecticut, and the Delaware rivers; in 1570 Spanish Jesuits established a mission in Virginia, decades before Roanoke and Jamestown. By the early 1540s they had sailed up the California coast as well, and other explorers—among them Albar Núñez Cabeza de Vaca and Esteban de Azamor (a black Moor), Hernando de Soto, Coronado—had walked across what are now Texas, New Mexico, Arizona, Oklahoma, Colorado, Tennessee, Alabama, Arkansas, Missouri, and Kansas (ubiquitous "Coronado was here" historic markers can still be found alongside roads in these states). By the time of the American Revolution, Spain had cast a wide net of Hispanic culture and communities stretching from San Diego and Los Angeles to San Francisco on the west coast; throughout the Southwest from Tucson to Santa Fé, El Paso, and San Antonio; along the Mississippi River from St. Louis to New Orleans; and eastward through towns that stretched to Florida's Atlantic coast by way of Mobile, Pensacola, and Tallahassee. Between the two coasts, as the historian David Weber has noted (1992), Spain claimed much of the American South and the entire Southwest—at least *half* of the present U.S. mainland—and Spain governed these areas for well over two centuries, a period longer than the United States has existed as an independent nation. When in 1763 Louisiana (until then French) came under Spanish rule, the Mississippi River divided most of what is now the continental United States into two enormous zones: one, to the east, English; one, to the west, Spanish.[9] In 1783, when Florida was returned to

[9]These events need to be placed in the context of the 18th century race for empire among Spain, Britain, and France. In 1763, as part of the Treaty of Paris that ended the French and Indian War (itself part of the wider Seven Years War in Europe), Britain gained Canada and all lands east of the Mississippi from France and gained Florida from Spain in exchange for

Spain, the entire southern corridor from California to Florida was once again Spanish-ruled—but Spain's hegemony in the Americas would decline soon after.

Thousands of place names, from Sacramento to Cape Cañaveral—including six states—silently testify to these Spanish antecedents, as well as others for whom the Spanish derivation is not so obvious: for instance, Key West derives from Cayo Hueso (literally Bone Key), words that English speakers would mispronounce and misspell (Weber, 1992). Coast to coast, there are regions of the country in which every town and village bears a Spanish name, and in them can be found the first missions, ranches, schools, churches, presidios, theatres, public buildings, and cities in U.S. history (Rumbaut, 1978). Spanish St. Augustine in Florida, founded in 1565, is the oldest city in the United States; San Miguel Church in Santa Fé, New Mexico, has been used for Catholic worship since 1610. The New Mexico missions, one for every pueblo, were flourishing by 1630. San Antonio was founded in 1718, with a mission that would play a key role in Texan and American history more than a century later: El Alamo. San Diego, California, was founded in 1769, with the first in a chain of 21 missions extending to San Francisco, founded in 1776.

In the United States, the collective memory of these silent antecedents remains clouded by remnants of prejudices and stereotypes whose roots go to colonial rivalries in the 16th century between Spanish America and English America. Anti-Spanish propaganda in Protestant Europe and America built into the *leyenda negra* (black legend), now centuries old, whose original intent was to denigrate Catholic Spanish culture throughout the world and to portray Spaniards as a uniquely cruel and depraved race (Jiménez, 1994; Maltby, 1968). That legend was kept alive whenever conflict arose between English- and Spanish-speaking societies in America in the 1800s, especially during the Texas Revolt (1836), the U.S.–Mexican War (1846–1848), and the Spanish American War (1898). Two wartime slogans—"Remember the Alamo!" and "Remember the Maine!"—and the

---

Havana (which the British armada had captured the year before). English Florida did not join its 13 sister colonies during the subsequent American Revolution of 1776; in fact, many English loyalists (Tories) fled to the Florida settlements at the time. When the Revolutionary War ended in 1783, Britain was forced to give up most of its American possessions; the Second Treaty of Paris returned Florida to Spain in return for the Bahamas (which had been captured by Spain after it declared war on England in 1779 during the American Revolution). The Tories who had earlier fled to Florida now moved to the Bahamas to remain under the British crown. In 1819, after years of diplomatic wrangling, Spain signed the Adams-Onis Treaty, ceding Florida to the United States and drawing a definite border between Spanish land and the Louisiana Territory; that treaty was not ratified by the United States and the new republic of Mexico until 1831.

first five words of the oldest song of the U.S. armed forces, the Marine Corps hymn, "From the halls of Montezuma"[10]—may be the most vivid remnants of these transformational wars in American memory. The Mexican War (largely forgotten in the United States but remembered in Mexico as *la invasión norteamericana*) was the first foreign war started by the United States and transformed the nation into a continental power; the treaty that ended it, along with the annexation of Texas that preceded it, expanded the territory of the United States by a million square miles, while severing nearly half of Mexico's. Five decades later, the Spanish American War gave the United States possession of Spain's last remaining colonies in Cuba, Puerto Rico, and the Philippines, transforming it into a global power.

The peoples of the conquered territories were absorbed into the expanding boundaries of the nation as second-class citizens. This was the case above all in the American (formerly the Mexican) Southwest: for a full century after the 1840s, Mexican Americans were subjected to laws, norms, and practices similar to the Jim Crow apartheid system that discriminated against blacks after the Civil War—injustices, most deeply rooted in Texas, that caused Mexicanos in the Southwest to see themselves as foreigners in a foreign land (Deutsch, 1987; Deverell, 2004; Foley, 2004; Montejano, 1987; Shipman, 1992; Weber, 1973, 1982).

The countries of the Caribbean Basin, and among them particularly Mexico, Puerto Rico, and Cuba, have felt most strongly the weight, and the lure, of the U.S. hegemonic presence. They include countries that, since the days of Benjamin Franklin (who already in 1761 suggested Mexico and Cuba as goals of American expansion) and Thomas Jefferson (who spoke Spanish fluently), were viewed as belonging as if by some "laws of political gravitation" (the phrase is John Quincy Adams' in 1823, who also crafted the Monroe Doctrine) to the manifest destiny of the United States, in a Caribbean long viewed as "the American Mediterranean" (the term is Alexander Hamilton's, writing in *The Federalist* in 1787). And they include countries whose ties with the United States are more recent, but who have emerged as major sources of Latin American immigration since the 1980s—notably the Dominican Republic, El Salvador, Guatemala, and Colombia, with other sizable flows from Nicaragua, Honduras, Perú, Ecuador, and elsewhere (Moncada and Olivas, 2003). Not surprisingly, given historical

[10]The reference is to the victory of General Winfield Scott at the battle of Chapultepec and the taking of Mexico City in September 1847. The imposing Castle of Chapultepec, built as a summer palace for Spanish viceroys, was seen by U.S. soldiers as the fabled Halls of the Montezumas, ancient home of Aztec kings (see Johannsen, 1985). (The accepted spelling of the name today is Moctezuma.)

patterns of economic, political, military, and cultural influence established over the decades,[11] it is precisely these countries whose people have most visibly emerged as a significant component of American society.

Origins and Destinies: Mexicans in the United States

Mexicans are by far the largest and the oldest of Hispanic ethnic groups, and they have been incorporated overwhelmingly as manual laborers (see Barrera, 1979; Gutiérrez, 1995). When the Treaty of Guadalupe-Hidalgo ceded the lands of the Southwest to the United States in 1848, there were perhaps 75,000 inhabitants of Mexican and Spanish origin residing in that vast territory—nearly three-fourths of them (Hispanos) in New Mexico, with smaller numbers of Tejanos and Californios (see Griswold del Castillo, 1984; Pitt, 1971). Toward the end of the century, with the rapid expansion of railroads, agriculture, and mining in the Southwest and with the exclusion of Chinese workers in 1882 and later the Japanese, Mexicans became preferred sources of cheap and mobile migrant labor—at about the same time that capitalist development in Mexico under the government of Porfirio Díaz was creating a landless peasantry. By the early 1900s railroad lines—which expedited deliberate labor recruitment by U.S. companies—had linked the interior of Mexico with Texas and other states, and large numbers of Mexican manual laborers called *braceros* were working from the copper and coal mines of Arizona and Colorado to the steel mills and slaughterhouses of Chicago, Detroit, and Pittsburgh (Vargas, 1993).

Not all these *braceros* returned to Mexico, and settler communities began to form and grow (Cardoso, 1980; Gamio, 1930; Sánchez, 1993). It has been estimated that as many as 1 million Mexicans, up to one-tenth of the Mexican population at the time, crossed the border to the United States at some point during the violent decade of the Mexican Revolution of

---

[11]The United States, under the Roosevelt Corollary to the Monroe Doctrine enunciated by Theodore Roosevelt in 1904, intervened frequently in the region, including at least 20 Marine landings in the Caribbean from 1905 to 1965. The United States took Panama in 1903 (then a province of Colombia) and built the canal between 1904 and 1914; the Panama Canal Zone operated thereafter as a U.S. territory until 1979. U.S. Marines occupied the Dominican Republic from 1915 to 1924 and again in 1965. The Marines were in Nicaragua almost continuously from 1912 to 1933; after the end of the Somoza dictatorship in 1979, the U.S. supported the opposition Contras from bases in Honduras in the 1980s. U.S.-backed coups in post–World War II Guatemala (1954) and Chile (1973), support for the governments of El Salvador and Guatemala during the wars of the 1980s, and other interventions—economic and cultural as well as military—have had the unintended consequence of further facilitating migration flows to the United States (see, e.g., Black, 1988; La Feber, 1993; Langley, 2001, 2003; Musicant, 1990; Schoultz, 1998; and Smith, 1999).

1910, while demand for their labor in the United States increased during World War I and the 1920s (all the more with immigration restrictions imposed on Southern and Eastern Europeans in the 1920s). The U.S. census in 1910 counted some 220,000 Mexicans in the country; that number more than doubled by 1920 and had tripled to over 600,000 by 1930. Largely at the urging of American growers, the passage of restrictive national-origins immigration laws in 1921 and 1924 placed no limits on countries in the Western Hemisphere in order to permit the recruitment of Mexican workers when needed—and their deportation when they were not (as happened, among other instances, during the 1930s when about 400,000 were repatriated to Mexico, including many U.S. citizens, and again during the much larger deportations of Operation Wetback in the mid-1950s).

The large increase in the Mexican-origin population in California dates to the World War II period, which saw the establishment of the Bracero Program (1942–1964) of contract labor importation negotiated by the U.S. and Mexican governments. The end of the Bracero Program, but not of a built-in, structural demand for immigrant labor—in conjunction with a sharp reduction in U.S. legal visas for Mexican immigrants and increasing population growth and economic downturns in Mexico—prompted increasing flows of illegal immigration, peaking in 1986 (when the Immigration Reform and Control Act, IRCA, was passed). It then declined briefly but increased and stabilized after 1989 and expanded further still after the mid-1990s. Indeed, the period from 1965 to 1985 has been labeled an "era of undocumented migration" that functioned as "a de facto guest worker program," bringing largely young male laborers from small Mexican towns and cities (Massey, Durand, and Malone, 2002). Nearly 3 million formerly undocumented immigrants were legalized under the amnesty provisions of IRCA, of whom over 2 million were Mexican nationals. By 2000, the undocumented population of the United States was estimated at about 8.5 million (Passel, 2002), of whom about 4.7 million were Mexicans—representing 55 percent of the total undocumented population in the country and about half of the total Mexican-born population.

The millions of Mexican immigrants and their children in the United States today are embedded in often intricate webs of transnational family ties and kinship networks, which can help sustain migration flows by reducing the risks and costs of migration (Massey, Alarcón, Durand, and González, 1987). By the end of the 1980s, national surveys in Mexico found that about *half* of adult Mexicans were related to someone living in the United States, and that one-third of all Mexicans had been to the United States at some point in their lives; later surveys suggest still larger proportions (Massey and Espinoza, 1997). Most of the adult immigrants living in the United States send remittances to their relatives in Mexico—estimated at over $13 billion in 2003 (Inter-American Development Bank, 2004).

Despite the large flows of both legal and unauthorized Mexican immigration in recent decades, however, the 2000 census found that nearly 60 percent of the Mexican-origin population of 22.3 million was U.S.-born; over 9 million were immigrants born in Mexico, about half of whom had come to the United States in the two decades since 1980. And their growing presence was spreading geographically: in 1990, Mexican immigrants were the largest foreign-born population in 18 of the 50 states; in 2000, they were the largest foreign-born population in 30 states. Yet two-thirds of all Mexican-origin persons still resided in California and Texas in 2000. (In both California and Texas, the Social Security Administration reported that the most popular baby boy's name in 1998 was no longer John, Michael, or David, but José—see Garvey and McDonnell, 1999; Pitts, 1999.) Significant numbers of Mexican Americans (over 1 million) were in Chicago—long a major center of Mexican immigration—and in Houston (nearly 1 million), and in Dallas, San Antonio, and Phoenix (over 650,000 in each), but none compared with the Mexican-origin population of greater Los Angeles, which, at more than 5 million in 2000 (the largest concentration of any ethnic minority in any U.S. metropolitan area), is exceeded only by Mexico City itself.

Puerto Ricans and Cubans in the United States

Puerto Rico was occupied by the United States in 1898 and formally acquired as part of the Treaty of Paris, which settled the Spanish-American War. The status of the islanders was left ambiguous until the passage of the Jones Act in 1917, at the time of U.S. entry into World War I, which gave Puerto Ricans U.S. citizenship and made them eligible for the military draft; these provisions essentially remained after 1947 when a new constitution defined commonwealth status for Puerto Rico (the first governor elected by popular vote took office in 1949). This status defines the island's relationship with the United States and distinguishes Puerto Ricans fundamentally from other Latin American peoples. As U.S. citizens by birth, Puerto Ricans travel freely—and frequently—between the island and the mainland without having to pass through the screens of the Immigration and Naturalization Service (now in the Department of Homeland Security) or the Border Patrol, as would foreign-born noncitizens coming to the United States.

Soon after the military occupation U.S. capital began flowing into Puerto Rico—then an island society based on subsistence agriculture and coffee exports—especially into a new and rapidly growing sugar industry, which displaced subsistence peasants into the cities and combined with high population growth to create urban unemployment. Capital-intensive industrialization and urbanization of the island continued and rapidly accelerated after the introduction of Operation Bootstrap in 1948 but failed to solve the urban unemployment and population growth problems, intensifying internal economic pressures for migration to the mainland. Labor recruitment (though it never reached the extent that it did with Mexican workers) began in 1900, when a large group of workers went to sugar cane plantations in Hawaii and later as farmworkers to the mainland. It became widespread among industrial employers only during and after World War II—at the same time that cheap air travel was instituted between San Juan and New York (a one-way ticket cost less than $50)—when mass immigration to New York reached its peak and made Puerto Ricans the first "airborne" migration in U.S. history.

The Puerto Rican population on the mainland grew from about 12,000 in 1920 to 53,000 in 1930, sextupled to 301,000 in 1950, then tripled (in a single decade) to 888,000 in 1960. Net Puerto Rican migration to the mainland during the 1950s (about 470,000) was higher than the immigration totals of any country, including Mexico, during that peak decade. Although net migration subsequently decreased, travel back and forth is incessant, averaging over 3 million people annually since the 1980s (Bonilla and Campos, 1981; Fitzpatrick, 1987; Moore and Pachón, 1985; Rivera-Batiz and Santiago, 1998; Rodríguez, 1991; Rumbaut, 1992; Sánchez Korrol, 1983, 1994). The 2000 census counted a mainland Puerto Rican population of over 3.5 million (almost as many as on the island). The pattern of concentration in New York City, which had accounted for over 80 percent of the total Puerto Rican population in the U.S. mainland in 1950, gradually declined to 62 percent in 1970, under 40 percent in 1990, and about 25 percent in 2000. Despite their relative dispersal in recent years, there are still twice as many Puerto Ricans in New York City (over 850,000) as in the capital of Puerto Rico, San Juan.

If Mexico was the first nation in the Americas to achieve its independence from Spain (in 1821), and Puerto Rico the only one that has never become an independent state, Cuba was the last in Spanish America, becoming formally independent in 1902 after almost four years of U.S. military occupation following the end of the second Cuban War of Independence (1895–1898), during which over 10 percent of the population died, and the Spanish-American War (1898). A notable Cuban presence in the United States goes back to the early 19th century, beginning what became a tradition for Cuban exiles to carry out their political work from bases in New York and Florida. At the same time, Cuba was the target of repeated efforts at annexation by the United States throughout the 19th century, and also a main focus of U.S. trade and capital investment—although it never became a recruiting ground for agricultural workers, as did Mexico and Puerto Rico. U.S. economic penetration of the island increased sharply after the war and the military occupation at the turn of the century, expanding its control over sugar production as well as other sectors of the Cuban economy, including transportation, mining, construction, and public utilities. By 1929 U.S. direct investment in Cuba totaled more than one-fourth of all U.S. investment in Latin America as a whole, more than was invested by U.S. capital in any Latin American country either on a per capita basis or in absolute terms. Moreover, Cuba remained subordinated to the United States after 1902 under the terms of the Platt Amendment, attached by the U.S. Congress to the Cuban Constitution. Not rescinded until 1934, the Platt Amendment formalized the right of the United States to intervene in Cuban internal affairs—and bred deep resentment of U.S. domination in various sectors of the Cuban population (see Pérez, 1990, 1999; Thomas, 1971). Nonetheless, an analyst of U.S.–Cuba relations and of the Americanization of the Cuban scene could write that, at least in the cities, "it is probably fair to say that by 1959, no other country in the world, with the exception of Canada, quite so resembled the United States" (Smith, 1991).

Still, at that time the Cuban population in the United States was just over 70,000. The waves of exiles that began in earnest in 1960, in the context of the Cold War, have continued to the present in several phases, from the daily flights that were suspended after the 1962 missile crisis, to the orderly "freedom flights" from 1965 to 1973, the boat flotillas from Camarioca in 1965 and Mariel in 1980, to the increasingly desperate crossings of *balseros* (rafters) in the 1980s and early 1990s, which became a full-fledged crisis in 1994 (when in less than one month 37,000 Cubans were rescued by the U.S. Coast Guard, most of whom detained for over a year in makeshift camps at the U.S. naval base in Guantánamo). An orderly migration quota was subsequently negotiated by the two governments, bringing almost 25,000 Cubans to the United States annually after the mid-1990s, but the bilateral accord and new high-level migration talks were suspended in late 2003 amid renewed intergovernmental conflict. Despite U.S. government efforts to resettle the exiles away from Miami, many eventually drifted back, adding to the original concentrations there and making the city in effect a majority Cuban community—and arguably the most politically powerful immigrant nationality in the country (García, 1996; Grenier and Pérez, 2003; Portes and Stepick, 1993). Cuban Americans have had consistently the lowest fertility rates among all Hispanic groups, as well as the oldest foreign-born population—it is estimated that more than 200,000 of those who came in the 1960s and early 1970s had died in exile by the year 2000. Still, the Cuban American population in the United States in 2000, at over 1.3 million, represented about 12 percent of the total on the island; nearly 50 percent of them are concentrated in metropolitan Miami, known as "Havana U.S.A." Among Cuban cities, only the real Havana is larger.

THE MAKING OF A PORTRAIT

Ethnic Identity and National Origin

I shift focus now from the past to the present and to a sketch of some key differences that, beyond the distinct histories of particular groups, most clearly distinguish the Hispanic population from non-Hispanics—national origin and ethnic identity, immigration and generation, racial classification, language, citizenship, and social status—and from each other. I also consider how the confluence of these factors shapes their modes of incorporation in American society. For this purpose, I rely principally on an analysis of the 5 percent PUMS of the 2000 U.S. census, supplementing the analysis from other data sources.

Despite growing diversification and accelerating immigration from a wider range of Latin American countries over the past two decades (see Table 2-1), persons of Mexican, Puerto Rican, and Cuban origin still comprised 77.1 percent of the 35.2 million Hispanics counted by the 2000 census.[12] Those of Mexican origin alone numbered 22.3 million—nearly two-thirds (63.3 percent) of the U.S. total (see Table 2-2). Thus, it should be underscored that aggregate statistics for the total Hispanic population reflect the predominant weight of the characteristics of the Mexican-origin population—a fact that shapes overall perceptions of the Hispanic population as a whole while obscuring its internal diversity.

Much of the remainder of this population is accounted for by six nationalities of relatively recent immigrant origin: Dominicans, Salvadorans, and Guatemalans make up another 7.2 percent of the Hispanic total, and Colombians, Peruvians, and Ecuadorians combine for nearly 4 percent more. Persons who trace their ethnic identities to the 10 other Spanish-speaking source countries of Central and South America, plus Spain, together comprised only 4 percent of the Hispanic total. Thus, 9 ethnic groups accounted for 9 of 10 (88 percent) Hispanics in the United States mainland. Their size and evolution reflect both the varied history of their incorporation in the United States and the relative geographical proximity of their source countries to the United States: Mexico, El Salvador, and Guatemala from Meso-America; Puerto Rico, Cuba, and the Dominican Republic from the Caribbean; Colombia, Perú, and Ecuador from South America. Only 7.9 percent of the 35.2 million Hispanics self-reported as "other Spanish, Hispanic or Latino" in the 2000 census, without indicating a particular

---

[12]If the Puerto Ricans on the island were added to the calculation, those three groups would comprise 80 percent of the total; the focus of this analysis, however, is on Hispanic and non-Hispanic populations on the U.S. mainland.

TABLE 2-2 Foreign-Born and Native-Born Generations of Hispanics and Non-Hispanics in the United States, 2000

Ethnic Identity (Self-Reported)		Generation		
		Foreign-Born First Generation	U.S.-Born Second+ Generations	Total Number
Not Hispanic	N	18,706,149	227,511,277	246,217,426
	%	7.6	92.4	100.0
Hispanic:	N	15,786,304	19,418,176	35,204,480
	%	44.8	55.2	100.0
Mexican	%	42.0	58.0	22,293,812
Puerto Rican[a]	%	39.7	60.3	3,537,351
Cuban	%	67.3	32.7	1,311,994
Dominican	%	68.5	31.5	994,313
Salvadoran, Guatemalan	%	77.5	22.5	1,532,512
Central American, other	%	76.5	23.5	903,574
Colombian	%	76.6	23.4	648,731
Peruvian, Ecuadorian	%	77.2	22.8	697,798
South American, other	%	78.3	21.7	494,186
Other Spanish, Hispanic, Latino[b]	%	5.7	94.3	2,790,209
Total	N	34,492,453	246,929,453	281,421,906
	%	12.3	87.7	100.0

[a]Puerto Ricans born in Puerto Rico are classified as "first generation"; those born in the U.S. mainland are classified as "second+ generations."

[b]Persons leaving "other" blank but specifying their country of birth or ancestry in other census questions were assigned to the appropriate national-origin group. This occurred in about 2 million cases.

SOURCE: 2000 U.S. Census, 5% Public Use Microdata Samples (PUMS).

national origin or ancestry.[13] Accordingly, for ease of presentation, the data tables that follow focus on the groups who account for the preponderant number of Hispanic Americans.

Hispanics as a whole are much more likely than non-Hispanics to consist of relatively recent newcomers to the United States. As noted, immigration and generation are central issues for understanding the Hispanic population of the United States: 45 percent of Hispanics are foreign-born, compared with only 7.6 percent of non-Hispanics; while 55 percent of Hispanics are U.S.-born, compared with 92.4 percent of non-Hispanics. Those figures refer to countries of birth, quite aside from citizenship status (e.g., Puerto Ricans born on the island are included under the foreign-born first generation, although they have birthright citizenship). Only the "other Spanish, Hispanic, Latino" are overwhelmingly a native-born population (94.3 percent)—some with ancestries that can be traced back many generations. Aside from that special case, the Mexicans and Puerto Ricans—the two populations of longest residence in the United States—are the only ethnic groups that consist mainly of natives (58 percent of the Mexicans and 60 percent of the Puerto Ricans were born on the U.S. mainland). All others are primarily first-generation immigrant populations—ranging from two-thirds of the Cubans and Dominicans to more than three-fourths of all the other groups.

Because the decennial census, which is the primary data source used in this chapter, no longer asks about parental nativity, it is not possible to break down the U.S.-born generations into those with foreign parentage (the second generation) and those with native parentage (that is, native-born of native parentage, the third+ generations). However, as noted, a decade ago the CPS restored the parental nativity question and thus makes possible multiple-generation comparisons (for that reason it is the data set of choice in several of the chapters that follow). Here, one finding from the CPS may be mentioned in passing because of its relevance to this discussion: fully 75 percent of the Hispanic population of the United States is of foreign parentage (first or second generation), compared with only 15 percent of the non-Hispanic population: a 5-to-1 ratio. About 95 percent of the Cubans, Central Americans, and South Americans are first or second genera-

---

[13]The 2000 census reported about 5 million persons who checked "other Spanish, Hispanic or Latino" but left the space blank without writing in a particular ethnicity or national origin. However, about 2 million of these in fact reported a specific Spanish-speaking Latin American country of birth or a Hispanic ancestry in other questions in the census form, permitting their assignment to one of the main national-origin Hispanic groups listed in the tables in this chapter. The figure of 2.8 million "other Spanish, Hispanic, or Latino" persons in Table 2-2 reflects this adjustment.

tion, as are 78 percent of the Puerto Ricans and 70 percent of the Mexicans, who have been in the United States longest. Among all Hispanics, those of Mexican origin account for 77 percent of the third+ generations, 68 percent of the second generation, and 58 percent of the first generation—suggesting the dominance of the Mexican population a few generations ago and its recent proportional decline as immigration from Central and South America and the Dominican Republic has accelerated sharply, especially over the past two decades.

Since 1970, census data on Hispanics have been based on subjective self-reports by respondents who check the "ethnic" question on Spanish origin (or "Hispanic or Latino" in the 2000 census)—and, if so, specify a particular Hispanic group. How closely do these subjective self-reports match objective markers, such as country of birth? At least among the foreign-born, who identifies as "Hispanic or Latino"?[14] Table 2-3 addresses that question, cross-tabulating that pan-ethnic self-identification (Hispanic or not) by principal countries of birth (distinguishing between Spanish-speaking countries—19 in Latin America, including the commonwealth of Puerto Rico, plus Spain—versus all other countries in the world). Of the 35.2 million self-identified Hispanics, 19.4 million (55 percent) were born in the United States. Among all foreign-born persons, 16 million were born in the 20 Spanish-speaking countries, and of them over 97 percent self-reported as "Hispanic or Latino." Another 18.4 million persons were born elsewhere in the world, and 99 percent of them indicated they were *not* "Hispanic or Latino."

The overwhelming majority (95 to 99 percent) of those born in each of the major Spanish-speaking countries of Latin America self-reported as "Hispanic or Latino" in 2000.[15] Among those born in non-Spanish-speaking countries, only minuscule proportions identified as Hispanic—for example, only 1 percent of those born in the Philippines, and—from

[14]Whether a particular ethno-national self-identification survives into the second or third-and-beyond generations, or shifts into a "Hispanic" or "Latino" pan-ethnicity, or fades altogether into non-Hispanic identities as a result of mixed parentage, ethnic intermarriage, racialization, or assimilation remain open empirical questions. The issue of intergenerational ethnic (and pan-ethnic) identity shifts is raised in other chapters of this volume (see especially Chapter 6 on Hispanic families).

[15]A third of those born in Spain and a third of those born in Panamá did not identify as "Hispanic or Latino"—nor did 19 percent of the Argentineans, 14 percent of the Venezuelans, and 9 percent of the Chileans—but those were the main exceptions. Among these groups—from Spain, Panamá, Argentina, Venezuela, and Chile—those not self-identifying as Hispanic were more likely to report their primary ancestry as "American," "African American," or a wide range of European origins, and to report their "race" as white or black (whereas those reporting as "Hispanic" from those countries were far more likely to indicate "other race" or "two or more races").

TABLE 2-3 Hispanic Ethnic Identity by Country of Birth, 2000

Country of Birth		Ethnic Identity: Hispanic	Ethnic Identity: Not Hispanic
Born in the United States:	N	19,418,176	227,511,262
	%	7.9	92.1
Foreign-born in:			
Spanish-speaking country	N	15,599,619	460,561
	%	97.1	2.9
Mexico	%	98.9	1.1
Puerto Rico[a]	%	95.3	4.7
Cuba	%	98.0	2.0
Dominican Republic	%	98.0	2.0
El Salvador, Guatemala	%	97.2	2.8
Central America, other	%	89.7	10.3
Colombia	%	97.0	3.0
Perú, Ecuador	%	96.0	4.0
South America, other	%	84.0	16.0
Spain	%	67.4	32.6
Born elsewhere in the world:	N	186,685	18,245,603
	%	1.0	99.0
Total	N	35,204,480	246,217,426
	%	12.5	87.5

[a]Figures refer to persons born in Puerto Rico.

SOURCE: 2000 U.S. Census, 5% PUMS.

non-Spanish "Latin" America—only 1.4 percent of those born in Haiti (on the island of Hispaniola), 1.8 percent of those born in Trinidad and Tobago, 1.8 percent of those born in Guyana, and 7.7 percent of those born in Brazil. In the first (immigrant) generation, clearly, there is a very strong correspondence between self-reported Hispanic ethnicity and national origin (being born in a Spanish-speaking country).

Hispanic Identity and "Race"

Much has been made in the media and even in academic discourse about "the browning of America," a misnomer based on popular stereotypes of phenotypes presumed to characterize peoples of Latin American origin. Does the Hispanic population differ significantly from non-Hispanics by "race," as it does by place and national origin? The American system of racial classification, employed variously since the first census of 1790, has been the sine qua non of externally imposed, state-sanctioned measures of group difference, distinguishing principally the majority white population from black and American Indian minority groups, and later from Asian-origin populations (see Snipp, 2003). "One drop rules" of hypodescent are but one illustration of the manner in which it is a sociohistorically constructed system, evolving fixed categories that concretize social hierarchies in supposed racial phenotypes. Yet as noted earlier, "Hispanics" were incorporated in official statistics as an "ethnic" category, and explicitly conceived as being "of any race."

Table 2-4 compares Hispanics and non-Hispanics, as well as the largest Hispanic ethnic groups, by the main racial categories employed in the 2000 census. Of the 246.2 million non-Hispanics counted by the census, 97 percent reported their race as either white (79 percent), black (13.7 percent), or Asian (4.1 percent). In sharp contrast, among the 35.2 million Hispanics, only half—49.9 percent—reported their race as either white (47.8 percent), black (1.8 percent), or Asian (0.3 percent). In both populations, only 1 percent reported their race as American Indian. However, there was a huge difference in the proportion of these two populations who indicated "other race": while scarcely any non-Hispanics (a mere 0.2 percent) reported being of some "other" race, among the Latin Americans that figure was 42.6 percent, a total of about 15 million persons—a reflection of more than four centuries of *mestizaje* (racial mixing) and miscegenation in Latin America and the Caribbean, as well as differing conceptions of "race." In addition, Hispanics were three times more likely to report an admixture of "two or more races"—6.4 percent of Hispanics versus only 2 percent of non-Hispanics—although among Hispanics who listed "two or more races" the overwhelming majority (85 percent) specified "white" plus another race.

Examining these results for the main Hispanic ethnic groups, the proportions who identified racially as white ranged from a low of 22 percent among Dominicans to a high of 84 percent among Cubans; the proportions who identified as black ranged from 1 percent or less among Mexicans, Salvadorans, Guatemalans, Colombians, Peruvians, and Ecuadorans, to a high of 8.2 percent among Dominicans, while the "other Spanish, Hispanic or Latino" were the most likely to identify as multiracial (10.7 percent). More than half of the Dominicans (59 percent) and of the Salvadorans and Guatemalans (55 percent) reported "another race," as did 46 percent of the Mexicans, 42 percent of the Peruvians and Ecuadorans, 38 percent of the Puerto Ricans, 28 percent of the Colombians, and less than 8 percent of the Cubans. The meaning of "race," however, is problematic for a number of reasons.

For example, one recent study found that, in addition to significant

TABLE 2-4 Hispanic Ethnic Identity by Race, 2000 Census

Ethnic Identity		Race (Self-Reported) White	Black	Asian	American Indian[a]	Other Race	Two or More Races	Total Number
Not Hispanic	N	194,527,123	33,706,554	10,088,521	2,437,149	443,304	5,014,775	246,217,426
	%	79.0	13.7	4.1	1.0	0.2	2.0	100.0
Hispanic:	N	16,832,198	651,282	102,833	390,465	14,982,091	2,245,611	35,204,480
	%	47.8	1.8	0.3	1.1	42.6	6.4	100.0
Mexican	%	46.8	0.7	0.2	1.2	45.8	5.2	22,293,812
Puerto Rican	%	46.9	5.8	0.4	0.7	38.1	8.1	3,537,351
Cuban	%	84.4	3.6	0.2	0.2	7.6	4.1	1,311,994
Dominican	%	22.4	8.2	0.2	0.9	58.8	9.4	994,313
Salvadoran, Guatemalan	%	35.8	0.6	0.1	1.1	55.2	7.2	1,532,512
Central American, other	%	44.7	7.1	0.2	0.9	37.7	9.5	903,574
Colombian	%	62.0	1.1	0.2	0.4	28.2	8.2	648,731
Peruvian, Ecuadorian	%	47.9	0.6	0.4	0.8	41.7	8.5	697,798
South American, other	%	70.0	0.8	0.3	0.4	20.6	8.0	494,186
Other Spanish, Hispanic, Latino	%	49.2	2.5	1.0	1.9	34.7	10.7	2,790,209
Total	N	211,359,321	34,357,836	10,191,354	2,827,614	15,425,395	7,260,386	281,421,906
	%	75.1	12.2	3.6	1.0	5.5	2.6	100.0

[a]Includes American Indian, Alaskan, and Hawaiian natives and other indigenous Pacific Islanders.

SOURCE: 2000 U.S. Census, 5% PUMS.

change in their ethnic self-identities over time and generation in the United States (as measured by open-ended questions), the offspring of Latin American immigrants were by far the most likely to define their racial identities in sharp contrast to their own parents (Portes and Rumbaut, 2001). During the 1990s in South Florida and Southern California, the Children of Immigrants Longitudinal Study (CILS) surveyed a sample of more than 5,200 1.5- and second-generation youths, representing 77 different nationalities, including all of the main Spanish-speaking countries of Latin America. Their immigrant parents were also interviewed separately. In one survey (conducted when the youths were 17 to 18 years old), the respondents were asked to answer a semistructured question about their "race" and were given the option to check one of five categories: "white," "black," "Asian," "multiracial," or "other;" if the latter was checked, they had to specify what that "other race" was. The results are presented in Table 2-5. Among the Latin American–origin youths, less than a fourth of the total sample checked the conventional categories of white, black, or Asian; 12 percent reported being multiracial; and over 65 percent checked "other." When those "other" self-reports were coded, it turned out that two-fifths of the sample (41 percent) wrote down "Hispanic" or "Latino" as their "race," and another fifth (19.6 percent) gave their nationality as their "race." The explicit racialization of the "Hispanic-Latino" category, as well as the substantial proportion of youths who conceived of their nationality of origin as a fixed racial category, are noteworthy both for their potential long-term implications in hardening minority group boundaries and for their illustration of the arbitrariness of racial constructions—indeed, of the ease with which an "ethnic" category developed for administrative purposes becomes externalized, diffused, objectified, and finally internalized as a putative biological marker of social difference.

The latter point is made particularly salient by directly comparing the youths' notions of their "race" with that reported by their own parents. The closest match in racial self-perceptions between parents and children were observed among the Haitians, Jamaicans, and other West Indians (most of whom self-reported as black), among the Europeans and Canadians (most of whom labeled themselves white), and among most of the Asian-origin groups (except for the Filipinos). The widest mismatches by far occurred among all of the Latin American–origin groups without exception: overall, about three-fifths of Latin parents defined themselves as white, compared with only one-fifth of their own children. More specifically, 93 percent of Cuban parents identified as white, compared with only 41 percent of their children; 85 percent of Colombian parents defined themselves as white, but only 24 percent of their children did so—proportions that were similar for other South Americans; two-thirds of the Salvadoran, Guatemalan, and Nicaraguan parents saw themselves as white, but only one-fifth of their children agreed; and about a third of the Dominican parents reported as white, more than twice the proportion of their children who did so. The children, instead, largely adopted "Hispanic" or "Latino" as a racial label (41 percent—the largest single response), whereas scarcely any of their parents did so (6.4 percent), or they gave their nationality as their race (19.6 percent of the children versus 6.3 percent of their parents). Indeed, well over half of the Dominican, Salvadoran, Guatemalan, Nicaraguan, Colombian, Peruvian, and Ecuadoran youth reported their race as "Hispanic" or "Latino." Among the Mexicans, whose pattern differed from all of the others, the children preponderantly racialized the national label, whereas Mexican parents were more likely to use "other" (*mestizo*) and "multiracial" as descriptors. These results point to the force of the acculturation process and its impact on children's self-identities. More fully exposed than their parents to American culture and its racial notions, and being incessantly categorized and treated as Hispanic or Latino, the children of immigrants learn to see themselves more and more in these terms—as members of a racial minority—and even to racialize their national origins. If these intergenerational differences between Latin immigrants and their U.S.-raised children can be projected to the third generation, the process of racialization may become more entrenched still.

In a related survey of more than 400 Dominican immigrants in New York City and Providence, Rhode Island, the adult respondents were asked a series of three questions about their racial self-identification (Itzigsohn, 2004). First, they were asked, in an open-ended format, how they defined themselves racially. Next they were given a close-ended question, asking if they were white, black, or other (and if other, to specify). Finally they were asked how they thought that "mainstream Americans" classified them racially. The results are summarized in Table 2-6. In response to the first open-ended question, 28 percent gave "Hispanic" as their "race," another 4 percent said "Latino," and still others offered a variety of mixed "Hispanic" or "Latino" answers; 13 percent said "Indio," and another 13 percent gave their Dominican nationality as their race. Only 6.6 percent chose "black," and 3.8 percent "white."

The rest of their responses showed the extraordinary range of racial categories and labels common in the Spanish Caribbean—as well as the very significant responses obtained depending on the question asked, even though all three were ostensibly getting at the same thing: the respondent's racial identity. When asked to choose from the closed-ended format of the second question, the largest response remained "Hispanic" (written in by 21 percent of the sample, in addition to 3 percent who chose "Latino"), although the categories "black" and "white" more than doubled to 16.8 and 11.6 percent, respectively. And when asked how they thought that others classified them racially, the category "black" dramatically increased

TABLE 2-5 Self-Reported Race of Children of Immigrants and Their Parents, by National Origin Groups, 1995–1996

National Origin	Respondent (Parent/Child)	White (%)	Black (%)
Latin America	Parent	58.1	1.5
	Child	21.9	0.8
Mexico	Parent	5.7	0.0
	Child	1.5	0.3
Cuba	Parent	93.1	1.1
	Child	41.2	0.8
Dominican Republic	Parent	30.6	11.1
	Child	13.9	2.8
El Salvador, Guatemala	Parent	66.7	4.2
	Child	20.8	0.0
Nicaragua	Parent	67.7	0.5
	Child	19.4	0.0
Other Central America	Parent	48.0	24.0
	Child	8.0	8.0
Colombia	Parent	84.6	1.1
	Child	24.2	1.1
Perú, Ecuador	Parent	61.8	0.0
	Child	32.4	0.0
Other South America	Parent	87.8	0.0
	Child	28.6	2.0
Afro-Caribbean	Parent	5.0	73.8
(Haiti, Jamaica, West Indies)	Child	2.0	70.3
Asia:	Parent	0.4	0.3
	Child	0.6	0.0
Europe, others	Parent	75.0	6.3
	Child	68.8	3.1

[a]Figures are row percentages. Interviews with immigrant parents and their teenage children were done separately, using the same question on racial identity. White, black, Asian, and multiracial were fixed responses; all others were open-ended entries.

SOURCE: CILS.

to 37 percent—reflecting the reverse way in which the "one drop rule" (whereby anyone with African ancestry is considered black) functions in the United States versus the Dominican Republic—while "white" decreased to 6.4 percent. "Hispanic" was still given by almost a third of the sample (30.4 percent) as the "racial" category that they perceived others used to classify them. Indeed, "Hispanic" was the label most consistently given by

Self-Reported Race[a]				
Asian (%)	Multiracial (%)	Hispanic, Latino (%)	Nationality (%)	Other (%)
1.1	14.7	6.4	8.3	9.8
0.0	12.1	41.0	19.6	4.6
2.1	21.6	15.9	26.1	28.5
0.0	12.0	25.5	56.2	4.5
0.3	2.5	1.1	0.5	1.4
0.0	11.5	36.0	5.5	4.9
0.0	44.4	0.0	5.6	8.3
0.0	13.9	55.6	8.3	5.6
4.2	16.7	8.3	0.0	0.0
0.0	12.5	58.3	4.2	4.2
1.6	22.0	5.4	0.5	2.2
0.0	9.7	61.8	2.7	6.5
4.0	20.0	0.0	4.0	0.0
0.0	40.0	44.0	0.0	0.0
0.0	9.9	2.2	0.0	2.2
0.0	9.9	58.2	1.1	5.5
0.0	26.5	2.9	2.9	5.9
0.0	11.8	55.9	0.0	0.0
0.0	6.1	2.0	2.0	2.0
0.0	14.3	40.8	14.3	0.0
3.5	5.0	0.0	6.4	6.4
4.5	12.4	0.0	5.9	5.0
69.3	4.4	0.0	23.3	2.2
77.5	7.7	0.0	13.0	1.2
6.3	6.3	3.1	0.0	3.1
6.3	9.4	9.4	0.0	3.1

the respondents to characterize their own *racial* identity, whether asserted by themselves or imposed upon them by others.[16]

[16]Similar results have been reported in a study of 1.5- and second-generation Dominican adolescents in Providence, Rhode Island (Bailey, 2001). For a relevant study of racial self-identification among Puerto Ricans on both the island and the mainland, see Landale and Oropesa (2002).

TABLE 2-6 Dominican Immigrants' Answers to Three Racial Self-identification Questions (Survey of Dominican Immigrants in New York City and Providence, N=418)

	Questions		
Responses	How Do You Define Yourself Racially? (Open-ended) (%)	Are You: White, Black, or Other? (If Other, specify) (Close-ended) (%)	How Do You Think Most Americans Classify You Racially? (%)
Black	6.6	16.8	36.9
White	3.8	11.6	6.4
Hispano/a (Hispanic)	27.5	21.1	30.4
Latino/a	4.1	2.8	3.2
Indio/a	13.1	18.8	4.0
Dominicano/a	12.8	2.0	0.2
Mestizo/a	4.7	8.0	1.0
Trigueño/a	4.1	4.5	2.0
Moreno/a	1.9	2.0	2.2
Mulato/a	0.3	1.5	0.0
Indio Hispano/a	4.1	1.0	0.2
Black Hispano/a	0.6	1.0	2.0
White Hispano/a	0.6	0.3	0.5
Mixed Hispano/a	0.6	1.3	0.2
Latino-Americano/a	0.6	0.5	0.0
Latino-Hispano/a	0.3	0.5	0.5
Java-India claro/a	0.3	1.3	0.2
Amarillo/a (yellow)	0.3	1.0	0.2
Oscuro, prieto, de color	0.3	0.8	1.0
American	0.6	0.0	0.5
Puerto Rican	0.0	0.0	0.2
Human race, other	6.9	1.5	0.7
Does not know	5.0	1.3	6.9

SOURCE: Adapted from Itzigsohn (2004).

Immigration and Citizenship

These data on national origin, ethnic identity, and racial categorization add to the earlier sketch of historical patterns of migration and settlement to show how the Hispanic population as a collectivity differs in distinctive ways from non-Hispanics generally. Citizenship patterns, reflective of the history, type, size, and recency of Latin American immigration to the United States, constitute another significant set of distinguishing characteristics. As depicted in Table 2-7, virtually all Puerto Ricans are U.S. citizens by birthright, compared with 58 percent of the Mexicans, a third of the Cubans and

TABLE 2-7 Citizenship Status of Hispanics and Non-Hispanics in the United States, 2000

Ethnic Identity		U.S. Citizenship: Citizen by Birthright[a]	U.S. Citizenship: Naturalized Citizen	U.S. Citizenship: Not a Citizen
Not Hispanic	N	229,216,195	8,616,047	8,385,184
	%	93.1	3.5	3.4
Hispanic:	N	21,072,230	3,917,885	10,214,365
	%	59.9	11.1	29.0
Mexican	%	58.9	9.2	31.9
Puerto Rican	%	98.7	0.6	0.8
Cuban	%	33.8	40.0	26.2
Dominican	%	32.9	24.5	42.6
Salvadoran, Guatemalan	%	23.2	18.7	58.1
Central American, other	%	25.8	23.9	50.3
Colombian	%	24.7	30.2	45.0
Peruvian, Ecuadorian	%	24.1	26.6	49.3
South American, other	%	23.8	28.1	48.0
Other Spanish, Hispanic, Latino	%	94.9	2.1	3.0
Total	N	250,288,425	12,533,932	18,599,549
	%	88.9	4.5	6.6

[a]Includes persons born in Puerto Rico and other U.S. territories and those born abroad with at least one parent who was a U.S. citizen.

SOURCE: 2000 U.S. Census, 5% PUMS.

Dominicans, and less than a fourth of all the rest. However, the likelihood of becoming a naturalized citizen—which generally requires living in the United States for a minimum of five years after gaining legal permanent residency (a "green card")—varies widely. In addition to the 33 percent of Cuban Americans who were born in the United States, another 40 percent have naturalized U.S. citizenship—by far the largest proportion among Hispanics—in part reflecting the large numbers who came as exiles to the United States after 1959 and the legal status accorded to them subsequently (at least until the chaotic Mariel boatlift of 125,000 in 1980, when the U.S. government created a new designation of "entrant, status pending"); most of the 26 percent of Cubans who are not U.S. citizens came to the United States in or after 1980. The Mexicans, Salvadorans, and Guatemalans have the lowest proportions of those who have become naturalized citizens—reflecting in part the undocumented status of many immigrants among these three groups (see Passel, 2002) and in part the recency of their arrival. The very high proportion of Hispanics who have not yet become U.S.

citizens—almost three out of five Salvadorans and Guatemalans, half of the Peruvians and Ecuadorans, more than two out of five Dominicans and Colombians, and a third of the Mexicans—have important political implications, suggesting the extent to which these populations are at present disenfranchised and limited in the extent to which they can participate in the electoral system.

Hispanics as a whole are not only much younger in their age profile as well as poorer and less educated than non-Hispanics (as elaborated in several of the chapters that follow), but also much more likely than non-Hispanics to consist of relatively recent newcomers to the United States—which in turns affects their eligibility and propensity for naturalization. Table 2-8 shows the timing of their immigration to the United States by decade of arrival. Not only are immigrants a much greater share of the total Hispanic population, as shown earlier, but they have also arrived more recently in greater numbers. Hispanic immigrants were disproportionately more likely to have come in the 1980s and 1990s—indeed, nearly half of the 15.8 million foreign-born Hispanics have arrived only since 1990—while non-Hispanic immigrants (especially those from Europe and Canada) were slightly more likely to have arrived in the 1960s and 1970s and much more likely to have come in the pre-1960 period. The main exceptions in this regard are the Puerto Ricans, who were much more likely than any other group, Hispanic or not, to have arrived during the 1950s, and the Cubans, who were much more likely than any other group, Hispanic or not, to have arrived during the 1960s. These patterns of migration and length of residence in the United States, in turn, help shape a central aspect of acculturation processes—language—to which we now turn. English proficiency has always been a key to socioeconomic mobility for immigrants, as well as to their full participation in their adoptive society.

Language and Acculturation

Unlike the mass migrations from Southern and Eastern Europe during the era from the 1880s to the 1920s, and unlike those from Asia since the 1965 amendments to U.S. immigration law reopened the doors to Eastern Hemisphere immigrants who had been effectively barred since the passage of national quota laws in the 1920s—the vast majority of whom spoke different languages—immigrants from the Spanish-speaking countries of Latin America, who now comprise nearly half of all immigration to the United States, speak a common language: Spanish. This fact—not place, not race, not religion, not citizenship—is the single most distinctive difference between Hispanics and non-Hispanics in the United States. It raises significant questions about their modes of acculturation and socioeconomic incorporation, and—in conjunction with their patterns of geographical con-

TABLE 2-8 Decade of Arrival of Foreign-Born Hispanics and Non-Hispanics in the United States, 2000

		Decade of U.S. Arrival				
Ethnic Identity		Pre-1960	1960s	1970s	1980s	1990s
Not Hispanic	N	2,163,245	1,818,758	2,963,728	4,678,592	7,230,753
	%	11.5	9.6	15.7	24.8	38.3
Hispanic:	N	702,943	1,265,481	2,314,159	4,482,200	7,036,411
	%	4.4	8.0	14.6	28.4	44.5
Mexican	%	3.0	5.0	15.3	27.9	48.7
Puerto Rican[a]	%	20.0	15.3	14.2	21.7	28.8
Cuban	%	7.0	31.9	14.4	19.7	27.0
Dominican	%	1.5	8.7	14.6	32.3	42.8
Salvadoran, Guatemalan	%	0.7	2.6	11.4	40.9	44.4
Central American, other	%	2.8	6.5	12.0	36.9	41.8
Colombian	%	1.9	10.2	14.3	28.3	45.4
Peruvian, Ecuadorian	%	1.8	8.5	13.5	29.0	47.2
South American, other	%	2.9	10.1	15.4	24.8	46.9
Other Spanish, Hispanic, Latino	%	7.4	14.3	17.5	24.0	36.8
Total	N	2,866,188	3,084,239	5,277,887	9,160,792	14,267,164
	%	8.3	8.9	15.2	26.4	41.2

[a]Puerto Ricans born in the island of Puerto Rico, by decade of arrival on the U.S. mainland.

SOURCE: 2000 U.S. Census, 5% PUMS.

centration—about the development of Hispanic media and marketing and Latino political mobilization. Altogether, more than 28 million persons older than age 5 in the United States in 2000 reported speaking Spanish at home. That figure is about 10 million more than the total number of persons who spoke all other languages combined. The next largest language communities in the United States were speakers of French and Chinese (2 million each), German and Filipino/Tagalog (less than 1.5 million speakers each), and Italian and Vietnamese (about 1 million speakers each).

Tables 2-9 to 2-12 present a linguistic profile of these populations relative to non-Hispanics and to each other, comparing the foreign-born first generation and the U.S.-born second+ generations.[17] Among the foreign-born, as Table 2-9 shows, a third of non-Hispanics age 5 and older speak English only (including those from English-speaking countries, from Australia and Canada to Jamaica and Britain itself), while two-thirds speak some other language at home; 93 percent of Hispanic immigrants speak Spanish at home, while only 6.3 percent speak English only. Among the U.S.-born, the contrast remains very sharp: 95.5 percent of non-Hispanics speak English only, compared with 36 percent of Hispanics; 63.5 percent of Hispanic natives still speak Spanish at home, especially Dominicans, Salvadoran, and Guatemalans.

All persons age 5 and older who reported speaking a language other than English at home were asked how well they spoke English ("very well," "well," "not well," or "at all"). The results are presented in Table 2-10, broken down by nativity (foreign-born versus U.S.-born). Among the foreign-born, only 30 percent of Hispanics speak English "very well" (compared with 50 percent of non-Hispanics), while 46 percent speak English "not well" (compared with only 21 percent of non-Hispanics). However, that pattern of linguistic disadvantage in English proficiency is erased by the U.S.-born second+ generations: now three-fourths of Hispanics and non-Hispanics alike report speaking English "very well," while the proportion who speak it "not well" is in single digits for both populations. Among both the first and second+ generations, Puerto Ricans emerge as the most English-proficient Hispanic group (English is an official language in Puerto Rico).

The evidence of linguistic assimilation between the foreign-born and the native-born is clear cut, but it leaves open the question of the degree of Spanish retention versus English acquisition among foreign-born Hispanics—a subject of considerable controversy in public commentary about a

[17]The CPS does not collect data on language, and therefore the 2000 census data presented here can examine differences only between the foreign-born and the U.S.-born; they cannot tease out the acculturative shifts in English language use and proficiency between the second and third+ generations.

TABLE 2-9 Language Spoken at Home of Foreign-Born and U.S.-Born Hispanics and Non-Hispanics, 2000 (Persons 5 Years and Older)

Ethnic Identity		First Generation (Foreign-Born) English Only	Spanish	All Other Languages	Second+ Generations (U.S.-Born) English Only	Spanish	All Other Languages
Not Hispanic	N	5,780,867	355,778	12,313,265	202,899,620	3,110,915	6,380,528
	%	31.3	1.9	66.7	95.5	1.5	3.0
Hispanic:	N	984,087	14,422,751	105,506	5,787,871	10,167,640	66,913
	%	6.3	93.0	0.7	36.1	63.5	0.4
Mexican	%	6.1	93.6	0.3	34.5	65.2	0.2
Puerto Rican[a]	%	8.4	91.2	0.5	37.1	62.4	0.5
Cuban	%	6.2	93.4	0.4	32.9	66.4	0.6
Dominican	%	5.7	94.0	0.3	11.7	88.0	0.4
Salvadoran, Guatemalan	%	4.9	94.4	0.6	14.2	85.2	0.6
Central American, other	%	6.8	92.6	0.6	32.7	66.8	0.5
Colombian	%	6.1	93.4	0.5	22.2	76.8	0.9
Peruvian, Ecuadorian	%	5.1	94.2	0.7	24.3	74.9	0.8
South American, other	%	7.9	89.9	2.2	35.1	63.4	1.5
Other Spanish, Hispanic, Latino	%	18.8	55.9	25.2	49.9	49.1	1.0
Total	N	6,764,954	14,778,529	12,418,771	208,687,491	13,278,555	6,447,441
	%	19.9	43.5	36.6	91.4	5.8	2.8

[a]For Puerto Ricans, "foreign-born" includes those born on the island of Puerto Rico, and "U.S.-born" refers to those born on the mainland.

SOURCE: 2000 U.S. Census, 5% PUMS.

TABLE 2-10 English Proficiency of Foreign-Born and U.S.-Born Hispanics and Non-Hispanics Who Speak a Language Other Than English at Home (Persons 5 Years and Older)

		First Generation (Foreign-Born)			Second+ Generations (U.S.-Born)		
Ethnic Identity		Very Well	Well	Not Well	Very Well	Well	Not Well
Not Hispanic	N	6,422,750	3,618,000	2,640,980	7,248,659	1,368,422	879,628
	%	50.6	28.5	20.8	76.3	14.4	9.3
Hispanic:	N	4,359,787	3,492,497	6,676,279	7,580,619	1,851,963	802,037
	%	30.0	24.0	46.0	74.1	18.1	7.8
Mexican	%	24.5	22.9	52.5	71.8	19.5	8.7
Puerto Rican	%	50.5	26.1	23.4	80.3	14.2	5.5
Cuban	%	36.0	20.6	43.4	87.3	8.9	3.8
Dominican	%	30.0	25.2	44.8	77.4	17.2	5.4
Salvadoran, Guatemalan	%	26.2	26.1	47.7	72.7	18.5	8.7
Central American, other	%	39.0	24.2	36.7	78.2	14.9	6.9
Colombian	%	35.1	29.1	35.8	84.5	11.3	4.3
Peruvian, Ecuadorian	%	35.7	28.0	36.2	84.2	11.7	4.1
South American, other	%	49.9	29.0	21.2	87.0	9.5	3.5
Other Spanish, Hispanic, Latino	%	50.0	28.0	21.9	75.7	17.4	6.9
Total	N	10,782,537	7,110,497	9,317,259	14,829,278	3,220,385	1,681,665
	%	39.6	26.1	34.2	75.2	16.3	8.5

SOURCE: 2000 U.S. Census, 5% PUMS.

presumed lack of a language shift to English among Hispanics, which in turn has raised questions about divided national loyalties and identities. Table 2-11 focuses on foreign-born Hispanics to examine in greater depth the dynamics of English acquisition and proficiency. The measure employed in the table—and illustrated in Figure 2-1—combines the percentage who speak English only with the ability to speak it very well or well into a single index of English fluency.

That degree of fluency is shaped by three main factors: length of time in the United States, age at arrival, and education. English fluency is only in part a function of length of time in the United States—46 percent of those who arrived in the United States in the 1990s were fluent in English by 2000, compared with 61 percent of those who entered in the 1980s, and 69 percent of those who came earlier—but much more powerfully it is a function of age at arrival and level of education. The capacity to learn and to speak a language like a native is especially good between age 3 and the early teens—which is why, of all the dimensions of assimilation, language acquisition is the one most likely to follow a straight-line trajectory. The younger the immigrant at the time of arrival—especially children under age 13—and the more educated the person, the greater the proficiency in English. For example, Spanish-speaking immigrants with a high school education or more who arrived before adolescence are almost universally English fluent (92 to 98 percent) regardless of decade of arrival in the United States, whereas only a minority (21 to 27 percent) of those with less than a high school education who arrived as adults age 35 or older were English proficient, regardless of how long they had been in the United States.

Table 2-12 presents data on a household measure of "linguistic isolation" (defined by the Census Bureau as households in which no one age 14 or older speaks English "very well"). By that measure, first-generation Hispanic households are twice as likely as non-Hispanic households to be linguistically isolated (39 to 19 percent), a disadvantage that remains in the second+ generations (13.8 to 0.6 percent). Again, within the Hispanic collectivity, significant differences were observed among different Hispanic ethnic groups, with U.S.-born Cuban households being the least likely to be linguistically isolated, and Salvadorans and Guatemalans the most.

The decennial census does not collect data on how well Hispanics speak Spanish, however, nor on their actual preference for or patterns of use of English versus Spanish, nor on their level of bilingualism (the sole question asked by the census about any language other than English is whether it is spoken in the home). Yet such data are indispensable to any analysis of linguistic assimilation, especially when examining the language status of those who immigrated as children or of the U.S.-born second generation. In Southern California and South Florida, the CILS collected relevant language data on large samples of 1.5- and second-generation

TABLE 2-11 English Fluency[a] of Foreign-Born Hispanics in the United States, 2000, by Age of Arrival, Education, and Length of Residence in the United States

% English Fluent[a]

(Speaks English Only, or Well, or Very Well)

Foreign-born Hispanics:		N %
Age at arrival:	0–12 years old	%
	13–34 years old	%
	35 and older	%
Education completed[b]:	College graduate	%
	High school graduate	%
	Less than high school	%
English fluency by:		
Age at arrival:	Education completed:	
0–12 years old	College graduate	%
	High school graduate	%
	Less than high school	%
13–34 years old	College graduate	%
	High school graduate	%
	Less than high school	%
35 and older	College graduate	%
	High school graduate	%
	Less than high school	%

[a]English fluency = Persons 5 years or older who speak English only, or well, or very well.

[b]Highest level of education completed for persons 25 years or older.

SOURCE: 2000 U.S. Census, 5% PUMS.

Mexican, Cuban, Colombian, Nicaraguan, Dominican, and other Latin American youth at three points in time across the decade from 1992 to 1995 to 2002, spanning ages 14 to 24 on average. The findings on linguistic assimilation are incontrovertible, even among the most presumably Spanish-retentive groups: Mexicans living along the U.S.-Mexico border in San Diego and Cubans in the most bilingual major city in the country, Miami. In 97 percent of the sample, Spanish was the primary language spoken at home. But among Mexican-born youth in San Diego, in the 1992 survey (when they were 14 years old on average) 32 percent already pre-

Decade of U.S. Arrival			
1990s	1980s	Pre-1980	Total
7,036,411	4,482,200	4,282,583	15,801,194
46	61	69	56.4
76	88	91	84.7
40	56	63	50.4
30	34	36	32.2
67	84	94	81.7
49	73	87	71.9
27	42	52	40.5

Decade of U.S. Arrival			
1990s	1980s	Pre-1980	Total
NA	96	98	98.1
NA	92	96	95.7
NA	68	80	77.1
71	85	93	82.1
52	73	83	69.0
29	43	50	40.8
57	69	71	62.0
40	52	55	45.5
21	24	27	23.6

ferred to speak English, and that preference rose to 61 percent by the 1995 survey and to 87 percent by the 2002 survey (when they were 24 years old on average); only 13 percent indicated a preference for Spanish by 2002. The proportions preferring English at the three surveys were even larger among the Mexican American second generation: 45 percent in 1992, 79 percent in 1995, and 96 percent by 2002. In Miami, only 2 percent of all of the Latin American groups combined, foreign-born and native-born, expressed a preference for Spanish over English by the last survey. A principal reason for this shift had to do with their levels of speaking, reading, and

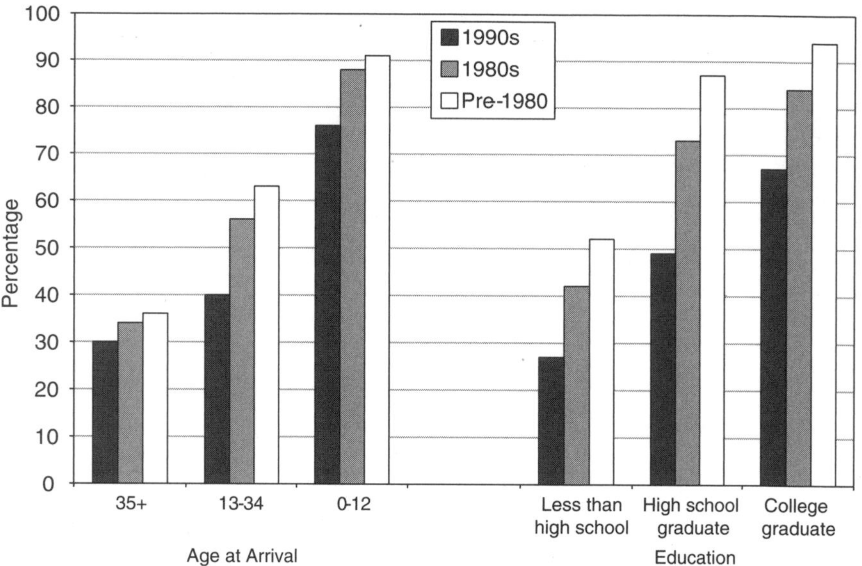

FIGURE 2-1 English fluency of foreign-born Hispanics in the United States, 2000, by age of arrival, education, and length of residence in the United States.
NOTE: English fluency = persons age 5 or older who speak English only, or well, or very well; education = highest level of education completed for persons age 25 or older.
LEGEND: Length of residence in the United States grouped by decade of arrival: 1990s, 1980s, before 1980.
SOURCE: 2000 U.S. Census, 5% PUMS.

writing proficiency in English and Spanish: over time, the degree of proficiency in English significantly outstripped their Spanish fluency, although nearly half of the sample managed to maintain a limited degree of bilingualism by their mid-20s—a pattern observed only among Spanish speakers, unlike Asian-origin children of immigrants, whose native languages atrophied at a much faster rate.

This pattern of rapid linguistic assimilation was constant across nationalities and socioeconomic levels and suggests that, over time, the use of and fluency in Spanish will inevitably decline. The appearance of language loyalty among Spanish speakers (especially Mexicans) is due largely to the effect of continuing high immigration to the United States. For example, a rare multigenerational study of a large representative sample of Mexican-origin couples in Los Angeles (López, 1978) found that among first-generation women, 84 percent used Spanish only at home, 14 percent used both languages, and 2 percent used English only; by the third genera-

TABLE 2-12 Linguistic Isolation in Hispanic and Non-Hispanic Households in the United States, by Generation, 2000 (Persons Five Years and Older)

		First Generation (Foreign-Born)		Second+ Generations (U.S.-Born)	
Ethnic Identity		Not Linguistically Isolated	Linguistically Isolated	Not Linguistically Isolated	Linguistically Isolated
Not Hispanic	N	14,842,048	3,505,125	219,177,673	1,244,351
	%	80.9	19.1	99.4	0.6
Hispanic:	N	9,474,134	6,000,378	16,289,498	2,610,582
	%	61.2	38.8	86.2	13.8
Mexican	%	57.3	42.7	84.7	15.3
Puerto Rican[a]	%	76.2	23.8	93.5	6.5
Cuban	%	61.5	38.5	94.0	6.0
Dominican	%	63.1	36.9	76.5	23.5
Salvadoran, Guatemalan	%	57.9	42.1	67.8	32.2
Central American, other	%	69.0	31.0	82.1	17.9
Colombian	%	65.8	34.2	84.4	15.6
Peruvian, Ecuadorian	%	67.5	32.5	83.6	16.4
South American, other	%	74.8	25.2	91.3	8.7
Other Spanish, Hispanic, Latino	%	78.9	21.1	90.6	9.4
Total	N	24,316,182	9,505,503	235,467,171	3,854,933
	%	71.9	28.1	98.4	1.6

NOTE: Linguistic isolation is defined by the U.S. Census Bureau as "a household in which no one age 14 or older speaks English very well."

[a]For Puerto Ricans, "foreign-born" includes those born on the island of Puerto Rico, and "U.S.-born" refers to those born on the mainland.

SOURCE: 2000 U.S. Census, 5% Integrated PUMS.

tion there was a complete reversal, with 4 percent speaking Spanish only at home, 12 percent using both, and 84 percent shifting to English only. Among the men, the pattern was similar except that their shift to English by the second generation was even more marked. More recently, the 2002 National Survey of Latinos—with a large representative sample of first-, second-, and third-generation adults age 18 and older—confirmed these generational differences in language preference and dominance, which in turn were found to shape attitudes and ethnic self-identities (Pew Hispanic Center/Kaiser Family Foundation, 2002). The findings of these studies strongly indicate that the linguistic outcomes for the third generation—the grandchildren of today's immigrants—will parallel the age-old pattern in American history: the grandchildren may learn a few foreign words and phrases as a vestige of their ancestry, but they are most likely to grow up speaking English only. The shift to English may actually be occurring at a more accelerated rate today. Arguably, the atrophy of these children's ability to maintain fluency in the language of their immigrant parents is a significant loss of scarce and valuable bilingual resources both for the individual and for the United States in a global economy.

Labor Migration and Human Capital

Group differences in acculturation and linguistic isolation are rooted in very significant differences in the overall educational attainment of Hispanics and non-Hispanics, especially among the foreign-born. By far, both the most educated and the least educated groups in the United States today are immigrants, a reflection of polar-opposite types of migrations embedded in very different historical contexts (Rumbaut, 1992, 1994). That point is made in Table 2-13, contrasting two poles of educational attainment among foreign-born and U.S.-born Hispanics and non-Hispanics age 25 or older: those with less than a high school education, and those with a four-year college degree or more.

Among the foreign-born, non-Hispanics (many of whom are Asian-origin professionals, such as the flows from India, Taiwan, China, and Korea, as well as others from Europe, the Middle East, and Africa) are four times more likely to have college degrees as Hispanics—36 compared with 9 percent. Conversely, nearly three-fifths of Hispanic adults have less than a high school education, compared with only one-fifth of non-Hispanic immigrants. This comparative disadvantage in human capital of Latin American immigrants vis-à-vis their non–Latin American counterparts is reduced but not eliminated by the U.S.-born generations. Intergroup differences in the Hispanic population are particularly pronounced, especially between Mexican, Salvadoran, and Guatemalan immigrants and other groups—although by the U.S.-born generations, these same groups (who in

TABLE 2-13 Educational Attainment of Foreign-Born and U.S.-Born Hispanics and Non-Hispanics in the United States, 2000 (Persons 25 Years and Older)

		First Generation (Foreign-Born)		Second+ Generations (U.S.-Born)	
Ethnic Identity		Less Than High School	College Graduate or More	Less Than High School	College Graduate or More
Not Hispanic	N	3,213,973	5,388,741	23,821,393	37,132,874
	%	21.3	35.7	16.0	25.0
Hispanic:	N	6,724,296	1,007,105	1,964,135	903,691
	%	58.5	8.8	29.1	13.4
Mexican	%	69.9	4.4	31.0	11.6
Puerto Rican	%	46.4	10.9	23.2	14.8
Cuban	%	40.9	18.8	13.3	34.2
Dominican	%	51.8	9.5	19.3	21.4
Salvadoran, Guatemalan	%	64.7	5.2	26.7	22.9
Central American, other	%	42.9	13.2	13.5	33.2
Colombian	%	27.9	22.0	10.7	38.3
Peruvian, Ecuadorian	%	29.5	17.6	9.3	36.1
South American, other	%	19.0	31.7	7.5	46.6
Other Spanish, Hispanic, Latino	%	28.2	28.5	30.1	12.8
Total	N	9,938,269	6,395,846	25,785,528	38,036,565
	%	37.4	24.0	16.6	24.4

SOURCE: 2000 U.S. Census, 5% PUMS.

the immigrant generation constitute the least educated population in American society) make a very substantial gain in educational attainment.

These intergroup differences in education are vividly reflected in their occupational status. Table 2-14 presents census data for employed persons age 16 and older, using the Duncan socioeconomic index (SEI) to rank occupations into two polar types: (1) professional, managerial, and technical occupations with SEI scores above 50 and (2) low-wage labor, indexing jobs with SEI scores below 25. It becomes immediately clear that the foreign-born Hispanic population of the United States is disproportionately concentrated at the bottom of the occupational structure, with 61.5 percent of workers in low-wage labor (more than twice the 30 percent of non-Hispanics working at these jobs). The presence of highly educated professionals from Mexico and elsewhere (Alarcón, 2000) is dwarfed within this overall profile.

It bears underscoring that this figure is driven by the extraordinarily high proportions of three nationalities in particular: Mexicans, among whom more than 4.5 million immigrants, or 69.7 percent of all Mexican-born workers, labor in the lowest paid jobs of the U.S. economy; and Salvadorans and Guatemalans, among whom two-thirds (65.6 percent) are low-wage laborers. Dominicans follow in this hierarchy (54 percent), then Peruvians, Ecuadorians, Colombians, and Puerto Ricans (all between 45 and 49 percent), Cubans (38 percent), and finally "other" South American and other Spanish (33 percent)—but even these latter groups have a higher proportion of low-status workers than do all non-Hispanic immigrants as a whole. That central fact—the entry of migrant workers into the bottom rungs of U.S. labor markets, who fill the vast demand for low-wage labor in an "hourglass" economy—is a defining characteristic of the Latin-origin foreign-born population, especially of its largest component (the flows from Mexico, El Salvador, and Guatemala, especially of undocumented laborers). It has profound long-term implications for the social and economic prospects of their children's generation, and it is also the basis for common stereotypes that disparage and stigmatize the population as a whole.

Still, among the U.S.-born generations, the gap between Hispanics and non-Hispanics in the proportion of all workers who are at the bottom of the occupational hierarchy closes substantially, to 36 versus 30 percent, respectively—a 6-point differential that is five times smaller than the 31-point gap observed among the foreign-born. Conversely, non-Hispanic immigrants as a whole are far more likely than Hispanics—by a 3-to-1 ratio (46 to 16 percent)—to be employed in professional status positions; indeed, their high levels of educational and professional attainment significantly surpass the norms for non-Hispanic white natives in the United States, and generally reflect the "brain drain" character of immigrant flows from these regions. That gap is also reduced by the U.S.-born generations between

TABLE 2-14 Occupational Status[a] of Foreign-Born and U.S.-Born Hispanics and Non-Hispanics in the United States, 2000 (Employed Persons 16 and Older)

		First Generation (Foreign-Born)		Second+ Generations (U.S.-Born)	
Ethnic Identity		Low-Wage Labor	Professional, Technical, Managerial	Low-Wage Labor	Professional, Technical, Managerial
Socioeconomic Index Score:		(SEI < 25)	(SEI > 50)	(SEI < 25)	(SEI > 50)
Not Hispanic	N	3,888,636	5,895,344	41,137,385	54,681,470
	%	30.1	45.7	30.2	40.1
Hispanic:	N	6,760,643	1,752,934	2,899,023	2,287,386
	%	61.5	15.9	36.4	28.7
Mexican	%	69.7	10.1	38.0	27.2
Puerto Rican	%	46.2	25.7	32.6	30.9
Cuban	%	38.2	34.1	21.2	44.3
Dominican	%	54.2	19.0	27.3	31.3
Salvadoran, Guatemalan	%	65.6	11.9	33.0	26.0
Central American, other	%	52.2	21.0	26.0	38.4
Colombian	%	45.0	29.5	23.5	40.3
Peruvian, Ecuadorian	%	49.6	24.4	22.8	41.6
South American, other	%	33.3	41.7	21.6	45.2
Other Spanish, Hispanic, Latino	%	34.3	41.4	38.3	28.9
Total	N	10,649,279	7,648,278	44,036,408	56,968,856
	%	44.6	32.0	30.5	39.5

[a]Occupations ranked by their SEI (Duncan socioeconomic index) scores.

SOURCE: 2000 U.S. Census, 5% PUMS.

Hispanics and non-Hispanics, to 40 versus 29 percent, but it is not eliminated. Again, as with education, intergroup differences within the Hispanic population are quite pronounced, especially between Mexican, Salvadoran, and Guatemalan immigrants on one hand (groups from three countries adjacent to the southern land border, with the fastest overall growth rates over the past two decades and the largest proportions of undocumented immigrants) and other groups on the other—although among the U.S.-born these ethnic groups make very substantial gains in occupational attainment overall. Nonetheless, the continuation of present trends portends widening social and economic inequalities in the Hispanic population, segmented by national origin and generation.

CONCLUSION

Four decades into a new era of mass immigration, it has become commonplace to observe that the United States is undergoing its most profound demographic transformation in a century. Whether in terms of its size, growth, composition, or spatial concentration, the sheer magnitude of the phenomenon is impressive. This new immigration is overwhelmingly non-European in national origin; half of it hails from Spanish-speaking Latin America. The immigrant stock population of the United States today numbers around 70 million people—that is, persons who are either immigrants or U.S.-born children of immigrants—a figure that accounts for nearly a fourth of the total national population and fully three-fourths of the Hispanic population. The latter has been growing much faster than the national population, both through continuing immigration and natural increase, and it will continue to do so for the foreseeable future.

This chapter has focused on factors that distinguish the Hispanic population of the United States from non-Hispanics—their histories and geographies of incorporation, national origins, racial categorization, immigration, citizenship, and especially language, as well as the crucial human capital disadvantages of the first generation compared with non-Hispanic immigrants generally and their implications for a rapidly growing U.S.-born second generation. The confluence of these factors, influencing one another in a process of cumulative causation, shapes a distinctive profile for Hispanics as a whole—a profile that reflects the numerical dominance of the Mexican-origin population, which accounts for nearly two-thirds of the total. However, I have also accented differences between the foreign-born and native-born generations, underscoring the dynamic changes taking place in their acculturation and integration, and among the largest Hispanic-origin ethnic groups, emphasizing that Hispanics or Latinos as a whole are not a homogeneous entity and should not be presumed to be so.

It is also true that the tens of millions of persons so categorized do share a common label symbolizing a minority group status in the United States. Although the official pan-ethnic category is only about three decades old, and the diverse peoples subsumed under it are largely newcomers who identify with their national origins, the labels "Hispanic" or "Latino" are now used pervasively throughout the society (alongside "Asian," "black," "non-Hispanic white"), entering into the popular culture and shaping the national racial-ethnic discourse and hierarchy.

Moreover, the Spanish roots of what is now the United States are older than those of Americans of European, African, and Asian descent. In that sense Hispanic Americans share the legacy of a distinct history that both precedes the founding of the nation, and, most notably as a consequence of two defining wars (the U.S.–Mexican War and the Spanish-American War), of the expansion of the nation in the 19th century. In particular, Mexican Americans and Puerto Ricans—the two largest Hispanic groups and two of the three largest ethnic minorities in the country—are peoples whose incorporation originated largely involuntarily through conquest, occupation, and exploitation, followed by mass immigration during the 20th century, setting the foundation for subsequent patterns of social and economic inequality. The Cubans, Dominicans, Salvadorans, Guatemalans, Nicaraguans, Colombians, and other Latin Americans are of more recent and varied vintage, but their distinct histories too shape their modes of incorporation.

The past, as William Faulkner observed, is never dead; it is not even past. But the past, while prologue, need not be the epilogue too. That epilogue is being written today largely by hard-working newcomers of diverse Latin origins seeking to make their way and looking ahead to their children's American futures. In the process they are transforming American society even as they themselves are being transformed into the newest Americans. This volume seeks to offer a systematic assessment of their collective enterprise.

REFERENCES

Alarcón, R. (2000). Skilled immigrants and *cerebreros*: Foreign-born engineers and scientists in the high technology industry of Silicon Valley. In N. Foner, R.G. Rumbaut, and S.J. Gold (Eds.), *Immigration research for a new century: Multidisciplinary perspectives* (pp. 301–321). New York: Russell Sage Foundation.

Bailey, B. (2001). Dominican-American ethnic/racial identities and United States social categories. *International Migration Review*, *35*(3), 677–708.

Barrera, M. (1979). *Race and class in the Southwest.* South Bend, IL: University of Notre Dame Press.

Bean, F.D., and Tienda, M. (1987). *The Hispanic population of the United States.* New York: Russell Sage Foundation.

Black, B. (1988). *The good neighbor*. New York: Pantheon.

Bonilla, F., and Campos, R. (1981). A wealth of poor: Puerto Ricans in the new economic order. *Daedalus*, *110*, 133–176.

Cardoso, L. A. (1980). *Mexican immigration to the United States, 1897–1931*. Tucson: University of Arizona Press.

Castillo, J. (2003). Latino? Hispanic? Chicano? *American Statesman*, July 26.

Choldin, H.M. (1986). Statistics and politics: The "Hispanic issue" in the 1980 census. *Demography, 23*(3), 403–418.

Collier, S., Blakemore, H., and Skidmore, T.E. (Eds.) (1985). *The Cambridge Encyclopedia of Latin America and the Caribbean* (pp. 127–160). New York: Cambridge University Press.

Deutsch, S. (1987). *No separate refuge: Culture, class, and gender on an Anglo-Hispanic frontier in the American Southwest, 1880–1940*. New York: Oxford University Press.

Deverell, W. (2004). *Whitewashed adobe: The rise of Los Angeles and the remaking of its Mexican past*. Berkeley: University of California Press.

Fears, D. (2003a). Latinos or Hispanics? A debate about identity. *Washington Post*, August 25.

Fears, D. (2003b). The roots of Hispanic: 1975 committee of bureaucrats produced designation. *Washington Post*, October 15.

Fernández-Shaw, C. M. (1972). *Presencia Española en los Estados Unidos*. Madrid: Ediciones Cultura Hispánica.

Fitzpatrick, J.P. (1987). *Puerto Rican Americans: The meaning of migration to the mainland* (2nd edition). Englewood Cliffs, NJ: Prentice-Hall.

Foley, N. (2004). Straddling the color line: The legal construction of Hispanic identity in Texas. In N. Foner and G. M. Frederickson (Eds.), *Not just white and black: Historical and contemporary perspectives on immigration, race, and ethnicity in the United States* (pp. 341–357). New York: Russell Sage Foundation.

Fuentes, C. (1992). *The buried mirror: Reflections on Spain and the New World*. New York: Houghton Mifflin.

Gamio, M. (1930). *Mexican immigration to the United States*. Chicago: University of Chicago Press.

García, M.C. (1996). *Havana USA: Cuban exiles and Cuban Americans in South Florida, 1959–1994*. Berkeley: University of California Press.

Garvey, M., and McDonnell, P.J. (1999). José moves into top spot in name game: Favorite choice for boys in California, Texas last year marks major shift. *Los Angeles Times*, January 8.

Grenier, G.J., and Pérez, L. (2003). *The legacy of exile: Cubans in the United States*. Boston: Allyn and Bacon.

Griswold del Castillo, R. (1984). *La familia: Chicano families in the urban Southwest, 1846 to the present*. South Bend, IL: University of Notre Dame Press.

Gutiérrez, D.G. (1995). *Walls and mirrors: Mexican Americans, Mexican immigrants, and the politics of ethnicity*. Berkeley: University of California Press.

Inter-American Development Bank. (2004, May). *Latin American immigrants in the United States to send $30 billion to homelands in 2004*. Available: http://www.iadb.org/exr/remittances/images/map2003English.pdf [accessed June 2004].

Itzigsohn, J. (2004). The formation of Latino and Latina panethnic identities. In N. Foner and G. Frederickson (Eds.), *Not just black and white: Historical and contemporary perspectives on immigration, race, and ethnicity in the United States* (pp. 197–216). New York: Russell Sage Foundation.

Jiménez, A. (Ed.) (1994). *Handbook of Hispanic cultures in the United States: History*. Houston: Arte Público Press.

Johannsen, R.W. (1985). *To the halls of the Montezumas: The Mexican War in the American imagination*. New York: Oxford University Press.

La Feber, W. (1993). *Inevitable revolutions: The United States in Central America*. New York: W.W. Norton.

Landale, N.S., and Oropesa, R.S. (2002). White, black, or Puerto Rican? Racial self-identification among mainland and island Puerto Ricans. *Social Forces, 81*, 231–254.

Langley, L.D. (2001). *The banana wars: United States intervention in the Caribbean, 1898-1934* (2nd cd.) Wilmington, DE: SR Books.

Langley, L.D. (2003). *The Americas in the modern age*. New Haven, CT: Yale University Press.

López, D.E. (1978). Chicano language loyalty in an urban setting. *Sociology and Social Research, 62*, 267–278.

Maltby, W.S. (1968). *The black legend in England: The development of anti-Spanish sentiment, 1558–1560*. Durham, NC: Duke University Press.

Massey, D.S. (1993). Latinos, poverty, and the underclass: A new agenda for research. *Hispanic Journal of Behavioral Sciences, 15*, 449–475.

Massey, D.S., and Espinosa, K.E. (1997). What's driving Mexico-U.S. migration? A theoretical, empirical, and policy analysis. *American Journal of Sociology, 102*(4), 939–999.

Massey, D.S., Alarcón, R., Durand, J., and González, H. (1987). *Return to Aztlán: The social process of international migration from Western Mexico*. Berkeley: University of California Press.

Massey, D.S, Durand, J., and Malone, N. (2002). *Beyond smoke and mirrors*. New York: Russell Sage Foundation.

Moncada, A., and Olivas, J. (2003). *Hispanos 2000*. Madrid: Ediciones Libertarias.

Montejano, D. (1987). *Anglos and Mexicans in the making of Texas, 1836–1986*. Austin: University of Texas Press.

Moore, J., and Pachón, H. (1985). *Hispanics in the United States*. Englewood Cliffs, NJ: Prentice-Hall.

Musicant, I. (1990). *The banana wars: A history of United States military intervention in Latin America from the Spanish American War to the invasion of Panama*. New York: Macmillan.

Passel, J. (2002). New estimates of the undocumented population in the United States. *Migration Information Source*. Available: http://www.migrationinformation.org/Feature/display.cfm?ID=19 [accessed May 22, 2002].

Pérez, L.A., Jr. (1990). *Cuba and the United States: Ties of singular intimacy*. Athens: University of Georgia Press.

Pérez, L.A., Jr. (1999). *On becoming Cuban: Identity, nationality, and culture*. Chapel Hill: University of North Carolina Press.

Pew Hispanic Center/Kaiser Family Foundation. (2002). *National survey of Latinos*. Available: http://www.pewhispanic.org/site/docs/pdf/LatinoSurveyReportFinal.pdf [accessed December 2002].

Pitt, L. (1971). *The decline of the Californios: A social history of the Spanish-speaking Californians, 1846–1890*. Berkeley: University of California Press.

Pitts, L., Jr. (1999). José is just as American as baseball, apple pie, and John. *Houston Chronicle*, January 15.

Portes, A., and Rumbaut, R.G. (2001). *Legacies: The story of the immigrant second generation*. Berkeley and New York: University of California Press and Russell Sage Foundation.

Portes, A., and Stepick, A. (1993). *City on the edge: The transformation of Miami*. Berkeley: University of California Press.

Rivera-Batiz, F.L., and Santiago, C.E. (1998). *Island paradox: Puerto Rico in the 1990s*. New York: Russell Sage Foundation.

Rodríguez, C. (1991). *Puerto Ricans: Born in the USA*. Boulder, CO: Westview Press.

Rodríguez, R. (1993). *Days of obligation: An argument with my Mexican father*. New York: Penguin.

Rumbaut, R.D. (1978). The Hispanic prologue. In D. Cardús (Ed.), *A Hispanic look at the bicentennial* (pp. 5–22). Houston, TX: Institute of Hispanic Culture.

Rumbaut, R.G. (1992). The Americans: Latin American and Caribbean peoples in the United States. In A. Stepan (Ed.), *Americas: New interpretive essays* (pp. 275–307). New York: Oxford University Press.

Rumbaut, R.G. (1994). Origins and destinies: Immigration to the United States since World War II. *Sociological Forum*, *9*(4), 583–621.

Sachs, S. (2001). What's in a name? Redefining minority. *New York Times*, March 11.

Sánchez, G.J. (1993). *Becoming Mexican American: Ethnicity, culture, and identity in Chicano Los Angeles, 1900–1945*. New York: Oxford University Press.

Sánchez, J.P. (1991). Hispanic American heritage. In H. J. Viola and C. Margolis (Eds.), *Seeds of change: A quincentennial commemoration* (pp. 173–185). Washington, DC: Smithsonian Institution Press.

Sánchez Korrol, V.E. (1983). *From colonia to community: The history of Puerto Ricans in New York City, 1917–1948*. Westport, CT: Greenwood Press.

Sánchez Korrol, V.E. (1994). In their own right: A history of Puerto Ricans in the USA. In A. Jiménez (Ed.), *Handbook of Hispanic cultures in the United States: History* (pp. 281–301). Houston, TX: Arte Público Press.

Schoultz, L. (1998). *Beneath the United States: A history of U.S. policy toward Latin America*. Cambridge, MA: Harvard University Press.

Shipman, D.E. (1992). *Spanish Texas, 1519–1821*. Austin: University of Texas Press.

Silverstein, S. (2003). Chancellor tackles image problems. *Los Angeles Times*, May 27.

Smith, P.H. (1999). *Talons of the eagle: Dynamics of U.S.-Latin American relations*. New York: Oxford University Press.

Smith, W.S. (1991). *Portrait of Cuba*. Atlanta, GA: Turner.

Snipp, C.M. (2003). Racial measurement in the American census: Past practices and implications for the future. *Annual Review of Sociology*, *29*, 563–588.

Thomas, H. (1971). *Cuba: The pursuit of freedom*. New York: Harper & Row.

U.S. Census Bureau. (1975). *Comparison of persons of Spanish surname and persons of Spanish origin in the United States*. Technical Paper No. 38. Washington, DC: U.S. Government Printing Office.

U.S. Census Bureau. (1997). *Revisions to the standards for the classification of federal data on race and ethnicity*. Available: http://www.census.gov/population/www/socdemo/race/Ombdir15.html [accessed May 2004].

U.S. Census Bureau. (2004a). *Census Bureau projects tripling of Hispanic population in 50 years*. Available: http://www.census.gov/Press-Release/www/releases/archives/population/001720.html [accessed May 2004].

U.S. Census Bureau. (2004b). *Hispanic and Asian Americans increasing faster than overall population*. Available: http://www.census.gov/Press-Release/www/releases/archives/race/001839.html [accessed June 2004].

Vargas, Z. (1993). *Proletarians of the North: A history of Mexican industrial workers in Detroit and the Midwest, 1917–1933*. Berkeley: University of California Press.

Wallman, K.K., Evinger, S., and Schechter, S. (2000). Measuring our nation's diversity. *American Journal of Public Health*, *90*(11), 1704–1708.

Walton, J. (2001). *Storied land: Community and memory in Monterey*. Berkeley: University of California Press.

Weber, D.J. (Ed.). (1973). *Foreigners in their native land: Historical roots of the Mexican Americans*. Albuquerque: University of New Mexico Press.

Weber, D.J. (1982). *The Mexican frontier, 1821–1846: The American Southwest under Mexico*. Albuquerque: University of New Mexico Press.
Weber, D.J. (1992). *The Spanish frontier in North America*. New Haven, CT: Yale University Press.
Williams, T., and Pietrusza, D. (2001). *My life in pictures*. Kingston, NY: Total Sports.
Wright, L. (1994). One drop of blood. *The New Yorker*, July 24.

3

The Demographic Foundations of the Latino Population

Jorge Durand, Edward Telles, and Jennifer Flashman

The news that Hispanics have become the nation's largest minority was no demographic surprise. Its fruition had been predicted at least 30 years ago. This news event, though, was important because the appearance of Latinos on the American scene could no longer be denied—neither in the nation's vital economic or educational policies nor in politics. Nowhere. Once considered a sleeping giant, the Latino population has not only grown tremendously but also now constitutes a significant presence throughout most of the United States. Once confined to a small number of states, the Latino population has migrated to new regions, including much of the South, moved into new sectors of the economy, and become an important voting bloc in many states. Its impact is heightened by the fact that it is considerably younger than an aging non-Latino America, making its potential impact on America's future all the greater.

This chapter reports on the factors that account for this growth. Overall, it describes how relatively high rates of immigration and fertility have shaped the growth and the creation of an especially youthful age structure among the Latino population. In particular, it examines how changing immigration policies, social networks, and other factors have led to immigration from Latin America and then how a changing labor market as well as immigration policies have affected migration patterns in the United States and prompted the regional dispersion of Latinos. These demographic foundations are fundamental for understanding nearly every aspect of Latino well-being covered in this book, including their spatial distribution and family structure, their position in the educational system and the labor market, and their access to health care and the political system. A notable example of the importance of this population was its role in the recent presidential election: the Hispanic vote may have influenced the outcome (Cobble and Velaquez, 2004). Given the demographic destiny of the Latino population, that influence is likely to grow with its dispersion into new states and as immigrants become citizens and their children reach voting age.

At the same time, the Latino population has become increasingly diverse by national origin. Mexicans continue to constitute the large majority of Latinos in the United States, driving the demographic behavior of Latinos in general as well as mainstream American attitudes toward the Hispanic group. However, many other groups have also become part of the new immigration from Latin America, as the previous chapter has shown. While Mexicans, Puerto Ricans, and Cubans constituted almost all Latinos in the United States just 30 years ago, Dominicans, Central Americans, and South Americans have doubled or tripled their numbers in the past two decades. This chapter also shows that Latino national groups vary greatly in their age structure and extent of regional dispersion. Specifically, Cubans have an old age structure and have become increasingly concentrated, two patterns that are unlike the rest of the Latino population, whereas Mexicans and Central Americans are especially young and have migrated throughout the United States.

COMPONENTS OF GROWTH

Demographic growth or decline is a result of births and deaths, also known as natural growth and net migration, which is the balance of immigration and emigration. The growth of the Latino population is mostly the result of two of these components, births or fertility and immigration. While many assume that the growth is due almost entirely to immigration, relatively high rates of Latino fertility now constitute roughly half of all population growth. That fertility is comprised largely of births to immigrants, but a sizeable component can also be attributed to the U.S.-born. Table 3-1 breaks down Latino population growth in the 1970s, 1980s, and 1990s into that resulting from either immigration or fertility to both immigrants and the U.S.-born.

The last row of the table shows that, in the 1990s, nearly half (48 percent) of Latino population growth was due to immigration, 28 percent can be attributed to fertility among immigrants, and the remaining 24 percent resulted from the fertility of U.S.-born Latinos. The same table also shows that, in relative terms, the share of Latino growth due directly to immigration in 1990–2000 declined compared with the decade before, when immigration accounted for fully 56 percent of growth. Even though immi-

TABLE 3-1 Percentage Components of Latino Population Growth by Decade, 1970–2000

Period	Foreign-Born (%)	U.S.-Born Children of Foreign-Born (%)	U.S.-Born Children of U.S.-Born (%)	(%)
1970–1980	40	21	39	100
1980–1990	56	27	17	100
1990–2000	48	28	24	100

SOURCE: Data from Table 5 of Bean et al. (2004).

gration increased in the 1990s in absolute numbers, its share of total Latino population growth declined, although fertility to immigrants continued at about the same rate. In both the 1980s and 1990s, at least three-quarters of Latino population growth has been due to immigrants, either by their own migration or through their childbearing.

Fertility went from accounting for 44 percent of all growth in the 1980s to representing 52 percent of growth in the 1990s. The growth from fertility to U.S.-born Latino parents represents the greatest growth share, increasing from 17 percent in the 1980s to 24 percent in the 1990s. This signals a reemergence of the so-called third generation, which begins to echo the presence of a large third generation, as in the period prior to 1980. Births to such parents had represented fully 39 percent of Latino growth in the 1970s but dropped steeply to less than half (17 percent) in the 1980s.

ORIGINS OF LATIN AMERICAN IMMIGRATION

The growth and increasing national diversity of immigration from Latin America was shown in Chapter 2, but in this chapter we seek to describe its sources. The volume and socioeconomic characteristics of the immigrant Latino population are largely related to economic and political factors and the social networks that have since perpetuated immigration. In the cases of Mexico and Puerto Rico, the current migration flows were initiated with intense labor recruitment, but once the process was set in motion, economic factors and social networks continued to fuel further immigration. In the Cuban case, the causes were, and continue to be, fundamentally political. For the Dominican Republic, political causes, including dictatorship and military intervention, played an important role at first but social and economic causes perpetuated the process. A similar process occurred in the cases of Guatemala, El Salvador, and Nicaragua, where immigration was political as well as economic. Finally, in the case of South America, socioeconomic factors have been predominant in immigration to the United States, although political violence in Colombia and Peru has been an important push factor for migration from those countries.

For more than a century, Mexican immigration to the United States was distinguished by two components: a migration that settled and another between Mexico and the United States that was circular, largely facilitated by the porosity of the border. Similar phenomena occurred in the case of the Puerto Ricans, who could easily go back and forth between Puerto Rico and the mainland, facilitated by low airfares and the fact that they are U.S. citizens. According to Massey, Durand, and Malone's (2002) theory of cumulative causation, each act of migration, especially through the large volume of return migration, alters the social context in which subsequent migration decisions are made, thus increasing the chances of future migration. Immigration from Mexico and Puerto Rico has advanced considerably through such social networks, although Puerto Rican immigration has slowed as the networks have already incorporated a large part of the eligible population in the immigration process. The other national groups are arguably at earlier stages.

Demographic, political, and economic factors in Latin America also help to account for the large increases in immigration from that region in the 1980s and 1990s. In the 1970s, many countries began birth control programs, as a demographic transition with continuing high fertility rates and decreasing mortality rates led to sharp population growth. The effects of Latin America's baby boom began to be felt in the labor force, as new entrants to the labor force had increasing difficulty finding work and thus opted for migration abroad. At the same time, the 1970s and 1980s were turbulent political times, especially in Central America, where civil wars and other types of armed conflict generated intense emigration (Hamilton and Stoltz Chinchilla, 2001; Menjivar, 2000).

Finally, it is important to recognize the continuing attraction of the United States, as Latin American countries struggle economically. Practically all Latin American countries have suffered recurring economic crises, currency devaluation, and runaway inflation that have left millions of people in poverty, many of them from sectors of the middle class who seek to maintain a decent quality of life through migration. The effect of neoliberal economic policies has been mixed across countries, with Chile being a successful case while Peru, Argentina, and Ecuador have had negative experiences thus far (Huber and Solt, 2004; Walton, 2004).

Effects of U.S. Immigration Law on Immigration from Latin America

If economic, political, and social factors provoked and perpetuated immigration from our southern neighbors, the history of immigration law may be most responsible for the diversity of Latino immigration in terms of legal status, class selectivity, and destination. With the exception of Puerto Rico, migratory flows from Latin American countries to the United States have been shaped, to varying degrees, by the opportunities, limitations, and exceptions that different laws and regulations concerning migration have offered since the turn of the 20th century. Among the national-level immigration laws that have been ratified in the United States, three deserve special attention because of their direct effects upon migration from Latin America:

1. The 1965 reform known as the Immigration and Nationality Act, and its numerous subsequent corrections;
2. The 1986 Immigration Reform and Control Act (IRCA); and
3. The 1996 Illegal Immigration Reform and Immigrant Responsibility Act (IIRAIRA).

In addition, there has been special legislation related to the specific cases of Cubans and Central Americans.

The Immigration Act of 1965, also known as the Hart-Celler Act, established an annual limitation of 170,000 visas from all Eastern Hemisphere countries with no more than 20,000 per country. The civil rights revolution in the 1960s sought to mitigate discrimination based on race and ethnicity, and thus the 1965 law sought to revoke the previous immigration policy, which favored European immigration and severely impeded Asian immigration. By replacing the old quotas with numerical country ceilings that were uniform across all Eastern Hemisphere countries, the change effectively eliminated the restrictions on immigration from Asia (Jasso and Rosenzweig, 1990). It also stressed family reunification as grounds for admission, along with a very inclusive definition of family relationships. Thus the 1965 act's legacy is to have opened the door to large-scale immigration from the Eastern Hemisphere. This law also ended the Bracero Program and created a general visa policy for the Western Hemisphere with no numerical limits.

In 1968, a limit of 120,000 visas for the Western Hemisphere was set, although this amendment does not determine fixed, per-nation quotas. For 10 years, Mexicans secured roughly half of all the Western Hemisphere visas under the quota. However, with a 1976 amendment, a quota of 20,000 visas per country was established and continues to the present (Jasso and Rosenzweig, 1990; Reimers, 1992, p. 87).

Consequently, this law greatly reduces the number of legally authorized immigrants who can come from Mexico and effectively increases the number of immigrants that can come from the rest of Latin America. Given historically high levels of legal Mexican immigration for the past century or more, a long common border with the United States and persistently great socioeconomic inequality between the two countries, the tightening of immigration restrictions for Mexico has generated greater levels of undocumented immigration.

This system of hemispheric limits soon was in crisis because of the almost 360,000 Cuban refugees who were allowed to enter the country between 1965 and 1978, a fact that came to modify the established ceiling for the Western Hemisphere. A case involving the exceptional number of visas given to Cubans was taken to court. The judge in that case, known as *Silva versus Levi*, ruled that the rights of 145,000 people, primarily Mexicans, had been violated. As a result, visas that came to be known as Silva Cards (*Cartas Silva*) were issued to the victors in the lawsuit (Reimers, 1992) and the immigration law was eventually reformed in 1980 to separate refugees from the per-country quota system.

In the next stage, the 1986 IRCA greatly affected the legal status of some 2.7 million undocumented migrants. This law outlined two amnesty programs, which included a general program named the Legally Authorized Worker (LAW) program for undocumented immigrants who had resided five years or more in the United States, and the Special Agricultural Workers (SAW) program for those who had worked in agriculture during the past six months. Fully 70 percent of those taking advantage of the LAW program and 81 percent of the SAW program were Mexicans. To some degree, Central Americans had a more difficult time qualifying for these programs, since many of these new immigrants did not meet the residency requirements (Donato, Durand, and Massey, 1992; Durand, 1998; Massey et al., 2002).

The major impact of this law was to improve the legal status of Latino immigrants in general (and Mexicans in particular), by regularizing the situation of most existing undocumented migrants. Legalization allowed Latinos to become more geographically dispersed throughout U.S. territory, because it permitted unrestricted movement. Undocumented workers tend not to move very far from their workplaces, because when traveling they become conspicuous and risk greater exposure to being detained by the Immigration and Naturalization Service (INS). However, once they were able to secure legal papers through IRCA, more than 3 million individuals were able to travel with greater ease to look for work or new opportunities in other areas. The economic crisis in California that resulted from the end of the Cold War and the decline of the local aerospace industry led to further immigration away from that state. At the same time, many immigrants who had taken advantage of the IRCA programs found better wages and opportunities in other states. The 1990s economic recovery in the rest of the United States increased the demand for workers (Donato et al., 1992).

The IIRAIRA of 1996 constituted a serious blow to the community of Latin American origin because it restricted a wide range of support programs and services to which the migrant population had previously had access, regardless of legal status. Undocumented workers consequently suffered, substantial hurdles were placed to prevent the entrance of refugees, and resident immigrants with work permits who were not citizens were penalized. In many ways, this federal law contained many of the same elements as California's Proposition 187, which voters in that state passed in 1994, although it avoided California's ban on K–12 education and emergency services for the undocumented, which had been ruled unconstitutional by the U.S. Supreme Court (Hood and Morris, 2000; Weintraub, 1997).

Nevertheless, as so often happens, laws bring unexpected consequences. In this case, the new restrictions on the immigrant community actually fostered the empowerment of that very group, as the number of applications for naturalization soon rose substantially. The year 1996 was a landmark in this regard, as the number of Mexican migrants who applied for naturalization tripled compared with the year before—an interesting development given this particular group's traditional reluctance to change its nationality, although it was expected from the amnesty program under IRCA. Similar patterns emerged among immigrants from Cuba, the Dominican Republic, El Salvador, Guatemala, Colombia, Ecuador, and Peru. Figure 3-1 shows that the number of naturalizations for immigrants from Latin America increased from 65,000 in 1991 to 529,000 in 1996.

Three factors were particularly responsible for the change in the number of naturalizations: (1) the 1986 IRCA legislation allowed residents to naturalize, (2) the 1996 IIRAIRA law placed restrictions on social benefits for illegal immigrants, and (3) the constitutional reforms in several Latin American nations, such as Mexico, Argentina, Costa Rica, and Peru, allowed migrants to acquire a new nationality without losing their original one. Of course, naturalization data are affected by bureaucratic rhythms, particularly the time required to process applications, but the large increase between the first and second half of the 1990s is indisputable. As in much of the data on Hispanics, the Mexican case drives these results. There were 22,000 naturalizations from that country in 1991, 254,000 in 1996, and an average of 150,000 in subsequent years.

In synthesis, there were no restrictions on immigration for Latin Americans prior to 1965. Hemispheric restrictions began in 1968 and by country in the hemisphere in 1976. Regardless of the quota system, this legislation did not impede the growth of the Latino population through immigration, although it clearly fueled increased diversification of national origins. Also, the 1986 IRCA legislation had transformed earlier undocumented Hispanics into permanent immigrants and encouraged greater geographical mobil-

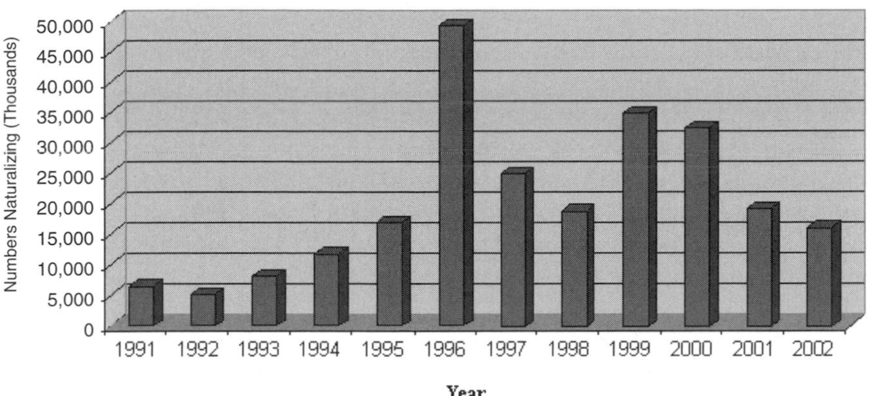

FIGURE 3-1 Number of Hispanics naturalizing each year from 1991 to 2002.
SOURCE: U.S. Immigration and Naturalization Service (2002).

ity within the country (Massey et al., 2002). The 1996 law stirred the Latino community to action, as many individuals decided to apply for naturalization in order to avoid losing a number of rights they had enjoyed up to that time. These changes consequently have implications for the nature of Latino political participation in the United States, as Chapter 11 discusses.

These different migration laws not only affected the Latino immigrant population directly, but also brought them into direct contact with governmental institutions and the U.S. legal system. Through personal procedures and collective social struggles—especially of a legal nature—Latinos began to interact with a variety of U.S. institutions. In short, they became more politically integrated as they learned how to operate in North American society. This dynamic of institutional interaction can be better appreciated through the analysis of some specific cases (Georges, 1990; Hamilton and Stoltz Chinchilla, 2001; Pessar, 1995).

U.S. immigration laws have treated specific Latin American countries distinctly, which may help explain why particular countries have sent more immigrants than others. For example, the only country to have ever experienced a guest-worker program on a large scale is Mexico. Without question, migration from Mexico has been subject to more exceptions to U.S. immigration law than that of any other country, beginning in 1917, when Mexican immigrants were exempted from the clause that required migrants to pass a literacy test (Cardoso, 1980; Jasso and Rosensweig, 1990). From 1942 to 1964, the Bracero Program allowed about 5 million Mexican agricultural workers to enter the United States to work legally on a seasonal basis (Calavita, 1992). In 1965, these former guest-workers (*braceros*) were offered the opportunity to legalize their migratory status if their employers or relatives were willing to support their applications, as there were no fixed limits or country quotas for Western Hemisphere nations.

It was not until 1978 that Mexico had to adapt to the quota system that the United States established at the world level (20,000 visas). This controlled migratory flow primarily involved people who tended to settle in particular cities, especially Los Angeles (Ortiz, 1996). Mexicans used the family reunification measures to bring their relatives into the country. According to Jasso and Rozenweig (1990), in 1985, 22.7 percent of spouses sponsored by native-born U.S. citizens were from Mexico, whereas the next highest group, Fillipinos, stood at 4.9 percent. Later still, in 1986, Mexican immigrants were also the main beneficiaries of the IRCA reforms, through which perhaps 2.3 million people succeeded in regularizing their migratory status. Finally, in the 1990s, almost 80,000 H2A and H2B visas were issued to Mexicans to enter the country legally as temporary agricultural and service workers, despite the fact that those particular visas had traditionally been granted to migrant workers from the Caribbean (Portes and Rumbaut, 1990; Smith-Nonini, 2002) (see Box 3-1).

Finally, the U.S. government initiated the Diversity Visa Program, also known as the Green Card Lottery, in 1990. It offers 55,000 visas each year to citizens of "under-represented countries" in order to facilitate immigration from countries other than those that send large numbers of migrants. This is the easiest and most cost-effective way to secure an immigration visa, because persons chosen under this system have the right to migrate with their families to the United States. In some cases, they are given pre-

BOX 3-1
H2A and H2B Visas

The H2A temporary agricultural visa is a nonimmigrant visa that allows foreign nationals to enter the United States to perform agricultural labor or services of a temporary or seasonal nature. Limits are not fixed and vary annually. The maximum annual limit has been 120,000.

The H2B nonimmigrant visa program permits employers to hire foreign workers to come to the United States and perform temporary nonagricultural work, which may be one-time, seasonal, peak load, or intermittent. There is a 66,000 per year limit on the number of foreign workers who may receive H2B status during each fiscal year (October through September). The process for obtaining H2B certification is similar to, but less extensive and time-consuming than, permanent certification.

paid airfare. In Latin America, citizens of Colombia, the Dominican Republic, El Salvador, and Mexico are considered ineligible.

Cuba became a special case beginning in 1959, both with respect to the entry of refugees and to the systems of quotas, lotteries, deportations, and regularization. What is most notable in the Cuban case is the series of advances and retreats that have characterized the migratory policies of the U.S. and Cuban governments, which open and close their doors as a function of changing political conjunctures. The Cuban government allowed several thousand emigrants to leave the island freely from the harbor at Camarioca in 1965, and in 1980 some 124,000 more were permitted to leave the country from the port of Mariel and were eventually received as refugees by the United States (Portes and Stepick, 1993). Beginning in the Johnson administration, air travel from Cuba was allowed, making it possible for 360,000 more Cubans to enter the country (Reimers, 1992, p. 124). Between 1961 and 1988, almost half a million Cubans (486,426) became permanent residents (Jasso and Rosenzweig, 1990). In the Cuban case, there has even been legislation (the Law of Adjustment) related to the so-called raft people, who are granted refuge only if they succeed in reaching American soil, a right that is denied to those who are captured or rescued while still at sea.

Dominicans also received preferential treatment after the fall of Trujillo, who governed as president from 1930 to 1961 and exercised an almost exclusively personal authority over the issuing of passports (Grasmuck and Pessar, 1991). During the 1965 U.S. invasion, President Johnson liberalized the authorization of visas as a kind of escape valve designed to diffuse social conflicts, so from 1965 to 1966 the number of resident visas increased by 74 percent. Those who benefited most were young men who had supported the opposition movement (Georges, 1990). Later, the economic reforms instituted by the Balaguer regime spurred an intense flow of migrants to the United States. Many of these Dominican migrants entered the country with legitimate tourist visas and then simply stayed on indefinitely, while others opted for an indirect emigration route that took them first to Puerto Rico, where they crossed the dangerous Strait of La Mona (Duany, 1990). During their stay in Puerto Rico, many Dominicans worked in agriculture or the informal economy, although others considered their time on the island as simply a stopover on their journey to the United States (Duany, Hernandez Angueira, and Rey, 1995).

Central American countries, such as Nicaragua and, to a lesser extent, El Salvador and Guatemala, have also benefited from special regularization programs. In the 1980s, President Reagan's support for the *contras* (anti-sandinistas) was manifested, among many other ways, by a very liberal policy for issuing tourist visas to Nicaraguans, many of whom later became illegal immigrants but were finally granted refugee status. After several years of legal struggles, Nicaraguans were granted refugee status in 1997, thereby earning the right to reside in the United States on a permanent basis, thanks to legislation called the Nicaraguan Adjustment and Central American Relief Act (NACARA). This particular act was also utilized by some Salvadoran, Guatemalan, and Cuban migrants (Menjivar, 2000).

Nonetheless, there was a clear reluctance to recognize most Salvadorans and Guatemalans as refugees even if they were fleeing civil wars, so they were classified as economic immigrants. Many of them were deported in the 1980s, while a few received asylum and others launched lawsuits with the support of a variety of nongovernmental and religious organizations (Hamilton and Stoltz Chinchilla, 2001). Finally, in 1990, a form of temporary protection was granted (temporary protected status, or TPS[1]), which gave those migrants permission to work, although it did not grant them permanent residence status, as had been the case with the Nicaraguans. This measure was renewed several times until 1997, when the courts established a legal status designed to protect all migrants who found themselves in similar situations. In this way, many Salvadorans and Guatemalans succeeded in regularizing their migratory status (Menjivar, 2000). If IRCA was for Mexicans the means of legal recourse that allowed many undocumented migrants in their communities to legalize their situation, for Central Americans the legislative processes provided by NACARA and TPS were fundamental to their establishing permanent residence on American soil.

Finally, migrants from South American countries depend mostly on the established quota system that allows them to enter the United States as tourists, although once there, they often take advantage of the family reunification provisions. Few South Americans have petitioned for refugee status, and there have been no cases of special legislation or programs related to these nations. Nonetheless, the number of migrants that decide to remain in the United States after their visas expire is increasing, adding to the ranks of undocumented migrants.

Undocumented Immigration

In effect, the limits on immigration from Latin America, which began in 1978, along with the growing demand for low-wage labor have led to the growth of an undocumented population. The Latino population in the United States today includes a high proportion of undocumented migrants, a situation that made regularization programs so significant in the past. In practice, there are now two main modalities of undocumented migration.

[1]The TPS provides nationals of certain regions or nationalities residing in the United States a temporary stay of removal and work authorization due to armed conflict or other extraordinary conditions in their home country.

The first is the preferred method of Mexican and Central American migrants, who enter the United States surreptitiously by crossing its southern border. The second is that used by individuals who first obtain a tourist visa to enter the country and then stay beyond the document's expiration date. Estimates for 2002 indicate that there are 9.3 million illegal migrants in the United States (Passel and Fix, 2004).

Careful demographic studies on the size of the undocumented population are relatively recent. At first, the INS estimated that there were between 8 and 12 millon undocumented in the 1970s but with no empirical evidence. This led to more careful examination by demographers. Systematic demographic studies began to be carried out based on the 1980 census, especially with respect to calculating the size of the Mexican-origin population. Demographers began to reach a consensus that, in 1980, the Mexican undocumented population was between 1.7 and 2.3 million and that other nationalities constituted roughly another 1.5 million (see Bean, Telles, and Lindsay Lowell, 1987, for a review of sources). This estimate appears to have been accurate, since IRCA legalized 2.3 millon Mexicans in 1986 and, on the basis of estimates by Massey et al. (2002), 600,000 undocumented immigrants remained. Thus, on the eve of IRCA in 1986, there were 2.9 million undocumented Mexicans. Soon after, the undocumented population began to grow again and now included a large Central American contingent. By 1997 with NACARA and with TPS in 2000, close to 3 million undocumented Central Americans in the United States had become legal residents (Hamilton and Stoltz-Chinchilla, 2001; Menjivar, 2000), so from 1986 to 2000, the undocumented population varied widely. By 2002, according to estimates by Passel and Fix (2004), the total undocumented population had grown to 9.3 million, the majority of whom are Hispanic. Mexicans constitute 57 percent of all undocumented, and other Latin Americans, primarily Central Americans, constitute 23 percent (Passel and Fix, 2004). Thus, four-fifths of all undocumented migration to the United States originates in Latin America.

Several factors explain the presence of many undocumented Hispanic immigrants. Historically, efforts were made to create a model of temporary migration from Mexico different from the flows that originated in Europe. On the other hand, the absence of specific legislation related to Mexico once the Bracero Program was eliminated clearly fostered undocumented immigration, which was tolerated by the U.S. government and used as a mechanism for regulating secondary labor markets where wages were low and working conditions poor.

Mexicans came to depend on a complex network of social relations to reduce the costs and risks associated with crossing the border and live as illegals. In the absence of official contracts, as during the Bracero Program period, these Mexicans sought the support of relatives and friends for finding work and a place to live. At the same time, employers, who could no longer seek workers from an official *bracero* system, began to utilize migrant networks to hire and train workers. As a result, the social networks matured and became increasingly complex. They served not only the migrants themselves but also employers' demand for low-cost and reliable labor (Durand, 1994; Durand and Massey, 2003; Massey, Alarcón, Durand, and González, 1987; Passel and Fix, 2004). Growing Mexican immigration, fostered through the networks of formerly unregulated migrants, simply overwhelmed the relatively small visa quotas suddenly imposed on Mexico in 1978.

Fertility

In addition to immigration from Latin America, the extent of Latino population growth in the United States depends on fertility or the childbearing rates of Hispanic women, which tend to be higher than for non-Hispanic whites and blacks. Also, Hispanic women vary widely by nationality in the number of children they bear. Table 3-2 shows total fertility rates and the mean number of children ever born to women ages 35 to 44 in 2000. The total fertility rate is an age-standardized measure of recent fertility among women ages 15 to 44 and has become the standard childbearing measure. All Latino groups shown have higher fertility rates than non-

TABLE 3-2 Total Fertility Rates by Ethnicity and Children Ever Born Rates to Women Ages 35 to 44 by Ethnicity and Generation Since Immigration, Women 35 to 44, 2000

		Children Ever Born to Women Ages 35 to 44			
Ethnicity	Total Fertility Rate	Total	Immigrants	2nd Generation	3rd Generation
Mexican	3.3	2.5	2.7	2.1	2.3
Puerto Rican	2.6	2.2	2.3	2.2	n.a.
Cuban	1.9	n.a.	n.a.	n.a.	n.a.
Central/South American	2.1	2.0	2.0	n.a.	n.a.
Non-Hispanic white	1.9	1.8	1.8	1.5	1.8
Non-Hispanic black	2.2	1.9	1.7	n.a.	2.0
Asian	1.9	1.7	1.7	n.a.	1.9

NOTE: n.a. = not available. Numbers are not shown when sample size is less than 50 women, which includes total Cubans.
SOURCES: Total fertility rates from Martin et al. (2002). Children ever born from fertility supplement of Current Population Survey (2000).

Hispanic white women in the United States. Mexican women clearly had the highest fertility, registering a rate of 3.3 in 2000 and at the other extreme, Cuban women had only 1.9 children. This compares with 1.9 for non-Hispanic whites and 2.2 for blacks.

We also computed the mean number of children ever born to women ages 35 to 44. This provides a measure of nearly complete fertility, although it misses the fertility experiences of younger women. However, it permits us to disaggregate fertility for various immigrant generations, since data are not available to break down the total fertility rate in this way. By limiting the age cohort to 35 to 44 rather than including all women of childbearing age, we avoid most, though not all, of the distortion caused by different age structures, especially problematic for the second generation, which tends to be very young.

Immigrant Mexican women in this age group have had 2.7 children compared with 2.1 for the children of immigrants and 2.3 for grandchildren and later generations. Thus, there is limited support for convergence toward the fertility of black and white native-born groups, although the second generation has even lower fertility than the third, which continues to have considerably higher fertility than black and white natives.[2] Interestingly, the fertility rates of white, black, and Asian immigrants are lower than those of the well-established and much more common third-generation black and white population. Non-Mexican Latino populations are generally too small to capture a reliable fertility index, except for the case of Puerto Ricans. The so-called Puerto Rican second generation, those who were born on the U.S. mainland of island-born parents, have only slightly lower fertility than those born in Puerto Rico.

Fertility rates for immigrants to the United States are often higher than those for their compatriots who stayed behind. This is especially true in the case of Mexicans, for whom an immigrant total fertility rate of 3.3 in 2000 was well above the 2.6 recorded for Mexico in the same year. The reasons for these differences are unclear, but perhaps Mexican immigration is selective of families and persons from rural areas where fertility is higher. A Cuban immigrant fertility rate of 1.9 is above that of 1.6 for Cuba; this may reflect the social status of those who immigrated as well as the profound changes that occurred on the island since the time when most Cubans immigrated. Puerto Rican immigrant fertility of 2.2 is also above that for

---

[2]It is important to note, however, that the so-called generations that we use are based on cross-sectional data and thus do not capture generational change. That is, the second generation in 2000, for example, consists not of children of the first generation in 2000 but rather children of a first generation cohort in earlier years. Also, the so-called Mexican third generation is actually comprised of many generations, including direct descendants of residents in the Southwest states prior to the U.S. occupation in 1848.

Puerto Rico, which recorded a total fertility rate of 1.9. Thus, although we might expect lower fertility among immigrants who migrate to the United States because they are coming to a more urban and modern destination and because the migration process itself may interrupt the likelihood of having children, their fertility tends to be higher.[3]

Age and Sex Distributions

We have shown that the Latino population is one of the fastest growing segments of the U.S. population, and that growth is fueled by a combination of fertility and immigration. However, the extent of fertility and the nature of immigration, specifically the age and sex of immigrants, have effects not only on the growth rate of the population but also on the population's age and sex structure. That is, it determines, along with mortality, how a population is distributed by age and the sex balance at each age. This age–sex distribution, represented in this section by population pyramids, reflects the importance of Latinos in different stages of the life cycle and thus the extent of their participation in such areas as education, family formation, the labor market, and their use of health care services.

The particular combination of relatively high fertility and the migration of persons at young working ages leads to a Latino population that is particularly young, as Figure 3-2 shows, especially when compared with the age structure of the non-Hispanic white and black populations (Figures 3-3 and 3-4). The population pyramids represent the age and sex distribution of these groups, and they are further broken down by generation since immigration. The Latino population pyramid's shape reveals a small middle-aged and senior population; the population under age 45 comprises the vast majority of the population. Almost 40 percent of the Latino population is under age 20, and 65 percent is under age 35. Foreign-born Latinos comprise 43 percent of the population, compared with 31 percent who are second generation and 26 percent in the third generation. However, the age distributions are quite diverse across generations. The foreign-born population, represented by the lightest shade, is diamond shaped around a middle band, comprised of 30- to 34-year-olds. This form characterizes a labor migrant population that brings few children with them. In terms of sex, the immigrant population is only slightly more male than female, making it more gender-balanced than earlier Latino immigrant waves.

By the second and third generations, there is little difference between the percentage distribution of males and females by age, as expected from a

---

[3]Fertility rates for Mexico, Cuba, and Puerto Rico in 2000 can be found in United Nations (2003).

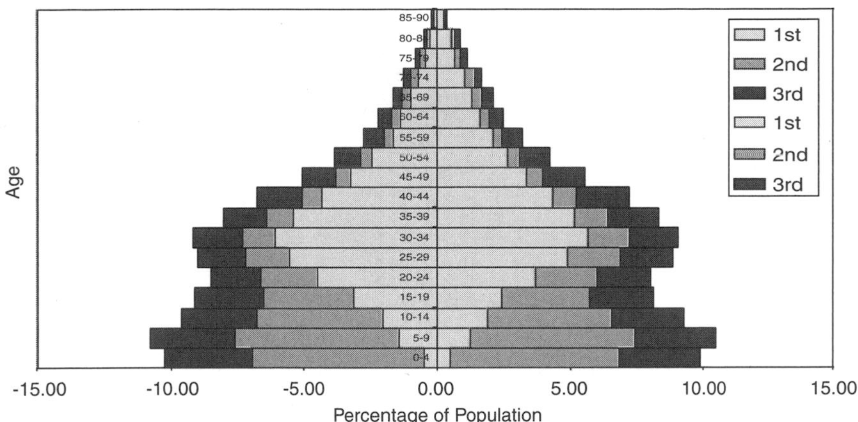

FIGURE 3-2 Age–sex composition of the Latino population of the United States, 1998–2002.
SOURCE: Data from Current Population Surveys, 1998–2002.

population that is no longer immigrant. For the third generation, the age–sex distribution is only slightly younger than the distribution for the entire U.S.-born population. In terms of age and sex, there is growing convergence with the rest of the U.S. population.

The youthfulness of the Latino population is especially apparent in comparison to the age pyramids for blacks and whites who are not His-

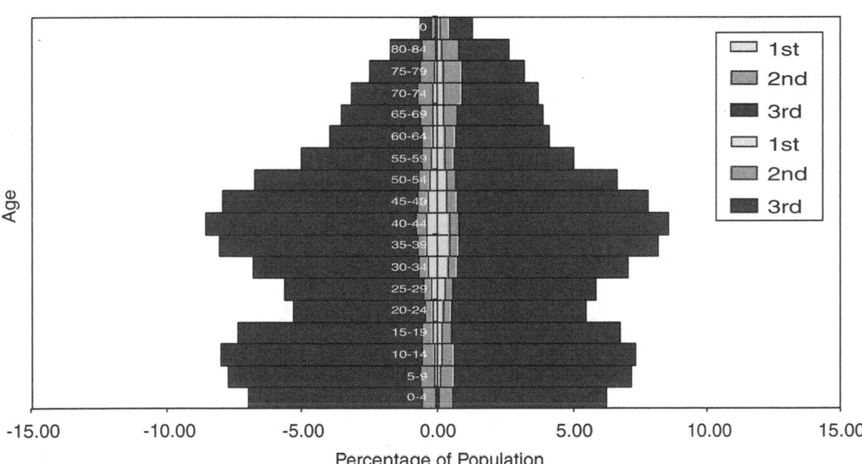

FIGURE 3-3 Age–sex distribution of the white population of the United States, 1998–2000.
SOURCE: Data from Current Population Surveys, 1998–2000.

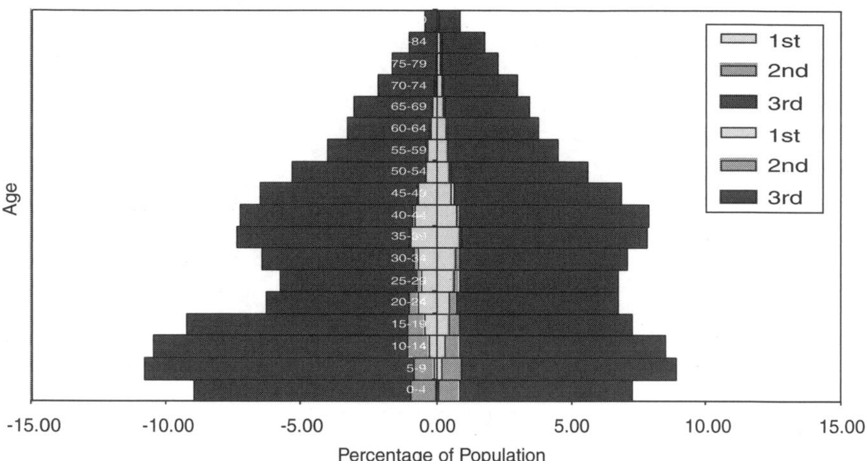

FIGURE 3-4 Age–sex distribution of the black population of the United States, 1998–2000.
SOURCE: Data from Current Population Surveys, 1998–2000.

panic. Their pyramids show the large bulge of a baby boom generation born for nearly 20 years after World War II. The bulge in the 40 to 54 age groups in the year 2000 for whites and blacks implies that a large group of U.S.-born will soon reach retirement age. Although the baby boom had had a significant echo effect, reflecting that generation's births, their fertility greatly declined compared with that of their parents. Latinos have thus largely supplanted non-Hispanic whites and blacks as new labor force entrants and increasingly constitute large numbers of the school-age population.

Figures 3-5, 3-6, and 3-7 show analogous population pyramids for three of the largest Latino national groups: Mexicans, Cubans, and Dominicans. These three groups illustrate the internal variation in the structure of the Latino population. The age–sex distribution of the Mexican population in the United States, shown in Figure 3-5, looks very similar to that of the Latino population. This is not surprising considering that Mexicans make up 63 percent of the Latino population. The Mexican population is also a young population: 42 percent are under age 20 and almost 70 percent are under age 35. First-generation immigrants constitute the largest percentage of the population over age 20, while second-generation immigrants dominate the population under age 20. Again, the male and female populations are relatively similar in terms of both age distribution and nativity, although there are slightly more first-generation males (41 percent) than females (36 percent). For the Mexican-origin population, the

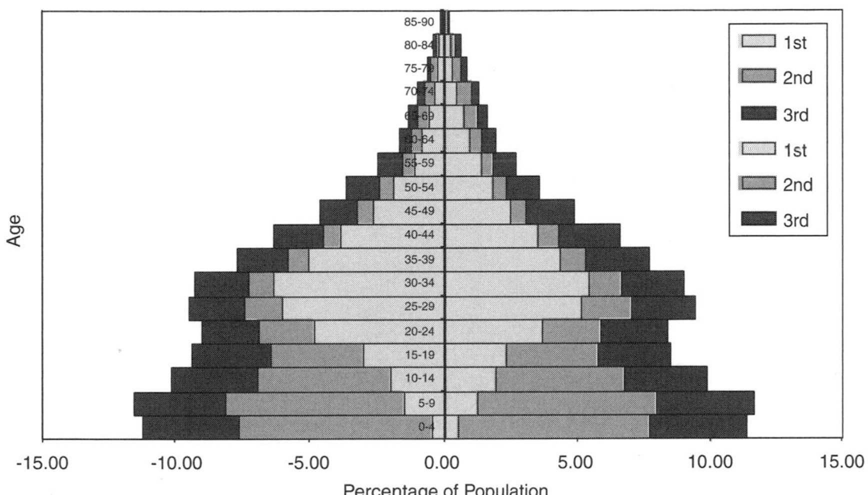

FIGURE 3-5 Age–sex composition of the Mexican-origin population by nativity, 1998–2002.
SOURCE: Data from Current Population Surveys, 1998–2002.

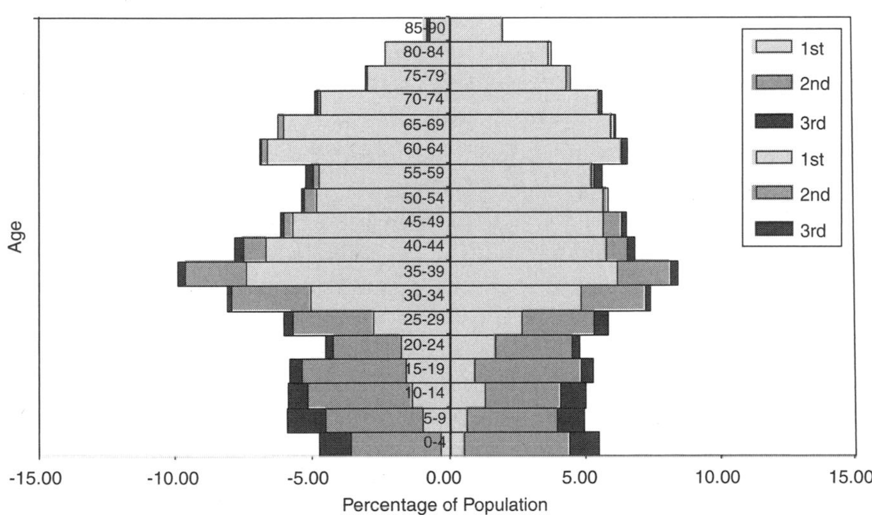

FIGURE 3-6 Age–sex composition of the Cuban-origin population by nativity, 1998–2002.
SOURCE: Data from Current Population Surveys, 1998–2002.

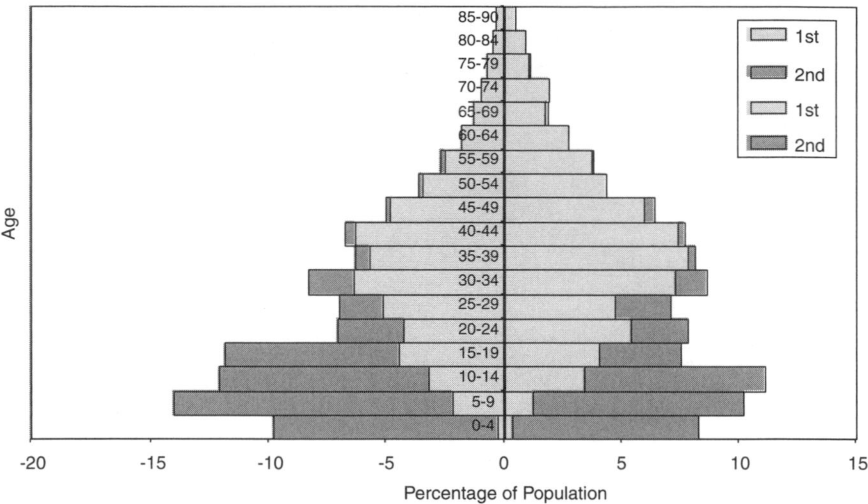

FIGURE 3-7 Age–sex composition of the Dominican-origin population by nativity, 1998–2002.
SOURCE: Data from Current Population Surveys, 1998–2002.

second and especially the third generation are significant in all age groups, reflecting an especially long-standing immigration.

Figure 3-6 demonstrates that the Cuban population in the United States departs markedly from the age–sex distributions of Mexicans and the general Latino population. While the shapes of the pyramids for all Latinos and for Mexicans specifically resemble triangles, reflecting young and gender-balanced populations, the Cuban graph shows a much older population, in which only 22 percent of Cubans are under age 20 and 40 percent are under age 35. This is consistent with their fertility levels, which are more similar to those of the mostly U.S. native black and white populations, which have similar distributions. These numbers provide a stark contrast to those for Mexicans, for whom the majority of the population is less than 35 years old.

Also, this graph shows that the vast majority of Cuban origin persons over the age of 40 are immigrants, apparently the result of refugee immigration flows concentrated in the 1960s. Only 6 percent of all Cubans in the United States are third generation, and these tend to be in the youngest age categories. This is in comparison to 27 percent who are second generation and 67 percent who are first generation. The sex distribution of the population is relatively equal, although there are slightly more first-generation males than females under age 20. Finally, the alternating periods of migratory flux and reflux, plus the age-related selectivity imposed by the Cuban government, which makes it more difficult for young people to migrate under the pretext of their obligation to perform military service, have left their mark on the peculiar distribution of ages and generations that make up the Cuban-origin community (Grenier and Pérez, 2003).

The other Latino national groups are nearly all part of the wave of new immigrants that came after 1970. Thus, the majority of adults of the new Latino subgroups (Dominicans, Central Americans, South Americans) are immigrants. The pyramids for Central Americans and South Americans are shown in Appendix Figures A3-1 and A3-2 at the end of this chapter. We show only a population pyramid for Dominicans in Figure 3-7.[4] The age distribution of Dominicans is particularly young, even more than other Latino groups, and, like the new immigration from Central and South America, the large majority of those over age 30 are immigrants. However, Dominicans are different from the other major Latino groups because of the preponderance of females, especially in the first generation: 64 percent of Dominican women are first-generation immigrants, compared with 54 percent of men. Although not shown, the age distribution for Central Americans is especially concentrated in the 25- to 45-year-old categories, which may reflect a sudden surge of immigration in the late 1970s and early 1980s, when civil wars broke out in Guatemala, El Salvador, and Nicaragua. Finally, the South American population, also not shown, is relatively old, apparently reflecting a largely middle-class immigration with low fertility.

With the exception of the Cubans, the Latino second generation is largely young and the offspring of the recently arrived immigrants. The white and black populations, in contrast, contain very few immigrants or children of immigrants and most of the non-Hispanic black and white immigrants are in the middle age ranges. Immigrants among the Latino population dominate the 20- to 39-year-old age bars, mostly with first-generation persons, while their second-generation U.S.-born children fill the ranks of the youngest age brackets. Thus, with continuing immigration in the next 20 years, the second generation will continue to dominate the under age 20 categories, while immigrants will compete for the 20- to 40-year-old brackets with the grown children of immigrants. Prior to 20 years ago, there were far fewer immigrants available to become mothers. Now, the rapidly growing population of immigrant mothers has contributed to a

[4]The age–sex pyramids for Dominicans, other Central Americans, and South Americans do not contain data on third-generation immigrants in the United States. The Current Population Survey contained only nativity data for the aggregated group of Central-South Americans. According to the cross-tabulation of nativity and country of origin, only 823 Central-South Americans, or 4 percent, are identified as third-generation Americans.

large and young second generation. Seen from another perspective, between ages 0 and 19, the Latino population is dominated by the children of immigrants. This baby boom caused by the growth in immigration portends a significant change in the ethnic composition of the U.S.-born adult population. A large Hispanic component born and socialized in the United States is entering the labor force and in certain parts of the country will dominate the blue-collar labor force in at least the next 40 years. The Latino proportion of the U.S. electorate is also certain to grow, which could have a large impact on U.S. leadership at the beginning of the 21st century. Overall, this infusion of young persons into the U.S. population will allow it to keep a relatively young age profile, in contrast to the aging populations of most industrialized countries.

The age structures of the Latino populations also have implications for education, the labor force, health care, and the future of the social security system, as subsequent chapters show. With time, the age structures demonstrate the progressive Hispanification of increasingly older age groups from children to adults to seniors, as Latinos themselves age. Also, massive industrial restructuring since the 1970s has removed and downgraded many formerly high-paying working-class jobs, and the new economy has taken advantage of the new infusion of low-cost labor provided by immigration, particularly from Latin America. The dispersion of Latinos into areas of new industrial growth may also reflect and fuel the changing spatial structure of industry. At the same time that young Latino immigrants are overrepresented and growing as a proportion of the young working population, their immigrant status means they are less likely to be qualified to vote. Thus, immigrants are contributing substantially to the well-being of the native population in several ways, but they are largely unable to participate in the electoral process, because of foreign birth or young age. For the children of these immigrants, who are automatically citizens, their relatively young age will prevent their electoral participation in the near future. The impact that Latinos will have on these institutions also depends on the extent to which they populate particular regions of the United States. Traditionally, they have been regionally concentrated, so their effects are often locally specific, but that is changing.

Geographical Dispersion

Traditionally, the Hispanic population in the United States has been concentrated near the southern border with Mexico, the Northeast, and Florida. Such concentration is typical of immigrant groups who build communities in a few areas before branching out. Also, in the case of Mexicans, the U.S. Southwest, their territorial area of concentration, was formerly Mexican territory that was annexed in the 19th century. Table 3-3 shows

TABLE 3-3 Top Three Places of Residence at the 2000 Census of the Foreign-Born Latino Population by Place of Birth

Place of Birth	First	%	Second	%	Third	%
North America						
Mexico	California	42.8	Texas	20.5	Illinois	6.7
Central America						
Costa Rica	Florida	18.3	New Jersey	17.2	California	17.0
Salvador	California	44.0	Texas	12.4	New York	9.4
Guatemala	California	44.0	New York	6.9	Florida	6.7
Honduras	Florida	18.7	California	16.5	New York	15.3
Nicaragua	Florida	44.5	California	29.2	New York	4.6
Panama	New York	24.9	Florida	17.3	California	11.5
Caribbean						
Cuba	Florida	73.7	New Jersey	6.3	California	4.7
Dominican Republic	New York	59.3	New Jersey	13.3	Florida	9.7
Puerto Rico	New York	30.7	Florida	14.1	New Jersey	10.8
South America						
Argentina	California	23.4	Florida	22.4	New York	14.3
Bolivia	Virginia	29.3	California	15.4	New York	10.7
Chile	Florida	19.7	California	19.4	New York	15.7
Colombia	Florida	30.9	New York	21.9	New Jersey	13.7
Ecuador	New York	46.6	New Jersey	17.9	Florida	9.7
Peru	Florida	19.4	California	19.1	New Jersey	16.2
Paraguay	New York	29.8	Florida	10.5	New Jersey	7.3
Uruguay	Florida	21.7	New Jersey	21.1	New York	16.7
Venezuela	Florida	44.2	New York	9.9	Texas	6.8

SOURCE: U.S. Census Bureau (2000).

the leading three states for several Latino national groups. California and Texas served as both ports of entry and areas of absorption for immigrants arriving from Mexico (and later Salvadorans and Guatemalans, the two largest Central American groups—Hamilton and Stoltz Chinchilla, 2001; Massey et al., 1987, Menjivar, 2000). On the East Coast, New York, New Jersey, and Florida are the preferred destinations of Caribbean and South American immigrants (Pessar, 1995; Portes and Stepick, 1993). As the traditional areas of settlement and because of the force of social networks that continues to draw immigrants to these states, 7 out of every 10 Hispanics reside in these five states. Other important immigrant-receiving states are Illinois, where Mexicans began to arrive in the 1920s and Puerto Ricans in the 1940s, and Arizona and New Mexico, which were, like Texas and California, formerly part of Mexican territory.

Despite the concentration of the Latino population in only a few states, we should also emphasize two more recent processes that are expanding with great intensity: (1) the diversification of national origin in urban areas once considered to be the capitals of migrants from particular countries and (2) a greater geographical dispersion in new destinations (Durand and Massey, 2003). New York City, for example, was well known as Puerto Rican territory, California and Texas has been home to numerous Mexican immigrants, and Florida was the preferred destination of Cubans. Today, however, these concentrations of migrants are being diluted, and there is an increasing diversity in the interaction among distinct national groups of Latino migrants.

The states of New York and, to a greater extent, Florida are paradigmatic cases regarding Latino concentration, where a process of diversification of the Hispanic population is taking place and there is potentially more interaction among Hispanics of different national groups. Although New York State, and especially the City of New York itself, have long been the main place of residence for Puerto Ricans, they are now the principal destination for Dominicans, Ecuadorians, Panamanians, and Paraguayans. In addition, New York is the second most common destination for Colombians, Guatemalans, and Venezuelans, and it is home to many Salvadorans, Hondurans, Nicaraguans, Argentineans, Chileans, Bolivians, Peruvians, and Cubans (Durand and Massey, 2003; Durand, Massey, and Charvet, 2000). Indeed, the fourth largest group is now Mexicans, who were of an almost negligible number in that city two decades ago (Smith, 1993).

A similar situation has developed in Florida. Although Cubans predominate there, this state is also the primary place of settlement for Honduran, Nicaraguan, and Colombian migrants and the second place for Peruvians, Dominicans, Guatemalans, Bolivians, and Ecuadorians. Meanwhile, many small cities and towns in the state of New Jersey have absorbed innumerable Hispanics from diverse places of origin in the Caribbean and South America, especially Cuba, the Dominican Republic, Peru, Ecuador, and Colombia. By contrast, in California and the border states, Mexicans continue to predominate, although a growing presence of Salvadorans and Guatemalans is increasingly evident, as are South Americans and even Caribbean migrants (Durand and Massey, 2003; Durand et al., 2000). This greater interaction among Hispanics of different nationalities could promote greater social and political ties among Latino national groups as well as stronger panethnic identities.

The geographical distribution of Hispanics in the 21st century no longer seems to obey the traditional patterns of concentration, in which networks of social relationships, ethnic enclaves, and niches in labor markets function as mechanisms of attraction and permanence for this population. The past experiences of earlier waves of European immigrants of diverse nationalities show that while they were initially attracted to a particular place, they tended to disperse and form new population centers in other areas, where they once again experienced processes of concentration and residential segregation. Table 3-4 shows the Latino populations of the top 20 states in 1990 and 2000. The top 9 states remain in roughly the same order over the course of the decade, but the next 11 states reveal Latino growth in places where they were few before. The table shows growth in new states that had only small Latino populations in 1990. Between 1990 and 2000, the Hispanic population more than tripled in Nevada, grew four times in Georgia, and nearly quintupled in North Carolina. It doubled in several others.

The new geography of the Latino population in the United States of the past two decades cannot be generalized for all Latinos. While Mexicans, Central Americans, Puerto Ricans, and Dominicans have dispersed in the past two decades, other national groups have not. Cubans, for example, have increased their residential concentration in Florida, from 60 percent in 1980 to 74 percent in 2000. As an example of residential stability, nearly 50 percent of Ecuadorians resided in New York in both 1980 and 2000.

TABLE 3-4 Latino Population (1000s) in 1990 and 2000 and Percentage Growth for Top 20 States in 2000

State	1990	2000	% Growth
California	7,688	10,967	42
Texas	4,340	6,670	53
New York	2,214	2,868	29
Florida	1,574	2,683	70
Illinois	904	1,530	69
New Jersey	740	1,117	51
Arizona	668	1,066	59
New México	579	765	32
Colorado	424	736	73
Washington	215	442	106
Georgia	109	435	299
Massachusetts	288	429	49
Pennsylvania	232	394	70
Nevada	124	394	218
North Carolina	77	379	392
Virginia	160	330	106
Michigan	202	324	60
Connecticut	213	320	50
Oregon	113	275	143
Maryland	125	228	82

SOURCE: U.S. Census Bureau, Census (2000) Summary File 1. Census of Population (1990), General Population Characteristics (CP-1-1).

The primacy of California and New York as Latino states is weakening, even though they continue to be the main ports of entry for immigrants from Latin America. In 1980, California was the residence of 58 percent of the Mexican population, but it fell by 15 percentage points to 43 percent in 2000. Similarly, 72 percent of Salvadorans lived in California in 1980 but only 44 percent in 2000. Guatemalans went from 58 percent in California in 1980 to 44 percent in 2000. California continues to be the principal place of residence for these three national groups, but the trend away from concentration in that state is substantial.

Similarly, New York was the state of residence for 47 percent of Puerto Ricans in 1980 but only 31 percent in 2000. At the same time, the total population of Puerto Ricans in New York declined. Just under 8 of 10 (77 percent) Dominicans lived in New York, but by 2000 only about 6 of 10 (59 percent) did. Finally, Cuban New Yorkers constituted 10 percent of all Cuban Americans in 1980 but only 4 percent in 2000. Thus, Latinos are moving away from the two traditional ports of entry. This includes both Latinos who first go to these states and then move to other states as well as a large number who are moving directly from their countries of origin to less traditional states.

The movement of these populations into these new regions has much to do with the profound structural changes that have taken place in U.S. labor markets, the availability of cheaper housing in the new regions, and processes of social and geographic mobility that affected the black and white populations (Durand and Massey, 2003; Hernández-León and Zúñiga, 2000; Stull, Broadway, and Griffith, 1995). For example, Latinos—and especially Mexicans—began to emigrate from Los Angeles to the state of Nevada in the 1980s in search of better wages. In the space of just 20 years, they have practically come to control the service industries linked to hotels, casinos, and restaurants, jobs that were previously held by native black and white workers and before that by Polish and Italian immigrants (Durand, 1994; Martinez Curiel, 2003). In addition to higher wages, Nevada offers migrants other advantages, such as ample opportunities to work double shifts and to bring their families, due to the availability of work for both men and women. Moreover, the arrival of Latinos in Nevada coincided with the recovery of the construction industry, which pursued a new phase of hotel and casino development.

Perhaps the most important industrial development for immigrants in the South is in the poultry industry, especially in chicken, duck, and turkey processing (Kandel and Parrado, 2004). There, processes of industrial conversion have been characterized by the relocation of plants to rural areas outside the cities and by efforts to reduce production costs, especially those of labor. As part of this process, older workers have been indemnified and labor unions dissolved, thus opening the way for the hiring of cheap, easily controlled workers (Griffith, 1995). New opportunities for employment have also emerged on the East Coast, especially in industries related to fish products. Fish, seafood, and crab processing plants have also gone through a process of conversion in which unionized black workers have been replaced by Latino migrants (Smith-Nonini, 2000).

Opportunities for employment also opened up in cities, especially in construction, the service sector, and manufacturing industries. The opening up of labor markets in the construction industry in Atlanta during the period leading up to the 1996 Olympic games is a particularly well-known case, because this sector had been a well-remunerated and specialized niche practically reserved for whites (Rosenfeld and Tienda, 1999). Over time, new Latino migrants have entered the construction industry and have come to occupy higher and better paid positions in it. In fact, many Latinos have become construction contractors themselves. Another example, also from the state of Georgia, is the revitalized carpet industry—in the city of Dalton—that hires only Latino migrants of Mexican and Central American origin, as Hernández-León and Zúñiga (2000) have documented.

Mexicans have gained a reputation as good workers in the agricultural labor markets in the South and on the East Coast, which have traditionally been dominated by black, poor white, and Caribbean workers. Today, almost the entire tobacco harvest depends on temporary workers who arrive from Mexico with H2A visas (see Box 3-1). Similarly, Mexican workers have begun to predominate in the agricultural belt between Florida and New Jersey by moving in a south-to-north direction in accordance with changing harvesting seasons (Griffith, 2000).

Finally, in the Midwest—especially in Minnesota, Iowa, and Nebraska—the growth of the Latino population has come largely as a response to the restructuring of the meat and poultry processing industries. As in the South, meat processing plants have been relocated outside the cities, many black and white workers have been laid off, and labor unions have been broken (Stull et al., 1995). These recently hired Latino workers have joined groups of earlier migrants who have lived and worked in this region since the 1920s and whose main points of reference are the cities of Chicago, Gary, Detroit, and St. Paul (Durand and Arias, 2000; Valdés, 1982, 1991, 2000).

Using the index of dissimilarity at the state level, Table 3-5 summarizes the extent of segregation or, alternatively, dispersion for several Hispanic subgroups across the 50 states. Dissimilarity indexes range from 0 to 100, in which 0 indicates complete dispersion into the general U.S. population and 100 indicates complete segregation. The table shows changes in state distribution from 1980 to 2000 and levels for foreign- and native-born in 2000. The first row shows the extent of dissimilarity for Hispanics with non-Hispanics since 1980 and reveals stability in the extent of segregation

TABLE 3-5 Dissimilarity Indexes at the State Level Between Hispanics and Hispanic Subgroups with the Remaining U.S. Population for 1980, 1990, and 2000 and by Foreign or U.S. Birth in 2000

Ethnicity	1980	1990	2000	U.S.-Born 2000	Foreign-Born 2000
Hispanic	48.9	48.6	43.8	45.8	40.6
Mexican	65.5	65.0	57.0	58.4	52.7
Puerto Rican	57.2	54.3	52.6	50.7	55.7
Cuban	63.2	64.6	65.2	51.8	73.3
Dominican	n.a.	75.0	73.2	72.4	74.0
Central American	n.a.	48.7	40.5	41.5	41.8
South American	n.a.	47.3	45.6	43.0	48.3
Other Hispanic	n.a.	38.2	41.2	44.1	39.7

NOTE: n.a. = not available.
SOURCE: Integrated Public Use Microdata Series (U.S. Census Bureau, 2000).

by state, when Hispanics are viewed as a single group. However, for subgroups, the patterns over time vary substantially. Mexican geographical dispersion remained fairly constant from 1980 to 1990 but then markedly dropped from 65 to 57, which reflects their recent emergence in nontraditional states. The last two columns show that dispersion is greater among the foreign-born. Thus, the cross-sectional evidence for 2000 demonstrates that Mexicans are bucking the trend of many other immigrant groups, who concentrate in the traditional ports of entry of earlier immigrants and then they or their descendants disperse, as they become incorporated into American society. In contrast, the dispersal of Mexicans is now being created in the immigrant generation, which is settling in new destinations and, to a great extent, eschewing traditional ones. These trends may have major implications for the way that Latinos are perceived and incorporated by American society in the future, as their geographic isolation diminishes.

Puerto Rican dispersion has increased slowly but steadily since 1980. Dominicans, for which no data are available in 1980, also became slightly more dispersed between 1990 and 2000. However, Cubans, the most concentrated subgroup in a single state, have continued to steadily increase their geographic isolation in each of the last two censuses. For all the Caribbean groups, immigrants are clearly more concentrated in fewer states than the U.S.-born, and this is especially true for Cubans. Thus, Puerto Ricans, Dominicans, and Cubans follow the traditional path of regional concentration followed by dispersion for later generations, and this is especially true for Cubans. Foreign-born Cubans, despite having been in the United States for a relatively long time compared with other immigrant groups, registered a full 73.3 dissimilarity rate, indicating extremely high concentration of immigrants, perhaps because of an exceptionally successful ethnic enclave in Southern Florida (Portes and Stepick, 1993). Still, U.S.-born Cubans had a rate of only 51.8, suggesting substantial movement of their children out of that state.

For the other groups, only 1990 and 2000 data are available. Rates of Central American segregation across states, like those for Mexicans, dropped sharply from 1990 to 2000. Central Americans registered the greatest dispersion among all of the subgroups. Dominicans and South Americans have registered barely noticeable declines in segregation, while Central Americans are increasingly dispersed, registering the lowest segregation by state among all Hispanic subgroups. South Americans as a whole follow the traditional path of dispersion by generation, while generational differences for Central Americans are small, suggesting a pattern that is between the traditional immigrant-native settlement path and the new settlement path of the Mexicans. Thus, the increasing distribution of Hispanics, as a group, is driven mostly by the new geographical trends in settlement among Mexican and Central American immigrants.

THE FUTURE

The Hispanic population is likely to continue its growth trend for at least the near future, especially considering that Latin America immigration has not ebbed. The labor market and political incentives appear to continue firmly in place. Based on the most likely future immigration scenario, in which immigration continues at about the current rate, Jeffrey Passel (2003) of the Urban Institute predicts that the Hispanic population will grow from 35 million in 2000 to 101 million by 2050, nearly a three-fold increase. Consequently, the Hispanic component will constitute fully 24.6 percent of the U.S. population, nearly double its 12.5 percent in 2000, meaning that Latinos are likely to account for about 45 percent of U.S. population growth in the next 50 years. Even if immigration were to suddenly end, the youthful composition and higher fertility rates of Latinos ensure continued growth.

Even if there were no immigration after 2000, the Latino population would still increase to 63 million in 2050 or to about 20 percent of the U.S. population. The extent to which immigration will continue at the same rate depends partly on the actions of the U.S. government to effectively conduct border control, as it has suggested in recent years. Also, immigration from Latin America may begin to slow, as new entrants to the labor force of sending countries begin to ebb as a result of rapidly decreasing fertility over the past 20 years. Finally, immigration may also decrease in an optimistic scenario in which Latin American economies recuperate and their labor force needs begin to increase.

Currently, 40 percent of the Latino population is foreign-born. However, under the middle immigration scenario, the share of immigrants among the population will decline to 24 percent. The children of immigrants or the second generation currently represents 28 percent of Latinos, but by 2050 their population will quadruple and will represent 39 percent. The so-called third generation (and beyond) will grow from 32 to 37 percent.

Regarding the national composition of the Latino population, the order by population size is likely to change in the near future as Dominicans and other national populations that have become part of the new immigration stream overtake the Cuban and Puerto Rican populations, which grew less than 20 percent each decade since 1980. Dominican immigrants, for example, grew at about 100 percent in each of the past two decades. Cuban immigration has had only intermittent immigration for the past 30 years. Similarly, Puerto Rican immigration cannot grow much, since a large portion of the island's population is already engaged in the immigration process to the mainland, making the pool of potential immigrants relatively small. Like Dominicans, the Mexican population also doubled in the 1980s and then again in the 1990s. The Central American countries of El Salvador, Guatemala, and Honduras grew even more.

Latin American immigrant populations, which seem to be small today, may grow in size, depending on the expansion of networks and especially the relative opportunities between their countries and the United States. This is particularly true for South Americans, who constitute the majority of the Latin American population and are only beginning to participate in the immigration process to the United States. Brazil, in particular, with a population of 170 million but less than 1 million immigrants in the United States, may potentially become a leading sender of immigrants to the United States, especially if conditions in that country greatly deteriorate. Brazilians are Latin Americans, and whether we consider them part of the Latino/Hispanic population will depend on how their identity in the United States is shaped, how others will consider them, especially the U.S. Census Bureau, and especially whether we use a Latino or Hispanic label. For now, the small size of that population makes their inclusion of little consequence.

It is hard to tell whether the growing spread of Latino populations is likely to continue, although we are inclined to think that they are. Apparently, these immigrants are gaining footholds in such nontraditional places as the South, but it is probably too early to tell how solid they will become. The experience of Cubans and Vietnamese, who were relocated throughout the United States but the majority of whom later resettled in one metropolitan area, may be telling. However, those immigrants were refugee populations, and decisions about their settlement were made by others. Today's Latino populations seem to be choosing these destinations for the economic opportunities they provide. With the integration process experienced by most immigrants and their descendants, the more common trend is residential dispersion, especially by the second and third generation.

An issue that is likely to increase in importance, especially with the emergence of a third generation, is identification as Latino or Hispanic. The data presented in official statistics depend on persons identifying as Latinos, Hispanic, or in one of the national subgroups. This does not seem to be a major issue for immigrants from Latin American countries. However, many of these second- and third-generation descendants of Latino immigrants may no longer identify as Latino or Hispanic, especially if their parents or grandparents include non-Latinos. The ability to identify as white rather than Latino may be especially appealing to light-skinned people and children of mixed marriages, given the higher status of (non-Hispanic) whites in American society. Eschbach and Gomez (1998), for example, found that as many as 20 percent of high school students identified as Hispanic in a survey during their sophomore year and as white in a survey two years later. These trends will surely vary by national group and the place of settlement. The experience in the South, with its historically important black–white dichotomy, will be especially interesting.

For the labor force, Passel expects the Latino labor force to grow from representing 11.5 percent of the labor force in 2000 to 25 percent in 2050. This is the middle immigration assumption, but the Latino share would increase under all of the immigration scenarios. Under the no-immigration assumption, the Latino labor force would still increase by 82 percent, while the non-Latino labor force would shrink. Regarding the educational composition of the labor force, Latinos with a college education will grow from 10 to 25 percent, which is greater than that for the overall labor force. At the end, the number of those without a high school diploma will shrink from 39 to 17 percent of the Latino workforce.

CONCLUSION

This chapter has emphasized differences among national groups, but we have also sought to stress commonalities where they occur. In addition, there are some signs that Latinos have begun to adapt and incorporate themselves in the United States as a pan-ethnic group. Despite class, race, and national differences, Latinos have found ways to coalesce to some extent based on a shared language and cultural traits and especially because of a common identity forged by categorization by U.S. natives as a single racial or ethnic group. The extent to which a Latino or Hispanic identity forms largely depends on similar interests and structural foundations, such as a common geography. The historically separate regional concentration of particular national groups represents a prime reason for separateness, but the growing dispersion of various national groups into overlapping places presents growing opportunities for pan-Latino identity. For now, though, Latinos tend to favor identities based on national origin.

One issue we have dealt with in this chapter but that does not arise in many of the subsequent chapters, largely because of the lack of data, is the issue of illegal status. Many Latinos continue to confront serious problems in their everyday lives because of their illegal and lower class status, and this may have particularly important implications for their future. Most Latinos are in the working class, have low levels of education, and receive low salaries, characteristics that impede their ability to assimilate into the country they have chosen. However, the undocumented among them especially suffer from these and also from the lack of access to formal institutions. The demographic foundations today have important implications for the future of the Latino population in various social dimensions, as the rest of the book shows.

The demographic trends outlined in this chapter have large and direct implications for all of the issues treated in subsequent chapters. Such demographic characteristics as population growth, concentration in young ages, significant rates of naturalization, and dispersion into new locales are important for understanding education, family life, labor force participation, voting, the criminal justice system, and health care. The changing geography of Latinos should also focus the attention of the public on their situation in places where they never existed before. The dispersion of the Latino population into new states may also suggest changing prospects for assimilation into American society. However, the next chapter shows that this dispersion has been accompanied by a resegregation in the cities of the new areas.

REFERENCES

Bean, F.D., Telles, E.E., and Lindsay Lowell, B. (1987). Undocumented migration to the United States: Perceptions and evidence. *Population and Development Review, 13*(4), 671–689.

Bean, F.D., Lee, J., Batalova, J., and Leach, M. (2004). Immigration and fading color lines in America. In E. Carnevale, M.M. Kent, and A. Tarmann (Eds.), *The American people*. New York: Russell Sage Foundation.

Calavita, K. (1992). *Inside the state: The Bracero Program, immigration, and the INS*. New York: Routledge.

Cardoso, L. (1980). *Mexican emigration to the United States, 1897–1931*. Tucson: University of Arizona Press.

Cobble, S., and Velaquez, J. (2004, December). Looking back, looking forward. *The Nation*, p. 11.

Donato, K.M., Durand, J., and Massey, D.S. (1992). Changing conditions in the U.S. labor market: Effects of the Immigration Reform and Control Act of 1996. *Population Research and Policy Review, 11*(2), 93–115.

Duany, J. (1990). *Los dominicanos en Puerto Rico: Migración en la semi-periferia*. San Juan, Mexico: Ediciones el Huracán.

Duany, J., Hernández Angueira, L., and Rey, C.A. (1995). *El barrio Gandul: Economía subterránea y migración indocumentada en Puerto Rico.* San Juan, Mexico: Ediciones Nueva Sociedad.

Durand, J. (1994). *Más allá de la línea: Patrones migratorios en el Occidente de México.* México D.F. CONACULTA.

Durand, J. (1998). *Política, modelo y patrón migratorios: El trabajo y los trabajadores mexicanos en Estados Unidos.* San Luis Potosí, El Colegio de San Luis, Serie Cuadernos del Centro.

Durand, J., and Arias, P. (2000). *La experiencia migrante: Historia e iconografía de la migración México Estados Unidos.* Guadalajara, Mexico: Universidad de Guadalajara.

Durand, J., and Massey, D.S. (2003). *Clandestinos: Migración México Estados Unidos en los albores del siglo XXI.* México D.F., Editorial Miguel Angel Porrua.

Durand, J., Massey, D.S., and Charvet, F. (2000). The changing geography of Mexican immigration to the United States: 1910–1996. *Social Science Quarterly, 81*(1), 1–15.

Eschbach, K., and Gomez, C. (1998). Choosing Hispanic identity: Ethnic identity switching among respondents to High School and Beyond. *Social Science Quarterly, 79*(1), 74–90.

Georges, E. (1990). *The making of a transnational community.* New York: Columbia University Press.

Grasmuck, S., and Pessar, P.R. (1991). *Between two islands. Dominican international migration.* Los Angeles: California University Press.

Grenier, G., and Pérez, L. (2003). *The legacy of exile: Cubans in the United States.* Boston, MA: Allyn and Bacon.

Griffith, D. (1995). Hay trabajo: Poultry processing, rural industrialization and the latinization of low-wage labor. In D.D. Stull, M.J. Broadway, and D. Griffith (Eds.), *Any way you cut it: Meat processing and small town America* (pp. 129–151). Lawrence: University Press of Kansas.

Griffith, D. (2000). Work and immigration: Winter vegetable production in South Florida. In R. Tardanico and M.B. Rosenberg (Eds.), *Poverty or development* (pp. 139–178). New York: Routledge.

Hamilton, N., and Stoltz Chinchilla, N. (2001). *Seeking community in global city: Guatemalans and Salvadorans in Los Angeles.* Philadelphia, PA: Temple University Press.

Hernández-León, R., and Zúñiga, V. (2000). Making carpet by the mile: The emergency of a Mexican immigrant community in an industrial region of the U.S. historic South. *Social Science Quarterly, 81*(1), 49–65.

Hood, M.V., III, and Morris, I.L. (2000). Brother, can you spare a dime? Racial/ethnic context and the Anglo vote on Proposition 187. *Social Science Quarterly, 81*(1), 194–206.

Huber, E., and Solt, F. (2004). Successes and failures of neoliberalism. *Latin American Research Review, 39*(3), 150–164.

Jasso, G., and Rosenzweig, M.R. (1990). *The new chosen people: Immigrants in the United States.* New York: Russell Sage Foundation.

Kandel, W., and Parrado, E. (2004). *U.S. industrial transformation and new Latino migration.* Prepared for publication by the Migration Policy Institute, Washington, DC, based upon a presentation at the 2003 Annual Meeting of the Population Association of America, Minneapolis, MN, May 1-3. Available: http://www.migrationinformation.org/Feature/display.cfm?ID=217 [accessed January 2006].

Martin, J.A., Hamilton, B.E., Ventura, S.J., Menacker, F., and Park, M.M. (2002). *Births: Final data for 2000.* (National Vital Statistics Reports, vol. 50, no. 5.) Hyattsville, MD: National Center for Health Statistics.

Martínez Curiel, E. (2003). *Hasta que la muerte nos separe.* Guadalajara, Mexico: Universidad de Guadalajara.

Massey, D., Alarcón, R., Durand, J., and González, H. (1987). *Return to Aztlán.* Berkeley: University of California Press.

Massey, D., Durand, J., and Malone, N. (2002). *Beyond smoke and mirrors.* New York: Russell Sage Foundation.

Menjívar, C. (2000). *Fragmented ties: Salvadoran immigrant networks in America.* Berkeley: California University Press.

Ortíz, V. (1996). The Mexican origin population: Permanent working class or emerging middle class? In R. Waldinger and M. Bozorgmehr (Eds.), *Ethnic Los Angeles* (pp. 247–278). New York: Russell Sage Foundation.

Passel, J.S. (2003). *Hispanic projections: The future and the past.* Presentation to the Panel on Hispanics in the United States, Washington, DC.

Passel, J.S., and Fix, M. (2004). *Undocumented immigrants: Facts and figures.* Urban Institute Immigration Studies Program, unpublished.

Pessar, P.R. (1995). *A visa for a dream.* London: Allyn and Bacon.

Portes, A., and Rumbaut, R. (1990). *Immigrant America: A portrait.* Los Angeles: University of California Press.

Portes, A., and Stepick, A. (1993). *City on the edge: The transformation of Miami.* Los Angeles: University of California Press.

Reimers, D.M. (1992). *Still the golden door.* New York: Columbia University Press.

Rosenfeld, M.J., and Tienda, M. (1999). Mexican immigration, occupational niches, and labor market competition: Evidence from Los Angeles, Chicago, and Atlanta, 1970–1990. In F.D. Bean and S. Bell-Rose (Eds.), *Immigration and opportunity.* New York: Russell Sage Foundation.

Smith, R. (1993). *Los ausentes siempre presentes: The imagining, making, and politics of a transnational community between New York City and Ticuani, Puebla.* Working Papers on Latin America, Institute for Latin American and Iberian Studies, Columbia University.

Smith-Nonini, S. (2002). Nadie sabe, nadie supo: El programa federal H2A y la explotación de mano de obra mediada por el estado. *Relaciones, 23*(90), 55–86.

Stull, D.D., Broadway, M.J., and Griffith, D. (1995). *Any way you cut it: Meat processing and small town America.* Lawrence: University Press of Kansas.

United Nations. (2003). *World population prospects 1950–2050: The 2002 revision.* Database, Department of Economic and Social Affairs, Population Division. New York: United Nations.

U.S. Census Bureau. (2000). *Index of census 2000 data sets.* Available: http://www2.census.gov/census_2000/datasets/Sim_Hispanic_Totals [accessed May 20, 2004].

U.S. Immigration and Naturalization Service. (2002). *Statistical yearbook of the Immigration and Naturalization Service.* Pittsburgh, PA: Superintendent of Documents.

Valdés, D. N. (1982). *El pueblo mexicano en Detroit y Michigan: A social history.* Detroit, MI: Wayne State University.

Valdés, D.N. (1991). *Al norte: Agricultural in the Great Lakes region, 1917–1970.* Austin: University of Texas Press.

Valdés, D.N. (2000). *Barrios norteños: St. Paul and Midwestern Mexican communities in the twentieth century.* Austin: University of Texas Press.

Walton, M. (2004). Neoliberalism in Latin America: Good, bad, or incomplete? *Latin American Research Review, 39*(3), 165–184.

Weintraub, S. (1997). U.S. policy and Mexican immigration. In F.D. Bean, R. de la Garza, B. Roberts, and S. Weintraub (Eds.), *At the crossroads: Mexican migration and U.S. policy* (pp. 283–298). New York: Rowman and Littlefield.

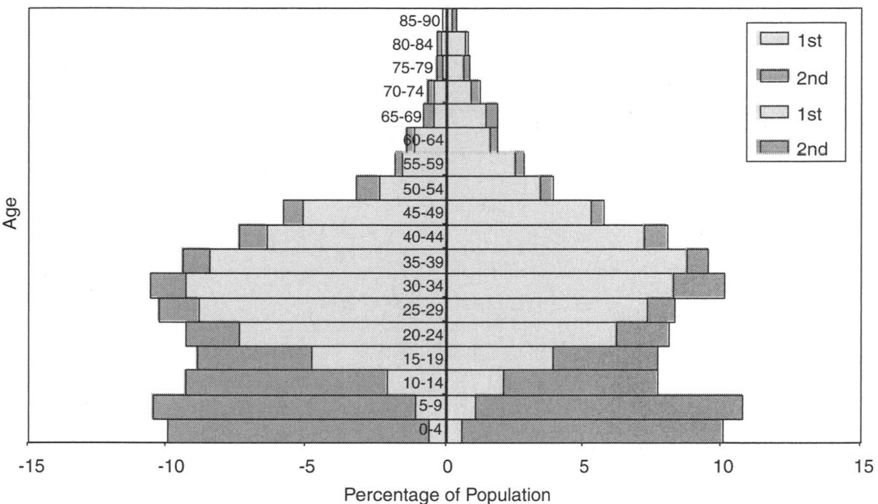

FIGURE A3-1 Age–sex composition of persons of Central American origin by nativity, 1998–2002.
SOURCE: Data from Current Population Surveys, 1998–2002.

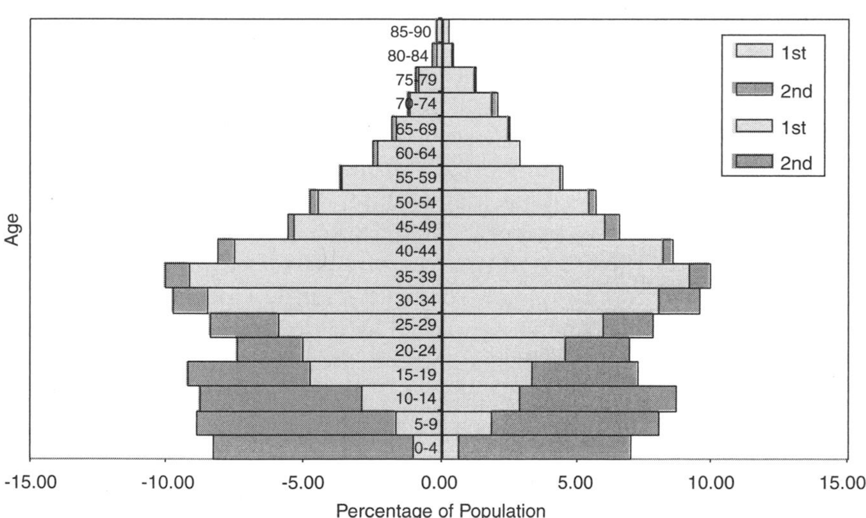

FIGURE A3-2 Age–sex composition of persons of South American origin by nativity, 1998–2000.
SOURCE Data from Current Population Surveys, 1998–2002.

4

Redrawing Spatial Color Lines: Hispanic Metropolitan Dispersal, Segregation, and Economic Opportunity

Mary J. Fischer and Marta Tienda

> In what might be a first for Georgia, students from one high school will attend three separate proms. Toombs County's dubious distinction demonstrates the evolving arithmetic of race in America, where white plus black plus brown doesn't add up to "one nation under God, indivisible, with liberty and justice for all." (Dan Chapman, *Atlanta Journal-Constitution*, April 11, 2004)

Toombs County, Georgia—a little town about 200 miles southeast of Atlanta—made national news when its local high school sponsored three senior proms instead of its usual two.[1] Principal Ralph Hardy, who is black, insisted that racism is not a serious problem at his school and that segregated proms are a matter of taste: "Latinos, blacks, and whites all prefer their own music and food." A prime example of communities, mostly in the South, that have experienced unprecedented Hispanic population growth, Toombs instantiates the growing complexity of the long-standing struggle for racial integration as newcomers from Mexico, Central America, and South America alter the ethno-racial landscape, forcing multiculturalism in places previously colored black and white. Whether the Hispanicization of metropolitan America redraws spatial color lines in urban places long divided into black and white into three-way splits is an empirical question with far-reaching implications for social integration and civic engagement.

More than at any time in the past, Hispanics have consolidated their national presence owing to their unprecedented geographic dispersal buttressed by growing numbers (Zúñiga and Hernández-León, 2005). Histori-

[1]Several counties in Georgia allow their students to plan their own proms independent of the school, in part to avoid problems arising from interracial dating. Hispanic students exercised their right to hold a separate prom because of what they described as a racist environment in the school and the ambiguity of choosing between the black and white proms. In 2004, whites made up just over half of the student population (56 percent); blacks just under one-third, and Hispanics the remainder (about 12 percent).

cally concentrated both regionally and in a few large metropolitan areas, Hispanics have scattered to nontraditional places since 1980, but with intensified force during the 1990s, redrawing ethno-racial landscapes along the way (see Chapter 3; Fischer et al., 2004; Logan, Stowell, and Oakley, 2002). Fueled by high levels of immigration from Mexico, Central America, and South America, the Hispanic geographic scattering presents the paradox of rising levels of regional and national integration combined with resegregation of old gateway cities and diverse settlement patterns in the new destinations (Alba and Nee, 1999; Logan, Stowell, and Oakley, 2002).

Residential location is a powerful indicator of social position because many economic opportunities and social resources, such as affordable housing, quality schools, public safety, transportation, and recreational and social amenities are unequally distributed across space. Where people live also influences access to jobs that pay family wages, the likelihood that racial and ethnic groups will commingle in schools, places of worship, and commercial establishments—in short, the prospects for minority group integration.

Accordingly, in this chapter we examine the implications of the Hispanic dispersal for segregation patterns, intergroup commingling, homeownership rates, and employment. Following a brief review of recent studies about race and ethnic residential segregation, we use the 100 largest metropolitan areas to document Hispanics' unprecedented geographic dispersal to new urban destinations; to portray trends in spatial segregation using measures of evenness and exposure; and to consider the social significance of the new residential patterns based on changes in school segregation, home ownership, and employment outcomes. Throughout we systematically compare Hispanics with blacks in order to understand whether, where, and how their new urban choices alter black spatial arrangements.

RESIDENTIAL DISPERSION AND METROPOLITANIZATION

Historically Hispanics have been highly concentrated regionally according to national origin, but their residential patterns differ from those of blacks and non-Hispanic whites in their high levels of early urbanicity and lower levels of spatial segregation from whites. As early as 1970, four out of five Hispanics resided in metropolitan areas, mostly in central cities (Bean and Tienda, 1987, pp. 146–147). Their highly urbanized residential history differentiates them from non-Hispanic whites, whose nonmetropolitan presence remains comparatively strong. Hispanics' metropolitanization experience also differs from that of blacks, whose mass exodus from the rural South after World War II resulted in very high levels of residential segregation (Massey and Denton, 1993; National Research Council, 1989).

Unlike blacks, Hispanics forged their urban imprints through intrametropolitan moves, including flows across international borders.

Despite a rise in racial integration during the 1990s, black–white residential segregation levels remain consistently above those of Hispanics nationally and in most metropolitan areas.[2] Even as Hispanics became more spatially integrated with whites in 86 of 210 metropolitan areas, their residential separation from whites actually *increased* in 124 metropolitan areas (Logan et al., 2004). This paradox of rising and falling segregation across metropolitan areas appears related to Hispanics' unprecedented geographic scattering to new regions of the country.

Los Angeles, New York, Chicago, and Miami have continued to serve as prominent gateways to U.S. job and housing markets during the recent mass migration. At the same time, the 2000 decennial census confirmed what many local school boards and governments already knew: that Hispanics, and recent immigrants in particular, are changing the face of America by making historically unprecedented residential choices (Kandel and Cromartie, 2004; Suro and Singer, 2002; Zúñiga and Hernández-León, 2005). Table 4-1, which summarizes changes in the residential distributions of Hispanics compared with the total U.S. population, illustrates the recentness and rising intensity of their geographic dispersal. Already under way during the 1980s, the Hispanic scattering gained considerable momentum during the 1990s.[3]

Metropolitanization of the total U.S. population inched up over the past two decades, but Hispanics are still more likely to live in metropolitan areas than the typical U.S. resident. Already in 1980, the largest 100 metropolitan areas housed over 3 in 4 Hispanics, and they did so for only 62 percent of all U.S. residents by 2000. An additional 13 percent of all Hispanics resided in metropolitan areas that were not among the largest 100 compared with 18 percent of the total population. Only 11 percent of Hispanics lived in nonmetropolitan areas in 1980 compared with nearly one-fourth of all U.S. residents; by 2000, these shares fell to 8 and 20 percent, respectively. Despite the declining share of nonmetropolitan Hispanic residents, the nonmetropolitan Hispanic population has doubled since 1980 and currently is the most rapidly growing segment of rural and small-town America (Kandel and Cromartie, 2004).

For ease of exposition and parsimony, we divide the 100 largest metropolitan areas into three strata: the Traditional Metros, New Hispanic Destinations, and a residual, designated Other Large Metros. The Traditional

---

[2]During the 1990s, blacks became more spatially integrated with whites in 240 of 265 metropolitan areas (Logan et al., 2004).

[3]Most of the analysis that follows focuses on the largest 100 metropolitan areas, but this tabulation also reports smaller metropolitan areas as well as nonmetropolitan areas.

Metros include 29 metropolitan areas located in the Southwest, as well as the past and current immigrant gateway cities of Miami, New York City, and Chicago. The stratum called New Hispanic Destinations represents 50 metropolitan areas outside the Southwest where the Hispanic presence rose appreciably since 1980. The remaining 21 Other Large Metros are those with relatively small Hispanic populations—less than 5 percent as late as 2000—including large rust belt cities with appreciable black populations, for example Philadelphia, Detroit, and St. Louis.[4]

Owing to faster demographic growth compared with native whites and blacks, the Hispanic proportion also increased in the largest 100 metropolitan areas, albeit unevenly. Between 1980 and 2000, Hispanic population shares rose from 18 to 30 percent in the Traditional Metros, while the black share declined slightly, from 14 to 12 percent of the stratum total. Hispanicization of the Traditional Metros is all the more impressive because many of these cities grew substantially during the period, with immigration driving up the foreign-born share of the population from 16 to 27 percent of the stratum total.[5]

The New Hispanic Destinations are of particular interest because of the number of places involved, their nationwide spread, their diverse growth rates, and the variable size of their black population. Unlike the Traditional Metros, where numerically dominant Hispanics further increased their population share over two decades, blacks remain numerically and proportionately dominant in both the New Hispanic Destinations and the Other Large Metros. In the New Hispanic Destinations, blacks outnumbered Hispanics by a ratio exceeding 6:1 in 1980, but by 2000, it plummeted to just under 2:1. By comparison, the black-to-Hispanic ratio in the Other Large Metros was higher both at the outset and the end of the period—8:1 in 1980 versus 4:1 in 2000. Still, the direction of change in population composition is clear.

The New Hispanic Destinations and Other Large Metros differ from each other in another important way, namely the salience of immigration in population diversification. In the New Hispanic Destinations, the foreign-

[4]Appendix Table A4-1 provides the detail for all 100 places corresponding to Table 4-1. Our strata are loosely based on the four-fold typology of Hispanic places of Suro and Singer (2002), which we have simplified into three categories that we think best represent the new Hispanic growth. We opted not to use the typology because it conflates growth of small and large places with relative changes in population composition.

[5]The GeoLytics Census CD Neighborhood Change Database lacks tables by birthplace for Hispanics. Therefore, we are unable to examine the growth of Hispanic immigrants across metropolitan area types. However, as documented for the 2000 period, the majority of Hispanics in the New Hispanic Destinations are recent arrivals.

TABLE 4-1 Total and Hispanic Population Distribution and Composition According to Metropolitan Area Type, 1980–2000

	1980 Population				
	Distribution		Composition		
Metropolitan Area Type	Total	Hispanic	% H	% B	% FB
Traditional Hispanic Metros	23	61	18	14	16
New Hispanic Destinations	24	12	2	13	6
Other Large Metros	12	4	2	17	5
Top 100 (P)MSA subtotal	59	77	8	14	10
All Other Small Metros	18	12	5	9	5
Nonmetropolitan Areas	23	11	3	8	3
Total	100	100	6	12	7
N (000s)	226,542	14,609			

NOTE: The "Total" and "Hispanic" columns represent group distribution; the % H, % B, and % FB columns are strata composition. MSA = metropolitan statistical area. FB = foreign-born.

born population share doubled (from 6 to 12 percent), but in the Other Large Metros, the foreign-born share remained relatively stable over the period. Ethno-racial profiles of nonmetropolitan and small metropolitan areas were also reconfigured as the Hispanic and black shares evened out. The rising Hispanic presence—from 5 to 9 percent in the remaining metropolitan areas and from 3 to 6 percent in nonmetropolitan areas—balanced the proportions of blacks and Hispanics. Large numbers of Hispanics settling in nonmetropolitan areas are recent immigrants with low levels of education; a significant segment are undocumented (Kandel and Cromartie, 2004).

Not only does the term "Hispanic" mask a great deal of *within*-group diversity, but also the ethnic make-up of the population varies considerably by metropolitan type. As the U.S. Hispanic population has become more diversified through immigration, the Cuban share of the total declined nationally and across all types of metropolitan areas, but especially the Traditional Metros and the New Hispanic Destinations. Concomitantly, the relative proportions of all "other" Hispanic nationalities rose from 19 to 27 percent in the Traditional Metros and from 34 to 37 percent of the Hispanics in the New Hispanic Destinations over the period (see Appendix table A4-2). Although the relative share of Puerto Ricans living in the Traditional Metros declined by half over the period, they still constituted over 1 in 3 Hispanics in the New York metropolitan area in 2000, down from nearly 60 percent in 1980. In the *New Hispanic Destinations*, no

1990 Population					2000 Population				
Distribution		Composition			Distribution		Composition		
Total	Hispanic	% H	% B	% FB	Total	Hispanic	% H	% B	% FB
24	62	24	13	22	25	59	30	12	27
24	12	4	14	8	26	16	7	15	12
11	3	2	17	5	11	4	4	17	7
59	77	12	14	13	62	79	16	14	18
18	13	6	9	7	18	13	9	10	13
23	10	4	9	3	20	8	6	9	6
100	100	9	12	9	100	100	13	12	12
248,710	22,354				281,422	35,306			

SOURCE: Data extracted from the GeoLytics Census CD Neighborhood Change Database 1970–2000 Tract Data.

single group comprises a clear majority, although Mexicans, whose share rose from 35 to 39 percent between 1980 and 2000, remain the largest single group.

Understanding the paradox of rising Hispanic residential segregation against the backdrop of their unprecedented geographic dispersal requires comparisons with the experiences of other groups. For instance, how does an influx of Hispanics affect the spatial patterns of blacks, Asians, and whites? It is not clear whether the decline in black segregation levels results because Hispanics' are sharing space with them, with whites, or with both. To examine this question, we use measures suited to portray spatial separation patterns in multiethnic contexts. Furthermore, considering how Hispanics' urban dispersal results in spatial isolation provides clues about their socioeconomic integration prospects in both old and new settings.

METROPOLITAN DIVERSIFICATION AND MULTIETHNIC SEGREGATION

Two countervailing forces activated by population moves—assimilation and succession—produce patterns of residential segregation. Before the onset of mass immigration during the 1970s, spatial assimilation trumped residential succession as the dominant mechanism driving Hispanic residential segregation. With the exception of Puerto Ricans living in New York, in 1980 Hispanics were only moderately segregated from Anglos—in sharp contrast with the apartheid levels experienced by blacks at the time (Massey, 1981).[6]

Segregation patterns began to change during the 1970s for two reasons. First, after nearly three decades of wage growth among unskilled workers, the wages of workers with college and high school educations began to diverge in the mid-1970s (Danziger and Gottschalk, 1995). Residential segregation tends to rise when the economy stagnates because immigrants and poor ethnics cluster into established neighborhoods where they can draw on social supports (Massey and Denton, 1987). Second, as the new era of mass migration gained momentum during the 1980s, residential clustering in ethnic and immigrant neighborhoods increased. Massey and Denton (1987) show that Hispanics' average segregation level across the 60 largest metropolitan areas remained moderate during the 1970s, around .44, but that segregation rose in metropolitan areas in which Hispanic immigrants settled. As Los Angeles became the primary destination of new Latin American immigrants, Hispanic residential segregation from whites there approached that of New York City, historically the most segregated city for Hispanics. Chicago's Hispanics also became more segregated from whites during the 1970s, as the volume of new immigrants rose (Bean and Tienda, 1987).

A third possible mechanism for the rise in Hispanic residential segregation is discrimination in housing markets. Because Hispanics were not included in the Housing Discrimination Survey until 1989, when the Department of Housing and Urban Development conducted its second national audit, it is not possible to evaluate this mechanism before this date. However, the 1989 survey revealed that Hispanics experienced adverse treatment relative to whites in almost 25 percent of their attempts to secure rental housing and in slightly over 25 percent of their home-buying inquiries (Turner et al., 2002). A third housing audit study conducted in 2000 found a slight *increase* in the adverse treatment of Hispanics in the rental housing market and, for the first time, registered higher levels of rental housing discrimination than blacks (Turner et al., 2002). Because Hispanic immigrants are more likely than their native-born counterparts to seek rental housing, they probably account for most of the registered increase in housing discrimination. However, the 2000 study showed that Hispanics experienced declines in adverse treatment in the sales market.

Several analyses of post-1980 residential patterns reveal lower levels of racial segregation in the most diverse metropolitan areas, yet without exception, blacks remained more spatially separated from whites than either

---

[6]In general, indices of dissimilarity below .3 are considered low, those between .3 and .6 are considered moderate, and those in excess of .6 are high.

Hispanics or Asians. Frey and Farley's (1996) study of segregation in 18 multiethnic metropolitan areas during the 1980s shows that segregation declined more rapidly for all groups in these contexts, as it did in places experiencing rapid growth in minority populations. Analyzing several hundred metropolitan areas, Logan et al. (2004) also showed a continuing decline in black–white segregation during the 1990s. Of the 255 metropolitan areas they examined, black–white segregation fell in all but 15 between 1980 and 2000. By contrast, aggregate Hispanic–white segregation remained relatively unchanged during the 1980s and registered a slight increase during the 1990s. However, this apparent stability concealed highly diverse experiences across areas, with some featuring greater integration and others resegregation. Informative binary comparisons with respect to whites in multiethnic settings cannot reveal whether and how color lines may be changing, and in particular whether a growing Hispanic presence in places historically divided along racial lines softens color boundaries in social space.

Not surprisingly, segregation measures based on multiple groups yield different insights about intergroup relations. Iceland and colleagues (2002) show that Hispanics (and Asians) experienced increases in three types of segregation between 1980 and 2000, namely evenness (dissimilarity), exposure (p* isolation index), and clustering (spatial proximity). However, despite sustained declines over two decades, black segregation remains above that of Hispanics and Asians in all three dimensions. Moreover, the drop in black segregation was insufficient to alter hypersegregation, defined as high levels of spatial separation on several dimensions. In 2000, blacks were hypersegregated in 29 metropolitan areas compared with only two for Hispanics—Los Angeles and New York City (Wilkes and Iceland, 2004). It is therefore noteworthy that, except for Chicago, black hypersegregated metropolitan areas lack large Hispanic populations.

It is conceivable that, except for the black hypersegregated metropolitan areas, population diversification facilitated the decline in racial residential segregation, particularly in locations that became more ethnically diverse. Because this is difficult to discern using segregation measures based solely on binary comparisons, several researchers have used multigroup entropy indices to examine the relationship between the growing diversity of places and patterns of segregation. Using entropy indices of overall diversity and segregation for all U.S. cities, Iceland (2003) concludes that increases in metropolitan area diversity between 1980 and 2000 resulted in *higher* segregation for all groups except blacks, which he (like Frey and Farley, 1996) interprets as evidence of a weakened racial divide.[7]

[7]Not everyone has found increasing segregation for Hispanics. For instance, Fischer (2003) found declining Hispanic segregation levels based on the 50 largest metropolitan areas plus

Using two measures of segregation—the dissimilarity and isolation indices—Iceland and Lake (2004) show that Hispanic segregation from whites differs by nativity and ethnicity. Their empirical support for the spatial assimilation hypothesis is bolstered by evidence that native-born Hispanics are less segregated from whites than their foreign-born counterparts, and that recent immigrants are more segregated than longer term residents. Although binary comparisons based on measures of evenness are less informative by themselves because Hispanics increasingly reside in multiethnic urban places, they indicate that immigrants are more socially segregated from whites than the native born.

To better appreciate the consequences of Hispanics' urban dispersal for intergroup contact, we examined their residential segregation with respect to blacks, Asians, and whites using measures of evenness and exposure and comparing outcomes by types of metropolitan areas. The following section first portrays how Hispanic segregation patterns evolved since 1980 compared with blacks in the largest 100 metropolitan areas. Subsequently we consider the implications of spatial arrangements for social isolation, school segregation, home ownership, and labor market integration.

Spatial Segregation by Types of Metropolitan Areas

Although multigroup indicators of segregation are advantageous for assessing residential trends for Hispanics, to maintain comparability with many prior studies we also use the dissimilarity index (D), which measures evenness in the distribution of two groups across neighborhoods (census tracts) in a metropolitan area. Segregation is minimized when each tract reflects the same proportion of each group as their representation in the city as a whole. Equation (1) shows the dissimilarity index, where x_i and y_i are the numbers of X and Y group members in tract i, while X and Y are the metropolitan area totals.

$$D_{XY} = .5 * \sum * \left| \left(\frac{x_i}{X} \right) - \left(\frac{y_i}{Y} \right) \right| \tag{1}$$

10 areas of high Hispanic concentration. The inconsistent conclusions of these two studies reflect differences in the sample of cities used (all cities versus the largest 60) and the methods. Fischer used the family income tables to calculate bivariate race and class multigroup entropy scores, while Iceland used the 100 percent person-level data to regress diversity on segregation measures.

A limitation of this binary measure is its inability to portray the overall status of segregation in multiethnic places. We minimize this bias by calculating segregation between minority groups (Hispanics and blacks in this case) and non-Hispanic whites ($D_{H/W}$ and $D_{B/W}$), as well as between both blacks and Hispanics and *all* other groups ($D_{H/O}$ and $D_{B/O}$). Because immigration is a driving force in Hispanic population growth and geographic dispersal, for comparative purposes we also compute segregation between foreign- and native-born residents ($D_{FB/O}$).[8] And, for the year 2000, we measure the degree to which foreign-born Hispanics are segregated from all others ($D_{HFB/O}$).[9]

A second dimension of Hispanic segregation examined is exposure, (P*), which measures the degree of potential contact between the members of two groups within the census tracts of a city. When the probability of contact is calculated with respect to one's own group, the exposure index measures isolation. Equation (2), the most commonly used measure of exposure, estimates the probability of contact between groups X and Y, where t_i is the total population of tract i and the other components are the ame as Equation (1).

$$xP^*y = \sum\left(\frac{x_i}{X}\right)*\left(\frac{y_i}{t_i}\right) \quad xP^*y = \sum\left(\frac{x_i}{X}\right)*\left(\frac{y_i}{t_i}\right) \tag{2}$$

Table 4-2 portrays temporal and spatial variation in Hispanic segregation levels for the three metropolitan types and, for illustration of variation across metropolitan areas, selected metropolitan areas within each type (see also Appendix Table A4-2). Segregation indices for blacks and all foreign-born provide comparison benchmarks. In Traditional Metros, Hispanics were moderately segregated from all other groups in 1980 (.446) and slightly more segregated from whites (.476). By 2000, these differentials appear to be heading in opposite directions. Over the 20-year period, the level of Hispanic segregation from all other groups fell 1 percent, but during the same time period their separation from whites increased 3 percent. This indicates that Hispanic population growth raises their likelihood of sharing residential space with groups other than whites. We address this issue in further depth below, after describing how segregation trends vary across types of metropolitan areas.

---

[8]Because the 1980 and 1990 data do not allow us to disaggregate the foreign-born into constituent race/ethnic groups, the foreign-born can be of any race/ethnicity. The foreign-born versus native entropy index therefore cannot be directly compared with the other entropy index calculations in Table 4-2 because there is no mutually exclusive relationship between the foreign-born measures and the other race/ethnic categorizations in the data.

[9]This is the only year for which we have this detailed information at the tract level.

TABLE 4-2 Segregation Trends (D) by Metropolitan Area Type for Hispanics, Blacks, and the Foreign Born: 1980–2000

	1980				
Metropolitan Area Type	$D_{H/O}$	$D_{H/W}$	$D_{B/O}$	$D_{B/W}$	$D_{FB/O}$
Traditional Metros	0.446	0.476	0.621	0.654	0.279
New York, NY	0.537	0.649	0.715	0.813	0.294
Chicago, IL	0.621	0.636	0.862	0.878	0.389
Los Angeles, CA	0.508	0.570	0.766	0.811	0.333
Miami, FL	0.547	0.526	0.772	0.788	0.418
New Hispanic Destinations	0.375	0.405	0.689	0.699	0.274
Allentown, PA	0.596	0.602	0.616	0.630	0.252
Providence, RI	0.505	0.520	0.721	0.733	0.336
Grand Rapids, MI	0.447	0.474	0.754	0.758	0.234
Minneapolis, MN	0.409	0.423	0.686	0.694	0.261
Atlanta, GA	0.297	0.347	0.769	0.772	0.321
Raleigh-Durham, NC	0.287	0.312	0.479	0.480	0.391
Nashville, TN	0.363	0.392	0.654	0.655	0.355
Tulsa, OK	0.297	0.288	0.748	0.752	0.330
Other Large Metros	0.393	0.430	0.715	0.717	0.270
Total top 100 MSAs	0.399	0.431	0.675	0.690	0.275

NOTE: MSA = metropolitan statistical area.
HH/O = Dissimilarity Hispanic vs others.
HH/W = Dissimilarity Hispanic vs white.
HB/O = Dissimilarity black vs others.

The largest increases in Hispanic segregation occurred in the New Hispanic Destinations, where their residential separation from other groups rose 10 percent—from .375 in 1980 to .412 in 2000. Although Hispanic segregation from all others and whites remained lower in New Hispanic Destinations compared with Traditional Metros, the countervailing trends have produced some convergence between strata. Moreover, the average level of segregation in New Hispanic Destinations masks considerable variability across specific metropolitan areas, reflecting variation in their size, their preexisting minority populations, and the timing of the Hispanic influx. For instance, as Atlanta's Hispanic population share increased tenfold between 1980 and 2000, their segregation from all other groups rose 56 percent, from .297 to .462. However, there does not appear to be a strict

1990					2000					
$D_{H/O}$	$D_{H/W}$	$D_{B/O}$	$D_{B/W}$	$D_{FB/O}$	$D_{H/O}$	$D_{H/W}$	$D_{B/O}$	$D_{B/W}$	$D_{FB/O}$	$D_{HFB/O}$
0.440	0.471	0.555	0.591	0.303	0.443	0.491	0.493	0.559	0.311	0.456
0.536	0.659	0.692	0.822	0.321	0.507	0.663	0.671	0.817	0.323	0.484
0.618	0.624	0.817	0.839	0.424	0.596	0.610	0.776	0.803	0.420	0.597
0.532	0.611	0.643	0.732	0.320	0.511	0.629	0.568	0.677	0.279	0.431
0.534	0.505	0.717	0.718	0.369	0.502	0.437	0.717	0.725	0.299	0.429
0.389	0.408	0.636	0.648	0.306	0.412	0.454	0.574	0.604	0.324	0.505
0.594	0.604	0.540	0.565	0.261	0.605	0.625	0.486	0.537	0.293	0.549
0.593	0.615	0.633	0.567	0.380	0.635	0.674	0.514	0.579	0.384	0.688
0.429	0.457	0.744	0.751	0.273	0.470	0.508	0.648	0.671	0.386	0.610
0.381	0.399	0.623	0.631	0.342	0.428	0.472	0.545	0.579	0.367	0.552
0.359	0.378	0.668	0.674	0.368	0.462	0.517	0.614	0.645	0.393	0.550
0.300	0.294	0.450	0.452	0.368	0.344	0.411	0.424	0.448	0.286	0.423
0.347	0.351	0.607	0.608	0.371	0.439	0.474	0.552	0.568	0.390	0.563
0.294	0.299	0.627	0.632	0.389	0.388	0.413	0.560	0.580	0.426	0.559
0.427	0.443	0.687	0.694	0.317	0.400	0.435	0.648	0.660	0.322	0.517
0.412	0.434	0.623	0.641	0.307	0.418	0.461	0.566	0.603	0.320	0.493

HB/W = Dissimilarity black vs white.
HFB/W = Dissimilarity foreign-born vs other.
HFB/O = Dissimilarity Hispanic foreign-born vs other (2000 only).
SOURCE: Data extracted from the GeoLytics Census CD Neighborhood Change Database 1970–2000 Tract Data.

relationship between the rate of Hispanic demographic growth and increases in segregation levels.[10]

To illustrate, both Minneapolis, Minnesota, and Providence, Rhode Island, have similar sized Hispanic populations (both slightly under 100,000 in 2000) that grew about 325 percent between 1980 and 2000. Yet during this period, Hispanic segregation increased far more in Providence than in Minneapolis. In Providence, Hispanic segregation from all other groups

[10]The correlation between the percentage increase in Hispanic population from 1980 to 2000 and the percentage increase in segregation from whites is .547, while the correlation between Hispanic population change and the percentage increase in segregation from all others is .490. Although both associations are positive and statistically significant, their magnitude suggests that other factors also contribute to increased segregation.

increased 26 percent, from .505 in 1980 to .635 in 2000, making them the most segregated of all groups living in Providence in 2000, including blacks. By contrast, in Minneapolis, Hispanics' residential segregation rose only about 5 percent over the same period. These disparities partly reflect differences in the ethnic composition of Hispanics in both cities. Unlike Minneapolis, Providence houses a relatively large number of Puerto Ricans, who tend to experience higher levels of segregation than other Hispanic groups (Massey, 1981).

Cross-group comparisons with other groups provide additional context for interpreting Hispanic segregation trends, especially in light of claims that the Hispanic geographic dispersal reshaped urban color lines. Table 4-2 suggests that blacks residing in the Traditional Metros have benefited from the continued influx of Hispanics over the past 20 years, as they experienced large average declines in segregation from Hispanics and all others and to a slightly lesser extent whites. Their moderately high 1980 segregation levels from whites (.654) and from all others (.621) were reduced by 15 and 21 percent, respectively, by 2000. These decreases were not uniform across places, however. In New York, for instance, segregation of blacks from whites was virtually unchanged and remained very high (.82) throughout the 20-year period. Moreover, black residential separation from others dropped a mere 6 percent in two decades, remaining high at .67.

Nevertheless, blacks remain *more* segregated from other groups in the New Hispanic Destinations compared with the Traditional Metros. They also experience higher average levels of segregation from others than do Hispanics. For the most part, the color lines in the New Hispanic Destinations were drawn in black and white through the 1970s because no other groups had significant representation in most of these cities. Consequently, average levels of racial segregation were high in 1980, with dissimilarity scores of .689 from all others and .699 from whites. The influx of Hispanics into these cities probably played a substantial role in the steady declines in racial segregation through the 1980s and 1990s. Over this period, the level of segregation between blacks and all others declined an average of 17 percent, while segregation from whites fell 14 percent.

Immigration is an important final piece of the changing residential puzzle over this 20-year period. As noted by other studies, segregation levels between native and foreign-born often increase following a substantial rise in immigration, as occurred in both the Traditional Metros and the New Hispanic Destinations. In the Traditional Metros, spatial separation between natives and immigrants rose over this time period from .279 in 1980 to .311 in 2000. Similarly, the foreign-born in New Hispanic Destinations experienced rising levels of segregation from natives since 1980, from .274 to .324 by 2000.

More fine-grained comparisons for Hispanic foreign-born in 2000 yield noteworthy insights. In the New Hispanic Destinations, foreign-born Hispanics not only are markedly more segregated than immigrants generally, but also are more segregated than their counterparts in the Traditional Metros. In 2000 the average dissimilarity of all foreign-born from natives was .311 in Traditional Metros compared with a score of .456 for foreign-born Hispanics, who also are 2.9 percent more segregated from others than all Hispanics are from other groups. In the New Hispanic Destinations, these differences are even more striking, as foreign-born Hispanics are 1.6 times more segregated from other groups compared with the foreign-born in general. In addition, foreign-born Hispanics are 22 percent more segregated from others than are Hispanics as a group. In short, increased Hispanic segregation in the New Hispanic Destinations appears to be largely driven by the higher degree of spatial separation experienced by the foreign-born.

The almost uniform increases in segregation for Hispanics settling in New Hispanic Destinations accompanied by substantial decreases in blacks' segregation from others in these metropolitan areas suggests the plausible hypothesis that the Hispanic dispersal is softening established color lines and weakening class divisions (Logan, 2003; Morenoff and Tienda, 1997). Logan (2003) and others have dubbed this phenomenon the "buffer hypothesis." In Chicago, for example, Morenoff and Tienda (1997) showed that the growth and residential concentration of Mexican immigrants transformed several inner-city neighborhoods experiencing succession into working class hubs rather than underclass ghettos. The changing exposure of blacks and Hispanics to other groups lends further support to the buffer hypothesis because, as the Hispanic presence increases the ethnic diversity of a place, segregation among all groups, and segregation of blacks from all others, decline, as demonstrated in the next section.

SOCIAL AND ECONOMIC TRANSFORMATION OF URBAN SPACES

Residential clustering results either when newcomers choose to live near ethnic compatriots or when groups are systematically excluded from selected neighborhoods and school districts via housing discrimination and discriminatory lending policies (Turner et al., 2002). Thus the social significance of the Hispanic scattering transcends physical space and influences prospects for social integration. In particular many immigrants congregate in high-density ethnic neighborhoods until they become familiar with U.S.

institutions and acquire proficiency in English, but over time they participate in residential assimilation. Accordingly, in this section we examine several correlates of spatial separation, including social isolation, school segregation, home ownership trends and labor force activity.

Social and Cultural Isolation

Tables 4-3a and 4-3b report (P*) indices depicting the exposure of Hispanics (3a) and blacks (3b) to whites, blacks, Hispanics, and others from 1980 to 2000, averaged across metropolitan types. The exposure index indicates the probability of sharing a tract with a member of a given race group, but when all possible combinations are represented, it reveals the average share of each group present in the typical neighborhood for that group. For instance, the exposure of Hispanics to whites at a level of .348 in the Traditional Metros indicates that, in 2000, the typical Hispanic in these metropolitan areas lived in a neighborhood that was 35 percent white. Isolation is the extent of exposure Hispanics had to other compatriots—namely, the probability of sharing a tract with a coethnic.

Hispanics became increasingly isolated in all metropolitan areas during the 1980s and 1990s, but there are large differences in the degree of isolation experienced by type of area and in specific metropolitan areas. For instance, in 2000 the average Hispanic isolation in Traditional Metros (.489) was over three times greater than the average for Other Large Metros (.082) but in 1980 the comparable ratio was seven-fold. Even within metropolitan types, there is considerable variability in isolation levels. In Los Angeles, second largest among the Traditional Metros, the average Hispanic lived in a neighborhood that was 63 percent Hispanic in 2000—up from 50 percent in 1980—while the average Hispanic in Chicago lived in a neighborhood that was only 48 percent Hispanic in 2000. Partly because Hispanics comprise relatively small population shares in the New Hispanic Destinations and especially in the Other Large Metros, their social isolation is considerably lower in these places: on average, their Hispanic compatriots comprised well below 20 percent of the neighborhood.

Besides other Hispanics, what other groups reside in the typical Hispanic's neighborhood? As Hispanic residential segregation from other groups, and particularly from whites, rose in the New Hispanic Destinations (Table 4-2), their exposure to whites declined. Table 4-3a reveals that in the New Hispanic Destinations, Hispanics' residential contact with whites is relatively high, with an exposure index value of .618. However, this represents an 18 percent decline since 1980. Hispanics in living in Traditional Metros not only average less exposure to whites than their counterparts residing in New Hispanic Destinations, but also the proportion of

TABLE 4-3a Segregation Trends (P*) by Metropolitan Area Type For Hispanics: 1980–2001

	1980				1990				2000			
Metropolitan Area Type	White	Black	Hispanic	Asian and Other	White	Black	Hispanic	Asian and Other	White	Black	Hispanic	Asian and Other
Traditional Metros	0.497	0.079	0.382	0.041	0.431	0.083	0.423	0.009	0.348	0.085	0.489	0.078
New York, NY	0.321	0.236	0.405	0.038	0.259	0.234	0.438	0.006	0.218	0.219	0.465	0.097
Chicago, IL	0.497	0.095	0.380	0.029	0.447	0.095	0.422	0.004	0.388	0.092	0.476	0.044
Los Angeles, CA	0.346	0.085	0.501	0.068	0.235	0.095	0.575	0.006	0.176	0.090	0.633	0.101
Miami, FL	0.340	0.068	0.583	0.010	0.233	0.083	0.672	0.002	0.183	0.090	0.710	0.016
New Hispanic Destinations	0.756	0.149	0.076	0.019	0.728	0.140	0.101	0.009	0.618	0.170	0.167	0.045
Allentown, PA	0.793	0.047	0.152	0.008	0.709	0.055	0.218	0.003	0.608	0.072	0.293	0.027
Providence, RI	0.798	0.094	0.076	0.032	0.625	0.114	0.186	0.024	0.489	0.120	0.315	0.076
Grand Rapids, MI	0.809	0.092	0.082	0.017	0.780	0.092	0.103	0.008	0.638	0.118	0.216	0.028
Minneapolis, MN	0.874	0.045	0.045	0.036	0.837	0.058	0.044	0.018	0.683	0.122	0.103	0.092
Atlanta, GA	0.748	0.217	0.022	0.013	0.704	0.210	0.050	0.003	0.498	0.253	0.187	0.061
Raleigh-Durham, NC	0.727	0.249	0.014	0.010	0.751	0.208	0.018	0.003	0.557	0.295	0.114	0.034
Nashville, TN	0.792	0.187	0.013	0.008	0.843	0.129	0.013	0.003	0.694	0.183	0.091	0.032
Tulsa, OK	0.853	0.064	0.022	0.061	0.816	0.072	0.036	0.065	0.702	0.112	0.105	0.082
Other Large Metros	0.732	0.176	0.053	0.039	0.732	0.155	0.068	0.005	0.680	0.182	0.082	0.056
Total top 100 MSAs	0.676	0.135	0.160	0.030	0.643	0.127	0.187	0.008	0.553	0.148	0.242	0.057

NOTE: MSA = metropolitan statistical area.
SOURCE: Data extracted from the GeoLytics Census CD Neighborhood Change Database 1970–2000 Tract Data.

TABLE 4-3b Segregation Trends (P*) by Metropolitan Area Type for Blacks: 1980–2000

	1980				1990				2000			
Metropolitan Area Type	White	Black	Hispanic	Asian and Other	White	Black	Hispanic	Asian and Other	White	Black	Hispanic	Asian and Other
Traditional Metros	0.379	0.365	0.216	0.041	0.378	0.297	0.255	0.008	0.337	0.255	0.317	0.091
New York, NY	0.160	0.629	0.191	0.020	0.130	0.626	0.214	0.006	0.116	0.604	0.232	0.049
Chicago, IL	0.126	0.827	0.039	0.009	0.159	0.773	0.055	0.002	0.172	0.722	0.083	0.023
Los Angeles, CA	0.166	0.602	0.189	0.043	0.175	0.425	0.333	0.006	0.171	0.344	0.403	0.082
Miami, FL	0.202	0.643	0.146	0.009	0.167	0.610	0.212	0.003	0.112	0.609	0.261	0.018
New Hispanic Destinations	0.436	0.508	0.039	0.018	0.462	0.455	0.055	0.008	0.453	0.410	0.095	0.041
Allentown, PA	0.828	0.076	0.085	0.100	0.785	0.070	0.127	0.003	0.697	0.085	0.191	0.027
Providence, RI	0.615	0.244	0.083	0.058	0.572	0.182	0.163	0.031	0.577	0.129	0.221	0.072
Grand Rapids, MI	0.451	0.508	0.032	0.009	0.462	0.482	0.040	0.010	0.487	0.391	0.097	0.026
Minneapolis, MN	0.634	0.294	0.021	0.050	0.635	0.243	0.023	0.031	0.585	0.233	0.067	0.114
Atlanta, GA	0.263	0.722	0.010	0.005	0.327	0.643	0.016	0.002	0.295	0.619	0.056	0.031
Raleigh-Durham, NC	0.480	0.505	0.008	0.006	0.511	0.464	0.010	0.003	0.480	0.414	0.078	0.028
Nashville, TN	0.428	0.558	0.008	0.006	0.463	0.520	0.006	0.003	0.485	0.458	0.037	0.021
Tulsa, OK	0.362	0.589	0.012	0.037	0.439	0.493	0.018	0.043	0.456	0.430	0.057	0.058
Other Large Metros	0.405	0.548	0.022	0.024	0.410	0.537	0.024	0.005	0.409	0.514	0.035	0.043
Total top 100 MSAs	0.413	0.475	0.087	0.026	0.427	0.426	0.107	0.007	0.410	0.387	0.147	0.056

NOTE: MSA = metropolitan statistical area.
SOURCE: Data extracted from the GeoLytics Census CD Neighborhood Change Database 1970–2000 Tract Data.

white in their average neighborhood dropped appreciably, from 50 percent white in 1980 to 35 percent white in 2000.

Hispanic contact with blacks also varied by metropolitan type. With an average neighborhood composition of 9 percent, Hispanics living in the Traditional Metros had a fairly constant, low probability of sharing residential space with blacks. By contrast, Hispanics in New Hispanic Destinations were increasingly likely to share residential space with blacks, as the average neighborhood percentage black rose from 15 to 17 percent. From the perspective of blacks living in New Hispanic Destinations, their probability of sharing residential space with Hispanics rose during the 1980s and 1990s, from an average neighborhood that was 4 percent Hispanic to one that was 10 percent Hispanic (see Table 4-3b).

Taken together, Tables 4-1 through 4-3 suggest that the rising Hispanic presence not only has forged new spatial imprints, but also has redrawn color lines by driving a wedge in the black–white residential dichotomy. However, it is important to note that we draw these inferences as descriptive rather than causal outcomes. Although black segregation declined in most metropolitan areas during the past two decades—in many places rather dramatically—their spatial integration was not due to increased contact with whites. Rather, blacks have, on average, reduced their contact with whites in Traditional Metros because their overall segregation has declined through greater contact with Hispanics and, to a lesser extent, Asians.[11]

Hispanics also experienced declining exposure to whites across *all* metropolitan types because they were more likely to share a neighborhood with coethnics in 2000 compared with 1980. In fact, over the past two decades, Hispanics grew more isolated in both Traditional Metros and New Hispanic Destinations. For example, in 2000 the average neighborhood composition for Hispanics in Traditional Metros was 49 percent Hispanic, 35 percent white, 9 percent black, and 8 percent other. However, in the New Hispanic Destinations and Other Large Metros, Hispanics experience much greater exposure to both whites and blacks.

The bewildering diversity of metropolitan transformation lends itself to several generalizations suggesting that the Hispanic dispersal was largely responsible for the ethno-racial reconfiguration of social space since 1980, but particularly during the 1990s. First, with very few exceptions, the largest metropolitan areas became more diverse over the past two decades, but the greatest ethno-racial diversification occurred during the 1990s and in the New Hispanic Destinations. Second, overall segregation levels were uniformly lower in 2000 compared with 1980, and the range of variation in average levels of spatial separation among metropolitan areas contracted as

[11]The correlation between black segregation and the percent Hispanic is –.372.

well.[12] Third, immigration has accentuated Hispanic resegregation patterns, but not uniformly among metropolitan areas because this impact depends on the highly variable sizes of the black and Hispanic populations before the upsurge in migration. Finally, by any measure used, widespread declines in overall black segregation, but particularly in areas where the Hispanic presence rose dramatically, are consistent with the "buffering" hypothesis, namely, that Hispanics serve as a buffer between blacks and whites. This inference is buttressed by evidence that falling black segregation is associated with an increased probability of contact with Hispanics and other nonwhites, which is facilitated by the increased presence of these groups.

Home Ownership

Housing exerts a powerful influence on social integration through school choices and work opportunities (Massey and Denton, 1993). Home purchases represent not only a commitment to place, but also financial investments that usually appreciate in value. Simply put, for working-class and low-income families, home ownership represents the realization of the American dream. Housing costs are a significant barrier to ownership, particularly in the large immigrant gateway cities (Papademetrious and Ray, 2004). As dwelling costs escalate in the largest of the Traditional Metros, affordable housing and jobs lure Hispanics, and immigrants in particular, to New Hispanic Destinations (Kelley and Chavez, 2004).

Table 4-4 summarizes trends and differentials in homeownership rates since 1990 by metropolitan area type. Hispanic homeownership rates inched up from 40 to 44 percent in the top 100 metropolitan areas, but remained about 27 percentage points below those of non-Hispanic whites. Black ownership rates also rose modestly, remaining slightly above the rate for all Hispanics in both periods. Nativity differentials explain the slight black advantage because native-born Hispanic ownership rates were three points higher than blacks. Over time, the ownership differential between native- and foreign-born Hispanics narrowed slightly.

Both the period-specific ownership rates and the pattern of change differ across metropolitan area types. Hispanic home ownership rates exceeded those of blacks in the Traditional Metros throughout the period, so that by 2000 nearly 2 in 5 blacks were homeowners in these metropolitan areas compared with 44 percent of Hispanics. Even foreign-born Hispanics

[12]The standard deviation for Hispanics from all others for the 100 metropolitan areas declined from .10 in 1980 to .09 in 2000 and fell from .11 in 1980 to .09 in 2000 for the Hispanic versus white index.

TABLE 4-4 Homeownership Rates by Race/Ethnicity and Metropolitan Area Type, 1990–2000

Metropolitan Area Type	1990						2000					
	Total	White	Hispanic	Foreign-Born Hispanic	Native-Born Hispanic	Black	Total	White	Hispanic	Foreign-Born Hispanic	Native-Born Hispanic	Black
Traditional Hispanic Metros	53.6	61.2	39.4	35.1	44.1	35.5	56.6	66.4	44.2	41.4	47.9	38.8
New Hispanic Destinations	65.3	69.8	43.3	43.0	43.6	43.1	67.3	73.3	44.0	41.3	47.2	47.3
Other Large Metros	67.6	72.2	47.6	50.6	46.7	48.0	69.3	75.1	47.0	43.7	48.1	49.2
Total top 100 MSAs	60.9	67.3	40.2	36.2	44.1	41.3	63.4	71.4	44.2	41.4	47.8	44.7

NOTE: MSA = metropolitan statistical area.
SOURCE: Data extracted from 5% Integrated Public Use Microdata System (IPUMS).

were more likely than blacks to own homes in the Traditional Metros, although this was not so in 1990. A rather different pattern characterizes the New Destination Metros, where black and Hispanic homeownership rates were identical in 1990, about 43 percent, but diverged in 2000 as blacks ascended to home ownership at a faster pace than Hispanics. The nativity breakdown reveals that the diverging ownership rate between Hispanics and blacks in these metropolitan areas results from nativity differentials in ownership. In 2000 immigrants were less likely to own homes in the New Destination Metros than they did in 1990. Thus, by 2000, black homeownership rates in the New Hispanic Destinations were slightly higher than those of Hispanics. The Hispanic–white homeownership gap widened even more because the white homeownership rate rose faster during the 1990s.

School Segregation

Residential choices have profound implications for life chances because of the school quality they afford. Following the historic *Brown versus Board of Education* decision in 1954, court-ordered school desegregation spawned a spate of social science research that tracked progress toward integration across schools and districts (Black, 1992; Coleman et al., 1966). Although the *Méndez versus Westminister School District* decision actually predated and served as a testing ground for the 1954 Supreme Court decision that outlawed school segregation (Ferg-Cadina, 2004), Hispanics were not even considered in school segregation litigation until 19 years after the Brown decision (Orfield and Lee, 2004). During the 1960s and 1970s, researchers primarily tracked trends in racial desegregation of schools and districts (Coleman et al., 1966; Taeuber, 1975; Taeuber, Sorensen, and Hollingsworth, 1975).

Ethnic diversification of inner-city urban schools after 1980 brought into sharp focus the growing concentration of Hispanic students (Orfield and Lee, 2004; Reardon and Yun, 2001). Although Hispanic youth are more integrated with whites compared with blacks (.58 versus .65 based on D), it is worrisome that both groups became more segregated during the 1990s, after districts were allowed to end their segregation plans (Logan et al., 2002). Social class segregation has also been on the rise (Logan et al., 2002).

The pernicious effects of school segregation stem from its divisive class underpinnings, namely that schools in which minorities are disproportionately concentrated are poorer, on average, than predominantly white schools (Tienda and Niu, 2004). Resource-poor schools have more unqualified teachers and offer more remedial courses and fewer advanced placement courses; hence their students—disproportionately black and Hispanic—

fare poorly on standardized achievement tests (see Chapter 6). In 2000, black and Hispanic students attended segregated schools where two out of three students were poor or near poor. Orfield and Lee (2004) note that 88 percent of the hypersegregated minority schools (i.e., with less than 10 percent whites) also concentrated poor students, but equally segregated white schools were only 15 percent poor.

That many financially well-off nonminority parents enrolled their children in private schools or moved to suburban neighborhoods undermined the spirit of court-ordered desegregation (Coleman, 1990). But even as minority youth become more suburbanized, their chances of enrolling in segregated schools are significantly higher than white youth, which suggests that school and residential segregation have become less strongly coupled. In documenting the reversal of several decades of school integration in the South during the 1990s, Reardon and Yun (2003) observe that schools located in southern metropolitan counties were 40 percent less segregated than housing markets in 1990, but a decade later the schools were only 27 percent less segregated. Their findings are pertinent for Hispanic youth in light of the growing Hispanic dispersal to New Hispanic Destinations in the South. That is, as minority spatial integration evolves in suburban areas, segregation rises rather than drops, as one would expect (Reardon and Yun, 2001).

However, the components of change, namely *within* versus *between* district segregation, operate differently among minority groups. For blacks, increases in school segregation mainly derive from changes in residential segregation between districts. However for Hispanics (and Asians), higher levels of school segregation are more complex because ethno-racial separation of students derives from uneven allocation across as well as within districts. The concentration of Hispanic suburbanization in the South and the West, where large, countywide districts are the norm, exacerbates this complexity. Both state of residence and school districts within states contribute to highly differentiated levels of Hispanic school segregation, but uneven enrollment *within* districts is the major source of division between white and Hispanic students in specific states. That changes in school segregation of blacks and Hispanics were driven by very different dynamics has important implications for future patterns of social integration, particularly in light of their recent geographic scattering. So too does evidence that school resegregation was largely driven by the reversal of social integration policies rather than changes in residential location. Because school segregation along ethnic lines is highly correlated with social class and school quality, evidence of a weakened association between school and residential segregation implies that social integration of future cohorts, including the rapidly growing second generation, may be thwarted.

Labor Force Consequences of the Hispanic Dispersal

Perhaps even more than affordable housing and better schools, jobs are the main draw to the New Hispanic Destinations (Zúñiga and Hernández-León, 2004). Total labor force growth averaged 25 percent in the largest 100 metropolitan areas between 1980 and 2000 and a whopping 39 percent in the smaller metropolitan and nonmetropolitan areas.[13] Uneven job growth across labor markets pulled Hispanics, and particularly the foreign-born, away from the traditional gateway cities toward rapidly growing southern labor markets. Labor force growth in the Traditional Metros was well above the 100-metropolitan-area average but slightly below the 34 percent employment growth registered in the New Hispanic Destinations. By contrast, in the large metropolitan areas with very small Hispanic populations (and very large black populations), the labor force contracted 4 percent over the two-decade period.

As Table 4-5 shows, immigration from Latin America fueled the changing ethno-racial composition of large urban labor markets, but smaller markets and nonmetropolitan areas also witnessed a trebling of their foreign-born population. In 1980, native-born Hispanic workers outnumbered their foreign-born counterparts in the 100 largest metropolitan areas, but by 2000 this scenario reversed, even as Hispanics doubled their labor force share from 7.5 to 14.5 percent of the total. Specifically in the 100 largest metropolitan areas, foreign-born Hispanics increased their labor force share from 3 to 8 percent of all workers, but the respective change for native-born Hispanics was far more modest—a mere 2.2 percentage points—which was nonetheless larger than the change witnessed by blacks. The white share of the labor force in the top 100 metropolitan areas contracted from 78 to 64 percent, although their absolute numbers remained constant because the total number of jobs increased.

Changes in the ethno-racial composition of the workforce were most striking in the New Hispanic Destinations, largely owing to the volume of recent immigrants—both Hispanics and others—where few had settled before. In 1980, foreign-born Hispanics comprised less than 1 percent of all workers in the New Hispanic Destinations, but their labor force share reached 4 percent by 2000, surpassing their native-born counterparts. Representation of blacks in the labor force of these metropolitan areas rose about 2 percentage points, while the share of whites in the workforce plummeted 11 points over the period. Immigration from Latin America continued to transform the ethnic contours of the labor force in the Traditional Metros as well. In 1980, native and foreign-born Hispanics consti-

[13]We base these analyses on the total labor force, which includes the unemployed, but trends are similar when only looking at the employed portion of the labor force.

tuted 8 and 7 percent, respectively, of the workforce in these markets, but by 2000, the immigrant share overtook that of the U.S.-born by 3 percentage points. The black workforce share in the Traditional Metros remained steady over the period, but that of non-Hispanic whites dropped nearly 17 points.

Expansion of unskilled jobs in construction and in personal and repair services, which include dwelling maintenance and private household workers, is largely responsible for luring Hispanics, and particularly the foreign-born, to the New Hispanic Destinations. As Table 4-6 shows, about 1 in 5 Hispanic workers residing in the largest 100 metropolitan areas worked in these industries, but by 2000 nearly 1 in 3 Hispanics were employed in these two industries. A similar trend was found in the smaller metropolitan areas and nonmetropolitan areas, where over 28 percent of Hispanic workers found jobs in these two industries. By comparison, just over 1 in 5 of the total workforce in the largest metropolitan areas held construction or personal and repair service jobs in 2000. These industries expanded as a share of total employment in the largest metropolitan areas, rising from 18 to 22 percent of all jobs over the two decades, which not only favored the absorption of unskilled immigrants, but also, as these jobs became typed as Hispanic or immigrant jobs, contributed to group-specific labor demand (Tienda and Wilson, 1991).

Changes in the industrial composition of employment in the New Hispanic Destinations favored the absorption of unskilled immigrant workers. Construction and personal and repair services, which absorb disproportionate shares of foreign-born workers, grew faster than the average for the largest metropolitan areas. In 2000, 36 percent of Hispanic workers in the New Hispanic Destinations were employed in either construction or personal and repair service industries, with over one quarter in the low-skill services alone. Two decades earlier, when the Hispanic workforce in the New Hispanic Destinations was one-fourth as large, only 21 percent worked in these two industries. Comparable shares employed in these two industries for the Traditional Metros were 20 and 30 percent in 1980 and 2000, respectively.

In the Traditional Metros, as Hispanic employment in nondurable manufacturing fell, from approximately 13 to 6 percent between 1980 and 2000, the representation of foreign-born Hispanic workers within the industry nearly doubled, rising from 15 to 29 percent (Table 4-7). That representation of native-born Hispanic workers in nondurable manufacturing remained steady suggests that this industry is becoming a niche for immigrant workers there. In the New Hispanic Destinations, the share of foreign-born Hispanics employed in nondurable manufacturing is considerably lower—about 7 percent in 2000—but the direction of change clearly

TABLE 4-5 Ethno-Racial Composition of the Civilian Labor Force by Metropolitan Area Type, 1980–2000

	Traditional Hispanic Metros			New Hispanic Destinations		
	1980	1990	2000	1980	1990	2000
Hispanic foreign-born	7.1	12.0	14.5	0.8	1.7	4.0
Hispanic native-born	8.3	9.5	11.3	1.3	1.9	2.9
Whites	68.7	59.7	52.1	84.6	81.3	73.5
Blacks	11.8	12.0	11.2	11.7	12.5	13.6
All others	4.1	6.8	10.9	1.5	2.7	6.0
Total %	100.0	100.0	100.0	99.9	100.1	100.0
Total N (000s)	24,943	29,515	33,028	22,686	29,845	30,390

[a]Ann Arbor, MI, and Mobile, AL, classified as "Other Large Metro" in 1980 and 1990 are contained in "All Other Metros/Nonmetropolitan Areas" for 2000.

SOURCE: IPUMS.

TABLE 4-6 Industry Distribution for the Hispanic Civilian Labor Force by Metropolitan Area Type, 1980–2000

	Traditional Metros		New Hispanic Destinations	
Industry Sector	1980	2000	1980	2000
Agriculture and mining	4.0	1.7	2.9	1.1
Construction	6.5	9.6	4.7	12.0
Nondurable manufacturing	13.2	6.4	10.8	5.7
Durable manufacturing	16.3	9.2	17.0	8.6
Wholesale trade	4.8	4.9	3.6	3.8
Retail trade	10.2	11.5	8.4	10.8
Transport and utilities	5.2	4.9	5.1	4.3
Information and communication	1.2	2.4	1.1	2.4
Finance, insurance, and real estate	5.3	5.5	5.5	5.5
Business and administrative services	2.9	5.2	4.0	5.9
Health, education, and professional services	12.2	15.0	14.9	13.1
Public administration	4.2	3.0	6.0	3.0
Personal and repair services	14.0	20.9	16.1	24.0
Total %	100.0	100.2	100.1	100.2
Ns (000s)	3,777	8,341	463	2,071

SOURCE: IPUMS.

Other Large Metros			Top 100 MSAs			Small Metropolitan and Nonmetropolitan Areas		
1980	1990	2000[a]	1980	1990	2000	1980	1990	2000
0.4	0.5	0.8	3.3	5.6	8.1	0.9	1.8	2.7
1.1	1.4	1.8	4.2	4.9	6.4	2.5	2.9	3.4
82.4	80.5	76.1	77.6	72.4	64.5	87.8	85.7	82.5
13.4	14.2	16.2	12.1	12.6	13.0	7.3	7.4	7.6
2.7	3.4	5.1	2.8	4.5	8.0	1.5	2.2	3.7
100.0	100.0	100.0	100.0	100.0	100.0	100.0	100.0	99.9
12,628	13,548	12,174	60,258	72,908	75,591	45,407	51,864	63,163

		Top 100 MSAs				Hispanic Labor Force	
Other Large Metros		Hispanic Labor Force		Total Labor Force		Small Metropolitan and Nonmetropolitan Areas	
1980	2000	1980	2000	1980	2000	1980	2000
1.9	1.5	3.8	1.6	1.8	0.7	13.3	9.2
4.8	8.2	6.2	10.0	5.6	6.4	8.0	9.1
10.5	6.7	12.9	6.3	7.8	4.2	9.9	8.2
20.1	12.1	16.6	9.1	13.9	8.2	12.9	8.1
3.7	3.3	4.6	4.6	4.7	3.9	3.2	3.4
10.6	11.6	10.1	11.4	11.8	11.6	10.0	10.6
6.2	3.5	5.2	4.7	6.1	5.3	5.1	3.8
1.0	2.5	1.1	2.4	1.6	3.7	0.9	1.5
3.3	5.2	5.2	5.5	7.0	7.9	2.9	3.5
3.2	5.1	3.0	5.3	4.8	8.7	1.9	3.7
15.7	17.9	12.6	14.7	17.4	20.3	14.5	16.4
5.3	4.0	4.5	3.0	5.5	4.5	5.1	3.9
13.9	18.5	14.2	21.5	11.9	14.7	12.4	18.6
100.2	100.1	100.0	100.1	99.9	100.1	100.1	100.0
172	304	4,413	10,717	58,971	74,411	1,469	3,776

TABLE 4-7 Hispanic Composition of Employment by Industry Sector and Metropolitan Area Type, 1980–2000

	Traditional				New Hispanic Destinations			
	1980		2000		1980		2000	
Industry Sector	% FB Hisp	% NB Hisp	% FB Hisp	% NB Hisp	% FB Hisp	% NB Hisp	% FB Hisp	% NB Hisp
Agriculture and mining	17.8	11.4	37.7	11.5	1.3	2.4	10.8	2.9
Construction	7.8	9.4	27.2	10.7	0.7	1.0	10.1	2.5
Nondurable manufacturing	15.2	10.0	28.9	10.0	1.4	1.6	7.1	3.3
Durable manufacturing	10.9	9.4	19.6	10.2	1.0	1.7	4.9	3.1
Wholesale trade	7.0	7.9	18.2	11.8	0.6	1.0	4.1	2.8
Retail trade	5.1	8.6	12.7	14.0	0.5	1.0	3.0	3.3
Transport and utilities	5.0	7.6	11.1	11.8	0.5	1.2	2.6	3.0
Information and communications	2.9	7.6	5.4	9.6	0.4	1.1	1.7	2.6
Finance, insurance, and real estate	4.4	6.1	7.2	10.4	0.7	1.0	2.1	2.6
Business and administrative services	3.5	4.8	6.5	8.3	0.7	1.1	2.2	2.5
Health, education, and professional services	3.7	7.5	7.9	11.4	0.7	1.1	2.0	2.5
Public administration	2.9	10.8	4.9	14.4	0.5	1.4	1.3	2.7
Personal and repair services	9.7	8.4	24.9	11.4	1.2	1.6	7.8	3.5
All industries	7.1	8.3	14.5	11.3	0.8	1.3	4.0	2.9

NOTE: FB = foreign-born. NB = native-born.
SOURCE: IPUMS.

indicates that the industry is becoming an employment niche for Hispanic immigrants here as well.

A comparable trend toward concentration of Hispanic immigrants is evident in rapidly growing industries, notably the personal and repair services. In Traditional Metros, native and foreign-born Hispanics made up, respectively, 8 and 10 percent of employment in personal and repair services in 1980, but two decades later, these shares rose to 25 and 11 percent,

Other Large Metros				Small Metropolitan and Nonmetropolitan Areas			
1980		2000		1980		2000	
% FB Hisp	% NB Hisp	% FB Hisp	% NB Hisp	% FB Hisp	% NB Hisp	% FB Hisp	% NB Hisp
0.7	1.2	4.9	2.3	2.8	3.4	12.9	3.5
0.3	0.9	1.4	2.1	0.9	2.9	4.1	3.2
0.5	1.3	1.2	2.4	1.0	2.3	5.4	2.9
0.4	1.1	1.0	1.8	0.9	2.1	2.4	2.5
0.3	0.9	0.8	1.5	0.7	2.2	4.0	3.3
0.4	0.8	0.6	1.9	0.5	2.4	1.6	3.7
0.3	1.3	0.3	1.5	0.6	2.7	1.6	3.2
0.2	0.9	0.4	2.0	0.3	2.1	1.2	3.0
0.3	0.5	0.3	1.6	0.5	1.7	1.0	3.0
0.4	0.8	0.5	1.3	0.4	2.3	1.6	3.0
0.3	0.9	0.5	1.6	0.5	2.3	1.2	3.4
0.3	1.4	0.3	2.0	0.5	3.1	0.8	4.1
0.5	1.2	1.2	2.1	0.9	2.7	3.8	4.2
0.4	1.1	0.8	1.8	0.9	2.5	2.7	3.4

respectively. Hispanic employment in these low-skill industries also surged in the New Hispanic Destinations, particularly for the foreign-born, which rose more than six-fold while the native-born share working in these industries only doubled. A similar change occurred in the smaller metropolitan areas and nonmetropolitan areas, where foreign-born Hispanics more than quadrupled their representation not only in the low-skilled personal and repair services and in construction, but also in agriculture and mining. The increasing concentration of Hispanic workers, and particularly recent immigrants, in rapidly growing unskilled industries, suggests both that the residential dispersal will continue well into the 21st century and possibly even gain momentum as high-tech and professional services employ unskilled workers for their labor needs.

CONCLUSIONS

The unprecedented Hispanic geographic scattering, which began during the 1970s and gained considerable momentum during the 1990s, is a significant agent of urban social transformation both because of its pace and the sheer number of persons and places involved. In addition to its potential for reconfiguring racially divided space, Hispanics' spatial scattering has broad ramifications for intergroup relations and the contours of ethnic stratification more generally.

Ethno-racial diversification of the largest 100 metropolitan areas during the 1980s and 1990s was accompanied by real declines in the spatial segregation of blacks, even as Hispanic segregation levels rose. However, changes in spatial separation differed appreciably across types of metropolitan areas. With one-third of all residents of Hispanic origin and 1 in 4 residents foreign-born, the Traditional Metros are among the most diverse, and they exhibit moderate segregation levels. Blacks and Hispanics are about equally segregated from other groups. Hispanics in these metropolitan areas average high levels of neighborhood isolation, which translates into relatively low exposure to blacks and Asians and only moderate contact with non-Hispanic whites. New Hispanic Destinations are experiencing rapid diversification and have moderate overall levels of segregation. Hispanics in these metropolitan areas are highly integrated with whites. The different spatial outcomes in these metropolitan areas compared with the Traditional Metros reflect several factors, including the pace of change, the large share of foreign-born among the newcomers, and the fact that blacks outnumber Hispanics by a 2:1 ratio.

The consequences of the Hispanic scattering for school segregation, homeownership, and employment are mixed because they are very much in flux. Immigration from Mexico, Central America, and South America not only was a driving force behind the Hispanic dispersal, but also transformed the ethno-racial composition of urban employment. In the largest 100 metropolitan areas, not only did the Hispanic share of total employment rise, but the foreign-born share also surpassed native-born workers in these urban areas. More generally, the Hispanic dispersal was accompanied by and facilitated changes in the industrial distribution of employment, as the expansion of construction and personal and repair services—industries viewed as immigrant niches in the Traditional Metros—allowed for the absorption of unskilled immigrant labor and lured unskilled immigrants to the New Hispanic Destinations.

Hispanic homeownership rates have risen slightly since 1980, but school segregation levels have been on the rise, particularly in the South—even without accounting for "soft" segregation. Whether high schools support one prom or several depends not only on settlement patterns, but also on whether black, Hispanic and white students interact socially within and beyond the school halls. Soft segregation as evidenced by Toombs County, Georgia, is not even broached by the vast literature about rising school segregation in the midst of increased residential diversity. Given the momentum of the Hispanic geographic dispersal and its broad reach across states and metropolitan areas, failure to reverse trends in resegregation could produce deleterious consequences for the well-being of the burgeoning second generation.

Although vestiges of long-standing regional concentration will persist for the foreseeable future, Hispanics' residential makeover is a potential harbinger of changes in intergroup relations. But much depends on how the newcomers are received in the nontraditional hubs. Many suburbanites welcome the new immigrants as hard-working people, but in other places the newcomers experience a backlash of discrimination. The consequences of Hispanics' changing spatial imprints will shape their futures in myriad ways, still to be played out and tallied even as they reshape the U.S. urban landscape.

Our descriptive foray into the contours and consequences of Hispanics' changing residential configuration cannot establish any causal connection with declines in racial segregation, but we do offer suggestive evidence to support the buffering hypothesis. Our work sets the stage for exploring the causal underpinnings of the changing urban ethno-racial landscape. In addition to developing a multivariate strategy to test this hypothesis in a causal framework, future research seeking to better understand the consequences of the Hispanics unprecedented geographic scattering should employ techniques that account for increasingly multiethnic character of the urban landscape, such as the entropy index.

REFERENCES

Alba, R., and Nee, V. (1999). Rethinking assimilation theory for a new era of immigration. In C. Hirschman, P. Kasinitz, and J. DeWind (Eds.), *Handbook of international migration* (pp. 137–160). New York: Russell Sage Foundation.

Bean, F.D., and Tienda, M. (1987). *The Hispanic population of the United States.* New York: Russell Sage Foundation.

Black, A.N., Jr. (1992). Segregation and desegregation. In E.F. Borgatta and M. Borgatta (Eds.), *Encyclopedia of sociology: Volume 4* (pp. 1728–1738). New York: Macmillan.

Chapman, D. (2004, April 11). Equal but separate in Lyons; The big dance: Hispanic, black, and white students at Toombs County High School all will hold their own proms. *Atlanta Journal-Constitution.*

Coleman, J.S. (1990). *Equality and achievement in education.* Boulder, CO: Westview Press.

Coleman, J.S., et al. (1966). *Equality of educational opportunity.* Washington, DC: U.S. Government Printing Office.

Danziger, S., and Gottschalk, P. (1995). *America unequal.* Cambridge, MA: Harvard University Press/Russell Sage Foundation.

Ferg-Cadina, J.A. (2004, May). *Black, white, and brown: Latino school desegregation efforts in the pre- and post-Brown v. Board of Education era.* Washington, DC: Maldef.

Fischer, C.S., Stockmayer, G., Stiles, J., and Hout, M. (2004). Distinguishing the geographic levels and social dimensions of U.S. metropolitan segregation. *Demography, 41*, 37–59.

Fischer, M.J. (2003). The relative importance of income and race in determining residential outcomes in U.S. urban areas. *Urban Affairs Review, 38*(5), 669–696.

Frey, W.H., and Farley, R. (1996). Latino, Asian, and black segregation in U.S. metropolitan areas: Are multiethnic metros different? *Demography, 33*(1), 35–51.

Iceland, J. (2003). Beyond black and white: Metropolitan residential segregation in a mutliethnic America. *Social Science Research, 33*(2), 248–271.

Iceland, J., and Lake, C. (2004). *The effect of immigration on residential segregation in U.S. metropolitan areas, 2000.* Boston, MA: Population Association of America.

Iceland, J., Weinberg, D.H., and Steinmetz, E. (2002). *Racial and ethnic residential segregation in the United States: 1980–2000.* (U.S. Census Bureau, Series CENSR-3.) Washington, DC: U.S. Department of Commerce.

Kandel, W., and Cromartie, J. (2004). *New patterns of Hispanic settlement in rural America.* (Rural Development Research Report No. 99, Economic Research Service.) Washington, DC: U.S. Department of Agriculture.

Kelley, D., and Chavez, C. (2004, 15 February). California dreaming no more. *Los Angeles Times*, A1.

Logan, J.R. (2003). *American newcomers.* Albany, NY: Lewis Mumford Center, SUNY-Albany.

Logan, J.R., Stowell, J., and Oakley, D. (2002). *Choosing segregation: Racial imbalance in American public schools, 1990–2000.* Albany, NY: Lewis Mumford Center for Comparative Urban and Regional Research, SUNY-Albany. Available at: http://mumford1.dyndns.org/cen2000/SchoolPop/SPReport/SPDownload.pdf.

Logan, J.R., Stults, B., and Farley, R. (2004). Segregation of minorities in the metropolis: Two decades of change. *Demography, 41*, 1–22.

Massey, D.S. (1981). Hispanic residential segregation: A comparison of Mexicans, Cubans, and Puerto Ricans. *Sociology and Social Research, 65*, 311–322.

Massey, D.S., and Denton, N.A. (1987). Trends in the residential segregation of blacks, Hispanics, and Asians: 1970–1980. *American Sociological Review, 52*, 802–825.

Massey, D.S., and Denton, N.A. (1993). *American apartheid.* Cambridge, MA: Harvard University Press.

Morenoff, J.M., and Tienda, M. (1997, May). Underclass neighborhoods in temporal and ecological perspective: An illustration from Chicago. *Annals of the American Academy of Political and Social Science, 551*, 59–72.

National Research Council. (1989). *A common destiny: Blacks and American society.* Committee on the Status of Black Americans. G.D. Jaynes and R.M. Williams, Jr. (Eds.). Washington, DC: National Academy Press.

Orfield, G., and Lee, C. (2004). *Brown at 50: King's dream or Plessy's nightmare?* Harvard Civil Rights Project. Available: http://www.civilrightsproject.harvard.edu/research/reseg04/brown50.pdf [accessed July 9, 2004].

Papademetriou, D., and Ray, B. (2004). *From homeland to home: Immigrants and homeownership in urban America.* (vol. 1, issue I, March). Washington, DC: Fannie Mae.

Reardon, S.F., and Yun, J.T. (2001). Suburban racial change and suburban school segregation, 1987–95. *Sociology of Education, 74*, 79–101.

Reardon, S.F., and Yun, J.T. (2003). Integrating neighborhoods, segregating schools: The retreat from school desegregation in the South, 1990–2000. *North Carolina Law Review, 81*, 1563–1596.

Suro, R., and Singer, A. (2002). *Latino growth in metropolitan America: Changing patterns, new locations.* Survey Series, Census 2000. Washington, DC: Brookings Institution.

Taeuber, K. (1975). Demographic perspectives on housing and school segregation. *Wayne Law Review, 21*, 833–850.

Taeuber, K., Sorensen, A., and Hollingsworth, L., Jr. (1975). Indexes of racial residential segregation for 109 cities in the United States, 1940 to 1970. *Sociological Focus, 8*, 125–142.

Tienda, M., and Niu, S. (2004, October). *Capitalizing on segregation, pretending neutrality: College admissions and the Texas top 10% law.* Paper presented at the Seminar on 50 years after *Brown*, Princeton University.

Tienda, M., and Wilson, F. (1991). Migration, ethnicity, and labor force activity. In J.M. Abowd and R.B. Freeman (Eds.), *Immigration, trade and the labor force* (pp. 135–163). Chicago, IL: University of Chicago Press.

Turner, M.A., Ross, S.L., et al. (2002). *Discrimination in metropolitan housing markets: National results from Phase I HDS 2000.* Washington, DC: U.S. Department of Housing and Urban Development.

Wilkes, R., and Iceland, J. (2004). Hypersegregation in the twenty-first century. *Demography, 41*, 23–36.

Zúñiga, V., and Hernández-León, R. (Eds.) (2005). *New destinations: Mexican migration in the United States.* New York: Russell Sage Foundation.

APPENDIX TABLE A4-1 Racial/Ethnic Composition Measures: 100 Largest Metropolitan Statistical Areas, 1980–2000

	1980			1990			2000		
Metropolitan Statistical Area	% H	% B	% FB	% H	% B	% FB	% H	% B	% FB
Traditional Hispanic Metros	18.0	13.6	16.6	24.0	12.8	22.4	29.8	12.4	26.8
Albuquerque, NM MSA	36.1	2.0	4.7	37.0	2.5	7.0	41.6	2.5	8.9
Austin, TX MSA	17.5	9.3	5.4	20.5	9.0	8.9	26.2	8.0	15.6
Bakersfield, CA MSA	21.6	5.2	8.6	28.0	5.3	13.8	14.5	6.0	19.4
Chicago, IL PMSA	8.1	20.0	12.0	12.1	21.7	14.8	17.1	18.9	18.5
Dallas, TX PMSA	8.9	16.0	5.0	14.5	15.8	9.8	23.0	15.1	18.9
Denver, CO PMSA	11.5	5.3	5.4	13.0	5.7	6.4	18.8	5.5	13.2
El Paso, TX MSA	61.9	3.8	22.3	69.6	3.5	27.4	78.2	3.1	30.2
Fort Worth–Arlington, TX PMSA	7.3	10.4	4.8	11.3	10.6	6.3	18.2	11.2	11.4
Fresno, CA MSA	29.0	4.8	11.0	35.5	4.6	18.2	44.0	5.1	20.6
Houston, TX PMSA	14.6	18.7	9.0	21.4	18.1	14.2	29.9	17.5	21.4
Jersey City, NJ PMSA	26.1	12.6	29.2	33.3	12.7	36.2	39.8	13.5	43.3
Los Angeles–Long Beach, CA PMSA	27.6	12.6	23.6	37.8	10.5	33.7	44.6	9.8	36.8
McAllen, TX MSA	81.3	0.2	20.0	85.2	0.1	28.0	88.3	0.5	31.5
Miami, FL PMSA	35.7	17.3	39.2	49.2	19.1	48.8	57.3	20.3	55.7
New York, NY PMSA	17.7	23.1	26.7	22.1	23.2	32.9	25.1	24.6	39.0
Newark, NJ PMSA	6.7	20.9	13.7	10.3	22.4	17.3	13.3	22.3	21.4
Oakland, CA PMSA	10.6	15.0	15.1	13.1	14.2	16.2	18.5	12.7	24.0
Orange County, CA PMSA	14.8	1.3		23.0	1.4		30.8	1.7	29.9
Phoenix–Mesa, AZ MSA	14.1	3.2	6.3	16.3	3.3	8.4	25.1	3.7	15.2
Riverside–San Bernardino, CA PMSA	18.6	5.1	8.8	26.5	6.5	15.5	37.8	7.7	19.2
Sacramento, CA PMSA	8.7	6.0	8.4	11.6	6.7	11.3	14.4	7.7	14.8
San Antonio, TX MSA	44.9	6.8	8.0	47.6	6.5	10.2	51.2	6.6	12.8
San Diego, CA MSA	14.8	5.5	13.9	20.5	6.0	18.7	26.7	5.7	23.7
San Francisco, CA PMSA	11.2	8.5	16.9	14.5	7.4	30.5	16.8	5.3	35.7

San Jose, CA PMSA	17.5	3.3	14.4	21.0	3.5	24.9	24.0	2.8	35.1
Stockton, CA MSA	19.3	5.5	11.7	23.5	5.2	16.4	30.5	6.7	20.7
Tucson, AZ MSA	20.9	2.7	8.0	24.4	2.9	10.8	29.3	3.0	13.6
Vallejo, CA PMSA	9.9	8.7	8.2	13.6	10.0	12.7	19.1	11.7	17.2
Ventura, CA PMSA	21.4	2.1	13.9	26.5	2.2	18.7	33.4	1.9	20.4
New Hispanic Destinations	2.4	12.9	5.8	3.8	13.8	7.5	7.0	14.8	12.4
Albany, NY MSA	1.0	3.6	5.3	1.8	4.6	5.3	2.7	6.1	6.3
Allentown, PA MSA	2.5	1.5	5.1	4.2	1.8	6.1	7.9	3.0	7.9
Atlanta, GA MSA	1.1	24.5	2.8	2.0	25.8	4.8	6.5	28.9	11.4
Baltimore, MD PMSA	0.9	25.5	4.0	1.3	25.7	4.6	2.0	27.4	6.8
Bergen–Passaic, NJ PMSA	7.0	7.1	20.0	11.6	7.5	21.1	17.3	8.1	28.1
Birmingham, AL MSA	0.7	28.8	1.2	0.4	27.0	1.2	1.8	30.1	3.4
Boston, MA–NH PMSA	2.3	5.3	11.5	4.5	6.8	14.0	5.9	7.0	18.4
Charlotte, NC–SC MSA	0.8	20.5	2.3	0.9	19.9	2.8	5.1	20.5	10.2
Columbus, OH MSA	0.7	11.2	2.6	0.8	11.9	2.5	1.8	13.4	6.4
Fort Lauderdale, FL PMSA	3.9	11.1	11.8	8.6	14.9	16.9	16.7	20.5	26.8
Gary, IN PMSA	7.2	19.6		7.9	19.2	3.7	10.5	19.7	4.8
Grand Rapids, MI MSA	2.1	6.3	4.1	3.3	5.8	3.6	6.3	7.3	6.5
Greensboro–Winston Salem, NC MSA	0.6	19.2	1.6	0.8	19.3	1.5	5.0	20.2	6.2
Greenville, SC MSA	0.7	17.1	2.0	0.7	17.2	2.1	2.7	17.5	
Harrisburg, PA MSA	1.1	6.1	3.1	1.7	6.5	3.0	3.1	7.8	3.9
Hartford, CT MSA	4.3	6.8	12.0	7.6	10.0	12.9	9.6	9.5	23.3
Indianapolis, IN MSA	0.8	12.8	1.8	0.9	13.7	1.8	2.7	13.9	4.6
Jacksonville, FL MSA	1.9	21.7	3.9	2.5	19.8	4.8	3.8	21.7	6.6
Kansas City, MO-KS MSA	2.4	12.9	2.5	2.9	12.7	2.6	5.2	12.8	4.6
Knoxville, TN MSA	0.6	6.9	2.0	0.5	6.0	1.9	1.3	5.8	2.9
Las Vegas, NV–AZ MSA	7.6	9.9	9.2	11.2	9.3	10.1	20.6	8.1	19.1
Little Rock, AR MSA	0.9	20.3	2.1	0.8	19.9	2.0	2.1	21.9	3.1
Louisville, KY–IN MSA	0.6	13.0	1.4	0.6	13.0	1.4	1.6	13.9	3.7

continues

APPENDIX TABLE A4-1 Continued

	1980			1990			2000		
Metropolitan Statistical Area	% H	% B	% FB	% H	% B	% FB	% H	% B	% FB
Memphis, TN–AR–MS MSA	1.0	40.1	1.6	0.8	40.5	1.9	2.4	43.4	5.0
Middlesex–Somerset–Hunterdon, NJ PMSA	4.4	5.3		7.1	6.5	14.7	11.2	8.0	22.0
Milwaukee, WI PMSA	2.5	10.8	4.6	3.6	13.6	4.4	6.3	15.7	6.8
Minneapolis–St. Paul, MN–WI MSA	1.1	2.3	3.7	1.5	3.6	4.5	3.3	5.3	8.4
Monmouth–Ocean, NJ PMSA	2.5	6.1		3.7	5.8	9.0	5.7	5.8	9.5
Nashville, TN MSA	0.6	16.1	1.5	0.8	15.4	2.3	3.3	15.6	6.7
Nassau-Suffolk, NY PMSA	4.0	6.2	9.8	6.3	7.0	11.3	10.3	8.5	15.6
New Haven, CT PMSA	3.7	10.4	9.0	6.2	11.7	9.0	9.8	13.1	8.5
Norfolk–Virginia Beach–Newport News, VA–NC MSA	1.5	28.5	4.5	2.3	28.2	5.7	3.1	30.9	6.7
Oklahoma City, OK MSA	2.3	9.0	3.0	3.5	10.4	4.7	6.7	10.6	9.6
Omaha, NE–IA MSA	2.2	7.5	3.7	2.6	8.3	2.8	5.5	8.3	7.3
Orlando, FL MSA	3.5	12.9	6.8	8.9	12.0	11.9	16.5	13.9	18.5
Portland–Vancouver, OR–WA PMSA	2.0	2.6	5.8	3.5	3.1	7.6	7.4	2.7	13.1
Providence, RI-MA MSA	2.0	2.3	9.7	4.8	4.1	10.0	7.9	4.0	18.7
Raleigh–Durham, NC MSA	0.8	24.7	3.3	1.2	24.9	4.8	6.1	22.7	11.3
Richmond, VA MSA	0.9	29.0	2.4	1.0	29.0	3.6	2.3	30.2	6.1
Seattle–Bellevue, WA PMSA	4.9	1.0	8.1	5.8	0.9	10.2	10.8	1.1	15.2
Salt Lake City, UT MSA	1.7	6.8	4.0	2.2	4.3	4.9	6.6	6.0	10.0
Sarasota, FL MSA	2.0	3.6	6.3	2.8	4.0	6.5	5.2	4.4	9.6
Springfield, MA MSA	4.4	5.2	9.3	9.1	6.2	10.6	12.5	6.7	13.5
Tacoma, WA PMSA	2.7	6.2	8.6	3.6	7.0	8.7	5.5	7.0	11.1
Tampa–St. Petersburg–Clearwater, FL MSA	5.1	9.2	7.5	6.7	8.8	8.9	10.4	10.2	12.1
Tulsa, OK MSA	1.5	7.8	1.7	2.0	8.2	2.5	4.8	8.8	5.5
Washington, DC–MD–VA–WV PMSA	2.9	26.7	9.5	5.7	26.2	14.8	8.8	26.0	20.9

West Palm Beach, FL MSA	4.9	13.7	10.8	7.8	11.9	13.9	12.4	13.8	20.0
Wichita, KS MSA	2.9	7.5	4.1	4.1	7.4	3.9	7.4	7.8	6.9
Wilmington, DE–MD PMSA	1.6	14.0	4.6	2.4	14.7	4.2	4.7	17.8	
Other Large Metros	1.7	15.8	5.4	2.1	16.7	5.2	2.9	17.5	6.5
Akron, OH PMSA	0.5	9.1	3.5	0.6	9.9	3.5	0.8	11.0	4.3
Ann Arbor, MI PMSA	1.4	11.0	6.0	2.1	11.0	6.1	3.1	7.3	6.8
Baton Rouge, LA MSA	1.8	27.9	2.2	1.4	29.5	1.8	1.8	31.9	3.2
Buffalo, NY MSA	1.3	9.3	6.8	1.8	10.0	5.6	2.9	11.7	5.9
Charleston, SC MSA	1.4	31.7	3.2	1.5	30.1	3.9	2.4	30.8	4.4
Cincinnati, OH–KY–IN PMSA	0.6	12.3	2.4	0.6	13.1	2.3	1.1	13.0	3.3
Cleveland, OH PMSA	1.8	16.2	6.9	1.9	19.3	6.8	3.3	18.5	6.0
Columbia, SC MSA	1.3	28.8	3.1	1.3	30.2	3.2	2.4	32.1	4.6
Dayton, OH MSA	0.6	12.6	2.6	0.8	13.2	2.6	1.2	14.2	3.2
Detroit, MI PMSA	1.6	20.3	6.8	1.9	21.4	5.9	2.9	22.9	8.5
Honolulu, HI MSA	7.2	2.2	18.1	6.8	3.0	18.6	6.7	2.4	23.3
Mobile, AL MSA	1.1	28.7	1.6	0.9	27.3	2.1	1.4	27.4	2.2
New Orleans, LA MSA	4.0	32.2	5.0	4.3	34.5	4.6	4.4	37.5	6.4
Philadelphia, PA–NJ PMSA	2.5	18.7	6.5	3.6	18.8	7.2	5.1	20.1	8.8
Pittsburgh, PA MSA	0.5	7.3	3.8	0.6	8.1	2.7	0.7	8.1	3.3
Rochester, NY MSA	2.0	8.0	6.2	3.1	9.1	6.6	4.3	10.3	9.9
Scranton, PA MSA	0.4	0.6	3.1	0.8	1.0	2.6	1.2	1.4	2.8
St. Louis, MO-IL MSA	0.9	17.0	2.7	1.1	17.3	2.5	1.5	18.3	3.6
Syracuse, NY MSA	1.0	4.8	4.8	1.4	5.8	4.8	2.1	6.5	4.9
Toledo, OH MSA	2.8	10.6	2.8	3.3	11.2	3.0	4.4	12.8	3.9
Youngstown, OH MSA	1.3	10.5	4.4	1.5	11.0	3.5	1.8	10.3	3.1
Top 100 MSA Averages	8.4	13.8	7.2	11.8	13.9	9.3	15.8	14.3	12.3

NOTE: MSA = metropolitan statistical area; PMSA = primary metropolitan statistical area; H = Hispanic; B = black; FB = foreign-born.
SOURCE: Data extracted from the GeoLytics Census CD Neighborhood Change Database 1970–2000 Tract Data.

APPENDIX TABLE A4-2 Hispanic Subgroup Composition by Metropolitan Area Type, 1980–2000

	1980 Population Composition (%)					
Metropolitan Area Type	N (000s)	HISP	MEX	PR	CUB	OTH
Traditional	9,363.5	18.0	60.2	13.8	6.9	19.0
Hispanic Metros						
New York, NY	1,465	17.7	1.8	59.9	4.7	33.6
Chicago, IL	581	8.1	63.0	22.3	3.2	11.5
Los Angeles, CA	2,065	27.6	79.6	1.8	2.2	16.4
Miami, FL	580	35.7	2.2	7.9	70.0	20.0
New Hispanic Destinations	1,268.5	2.4	35.1	23.2	7.5	34.1
Allentown, PA	14	2.5	8.0	70.8	1.8	19.4
Providence, RI	22	2.0	7.2	19.0	3.0	70.8
Grand Rapids, MI	18	2.1	71.2	9.6	3.9	15.4
Minneapolis, MN	23	1.1	63.4	5.9	2.4	28.4
Atlanta, GA	23	1.1	32.6	11.3	16.9	39.3
Raleigh-Durham, NC	5.3	0.8	42.9	7.5	7.1	42.5
Nashville, TN	5.5	0.6	49.1	5.7	4.5	40.6
Tulsa, OK	10	1.5	59.3	4.7	4.0	32.0
Other Large Metros	484.6	1.7	25.0	37.2	4.0	33.8
Top 100 (P)MSA	11,116.6	8.4	55.4	16.1	6.9	21.6

NOTE: N= Hispanic population absolute size (000s).
HISP = Hispanics as a percent of that city's population.
MEX = % of Hispanics that are Mexican.
PR = % of Hispanics that are Puerto Rican.
CUB = % of Hispanics that are Cuban.
OTH = % of Hispanics that are other.
MSA = metropolitan statistical area.

1990 Population Composition (%)						2000 Population Composition (%)					
N (000s)	HISP	MEX	PR	CUB	OTH	N (000s)	HISP	MEX	PR	CUB	OTH
14,416.5	24.1	63.4	9.9	5.7	21.0	21,516.8	29.8	62.0	6.6	4.1	27.3
1890	22.1	3.5	48.8	3.5	44.2	2,338	25.1	9.2	35.7	2.0	53.1
735	12.1	69.5	17.4	2.0	11.1	1,415	17.1	75.0	10.7	1.2	13.1
3351	37.8	76.2	1.2	1.4	21.2	4,245	44.6	71.7	0.9	0.9	26.5
950	49.2	2.4	7.2	59.2	31.2	1,292	57.3	2.9	6.2	50.4	40.5
2,223.2	3.8	33.1	24.3	6.9	35.7	5,022.4	6.8	38.8	18.9	4.8	37.5
29	4.2	5.6	72.8	2.0	19.6	50	7.9	7.0	66.3	1.5	25.2
31.5	4.8	4.7	28.6	2.3	64.4	94	7.9	6.3	28.9	1.2	63.6
23	3.3	72.1	11.6	3.7	12.6	69	6.3	68.0	7.4	2.4	22.2
37.5	1.5	64.6	7.9	3.3	24.2	98	3.3	65.9	5.4	1.9	26.8
57	2.0	39.8	13.9	11.0	35.3	267	6.5	61.5	7.1	3.4	28.0
9	1.2	41.3	14.8	6.3	37.6	72	6.1	66.2	5.8	2.0	26.0
8	0.8	48.1	12.5	5.7	33.7	41	3.3	63.0	7.3	2.9	26.8
14.5	2.0	67.4	7.2	2.2	23.2	39	4.8	72.3	4.9	1.3	21.5
586.5	2.0	23.5	45.0	3.7	27.8	1,050.4	2.9	27.4	42.3	3.2	27.1
17,226.2	11.8	57.7	13.2	5.8	23.3	27,589.6	15.9	56.4	10.2	4.2	29.2

5

Hispanic Families in the United States: Family Structure and Process in an Era of Family Change

Nancy S. Landale, R. Salvador Oropesa, and Cristina Bradatan

The last decades of the 20th century were a period of significant change in family life in the United States. Among the well-documented changes are a rising age at marriage, an increase in cohabitation, and a dramatic shift in the proportion of children born outside marriage (Bramlett and Mosher, 2002; Casper and Bianchi, 2002; Wu and Wolfe, 2001). Coupled with a high divorce rate, these trends have led to high rates of female family headship and a growing share of children with restricted access to their fathers' resources.

These changes in family patterns have taken place alongside rapid growth in immigration and concomitant changes in the racial and ethnic composition of the U.S. population. The average annual inflow of immigrants more than doubled between the 1970s and 1990s, and the share of immigrants from Latin America increased at the same time (Martin and Midgley, 2003). Thus, the Hispanic population grew from 5 percent of the total U.S. population in 1970 to 13 percent in 2000. Furthermore, population projections suggest that Hispanics will comprise 20 percent of the U.S. population in 2030 (National Research Council, 1997).

This chapter addresses the intersection of these two domains of rapidly changing demographic behavior. Specifically, we analyze the family patterns of Hispanics, focusing on several key issues. First, to place the present in a larger context, we document trends in several indicators of family change. Comparisons between Hispanic subgroups, non-Hispanic whites, and non-Hispanic blacks provide information on the extent to which Hispanics have shared in the general shifts in family configurations that took place during the past several decades. This issue is fundamental to understanding the nature of family life among Hispanics as well as links between changing family processes and family members' access to social and economic resources. As noted by Vega (1995, p. 6), "Changing family structures, including marital disruption and cohabitation, could represent the most important issue for Latino family theory and research in the decade ahead."

A second issue addressed in the chapter is generational variation in family patterns within Hispanic subgroups. Our descriptive analyses demonstrate that Hispanics—like other racial/ethnic groups—exhibit many behaviors that are consistent with what some scholars call "family decline" (Popenoe, 1993). At the same time, Hispanics (especially Mexican Americans) are typically described as oriented toward family well-being, rather than individual well-being (Sabogal, Marin, Otero-Sabogal, VanOss Marin, and Perez-Stable, 1987; Valenzuela and Dornbusch, 1994; Vega, 1995). To the extent that such "familism" remains alive among U.S. Hispanics, one would expect it to reduce the erosion of traditional family patterns or to contribute to new family forms in which family support remains high. However, it is possible that the process of assimilation reduces familism and encourages the individualism that some have argued is at the heart of recent changes in family behavior. After describing racial/ethnic differences in the characteristics of family households and the living arrangements of individuals of various ages, we focus on differences *within* Hispanic groups by generational status. Our comparisons of the family patterns of the first generation (foreign-born), the second generation (native-born of foreign parentage), and the third or higher generations (native-born of native parentage) will shed light on the dynamics of assimilation with respect to family patterns.

A third topic considered in the chapter is racial/ethnic mixing in sexual partnerships of various types, including marriage, cohabitation, and parenthood. Intermarriage is a long-standing theme in the study of assimilation. It has been considered both an indicator of assimilation and a means by which assimilation is achieved (Gordon, 1964; Lieberson and Waters, 1988). According to the classic assimilation theory, intermarriage between an immigrant group and the dominant population reduces social boundaries and eventually leads to a reduction in the salience of an ethnic identity. Because the offspring of intermarried couples may opt out of defining themselves as members of an ethnic group, intermarriage may affect the future size and shape of an ethnic population. Among Hispanics, intermarriage with non-Hispanic whites or non-Hispanic blacks may ultimately lead to a blurring of racial/ethnic boundaries. At the same time, intermarriage between members of different Hispanic subgroups may *strengthen* panethnicity, or the adoption of a "Hispanic" identity instead of an identity as a member of a specific national-origin group. While recognizing the importance of intermarriage, we contend that in the current era of what is called the "retreat from marriage," the study of racial/ethnic mixing in sexual partnerships must be expanded to include unions other than traditional marriages. Thus, we examine ethnic endogamy and exogamy among Hispanics in both marriage and cohabitation. Given the growing separation of marriage and childbearing, we also examine racial/ethnic mixing in both marital and nonmarital childbearing.

It is now widely recognized that Hispanic national-origin groups differ markedly with respect to their histories of immigration, settlement patterns, socioeconomic position, and other circumstances (Bean and Tienda, 1987; Oropesa and Landale, 1997; Portes and Rumbaut, 2001). There is a general consensus among experts on the Hispanic population that, to the extent possible, research should disaggregate the generic category "Hispanic" into specific national-origin groups. Thus, all of our analyses present information separately for Mexicans, Cubans, Puerto Ricans, Central/South Americans, and other Hispanics.[1] In addition to addressing differences between Hispanics and non-Hispanics, we examine the diversity of family patterns among the specific Hispanic groups.

Several broad conclusions are supported by our analyses. First, Hispanics exhibit high levels of familism relative to non-Hispanics on a variety of structural/demographic indicators. However, they are also participating in the general changes in family life that are under way in the United States. Second, analyses conducted separately by national origin suggest declining familism across generations (with some exceptions). Third, all Hispanic subgroups exhibit substantial declines in ethnic endogamy across generations. This pattern suggests that assimilation is occurring and that racial/ethnic boundaries for Hispanics are not sharp. Nonetheless, the Mexican-origin population stands out for its high levels of ethnic endogamy in marriage, cohabitation, and parenthood.

TRENDS IN FAMILY LIFE AMONG HISPANICS

One of the most significant changes in family behavior that occurred during the past several decades is the retreat from marriage. Although most individuals marry eventually, a declining percentage of men and women are entering marriage in their teens and early 20s (Ventura and Bachrach, 2000). At the same time, most young people begin having sex in their mid-

[1] In some cases, additional information on the subgroups that comprise the Census Bureau's Central/South American category is provided. These subgroups include Dominicans, Guatemalans/El Salvadorans, other Central Americans, Colombians, Ecuadorians/Peruvians, and other South Americans.

to late teens (Alan Guttmacher Institute, 1999), and cohabitation has become so widespread that it has largely offset the decline in marriage (Bumpass and Lu, 2000). Thus, the process of union formation has changed substantially. In addition, divorce rates remain high, although they have declined slightly since their peak around 1980 (Casper and Bianchi, 2002). The growing proportion of women who are unmarried (but sexually active and often cohabiting), increasing birth rates among unmarried women, and decreasing birth rates among married women have all contributed to a striking increase in the proportion of births occurring outside marriage (Wu et al., 2001).

Table 5-1 summarizes information on trends in several family-related behaviors from 1980 to 2000. The top panel shows the percentage married among females ages 20 to 24. At each time point, Mexican-origin females were the most likely to be married and non-Hispanic black females were the least likely to be married. For example, in 1980 roughly half of Mexican females ages 20 to 24 were married compared with one-fourth of their non-Hispanic black counterparts. The figures for non-Hispanic whites (45 percent), Cubans (40 percent), and Puerto Ricans (38 percent) are intermediate between those for Mexicans and non-Hispanic blacks. Between 1980 and 2000, there was a marked decline in early marriage for each of the racial/ethnic groups shown. However, the percentage change in the percentage married was weaker for Mexican women (–20 percent) than for Cubans (–31 percent), Puerto Ricans (–37 percent), non-Hispanic whites (–39 percent), and non-Hispanic blacks (–44 percent).[2] Thus, while all groups have shared in the retreat from early marriage, young Mexican women are more likely to enter marriage by their early 20s than the other Hispanic and non-Hispanic groups.

The second through fourth panels of the table focus on various aspects of fertility. The total fertility rates (TFRs) presented in the second panel describe the number of children the typical woman in a particular racial/ethnic group would have if her fertility throughout her reproductive period reflected the prevailing age-specific fertility rates for the racial/ethnic group at a given point in time. In 1980, the TFR for each Hispanic subgroup except Cubans was higher than that for non-Hispanic whites (1.7), but only Mexicans exhibited substantially higher fertility (TFR = 2.9). The TFRs for Puerto Ricans and other Hispanics (both 2.1) were slightly higher than the non-Hispanic white rate (1.7), but slightly lower than the non-Hispanic black rate (2.4).

[2] The figures for the percentage change between 1980 and 2000 were calculated from more precise information (i.e., rounded to hundredths rather than tenths) than that presented in the table. Thus, in some cases, they differ slightly from calculations based on the numbers in the first and third columns of the table.

TABLE 5-1 Selected Indicators of Family Change, by Race and Ethnicity

	Period			% Change
Indicators	1979–1980	1989–1990	2000–2001	1980–2000
Percentage married, females, ages 20–24[a]				
Mexican	52.0	41.2	41.4	–20.5
Puerto Rican	38.2	28.3	24.0	–37.1
Cuban	40.5	31.1	27.8	–31.2
Central/South American	n.a.	32.7	30.7	n.a.
Other Hispanic	n.a.	29.5	31.7	n.a.
Non-Hispanic white	44.6	32.2	27.4	–38.7
Non-Hispanic black	24.8	15.4	13.7	–44.5
Total fertility rate[b]				
Mexican	2.9	3.2	3.3	12.8
Puerto Rican	2.1	2.3	2.6	25.9
Cuban	1.3	1.5	1.9	43.9
Other Hispanic	2.1	2.9	3.0	44.2
Non-Hispanic white	1.7	1.9	1.9	11.2
Non-Hispanic black	2.4	2.6	2.3	–3.8
Percentage of births to unmarried mothers[c]				
Mexican	20.3	33.3	40.8	101.0
Puerto Rican	46.3	55.9	58.9	27.2
Cuban	10.0	18.2	27.3	173.0
Central/South American	27.1	41.2	44.3	63.5
Other/unknown Hispanic	22.4	37.2	44.2	97.3
Non-Hispanic white	9.6	16.9	22.5	134.4
Non-Hispanic black	57.3	66.7	68.6	19.7
Percentage of births to mothers under 18[d]				
Mexican	7.7	6.9	6.2	–19.5
Puerto Rican	10.0	9.1	7.4	–26.0
Cuban	3.8	2.7	2.7	–28.9
Central/South American	2.4	3.2	3.1	29.2
Other/unknown Hispanic	6.5	8.0	6.8	4.6
Non-Hispanic white	4.0	3.0	2.3	–42.5
Non-Hispanic black	12.7	10.2	7.3	–42.5
Percentage female householder, no spouse present				
Mexican[e]	14.8	19.0	21.1	42.6
Puerto Rican[e]	38.2	39.6	35.8	–6.3
Cuban[e]	n.a.	17.7	18.3	n.a.

TABLE 5-1 Continued

	Period			% Change
Indicators	1979–1980	1989–1990	2000–2001	1980–2000
Central/South American[e]	n.a.	25.0	24.6	n.a.
Other/unknown Hispanic[e]	n.a.	26.4	27.4	n.a.
White[f]	11.6	12.9	13.9	19.8
Black[f]	40.3	43.8	45.1	11.9

NOTE: For figures based on vital statistics, states without a Hispanic-origin item on the birth certificate were excluded prior to 1993. n.a. = not available.

[a]Authors' calculations; Integrated Public Use Microdata Series.

[b]Martin, Hamilton, Ventura, Menaker, and Park (2002); National Center for Health Statistics (2003), Ventura (1980).

[c]National Center for Health Statistics (2003, Table 9).

[d]National Center for Health Statistics (2003, Table 8).

[e]For 1980, Statistical Abstracts (1981) (Current Population Reports, P-20, No. 361); for 1989, Statistical Abstract 1992: Table 45 (Current Population Reports, P-20, No. 444); for 2000, Statistical Abstract, 2001: Tables 38 and 41 (Current Population Reports P-20, No. 535, P-60, No. 209, and P-60, No. 210).

[f]Statistical Abstract 2001, Table 38.

Despite the long-term trend toward lower fertility, the TFR increased between 1980 and 2000 for all groups except non-Hispanic blacks. The TFR rose by 11 percent for non-Hispanic whites (from 1.7 to 1.9), 13 percent for Mexicans (from 2.9 to 3.3), 26 percent for Puerto Ricans (from 2.1 to 2.6), and 44 percent for Cubans (from 1.3 to 1.9) and other Hispanics (from 2.1 to 3.0). The generally greater increase in fertility among Hispanics compared with non-Hispanic whites resulted in more diversity in fertility in 2000 than in 1980. Currently, the average Mexican, Puerto Rican, and other Hispanic woman can expect to have about one more child than the average non-Hispanic white woman.[3] Cubans are an exception, with a TFR that is nearly identical to that of whites. The TFRs for all Hispanic groups except Cubans also exceed that for non-Hispanic blacks.

The third panel presents figures on nonmarital childbearing. In 1980, the percentage of births to unmarried women was more than twice as high for each Hispanic subgroup (except Cubans) as it was for non-Hispanic whites (10 percent). The figures range from 20 percent for Mexicans to 46 percent for Puerto Ricans. Over the subsequent 20 years, all groups experi-

[3]Because the TFR is based on age-specific fertility rates, it essentially "controls" for the age distribution of groups. Consequently, the youthful age structures of the Hispanic subgroups, relative to non-Hispanic whites, do not explain their relatively high fertility.

enced a substantial increase in nonmarital childbearing. The percentage of births to unmarried women more than doubled for non-Hispanic whites (percentage change of 134 percent), Mexicans (101 percent), and Cubans (173 percent), and increased by more than half for Central/South Americans (64 percent) and other Hispanics (97 percent). The two groups that showed less growth over the 20-year period (Puerto Ricans and non-Hispanic blacks) had relatively high shares of nonmarital births at the first point in time (46 and 57 percent, respectively). Overall, these figures indicate that each Hispanic subgroup has experienced the trend toward nonmarital childbearing that has been documented for the general U.S. population. Nonetheless, there remain substantial racial/ethnic differences in the percentage of births to unmarried mothers in 2000. Non-Hispanic whites (22 percent) and non-Hispanic blacks (69 percent) fall at the two extremes of the distribution. While Cubans are closer to non-Hispanic whites (27 percent) and Puerto Ricans are closer to non-Hispanic blacks (59 percent), Mexicans (41 percent) and Central/South Americans (44 percent) are equidistant from the extremes.[4]

The fourth panel sheds light on differences and similarities in the timing of entry into motherhood across the groups. In 1980, less than 5 percent of births to non-Hispanic whites, Cubans, and Central/South Americans were to women under 18 years of age. The figures were slightly higher for other Hispanics (7 percent) and Mexicans (8 percent), and substantially higher for Puerto Ricans (10 percent) and non-Hispanic blacks (13 percent). Consistent with the well-established decline in teenage childbearing in the United States, the trend from 1980 to 2000 shows a substantial decrease in the percentage of births to young teen mothers for almost all groups. However, the decline has not been as great for most Hispanic subgroups as it has been for non-Hispanic whites and non-Hispanic blacks. In 2000, Mexican (6 percent), Puerto Rican (7 percent), and other Hispanic (7 percent) infants were more likely than Cuban (3 percent) and Central/South American (3 percent) infants to have a teenage mother. The figures for the former groups are more similar to that for non-Hispanic blacks (7 percent), while those for the latter are similar to that for non-Hispanic whites (2 percent).

The last panel of the table focuses on the structure of family households. Available data for 1980 show that whites (12 percent) and Mexicans (15 percent) had relatively low levels of female family headship, but Puerto Ricans (38 percent) and non-Hispanic blacks (40 percent) had substantially

---

[4]In 2000, roughly 50 percent of nonmarital births to both Hispanic and non-Hispanic white women occurred within cohabitation, compared with 22 percent for non-Hispanic blacks (Bumpass and Lu, 2000). The role of cohabitation in nonmarital childbearing also varies across Hispanic subgroups; however, comparable information is not available for specific Hispanic groups.

higher levels. An increase in the percentage of female householders is evident for three of the four groups for which complete data are shown (non-Hispanic whites, non-Hispanic blacks, and Mexicans). Puerto Ricans are the exception, showing a slight decline in the percentatge of family households with a female head over the two-decade period. In 2000, the various Hispanic subgroups fall between the extremes occupied by non-Hispanic whites and blacks with respect to family structure. About 14 percent of white families had a female householder, compared with about 20 percent of Mexican and Cuban families, 25 percent of Central and South American families, 36 percent of Puerto Rican families, and 45 percent of non-Hispanic black families.

In summary, Table 5-1 shows that trends for each dimension of family life are generally similar for Hispanic subgroups and the non-Hispanic majority. However, consistent with differences in their histories and social locations (see Chapter 2), there are substantial differences across Hispanic subgroups—and between Hispanic subgroups and non-Hispanics—in specific aspects of family behavior. Moreover, there are a few instances of divergence (i.e., widening of group differences) over time between Hispanic and non-Hispanic groups. For example, the 1980–2000 increase in fertility (as measured by the TFR) was somewhat greater for Hispanic groups than for non-Hispanic whites. In addition, there was a weaker decline in teenage childbearing among Hispanics compared with non-Hispanics. The growing divergence between Hispanic and non-Hispanic fertility patterns is undoubtedly linked to the relatively rapid growth of the immigrant population (Suro and Passel, 2003). Since Latin American immigrants have higher fertility and tend to bear their children earlier than native-born Hispanics, a shift in the generational composition of the Hispanic population would contribute to such a pattern. Also noteworthy is the considerably greater increase in female family headship among Mexican Americans compared with non-Hispanic whites and blacks.

CURRENT FAMILY PATTERNS: VARIATION BY ETHNICITY AND GENERATION

Recent scholarship on current family patterns among Hispanics emphasizes several distinct themes, which can be broadly classified as stressing either the structural conditions in which Hispanics live or the role of culture in shaping values and behavior. We discuss each in turn.

The Role of Structural Conditions

One recurrent theme in the study of Hispanic families is the impact of socioeconomic disadvantage on family life (Baca Zinn and Wells, 2000;

Massey, Zambrana, and Bell, 1995; Oropesa and Landale, 2004; Vega, 1995). Due to a complex set of factors, including the hardships of immigration, low levels of human capital, racial discrimination, and settlement patterns, Hispanic poverty rates remain high. In 2002, about 22 percent of Hispanics were poor, a figure roughly comparable to that for blacks (24 percent) and almost three times that for non-Hispanic whites (8 percent) (Proktor and Dallaker, 2003).[5] A constellation of behaviors and conditions that are associated with poverty, especially low skill levels, job instability, and inadequate earnings for males, play a central role in recent explanations of the retreat from marriage, nonmarital childbearing, and female family headship (Oppenheimer, 2000; Sweeney, 2002; Wilson, 1987). Contemporary scholarship on Hispanic families is highly critical of a "culture of poverty" interpretation of the link between poverty and family patterns. Rather, it emphasizes a "social adaptation" paradigm, in which individuals and families adapt to the situations they face as a result of their social and economic position in U.S. society (Baca Zinn and Wells, 2000; Vega, 1995).

An issue that has received attention is whether links between poverty and family processes among Hispanics can be understood using frameworks developed to study the experience of other disadvantaged groups (i.e., blacks). Massey et al. (1995) argue that the Hispanic experience is fundamentally different from that of blacks in five important ways. First, consistent with Bean and Tienda's seminal work (1987), they contend that Hispanics cannot be understood as a single group; analyses must be conducted separately for each Hispanic subgroup because of differences in their histories and current situations. Second, Hispanics are heterogeneous with respect to race, while blacks are relatively homogeneous. Furthermore, foreign-born Hispanics experience a marked disjuncture between the way race is viewed in Latin America and the racial dynamics they encounter in the United States. Third, related to their diverse racial features, Hispanics experience more varied levels of segregation (and consequently, more varied opportunities) than do non-Hispanic blacks, but this is changing. Fourth, the Hispanic experience remains bound up with immigration. Massey et al. (1995) argue that the dynamics of immigration must be explicitly considered in studies of Hispanic family patterns. This requires attention to the complexities of international migration (e.g., selective migration) as well as consideration of issues related to the assimilation process. Finally, Hispanics differ from blacks in that their experience is influenced by their use of the Spanish language. Given these differences, Massey and colleagues argue

[5]There is considerable variation among Hispanic subgroups in poverty. In 2001, about 23 percent of Mexicans, 26 percent of Puerto Ricans, 16 percent of Cubans, 15 percent of Central/South Americans, and 18 percent of other Hispanics were poor (Ramirez and de la Cruz, 2002).

that studies of Hispanic families cannot simply adopt theories developed to explain the experience of other disadvantaged groups. Although socioeconomic disadvantage is central to the Hispanic experience, its effects on family patterns must be understood in the context of more complex frameworks that simultaneously consider the aforementioned issues.

The Role of Culture

Another theme that is widespread in studies of Hispanic families is the idea that Hispanics are characterized by familism or a strong commitment to family life that is qualitatively distinct from that of non-Hispanic whites (Vega, 1995). The concept of familism can be found in the sociological literature as early as the mid-1940s (Burgess and Locke, 1945; Ch'Eng-K'Un, 1944). Although it has been used in somewhat varied ways since that time, there is general agreement that familism entails the subordination of individual interests to those of the family group. Some authors have stressed the attitudinal foundations of familism (Bean, Curtis, and Marcum, 1977; Burgess and Locke, 1945; Gaines et al., 1997; Lesthaeghe and Meekers, 1986; Rodriguez, Kosloski, and Kosloski, 1998; Oropesa and Gorman, 2000), while others have emphasized behavioral manifestations (Tienda, 1980; Winch, Greer, and Blumberg, 1967). Recent scholarship puts forth the view that familism is a multidimensional concept encompassing at least three features: a structural/demographic dimension,[6] a behavioral dimension, and an attitudinal dimension (Valenzuela and Dornbusch, 1994). The structural dimension is evident in such family configurations as family size, family structure (including the presence or absence of nuclear and extended kin), and fertility patterns. The behavioral dimension includes behaviors that indicate the fulfillment of family role obligations, such as the sharing of economic resources, mutual assistance and social support, and frequent contact among family members. The attitudinal (or normative) dimension entails values that emphasize the importance of the family and prescribe loyalty, reciprocity, and solidarity among family members (Sabogal et al., 1987; Steidel, Contreras, and Contreras, 2003).

Early scholarship often regarded familism as an impediment to socioeconomic advancement in urban industrial societies because such societies emphasize individualism, competition, and geographic mobility. For example, some studies argued that familism hindered the socioeconomic success of Mexican Americans (Valenzuela and Dornbusch, 1994). More re-

[6]For ease of presentation, we refer to the structural/demographic dimension as the structural dimension in the remainder of the text. A similar shorthand is used when discussing the variables used to measure this dimension of familism.

cently, however, this view has been turned on its head and familism is generally viewed as a protective factor. Studies of a variety of outcomes (e.g., physical and mental health, education) among Hispanics propose that extended family networks, family cohesion, and high levels of social support reduce the adverse consequences of poverty (Guendelman, 1995; Landale and Oropesa, 2001; Rumbaut and Weeks, 1996; Sabogal et al., 1987; Zambrana, Scrimshaw, Collins, and Dunkel-Schetter, 1997). Thus, recent scholarship regards familism as a positive attribute of Hispanic families that may decline with acculturation to U.S. family norms and adaptation to life in the United States.

Although a comprehensive assessment of the three dimensions of familism is beyond the scope of this chapter, we focus on the structural dimension in Tables 5-2 through 5-5. Based on weighted data from the 1998–2002 March Current Population Surveys (pooled across years), we provide descriptive information on the characteristics of Hispanic families and the living arrangements of individuals in different age groups. Comparisons are made across racial/ethnic groups and within Hispanic subgroups by generational status.[7]

Characteristics of Family Households

Table 5-2 addresses a fundamental question: What percentage of all households are family households? The U.S. Census Bureau defines a family household as a household maintained by a householder who is in a family; a family is a group of two or more people (one of whom is the householder) who are related by birth, marriage, or adoption and reside together (U.S. Census Bureau, 2000).[8] It is important to note that the Census Bureau does not regard cohabitation as a family status. Given the growing role of cohabitation in U.S. family life (Bramlett and Mosher, 2002; Bumpass and Lu, 2000) and its prominence among some Hispanic subgroups, we believe it is important to recognize cohabiting unions. Thus, we depart from the Census Bureau's definition of a family household by treating cohabitation as a family status. Households in which the householder is cohabiting with a partner are therefore included as family households in Tables 5-2 and 5-3.[9]

---

[7]To simplify the presentation of results, the text reports numbers that have been rounded to the nearest whole number. The rounding is based on more precise data than the information that appears in the tables (i.e., rounded to hundredths rather than tenths).

[8]A householder is the first adult household member listed on the census form. The instructions indicate that this should be the person (or one of the people) in whose name the home is owned or rented.

[9]To allow for comparisons with prior studies, we also provide tables in the appendix that are based on the Census Bureau's definition of a family household. Appendix Table A5-1 is comparable to Table 5-2 and Appendix Table A5-2 is comparable to Table 5-3. Using the

TABLE 5-2 Percentage Family Households by Race/Ethnicity and Generational Status of Householder[a]

Household	Mexican	Puerto Rican	Cuban	Central/ South American	Other Hispanic	Non-Hispanic White	Non-Hispanic Black
All households	85.1	76.3	75.0	81.6	77.6	69.5	68.3
1st generation	88.6	74.5	74.5	83.2	79.4		
2nd generation	81.7	79.6	80.5	69.0	76.1		
Native-born of native parentage	80.9	76.7	66.9	67.0	76.5	70.4	68.3
Standardized for Age of Householder[b]							
All households	81.7	72.4	76.0	76.9	74.1	69.5	65.8
1st generation	84.2	73.8	77.5	78.3	73.6		
2nd generation	80.9	71.6	80.3	64.1	72.8		
Native-born of native parentage	77.7	64.9	71.8	60.6	74.0	69.6	61.2

[a]Based on revised definition of family household in which cohabitation is treated as a family status that is equivalent to marriage.

[b]Age distribution of non-Hispanic white family householders (5 year age groups) used as standard.

SOURCE: Pooled March 1998–2002 Current Population Survey (CPS) Files.

TABLE 5-3 Characteristics of Family Households by Race/Ethnicity and Generation of Householder[a]

Household	Mexican	Puerto Rican	Cuban	Central/ South American	Other Hispanic	Non-Hispanic White	Non-Hispanic Black
Percentage married couple							
All family households	69.0	53.1	75.2	65.3	62.0	79.5	46.3
1st generation	72.4	56.9	74.7	65.8	55.0		
2nd generation	64.7	48.1	80.9	55.4	59.8		
Native-born of native parentage	64.8	47.6	—	—	68.6	79.3	45.8
Percentage cohabiting couple							
All family households	5.9	7.4	4.0	6.3	6.0	5.1	5.7
1st generation	5.0	5.7	3.6	5.9	5.1		
2nd generation	6.0	10.1	4.2	11.0	7.0		
Native-born of native parentage	7.5	8.6	—	—	6.5	5.3	5.6
Percentage female householder, no partner							
All family households	18.2	33.5	15.8	21.2	25.8	11.4	41.4
1st generation	14.8	32.4	16.9	21.2	33.8		
2nd generation	22.6	34.4	8.8	24.8	25.5		
Native-born of native parentage	22.1	36.6	—	—	19.0	11.4	42.2

Mean number of persons in household							
All family households	4.0	3.4	3.1	3.7	3.4	3.0	3.3
1st generation	4.4	3.3	3.1	3.8	3.7		
2nd generation	3.6	3.5	3.3	3.3	3.3		
Native-born of native parentage	3.6	3.4	—	—	3.2	3.0	3.3
Percentage extended family household							
All family households	8.4	7.2	6.5	9.6	6.4	2.6	7.2
1st generation	9.6	8.7	6.3	10.2	6.9		
2nd generation	7.8	5.6	8.9	3.9	10.0		
Native-born of native parentage	6.5	4.4	—	—	5.1	2.5	7.0
Unweighted number of cases							
All family households	17,255	3,176	1,432	4,370	2,582	145,425	19,848
1st generation	9,507	1,786	1,178	3,953	884		
2nd generation	2,860	1,004	213	272	269		
Native-born of native parentage	4,888	386	41	145	1,429	127,611	17,919

NOTE: — = fewer than 200 cases in racial/ethnic-generation group.

[a]Based on revised definition of family household in which cohabitation is treated as a family status that is equivalent to marriage.

SOURCE: Pooled March 1998–2002 CPS files.

The top panel of Table 5-2 presents unadjusted percentages for all households and for households broken down by the generational status of the householder. Because the propensity to live in family versus nonfamily households varies by age, we also present comparable information standardized for the age of the householder. The age-standardized percentages are especially important for comparisons between Hispanic subgroups and non-Hispanic whites, since the former are relatively young populations.

Both the unstandardized and age-standardized percentages for *all households* (i.e., not disaggregated by generation) show that all Hispanic subgroups are more likely to reside in family households than are non-Hispanic whites and non-Hispanic blacks. The age-standardized percentages for Hispanic groups range from 72 percent (Puerto Ricans) to 82 percent (Mexicans), while those for non-Hispanic whites and non-Hispanic blacks are 69 and 66 percent, respectively.[10] This is consistent with the thesis of relatively high levels of familism among Hispanics, especially Mexican Americans. Focusing on *within-group differences by generation*, the age-standardized pattern is similar for Mexicans, Puerto Ricans, and Central/South Americans: households in which the householder is foreign-born are more likely to be family households than those in which the householder is native-born (of native or foreign parentage). For example, 84 percent of households headed by a first-generation Mexican are family households, compared with 81 percent of households headed by a second-generation Mexican and 78 percent of households headed by a Mexican in the third (or higher) generation. Although the pattern for Cubans is not linear, households in which the householder is third (or higher) generation are the least likely to be family households.

Table 5-3 provides information on various structural characteristics of family households. We distinguish between married-couple households, cohabiting-couple households, and households with a female householder who does not live with a partner.[11] The figures for *all family households*

Census Bureau definition, households in which the householder is cohabiting are defined as family households only if there are other relatives of the householder living in the dwelling unit. Thus, a householder living with a cohabiting partner and her children would not be defined as a family household.

[10]Additional analyses (not shown) examined first- and second-generation Dominicans, Guatemalans/El Salvadorans, other Central Americans, Colombians, Ecuadorans/Peruvians, and other South Americans. Because of the recency of immigration from these countries, the third generation was not of sufficient size for inclusion in the analysis. Each of these groups exhibited considerably higher age-standardized percentages of family households than non-Hispanic whites (ranging from 74 percent for other South Americans to 78 percent for Colombians, compared with 69 percent for non-Hispanic whites).

[11]Because of space limitations, we do not present information on the percentage of family households headed by a male householder who does not live with a partner.

(i.e., not disaggregated by generation) show considerable variation across Hispanic subgroups in household type. Cuban and Mexican households are the most likely to be headed by a married couple (75 and 69 percent, respectively, compared with 79 percent for non-Hispanic whites) and the least likely to be headed by a female with no spouse or partner present (16 and 18 percent, respectively, compared with 11 percent for non-Hispanic whites). Puerto Ricans represent the other extreme: 53 percent of Puerto Rican family households are headed by a married couple and 34 percent are headed by a female with no spouse or partner present. Cohabitation is the least common arrangement shown, but it is significant for all groups. About 6 to 7 percent of Hispanic family householders in all subgroups except Cubans (4 percent) live with a cohabiting partner. These percentages are slightly higher than that for non-Hispanic whites (5 percent) and roughly comparable to that for non-Hispanic blacks (6 percent).

Other noteworthy group differences for *all family households* are the slightly larger household size and the greater prevalence of extended families[12] among Hispanics, relative to non-Hispanic whites. With respect to the latter, about 6 to 10 percent of family households in each Hispanic subgroup are extended, compared with 3 percent of non-Hispanic white family households. The figure for non-Hispanic blacks (7 percent) is comparable to those presented for the Hispanic groups.[13]

As noted earlier, there are two major explanations for differences in family patterns between Hispanic subgroups and the comparison groups (non-Hispanic whites and non-Hispanic blacks). One explanation points to differences in the structural positions of the groups, especially the disadvantaged socioeconomic status of some Hispanic subgroups (and non-Hispanic blacks) relative to non-Hispanic whites. The other emphasizes cultural orientations and values vis-à-vis the family. Evaluation of these perspectives is complex and beyond the scope of the present study; however, to provide some information on the role of structural characteristics, we standardized the educational distributions of the groups being compared. Specifically, using direct standardization, we calculated what the family characteristics of each group would be if the educational distribution of its householders

[12]We define extended family households as households that are extended vertically or laterally to include relatives who are not part of the nuclear family.

[13]Additional analyses (not shown) that disaggregated Central/South Americans into Dominicans, Guatemalans/El Salvadorans, other Central Americans, Colombians, Ecuadorans/Peruvians, and other South Americans showed that Dominican families were more likely than all other Hispanic families (including Mexicans, Puerto Ricans, and Cubans) to be headed by a female householder with no partner present (42 percent) and to be extended (12 percent). Because of the recency of immigration from Central and South America, the additional analyses were restricted to the first and second generations.

was the same as that of non-Hispanic white householders.[14] With education controlled, similar patterns were evident, although differences were attenuated (results not shown). For example, the percentage of family households with a female householder was 15 percent for Cubans, 17 percent for Mexicans, and 29 percent for Puerto Ricans in the standardized analysis, compared with 11 percent for non-Hispanic whites. In the unstandardized analysis, it was 16 percent for Cubans, 18 percent for Mexicans, and 34 percent for Puerto Ricans.

Table 5-3 also shows differences in family household characteristics by the generational status of the householder. Although there are some inconsistencies across national-origin groups, the pattern for several Hispanic subgroups suggests declining familism across generations. For example, among Mexicans, foreign-born householders are more likely to be married and less likely to cohabit or to be female family heads than their native-born counterparts. Among the foreign-born, 72 percent are married, 5 percent are cohabiting, and 15 percent are single female householders; the comparable figures for the native-born of native parentage are 65 percent married, 7 percent cohabiting, and 22 percent single female householders. In addition, the mean household size and the percentage of extended family households are higher among foreign-born Mexicans than native-born Mexicans. For example, among the foreign-born, 10 percent of households are extended, compared with 7 percent among the native-born of native parentage. Similar generational patterns are found among Puerto Ricans and Central/South Americans, except that family size does not vary by generation for Puerto Ricans. However, there are irregular or opposite patterns for Cubans and other Hispanics. When the educational distribution of household heads is standardized (each generation of each Hispanic subgroup given the educational distribution of the total non-Hispanic white population), the generational patterns remain unchanged (results not shown).

Living Arrangements

The structure and composition of households are experienced by individuals in different ways as they move through the life course. Thus we summarize in Table 5-4 the living arrangements of individuals in four broad age groups (0–17; 18–24; 25–64; 65+). Some of the largest differences in living arrangements by race and ethnicity are found for children. Among Hispanics, the percentage living with both parents ranges from 42 percent for Puerto Ricans to 69 percent for Cubans (with the figures for

---

[14]The educational categories used in the standardization were: less than high school; high school graduate; some college; college graduate.

Mexicans and Central/South Americans about 67 percent). Again, the figures for Hispanics fall between the extremes represented by the experience of non-Hispanic whites (77 percent) and non-Hispanic blacks (37 percent), although Hispanics are generally closer to whites. As one would expect, Puerto Rican (46 percent) and non-Hispanic black children (49 percent) are the most likely to live in a mother-only family. Both groups are more than twice as likely to live in such a family arrangement as non-Hispanic white, Mexican, Cuban, and Central/South American children.[15]

There is less racial and ethnic variation in living arrangements in early adulthood (18 to 24) and the middle adult years (25 to 64). However, several group differences are noteworthy. In early adulthood, Cubans stand out for their comparatively low rates of household headship and high propensity to remain in the parental home. Fully 62 percent of Cubans ages 18 to 24 live in their parent's household, compared with less than 50 percent for all other Hispanic groups. This living arrangement may facilitate the relatively high levels of education attained by Cubans in young adulthood. Also noteworthy are the considerably greater shares of Hispanic and black young adults living with "other relatives," compared with white young adults. This pattern carries over to middle adulthood (ages 25 to 64), and in fact is one of the major ways in which living arrangements vary by race and ethnicity during the middle adult years. For example, while only 2 percent of non-Hispanic whites ages 25 to 64 live with other relatives, fully 10 percent of Mexicans and 12 percent of Central/South Americans do so. Doubling up with relatives may be an economic strategy that is employed under conditions of economic disadvantage.

Among the elderly (ages 65+), the most striking differences in living arrangements are between Hispanics and non-Hispanic whites, rather than among Hispanic subgroups. In particular, Hispanics are considerably more likely to live with other relatives and less likely to live alone than are non-Hispanic whites. For example, only 5 percent of non-Hispanic whites live with other relatives, compared with 19 percent of Mexicans and Cubans, 15 percent of Puerto Ricans, and 33 percent of Central/South Americans. These differences undoubtedly reflect both differences in economic resources and cultural preferences regarding the care of the elderly.

Information on living arrangements by race/ethnicity and generational status for each age group cannot be presented, given space constraints. However, in Table 5-5 we provide data for Mexican Americans on genera-

---

[15]It should be noted that the Current Population Survey variables on children's living arrangements do not consider the parent's cohabitation status. Estimates suggest that 12 percent of Hispanic children in mother-only families are living with a single cohabiting mother. The comparable figures for non-Hispanic whites and non-Hispanic blacks are 14 percent and 6 percent, respectively (Fields, 2003).

TABLE 5-4 Living Arrangements by Age and Ethnicity

Living Arrangements	Mexican	Puerto Rican	Cuban	Central/ South American	Other Hispanic	Non-Hispanic White	Non-Hispanic Black
Ages 0–17[a]							
Both parents	67.2	42.4	69.5	66.7	53.6	76.8	36.9
Mother only	22.8	45.6	21.9	22.5	35.6	16.0	49.4
Father only	4.4	5.0	2.7	5.0	5.9	4.4	4.5
Other relatives	3.7	4.4	4.1	3.0	3.2	1.7	7.4
Nonrelatives	1.5	2.0	1.3	2.6	1.2	0.9	1.6
Ages 18–24							
Family householder	19.1	23.3	10.1	14.8	20.5	16.4	19.8
Spouse/partner of householder	12.6	10.1	12.4	9.4	10.0	10.5	5.3
Child of householder	40.1	48.4	62.1	48.8	49.9	54.1	51.9
Other relatives	16.8	9.3	9.3	14.4	9.6	4.3	12.2
Alone	2.0	2.7	3.7	2.7	3.5	5.3	5.5
Nonrelatives	9.5	6.3	2.4	9.9	6.6	9.4	5.3

Ages 25–64							
Family householder	42.4	45.6	42.3	40.1	45.2	43.2	43.1
Spouse/partner of householder	32.5	26.9	32.0	31.5	29.2	35.9	22.6
Child of householder	6.1	6.3	8.4	4.7	6.3	4.7	9.7
Other relatives	10.0	6.5	7.0	11.8	6.7	1.9	5.8
Alone	4.4	10.5	7.1	5.5	8.1	11.6	15.4
Nonrelatives	4.6	4.2	3.3	6.4	4.5	2.8	3.5
Age 65+							
Family householder	38.7	36.9	32.0	30.0	33.6	36.3	36.4
Spouse/partner of householder	22.7	20.9	23.6	19.0	19.7	26.4	17.8
Other relatives[b]	19.3	15.0	19.3	32.7	16.5	5.1	10.9
Alone	18.3	26.4	23.9	16.1	28.6	31.4	32.9
Nonrelatives	1.0	1.0	1.3	2.2	1.6	0.9	2.0

[a]Categories "Householder," "Spouse of householder," and "Cohabiting partner of householder" not shown because fewer than 1 percent of children are in these categories combined.

[b]Category "Other relatives" includes children of householder.

SOURCE: Pooled March 1998–2002 CPS Files.

TABLE 5-5 Living Arrangements by Generation, Mexican Children, and Elderly Persons

Living Arrangements	Children Ages 0–17			
	All Children	1st Generation	2nd Generation	NBNP
Both parents	67.2	73.6	72.3	56.0
Mother only	22.8	13.8	20.1	30.9
Father only	4.4	3.0	3.8	6.2
Other relatives	3.7	5.4	2.5	5.0
Nonrelatives	1.5	2.9	1.0	1.7
Unweighted number	28,503	3,916	15,555	9,032
	Elderly Persons (65+)			
	All Elderly Persons	1st Generation	2nd Generation	NBNP
Family householder	38.7	34.1	43.4	39.9
Spouse/partner of householder	22.7	20.0	25.5	23.4
Other relatives[a]	19.3	30.3	9.5	14.0
Alone	18.3	14.9	20.4	21.5
Nonrelatives	1.0	0.7	1.2	1.3
Unweighted number	3,033	1,245	1,027	761

NOTE: NBNP = native-born with native parents.

[a]Includes children of householder.

SOURCE: Pooled March 1998–2002 CPS files.

tional differences in living arrangements among children and the elderly. The top panel shows a striking difference between children with foreign-born parents (first- and second-generation children) and children with native-born parents. Children in the former groups are much more likely to live with both parents (72–73 percent) than children in the latter group (56 percent). About 17 percent of first-generation children live with only one parent (14 percent with mother and 3 percent with father), compared with 24 percent of second-generation children and 37 percent of native-born children with native-born parents. Thus, children of the foreign-born experience greater parental union stability than children of the native-born.

The situation of Mexican American elderly persons also varies by generation. First, foreign-born elderly persons are less likely to be the householder or the spouse or partner of the householder (54 percent) than the native-born of foreign parentage (69 percent) or the native-born of native parentage (63 percent). They are also less likely to live alone (15 percent, compared with about 20–21 percent for the native-born groups). Instead, the foreign-born are considerably more likely to live with other relatives (30 percent), such as their children, than the native-born of foreign percentage (9 percent) and native parentage (14 percent).

Overall, Hispanics exhibit higher levels of familism than non-Hispanics on most of the structural indicators examined. A notable exception is female family headship, which is considerably more prevalent in all Hispanic subgroups than among non-Hispanic whites. At the same time, there is considerable diversity in the family characteristics of Hispanics by both national origin and generation. Although the findings are not entirely consistent across Hispanic groups, within-group generational differences generally suggest declining familism across generations. This is especially the case for Mexican Americans, a group that exhibits lower levels of family-oriented behavior on every indicator among the native-born compared with the foreign-born.

RACIAL/ETHNIC MIXING IN SEXUAL PARTNERSHIPS

As is common practice in social demographic research, our analysis to this point has assumed that racial/ethnic categories are fixed and reflect unambiguous distinctions among individuals. However, the social construction of race and ethnicity—and the complexities involved in racial and ethnic identities—are increasingly emphasized by contemporary social scientists. The dominant view is that racial and ethnic categories reflect shared social meanings, rather than biological differences between groups, and that social interpretations of the categories are tied to long-standing power differentials (Waters, 2002). In addition, the fluidity of racial and ethnic identities across situations, over time, and across generations is stressed.

One important factor in the fluidity of racial/ethnic boundaries is intermarriage, which has long been considered an indicator of the social distance between groups (Rosenfeld, 2002). The prevalence of intermarriage is strongly influenced by two factors: the strength of preferences for endogamy and demographic factors that govern opportunities for in-group and out-group marriage (e.g., the relative size of groups, the sex ratio, residential segregation) (Stevens and Tyler, 2002). Some studies of intermarriage have taken as their primary question the extent to which social boundaries exist between groups (i.e., there is a preference for in-group versus out-group marriage) and thus have attempted to control for opportunities and constraints imposed by demographic factors when examining patterns of intermarriage. In this chapter, our aim is descriptive and thus does not require controlling for demographic factors. Our goal is to describe patterns of ethnic mixing in marriage, cohabitation, and parenthood. Regardless of

TABLE 5-6 Ethnic Endogamy Versus Exogamy in Coresidential Unions, by Female Partner's Ethnicity and Generation

	Marriages		
Ethnicity and Generation	Endogamous (%)	Exogamous Hispanic (%)	Exogamous Non-Hispanic White (%)
Mexican total	84.3	2.4	12.3
1st generation	91.5	2.6	5.6
2nd generation	79.4	3.1	15.7
Native-born of native parentage	72.5	1.8	24.2
Puerto Rican total	62.0	11.9	21.5
1st generation	70.6	12.0	15.2
2nd generation	52.7	12.0	29.0
Native-born of native parentage	42.6	10.7	33.8
Cuban total	74.4	8.8	15.9
1st generation	82.5	7.6	9.2
2nd generation	32.6	17.1	49.0
Native-born of native parentage	—	—	—
Central/South American total	65.3	13.2	19.5
1st generation	68.2	13.2	17.0
2nd generation	37.2	16.7	42.1
Native-born of native parentage	38.0	8.3	46.7
Other Hispanic total	55.3	11.8	30.5
1st generation	68.3	16.9	13.7
2nd generation	43.7	8.6	43.4
Native-born of native parentage	48.1	9.3	40.3

NOTE: — = fewer than 50 cases in racial/ethnic-generation group.
SOURCE: Pooled March 1998–2002 CPS files.

whether preferences or demographic factors underlie patterns of interethnic mating, the long-term consequences for racial/ethnic identities are likely to be the same. Higher rates of ethnic mixing between Hispanic subgroups and other groups will potentially reduce racial/ethnic boundaries. One important mechanism through which this potentially occurs is fertility. For instance, offspring with one Hispanic parent and one non-Hispanic white parent are likely to identify more weakly with a specific Hispanic subgroup or with the pan-ethnic Hispanic or Latino labels than offspring with two Hispanic parents, especially coethnic parents (Duncan and Trejo, 2004; Hirschman, 2002).

	Cohabiting Unions			
Exogamous Non-Hispanic Black (%)	Endogamous (%)	Exogamous Hispanic (%)	Exogamous Non-Hispanic White (%)	Exogamous Non-Hispanic Black (%)
0.7	73.8	5.4	17.8	2.4
0.3	89.4	5.5	3.2	1.7
1.4	62.7	9.3	24.8	2.0
1.2	60.3	3.5	31.9	3.5
4.0	58.2	14.7	18.0	8.1
1.8	64.6	19.4	13.9	2.2
5.2	57.5	10.2	19.4	10.6
12.6	—	—	—	—
0.9	38.8	10.5	50.8	0.0
0.7	—	—	—	—
1.4	—	—	—	—
—	—	—	—	—
1.8	57.8	19.8	18.8	3.5
1.5	63.3	19.1	14.7	2.9
4.1	—	—	—	—
5.9	—	—	—	—
2.0	55.4	17.0	24.1	2.6
1.9	74.6	18.4	6.5	0.0
4.2	—	—	—	—
1.7	43.0	11.1	37.3	6.4

In Table 5-6, we present summary information on ethnic endogamy[16] versus exogamy in marriages and cohabiting unions.[17] The data are broken

[16]A marriage (or partnership) is defined as ethnically endogamous if the partners are members of the same Hispanic-origin group (e.g., a Mexican woman is married to a Mexican man).

[17]Intermarriage can be examined using prevalence measures (based on the stock of marriages at a given point in time) or incidence measures (based on marriages that occur during a given period of time) (Kalmijn, 1998). Because our analysis is based on cross-sectional data that describe the characteristics of the general population, we examine intermarriage with prevalence measures.

down by the female partner's ethnicity and generational status. For marriages, there are differences in *levels* of ethnic endogamy across Hispanic groups, with Mexican Americans exhibiting a higher level of endogamy than all other groups. Among married Mexican women, 84 percent have a Mexican husband; the corresponding figures are 74 percent for Cubans, 65 percent for Central Americans and South Americans, 62 percent for Puerto Ricans, and 55 percent for other Hispanics. The higher level of in-group marriage among Mexican Americans is undoubtedly influenced by the size of the U.S. Mexican population, which allows for relatively high levels of contact with other Mexican Americans. The *generational pattern* with respect to ethnic endogamy in marriage is very similar across Hispanic groups. In each Hispanic subgroup, there is a marked decline in ethnic endogamy from the first generation to the second. Among Mexicans and Puerto Ricans, a decline is also evident between the second generation and the native-born with native parents; however, among Central Americans and South Americans and other Hispanics, roughly comparable percentages of second- and third (or higher)-generation women are married to partners with similar national origins.

The other side of endogamy is exogamy, and the data for each Hispanic subgroup indicate that married Hispanic women who do not have a coethnic husband are relatively likely to be married to a non-Hispanic white.[18] For example, 12 percent of married Mexican American women have a non-Hispanic white husband, while only 2 percent are married to a non-Mexican Hispanic and less than 1 percent are married to a non-Hispanic black. Exogamous marriages represent 16 percent (100 – 84) of all marriages among Mexican American women; in such marriages, 78 percent (12.3/15.7) of husbands are non-Hispanic white. The *generational pattern* with respect to marriages between Hispanics and non-Hispanic whites is also important. In each Hispanic subgroup, the percentage of women with a non-Hispanic white husband rises dramatically across generations.

The second most common type of exogamous marriage involves Hispanic spouses from dissimilar national origins. While such marriages are not very common among Mexicans (2 percent of all marriages), they constitute between 9 percent (Cubans) and 13 percent (Central/South Americans) of all marriages among Hispanic women in other groups. Marriages with Hispanic (but not coethnic) husbands constitute 15 percent (2.4/15.7) of all exogamous marriages among Mexican Americans, compared with 26 per-

[18]Table 5-6 provides information on exogamous unions with Hispanics, non-Hispanic whites, and non-Hispanic blacks. The rows do not sum to 100 percent because information on exogamous unions with partners from other ethnic groups (e.g., Asians, Native Americans) is omitted from the table.

cent (11.8/44.7) for other Hispanics, 31 percent (11.9/38.0) for Puerto Ricans, 34 percent (8.8/25.6) for Cubans, and 38 percent (13.2/34.7) for Central/South Americans.

Table 5-6 also presents information on cohabiting unions. With few exceptions, the overall *level* of ethnic endogamy is lower for cohabiting unions than for formal marriages. Among Mexican Americans, for example, 74 percent of all cohabiting unions are endogamous, compared with 84 percent of marriages. In addition, using exogamous unions as the base, the distribution of unions by the race/ethnicity of the partner differs somewhat from that for marriages. In particular, exogamous cohabiting unions are generally less likely to involve a non-Hispanic white partner and more likely to involve a Hispanic partner or a black partner than are exogamous marriages. The figures for black partners are especially striking. Among Mexican American women, for example, about 4 percent (.7/15.7) of exogamous marriages involve a black spouse, while 9 percent (2.4/26.2) of exogamous cohabiting unions involve a black partner. Similarly, among Puerto Ricans, 11 percent (4.0/38.0) of exogamous marriages involve a black partner, compared with 19 percent (8.1/41.8) of exogamous cohabiting unions.

Due to sample size limitations, the full array of *generational differences* in endogamy in cohabiting unions can be presented only for Mexican Americans. Among Mexican Americans, the generational pattern of endogamy is similar to, albeit stronger than, that observed for marriages—declining percentages in endogamous unions across generations. In addition, exogamous unions involving Mexican American women and non-Hispanic white partners become more common in each successive generation. This is also the case for unions with non-Hispanic black partners, but the overall percentage of unions with non-Hispanic blacks is small.

Interethnic unions are of interest in their own right, but their consequences for ethnic boundaries are greatest when they produce children. Children of mixed unions face complex identity issues, one of which is whether to retain a mixed identity or to adopt one parent's racial/ethnic identity or the other's. We have seen that mixed unions among Hispanic women most commonly involve a non-Hispanic white partner. Because such unions both signal and facilitate assimilation into mainstream white society, their offspring are likely to identify less strongly with their Hispanic national origins than children with two coethnic parents. Although numerous factors affect the size and composition of Hispanic groups (e.g., rates of immigration and return migration, socioeconomic mobility), ethnic mixing undoubtedly will contribute to greater fluidity in ethnic identities and therefore play an important role (Hirschman, 2002; Waters, 2002).

In Table 5-7, we expand our analysis by examining interethnic mating among parents of children born in 2000, using data from the 2000 Detail

TABLE 5-7 Ethnic Endogamy Versus Exogamy in Parenthood, by Mother's Ethnicity and Generation

Ethnicity and Generation	Endogamous (%)	Exogamous Hispanic (%)	Exogamous Non-Hispanic White (%)	Exogamous Non-Hispanic Black (%)	Missing (%)
All Births					
Mexican total	85.9	4.0	7.8	1.5	12.7
1st generation	92.8	3.8	2.7	0.4	11.4
Native-born	73.8	4.2	16.8	3.3	14.7
Puerto Rican total	51.8	18.0	16.0	11.5	17.0
1st generation	60.5	19.9	12.1	6.1	16.1
Native-born	46.9	17.0	18.2	14.5	17.4
Cuban total	56.7	17.4	22.4	2.5	8.4
1st generation	70.3	13.7	14.4	1.1	7.9
Native-born	37.8	22.6	33.4	4.6	9.1
Central/South American total	64.4	19.1	12.6	2.8	15.6
1st generation	68.2	18.1	10.6	2.2	15.9
Native-born	34.5	27.3	27.8	8.1	13.5
Other Hispanic total	51.8	16.8	23.3	4.5	19.2
1st generation	67.6	11.8	15.8	3.0	14.3
Native-born	46.5	18.4	26.0	4.9	20.0
Births to Married Mothers					
Mexican total	85.7	3.5	9.1	0.9	1.0
1st generation	92.8	3.3	3.3	0.3	0.7
Native-born	71.7	3.8	20.6	2.2	1.7
Puerto Rican total	46.6	18.9	24.3	7.9	1.9
1st generation	56.0	20.3	18.2	4.3	1.8
Native-born	40.5	18.0	28.3	10.2	1.9

Cuban total	56.9	14.8	25.7	1.6	1.1
1st generation	68.9	12.8	16.8	0.9	1.3
Native-born	40.6	17.6	37.7	2.6	1.8
Central/South American total	62.2	17.4	16.9	2.3	1.2
1st generation	66.1	16.7	14.3	1.9	1.2
Native-born	30.9	23.8	37.6	5.4	1.2
Other Hispanic total	49.3	15.6	28.8	3.1	1.7
1st generation	63.4	11.1	20.6	2.7	1.0
Native-born	44.2	17.2	31.8	3.2	1.8
Births to Unmarried Mothers					
Mexican total	86.1	5.0	5.3	2.5	29.7
1st generation	92.8	5.1	1.3	0.5	29.5
Native-born	77.3	4.8	10.7	5.1	29.7
Puerto Rican total	56.5	17.2	8.4	14.9	27.2
1st generation	65.5	19.4	5.4	8.1	27.7
Native-born	52.2	16.1	9.9	18.2	26.9
Cuban total	55.6	26.9	10.4	6.0	27.8
1st generation	75.0	16.8	5.9	1.8	25.4
Native-born	27.0	42.0	17.1	12.1	31.0
Central/South American total	68.3	22.2	4.6	3.9	33.5
1st generation	72.1	20.8	3.7	2.7	34.2
Native-born	40.4	33.1	11.6	12.6	28.2
Other Hispanic total	56.7	18.9	13.1	7.1	39.6
1st generation	76.7	13.1	5.1	3.7	33.8
Native-born	50.7	20.5	15.5	8.1	40.0

SOURCE: 2000 Natality File, National Center for Health Statistics.

Natality File.[19] We first present information on all births and then disaggregate the data into births to married and unmarried mothers. As was the case in the previous table on union patterns, we organize the data by the mother's ethnicity and generation. However, due to the limited information collected on the birth certificate, we are able to distinguish only between foreign-born mothers and native-born mothers. For mothers in each Hispanic subgroup, the percentages of births in which the father is coethnic, from a different Hispanic group, non-Hispanic white, and non-Hispanic black are shown. These percentages are based on cases in which the father's race and ethnicity are known; however, since missing information on fathers is problematic in birth certificate data, we also show the percentage of cases in each group with missing information on the father's ethnicity.

Focusing first on all births, there are substantial differences in intermating patterns by Hispanic ethnicity and generation. As was the case in our analysis of marital and cohabiting unions, the *level* of ethnic endogamy is higher among Mexican Americans than for other Hispanic groups. Moreover, for all groups except Mexican Americans, coethnicity of parents is considerably lower than coethnicity of married or cohabiting partners. For example, among Puerto Ricans, 62 percent of married partners and 58 percent of cohabiting partners have similar Hispanic origins; however, only 52 percent of births can be attributed to coethnic parents. The most striking pattern shown in the table, however, is that for *generation*: infants of foreign-born mothers are substantially more likely to have coethnic parents than infants of native-born mothers. The percentages of children born to coethnic parents for foreign-born and native-born mothers, respectively, are 93 and 74 for Mexicans, 61 and 47 for Puerto Ricans, 70 and 38 for Cubans, 68 and 34 for Central American and South American mothers, and 68 and 46 for other Hispanic mothers. Exogamous unions producing children are highly likely to be with Hispanic fathers (from other national-origin groups) or with non-Hispanic white fathers, with one exception. Mexican-origin women are considerably more likely to bear a child with a non-Hispanic white partner than with a non-Mexican Hispanic partner.

When births are broken down by the marital status of the mother, several important differences in ethnic mixing are evident. First, considerably fewer births to unmarried Hispanic mothers involve partnerships with non-Hispanic white males than is the case for births to married Hispanic mothers. Second, births outside marriage are more likely to involve a non-Hispanic black father than births within marriage. For example, about 8

[19]The natality public-use data files include information on all births occurring in the United States. Data are obtained from birth certificates for births occurring in each state and the District of Columbia. The data are compiled and released in electronic format by the National Center for Health Statistics.

percent of infants of unmarried Puerto Rican mothers had non-Hispanic white fathers, compared with 24 percent of infants of married Puerto Rican mothers. Children born to unmarried Puerto Rican women were much more likely to have a black father (15 percent) than children born to married Puerto Rican women (8 percent). This pattern is similar across all Hispanic groups. Given the relatively high propensity of non-Hispanic whites to bear children within marriage and the relatively high propensity of non-Hispanic blacks to bear children outside marriage, these patterns appear to reflect the preferences and circumstances of fathers.

In summary, several broad conclusions can be drawn from our analyses of ethnic mixing. First, there are substantial differences across Hispanic groups in the level of ethnic endogamy in marriages, cohabiting unions, and parenthood. The most significant differences are those between Mexican Americans and all other groups: Mexican Americans are substantially more likely to be paired with a coethnic partner in marriage, cohabitation, and parenthood than are Puerto Ricans, Cubans, Central/South Americans, or other Hispanics. Second, in all Hispanic groups, there are marked declines in ethnic endogamy in marriage, cohabitation, and parenthood across generations. This is consistent with a large body of research that shows that intermarriage is a sensitive indicator of assimilation. Finally, the most provocative findings emerge from a comparison of results for marriage, cohabitation, and parenthood. In marriage, there is a higher level of ethnic endogamy than in cohabitation and parenthood. Moreover, among exogamous unions, matches with non-Hispanic white partners are more common in marriage than in cohabitation or parenthood. Unions among partners from different Hispanic origins or between Hispanics and non-Hispanic blacks are considerably more evident in cohabitation and parenthood than they are in marriage. In particular, unions between Hispanics and non-Hispanic blacks are prominent in parenthood, especially nonmarital births.

CONCLUSIONS

Portrayals of U.S. Hispanics consistently emphasize their relatively high level of familism and links between familism and traditional family patterns in Latin American- and Caribbean-origin countries. Familism is typically regarded as a multidimensional concept that reflects both values and behaviors that emphasize the needs of the family over the needs of individuals (Vega, 1995). Key questions for understanding family life among Hispanics are (1) whether familistic values and behaviors are more prominent among Hispanics than among other racial and ethnic groups and (2) whether familism wanes with exposure to the U.S. social context (i.e., duration of U.S. residence for the foreign-born or generational status for all members of a Hispanic group). Evaluations of Hispanic familism, however, are complicated by the fact that family behavior is not shaped solely by normative orientations and values; it is also strongly influenced by socioeconomic position and the structure of economic opportunities in the broader society. Thus, contemporary scholars generally argue that Hispanic family patterns can best be understood within a social adaptation framework, which stresses the interplay between familistic values and the circumstances experienced by Hispanics in their everyday lives.

Because the data presented in this chapter are descriptive, we cannot evaluate the relative importance of the aforementioned factors in shaping family behavior among Hispanics. Instead, we identify structural characteristics of families that suggest variation in familism by race/ethnicity and generational status. Several patterns are consistent with the idea that Hispanics are family oriented, relative to non-Hispanics. First, with the exception of Cubans, Hispanics have higher fertility than non-Hispanics. Childbearing also begins earlier in Hispanic women's lives than it does for non-Hispanic white women. Second, Hispanics are more likely to live in family households than are non-Hispanic whites and blacks. Third, the family households of Hispanics are slightly larger and much more likely to be extended than those of non-Hispanic whites. At the same time, the figures for family structure and children's living arrangements show that traditional two-parent families are not more common among Hispanics than non-Hispanic whites. In fact, female family headship and one-parent living arrangements for children are considerably more prevalent among Hispanics than non-Hispanic whites, although less prevalent than among non-Hispanic blacks.

A related issue is whether familism declines as Hispanic groups spend more time in the United States. Although comparisons across generations using cross-sectional data must be used cautiously to address this question,[20] our analysis of structural measures of familism shows some support for the declining familism thesis. The support is strongest for the Mexican-origin population. On every indicator, the second and third (or higher) generations exhibit less traditional family behavior than the first generation. For instance, in 15 percent of households headed by a first-generation Mexican, the householder is a female with no partner present, compared with 23 percent of households headed by a second- or third (or higher)-generation Mexican. The implications of these differences are particularly striking for children: about 14 percent of first-generation Mexican children live in a mother-only family, compared with 20 percent of second-generation children and 31 percent of third (or higher)-generation chil-

[20]Generational differences found in cross-sectional data can be influenced by in the characteristics of immigrants arriving in the United States at different points in time, as well as differences in the context of reception at the time of arrival.

dren. A similar but somewhat weaker pattern of declining familism across generations is shown for Puerto Ricans, but the evidence is considerably more mixed for the other Hispanic subgroups.

A limitation of this study is that we have only examined the structural dimension of familism. This is due, in part, to the absence of national-level databases that include both information on other dimensions of familism and sufficient numbers of the various Hispanic subgroups to allow for analysis. Future research on attitudinal and behavioral aspects of familism is needed, given the unevenness of conclusions that can be drawn from the existing literature and data. For example, perhaps the best general-purpose survey for describing the attitudinal and behavioral dimensions of familism is the National Survey of Families and Households (NSFH). This survey includes numerous questions that tap normative beliefs about the obligations of parents to support their adult children and the obligations of adult children to support aging parents. It suggests that members of Hispanic groups are more likely than non-Hispanic whites to recognize both parental and filial obligations (results available upon request), although the difference may be due in part to nativity differences between groups and the tendency of the foreign-born to value parental and filial duties. Indeed, Hispanics are more likely than non-Hispanic whites to say they would rely on their children or their parents for emergency help, for a loan, or advice (Kim and McKenry, 1998). These findings are consistent with research based on other data sets, which show that Hispanic adolescents, irrespective of nativity, more strongly respect their parents and feel more obligated to provide their parents with support in the future than non-Hispanic whites (Fuligni, Tseng, and Lam, 1999).

Such findings on the *attitudinal* dimension of familism stand in sharp contrast to a more complicated set of findings from NSFH-based studies that focus on the *behavioral* dimension of familism, in particular social participation and both instrumental (money/help) and noninstrumental (advice/support) transfers within families. A concise summary of this literature is complicated by the fact that there is little consistency across studies in research methodology. For example, only some studies disaggregate Hispanics by national origin and generational status, and many studies are restricted to particular stages of the life course (e.g., old age). In addition, there are inconsistencies in the types of support examined as well as whether information is provided on the direction of exchanges (i.e., the providers and recipients of support are identified) (Hogan, Eggebeen, and Clogg, 1993; Lee and Aytec, 1998; Spreizer, Schoeni, and Rao, 1996). Nonetheless, whether one focuses on Hispanics as a generic category or specific subgroups such as Mexican Americans, there is some indication that Hispanics tend to socialize more frequently with relatives than others (Kim and McKenry, 1998). As for giving and receiving support within families, the

NSFH suggests that ethnic differences are either trivial or various Hispanic groups tend to participate in fewer exchanges than others. This may be due, in part, to the role of migration in separating family members (Hogan et al., Clogg, 1993) or to the relative lack of resources to give (Lee and Aytac, 1998). More systematic attention to differences in family relations and exchanges by national origin and generation is needed before firm conclusions about these issues can be drawn.[21]

Another topic considered in this chapter is ethnic mixing in family formation. The future size and composition of the Hispanic population will be shaped by the processes that constitute the well-known demographic balancing equation: population change = births – deaths + net migration. High rates of immigration and relatively high fertility will continue to fuel the rapid growth of the Hispanic population. While these factors are fundamental, there are additional complications in the situation of Hispanics that are not taken into account in population projections based on the balancing equation. Specifically, the equation assumes that there is no intermarriage and that the racial and ethnic identities of children are identical to those of their mothers (National Research Council, 1997). As we have seen, the assumption of full ethnic endogamy is untenable, as is the premise of fixed identities across generations.

Recent changes in family formation behavior and the complexities of ethnic mixing will play significant roles in the future size and composition of Hispanic subgroups. Hispanics have shared in the trend toward cohabitation and nonmarital childbearing that has characterized the general U.S. population. Currently, more than 40 percent of births to Hispanic mothers take place outside marriage (National Center for Health Statistics, 2003), and roughly half of those births are to cohabiting couples (Bumpass and Lu, 2000). Our analysis shows that ethnic exogamy is common in marriage and in marital births among Hispanics—but exogamy is even more prominent in cohabiting unions and in nonmarital childbearing. Thus, recent shifts in the union context of childbearing are linked to growth in the population of children with mixed ethnic backgrounds and to a blurring of boundaries between specific Hispanic subgroups and both other Hispanic subgroups and non-Hispanics.

Importantly, there are differences *between* Hispanic subgroups and *within* Hispanic subgroups by generational status in the extent of ethnic mixing. The most consequential differences are those between the Mexican-origin population and all other Hispanic groups. Relative to the other Hispanic subgroups, the Mexican-origin population exhibits much higher

[21]For studies of the elderly population using data sources other than the NSFH, see Angel, Angel, and Markides (2002); Angel, Angel, Lee, and Markides (1999); Angel, Angel, McClellan, and Markides (1996).

levels of ethnic endogamy in marriage, cohabitation, and parenthood. Moreover, while ethnic endogamy in parenthood is lower for native-born mothers than for foreign-born mothers in each Hispanic group, the level of endogamy among *native-born Mexican mothers* exceeds that for *foreign-born* mothers in the other groups. Thus, the Mexican-origin population is unique among Hispanics in its high level of ethnic endogamy in marriage, cohabitation, and parenthood. This suggests that there will be fewer exits from the Mexican American population due to mixed racial/ethnic backgrounds of offspring (and consequent identity shifts) than is the case for other groups.

A question that remains unanswered is: What are the implications of these interethnic mating patterns for the future of racial and ethnic boundaries in the United States? Some scholars argue that race and ethnicity are in the process of being reconfigured in U.S. society. Due to the large-scale immigration of groups that are not readily classified as whites or blacks—and to the growth of the mixed-race population—the old black–white dualism is being transformed into a black–nonblack dualism (Gans, 1999). According to Gans (1999), Hispanics and Asians are "in reserve" as a residual category that will be sorted into the principal categories over time by the dominant white society. This sorting process is likely to depend on the socioeconomic position and phenotypic characteristics of Hispanic- and Asian-origin individuals.

Several features of ethnic mixing among Hispanics are consistent with the idea that Hispanics will be classified with whites into the nonblack category of the new racial dualism. First, with the exception of Mexican Americans, the level of exogamy among Hispanics is high and sizeable proportions of exogamous unions are with non-Hispanic whites. Second, very low proportions of exogamous unions are with non-Hispanic blacks. And third, the level of intermixing with non-Hispanic whites increases markedly across generations. In all Hispanic groups except Mexican Americans, more than half of the unions of native-born women are exogamous,[22] and such unions frequently involve non-Hispanic white partners. At the same time, there are features of ethnic mixing that are not consistent with the idea of a growing black–nonblack dichotomy in which Hispanics are blending into an undifferentiated nonblack group. One such feature is the relatively high level of ethnic endogamy among Mexican Americans, which will undoubtedly contribute to the persistence of a Mexican ethnic identity and culture. Given the size of the Mexican-origin population and continued high rates of immigration from Mexico, this pattern suggests that "Mexi-

[22]This is the case for all coresidential unions combined (marriages and cohabiting unions) and partnerships producing children born in 2000.

can" or "Hispanic" may continue to be quasi-racial categories for many years to come. Another important factor is the shift in ethnic mixing that has accompanied the trends toward cohabitation and nonmarital childbearing. Cohabitation and nonmarital childbearing among Hispanics are more likely to entail partnerships with non-Hispanic blacks than are marriage and marital childbearing. This is especially the case for some Hispanic subgroups, including Puerto Ricans, Central/South Americans, and Cubans.

In sum, the overall pattern of ethnic mixing among Hispanics does not have unambiguous implications for the future of racial and ethnic boundaries in the United States. Mexican Americans are likely to maintain a distinct ethnic identity, although some blurring of boundaries will occur due to unions with non-Hispanic whites. Other Hispanic subgroups are less likely to sustain distinct identities over time. Furthermore, their higher levels of ethnic mixing with other Hispanic groups and non-Hispanic blacks suggest somewhat greater ambiguity with regard to their placement in a black–nonblack racial system. In short, while current patterns of immigration and ethnic mixing are contributing to a softening of some racial/ethnic boundaries, both race and ethnicity are likely to remain salient and to intersect in complex ways.

REFERENCES

Alan Guttmacher Institute. (1999). *Teen sex and pregnancy. Facts in brief.* Available: http://www.agi-usa.org [accessed March 2004].

Angel, J.L., Angel, R.J., and Markides, K.S. (2002). Later-life immigration: Changes in living arrangements, and headship status among older Mexican-origin individuals. *Social Science Quarterly*, *81*(1), 389–403.

Angel, R.J., Angel, J.L., Lee, G.-Y., and Markides, K.S. (1999). Age at migration and family dependency among older Mexican immigrants: Recent evidence from the Mexican American EPESE. *The Gerontologist*, *39*, 59–65.

Angel, R.J., Angel, J.L., McClellan, J.L., and Markides, K.S. (1996). Nativity, declining health, and preferences in living arrangements among elderly Mexican Americans. *The Gerontologist*, *36*, 464–473.

Baca Zinn, M., and Wells, B. (2000). Diversity within Latino families: New lessons for family social science. In D.H. Demo, K.R. Allen, and M.A. Fine (Eds.), *Handbook of family diversity* (pp. 252–273). New York: Oxford University Press.

Bean, F.D., and Tienda, M. (1987). *The Hispanic population of the United States.* New York: Russell Sage Foundation.

Bean, F.D., Curtis, R.L., and Marcum, J.P. (1977). Familism and marital satisfaction among Mexican Americans: The effects of family size, wife's labor force participation, and conjugal power. *Journal of Marriage and the Family*, *39*(4), 759–767.

Bramlett, M.D., and Mosher, W.D. (2002). Cohabitation, marriage, divorce, and remarriage in the United States. National Center for Health Statistics. *Vital Health Statistics*, *23*(22).

Bumpass, L., and Lu, H. (2000). Trends in cohabitation and implications for children's family contexts in the United States. *Population Studies*, *54*, 29–41.

Burgess, E.W., and Locke, H.S. (1945). *The family: From institution to companionship*. New York: American Book.

Casper, L.M., and Bianchi, S.M. (2002). *Continuity and change in the American family*. Thousand Oaks, CA: Sage.

Ch'Eng-K'Un, C. (1944). Familism the foundation of Chinese social organization. *Social Forces, 23*(1), 50–59.

Duncan, B., and Trejo, S.J. (2004, April). *Ethnic choices and the intergenerational progress of Mexican-Americans*. (Working Paper #04-05-02.) Austin: University of Texas Population Research Center.

Fields, J. (2003). *Children's living arrangements and characteristics*. (Current Population Reports, P20-547.) Washington, DC: U.S. Census Bureau.

Fuligni, A.J., Tseng, V., and Lam, M. (1999). Attitudes toward family obligations among American adolescents with Asian, Latin American, and European backgrounds. *Child Development, 70*, 1030–1044.

Gaines, S.O., Jr., Barajas, L., Hicks, D., Lyde, M., Takahashi, Y., Yum, N., Garcia, B.F., Marelich, W.D., Bledsoe, K., Steers, W.N., Henderson, M.C., Granrose, C.S., Rios, D., Farris, K.R., and Page, M.S. (1997). Links between race/ethnicity and cultural values as mediated by racial/ethnic identity and moderated by gender. *Journal of Personality and Social Psychology, 72*(6), 1460–1476.

Gans, H.J. (1999). The possibility of a new racial hierarchy in the twenty-first century United States. In M. Lamont (Ed.), *The cultural territories of race: Black and white boundaries* (pp. 371–390). Chicago, IL: University of Chicago Press.

Gordon, M. (1964). *Assimilation in American life: The role of race, religion, and national origins*. New York: Oxford University Press.

Guendelman, S. (1995). *Immigrants may hold clues to protecting health during pregnancy: Exploring a paradox*. (Wellness Lecture Series 5.) Oakland: University of California.

Hirschman, C. (2002). The meaning of race and ethnic population projections. In N.A. Denton Stewart and E. Tolnay (Eds.), *American diversity: A demographic challenge for the twenty-first century* (pp. 51–72). Albany: State University of New York Press.

Hogan, D.P., Eggebeen, D.J., and Clogg, C.C. (1993). The structure of intergenerational exchanges in American families. *American Journal of Sociology, 98*, 1428–1458.

Kalmijn, M. (1998). Intermarriage and homogamy: Causes, patterns, trends. *Annual Review of Sociology, 24*, 395–421.

Kim, H.K., and McKenry, P.C. (1998). Social networks and support: A comparison of African Americans, Asian Americans, Caucasians, and Hispanics. *Journal of Comparative Family Studies, 29*, 313–334.

Landale, N.S., and Oropesa, R.S. (2001). Migration, social support and perinatal health: An origin-destination analysis of Puerto Rican women. *Journal of Health and Social Behavior, 42*, 166–183.

Lee, Y.-J., and Aytac, I.A. (1998). Intergenerational financial support among whites, African Americans, and Latinos. *Journal of Marriage and the Family, 60*, 426–441.

Lesthaeghe, R., and Meekers, D. (1986). Value changes and the dimensions of familism in the European community. *European Journal of Population, 2*, 225–268.

Lieberson, S., and Waters, M.C. (1988). *From many strands: Ethnic and racial groups in contemporary America*. New York: Russell Sage Foundation.

Martin, J.A., Hamilton, B.E., Ventura, S.J., Menaker, F., and Park, M.M. (2002). *Births: Final data for 2000*. (National Vital Statistics Reports 50(5).) Hyattsville, MD: National Center for Health Statistics.

Martin, P., and Midgley, E. (2003). Immigration: Shaping and reshaping America. *Population Bulletin, 58*(2), 5–42.

Massey, D.D., Zambrana, R.E., and Bell, S.A. (1995). Contemporary issues in Latin families. In R. Zambrana (Ed.), *Understanding Latino families: Scholarship, policy and practice* (pp. 190–203). Thousand Oaks, CA: Sage.

National Center for Health Statistics. (2003). *Health: United States, 2003*. Hyattsville, MD: U.S. Department of Health and Human Services.

National Research Council. (1997). *The new Americans: Economic, demographic, and fiscal effects of immigration.* Panel on the Demographic and Economic Impacts of Immigration Committee on Population and Committee on National Statistics, J.P. Smith and B. Edmonston (Eds.). Washington, DC: National Academy Press.

Oppenheimer, V.K. (2000). The continuing importance of men's economic position in marriage formation. In L.J. Waite (Ed.), *The ties that bind: Perspectives on marriage and cohabitation* (pp. 283–301). New York: Aldine de Gruyter.

Oropesa, R.S., and Gorman, B.K. (2000). Ethnicity, immigration, and beliefs about marriage as a "tie that binds." In L.J. Waite (Ed.), *The ties that bind: Perspectives on marriage and cohabitation* (pp. 188–226). New York: Aldine de Gruyter.

Oropesa, R.S., and Landale, N.S. (1997). Immigrant legacies: Ethnicity, generation, and children's familial and economic lives. *Social Science Quarterly*, *78*(2), 399–416.

Oropesa, R.S., and Landale, N.S. (2004). The future of marriage and Hispanics. *Journal of Marriage and Family*, *66*, 901–920.

Popenoe, D. (1993). American family decline, 1960–1990: A review and appraisal. *Journal of Marriage and Family*, *55*, 527–555.

Portes, A., and Rumbaut, R.G. (2001). *Legacies: The story of the immigrant second generation.* New York: Russell Sage Foundation.

Proktor, B.D., and Dalaker, J. (2003). *Poverty in the United States, 2000.* (Current Population Reports, P60-222.) Washington, DC: U.S. Census Bureau.

Ramirez, R.R., and de la Cruz, P. (2002). *The Hispanic population in the United States.* (Current Population Reports, P20-545.) Washington, DC: U.S. Census Bureau.

Rodriguez, J., Kosloski, M., and Kosloski, K. (1998). The impact of acculturation on attitudinal familism in a community of Puerto Rican Americans. *Hispanic Journal of Behavioral Sciences*, *20*(3), 375–390.

Rosenfeld, M.J. (2002). Measures of assimilation in the marriage market: Mexican Americans, 1970–1990. *Journal of Marriage and Family*, *64*, 152–162.

Rumbaut, R.G., and Weeks, J.R. (1996). Unraveling a public health enigma: Why do immigrants experience superior perinatal health outcomes? *Research in the Sociology of Health Care*, *13B*, 337–391.

Sabogal, F., Marin, G., Otero-Sabogal, R., VanOss Marin, B., and Perez-Stable, E.J. (1987). Hispanic familism and acculturation: What changes and what doesn't? *Hispanic Journal of Behavioral Sciences*, *9*(4), 397–412.

Spreitzer, E., Schoeni, R., and Rao, K.V. (1996). Tracing intergenerational relations through reports of transfers of time and money: A comparative study of African Americans, Hispanics, and whites. *International Journal of Sociology and Social Policy*, *16*, 11–34.

Steidel, A.G., Contreras, L., and Contreras, J.M. (2003). A new familism scale for use with Latino populations. *Hispanic Journal of the Behavioral Sciences*, *25*(3), 312–330.

Stevens, G., and Tyler, M.K. (2002). Ethnic and racial intermarriage in the United States: Old and new regimes. In N.A. Denton and S.E. Tolnay (Eds.), *American diversity: A demographic challenge for the twenty-first century* (pp. 221–243). Albany: State University of New York Press.

Suro, R., and Passel, J. (2003). *The rise of the second generation: Changing patterns in Hispanic population growth.* Washington, DC: Pew Hispanic Center.

Sweeney, M.M. (2002). Two decades of family change: The shifting economic foundations of marriage. *American Sociological Review*, *67*, 132–147.

Tienda, M. (1980). Familism and structural assimilation of Mexican Americans in the United States. *International Migration Review*, *14*(3), 383–408.

U.S. Census Bureau. (2000). *Population profile of the United States: 2000.* Available: http://www.census.gov/population/www/pop-profile/profile2000.html [accessed November 2003].

Valenzuela, A., and Dornbusch, S.M. (1994). Familism and social capital in the academic achievement of Mexican origin and Anglo adolescents. *Social Science Quarterly*, *75*, 18–36.

Vega, W.A. (1995). The study of Latino families. In R. Zambrana (Ed.), *Understanding Latino families: Scholarship, policy, and practice* (pp. 3–17). Thousand Oaks, CA: Sage.

Ventura, S.J. (1980, May). Trends and differentials in births to unmarried women: United States, 1970–1976. *Vital and Health Statistics*, Series 21, No 36. Hyattsville, MD: U.S. Department of Health and Human Services.

Ventura, S.J., and Bachrach, C.A. (2000). *Nonmarital childbearing in the United States, 1940–1999.* (National Vital Statistics Reports, vol. 48, No. 16.) Hyattsville, MD: National Center for Health Statistics.

Waters, M.C. (2002). The social construction of race and ethnicity: Some examples from demography. In N.A. Denton and S.E. Tolnay (Eds.), *American diversity: A demographic challenge for the twenty-first century* (pp. 25–49). Albany: State University of New York Press.

Wilson, W.J. (1987). *The truly disadvantaged.* Chicago, IL: University of Chicago Press.

Winch, R.F., Greer, S., and Blumberg, R.L. (1967). Ethnicity and extended familism in an upper middle-class suburb. *American Sociological Review*, *32*(2), 265–272.

Wu, L.L., and Wolfe, B. (Eds.) (2001). *Out of wedlock: Causes and consequences of nonmarital fertility.* New York: Russell Sage Foundation.

Wu, L.L., Bumpass, L.L., and Musick, K. (2001). Historical and life course trajectories of nonmarital childbearing. In L.L. Wu and B. Wolfe (Eds.), *Out of wedlock: causes and consequences of nonmarital fertility* (pp. 3–48). New York: Russell Sage Foundation.

Zambrana, R.E., Scrimshaw, S.C.M., Collins, N., and Dunkel-Schetter, C. (1997). Prenatal health behaviors and psychosocial risk factors in pregnant women of Mexican origin: The role of acculturation. *American Journal of Public Health*, *87*, 1022–1026.

APPENDIX TABLE A5-1 Percentage Family Households by Race/Ethnicity and Generational Status of Householder[a]

Generational Status	Mexican	Puerto Rican	Cuban	Central/ South American	Other Hispanic	Non-Hispanic White	Non-Hispanic Black
All households	83.5	74.1	73.0	80.0	75.4	67.1	66.6
1st generation	87.4	72.7	72.7	81.9	78.0		
2nd generation	79.8	76.9	78.0	65.9	72.6		
Native-born of native parentage	78.5	73.9	58.5	63.6	73.9	67.9	66.6
Standardized for Age of Householder[b]							
All households	80.5	70.7	73.7	75.6	72.3	67.9	64.2
1st generation	83.3	72.1	75.6	77.2	72.6		
2nd generation	79.5	69.8	78.5	62.9	70.6		
Native-born of native parentage	75.9	63.6	67.0	58.0	71.8	67.2	64.4

[a]Based on standard Census Bureau definition of family household.
[b]Age distribution of non-Hispanic white family householders (5 year age groups) used as standard.

SOURCE: Pooled March 1998–2002 CPS files.

APPENDIX TABLE A5-2 Characteristics of Family Households by Race/Ethnicity and Generation of Householder[a]

Household and Generation	Mexican	Puerto Rican	Cuban	Central/ South American	Other Hispanic	Non-Hispanic White	Non-Hispanic Black
Percentage married couple							
All family households	70.4	54.6	77.4	66.6	63.8	82.4	47.5
1st generation	73.3	58.3	76.5	66.9	55.9		
2nd generation	66.3	49.9	83.5	58.1	62.6		
Native-born of native parentage	66.8	49.4	—	—	71.0	82.3	46.9
Percentage cohabiting couple							
All family households	4.0	4.7	1.3	4.4	3.3	1.7	3.3
1st generation	3.8	3.4	1.3	4.3	3.5		
2nd generation	3.7	6.8	1.2	6.8	2.7		
Native-born of native parentage	4.6	5.1	—	—	3.3	1.8	3.2
Percentage female householder, no partner							
All family households	18.5	34.5	16.2	21.7	26.6	11.9	42.5
1st generation	15.0	33.2	17.3	21.5	34.4		
2nd generation	23.2	35.6	9.1	26.0	26.7		
Native-born of native parentage	22.8	38.1	—	—	19.7	11.9	43.3
Mean number of persons in household							
All family households	4.1	3.4	3.1	3.8	3.5	3.0	3.3
1st generation	4.4	3.3	3.1	3.8	3.7		
2nd generation	3.6	3.5	3.4	3.4	3.4		
Native-born of native parentage	3.7	3.5	—	—	3.3	3.1	3.3

continues

APPENDIX TABLE A5-2 Characteristics of Family Households by Race/Ethnicity and Generation of Householder[a]

Household and Generation	Mexican	Puerto Rican	Cuban	Central/ South American	Other Hispanic	Non-Hispanic White	Non-Hispanic Black
Percentage extended family household							
All family households	8.6	7.4	6.7	9.8	6.6	2.7	7.4
1st generation	9.7	8.9	6.5	10.4	7.0		
2nd generation	8.0	5.8	9.2	4.1	10.4		
Native-born of native parentage	6.7	4.5	—	—	5.2	2.6	7.1
Unweighted number of cases							
All family households	16,924	3,084	1,393	4,287	2,507	140,639	19,360
1st generation	9,394	1,741	1149	3,888	867		
2nd generation	2,788	970	207	259	258		
Native-born of native parentage	4,742	373	37	140	1382	123,304	17,485

NOTE: — = fewer than 200 cases in racial/ethnic generation group.

[a]Based on standard Census Bureau definition of family household.

SOURCE: Pooled March 1998–2002 CPS files.

6

Barriers to Educational Opportunities for Hispanics in the United States

Barbara Schneider, Sylvia Martinez, and Ann Owens

For Hispanics in the United States, the educational experience is one of accumulated disadvantage. Many Hispanic students begin formalized schooling without the economic and social resources that many other students receive, and schools are often ill equipped to compensate for these initial disparities. For Hispanics, initial disadvantages often stem from parents' immigrant and socioeconomic status and their lack of knowledge about the U.S. education system. As Hispanic students proceed through the schooling system, inadequate school resources and their weak relationships with their teachers continue to undermine their academic success. Initial disadvantages continue to accumulate, resulting in Hispanics having the lowest rates of high school and college degree attainment, which hinders their chances for stable employment. The situation of Hispanic educational attainment is cause for national concern.

Today, most parents and their children believe that a college degree is necessary for obtaining stable and meaningful work (Schneider and Stevenson, 1999). This attitude is reflected in the educational expectations parents hold for their children and in the expectations that young people have for themselves (U.S. Department of Education, 1995b, p. 88). High educational expectations can be found among all racial and ethnic groups regardless of their economic and social resources (p. 73). Although parents and children share high educational aims, their aspirations do not necessarily translate into postsecondary matriculation. This is especially the case for Hispanic high school students, particularly those whose parents have not attended college (Nuñez, Cuccaro-Alamin, and Carroll, 1998).

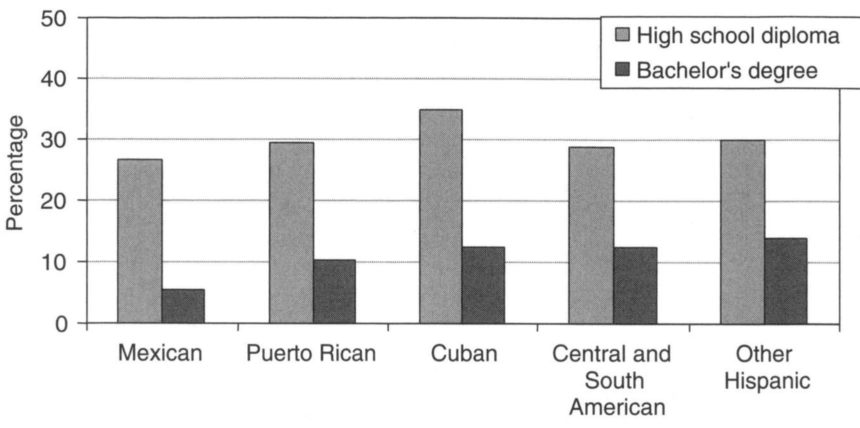

FIGURE 6-1 Educational attainment of the population 25 years and over by country of origin (percentage), 2002.
SOURCE: U.S. Census Bureau (2002a).

Despite high educational expectations, Hispanics are among the least educated group in the United States: 11 percent of those over age 25 have earned a bachelor's degree or higher compared with 17 percent of blacks, 30 percent of whites, and 49 percent of Asian Americans in the same age group (U.S. Census Bureau, 2003).[1] Even more troubling, more than one-fourth of Hispanic adults have less than a ninth-grade education (U.S. Census Bureau, 2002b). These numbers represent all Hispanic groups and include recent immigrants. When examined by country of origin, educational attainment for Hispanics varies. As shown in Figure 6-1, Mexican Americans, who are the largest and fastest growing Hispanic subgroup in the United States, have the lowest rates of educational attainment compared with other groups. Cuban Americans report the highest levels of high school completion, and "other Hispanics" report the highest levels of bachelor's degree attainment. Most data sets do not distinguish among Hispanic subgroups, disregarding important cultural and economic differ-

[1]Mexican Americans constitute the largest proportion of Hispanics in the United States as shown in the 2000 census. The composition of the Hispanic population is as follows: 66 percent Mexican, 15 percent Central and South American, 9 percent Puerto Rican, 6 percent other Hispanic, and 4 percent Cuban (U.S. Census Bureau, 2002b). Reported percentages have been rounded to the nearest whole number.

ences among them. Whenever possible, analyses in this chapter attend to such differences.

Given the growth of the Hispanic population in the United States, most notably in the past decade (U.S. Census Bureau, 2001a), and the increasing importance of a college degree even for entry-level jobs (Carnoy, 2000), the barriers Hispanics face in realizing their educational ambitions is a major policy concern (see Chapter 4). This chapter presents the current state of educational opportunities available to the majority of Hispanic students in elementary, secondary, and postsecondary schools. Similar to other chapters in this volume, this chapter moves beyond the descriptive and explores some of the institutional and student-level factors that appear to be hindering Hispanic educational success. The goal is to identify some of the barriers to educational advancement experienced by Hispanic students in the United States, including entering school at a disadvantage because of a lack of exposure to literacy activities at home and in early formalized school settings, teacher assessments of students' language proficiency unduly influencing instructional practices, how the relationship between Hispanic students and their predominantly non-Hispanic teachers encourages disengagement from academic work, and how the lack of academic guidance pertaining to course selections and college choice impedes Hispanics from attending four-year colleges.

TAKING THE FIRST STEPS: ACTIVITIES AT HOME

One of the most important factors in school success is the extent to which parents actively participate in their children's education prior to their entry into formal preschool or kindergarten programs (U.S. Department of Education, 2003d). Specific activities, such as reading to children, have been shown to enhance children's language acquisition, early reading performance, social development, and later success in school (Loeb, Fuller, Kagan, and Carrol, 2004; National Research Council, 1998). National trend data from the National Household and Education Survey (NHES) from 1993 to 1999 indicate that Hispanic children age 3 to 5 are less likely to be read to compared with non-Hispanic children. Families in which parents' primary language at home is Spanish have especially low rates of participation in literacy activities. With respect to reading to children three or more times per week, Hispanic families in which both parents speak only Spanish at home had participation rates that were nearly 50 percentage points lower than white families in 1999. By contrast, for Hispanic families in which both parents speak English at home, participation rates were only 15 percentage points lower than white families. Hispanic households are also less likely than white households to participate in other prekindergarten literacy activities, such as telling their child a story or visiting a library, again with a pronounced difference between Hispanic families who speak English in the home and those who do not.

Families with limited economic, educational, and social resources are often less likely to participate in literacy activities than those with greater resources. Using data from the NHES, families were categorized by income level to determine whether literacy activities still differ by race/ethnicity when resources are taken into account.[2] Figure 6-2 suggests a statistically significant association between literacy activities and family resources across racial/ethnic groups.[3] However, at all income levels except the highest, Hispanic families are less likely than other groups to participate in literacy activities (see Figure 6-2), indicating that lower participation in literacy activities can be partially explained by lack of financial resources. An additional mechanism explaining different rates of participation is language: within each income bracket except the highest, Hispanic families in which neither parent speaks English were less likely to read to their children, tell a story, or visit a library than Hispanic families in which both parents speak English in the home.[4] The rates of literacy participation for Hispanic families who speak English at home more closely resemble those of white and black families, suggesting that bilingual families may be more assimilated into American culture, and specifically into practices that increase school performance.

It is difficult to draw causal conclusions regarding the effects of language spoken at home across racial/ethnic groups and within the Hispanic population due to methodological shortcomings of existing data sets: the small numbers of non-English speakers in the existing samples, some surveys not being administered bilingually, and questions regarding literacy activities not differentiating between reading to a child in Spanish and doing so in English. However, multivariate analyses based on these NHES data show that, regardless of mother's educational attainment and household income, Hispanic parents who speak only Spanish at home are less likely to read to their children than other Hispanic parents (both bilingual parents and those who speak only English).[5] However, NHES data indicate

[2]Income brackets were constructed by recoding the NHES household income variable into quartiles. NHES does not provide a more comprehensive measure of socioeconomic status, such as a construct that includes parental level of education.

[3]The language variable was constructed from questions about the mother's and father's first language and the language spoken at home. The three language categories are (1) both parents' main language is English, (2) one of two parents speaks a language other than English in the home, and (3) both parents speak a language other than English in the home.

[4]While the language variable is not specific, we can infer that for the majority of Hispanic families, Spanish is the other language spoken in the home.

[5]Multivariate analyses, using NHES, are not shown but are available from authors upon request.

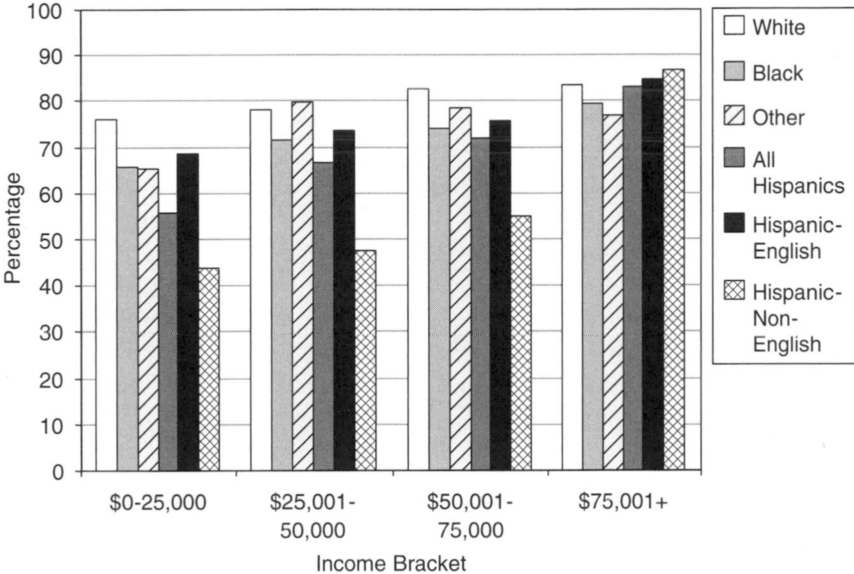

FIGURE 6-2 Average rates of participation for 3- to 5-year-olds not yet enrolled in kindergarten in being read to by a family member, by race/ethnicity according to income.
NOTES: Differences between racial groups and language status are statistically significant ($p < .001$). The difference between racial groups was not significant within the highest income bracket for this measure. "Read to" refers to being read to at least three times in the past week.
SOURCE: U.S. Department of Education (1999).

that parents who are bilingual are more likely to engage their child in literacy activities than parents who speak only Spanish, but their children are still at a disadvantage in reading compared with children whose parents speak only English. While participating in literacy activities in English is the optimal preparation for schooling, being read to in Spanish also exposes children to literacy strategies that will be beneficial as they start school. Students who are successful readers in their native language employ the same strategies to help them read in English (Jiminez, Garcia, and Pearson, 1996; Saville-Troike, 1984). However, parents who speak only Spanish in the home are more likely to be recent immigrants, live in disadvantaged communities, be unfamiliar with American cultural and educational practices, and have lower levels of education and less income. Taken together, this confluence of language, nativity, and environment creates obstacles for young children as they prepare to enter school.

Preschool Attendance

Most young children will attend some type of preschool program before entering kindergarten. Increasingly, scholars have pointed to the importance of having children attend preschool, arguing that it produces persistent gains on achievement tests and reduces the likelihood of grade retention and placement in remedial programs, especially for low-income children (Barnett and Camilli, 2002). Quality preschool and kindergarten experiences provide the basic foundation for children's later cognitive and social development (Elkind, 1981; Wadsworth, 1989). Specifically, for Hispanic children, preschool can serve as a mediator between home and school. By exposing children to English and by socializing them into academic and cultural norms, even early schooling can reinforce the importance of education for future job success (Currie and Thomas, 1996). Despite evidence showing the benefits of preschool attendance, Hispanic children are the least likely to be enrolled in preschool. In 1999, 60 percent of white children who were 3 years old attended preschool, whereas only 26 percent of Hispanic children had started their education at this age (U.S. Department of Education, 2003d, p. 23). Among Hispanic 4- and 5-year-olds, enrollment rates were slightly higher and more closely resemble those of white and black children: 64 percent of Hispanic 4-year-olds attended preschool, compared with 69 percent of white and 81 percent of black 4-year-olds; among 5-year-olds, 89 percent of Hispanic, 93 percent of white, and 99 percent of black children attended preschool. Black children, however, are significantly more likely to attend preschool than Hispanic children in all age groups.

Some positive changes in Hispanic attendance in preschool programs can be seen by looking at participation in Head Start, which is specifically designed to serve disadvantaged children and uses federal poverty guidelines as a key factor for assessing eligibility. In 1998, black children age 5 and under had an attendance rate that was almost 10 percent higher than eligible Hispanics. By 2003, however, black children had an attendance rate that was only about 1 percent higher than Hispanic children (see Table 6-1). The higher attendance rates of Hispanic children may be the result of more parents taking advantage of Head Start, or it may merely reflect increases in the numbers of Hispanic children eligible for the program.

Attending Head Start appears to be a positive experience for most Hispanic children. Currie and Thomas (1996) have shown that Hispanic children who are enrolled in Head Start perform slightly better on a series of cognitive tests than those who do not attend any preschool program. However, the effects of participating in Head Start differ across Hispanic subgroups. The advantages of attending Head Start are the greatest among children of Mexican origin; Puerto Rican children appear to reap fewer benefits, although they do perform better than those who attend other types

TABLE 6-1 Head Start Enrollment Trends for Children Age 5 and Under by Race/Ethnicity, 1998–2003

	Year					
Race/Ethnicity	1998 (%)	1999 (%)	2000 (%)	2001 (%)	2002 (%)	2003 (%)
Black	35.8	35.1	34.5	33.8	32.6	31.5
White	31.5	30.5	30.4	29.9	28.4	27.6
Hispanic	26.4	27.8	28.7	29.7	29.8	30.6
Asian	2.9	2.1	2.0	2.0	2.0	1.8
American Indian	3.4	3.4	3.3	3.6	2.9	3.2
Hawaiian/Pacific Islander	1.0	1.0	1.0	1.0	1.1	

SOURCE: Head Start Bureau Fact Sheets (2004).

of preschool programs. One explanation for this difference may be the poor quality of other available preschool programs (Currie and Thomas, 1996).[6] While attending Head Start programs appears to provide some benefits, lack of available quality preschool programs remains an obstacle for some Hispanic children. Currently, programs such as universal preschool are being implemented in several states, including California. However, critics of such programs argue that while state-funded preschool allows access to preschool to more children, it detracts from creating *quality* preschools (Olsen, 1999).

Risk Factors for Kindergartners

Limited success in early schooling can be traced to several family background characteristics. Specific factors, such as having a mother who did not complete high school (Bianchi and McArthur, 1993), living in a single-parent home (McLanahan and Sandefur, 1994), living in a low-income or welfare-dependent household (U.S. Department of Education, 1995a), and having parents who speak a language other than English in the home (Kao, 1999; Rumberger and Larson, 1998) place children at risk of not succeeding academically (Pallas, Natriello, and McDill, 1989). These broad indicators, several of which are interrelated, do not necessarily predict that a student is destined for school failure. However, students whose families have combinations of these factors are more likely to have diffi-

[6]In examining the benefits of Head Start attendance, the comparison group is siblings who either did not attend a preschool program or attended other types of preschool programs.

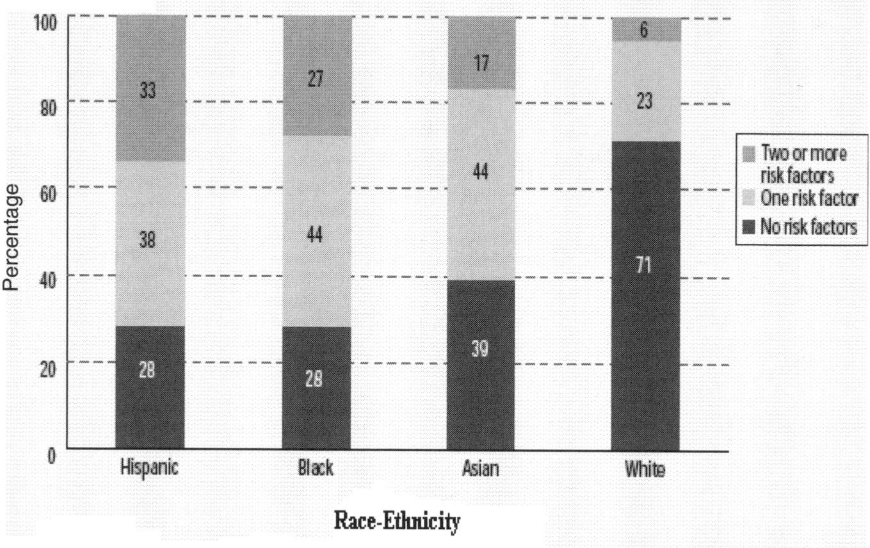

FIGURE 6-3 Percentage distribution of kindergartners by number of risk factors and race/ethnicity: Fall 1998.
NOTE: Percentage may not add to 100 due to rounding.
SOURCE: U.S. Department of Education (1998).

culty in school. Hispanic and black children entering kindergarten are disproportionately from families with one or more of these risk factors (see Figure 6-3). The proportion of children with two or more risk factors is five times larger among Hispanics (33 percent) and four times larger among blacks (27 percent) than among whites (6 percent) (U.S. Department of Education, 2001a).

To examine the risk factors for first-time kindergartners of different racial/ethnic backgrounds, several analytic models were constructed distinguishing among whites, blacks, Asians, and Hispanics (categorized by the language parents report is primarily spoken at home).[7] The three models, in Appendix Table A6-1, show that race/ethnicity is differentially associated with each risk factor, and that Hispanics who speak English at home face different risks than those who speak Spanish at home. Hispanics, especially those who speak Spanish at home, are much less likely than blacks to be in a single-parent family relative to whites. There is a strong sense of family among Hispanics that is reinforced by religion, perhaps making single parenthood less likely to occur. For example, only 47 percent of Hispanics who

[7]Appendix Table A6-1 presents three logistic regression models in which each of three risk factors serves as the dependent variable.

primarily speak Spanish find divorce acceptable, compared with 72 percent of the U.S. population as a whole (Pew Hispanic Center Survey Brief, 2004). However, as shown in Chapter 5, single parenting is now rising among Hispanic families; if this trend continues, it may place more Hispanic students at risk.

The picture changes, however, when examining the likelihood of having a mother who does not have a high school diploma or being raised in a low-income family. Hispanics are between two (those who speak English at home) and three times (those who speak Spanish at home) more likely to have a mother with low educational attainment compared with whites, even when other risk factors and socioeconomic status have been taken into account. In addition, Hispanic families in which the parents speak Spanish at home are more than twice as likely to be below the poverty threshold as non-Hispanic whites.[8] The risk factors seem to interact or be predictive of one another as well. Parents in Spanish-dominant families tend to be both less well educated and more likely to be poor. In general, these findings suggest that, although there are large numbers of Hispanics with two or more risk factors, the pattern of risk differs considerably for Hispanics who speak English at home and those who speak Spanish at home.[9]

As with literacy activities that occur prior to formal schooling, parental education and limited English proficiency play an important role in academic success when examining risk factors contributing to school performance. A parent's primary language has implications for how involved he or she can be in their child's education. Even a bilingual parent may have trouble with reading comprehension if he or she has not completed high school (Huerta-Macias, 2003; Zulmara and Necochea, 2003). Visiting the library or enrolling one's child in a preschool program requires knowledge of what is available, where it is located, and how to get there. The most economically advantaged parent still needs logistical and organizational support to enroll and transport their young child to a preschool program. Furthermore, with respect to formal schooling, if kindergarten is not required, then parents may not even receive information about available programs.[10]

---

[8]As expected, once other risk factors and socioeconomic status have been controlled, the coefficient for Hispanics drops significantly.

[9]Partial linear regressions (not shown) predicting the total number of risk factors were conducted for each racial/ethnic group to determine the additive effects of these risk factors. These regressions resulted in different patterns for these groups, confirming results presented in Appendix Table A6-1.

[10]Kindergarten is commonly regarded as the first step in the formal schooling process (Barnett, 1998), although in many states being enrolled in kindergarten is not mandatory (U.S. Department of Education, 2002d). Several states with a high proportion of Hispanic residents (California, New York, and Texas) do not have mandatory kindergarten enrollment (U.S. Department of Education, 1996a).

Most existing data do not indicate whether Hispanic children in preschool or formal school are taught in English or Spanish. However, because of the monolinguistic nature of the U.S. school system, encouraging English proficiency in students and parents at the earliest possible stage is likely to lead to a stronger foundation for school learning and later academic success. Parents with young children, especially those who are first-generation immigrants, are likely to benefit if their schools and communities worked together to provide parent literacy programs, translators at school-related activities, advice on how to assist children in homework or engage them in academic activities, before- and after-school child care, and community outreach programs.

ACADEMIC PERFORMANCE IN THE PRIMARY GRADES, MIDDLE SCHOOL, AND HIGH SCHOOL

By the time they enter kindergarten, Hispanic students for the most part already trail their classmates in reading and mathematics achievement. Results from a recent national study of kindergartners, the Early Childhood Longitudinal Study Kindergarten Class of 1998–1999 (ECLS–K), point to a problematic academic future for Hispanic children. Non-Hispanic white children were more likely to score in the highest quartile in reading, mathematics, and general knowledge than black or Hispanic children (U.S. Department of Education, 2000a). Examining early literacy skills, Asian and non-Hispanic white children were more likely to recognize letters, beginning sounds, ending sounds, and sight words than blacks or Hispanics (see Table 6-2). With the exception of American Indians, Hispanic children whose parents do not speak English at home were the least likely to have passing reading proficiency scores across all tasks.

Results for mathematics proficiency were similar to those for language proficiency (see Table 6-3). Hispanic students whose parents primarily speak Spanish at home were the least likely to have passing scores for number and shape recognition, relative size, ordinal sequence, and addition and subtraction. In this instance, passing rates were lower than those for American Indians in all categories. The academic achievement gap between Hispanics and other groups at the onset of schooling continues through the primary grades, suggesting that the effects of family background characteristics, including language, create an initial barrier that is difficult to overcome.

Primary Grades

Using ECLS data from kindergarten and first grade, Reardon and Galindo (2003) conducted a series of multivariate analyses that show substantial variation in mathematics achievement scores among Hispanic sub-

TABLE 6-2 Percentage of First-Time Kindergartners Passing Each Reading Proficiency Level, by Child's Race/Ethnicity, Fall 1998

Characteristic	Letter Recognition	Beginning Sounds	Ending Sounds	Sight Words
Child's race/ethnicity				
White, non-Hispanic	70.2	34.3	20.7	4.2
Black, non-Hispanic	61.7	20.4	11.8	2.3[a]
Asian	82.8	44.2	29.5	12.1
Hispanic, speak English at home	51.2	24.4	13.1	2.9[a]
Hispanic, speak Spanish at home	38.3[a]	15.3[a]	6.6[a]	1.4[a]
Hawaiian native/Pacific Islander	62.1	29.5	13.1	7.0[a]
American Indian/Alaska native	37.1	14.4	6.4	1.3[a]
More than one race, non-Hispanic	61.0	26.6	15.5	5.2

NOTES: Only students with complete assessments were included. Sixty percent of the Hispanic students who speak Spanish at home were assessed in Spanish.

[a]These numbers include students who scored below the cutoff on the Oral Language Development Scale.

SOURCE: U.S. Department of Education (1998).

TABLE 6-3 Percentage of First-Time Kindergartners Passing Each Mathematics Proficiency Level, by Child's Race/Ethnicity, Fall 1998

Characteristic	Number and Shape	Relative Size	Ordinal Sequence	Add/ Subtract
Child's race/ethnicity				
White, non-Hispanic	94.1	66.2	27.7	5.9
Black, non-Hispanic	88.1	45.7	9.8	1.2
Asian	95.6[a]	71.1	30.3	7.6
Hispanic, speak English at home	88.2	41.1	12.0	2.3
Hispanic, speak Spanish at home	74.8	22.6	4.0	0.7
Hawaiian native/Pacific Islander	92.4	52.3	14.2	1.7
American Indian/Alaska native	80.3	37.0	7.3	1.0
More than one race, non-Hispanic	90.5	55.5	18.6	4.0

NOTES: Only students with complete assessments were included. Sixty percent of the Hispanic students who speak Spanish at home were assessed in Spanish.

[a]This number represents variables with high percentages of missing or not-applicable data.

SOURCE: U.S. Department of Education (1998).

groups (see Figure 6-4). Cuban Americans are the most similar to non-Hispanic whites, with Mexican Americans and Central Americans scoring nearly one standard deviation below their white classmates. This trend persists over time: by the end of first grade, Cuban Americans catch up to whites while Puerto Ricans, Mexican Americans, and Central Americans fall further behind. The achievement gap in mathematics is especially troubling because both instruction and performance in mathematics tend not to be dependent on language, in contrast to reading. One might expect that academic performance would improve as English language proficiency increases. However, this does not appear to be the case.

In the next set of analyses, Reardon and Galindo (2003) examined mathematics performance from kindergarten to first grade among first-, second-, and third-generation Mexican Americans and non-Hispanic whites. First- and third-generation Mexican immigrant students started kindergarten with lower levels of math skills than second-generation students, and that pattern did not change over time (see Figure 6-5).

The language barrier seems to place first-generation immigrant students at a decided disadvantage compared with second-generation Mexican Americans and whites. What is surprising is that this performance gain by second-generation immigrants does not hold for those who are third gen-

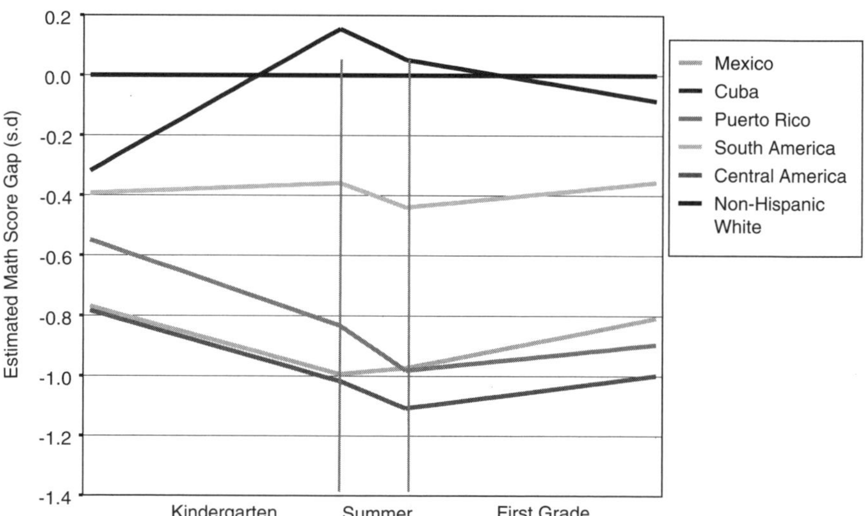

FIGURE 6-4 Hispanic mathematics achievement gap by country of origin, kindergarten and first grade.
SOURCE: U.S. Department of Education (1998).

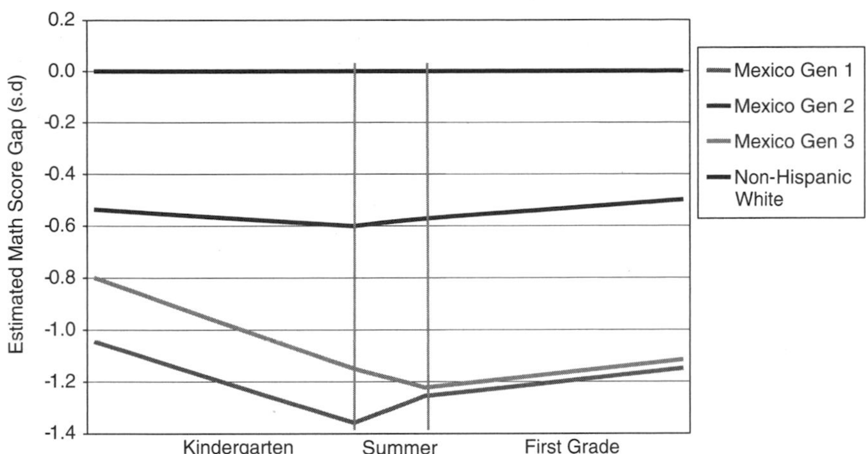

FIGURE 6-5 Hispanic mathematics achievement gap by generational status, kindergarten and first grade.
SOURCE: U.S. Department of Education (1998).

eration. One explanation may be that parents of second-generation students are motivated to succeed and instill those values in their children. The parents of third-generation students, particularly those who continue to speak only Spanish and who live in barrio communities with limited economic resources and poor schools, may become disillusioned with education as a path to social mobility and transmit these attitudes to their children.

Another problem may be teachers' perceptions of their students' abilities. Reardon and Galindo (2003) found that Hispanic students entering kindergarten were rated lower than white students by their teachers, regardless of their academic ability. In the ECLS kindergarten survey, teachers were asked to rate the math and literacy readiness and proficiency of each of the students in the sample in math and literacy skills. Each student was also tested in mathematics and reading by a trained ECLS assessor. Reardon and Galindo (2003) conducted a series of multivariate analyses to look for evidence of teacher bias. Given students of equal ability from the same classroom, they estimated the extent to which the teachers rated Hispanic students lower than non-Hispanic whites. Table 6-4 shows, that, in the fall of the kindergarten year, the Hispanic students were rated, on average, more than one-eighth of a standard deviation below the non-Hispanic white students. This rating gap was reduced by one-half to two-thirds by the spring of the kindergarten year and completely disappeared by the spring of first grade.

TABLE 6-4 Average Difference in Standardized Teachers' Ratings of Hispanic and Non-Hispanic White Students in the Same Classroom, by Subject and Grade

	Subject	
Classroom	Math	Reading
Fall kindergarten	–0.129***	–0.146***
Spring kindergarten	–0.084***	–0.074*
Spring first grade	-0.049^{ns}	-0.006^{ns}

NOTE: ns = not significant. Sample includes all Hispanic and non-Hispanic white students who had both teacher ratings and test scores at each wave. Reading sample includes only students who passed the English Oral Language Development Scale Assessment in the fall of kindergarten. Models include controls for test scores, age, kindergarten repeat status, classroom Hispanic composition, average classroom test scores, and teacher's ethnicity.

*p < .05
***p < .001

It appears that some teachers base their initial ratings of students, in part, on the student's ethnicity. This teacher bias is reduced as teachers come to know students better over time, explaining the substantial initial rating gap and its decline over kindergarten and first grade. Furthermore, it is possible that this bias acts as a self-fulfilling prophecy, so that students' test scores come to more closely match their teachers' ratings over time. This could be the result of subtle or overt differences in instructional practices directed toward Hispanic students who are rated lower than their white classmates. Another possible explanation is that the teacher ratings are unbiased measures of some aspect of mathematics and reading skills that is not measured by the tests, but on which non-Hispanic white students rate higher than Hispanic students.[11] Whatever the explanation for the closer match between student performance and teacher ratings over time, the initial gap in teacher assessment between white and Hispanic students does point to teacher bias. Such bias at the onset of formal schooling sets the stage for lower expectations and underperformance by Hispanic students.

[11]The size of the rating gap when the teacher is Hispanic was examined, but no differences were found. However, it was discovered that teachers rated all students lower, on average, in classrooms with larger percentages of Hispanic students. Since the composition of the student body is correlated with other factors, however, it is not clear what to make of this.

Persisting Problem

The initial achievement gap between Hispanic and white students persists throughout middle school and high school. Tracing the academic performance of Hispanic students over the past 20 years using trend data from the National Assessment of Educational Progress (NAEP) shows that Hispanic students continue to lag behind non-Hispanic whites (U.S. Department of Education, 2003d). Figure 6-6 indicates that for fourth, eighth, and twelfth graders, differences in average reading scores between Hispanic and non-Hispanic white students are evident, and this pattern is consistent across Hispanic subgroups.

In 2002, Hispanic fourth graders scored close to 30 points lower than their white classmates in reading (see Figure 6-6). Although there have been some fluctuations in the scores of Hispanics and non-Hispanic whites, a 30-point differential after several decades of school reform is clearly problematic. The situation for eighth-grade students closely resembles that for fourth graders. By twelfth grade, Hispanic students have closed the gap somewhat, with Hispanics scoring an average of 18 points lower than whites. However, since Hispanics have a higher dropout rate, these averages are probably inflated because they reflect only the scores of more promising students who have stayed in school through twelfth grade. Compared with black students, Hispanic students are doing slightly better at all three grade levels, although the differences are small. The lower test scores of blacks and Hispanics suggest that low socioeconomic status may play a role in creating this achievement gap.[12]

When Hispanic reading scores are examined by subgroup, Mexican Americans and Puerto Ricans tend to score the lowest. This is cause for concern, because Mexican American immigrants are the largest and fastest growing minority group among young elementary school students. Assuming there is no immediate and effective intervention strategy to improve their reading skills, it is reasonable to expect that by eighth grade, these students' levels of achievement will continue to be low, which may contribute to their higher dropout rates.[13]

[12]NAEP data do not include a measure of socioeconomic status or income. While the surveys do include variables assessing resources in the home and a measure of urbanicity, parent education and income are not measured. The urbanicity variable is difficult to analyze because it defines urbanicity in terms of being in a large city, midsize city, fringe of a large city, fringe of a midsize city, large town, small town, or rural with no census data available. Zip codes for respondents are not available for the 1990s, making linking the data sets used in this paper to census data difficult.

[13]When Hispanic respondents are analyzed according to their immigrant status and language spoken in the home, there are no significant differences between first- and second-generation immigrants for both math and reading scores (analyses not shown). Because iden-

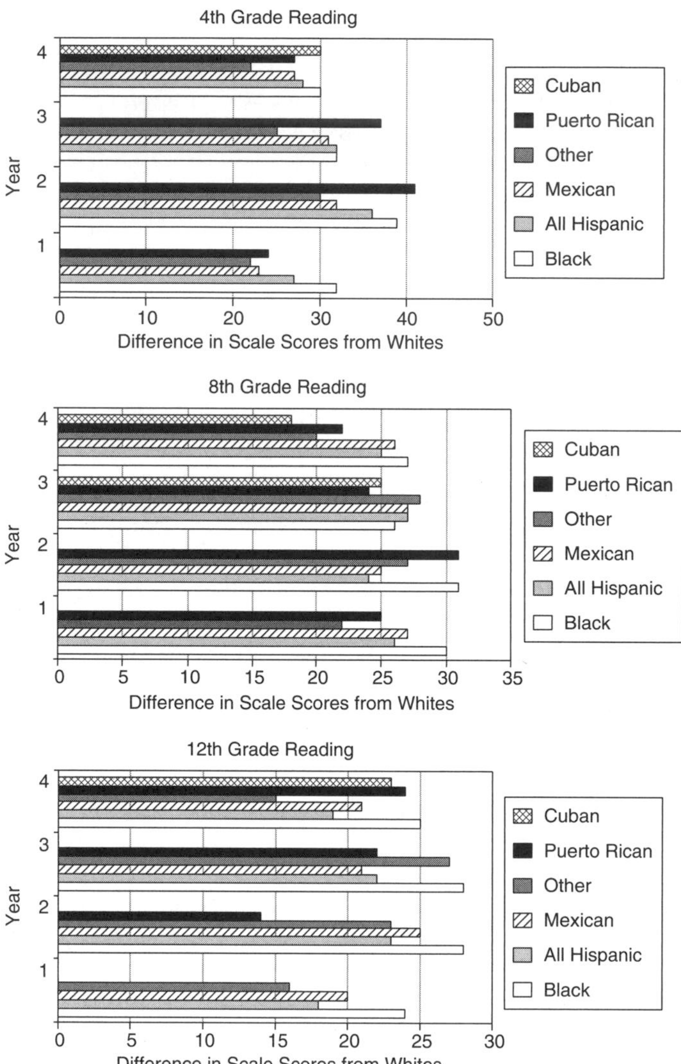

FIGURE 6-6 Differences between white, non-Hispanic, and minority students' average NAEP reading scale scores, by age: Selected years, 1992–2002.

NOTES: Year 1 = 1992, Year 2 = 1994, Year 3 = 1998, Year 4 = 2002. The scale scores reported are plausible value scores, imputed by random draws from respondents' scores. Data for fourth- and twelfth-grade Cuban respondents were not available until 2002; data for eighth-grade Cuban respondents were not available until 1998. Data for Puerto Rican twelfth-grade respondents were not available until 1994.

SOURCE: U.S. Department of Education (2003e).

The mathematics achievement gap between Hispanics and non-Hispanic whites is similar to that for reading scores (see Figure 6-7). Across all grades, Hispanic students scored higher than blacks, but lower than whites, in mathematics. For twelfth graders, the gap between Hispanic and non-Hispanic white students is smaller than in earlier grades, most likely because Hispanic students with poor academic records and low test scores tend to leave school before twelfth grade.

In looking at NAEP data over time, it appears that Hispanic children have been making achievement gains, but so have other groups, including whites; thus the achievement gap is not narrowing (Pew Hispanic Center Fact Sheet, 2004b). In the 1990s, even though Hispanic scores in reading and mathematics increased overall, the achievement gap actually increased, suggesting that this gap will widen by the time this cohort of students reaches twelfth grade. Overall, achievement results from kindergarten through twelfth grade show differences in test scores among Hispanic subgroups and across generations. However, not all data sets include sufficient information on generational status or Hispanic subgroups to identify interventions that would be most effective for different groups. Better national longitudinal data must be collected that distinguishes between Hispanic subgroups, English as a second language (ESL) versus non-ESL curricula, and immigrant status. Data should also be collected on the types of students who drop out between eighth and twelfth grade. Nonetheless, even these broad indicators point to the need for immediate academic interventions at the primary and middle school levels.

Elementary and Middle School Contexts

As illustrated by growing gaps in achievement from fourth to eighth grade, school characteristics can play a role in student achievement, especially during middle school, when students form attachments to their teachers and schools.[14] Fostering attachment and a sense of belonging is particularly problematic in large school environments. Hispanics are the most likely to be enrolled in large schools with large class sizes, and these schools are also more likely to be underfunded and deficient in resources.[15] The

---

tifying Hispanics by country of origin is a more recent practice, trend data are unavailable for comparison before 1990.

[14]Resources include such factors as teacher quality, quality of school infrastructure, safety measures, and library and computer resources.

[15]The availability of computers at school is another resource that appears disproportionately denied to Hispanics and blacks compared with whites. Computers are an essential learning tool and are increasingly being used for instructional and assessment purposes. Hispanics and blacks are less likely than non-Hispanic whites to have access to a computer at

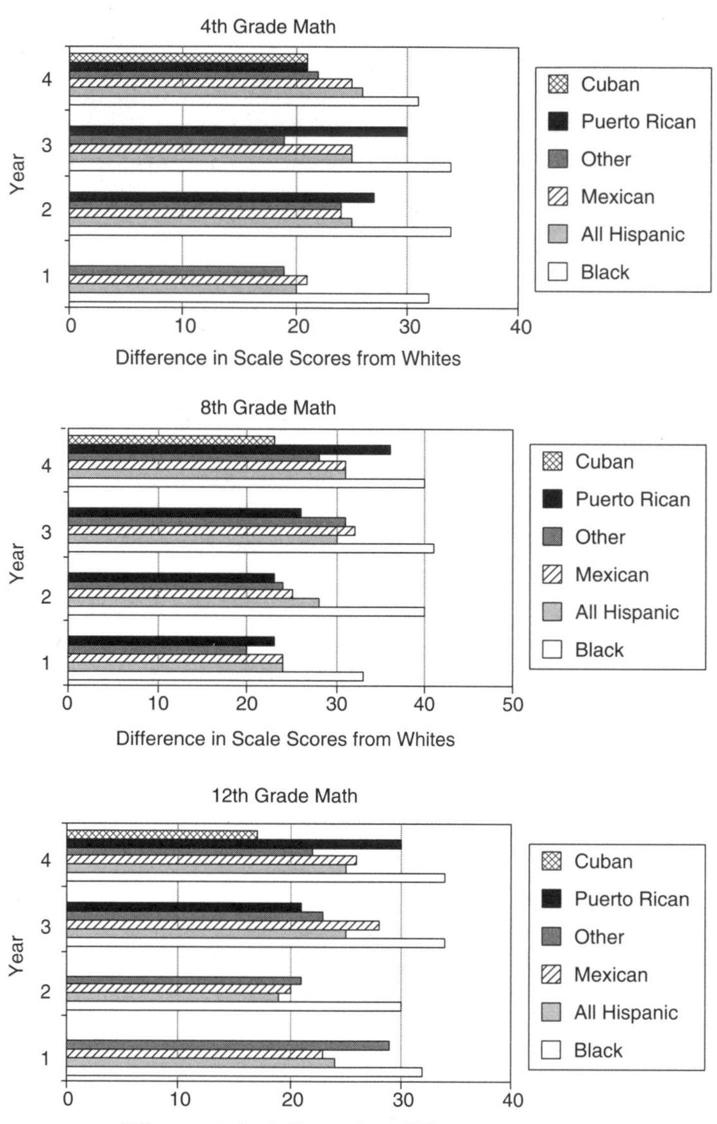

FIGURE 6-7 Differences between white, non-Hispanic, and minority students' average NAEP mathematics scale scores by age: selected years 1990 to 2000.
NOTES: Year 1=1990, Year 2=1992, Year 3=1996, Year 4=2000. Data for Cuban respondents were not available until 2000. Data for Puerto Rican fourth-grade respondents were not available until 1992; Puerto Rican twelfth-grade respondents were not available until 1996.
SOURCE: U.S. Department of Education (2003e).

majority of Hispanic students at both the elementary and secondary levels attend urban schools that are above average in size (U.S. Department of Education, 1996b). Hispanics comprise one-quarter of the student population in central-city schools (ERIC Clearinghouse on Urban Education, 2001).[16] Compared with other groups, Hispanic students disproportionately attend schools with the highest levels of poverty, as measured by the proportion of students who qualify for a free or reduced price lunch, and are enrolled in the most highly segregated schools (Orfield and Yun, 1999). Approximately 75 percent of Hispanic students attend schools with over 50 percent minority student populations, and a little over 35 percent of Hispanic students attend schools with over 90 percent minority student populations (Orfield and Yun, 1999).

Hispanics are also more likely to be in schools with inexperienced or noncertified teachers (U.S. Department of Education, 2003a; Valencia, 2002). Public and private schools with the highest percentages of minority and limited-English proficient students are more likely to employ beginning teachers than schools with lower percentages of minority limited-English proficient students, thus virtually ensuring that a high proportion of Hispanic youth, who most need experienced teachers, are taught by less-qualified instructors. Furthermore, these schools often have too few bilingual teachers certified in ESL (Hacsi, 2002; U.S. Department of Education, 1996b). The quality of bilingual programs also varies across schools and districts and may in some instances interfere with, rather than enhance, students' ability to master both Spanish and English.

Finally, many urban schools have very few Hispanic teachers compared with the number of Hispanic students they instruct: only 4 percent of public school teachers are Hispanic, whereas Hispanic students at the elementary school level constitute about 15 percent of the student body nationally (U.S. Department of Education, 1997). This sometimes makes it difficult for Hispanic students to identify with teachers and view them as role models. By sharing a cultural identity with their teachers, Hispanic students might benefit by seeing someone from their own cultural background succeed. Having a teacher who is sensitive to cultural differences may also help

---

school: 68 percent of Hispanics report using a computer at school compared with 70 percent of blacks and 84 percent of whites. In addition, only 18 percent of Hispanics and 19 percent of blacks report using a computer at home compared with 52 percent of whites (ERIC Clearinghouse on Urban Education, 2001). One of the reasons that the computer disadvantage is so important is that the most recent advanced placement tests are being given on the computer. It is expected that most college admission tests will also be administered by computer.

[16]The majority of Hispanic students attend public schools, although the fastest growing population among private religious/Catholic elementary and secondary schools are Hispanics (McDonald, 2003).

students feel more engaged and less alienated (Graham, 1987; Valencia and Aburto, 1991). Therefore, it is important for schools serving Hispanic students to recruit more Hispanic principals and teachers to act as role models. Some strategies for recruiting minority students into the teaching profession have been recommended, for example, a forgiveness loan program in which minority students who pursue teaching need not repay student loans, credentialing of experienced minority teacher aides, and early identification and recruitment of minority students (Valencia and Aburto, 1991).

Teacher–Student Interactions

One of the most important findings of the 1980s was the recognition of the significance of the middle school experience and its lasting effects on students' schooling careers (Carnegie Council on Adolescent Development, 1989). The experiences Hispanics have in middle school often follow them through high school, creating obstacles for future schooling success. Specifically, it appears that teacher interactions and the less than optimal school contexts that Hispanic students encounter in middle school contribute to their academic and social difficulties in later years.

Finn (1989) claims that school success depends on students' sense of a close connection with their schools. Students who identify with their schools have an internalized sense of belonging; that is, they feel they are a part of the school community and that school constitutes an important aspect of their own experience. Students who feel this way are more likely to value and pursue academic or school-relevant goals and thus are more likely to participate in the classroom (Finn, 1989). In studying student–teacher relationships, Payne (1994) and Valenzuela (1999) have found that negative attitudes or teacher stereotypes of minority students may weaken bonds necessary for learning. These findings indicate that success in the classroom depends on students' ability to accept their teacher as a credible source of information. Students have to believe that the teacher respects and cares about their well-being. When this bond is not established or fully developed, students resist teachers both personally and academically, become detached from school, and consequently are less likely to succeed in school. The ability to form these types of bonds with minority students is particularly difficult for white middle-class teachers working in urban schools (Buriel, 1983; Katz, 1999; Rosenbloom and Way, 2004). Payne (1994) found that when these teachers avoid or reject negative attitudes and stereotypes, they are able to offer minority students the respect and high expectations that facilitate academic success. Prior research indicates that when minority students are aware of negative stereotypes regarding their academic ability, "stereotype threat" is activated. This heightened awareness of negative stereotypes may cause Hispanics to underperform, particularly on aptitude or cognitive ability tests, and score lower than white students (McKown and Weinstein, 2003; Steele and Aronson, 1995).

Teachers and administrators who lack an understanding of cultural differences can also hinder the academic success of Hispanics by misassigning bilingual students to remedial programs. This inaccurate assessment of student abilities has more recently been found even among kindergarten students, whose teachers tend to underestimate the literacy skills among Hispanic kindergarteners (Reardon and Galindo, 2003). When teachers or administrators use lack of English proficiency to signal special needs, language-minority students are overrepresented in special education classes, in which academic performance is underemphasized in favor of social adjustment (Schmid, 2001).

Bryk and Schneider (2002) found that many teachers, particularly those working in urban schools, do not know their students well and lack an empathetic understanding of their situations or the interpersonal skills to engage them—conditions that are necessary for a trusting relationship to evolve and be sustained. Martinez (2003) found that Mexican Americans more than other students feel better when they are not with their teachers. Data from 625 students who participated in the Alfred P. Sloan Study of Youth and Social Development, a longitudinal study of how young people form ideas about postsecondary school and work, show that when Mexican American students are not with their teachers, they are happier and more excited, feel better about themselves, and believe that they are living up to their own expectations (Csikszentmihalyi and Schneider, 2000). In addition, when in the company of a teacher, Mexican American students also are more likely to believe that teachers have more unfavorable thoughts about them than about other racial/ethnic groups. In contrast, when white students are with their teachers, they report feeling that they are meeting their own expectations, are relaxed and challenged, and indicate that what they are doing is important to their future goals. Like Mexican American students, black students feel happier and more relaxed when not with their teachers. Black students, however, experience higher levels of challenge when they are with teachers, much like white students.

Weak relational ties between Hispanic students and their teachers may diminish motivation or engagement in academic work, which in turn can undermine academic achievement. When weak relational ties exist between students and teachers, students may feel that teachers have low expectations of them or do not care about them, which can be highly discouraging and cause Hispanic students to disengage from classroom activities or ultimately withdraw. When disengaged in the classroom, Hispanic students are less likely to see the relevance of what is being taught to their future schooling or careers. It seems particularly important for Hispanic students to have teachers who have high expectations for their academic performance, strengthen personal ties between themselves and their students, and point out the relevance of schoolwork to future opportunities in both school and the labor market.

Transitioning into High School

Moving from middle school to high school is a challenging and uncertain process for many students, even under optimal circumstances (Schiller, 1995). This transition is especially problematic for Hispanics and blacks living in urban areas. These students are more likely than Asians and whites to be uncertain about what high school they will attend and seem to have the most difficulty adjusting to a new school. Based on these findings, Schiller (1995) concludes that Hispanics and blacks require assistance in making the transition from middle school to high school. Not only do they require social and psychological support, but they especially need early guidance about the consequences of taking specific courses for postsecondary school options.

One school organizational factor that is strongly related to academic performance is curricular differentiation, that is, how students are sorted into different ability groups and courses (Hallinan, 1994; Smith, 1995; Stevenson, Schiller, and Schneider, 1994). The course selection process, especially in the eighth grade, affects standardized test scores and college attendance and completion (Schneider and Stevenson, 1999; Stevenson et al., 1994). For example, unlike English and social studies, the mathematics curriculum becomes sharply differentiated beginning in middle school (Usiskin, 1987). Students given instruction in algebra rather than general mathematics in eighth grade are at an advantage as they can take more advanced courses in high school and move through the high school mathematics curriculum more quickly. Smith (1995) also finds that students who took algebra in eighth grade had higher mathematics achievement scores and expressed higher educational aspirations in the tenth grade. That Hispanic students are less likely than Asians, whites, and blacks to take algebra in the eighth grade greatly limits their future curricular options (U.S. Department of Education, 1990).

Before eighth graders enter high school, they are given the opportunity to select a specific curricular program from several different options, commonly labeled college preparatory, general or comprehensive, and vocational. These programmatic choices are not benign with respect to students' schooling careers and academic achievement. Data from High School and Beyond and the National Education Longitudinal Study of 1988–2000 (NELS: 88-2000) have linked high school curricular placement to achievement, educational expectations, and occupational aspirations (Gamoran and Mare, 1989; Oakes, Gamoran, and Page, 1992; Schneider and

Stevenson, 1999). By spring of eighth grade, only 23 percent of Hispanic students plan to enroll in a college preparatory curriculum, compared with 25 percent of blacks, 31 percent of whites, and 37 percent of Asian Americans (U.S. Department of Education, 1990). However, Hispanics also comprise 29 percent of eighth graders who are unsure about their high school curriculum program.

Part of the uncertainty Hispanic students and their parents feel about educational practices can be traced to parents' limited experiences with the U.S. education system and the trust they place in the authority and knowledge of teachers. Mexican American immigrant parents are particularly vulnerable and more likely to defer to teachers and administrators, rarely questioning their decisions (Bryk and Schneider, 2002). Curricular counseling for college, especially for recent immigrants who may be unfamiliar with the complexities of the U.S. education system, must begin before high school. For this reason, providing Hispanic eighth graders early and more detailed information about which curricular programs lead to college admission would greatly assist many students in making choices that promote higher levels of educational attainment.

High School Course Selection

Schools play a critical role in influencing what courses students will take by deciding what courses will be offered, establishing procedures for admission to particular courses, and creating a climate whereby teachers and counselors are encouraged to adopt a selective or universal approach to student counseling and academic planning. Taking specific course sequences has certain educational advantages. For example, students who successfully complete courses in algebra, geometry, and trigonometry are much more likely to take the next advanced level of mathematics than their classmates who take other course sequences. In certain subjects, such as mathematics, students are typically not allowed to take advanced courses out of sequence. This makes it difficult for students to take a high-level course if they lack the necessary prerequisites. Courses taken in high school better predict who attends college than family background, school characteristics, or educational expectations. Course selection decisions are in turn more influenced by student academic ability and prior achievement than by family background characteristics, such as parents' educational attainment (Stevenson et al., 1994).

Hispanic students are less likely than white students to complete advanced mathematics; they are also less likely than both white and black students to take certain advanced science courses. Table 6-5 shows that Hispanics are about 20 percent less likely than whites to take advanced course work in mathematics. The low numbers of Hispanics taking ad-

TABLE 6-5 Percentage Distribution of High School Graduates, by Highest Levels of Mathematics Courses Completed and Race/Ethnicity, 1998

Race/Ethnicity	No Mathematics[a]	Nonacademic[b]	Low Academic[c]	Middle Academic[d]	Advanced Academic[e]
Total	0.8	3.6	5.3	48.9	41.4
White, non-Hispanic	0.8	3.2	4.6	46.3	45.1
Black, non-Hispanic	0.9	3.6	8.3	56.8	30.4
Hispanic	0.9	6.3	7.5	59.1	26.2
Asian/Pacific Islander	0.2	2.8	2.6	38.8	55.5
American Indian/Alaska native	0.7	8.6	6.3	57.4	26.9

NOTE: Students classified at any particular level need not have taken courses at a lower level and may have taken more than one course at that level. For more detailed descriptions of these categories, please see supplement note 5 in the Condition of Education (2002). Detail may not add to 100.0 due to rounding.

[a]Students in this category may have taken some mathematics courses, but these courses are not defined as mathematics courses according to the classification used in this analysis.

[b]Students who took general mathematics or basic skills mathematics courses.

[c]Students who took algebra taught over the course of 2 years, prealgebra, or informal geometry.

[d]Students who took algebra I or unified mathematics I and took 3 full-year courses of mathematics (e.g., algebra I, algebra II, and geometry).

[e]Students who took precalculus, calculus, or other courses labeled as "advanced" such as trigonometry.

SOURCE: U.S. Department of Education (2002c).

vanced mathematics courses are of serious concern because advanced mathematics course-taking, more than any other subject, appears to have the strongest relationship to whether a student matriculates to a two-year or a four-year college (Riegle-Crumb, 2003).

Several subjects, including mathematics, are often offered as advanced placement (AP) courses. Students who enroll in AP classes may elect to take an examination in that subject, and if they score above a designated threshold, can earn college credit for that course. Minority students, with the exception of Asian Americans, are less likely than white students to take AP examinations (see Table 6-6). While the proportion of Hispanic test takers increased after 1997, only 9 percent of AP test takers in 2002 were Hispanic, half of whom were Mexican American (see Table 6-6). The increase among Hispanic twelfth graders taking AP exams appears to be driven mainly by the population growth of Hispanics, especially Mexican Americans, in the United States who are now staying in high school through twelfth grade. In 1997, 10 percent of all twelfth graders were Hispanic; by 2001, 12 percent of the twelfth-grade population was Hispanic (Common Core of Data, the Department of Education's database on public elementary and secondary U.S. schools, which contains basic information and descriptive statistics on schools, school districts, students, staff, and fiscal data).

Perhaps one of the most significant indicators of preparedness for college is one's score on college entrance examinations such as the ACT and

TABLE 6-6 Proportion of Twelfth-Grade Students Who Took Advanced Placement Examinations by Race/Ethnicity, 1997, 2001, 2002

Ethnic Group	1997 (%)	2001 (%)	2002 (%)
Not stated	6.4	2.2	2.3
American Indian/Alaskan native	0.5	0.4	0.4
Asian/Asian American	10.6	10.9	10.9
Black/African American	4.6	5.2	5.2
Hispanic/Latino	7.6	9.2	9.4
Chicano/Mexican American	3.6	4.7	4.8
Puerto Rican	0.7	0.7	0.7
Other Hispanic/Latino	3.2	3.8	3.9
White	67.7	68.7	68.6
Other	2.6	3.3	3.1
Total students	301,047	407,572	440,916

SOURCE: College Board (2004).

SAT, which measure students' verbal, mathematical, and analytic skills. Over the past decade the number of minority students taking the SAT has risen dramatically. Hispanics accounted for 9 percent of the SAT-taking population in 2001 (U.S. Department of Education, 2003d, p. 62; see Table 6-7); however, they constituted 14 percent of the U.S. high school population enrolled as juniors or seniors (U.S. Census Bureau, 2001b).

With respect to SAT performance, Hispanics, although scoring higher than blacks, continue to lag behind whites and Asians on the SAT in both the math and verbal components of the exam (see Figure 6-8). Low test scores coupled with fewer college preparatory courses decrease the chance that Hispanics will be accepted into highly selective colleges.

Hispanic students are the least likely group to take college entrance examinations and to apply to college (Fry, 2004). To further explore the relationship between race/ethnicity and academic preparation, particularly among Hispanics, a series of analyses predicting the likelihood of taking advanced course sequences and college admission tests was conducted with data from the second follow-up of NELS: 88-2000. Figure 6-9 shows the probabilities that a student will take an advanced math course (e.g., trigonometry or above), an advanced science course (e.g., physics, advanced biology, or chemistry), or the SAT by the end of high school. These prob-

TABLE 6-7 Percentage Distribution of Students Who Took the Scholastic Assessment Test (SAT), by Race/Ethnicity, 1991 and 2001

	% Distribution of Students Who Took the SAT	
Race/Ethnicity	1991	2001
Total	100	100
White	72	66
Black	10	11
Hispanic	7	9
Mexican American	3	4
Puerto Rican	1	1
Other Hispanic/Latino	3	4
Asian/Pacific Islander	8	10
American Indian/Alaskan native	1	1
Other	2	4

NOTE: Detail may not add to 100 due to rounding.
SOURCE: College Board (2002).

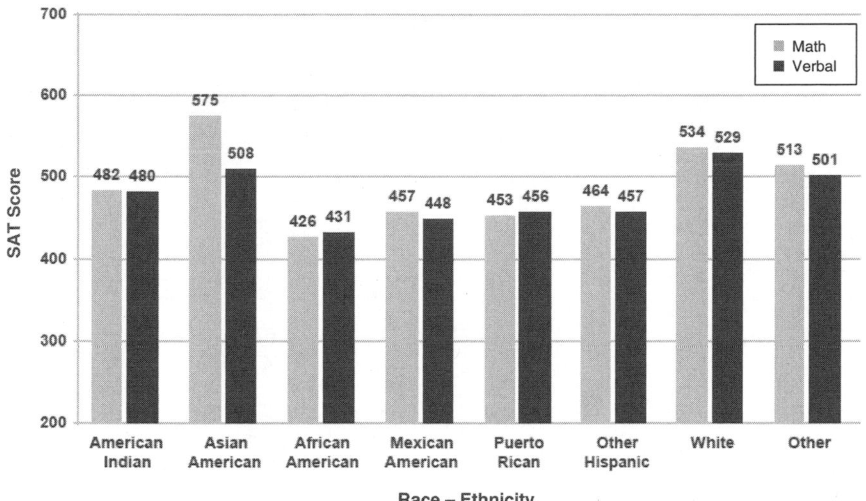

FIGURE 6-8 Average scholastic assessment test (SAT) scores (verbal and math) for college-bound seniors, by race/ethnicity, 2003.
SOURCE: College Board (2003).

abilities are estimated taking into account racial/ethnic background and language spoken in the home. When background characteristics are not accounted for, there are pronounced differences between groups with respect to academic preparation, with Hispanics among the least likely to be engaged in college preparatory activities.[17] Once background characteristics are taken into account, Hispanics who are bilingual are more likely than whites to take advanced courses and the SAT (see Figure 6-9). Bilingual students have the advantage of having parents who are proficient in both English and Spanish and who are thus able to bridge cultural and language barriers to secure educational opportunities for their children (see Kim and Schneider, 2004).

The next set of analyses shows the probability of attending a four-year

[17]Appendix Figure A6-1 shows the individual effects of family and student characteristics on the likelihood of taking advanced math and science courses and taking the SAT. The gap between whites and Hispanics for whom English is not spoken in the home is largest in Model 3, in which having a traditional mother–father family is taken into account. The most equalizing variable is prior academic achievement, as measured by eighth-grade math and reading scores (see Model 8). This finding suggests that Hispanics who do well academically early in their schooling careers are more likely to succeed in high school and to prepare for college.

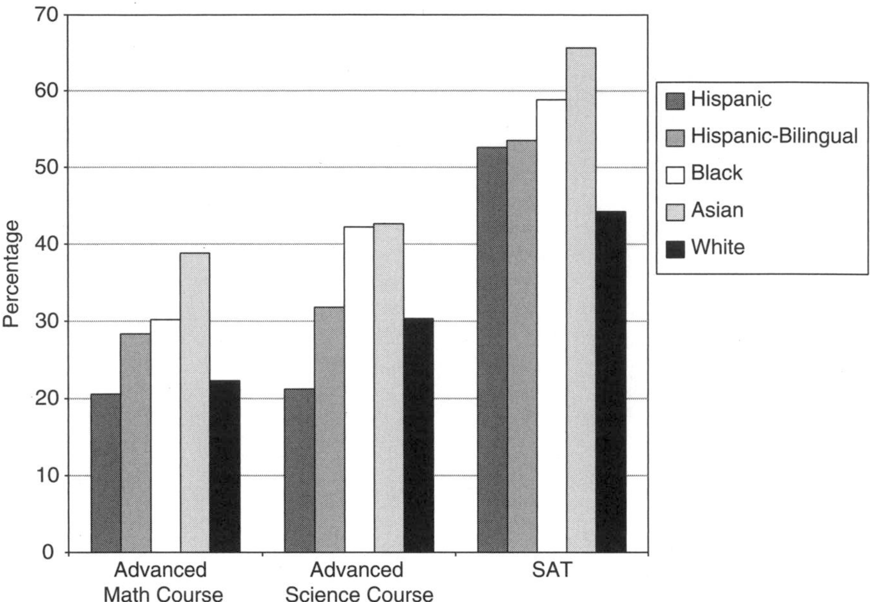

FIGURE 6-9 Probability of taking advanced math courses, advanced science courses, and the SAT by the end of high school by race/ethnicity, controlling for various family and student characteristics.
NOTES: Probabilities are based on equations from logistic regression models. The imputation program AMELIA was used for missing values. Figure is based on models in which all family and student characteristics are included as controlled (see Appendix Figure A6-1 for list of control variables).
SOURCE: U.S. Department of Education, National Center for Education Statistics, National Education Longitudinal Study of 1988–2000 (NELS: 88-2000), Second Follow-Up, 1992, restricted-use data (with imputed values).

college for all racial/ethnic groups, taking into account academic course preparation and having taken the SAT. Figure 6-10 shows that the probability of matriculating to a four-year college is higher among students who have taken the SAT and advanced coursework in mathematics and science compared with those who are not so prepared. The second panel predicts the probability of attending a four-year versus a two-year college by academic preparation and race/ethnicity. The likelihood that Hispanics and whites will attend a four-year college increases by about 30 percentage points when academic preparation is taken into account. Hispanics from Spanish-speaking families are nearly as likely as blacks to attend four-year colleges when they have high levels of academic preparation. Highly pre-

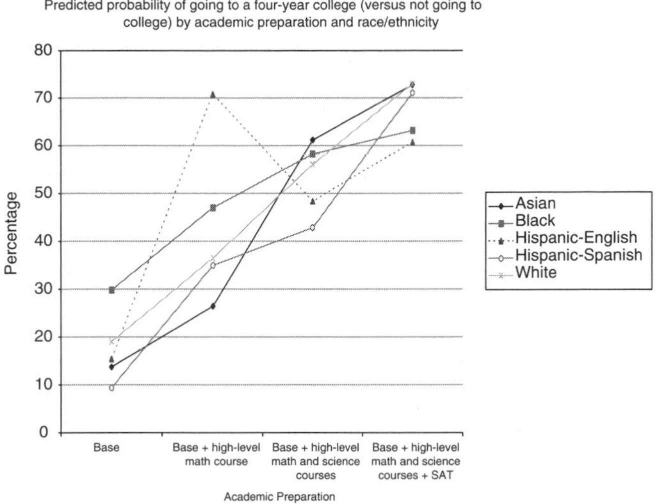

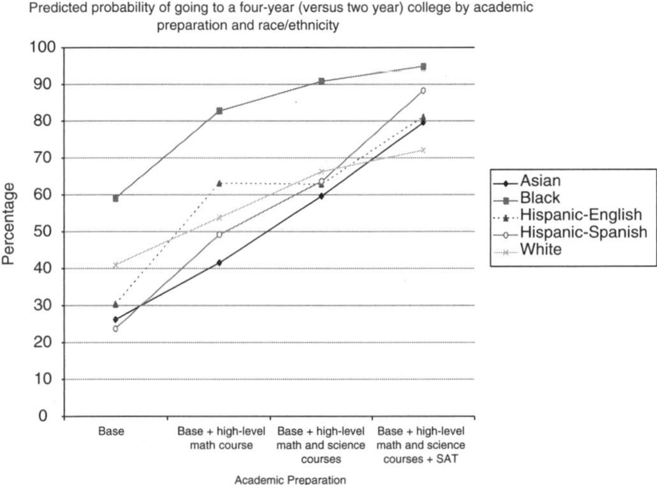

FIGURE 6-10 Predicted probabilities (in percentages) of going to a four-year college versus a two-year college or not going to college by academic preparation (advanced math course, advanced science course, and taking the SAT) and race/ethnicity.

NOTES: Probabilities are based on logistic regression models. The imputation program AMELIA was used for missing values. All models include control variables listed in Appendix Figure A6-1. Additionally, the interactions of each race/ethnic group and course sequences have been included as controls.

SOURCE: U.S. Department of Education, National Center for Education Statistics, National Education Longitudinal Study of 1988–2000 (NELS: 88-2000), Second Follow-up 1992, restricted-use data (with imputed data).

pared Hispanics are even more likely than comparable whites to attend a four-year versus a two-year college. These analyses suggest that one reason why Hispanics are more likely to matriculate to two-year rather than four-year colleges is poor academic preparation. Therefore, for Hispanics, especially those who are first-generation college-goers, it is imperative that schools offer programs explaining the importance of college preparatory curricula, SAT preparation, and advanced course-taking.

High School Noncompleters

Despite high educational expectations, Hispanics have the highest high school dropout rate (28 percent in 2000) compared with blacks and whites (U.S. Department of Education, 2000b). While the percentage of 16- to 24-year-old Hispanics without a high school diploma has decreased over the past 30 years, the status dropout rate of Hispanics is still more than double the rate of both whites and blacks (see Figure 6-11).[18]

However, this status dropout rate is inflated by recent increases in teenage Hispanic immigrants who never enroll in U.S. schools (Fry, 2003). Hirschman (2001) estimates that almost half of Mexican 15- to 17-year-olds who arrived in the United States between 1987 and 1990 did not enroll in school. These numbers are considerable, especially when compared with the dropout rates of Mexican Americans born in the United States. In 2001, 43.1 percent of foreign-born Hispanics did not complete high school compared with only 15 percent of U.S.-born Hispanic students (U.S. Department of Education, 2004a).

Figure 6-12 displays the differences between the dropout rates of foreign- and U.S.-born Hispanics. Rates for foreign-born Hispanics are double those of their U.S.-born counterparts, with the exception of South Americans. The dropout rate among U.S.-born Hispanics decreased from 1990 to 2000; however, the dropout rate among this group (14 percent) is still higher than that of blacks or whites (12 and 8 percent, respectively; Fry, 2003). One positive finding is that immigrant children who do enroll in high school are not more likely to drop out than U.S.-born students (Pew Hispanic Center Fact Sheet, 2004a).

Some students may temporarily "stop out" of high school and later return to receive their degree through alternative programs or by earning

---

[18]The dropout rate reported by the U.S. Census Bureau, reported in the table above, is the "status dropout rate." This rate measures the proportion of the population who has not completed high school and are not enrolled, regardless of when they dropped out. It includes immigrants who were never enrolled in the United States (Hispanic Dropout Project Databook, 1998).

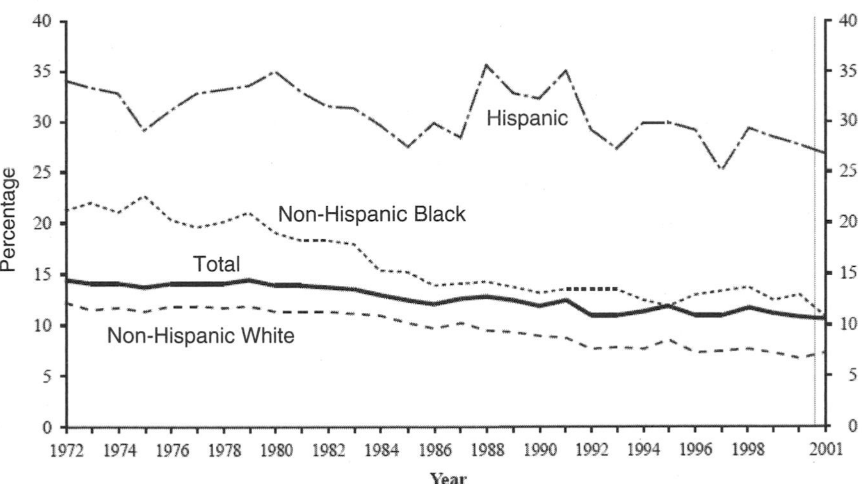

FIGURE 6-11 Status dropout rates of 16- through 24-year-olds, by race/ethnicity: October 1972 through October 2001.
NOTES: Due to small sample size, American Indians/Alaska natives and Asians/Pacific Islanders are included in the totals but are not shown separately. In addition, the erratic nature of the Hispanic status rates reflects, in part, the small sample size of Hispanics in the Current Population Survey. Numbers for years 1987 through 2001 reflect new editing procedures instituted by the U.S. Census Bureau for cases with missing data on school enrollment items. Numbers for years 1992 through 2001 reflect new wording of the educational attainment item in the Current Population Survey beginning in 1992. Numbers for years 1994 through 2001 reflect changes in the Current Population Survey due to newly instituted computer-assisted interviewing and the change in population controls used in the 1990 Census-based estimates, with adjustment for understanding in the 1990 Census. See Appendix C of the source document for a fuller description of the impact of these changes on reported rates.
SOURCE: U.S. Department of Commerce, Census Bureau, Current Population Survey, October 1972–2001.

general educational development (GED) certification. In 2001, the national high school completion rate for Hispanics was 64 percent, compared with 92 percent for whites. Such low completion rates are typical of urban schools that serve large numbers of minority students, many of whom come from low-income families (U.S. Department of Education, 2004b).[19] His-

[19]The Common Core of Data calculates high school completion rate based on students who completed their GED or received a high school diploma within four years of entering high school.

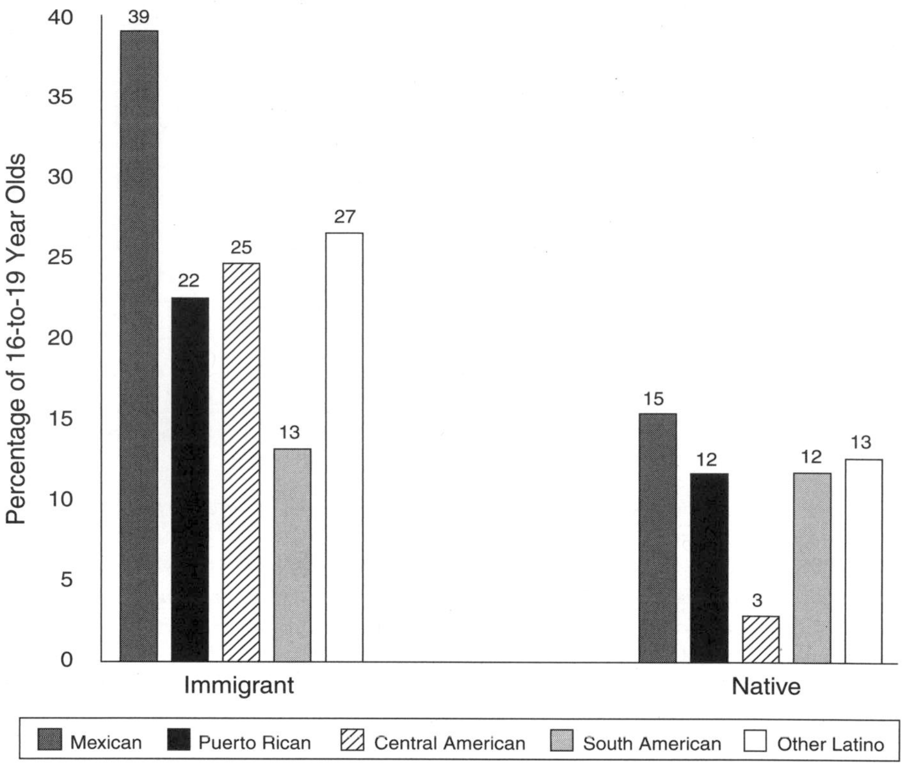

FIGURE 6-12 Dropout rates according to Hispanic subgroups by immigrant and U.S.-born status.
SOURCE: Census 2000 Supplementary Survey.

panic students remain concentrated in large urban school systems, such as Los Angeles, Chicago, and New York, where overall graduation rates are less than 60 percent. Overall, almost 40 percent of Hispanic students attend high schools in which the graduation rate is less than 60 percent (Balfanz and Letgers, 2004). Educators and policy makers remain acutely aware of the difficulties facing Hispanic students, and a variety of retention programs have been instituted in high schools with large numbers of noncompleters. The most effective intervention programs for high school completion are those that link graduation to college matriculation by including college-based or college-level courses or programs, after-school academic preparation, SAT test preparation, and tutoring. While there is a documented relationship between these programs and academic success, most have not been thoroughly evaluated and have been criticized for not accounting for selection bias—that is, the most talented students are those most likely to seek out these programs. Evidence suggests a causal relationship between program participation and college matriculation; however, systematic evaluations including clinical randomized trials pertaining to these interventions are limited (U.S. Department of Education, 2001b). These types of scientifically rigorous evaluations need to be designed and conducted.[20]

Pathways After High School

Although the high school completion rates of Hispanic students have risen over the past decade, their job prospects remain weak because the standard requirement for stable employment in many fields is a baccalaureate degree.[21] Many Hispanic students will enter the labor force immediately after high school, a pathway that economists have estimated will eventually lead to unstable employment and low wages (Levy, 1995). Some Hispanics will also enter the military, a pathway that few high school graduates are taking. It appears that Hispanic entry into the military has increased significantly; Hispanics constituted just 4 percent of military personnel in 1985, but that number rose to 11 percent in 1999 (U.S. Department of Defense, 2000). However, data are not available as to whether Hispanics are taking advantage of the educational benefits offered to military personnel.

Even though a large percentage of Hispanics choose to work after high school, over half of Hispanic high school seniors plan to attend a four-year college. College expectations of Hispanic students doubled from 24 percent in 1972 to 50 percent in 1992; actual college enrollment for Hispanics has increased, as it has for other racial/ethnic groups (U.S. Department of Education, 1995b). In 1972, over 14 percent of Hispanic high school graduates matriculated to four-year colleges (Olivas, 1979); by 2000, 36 percent of Hispanic graduates were enrolled in four-year colleges (U.S. Department of Education, 2003d). Although the number of high school graduates attending college has risen, Hispanics constitute a disproportionately small portion of those attending four-year colleges: 12.5 percent of the U.S. population in 2000 identified themselves as Hispanic, and only 7 percent of

[20]Fry (2004) found no difference in college enrollment rates among Hispanic children of immigrant or native parents, indicating that the students' background characteristics were not as influential as the bridge programs on their academic success.

[21]The proportion of the Hispanic population age 25 and over with a high school diploma or higher degree increased from 50.8 percent in 1990 to 55.5 percent in 1998 (U.S. Census Bureau, 2002b).

four-year college students were Hispanic (U.S. Census Bureau, 2002b; U.S. Department of Education, 2003b). The burgeoning number of first-generation Mexican Americans may account in part for the low rates of college attendance among Hispanics. First-generation immigrant parents may be unfamiliar with the complex policies and practices of the U.S. education system, which require a high level of parent knowledge and involvement, particularly with respect to academic preparation for college.

However, the enrollment rates for Hispanics are misleading, since they are more likely to enroll in two-year rather than four-year institutions, especially first-generation college-goers. In 2000, Hispanics accounted for 14 percent of students enrolled in two-year colleges and only 7 percent of those enrolled in four-year institutions (see Table 6-8).

One of the primary missions of the two-year community college is to provide low-cost local access to postsecondary education. Many students choose to attend two-year colleges because of financial limitations or inadequate preparation and with the intention of transferring to a four-year college. However, the majority of high school graduates who begin their postsecondary education at a two-year institution do not transfer to a four-year institution (Rendon and Garza, 1996; Schneider and Stevenson, 1999). This problem is not unique to Hispanics; for example, only 36 percent of white students who attend community college transfer to four-year colleges or complete a bachelor's degree. However, the transfer or completion rates for Hispanic students at two-year colleges are even lower; only 25 percent

TABLE 6-8 Percentage Distribution of Enrollment in Two-Year Versus Four-Year Colleges, by Race

	% Distribution of Enrollment in College and Universities					
	1980			2000		
Race/Ethnicity	Total	2-Year	4-Year	Total	2-Year	4-Year
Total	100	100	100	100	100	100
White, non-Hispanic	81	79	83	68	64	71
Black, non-Hispanic	9	10	8	11	12	11
Hispanic	4	6	3	10	14	7
Asian/Pacific Islander	2	3	2	6	7	6
American Indian/Alaskan native	1	1	0	1	1	1
Nonresident alien	8	1	3	3	1	5

NOTE: Includes 2-year and 4-year degree granting institutions that were participating in the IV federal financial aid programs. Detail may not add to 100 due to rounding.
SOURCE: U.S. Department of Education (2002d).

will go on to a four-year institution or eventually complete a bachelors degree (Fry, 2004). Schneider and Stevenson (1999) refer to this discrepancy as an ambition paradox—students with high ambitions choosing an educational route with low odds of success. Given the low transfer rates and length of time young adults spend in community college without receiving a degree, transition programs are needed to assist Hispanic students considering transferring to four-year institutions. These types of programs may also be subject to selection bias, in that students who seek out assistance may be more motivated to transfer regardless of the presence of extra help. Key features of these programs, including academic counseling and guidance about the transfer process and requirements, have been shown to help students who are unsure about the college process and may be one strategy for increasing Hispanic students' access to information (Schneider and Stevenson, 1999).

Compared with white students with similar abilities and levels of preparation, fewer Hispanic students enter highly selective colleges, attending less rigorous postsecondary institutions instead (Fry, 2004). Even more problematic, Hispanics have the lowest degree completion rate of any racial group four years after high school (U.S. Department of Education, 2003c). In the 1999–2000 academic year, Hispanics earned only 9 percent of all associate degrees, 6 percent of bachelor's degrees, 4 percent of master's degrees, 3 percent of doctoral degrees, and 5 percent of professional degrees (see Table 6-9). Overall, Hispanics tend to earn relatively more associate degrees and fewer advanced degrees than Asians, blacks, or whites.

As Hispanic enrollment in postsecondary institutions increases, Hispanic-serving institutions (HSIs) play an important role in providing Hispanics with access to college education. HSIs are public or private degree-granting institutions in which Hispanics comprise 25 percent or more of the undergraduate full-time-equivalent enrollment. According to the U.S. Department of Education (2004), at least 50 percent of Hispanic students who are enrolled in these institutions have low family income. There are approximately 242 HSIs located in 14 different states and Puerto Rico (U.S. Department of Education, 2004b). Nearly 46 percent of all HSIs are located in Texas and California. About half of the HSIs are four-year institutions. In 1999, nearly one-half of the total Hispanic undergraduate enrollment in colleges and universities was in HSIs (U.S. Department of Education 2003d, p. 96). Much like historically black colleges and universities, HSIs also enroll a considerable population of first-generation college-goers. There are limited evaluations of the effectiveness of HSIs in terms of their matriculation rates, graduation rates, and job placement. Further research should be conducted to understand how successful these institutions are in serving Hispanic college students.

TABLE 6-9 Percentage Distribution of Degrees Conferred by Colleges and Universities, by Race/Ethnicity and Degree Level, 1999–2000

	Race and Ethnicity		
Degree Level	Total	White, Non-Hispanic	Black, Non-Hispanic
Associate degree	100.0	72.3	10.7
Bachelor's degree	100.0	75.0	8.7
Master's degree	100.0	69.6	7.8
Doctor's degree	100.0	61.4	5.0
First professional	100.0	74.4	6.9

NOTE: Includes 2-year and 4-year degree granting institutions that were participating in the IV federal financial aid programs. Detail may not add to 100 due to rounding.
SOURCE: U.S. Department of Education (2001c).

TAKING THE NEXT STEPS

Factors that are most predictive of educational success among Hispanic students vary across stages in the schooling process. Before Hispanic students begin formalized schooling, family resources are critically important. The confluence of limited English proficiency, low educational attainment, and other economic resources hinder many Hispanic parents from engaging their children in early literacy activities that have been shown to be important for later academic success. Once enrolled in schools, the academic performance of Hispanic students compared with whites is alarmingly low. Moreover, low achievement scores are found as early as kindergarten and continue through middle school. The lowest scores are found among Mexican Americans who are recent immigrants or who live in segregated and disadvantaged communities. Teacher stereotyping and low expectations for Hispanic students are also associated with the achievement gap between Hispanic students and other groups. This teacher bias contributes to Hispanic students' disengagement in academic classes and their failure to form strong attachments to schools and teachers. This particular pattern of disengagement appears to be unique to Hispanic students, resulting in a failure to see the importance of schoolwork to their futures.

Many Hispanic students preparing to enter high school are uncertain about what programs or courses to take and are less likely to have taken courses, such as algebra, that would prepare them for advanced high school

Hispanic	Asian/Pacific Islander	American Indian/ Alaska Native	Nonresident Alien
9.1	4.9	1.1	1.8
6.1	6.3	0.7	3.3
4.2	5.0	0.5	13.0
2.9	5.3	0.4	25.1
4.8	10.7	0.7	2.4

course sequences. The importance of high school academic preparation—in the form of high-level course sequences and college entrance exams—is crucial in predicting postsecondary enrollment in four-year versus two-year colleges. Hispanic students are among the least likely to take high-level math and science course sequences or to enroll in four-year colleges. However, Hispanic students who are academically prepared when they enter high school are more likely to stay in school, to succeed academically, and to matriculate to four-year colleges. Among those attending college, however, Hispanic students tend to enroll in two-year versus four-year institutions. Research has shown that students who enroll in a two-year college with the expectation of transferring to a four-year college are unlikely to do so. Perhaps most troubling is the fact that Hispanic students have the lowest college completion rates of any other racial/ethnic group—even after surmounting the obstacles on the path to college, further barriers, such as low financial resources and inadequate career guidance, remain.

It is critical that academic interventions for Hispanic youth become a national priority. Implementation and evaluation of these interventions must be sensitive to generational status and differences among Hispanic subgroups. Because of the inconsistencies across data sets and the frequent omission of such important factors as generational status, ethnic subgroup, and language proficiency, causal conclusions and specific policy recommendations are not possible at this time or in the scope of this chapter. However, the current data indicate that at every level of education, Hispanic families would benefit from and are especially in need of strategies for helping their children achieve academic success. These strategies are not hidden; many socially and economically advantaged families and schools effectively help children make successful transitions into postsecondary school and the labor force. The problem, then, is not one of what is unknown, but rather how to take what is known and make it accessible to Hispanic families and their communities.

REFERENCES

Balfanz, R., and Letgers, N. (2004). *Locating the dropout crisis.* Baltimore, MD: Johns Hopkins University.

Barnett, W.S. (1998). Long-term effects on cognitive development and school success. In W.S. Barnett and S.S. Boocock (Eds.), *Early care and education for children in poverty: Promises, programs, and long-term results* (pp. 11–44). Albany: State University of New York Press.

Barnett, W.S., and Camilli, G. (2002). Compensatory preschool education, cognitive development, and race. In J.M. Fish (Ed.), *Race and intelligence: Separating science from myth* (pp. 369–406). Mahwah, NJ: Erlbaum.

Bianchi, S., and McArthur, E. (1993). *Characteristics of children who are "behind" in school.* Paper presented at the Annual Meeting of the American Statistical Association, San Francisco, CA.

Bryk, A.S., and Schneider, B. (2002). *Trust in schools: A core resource for improvement.* New York: Russell Sage Foundation.

Buriel, R. (1983). Teacher student interactions and their relationship to student achievement: A comparison of Mexican American and Anglo-American children. *Journal of Educational Psychology, 75*, 889–897.

Carnegie Council on Adolescent Development. (1989). *Turning points: Preparing American youth for the 21st century.* New York: Carnegie Corporation of New York.

Carnoy, M. (2000). *Sustaining the new economy: Work, family, and community in the information age.* Cambridge, MA: Harvard University Press.

College Board. (2002). *How have college-bound students changed in 10 years* (News 2000–2001, Table 1). New York: College Entrance Examination Board.

College Board. (2003). *College-bound seniors 2003: A Profile or SAT Program Test Takers.* New York: Author. Available: http://www.collegeboard.com/about/news_info/cbsenior/yr2003/html/2003reports.html [accessed May 6, 2005].

College Board. (2004). *Advanced Placement Program national summary reports, 1997, 2001, 2002.* New York: Author.

Csikszentmihalyi, M., and Schneider, B. (2000). *Becoming adult: How teenagers prepare for the world of work.* New York: Basic Books.

Currie, J., and Thomas, D. (1996). *Does Head Start help Hispanic children?* (Working Paper.) Cambridge, MA: National Bureau of Economic Research.

Elkind, D. (1981). *The hurried child: Growing up too fast too soon.* Reading, MA: Addison-Wesley.

ERIC Clearinghouse on Urban Education. (2001, February). *Latinos in school: Some facts and findings.* ERIC Online Digest, 162. Available : http://www.ericfacility.net/databases/ERIC_Digests/ed449288.html [accessed July 16, 2004].

Finn, D.J. (1989). Withdrawing from school. *Review of Educational Research*, *59*(2), 117–142.

Fry, R. (2003). *Hispanic youth dropping out of U.S. schools: Measuring the challenge.* Washington, DC: Pew Hispanic Center.

Fry, R. (2004). *Improving young Hispanic college graduation rates: Beyond preparation and affirmative action.* Washington, DC: Pew Hispanic Center.

Gamoran, A., and Mare, R.D. (1989). Secondary school tracking and educational inequality: Compensation, reinforcement, or neutrality? *American Journal of Sociology*, *94*, 1146–1183.

Graham, P.A. (1987). Black teachers: A drastically scarce resource. *Phi Delta Kappan*, *68*, 598–605.

Hacsi, T. (2002). *Children as pawns: The politics of educational reform.* Cambridge, MA: Harvard University Press.

Hallinan, M. (1994). Tracking: From theory to practice. *Sociology of Education*, *67*, 79–84.

Head Start Bureau Fact Sheets. (2004). Available: http://www.acf.hhs.gov/programs/hsb/research/factsheets [accessed July 21, 2004].

Hirschman, C. (2001). The educational enrollment of immigrant youth: A test of the segmented-assimilation hypothesis. *Demography*, *3*, 317–336.

Hispanic Dropout Project Databook. (1998). Available: http://bingaman.senate.gov/databook.pdf [accessed March 15, 2004].

Huerta-Macias, A. (2003). Meeting the challenge of adult education: A bilingual approach to literacy and career development. *Journal of Adolescent and Adult Literacy*, *47*(3), 218–226.

Jimenez, R., Garcia, G., and Pearson, P. (1996). The reading strategies of bilingual Latina/o students who are successful English readers: Opportunities and obstacles. *Reading Research Quarterly*, *31*(1), 90–112.

Kao, G. (1999). Psychological well-being and educational achievement among immigrant youth. In National Research Council, *Children of immigrants: Health, adjustment, and public assistance* (pp. 410–477). Committee on the Health and Adjustment of Immigrant Children and Families, D.J. Hernandez (Ed.). Washington, DC: National Academy Press.

Katz, S.R. (1999). Teaching in tensions: Latino immigrant youth, their teachers, and the structures of schooling. *Teachers College Record*, *100*, 809–840.

Kim, D., and Schneider, B. (Forthcoming). Social capital in action: Alignment of parental support in adolescents' transition to postsecondary education. *Social Forces.*

Levy, P. (1995). *Puerto Rico.* New York: M. Cavendish.

Loeb, S., Fuller, B., Kagan, S., and Carrol, B. (2004). Child care in poor communities: Early learning effects of type, quality, and stability. *Child Development*, *75*(1), 47–65.

Martinez, S. (2003). *Explaining patterns of disengagement of Mexican Americans in high school.* Unpublished Ph.D. dissertation, University of Chicago.

McDonald, D. (2003). *Annual report on Catholic elementary and secondary schools: United States Catholic elementary and secondary school statistics 2002–2003.* Washington, DC: The National Catholic Educational Association.

McKown, C., and Weinstein, R. (2003). The development and consequences of stereotype consciousness in middle childhood. *Child Development*, *74*(2), 498–515.

McLanahan, S.S., and Sandefur, G. (1994). *Growing up with a single parent: What hurts, what helps?* Cambridge, MA: Harvard University Press.

National Research Council. (1998). *Preventing reading difficulties in young children.* Committee on the Prevention of Reading Difficulties of Young Children, C.E. Snow, M.S. Burns, and P. Griffin (Eds.). Washington, DC: National Academy Press.

Nuñez, A., Cuccaro-Alamin, S., and Carroll, C.D. (1998). *First-generation students: Undergraduates whose parents never enrolled in postsecondary education.* Washington, DC: U.S. Department of Education, Office of Education Research and Improvement.

Oakes, J., Gamoran, A., and Page, R.N. (1992). Curriculum differentiation: Opportunities, outcomes, and meanings. In P.W. Jackson (Ed.), *Handbook of research on curriculum: A project of the American educational research association* (pp. 570–608). New York: Macmillan.

Olivas, M.A. (1979). *The dilemma of access: Minorities in two year colleges.* Washington, DC: Howard University Press.

Olsen, D.A. (1999). *Universal preschool is no golden ticket.* (Policy Analysis Brief No. 333.) Washington, DC: Cato Institute. Available: http://www.cato.org/pubs/pas/pa-333es.html [accessed September 2, 2004].

Orfield, G., and Yun, J.T. (1999). *Resegregation in American schools.* Cambridge, MA: Harvard University, the Civil Rights Project. Available: http://www.civilrightsproject.harvard.edu/research/deseg/Resegregation American_Schools99.pdf [accessed January 25, 2004].

Pallas, A., Natriello, G., and McDill, E. (1989). The changing nature of the disadvantaged population: Current dimensions and future trends. *Educational Researcher, 18*, 16–22.

Payne, K. (1994). *Influences on parental choice of children's early educational experiences.* Ph.D. dissertation, Michigan State University.

Pew Hispanic Center Fact Sheet. (2004a). *Latino teens staying in high school: A challenge for all generations.* Available: http://pewhispanic.org/site/docs/pdf/persistence%20Jan%2026%202004.pdf [accessed April 17, 2004].

Pew Hispanic Center Fact Sheet. (2004b). *Hispanic school achievement: Catching up requires running faster than white youth.* Available: http://pewhispanic.org/site/docs/pdf/achievement%20Jan%2026%202004.pdf [accessed April 17, 2004].

Pew Hispanic Center Survey Brief. (2004). *Assimilation and language.* (Publication No. 7052.) Available: http://www.pewhispanic.org/site/docs/pdf/ASSIMILATION%20AND%20LANGUAGE-031904.pdf [accessed May 2, 2004].

Reardon, S., and Galindo, C. (2003). H*ispanic children and the initial transition to schooling: Evidence from the Early Childhood Longitudinal Study.* Presentation to the National Academies/National Research Council, Panel on Hispanics in the United States.

Rendon, L.I., and Garza, H. (1996). Closing the gap between two- and four-year institutions. In L.I. Rendon and R.O. Hope (Eds.), *Educating a new majority: Transforming America's educational system for diversity* (pp. 289–308). San Francisco, CA: Jossey-Bass.

Riegle-Crumb, C. (2003). *International gender inequity in math and science education: The importance of gender stratification.* Ph.D. dissertation, University of Chicago.

Rosenbloom, S.R., and Way, N. (2004). Experiences of discrimination among African American, Asian American, and Latino adolescents in an urban high school. *Youth and Society, 35*(4), 420–451.

Rumberger, R.W., and Larson, K.A. (1998). Toward explaining differences in educational achievement among Mexican American language-minority students. *Sociology of Education, 71*, 69–93.

Saville-Troike, M. (1984). What really matters in second language learning for academic achievement. *TESOL Quarterly, 18*, 199–219.

Schiller, K. (1995). *Organizations, individuals, and uncertainty: The transition to high school.* Ph.D. dissertation, University of Chicago.

Schmid, C.L. (2001). Educational achievement, language-minority students, and the new second generation. *Sociology of Education, 74*, 71–87.

Schneider, B., and Stevenson, D. (1999). *The ambitious generation: America's teenagers, motivated but directionless.* New Haven, CT: Yale University Press.

Smith, J.B. (1995). Does an extra year make any difference? The impact of early access to algebra on long-term gains in mathematics attainment. *Educational Policy and Policy Analysis, 18*(2), 141–153.

Steele, C., and Aronson, J. (1995). Stereotype threat and the intellectual test performance of African Americans. *Journal of Personality and Social Psychology, 69*(5), 797–811.

Stevenson, D.L., Schiller, K., and Schneider, B. (1994). Sequences of opportunities for learning. *Sociology of Education, 67,* 184–198.

U.S. Census Bureau. (2001a). *Population by race and Hispanic or Latino origin for the United States: 1990 and 2000* (PHC-T-1). Washington, DC: Author, Population Division.

U.S. Census Bureau. (2001b, October). *Current Population Survey.* School enrollment: Social and economic characteristics of students. Detailed Tables, Table 7. Available: http://www.census.gov/population/www/socdemo/school/cps2001.html [accessed June 5, 2004].

U.S. Census Bureau. (2002a, March). *Current Population Survey.* Washington, DC: Author, Ethnic and Hispanic Statistics Branch, Population Division. Available: http://www.census.gov/population/socdemo/hispanic/ppl-165/tab07-2.txt [accessed March 24, 2004].

U.S. Census Bureau. (2002b). *The Hispanic population in the United States: March 2000* (Current Population Reports, P20-535). Washington, DC: Author.

U.S. Census Bureau. (2003). *Current Population Survey.* Annual Social and Economic Supplement. Washington, DC: Author.

U.S. Department of Defense. (2000). *Population representation in the military services, Fiscal year 1999.* Washington, DC: Author.

U.S. Department of Education. (2004). *Title V: Developing Hispanic-serving institutions program.* Washington, DC: Author.

U.S. Department of Education, National Center for Education Statistics. (1988). *National Education Longitudinal Study.* Washington, DC: Author.

U.S. Department of Education, National Center for Education Statistics. (1990). *A profile of the American eighth grader: NELS: 88 student descriptive summary* (NCES 90-458). Washington, DC: Author.

U.S. Department of Education, National Center for Education Statistics. (1995a). *Approaching kindergarten: A look at preschoolers in the United States* (NCES 95-280). Washington, DC: Author.

U.S. Department of Education, National Center for Education Statistics. (1995b). *A profile of the American high school senior in 1992* (NCES 95-384). Washington, DC: Author.

U.S. Department of Education, National Center for Education Statistics. (1996a). *Digest of education statistics, 1996* (Table 149). Ages for compulsory school attendance, special education services for students, policies for kindergarten programs, and year-round schools, by state: 1995 and 1996 (NCES 96-133). Washington, DC: Author.

U.S. Department of Education, National Center for Education Statistics. (1996b). *School and staffing in the U.S.: A statistical profile, 1993–94* (NCES 96-124). Washington, DC: Author.

U.S. Department of Education, National Center for Education Statistics. (1997). *America's teachers: Profile of a profession, 1993–94* (NCES 97-460). Washington, DC: Author.

U.S. Department of Education, National Center for Education Statistics. (1998, Fall). *Early childhood longitudinal study: Kindergarten class of 1998–99.* Washington, DC: Author.

U.S. Department of Education, National Center for Education Statistics. (1999). *National Household Education Survey* (Parent Interview Component), public-use data (weighted). Washington, DC: Author.

U.S. Department of Education, National Center for Education Statistics. (2000a). *America's kindergartners* (NCES 2000-070). Washington, DC: Author.

U.S. Department of Education, National Center for Education Statistics. (2000b). *Dropout rates in the United States, 2000* (NCES 2002-114). Washington, DC: Author.

U.S. Department of Education, National Center for Education Statistics. (2001a). *Findings from the condition of education 2000: Entering kindergarten* (NCES 2001-035). Washington, DC: Author.

U.S. Department of Education, National Center for Education Statistics. (2001b). *Paving the way to postsecondary education: K–12 intervention programs for underrepresented youth* (NCES 2001-205). Washington, DC: Author.

U.S. Department of Education, National Center for Education Statistics. (2001c). *Digest of education statistics.* Based on Integrated Postsecondary Education Data System (IPEDS), "Completion" Survey, 1999–2000. Washington, DC: Author.

U.S. Department of Education, National Center for Education Statistics. (2002a). *New directions for program evaluation at the U.S. Department of Education.* Washington, DC: Author. Available: http://www.ed.gov/print/news/pressreleases/2002/04/evaluation.html [accessed June 16, 2004].

U.S. Department of Education, National Center for Education Statistics. (2002b). *Digest of education statistics, 2001* (NCES 2002-130). Washington, DC: Author.

U.S. Department of Education, National Center for Education Statistics. (2002c). *The condition of education.* Based on 1998 High School Transcripts Study. Washington, DC: Author.

U.S. Department of Education, National Center for Education Statistics. (2002d). *Digest of education statistics.* Based on Higher Education General Information Survey (HEGIS), Fall Enrollment in Colleges and Universities Survey, 1980–81, and Integrated Postsecondary Education Data System (IPEDS), Fall Enrollment Survey, 2000–01. Washington, DC: Author.

U.S. Department of Education, National Center for Education Statistics. (2003a). *The condition of education 2003* (NCES 2003-067). Washington, DC: Author.

U.S. Department of Education, National Center for Education Statistics. (2003b). *Digest of education statistics, 2002* (NCES 2003-060). Washington, DC: Author.

U.S. Department of Education, National Center for Education Statistics. (2003c). *Racial/ethnic differences in the path to a postsecondary credential* (NCES 2003-005). Washington, DC: Author.

U.S. Department of Education, National Center for Education Statistics. (2003d). *Status and trends in the education of Hispanics* (NCES 2003-008). Washington, DC: Author.

U.S. Department of Education, National Center for Education Statistics. (2003e). *National Assessment of Educational Progress (NAEP).* Washington, DC: Author.

U.S. Department of Education, National Center for Education Statistics. (2004a). *Dropout rates in the United States: 2001* (NCES 2005-045). Washington, DC: Author.

U.S. Department of Education, National Center for Education Statistics. (2004b). *Public high school dropouts and completers from the Common Core of Data: School year 2000–01* (NCES 2004-310). Washington, DC: Author.

Usiskin, Z. (1987). Why elementary algebra can, should, and must be an eighth grade course for average students. *Mathematics Teacher, 80,* 428–438.

Valencia, R. (2002). *Chicano school failure and success: Past, present, and future.* New York: Routledge/Falmer Press.

Valencia, R., and Aburto, S. (1991). Contemporary testing and Latino student access to the teaching profession: An overview of issues. In G. Keller, J. Deneen, and R. Magallan (Eds.), *Assessment and access: Hispanics in higher education* (pp. 195–232). Albany: State University of New York Press.

Valenzuela, A. (1999). *Subtractive schooling: U.S. Mexican youth and the politics of caring.* Albany: State University of the New York Press.

Wadsworth, B.J. (1989). *Piaget's theory of cognitive and affective development* (fourth edition). New York: Longman.

Zulmara, C., and Necochea, J. (2003). My mother never read to me. *Journal of Adolescent and Adult Literacy*, 47, 122–126.

APPENDIX TABLE A6-1 Logistic Regression Predicting the Likelihood of Having a Risk Factor (One of Three) by Race/Ethnicity and the Other Risk Factors

Single Parent Family Risk Factor

	Model 1		Model 2		Model 3	
Predictor	Beta	Odds Ratio	Beta	Odds Ratio	Beta	Odds Ratio
Constant	–1.871***		–2.063***		–1.077***	
Black	1.946***	6.998	1.611***	5.007	1.518***	4.561
Hispanic, speaks English at home	.864***	2.372	.621***	1.861	.559***	1.749
Hispanic, speaks Spanish at home	.326***	1.386	–.275	.760	–.401***	.670
Asian	–.338**	.713	–.440**	.644	–.349**	.706
Other	.942***	2.566	.671***	1.956	.608***	1.837
Below poverty level (risk)			1.368***	3.929	1.017***	2.766
Low educational attainment for mother (risk)			.064	1.066	–.300***	.741
Socioeconomic status (quintiles)					–.282***	.754
Chi-square	3234.50***		4689.61***		5049.38***	
–2 Log-likelihood	27874.65		26419.55		26059.78	

Family Income Below the Poverty Threshold Risk Factor

	Model 1		Model 2		Model 3	
Predictor	Beta	Odds Ratio	Beta	Odds Ratio	Beta	Odds Ratio
Constant	–2.301***		–2.769***		.964***	
Black	1.860***	6.423	1.287***	3.620	.955***	2.599
Hispanic, speaks English at home	1.219***	3.384	.840***	2.316	.658***	1.932
Hispanic, speaks Spanish at home	2.079***	8.000	1.523***	4.585	.857***	2.356

Asian	.435***	1.545	.439***	1.552	.816***	2.262
Other	1.354***	3.873	1.129***	3.093	.915***	2.497
Low educational attainment for mother (risk)			1.526***	4.598	–.220***	.803
Single parent family (risk)			1.370***	3.935	1.024***	2.785
Socioeconomic status (quintiles)					–1.317***	.268
Chi-square	3261.36***		5929.60***		10722.43***	
–2 Log-likelihood	25066.33		22398.08		17605.26	

Low Educational Attainment for Mother (Less Than a High School Diploma) Risk Factor

	Model 1		Model 2		Model 3	
Predictor	Beta	Odds Ratio	Beta	Odds Ratio	Beta	Odds Ratio
Constant	–2.635***		–2.897***		2.495***	
Black	1.084***	2.955	.515***	1.673	.065	1.067
Hispanic, speaks English at home	1.292***	3.638	1.015***	2.759	.759***	2.136
Hispanic, speaks Spanish at home	2.609***	13.585	2.183***	8.875	1.109***	3.033
Asian	.577***	1.781	.504***	1.655	.880***	2.410
Other	.689***	1.992	.309***	1.362	–.011	.989
Below poverty level (risk)			1.519***	4.565	–.407***	.665
Single parent family (risk)			.095*	1.099	–.280***	.756
Socioeconomic status (quintiles)					–2.191***	.112
Chi-square	2291.68***		3626.14***		9830.56***	
–2 Log-likelihood	19850.60		18516.13		12311.72	

NOTES: This is a weighted data set. The reference category for race/ethnicity is white, non-Hispanic.
+ p < .10, *p < .05, **p < .01, ***p < .001.
SOURCE: U.S. Department of Education (1998).

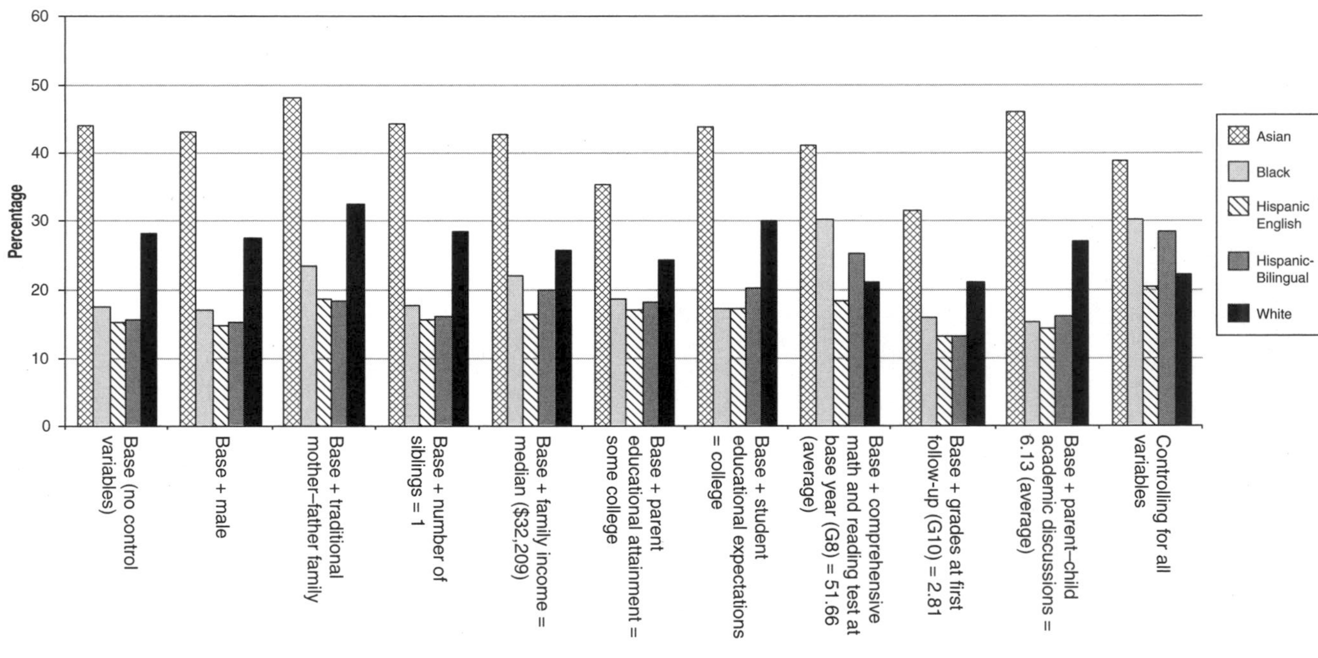

FIGURE A6-1a Probability (in percent) of taking high math courses (trigonometry or above) for each race/ethnicity by different control variables.
SOURCE: U.S. Department of Education, National Center for Education Statistics, NELS 88-2000, Second Follow-Up, 1992, restricted-use data (with imputed values).

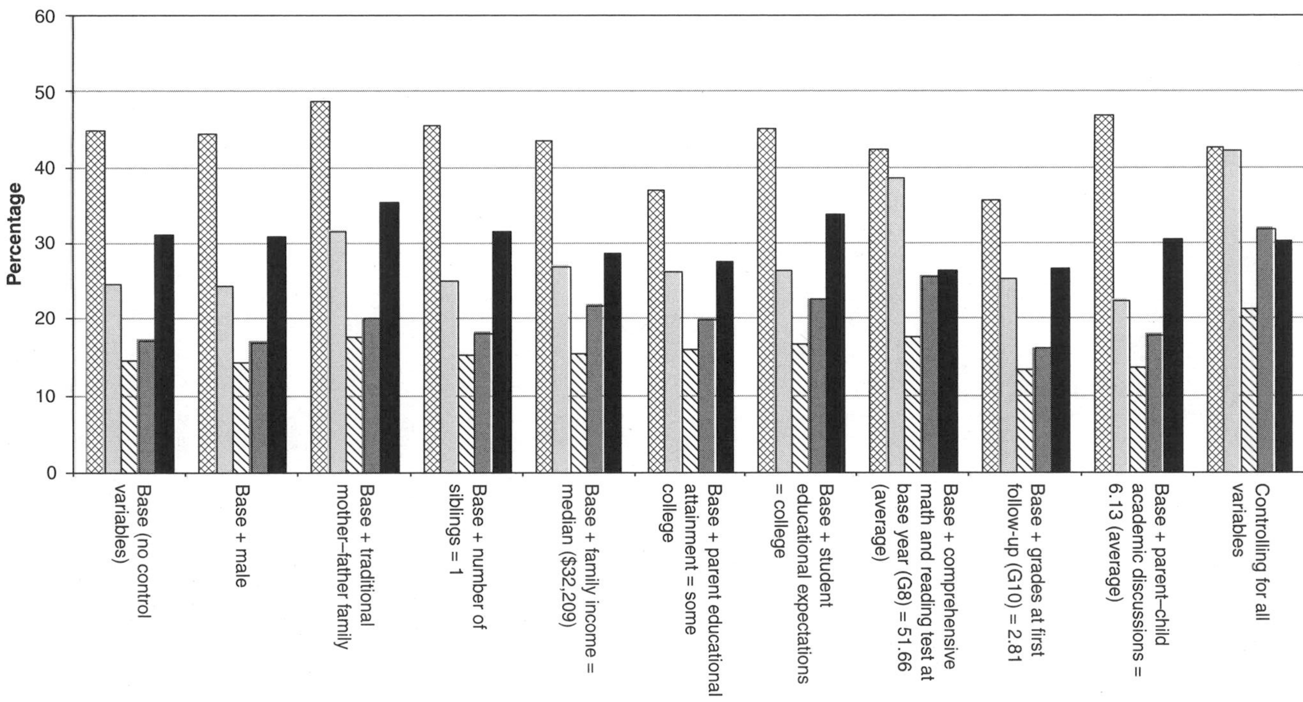

FIGURE A6-1b Probability (in percent) of taking a high science course for each race/ethnicity by different control variables.
SOURCE: U.S. Department of Education, National Center for Education Statistics, NELS 88-2000, Second Follow-Up, 1992, restricted-use data (with imputed values).

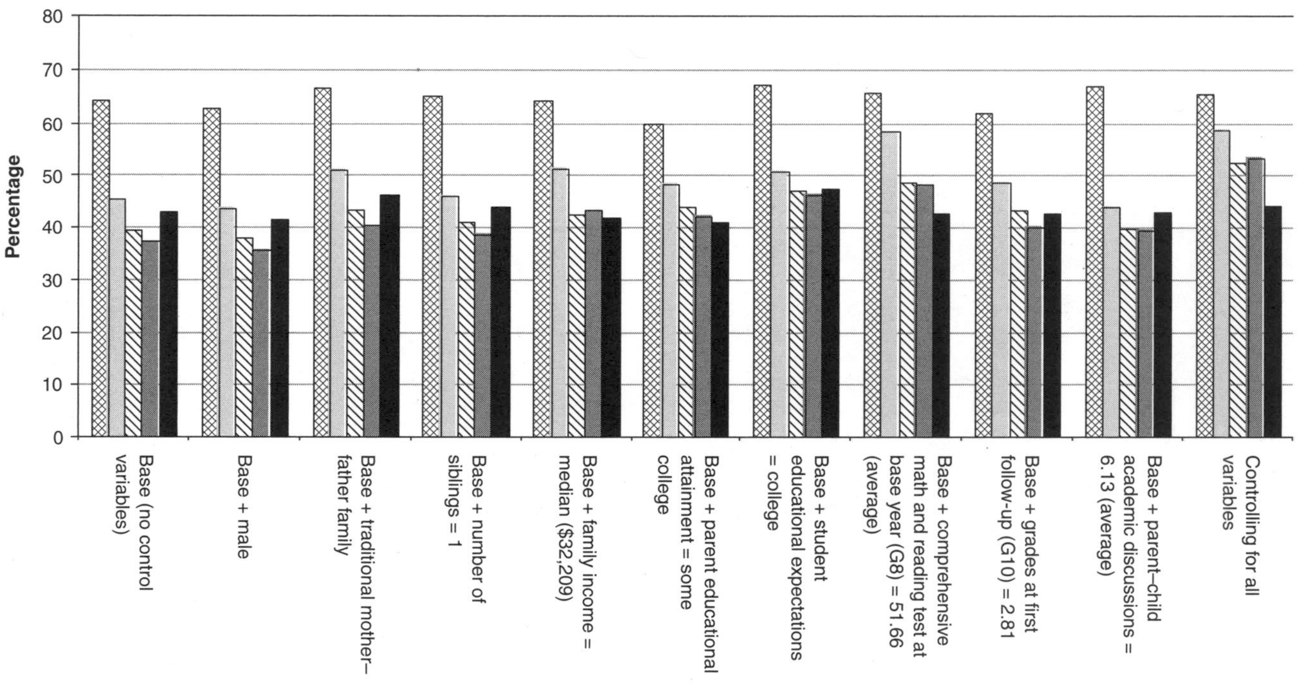

FIGURE A6-1c Probability (in percent) of taking the SAT for each race/ethnicity by different control variables.
SOURCE: U.S. Department of Education, National Center for Education Statistics, NELS 88-2000, Second Follow-Up, 1992, restricted-use data (with imputed values).

APPENDIX FIGURE A6-1
NOTES:
Model 1: Base (no control variables)
Model 2: Base + male
Model 3: Base + traditional mother–father family
Model 4: Base + number of siblings = 1
Model 5: Base + family income = median ($32,209)
Model 6: Base + parent educational attainment = some college
Model 7: Base + student educational expectations = college
Model 8: Base + comprehensive math and reading test at base year (G8) = 51.66 (average)
Model 9: Base + grades at first follow-up (G10) = 2.81
Model 10: Base + parent–child academic discussions = 6.13 (average)
Model 11: Controlling for all variables

7

Hispanics in the U.S. Labor Market

Brian Duncan, V. Joseph Hotz, and Stephen J. Trejo

As the first two chapters of this volume have noted, Hispanics constitute a large and rapidly growing segment of the U.S. population. Much of the public debate and controversy concerning Hispanics focuses on their integration and success in the U.S. labor market. In this chapter, we summarize some of what is currently known about these issues. We focus on employment and earnings as measures of labor market success. We also examine the educational attainment of Hispanics, given its crucial role in labor market success. We consider four different but complementary perspectives.

We begin by examining Hispanics and their subgroups that currently reside in the United States, on the basis of data from the 2000 Census of Population. We focus on how foreign-born versus U.S.-born Hispanics differ in an important indicator of human capital, namely their educational attainment. We then document the differences that exist among Hispanics, their subgroups, whites, and blacks in employment and earnings. Finally, we ask how much of these differences can be accounted for by differences in years of schooling, English language proficiency, and potential work experience. Two conclusions emerge from this analysis. First, we confirm the findings in Chapter 6 as well as numerous other studies that Hispanics have markedly lower levels of educational attainment than do whites or blacks and that these educational deficits are more pronounced for the foreign-born. Second, while the employment and earnings of Hispanics tend to lag behind those of whites, almost all of the differences relative to whites can be accounted for by a relatively small number of measures of human capital, namely, years of schooling, English proficiency, and potential work experience.

We next examine the early life-cycle patterns of schooling and work for Hispanics relative to blacks and whites, using data on cohorts who reached adulthood during the late 1980s and 1990s. In this analysis, we focus on two issues arising from the role that the Hispanic educational deficit plays in accounting for their relative employment and earnings differentials. First, we examine exactly what sorts and amounts of work experience Hispanics accumulated during early adulthood. We know that they accumulated less education over their early adulthood. But do they compensate by accumulating more work experience to offset some of their educational deficit? Second, we examine whether Hispanics realized the same financial returns from their accumulated work experience and schooling. Previous studies of other minority groups suggest that they do not realize the same gain from an additional year of schooling or work experience as do whites. Whether these differences reflect evidence of labor market discrimination or unmeasured differences in the quality of schooling and the amount of actual work experience is less certain. But at issue is whether observed measures of human capital have different impacts on the degree of labor market success by race or ethnicity.

In the final section of the chapter, we focus on how the labor market attainment of Hispanics in the United States has changed over time and across generations. Analyzing whether there has been secular and generational progress among Hispanics in the United States is important for at least three reasons. First, our analysis was performed on Hispanics during a period of substantial change in the structure of the U.S. labor market, which tended to be decidedly less favorable for less-skilled workers in the United States. As a result, it is important to assess, if only somewhat speculatively, how important this restructuring was for the lower levels of labor market attainment experienced by Hispanics. Second, knowing how things have changed is an essential ingredient for forecasting what will happen to the labor market attainment of this growing and increasingly important segment of the U.S. population. Third, assessing how things have changed across generations is essential because of the immigrant nature of Hispanics. The immigrants of today will be the parents and grandparents of future generations of Hispanics, and it is of critical importance to understand the degree of their intergenerational assimilation into the U.S. labor market.

THE CURRENT SCENE: THE LABOR MARKET ATTAINMENT OF HISPANICS

Human Capital

Time and time again, researchers have found that indicators of labor market disadvantage for U.S. Hispanics, such as earnings deficits or em-

TABLE 7-1 Average Years of Schooling, by Gender, Ethnicity, and Nativity

	Men, by Nativity			Women, by Nativity		
Ethnicity	All	Foreign-Born	U.S.-Born	All	Foreign-Born	U.S.-Born
Whites			13.6			13.6
Blacks			12.4			12.8
All Hispanics	10.5	9.5	12.2	10.8	9.8	12.4
Mexicans	9.8	8.5	12.1	10.1	8.6	12.2
Puerto Ricans	11.7	11.2	12.4	12.0	11.4	12.7
Cubans	12.7	12.4	13.6	12.9	12.5	14.2

NOTE: The samples include individuals ages 25 to 59. See Appendix Table A7-1 for standard errors and sample sizes, as well as for analogous calculations for other Hispanic subgroups.
SOURCE: 2000 Census, 5% Public Use Microdata Samples (PUMS).

ployment gaps with respect to white workers, are in large part explained by relatively low levels of human capital.[1] Accordingly, we begin by describing, in broad terms, the labor market skills possessed by Hispanic Americans and how these skills compare with those of non-Hispanics.

One of the most important and easiest to observe dimensions of human capital is educational attainment, and Chapter 6 has documented the obstacles faced by Hispanic children in U.S. schools. Table 7-1 shows the substantial gaps in completed education that exist for Hispanic adults. Based on microdata from the 2000 census, the table reports average years of schooling—by gender, ethnicity, and nativity—for individuals between the ages of 25 and 59.[2] In addition to presenting statistics for Hispanics as an aggregate group, we display separate results for Mexicans, Puerto Ricans, and Cubans, the three Hispanic national-origin groups with the largest U.S.-born populations.[3] We also present comparable statistics for non-

[1]See, for example, Altonji and Blank (1999); Antecol and Bedard (2002, 2004); Bean and Stevens (2003); Bean and Tienda (1987); Bean, Trejo, Capps, and Tyler (2001); Carlson and Swartz (1988); Carnoy, Daley, and Hinojosa-Ojeda (1993); Cotton (1985); Darity, Guilkey, and Winfrey (1995); DeFreitas (1991); Grogger and Trejo (2002); Gwartney and Long (1978); McManus, Gould, and Welch (1983); Reimers (1983); Smith (1991, 2001); Trejo (1996, 1997, 2003).

[2]We focus on individuals in this age range because they are old enough that virtually all of them have completed their schooling, yet they are young enough that observed labor market outcomes reflect their prime working years.

[3]Appendix Table A7-1 reports standard errors and sample sizes for the estimates in Table 7-1, as well as analogous calculations for other Hispanic subgroups. Throughout this chapter, appendix tables provide further details of the tables and charts presented in the text. All statistics reported in this chapter make use of the relevant sampling weights.

Hispanic whites and non-Hispanic blacks, with both of these latter groups restricted to individuals who were born in the United States.[4] U.S.-born whites provide a yardstick for measuring Hispanic outcomes against those of the primary native majority group in American society, whereas U.S.-born blacks are an important native minority group that is instructive to compare with Hispanics.

Table 7-1 shows that educational patterns are very similar for men and women. For Hispanics overall, immigrants average less than 10 years of schooling, but mean educational attainment rises sharply to over 12 years for U.S.-born Hispanics. Despite this sizeable improvement associated with nativity, U.S.-born Hispanics trail the average educational attainment of whites by more than a year, and they even trail the educational attainment of blacks. Consequently, Hispanic educational attainment is low not only in comparison with advantaged groups in American society such as whites, but also in comparison with disadvantaged minority groups such as blacks.

Among the Hispanic subgroups, Mexicans and Puerto Ricans display the same general patterns as Hispanics overall, with substantial schooling growth between immigrants and the U.S.-born, yet a large educational deficit relative to whites that persists even for the U.S.-born. Average education levels among the foreign-born, however, are much lower for Mexicans than for Puerto Ricans (8.5 years versus more than 11 years, respectively), but Mexicans experience bigger gains for the U.S.-born, thereby shrinking to a half year or less the educational gap between U.S.-born Mexicans and Puerto Ricans. Cubans stand out from the other groups with notably high levels of educational attainment. In terms of average schooling, Cuban immigrants exceed U.S.-born Mexicans and approach the level of U.S.-born Puerto Ricans, and U.S.-born Cubans equal (for men) or surpass (for women) the educational attainment of whites. More detailed tabulations reveal that the schooling deficits (relative to whites) of U.S.-born Hispanics, in general, and of Mexican Americans and Puerto Rican Americans, in particular, emanate from differences at the extremes of the education distribution. U.S.-born Mexicans and Puerto Ricans are much more likely to be without a high school diploma and much less likely to earn a bachelor's degree than are non-Hispanic whites (Bean et al., 2001).

For Hispanic immigrants, a critical aspect of their human capital is that much of it was acquired outside the United States. The foreign schooling

[4]We identify Hispanics and Hispanic subgroups using the census information regarding country of birth, Hispanic origin, and ancestry. Among non-Hispanics, we identify whites and blacks using the census information on race. For Hispanics and blacks, we employ the full 5 percent samples of the population available in census microdata, but to lighten the computational burden we randomly sample whites (at a 1 in 10 rate) so as to end up with a 0.5 percent sample of the white population.

and work experience that Hispanic immigrants bring with them transfer imperfectly to the U.S. labor market, in that U.S. employers typically place a lower value on human capital acquired abroad than on that acquired here (Chiswick, 1978; Schoeni, 1997). As a result, even after conditioning on age, education, and other observable indicators of human capital, labor market outcomes are likely to differ between foreign-born Hispanics and U.S.-born Hispanics (or between foreign-born Hispanics and U.S.-born whites), because of differences in the returns to human capital for foreign-born and U.S.-born workers. For this reason, nativity plays a key role in shaping the labor market success of Hispanics, and it is essential that labor market analyses of U.S. Hispanics distinguish between immigrants and the U.S.-born.

English language proficiency is an important dimension of human capital closely related to nativity. Census microdata provide self-reported information on English ability, and we display some of this information in Figure 7-1.[5] All respondents were asked whether they "speak a language other than English at home," and only those who answered affirmatively were asked how well they speak English, with possible responses of "very well," "well," "not well," or "not at all." For the tabulations presented in Figure 7-1, English monolinguals are presumed to speak English "very well" and are grouped together with bilinguals who indicated the highest level of English proficiency.

By this accounting, only a third of Hispanic immigrants speak English very well, but the proportion approaches 90 percent for U.S.-born Hispanics. Even among U.S. natives, however, the English proficiency of Hispanics falls somewhat short of the 99 percent rates observed for blacks and whites. Given the substantial penalties that the U.S. labor market assesses for English deficiencies (Bleakley and Chin, 2004; Grenier, 1984; McManus et al., 1983; Mora, 1998), the language gaps observed in Figure 7-1 can explain a considerable portion of Hispanic employment and earnings deficits, especially for immigrants, but also to some extent for U.S.-born Hispanics. In addition, English language proficiency varies across Hispanic subgroups. Among immigrants, Mexicans have the lowest rate of English proficiency (with 26 percent speaking the language very well), whereas the corresponding rate is around 50 percent for Cubans and still higher for Puerto Ricans. Differences are much less pronounced for U.S.-born Hispanics, with rates just under 90 percent for Mexicans and Puerto Ricans and a somewhat higher rate for Cubans.

A key feature of Hispanic immigration is that much of it is undocumented. Given the clandestine nature of undocumented immigration, this

[5] More detailed information is reported in Appendix Table A7-2.

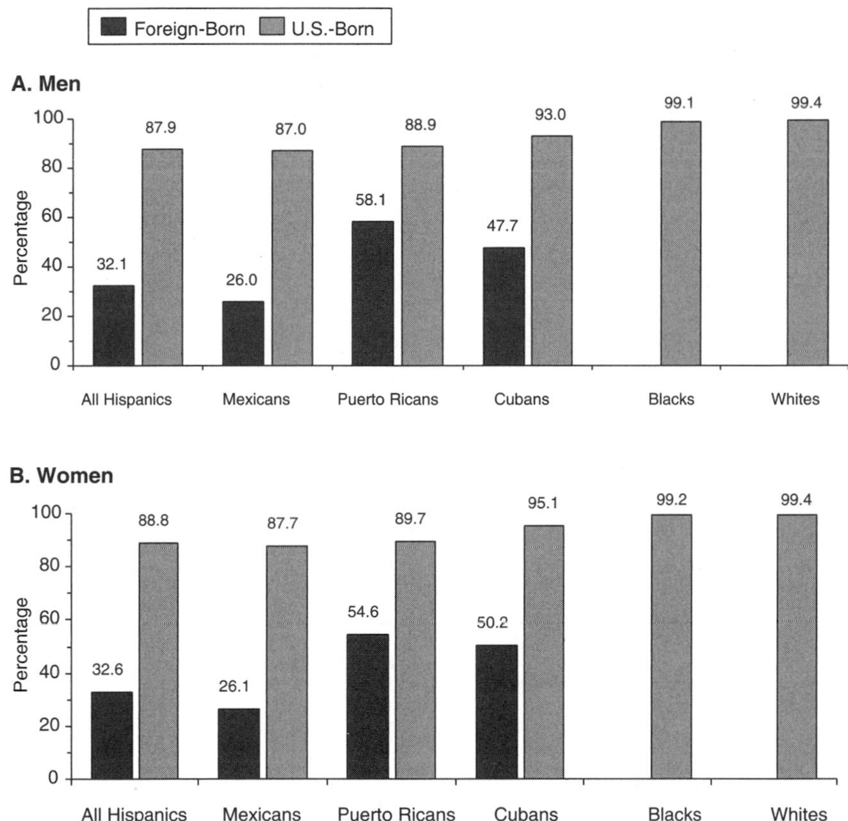

FIGURE 7-1 Percentage speaking English very well, by gender, ethnicity, and nativity.
NOTE: The samples include individuals ages 25 to 59. In these tabulations, those who speak only English are presumed to speak English "very well." See Appendix Table A7-2 for further details.
SOURCE: 2000 census, 5% PUMS.

population is difficult to observe, but some credible information is available nonetheless. Passel, Capps, and Fix (2004) estimate that Latin Americans made up 80 percent of the undocumented immigrants living in the United States as of March 2002, with Mexicans alone accounting for 57 percent of the undocumented population. Moreover, these same authors estimate that undocumented immigrants represent a quarter of the total foreign-born population in the United States, and Passel (2004) indicates that the share of undocumented immigrants is much higher among foreign-born Hispanics, particularly for recent immigrants. Indeed, Passel (2004) reports that over 80 percent of all Mexican immigrants who arrived in the United States after 1990 were undocumented as of March 2002.

Does undocumented status, by itself, hurt the labor market opportunities of Hispanic immigrants? If so, by how much? Most sources of information about U.S. immigrants, including the decennial census and Current Population Survey data that we analyze in this chapter, do not identify undocumented immigrants, so our analyses will not be able to control for the legal status of Hispanic immigrants. Other studies, however, have exploited unique surveys to shed light on this issue. Massey (1987), for example, compared the U.S. wages earned by legal and illegal immigrants originating in four Mexican communities. He reports that undocumented Mexican immigrants earn substantially less, on average, then legal Mexican immigrants, but he also shows that this wage gap is explained by the lower human capital possessed by undocumented immigrants, particularly with regard to English proficiency and U.S. work experience. After controlling for observable determinants of earnings, Massey finds that legal status per se has little direct effect on U.S. wages for the Mexican immigrants in his sample. Donato and Massey (1993), however, obtained a different result when they conducted a similar analysis of later and more extensive data from 13 Mexican communities. In these later data, undocumented status reduced wages by about 20 percent, even after controlling for observables.

Perhaps the best evidence on the labor market impact of undocumented status comes from a survey that tracked the experiences of initially undocumented immigrants before and after they were granted permanent legal resident status through the amnesty provisions of the 1986 Immigration Reform and Control Act. Despite using somewhat different approaches, Rivera-Batiz (1999) and Kossoudji and Cobb-Clark (2002) reach similar conclusions. First, holding observable skills constant, estimates suggest that legalization raised the wages of these workers by about 5–10 percent relative to what their wages would have been had the workers remained undocumented. Second, by increasing the incentives for these workers to invest in human capital, legalization also may have induced greater skill acquisition and thereby boosted wages through this indirect channel. Clearly, legal status is an important factor underlying the huge earnings deficits for Hispanic immigrants (relative to U.S.-born whites) that we document below, and this is especially true for recent immigrants from Mexico and Central America. Nevertheless, undocumented immigration assumes a minor role in the Hispanic labor market story compared with the leading role played by human capital. Indeed, we show below that, even without controlling for legal status, all or most of the earnings deficits of Hispanic immigrants can be explained by their low levels of education and English proficiency.

TABLE 7-2 Annual Employment Rates (Percentages), by Gender, Ethnicity, and Nativity

	Men, by Nativity			Women, by Nativity		
Ethnicity	All	Foreign-Born	U.S.-Born	All	Foreign-Born	U.S.-Born
Whites			91.8			80.2
Blacks			77.4			77.7
All Hispanics	86.8	87.5	85.6	67.0	61.2	76.3
Mexicans	87.8	88.5	86.5	64.7	56.1	76.4
Puerto Ricans	80.0	76.6	83.8	67.7	60.8	75.5
Cubans	87.3	86.8	89.1	74.7	72.5	82.5

NOTE: The samples include individuals ages 25 to 59. See Appendix Table A7-3 for standard errors, as well as for analogous calculations for other Hispanic subgroups.
SOURCE: 2000 census, 5% PUMS.

Employment

The success of Hispanics in the U.S. labor market heavily depends on their propensity to work and the kinds of jobs they are able to secure. We now turn to a discussion of these issues, highlighting the important influence of human capital.

Table 7-2 reports annual employment rates for whites, blacks, and Hispanics, by gender and nativity. The annual employment rate is defined as the percentage of individuals who worked at all during the calendar year preceding the census.[6] For men, the overall Hispanic employment rate of 87 percent is somewhat lower than the 92 percent rate for U.S.-born whites but well above the 77 percent rate for U.S.-born blacks. Among Hispanic men, Mexicans and Cubans are employed at similar rates, and these rates vary only modestly with nativity, whereas the lower rates observed for Puerto Ricans (80 percent, overall) are markedly higher for the U.S-born (84 percent) than the foreign-born (77 percent).[7]

For Hispanic women, Table 7-2 highlights the important role that nativity plays in employment determination. For every national-origin

[6]See Appendix Table A7-3 for further details. Another possible measure of labor supply is annual hours of work. Compared with the employment rate, this measure has the advantage of reflecting the intensity as well as the incidence of work. It turns out, however, that the relevant patterns for annual hours are similar to those for employment, so we present only the results for employment.

[7]Appendix Table A7-3 shows that Dominican men also have relatively low employment rates. Unlike the situation for Puerto Ricans, however, employment rates are similar for foreign-born and U.S.-born Dominicans.

group, employment rates are at least 10 percentage points lower for immigrants than for U.S. natives, with this immigrant-native gap reaching 20 percentage points for Mexicans. Among U.S.-born women, the employment rates of 76 percent for Mexicans and Puerto Ricans are close to the corresponding rates for blacks (78 percent) and whites (80 percent), and the 83 percent rate for Cubans is highest of all.

How much does the human capital deficit of U.S. Hispanics contribute to their employment gap? The next two graphs address this question, with results for men presented in Figure 7-2 and those for women in Figure 7-3.

A. Not Controlling for Education or English Proficiency:

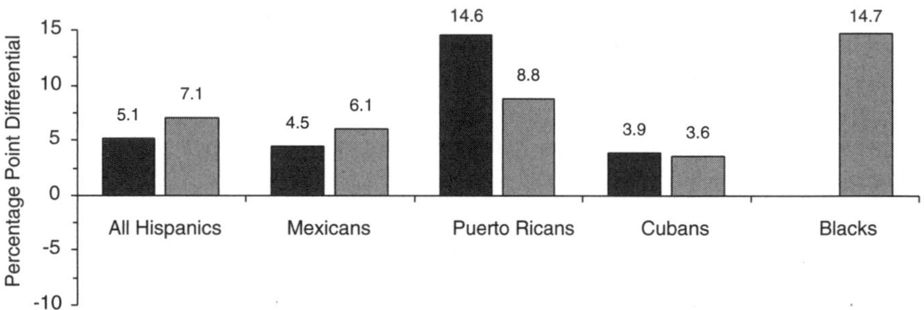

B. Controlling for Education and English Proficiency:

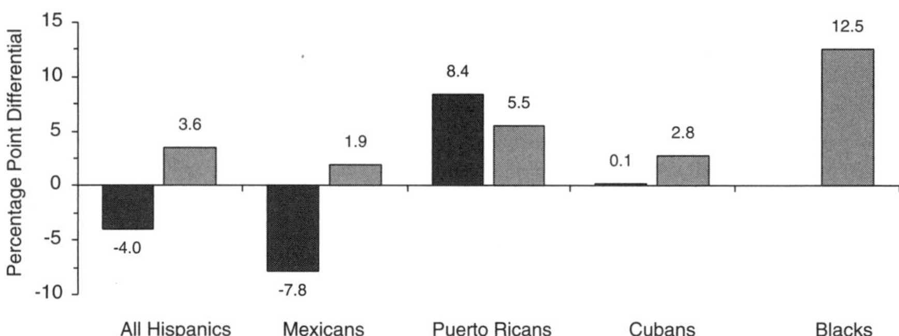

FIGURE 7-2 Male employment deficits relative to U.S.-born whites, by ethnicity and nativity.

NOTE: The samples include individuals ages 25 to 59. All of the reported differentials control for geographic location and age. See Appendix Table A7-4 for further details.

SOURCE: 2000 census, 5% PUMS.

A. Not Controlling for Education or English Proficiency:

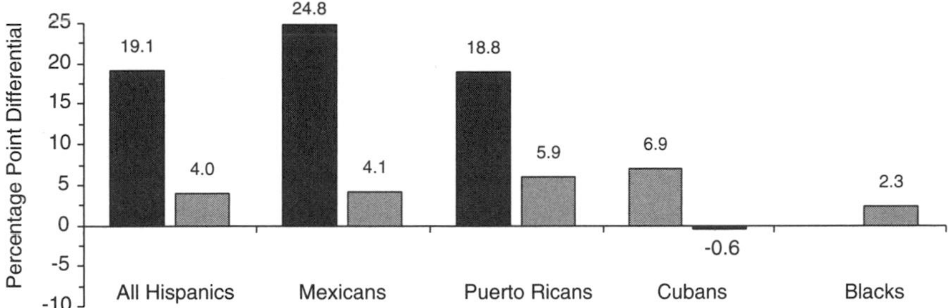

B. Controlling for Education and English Proficiency:

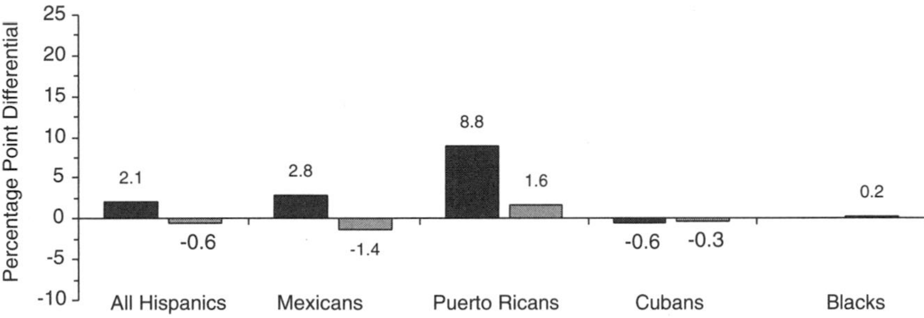

FIGURE 7-3 Female employment deficits relative to U.S.-born whites, by ethnicity and nativity.
NOTE: The samples include individuals ages 25 to 59. All of the reported differentials control for geographic location and age. See Appendix Table A7-4 for further details.
SOURCE: 2000 census, 5% PUMS.

To highlight ethnic differences, these graphs show the percentage point gap between the employment rate of each group and the corresponding rate for U.S.-born whites. A positive gap implies that whites have a higher employment rate than the group in question, whereas a negative gap indicates the opposite.[8] The top panel of each figure displays the employment gaps that

[8]The employment gaps shown in Figures 7-2 and 7-3 are based on the estimates reported in Appendix Table A7-4. In the graphs, however, the estimates in Table A7-4 have been first multiplied by 100 to transform them into percentage point differentials, and then their signs have been reversed so that they represent employment *deficits*, rather than *differences*, relative to U.S.-born whites.

remain after using regression analysis to control for the influence of geographic location and age.[9] The bottom panel of each figure shows what happens to the estimated employment gaps when the underlying regressions also control for completed years of schooling and English language proficiency.[10]

The main lesson from these figures is that the human capital disadvantage of Hispanics can account for most of their employment deficit. Indeed, after conditioning on educational attainment and English proficiency, Hispanic employment gaps (relative to U.S.-born whites) tend to vanish. For example, after adjusting for age and geographic location, Mexican men have employment deficits of 5–6 percentage points, but controlling for human capital lowers the deficit to 2 percentage points for U.S.-born Mexican Americans and creates a large employment advantage for Mexican immigrants. Foreign-born Mexican women provide an even more striking case, as controlling for education and language cuts their employment deficit from 25 percentage points down to just 3 percentage points. Puerto Ricans are an exception to this pattern, however. For immigrants, both men and women, and for U.S.-born men, large Puerto Rican employment gaps shrink substantially after conditioning on human capital, but even the adjusted gaps remain sizeable.[11]

Do Hispanic workers fill particular roles in the U.S. economy? Table 7-3 examines one facet of this question: the propensity to be self-employed. Among individuals ages 25–59 who were employed during the census reference week, Table 7-3 reports the percentage that mainly worked in their own business (whether incorporated or not).[12] Overall, Hispanic self-employment rates lie between the corresponding rates of blacks and whites, with substantial variation across Hispanic subgroups. Cubans, both men and women, are self-employed at relatively high rates, with the rate for

---

[9]Separate least-squares regressions were run for men and women. The dependent variable is a dummy variable indicating whether the respondent worked at all during the calendar year preceding the census. These regressions allow intercepts to differ across ethnicity/nativity groups (with U.S.-born whites as the reference group), but the coefficients of the control variables are restricted to be the same for all groups. The control variables include indicators for geographic location and age. The geographic indicators are dummy variables identifying the nine census divisions, eight states that are home to a large proportion of the Hispanic population in the United States (Arizona, California, Florida, Illinois, New Jersey, New Mexico, New York, and Texas), and whether the respondent resides in a metropolitan area. The age indicators are dummy variables identifying the five-year age group (i.e., 25–29, 30–34, . . . , 55–59) to which each respondent belongs.

[10]The controls for English proficiency are a set of dummy variables identifying whether respondents speak a language other than English at home, and, if so, how well such individuals report being able to speak English: "very well," "well," "not well," or "not at all."

[11]Appendix Table A7-4 shows that U.S.-born Dominican men display a similar pattern.

[12]See Appendix Table A7-5 for further details.

TABLE 7-3 Self-Employment Rates (Percentages), by Gender, Ethnicity, and Nativity

	Men, by Nativity			Women, by Nativity		
Ethnicity	All	Foreign-Born	U.S.-Born	All	Foreign-Born	U.S.-Born
Whites			13.9			8.1
Blacks			5.8			3.4
All Hispanics	8.2	8.4	7.9	6.6	8.0	5.0
Mexicans	7.5	7.4	7.7	6.1	7.6	4.8
Puerto Ricans	5.6	5.7	5.5	4.0	4.2	3.8
Cubans	15.9	16.9	12.7	7.4	7.6	7.1

NOTE: The samples include individuals ages 25 to 59 who were employed during the census reference week. See Appendix Table A7-5 for standard errors, as well as for analogous calculations for other Hispanic subgroups.
SOURCE: 2000 census, 5% PUMS.

foreign-born Cuban males (17 percent) exceeding the rate for U.S.-born white males (14 percent). Puerto Ricans, both island-born and U.S.-born, have low self-employment rates (6 percent for men and 4 percent for women) that are similar to those of blacks. Mexican self-employment rates generally fall between the rates of the other two Hispanic groups, although foreign-born Mexican women have a relatively high rate (8 percent), as do several other groups of immigrant women such as Salvadorans/Guatemalans (11 percent), other Central Americans (8 percent), Colombians (12 percent), Peruvians/Ecuadorans (9 percent), and other South Americans (12 percent).[13] Much of this self-employed work by Hispanic immigrant women is in domestic service.

For self-employment rates, it turns out that controlling for geographic location and human capital (i.e., age, education, and English proficiency) accounts for little of the differences between Hispanics and whites or of the variation across Hispanic subgroups.[14] Several theories have been advanced to explain why self-employment rates vary across immigrant national-origin groups and across native ethnic groups, but these theories all have trouble providing a consistent explanation for the differences observed over a wide range of groups (Fairlie and Meyer, 1996; Portes and Rumbaut, 1990, pp. 71–79).

Table 7-4 examines another aspect of how Hispanic workers fit into the U.S. labor market: the kinds of jobs that they fill. For individuals ages 25 to 59 who were employed during the census reference week, Table 7-4

[13]See Appendix Table A7-5.

[14]See Appendix Table A7-6. Also see Fairlie and Meyer (1996).

TABLE 7-4 Industry and Occupation Distributions (Percentages), by Gender, Ethnicity, and Nativity

	Men, by Ethnicity and Nativity				Women, by Ethnicity and Nativity			
	Foreign-Born	U.S.-Born			Foreign-Born	U.S.-Born		
Definitions	Hispanics	Hispanics	Blacks	Whites	Hispanics	Hispanics	Blacks	Whites
Industry								
Agriculture and forestry	10.9	4.4	2.2	4.3	2.7	0.9	0.3	1.4
Construction	18.0	12.9	8.4	12.6	1.1	1.4	0.7	1.8
Manufacturing	20.6	16.4	21.2	21.3	18.9	9.4	12.1	11.0
Transportation and communications	5.4	8.5	10.6	7.9	2.5	3.7	4.7	3.1
Trade	20.4	18.4	15.4	16.3	20.6	17.5	12.6	17.2
Finance, insurance and real estate	2.7	4.3	4.0	5.1	5.0	8.6	7.6	8.6
Services	20.0	26.5	28.8	26.0	46.4	50.8	51.7	51.3
Public administration	2.0	8.5	9.5	6.6	2.8	7.7	10.4	5.5
	100.0	100.0	100.0	100.0	100.0	100.0	100.0	100.0
Occupation								
Managerial and professional	12.2	24.3	21.4	35.8	22.7	37.7	38.8	44.9
Technical and sales	10.3	17.3	15.9	16.2	23.6	39.2	32.0	35.6
Service	18.5	13.4	16.3	7.9	27.7	14.0	15.6	11.0
Farming and forestry	5.8	1.4	0.9	0.9	2.9	0.4	0.2	0.3
Precision, craft, and repair	24.0	20.4	14.8	18.9	1.1	0.8	0.9	0.8
Operators and laborers	29.3	23.2	30.8	20.3	22.1	7.8	12.5	7.5
Total	100.0	100.0	100.0	100.0	100.0	100.0	100.0	100.0

NOTE: The samples include individuals ages 25 to 59 who were employed during the census reference week.
SOURCE: 2000 census, 5% PUMS.

presents their percentage distributions across eight major industry and six major occupation categories.[15] In each column, the industry percentages sum to 100 percent and the occupation percentages sum to 100 percent, except for rounding error.

At this broad level of aggregation, the important sectoral differences are related to nativity rather than to ethnicity. The industry and occupation distributions of Hispanic immigrants are quite distinct from those of any of the native groups, whereas much smaller differences exist between U.S.-born Hispanics and whites. Hispanic immigrant men disproportionately work in agriculture (11 percent) and construction (18 percent), and Hispanic immigrant women are particularly overrepresented in manufacturing (19 percent). Foreign-born Hispanics of both sexes are underrepresented in the managerial/professional and technical/sales occupations, which is not surprising given the low education levels and imperfect English skills of many Hispanic immigrants, and they are overrepresented in the service and operators/laborers occupations.

The index of dissimilarity (Duncan and Duncan, 1955) provides a useful summary measure of the extent to which two distributions differ. In the current context, for example, the dissimilarity index comparing the industry distributions of U.S.-born Hispanics and whites represents the percentage of Hispanic workers (or, equivalently, white workers) who would have to change industries in order to make the industry distributions identical for these two groups of workers. The index can range between 0 and 100 percent, with higher values indicating larger differences between the two industry distributions. In practice, the index values obtained in a particular application depend on how coarsely or finely sectors are defined, with broad industry and occupation categories such as those used here producing lower values of the index.

Dissimilarity indices comparing the industry or occupation distributions of U.S.-born whites with the corresponding distributions for each of the other ethnicity/nativity groups confirm the visual impression from Table 7-4 that U.S.-born Hispanics are the most similar to whites, followed by blacks, and then by Hispanic immigrants. For the industry comparisons, the dissimilarity indices for male workers are 5.7 for U.S.-born Hispanics,

---

[15]The complete names of the industry and occupation categories are as follows. The eight major industry categories are (1) agriculture, forestry, fishing, hunting, and mining; (2) construction; (3) manufacturing; (4) transportation, communications, and other public utilities; (5) wholesale and retail trade; (6) finance, insurance, real estate, and rental and leasing; (7) services; and (8) public administration. The six major occupation categories are (1) managerial and professional specialty occupations; (2) technical, sales, and administrative support occupations; (3) service occupations; (4) farming, forestry, and fishing occupations; (5) precision production, craft, and repair occupations; and (6) operators, fabricators, and laborers.

8.5 for blacks, and 16.1 for foreign-born Hispanics. For women, the analogous indices are 3.0 for U.S.-born Hispanics, 7.9 for blacks, and 12.5 for foreign-born Hispanics. Similar patterns emerge for the occupational distributions, with male indices of 11.5 for U.S.-born Hispanics, 18.9 for blacks, and 29.5 for foreign-born Hispanics, and indices of 7.2, 9.7, and 34.2 for U.S.-born Hispanic, black, and foreign-born Hispanic women, respectively.

Earnings

Perhaps the ultimate indicator of labor market success is earnings, since earnings reflect the market's valuation of a worker's entire package of abilities and attributes, including those abilities and attributes for which data are often lacking (e.g., family background, the quality of schooling). Researchers have consistently found that, after controlling for human capital and observable skills, Hispanic workers enjoy earnings opportunities roughly similar to those of non-Hispanic whites (e.g., Antecol and Bedard, 2002; Bean et al., 2001; Grogger and Trejo, 2002; McManus et al., 1983; Reimers, 1983; Smith, 1991; Trejo, 1997). This finding for Hispanics contrasts with analogous research that shows that the earnings deficits of black men shrink only modestly upon adjusting for standard control variables (Altonji and Blank, 1999; Neal and Johnson, 1996).

To illustrate these patterns, Figures 7-4 and 7-5 display annual earnings gaps for Hispanics and blacks.[16] The graphs show the estimated percentage earnings deficits for each group relative to U.S.-born whites.[17] The samples include individuals ages 25 to 59 who worked during the calendar year preceding the decennial census.[18] Figure 7-4 presents the results for men

[16]Our measure of earnings includes any income from self-employment. Annual earnings variation across ethnicity/nativity groups reflects differences in annual hours of work as well as differences in hourly wages. Patterns for hourly wages, however, are similar to those we report here for annual earnings.

[17]The estimated deficits come from regressions similar to those that underlie Figures 7-2 and 7-3 except that now the dependent variable is the natural logarithm of annual earnings. The key estimates from these log earnings regressions are reported in Appendix Table A7-7. For ease of exposition, in the text and in Figures 7-4 and 7-5, we refer to the estimated log earnings differentials from Table A7-7 as if they represented percentage earnings gaps. Strictly speaking, however, log earnings differentials closely approximate earnings gaps only when the log earnings differentials are on the order of .25 or less in absolute value. For larger differentials, the implied percentage earnings gap can be calculated as $e^c - 1$, where c is the log earnings differential (i.e., the relevant estimate from Table A7-7).

[18]The fact that earnings information is unavailable for those without jobs can distort earnings comparisons like those shown in Figures 7-4 and 7-5. For example, suppose that individuals with lower earnings potential are less likely to be employed than those with higher skills and better labor market opportunities. In this case, the average earnings we observe, in the sample of people with jobs, are higher than what they would be if we somehow had

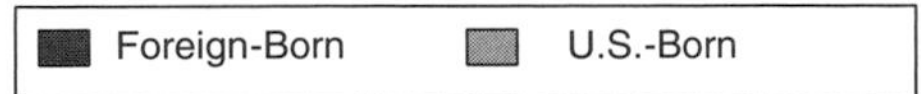

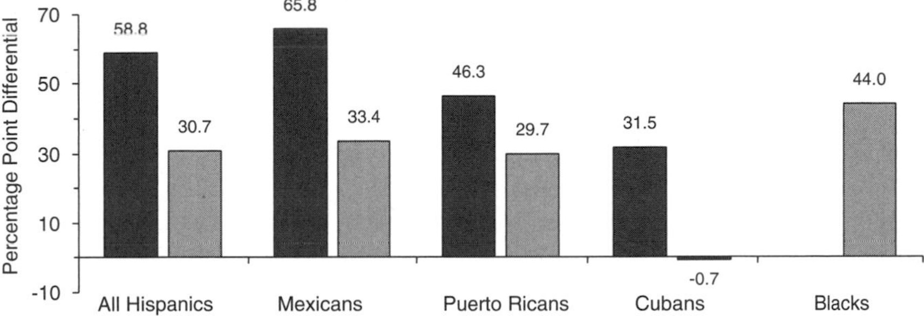

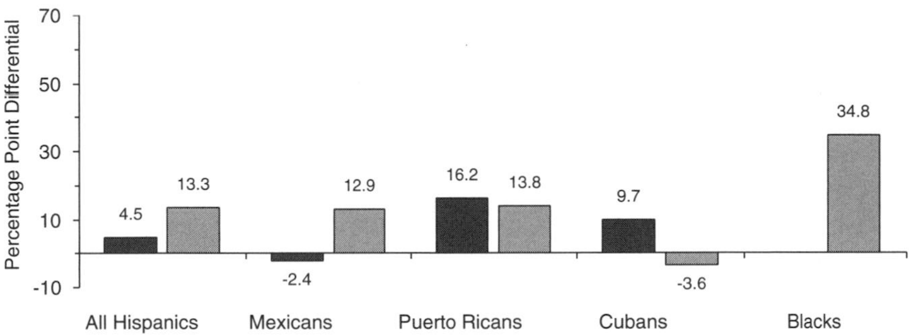

FIGURE 7-4 Male annual earnings deficits relative to U.S.-born whites, by ethnicity and nativity.
NOTE: The samples include individuals ages 25 to 59 who worked during the calendar year preceding the survey. All of the reported differentials control for geographic location and age. See Appendix Table A7-7 for further details.
SOURCE: 2000 census, 5% PUMS.

---

information on the earnings potential of all individuals, including those without jobs. Most importantly, the upward bias in observed average earnings will be larger for groups with relatively low employment rates, such as black and Puerto Rican men and immigrant Hispanic women, because for these groups a larger share of potentially low-earnings individuals will be excluded from the analysis samples. In an attempt to mitigate this problem, we present earnings comparisons that control for observable indicators of skill, such as age, education, and English proficiency, but the potential for bias remains to the extent that there are other important, unobserved determinants of labor market skills and earnings that are correlated with employment rates. This point should be kept in mind when interpreting the results reported in Figures 7-4 and 7-5. Under certain circumstances, statistical techniques can be

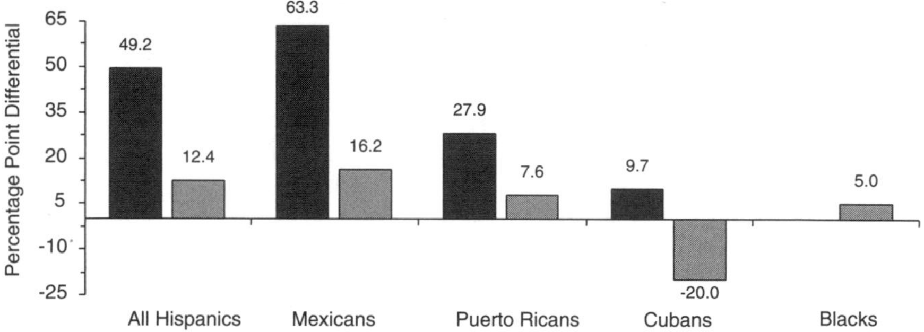

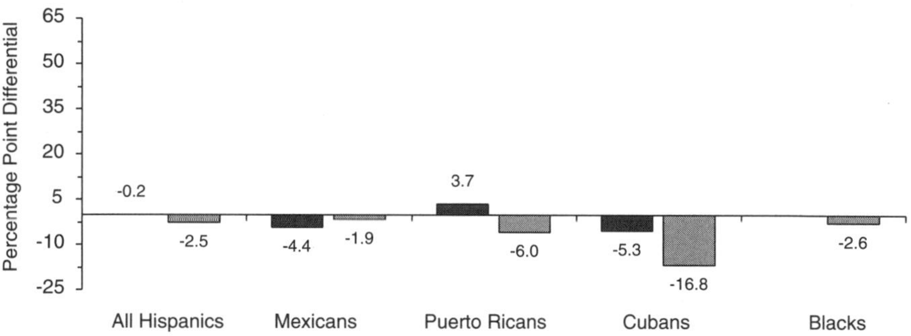

FIGURE 7-5 Female annual earnings deficits relative to U.S.-born whites, by ethnicity and nativity.
NOTE: The samples include individuals ages 25 to 59 who worked during the calendar year preceding the survey. All of the reported differentials control for geographic location and age. See Appendix Table A7-7 for further details.
SOURCE: 2000 census, 5% PUMS.

used to adjust earnings averages for the effects of employment differences across groups (Heckman, 1979), but the census data analyzed here do not provide the information necessary to make credible adjustments of this type. Later in this chapter, however, when we present estimates from longitudinal data of life-cycle patterns of human capital accumulation and wage growth, we discuss findings from research that does attempt to control for this form of selection bias as well as the endogeneity of work experience.

and Figure 7-5 gives the corresponding results for women. As with the similar graphs of employment deficits shown earlier (Figures 7-2 and 7-3), the top panel of each figure displays earnings gaps after adjusting only for geographic location and age, whereas the bottom panel also adjusts for education and English proficiency.

Without controls for human capital (i.e., the top panels of Figures 7-4 and 7-5), earnings gaps narrow sharply as we move from Hispanic immigrants to U.S.-born Hispanic Americans. For Hispanics overall, the male earnings deficit falls from 59 percent for immigrants to 31 percent for U.S. natives, and the corresponding reduction is even larger for Hispanic women, from 49 to 12 percent. Among both men and women, Mexicans exhibit the largest earnings growth between immigrants and natives, but substantial growth of this sort also occurs for Puerto Ricans and Cubans, as well as for the other Hispanic subgroups reported in Appendix Table A7-7. U.S.-born Cubans, in particular, have relatively high earnings. Indeed, even without adjustments for education and English proficiency, Cuban American men earn the same as native white men, on average, and Cuban American women earn 20 percent *more* than their white counterparts. Finally, note that the earnings deficit of 44 percent for black men is considerably larger than that for U.S.-born men from any Hispanic subgroup.

The bottom panels of Figures 7-4 and 7-5 show what happens to these earnings gaps when we condition on schooling and language. For every Hispanic group with a sizeable initial earnings deficit, controlling for education and English proficiency produces a dramatic reduction in their deficit. For men, Figure 7-4 reveals that this adjustment shrinks the earnings gap from 59 to 5 percent for Hispanic immigrants and from 31 to 13 percent for U.S.-born Hispanics. In contrast, the same adjustment reduces the earnings deficit of black men only from 44 percent to 35 percent. Consequently, low human capital explains a much bigger portion of the earnings disadvantage of Hispanic men (relative to whites) than it does for black men. Moreover, after accounting for the admittedly crude measures of labor market skill available in census data—age, educational attainment, and English proficiency—the annual earnings gap of U.S.-born Hispanic men falls to 13 percent, whereas the corresponding earnings gap for black men is 35 percent. In other words, after conditioning on observable skills, Hispanics face labor market opportunities much more similar to those faced by whites than do blacks.

Figure 7–5 shows that the earnings patterns are largely the same for women. In fact, the effects of controlling for human capital are even more striking in this case, as the adjusted earnings deficit vanishes for every group of Hispanic women, regardless of nativity or national origin. Therefore, after adjusting for differences in schooling and English proficiency, all groups of Hispanic women have average annual earnings as high as those of

U.S.-born white women. In contrast to the situation for black men, however, black women display a modest earnings disadvantage relative to white women that disappears after conditioning on schooling.

We have seen that, for both employment and earnings, Hispanic–white differences are in large part explained by the relatively low human capital of most Hispanic groups. The estimates reported in the bottom panels of Figures 7-2 to 7-5, however, derive from regression specifications that constrain the impact of schooling and other measures of human capital to be the same for all ethnicity/nativity groups. Because U.S.-born whites make up the bulk of the population, the estimated labor market returns to our measures of human capital mainly reflect the returns for this dominant group. As a result, the education-adjusted employment and earnings deficits presented here reflect the quality as well as the quantity of schooling. These deficits represent the gaps relative to U.S.-born whites that would exist if Hispanics possessed as much education as whites and also earned the same labor market reward for education as whites. To the extent that differences in the returns to schooling across ethnicity/nativity groups arise from labor market discrimination rather than from differences in the quality of schooling, however, the education-adjusted employment and earnings gaps we present may overstate the role that human capital disparities play in the economic disadvantage of Hispanics. We return to the issue of differences in the returns to human capital by ethnicity and nativity in the next section.

Another issue that arises when attempting to adjust for human capital differences between workers is how to control for work experience. The results presented in the bottom panels of Figures 7-2 to 7-5 control for age, as well as years of schooling and English proficiency. By simultaneously controlling for age and education, these regressions implicitly hold constant *potential* work experience, which is typically measured as "Age-Years of Schooling-6."[19] The popularity of this means of controlling for differences in work experience is rooted largely in the lack of information on actual work experience in many data sources, including the decennial census and the Current Population Survey. Nonetheless, the issue is whether measures of potential work experience accurately represent the actual work experiences of various demographic groups, and whether the use of potential rather than actual work experience biases estimated earnings regressions.[20] The employment rates reported in Table 7-2 (and Appendix Table A7-3)

[19]Following the influential work of Mincer (1974), potential work experience is often entered as a quadratic function in logarithmic earnings regressions. Murphy and Welch (1990) and Heckman, Lochner, and Todd (2003) provide critical assessments of Mincer's specification of the earnings function.

[20]See Antecol and Bedard (2002, 2004) for recent treatments of this issue.

indicate notable differences across racial and ethnic groups and especially by gender. Moreover, the extent to which work experience is systematically related to years of schooling can generate bias in estimated returns to education.[21] In the next section, we explore these issues by investigating how Hispanic men and women differ relative to whites and blacks using longitudinal data for a set of birth cohorts who began their transition from school to work during the 1980s. We also discuss findings on whether the returns to schooling and work experience for Hispanics differ from those of whites or blacks.

LIFE-CYCLE PATTERNS IN LABOR MARKET EXPERIENCES AND THEIR CONSEQUENCES FOR LIFE-CYCLE WAGE GROWTH[22]

We now turn to a more detailed assessment of the life-cycle patterns of educational and labor market experiences of young Hispanic men and women and examine how these experiences have affected their earnings attainment. These estimates are derived for a nationally representative sample of young men and women between the ages of 13 and 16 in 1978 drawn from the National Longitudinal Survey of Youth 1979 (NLSY79).[23] We note that all of the young adults enrolled in this sample resided in the United States in 1978. As a result, the sample members, including the Hispanics, had access to U.S. schools for much, if not all, of their adolescent years. As a result, we should expect to find differences in educational attainment by nativity for Hispanics between these data and those from the 2000 census presented above. Below, we present estimates for Hispanics, both U.S.-born and foreign-born, as well as blacks and whites. The information available in the NLSY79 does not permit identification of the Hispanic subgroups considered in the rest of this chapter.

Accumulated Labor Market–Related Experiences in Early Adulthood

Table 7-5 tabulates the high grades completed, high school and college graduation rates, and years spent in various work and other activities between the ages of 13 and 27 by gender and ethnicity and race.[24] Consistent

---

[21]See Heckman et al. (2003) for evidence that the shape, as well as the level, of age-earnings profiles do differ by years of schooling over the latter part of the 20th century.

[22]This section draws heavily on results from Ahituv and Tienda (2004), Bacolod and Hotz (2004), and Hotz, Xu, Tienda, and Ahituv (2002).

[23]Details of this sample and its construction can be found in Bacolod and Hotz (2004). This sample closely parallels those used in Hotz et al. (2002) and Ahituv and Tienda (2004).

[24]See Bacolod and Hotz (2004) for a description of the year-by-year work, schooling, and other activities used to construct these accumulated "years spent" measures.

TABLE 7-5 Graduation Rates and Years Spent in Various School, Work, and Other Activities

Ages 13–27									
Young Men					Young Women				
	Hispanics					Hispanics			
All	Foreign-Born	U.S.-Born	Blacks	Whites	All	Foreign-Born	U.S.-Born	Blacks	Whites
Highest grade completed									
12.15	11.88	12.22	12.50	13.32	12.39	11.81	12.54	12.86	13.36
1.17	*1.44*	*1.10*	*0.82*		*0.97*	*1.55*	*0.82*	*0.50*	
Proportion graduated from high school									
0.73	0.71	0.74	0.84	0.88	0.79	0.65	0.83	0.87	0.91
0.15	*0.17*	*0.14*	*0.04*		*0.12*	*0.26*	*0.08*	*0.04*	
Proportion graduated from college									
0.11	0.08	0.12	0.11	0.26	0.11	0.12	0.11	0.13	0.27
0.15	*0.18*	*0.14*	*0.15*		*0.16*	*0.15*	*0.16*	*0.14*	
Years spent working since age 13, all types									
9.98	10.41	9.85	9.09	10.48	9.09	8.62	9.21	8.35	10.30
0.50	*0.06*	*0.63*	*1.39*		*1.21*	*1.68*	*1.09*	*1.95*	
Years spent working while in school since age 13									
2.75	2.91	2.71	2.50	3.65	2.71	2.44	2.78	2.65	3.56
0.90	*0.75*	*0.95*	*1.15*		*0.84*	*1.11*	*0.78*	*0.90*	
Years spent working part-time (and not in school) since age 13									
3.39	3.27	3.43	3.29	2.57	3.60	3.50	3.63	3.44	3.50
–0.82	*–0.70*	*–0.86*	*–0.72*		*–0.11*	*0.00*	*–0.13*	*0.06*	
Years spent working full-time									
3.83	4.24	3.72	3.30	4.26	2.77	2.68	2.80	2.26	3.24
0.42	*0.01*	*0.54*	*0.96*		*0.47*	*0.56*	*0.45*	*0.99*	
Years of military service									
0.57	0.28	0.65	0.91	0.71	0.04	0.09	0.03	0.13	0.08
0.14	*0.43*	*0.06*	*–0.21*		*0.04*	*–0.01*	*0.05*	*–0.05*	
Years spent in other nonschool, nonwork activities since age 13									
0.67	0.41	0.74	0.96	0.31	1.87	2.16	1.80	2.24	1.12
–0.36	*–0.10*	*–0.43*	*–0.65*		*–0.75*	*–1.04*	*–0.68*	*–1.12*	
Number of observations (persons)									
488	111	377	769	1,588	493	103	390	720	1,523

NOTE: Italicized values below average accumulated years and proportions are deficits relative to whites.
SOURCE: NLSY79.

with our findings based on data from the 2000 U.S. Census of Population, Hispanics, both U.S.- and foreign-born, had lower levels of education than do their black and white counterparts. This is true, regardless of what measure of education (e.g., graduate rates or highest grades completed) is used. We note that the deficits in highest grades completed for U.S.-born Hispanics are almost identical to those presented in Table 7-1 using census data.

The high grade completed for foreign-born Hispanics in Table 7-5 is almost two grades higher, for both men and women, than the estimates presented in Table 7-1. This difference is consistent with the fact that the sample members in the NLSY79 had already entered the United States by the time they were adolescents, whereas no such restriction holds for the respondents in the 2000 census. With respect to rates of graduation from high school, the rates for Hispanic men are 15 percentage points lower than those of white men, with deficits of 17 percentage points for foreign-born Hispanic males. While the high school graduation rate deficits for all Hispanic women relative to white women are slightly lower than those for men (12 percentage points), foreign-born Hispanic women have graduation rates that were even larger than those of men (26 percentage points). The fact that we have sizeable deficits in graduation rates for foreign-born Hispanics relative to their white counterparts is all the more notable, given that the NLSY79 respondents resided in the United States during their adolescent years.

With respect to accumulated work experience, Hispanic men accumulated half a year less in the number of years they engaged in some work for pay between the ages of 13 and 27 than their white counterparts (9.98 years versus 10.48 for white men) and almost a year more than black men (9.09 years). Furthermore, we found no difference in accumulated years of work over this age range between foreign-born Hispanic men and whites. Among women, Hispanics accumulated a little more than a year less work experience than whites (9.09 versus 10.30 years for white women) and three quarters of a year more than blacks. Contrary to the findings for men, foreign-born Hispanic women worked 1.68 years less than white women over this age range.

Table 7-5 also records accumulated years spent working part-time, while both in and out of school, and working full-time during a given year. With respect to full-time work, Hispanic men worked 0.42 fewer years or 10 percent less than white men, and Hispanic women worked 0.47 years or 14.5 percent less than their white counterparts. As with overall work experience, foreign-born Hispanic men worked almost as many years between the ages of 13 and 27 as did native-born white men, but foreign-born Hispanic women were less likely to acquire full-time work experience than either U.S.-born Hispanic or white women. With respect to working part-time in years that they were not in school, Hispanics, especially men, actually accumulated more of this type of work experience than did whites, with Hispanic men working 0.82 (or 32 percent) more years and virtually no differences between Hispanic women and their white counterparts. Finally, both Hispanic men and women, regardless of their nativity status, spent less time working while in school than did whites, although both accumulated more years of working while in school than did their black counterparts. This deficit in working-while-in-school for Hispanics relative to whites is largely due to the fact that Hispanics spent less time in school (and thus accumulated less education) than did whites. In sum, Hispanics gained less work experience in their transition from school to the world of work, and their work experience tended to be part-time rather than full-time work experience. To the extent that full-time work experience reflects greater attachment to the labor force and is more likely to enhance one's human capital than part-time experience, these differences may play an important role in the subsequent success Hispanics had in earnings and the growth of earnings over their life-cycle.

We also present in Table 7-5 estimates of the years Hispanics spent in military service and compare them to whites and blacks. With respect to military experience, we note that since the Vietnam War, the U.S. military has been staffed by an all-volunteer force and studies have shown that military service provides an important employment and skill-enhancing opportunity for less-educated young adults, especially minority men (Kilburn, 1993). Partially consistent with the latter view, we found that black men and women spent more years in the military than their white counterparts, although relatively few young adults spent any time in the military, regardless of their race or ethnicity. However, both Hispanic men and women spent less time in the military than either blacks or whites. While this trend may have changed for more recent cohorts of young men, these statistics suggest that Hispanics did not make use of this alternative route into the U.S. labor force, which was used by less-educated blacks.

Finally, we examine the time that Hispanics and their black and white counterparts spent in an omnibus category of other nonwork, nonschool activities during their adolescent and early adult years. For young women, some of this time reflects time spent bearing and rearing children. For young men, it is less clear what activities they were engaged in, although one might presume that spending large amounts of one's early adulthood in activities other than school, work, or the military did not enhance their success in the labor market. As recorded in Table 7-5, we found that women spent more time in this activity category than did men, and Hispanic and black women spent more of their years than did white women, consistent with both the greater time commitment of women relative to men to childrearing and the higher fertility rates of minority women relative to white women. Among men, we also found that Hispanics spent more time not working, going to school, or serving in the military than whites but spent less of their adolescent and early adult years doing so than black men.

Wages in Early Adulthood

An important indicator of an individual's labor market success, in addition to employment, is the wages they can command in the marketplace. Standard models of human capital accumulation (Mincer, 1974) argue that individuals acquire human capital through schooling and from the on-the-job training and experiences that are a by-product of early work experiences. Furthermore, these theories suggest that market wages received by individuals reflect the market rewards, or returns, to the amount of human capital one acquires over the life-cycle. In this section, we examine the life-cycle patterns in market wage rates received by Hispanic young men, as well as their black and white counterparts. We examine the wages and wage growth of Hispanics relative to whites and blacks during their early adulthood, focusing on ages 16 through 27. Note that these estimates are calculated using data for individuals who were employed at a particular age (more on the potential selectivity of these subsamples and their implications for estimating wages below).

Focusing on average hourly wage rates for ages 23 to 27, we found that Hispanic men and women earned $1.46 (16 percent) and $1.09 (14 percent) lower hourly wage rates, respectively, than did their white counterparts. For the same ages, Hispanic men had slightly higher wages than blacks, while Hispanic women had wage rates over a dollar lower than black women. U.S.-born Hispanics had slightly lower wages over these ages than did their foreign-born counterparts. Overall, these wage rate differentials between Hispanics and whites and blacks are consistent with those found for broader age ranges using 2000 census data.

Hispanics also experienced lower rates of growth in wages relative to whites and blacks during early adulthood. Wages over the age range 16 to 27 grew at an annual rate of 7.9 percent for Hispanic men, while the corresponding rates for white and black men were 9.2 and 8.2 percent, respectively. Among Hispanic women, wages over this same age range grew at an annual rate of 7.7 percent, compared with 8.5 and 6.9 percent per year for white and black women, respectively.[25]

---

[25]We note, however, that the wages of foreign-born Hispanic men had an annual rate of growth that was essentially the same as their white counterparts.

Differences in Returns to Schooling and Work Experience for Earnings

The evidence on wage levels and growth in Table 7-6, along with that on annual earnings, indicates that over the life-cycle almost all Hispanics experienced a growing differential in wage rates between themselves and whites. As noted earlier, differences in wages between Hispanics and whites (or between Hispanics and blacks) can result from two factors: differences in the *amounts* of human capital—e.g., schooling, English language proficiency, and the amount and types of accumulated work experience—and differences in the *returns* to human capital across groups. We have already seen that a key difference between Hispanic young men and their black and white counterparts is the markedly lower levels of educational attainment for the former group. These findings are consistent with those in a large number of other studies of differences in labor market earnings by race and ethnicity.

However, a central issue in the literatures on labor market discrimination and educational quality has been the extent to which differences in labor market earnings are driven by differences across groups in the returns to skills, that is, differences by race and ethnicity in the way that labor markets reward skills.[26] Several studies that have examined this issue (Grogger and Trejo, 2002; Smith, 1991; Trejo, 1997) have found that estimates of returns to additional years of schooling in terms of labor market earnings are similar for U.S.-born whites, blacks, and Hispanics. At the same time, estimated returns to years of schooling are typically much lower for immigrants. That the U.S. labor market pays less for years of schooling acquired outside the United States is a common finding that also applies to non-Hispanic groups, including whites (Borjas, 1995; Schoeni, 1997; Trejo, 2003). This finding is usually interpreted as evidence that the schooling immigrants acquire in their home country transfers imperfectly to the U.S. labor market (Chiswick, 1978).

In drawing conclusions about differences in the returns to acquired skills across racial and ethnic groups, it is important to take account of why individuals and groups differ in their accumulation of human capital (e.g., their acquisition of schooling and work experience) and how these processes relate to the generation of their labor market earnings. The central issue here is whether or not years of schooling and work experience used to measure an individual's accumulation of human capital are *exogenous* with respect to one's labor market earnings. Economic models of schooling acquisition (as well as the accumulation of work experience) assume that individuals (and families) choose these components of human capital so as

[26]See Altonji and Blank (1999) for a survey of this literature.

TABLE 7-6 Average Hourly Wage Rates by Age, Ages 16 to 27

	Young Men					Young Women				
		Hispanics					Hispanics			
Age	All	Foreign-Born	U.S.-Born	Blacks	Whites	All	Foreign-Born	U.S.-Born	Blacks	Whites
16	4.39	1.65	4.81	3.53	3.79	7.11	4.94	7.60	12.20	3.56
17	4.08	3.26	4.34	3.98	3.91	3.39	3.25	3.42	4.50	3.65
18	4.24	4.50	4.17	3.76	4.42	3.69	3.90	3.64	3.33	3.95
19	5.05	5.26	4.98	4.14	5.22	4.05	4.11	4.03	4.06	4.19
20	5.58	6.56	5.28	4.55	5.46	4.28	4.02	4.34	4.17	4.80
21	5.57	5.50	5.59	5.07	5.69	5.39	4.99	5.48	4.55	5.10
22	6.22	6.60	6.10	5.77	6.73	5.91	6.42	5.79	4.97	9.62
23	6.71	6.71	6.71	6.33	8.09	5.90	5.10	6.09	4.81	6.42
24	7.17	7.00	7.23	6.64	7.98	6.34	7.41	6.11	5.88	7.06
25	7.62	7.49	7.67	7.50	8.57	6.43	6.52	6.41	6.17	7.14
26	8.19	7.84	8.29	7.13	10.65	6.88	6.95	6.87	8.75	7.34
27	8.44	9.80	8.02	9.21	10.04	7.09	6.45	7.23	10.14	9.56
Average ages 24–27	7.86	8.03	7.80	7.62	9.31	6.69	6.83	6.66	7.74	7.78
Different from whites, ages 24–27	1.46	1.28	1.51	1.69		1.09	0.94	1.12	0.04	
Annual growth rate	0.079	0.095	0.074	0.082	0.092	0.077	0.062	0.081	0.069	0.085

NOTE: All wages are deflated to be in 1982–1984 dollars. Averages were taken over respondents who reported working at a particular age.
SOURCE: NLSY79.

to maximize, in part, their subsequent earnings (Becker, 1975; Card, 2001; Heckman et al., 2003; Mincer, 1958, 1974; Rosen, 1977; Willis, 1986).

In such models, for example, the amount of schooling an individual acquires will depend on two sets of factors: (a) individual "ability," that is, one's capacity to generate labor market earnings in the absence of any further skill acquisition and/or their productivity in converting schooling and work experience into market earnings and (b) "opportunities," that is, the nontime costs of acquiring human capital and/or the ability to finance these costs. To the extent that there are differences in ability or opportunities or both across individuals, both within and across ethnic and racial groups, and that these differences are unobserved, simple (ordinary least-squares) regression methods for estimating the "average" returns to schooling and work experience—such as those used to produce the adjusted earnings in Figure 7-4 and 7-5 and as used in most simple analyses of racial, gender, and ethnic differences in earnings—are likely to be biased.[27] More generally, this potential for *endogeneity* or *self-selection* bias can compromise the conclusions about ethnic and racial differences in the returns to schooling and work experience in previous empirical investigations.

In a recent paper, Hotz et al. (2002) exploit the richness of the longitudinal data in the NLSY79 to estimate the returns to educational attainment and a detailed set of accumulated work experiences, such as those presented in Table 7-5 for Hispanic, black, and white young men. The authors use a factor analytic, dynamic selection model developed by Cameron and Heckman (1998, 2001) to account for the endogenous acquisition of schooling and work experience of young white, black, and Hispanic men when estimating their returns in wages over their early careers. There are two notable findings in Hotz et al. (2002) with respect the rates of return to different forms of work and schooling experiences. First, once one controls for various forms of self-selection in the accumulation of years of schooling and work experience, one finds that spending an extra year in school (and completing an additional grade) has a higher rate of return than spending that year in full-time or part-time work or in the military. Second, there is no evidence that the returns for wages to various forms of human capital are systematically different across Hispanic and white young men once one controls for self-selection.[28] These findings add further credence to the

[27]See Griliches (1977) for a discussion of the problem of "ability" bias in estimating the returns to schooling and Willis (1986) and Heckman and Vytlacil (1998) for discussions of the more general nature of the biases in estimating returns to acquired human capital in earnings equations.

[28]Differences in the returns to schooling and work for blacks relative to the other two groups persist, although the selection-correction methods reduce these differences compared with standard ordinary least-squares estimates.

conclusion drawn earlier—and that drawn by a number of other previous studies: the fact that Hispanics have lower labor market outcomes than whites is the result of having acquired less human capital and their lower levels of skill and not because comparably skilled Hispanics are treated differently from whites in the U.S. labor market.

TEMPORAL AND GENERATIONAL CHANGES IN THE LABOR MARKET ATTAINMENT OF HISPANICS

Our discussion of the labor market attainment of Hispanics in the United States to this point has focused either on the recent experiences (as of 2000) of Hispanics or on those of a recent cohort. But have the attainments of Hispanics in the United States improved or deteriorated over time? Have they improved across generations? In the following two sections, we address each of these questions in turn, examining whether Hispanics made progress in terms of educational attainment, employment, and earnings over the latter part of the 20th century and whether later cohorts of Hispanics show improvement relative to earlier generations. Examining the secular and generational changes in Hispanic labor market attainment is important for at least two reasons.

First, an essential part of the story of Hispanics in the United States is immigration. As has been noted by Rumbaut in Chapter 2, the United States has undergone a wave of immigration over the last 25 years that has increased the size of the Hispanic population as well as changed its composition. Both have potentially important impacts on the secular and generational trends in Hispanic attainment and on the ways they are likely to change in the future.

Second, the U.S. labor market and economy have undergone several important secular changes with important consequences for different skill groups in the U.S. workforce, including Hispanics. The past 30 years have witnessed a large rise in overall wage inequality among American workers that has resulted from substantial increases in the returns to skills (see Katz and Murphy, 1992). For example, from 1979 to 1988 the average wage rate of college graduates increased relative to that of high school graduates by 15 percentage points (Bound and Johnson, 1992, p. 371). In addition, since 1975, the United States has also experienced a significant decline in the share of employment in the manufacturing sector and a noticeable increase in the share of service-sector jobs (Levy and Murnane, 1992, Table 7). Jobs in the manufacturing sector in the United States traditionally paid relatively high wages to lower skilled workers; service-sector jobs, especially for less-skilled workers, have tended to pay lower wages and exhibit lower rates of improvement with experience and seniority. Given the lower levels of educational attainment of Hispanics relative to their white and black counterparts, these changes in the structure of the U.S. labor market over the past 30 years have had a substantial impact on the likelihood of secular improvements for Hispanics over this period. Thus, a closer look at how Hispanics fared in the labor market over time and across generations is clearly in order.

Changes in Educational Attainment and Labor Market Earnings Over Time

We begin by discussing what happened to the educational attainment of Hispanics over the latter part of the 20th century. Whenever analyzing intertemporal trends for U.S. Hispanics, it is imperative to recognize that immigration is a fundamental source of change for this population. High rates of immigration imply that change can occur rapidly, not only in terms of the size of this group, but also with respect to its composition. As we have shown, foreign-born and U.S.-born Hispanics differ dramatically in their labor market skills and outcomes, and therefore it is essential to disaggregate by nativity when analyzing Hispanics. Immigration-induced shifts in the composition of the Hispanic population make this even more relevant when examining changes over time.

To illustrate this point, Figure 7-6 shows average years of schooling for Mexican and white men in the 1980, 1990, and 2000 censuses. If we compare *all* Mexicans (i.e., foreign-born and U.S.-born combined) with U.S.-born whites, the story that emerges is one of educational stagnation. Between 1980 and 2000, average schooling rose by just 0.4 years for all Mexicans (from 9.4 to 9.8), which is only half of the 0.8-year increase experienced by whites (from 12.8 to 13.6), so the educational disadvantage of Mexicans appears to have widened. Looking at the trends by nativity, however, leads to exactly the opposite conclusion. Over these two decades, average schooling climbed by 1.2 years for foreign-born Mexicans (from 7.3 to 8.5) and by 1.5 years for U.S.-born Mexicans (from 10.6 to 12.1), so both groups actually made some progress in closing their educational gaps relative to whites.

Why is the overall trend for Mexicans much less favorable than the nativity-specific trends? Because immigrants, with their relatively low education levels, constitute an increasingly large share of U.S. Mexicans. In the samples of men ages 25 to 59 used in Figure 7-6, the percentage foreign-born among Mexicans shot up from 37 percent in 1980 to 51 percent in 1990 and 63 percent in 2000. With the potential for profound compositional changes such as this, trends for Hispanic groups that do not distinguish by nativity are likely to provide a misleading portrait of what is really happening to these groups.

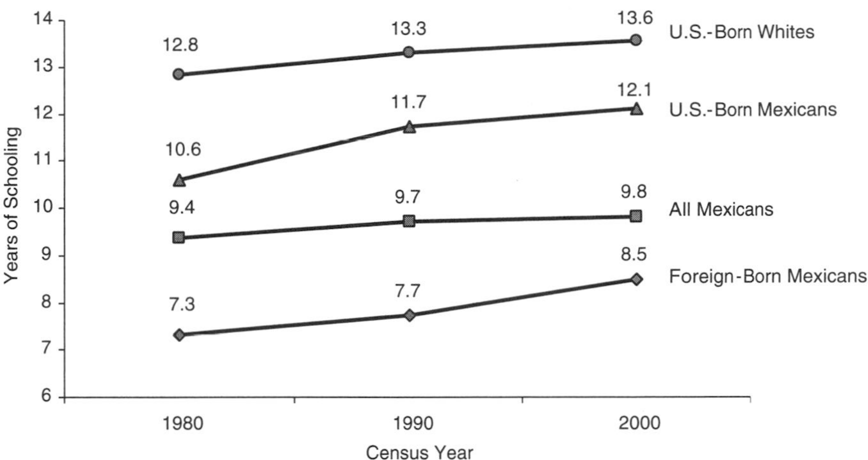

FIGURE 7-6 Average years of schooling for men, 1980–2000, by ethnicity and nativity.
NOTE: The samples include men ages 25 to 59.
SOURCE: 1980, 1990, and 2000 census, 5% PUMS.

We next turn to what happened to labor market earnings for Hispanics relative to whites and blacks over the latter part of the 20th century. In Table 7-7, we present estimates of the annual earnings of Hispanic men and women, for all Hispanics and subgroups, as a percentage of the earnings of whites and blacks for 1980, 1990, and 2000. On average, the gap in earnings between Hispanic men and women relative to U.S.-born whites grew from 1980 to 2000, with most of the change occurring between 1980 and 1990. In 1980, the earnings of Hispanic men were 58.5 percent of those of white men; by 2000, the earnings of Hispanic men had declined to 50.8 percent of white men. The declines in the earnings of Hispanic women relative to their white counterparts were even larger, declining by 18.5 percentage points from 1980 to 2000. Notably, the earnings of Hispanic men and women also declined relative to U.S.-born blacks, with the declines being steeper for men relative to women. As shown in Table 7-7, there is some variation in this pattern when comparing Hispanic subgroups to whites and blacks. Mexicans show steeper declines in earnings, relative to whites and blacks for both men and women. In contrast, the earnings of Puerto Rican men actually improved relative to whites and blacks, while the earnings of Puerto Rican women relative to whites declined slightly but remained largely unchanged relative to their black counterparts. The earnings of Cuban men remained largely unchanged relative to white men and

TABLE 7-7 Annual Earnings of Hispanics Relative to Black and Whites, 1980–2000

	Men						Women					
	Annual Earnings as Percentage of U.S.-Born Whites			Annual Earnings as Percentage of U.S.-Born Blacks			Annual Earnings as Percentage of U.S.-Born Whites			Annual Earnings as Percentage of U.S.-Born Blacks		
Ethnicity/Nativity	1980	1990	2000	1980	1990	2000	1980	1990	2000	1980	1990	2000
U.S.-born blacks	54.8	49.5	56.0				105.3	99.6	95.0			
All Hispanics												
All	58.5	49.8	50.8	106.8	100.6	90.7	85.2	73.0	66.7	80.9	73.3	70.2
Foreign-born	48.4	37.5	41.2	88.3	75.8	73.6	82.1	59.0	50.8	78.0	59.2	53.5
U.S.-born	68.9	67.9	69.3	125.7	137.2	123.8	88.0	88.9	87.6	83.6	89.3	92.2
Mexicans												
All	55.8	45.4	45.8	101.8	91.7	81.8	77.8	65.9	60.3	73.9	66.2	63.5
Foreign-born	38.1	26.3	34.2	69.5	53.1	61.1	63.8	37.8	36.7	60.6	38.0	38.6
U.S.-born	66.3	65.1	66.6	121.0	131.5	118.9	83.7	83.8	83.8	79.5	84.1	88.2
Puerto Ricans												
All	50.1	53.5	62.0	91.4	108.1	110.7	89.7	85.3	82.8	85.2	85.6	87.2
Foreign-born	44.8	45.8	53.7	81.8	92.5	95.9	85.6	75.8	72.1	81.3	76.1	75.9
U.S.-born	69.5	66.0	70.3	126.8	133.3	125.5	101.7	98.6	92.4	96.6	99.0	97.3
Cubans												
All	77.4	76.7	75.8	141.2	154.9	135.4	110.3	104.8	97.9	104.7	105.2	103.1
Foreign-born	76.9	73.7	68.5	140.3	148.9	122.3	109.5	102.5	90.3	104.0	102.9	95.1
U.S.-born	83.1	95.7	100.7	151.6	193.3	179.8	122.3	118.5	120.0	116.1	119.0	126.3

NOTE: The estimates for 1980 and 1990 are constructed in an analogous way, using data from the 1980 and 1990 5% PUMS, census files. The estimates for 2000 are taken from Appendix Table A7-7, Columns (1) for Men and Women.
SOURCE: 1980, 1990, 2000 censuses 5% PUMS.

improved relative to blacks, while Cuban women saw their earnings decline relative to white women and remain largely the same relative to black women.

The trends in the relative labor market earnings of Hispanics are markedly different for those who are foreign-born and U.S.-born. For Hispanics taken as a group and for all subgroups but Puerto Ricans, the earnings of foreign-born Hispanics either declined or remained unchanged relative to the earnings of whites and blacks. The relative declines in earnings for the foreign-born were more pronounced among all groups of Hispanic women. In contrast, the earnings of U.S.-born Hispanics tended to either improve or remain the same, compared with those of whites and blacks over the last 30 years of the 20th century. Thus, consistent with the trends in years of schooling—and probably as a result of the changes in educational attainment—the story of what happened to Hispanics over the latter part of the 20th century with respect to their success in the labor market is largely driven by immigration and where these groups were educated. The more recent waves of immigrants have fallen behind their white and black counterparts, while those educated in the United States tended to hold their position but not improve, relative to whites and blacks. In short, the education deficits of Hispanics, primarily those of the foreign-born, appear to have been an increasing liability over time as the U.S. labor market restructured and put a greater premium on work-related skills.

Intergenerational Changes in Attainment

As noted above, a distinguishing feature of the U.S. Hispanic population is the preponderance of those who are relatively new to this country. Because of the large volume of immigration from Spanish-speaking countries over the past several decades, most Hispanic workers in the United States come from families that have been in the country for no more than two generations. Previous waves of predominantly unskilled immigrants, such as the Italians and the Irish, experienced substantial intergenerational progress that ultimately enabled their descendants to join the economic mainstream of American society, but this process took two or three generations to unfold (Borjas, 1994; Chiswick, 1977; Neidert and Farley, 1985; Perlmann and Waldinger, 1997). When analyzing labor market outcomes for U.S. Hispanics, it is therefore of interest to examine differences not just between the foreign-born and U.S.-born, but also, when possible, across generations of the U.S.-born. In this section, we explore what available data can tell us about such intergenerational patterns.

Beginning in 1980, the decennial census stopped asking respondents where their parents were born. Starting in 1994, the Current Population Survey (CPS) began collecting this information on a regular basis from all respondents. As a result, the CPS is currently the best large-scale U.S. data set for investigating how Hispanic labor market outcomes vary by immigrant generation.

The CPS is a monthly survey of about 50,000 households that the U.S. government uses to estimate unemployment rates and other indicators of labor market activity. Every March, the CPS includes a set of additional questions, known as the annual demographic supplement, that collects detailed information on respondents' labor supply and sources of income for the preceding calendar year. We analyzed microdata from these March CPS files for the years 1998–2002, and the earnings measures that we constructed pertain to calendar years 1997–2001.[29]

As before, we restricted our analysis to individuals in the age range of 25 to 59. Using the CPS information on the nativity of each individual and his or her parents, we define three broad categories of immigrant generation. The first generation consists of immigrants: foreign-born individuals whose parents were also born outside the United States. The second generation includes U.S.-born individuals who have at least one foreign-born parent. The "third and higher generation" is the designation applied to U.S. natives whose parents are also natives. For ease of exposition, we often refer to this last group as the "3rd+ generation" or simply the third generation. Compared with the census data presented earlier, the main advantage of the CPS is this ability to distinguish between the second and third+ generations of U.S.-born individuals. For our purposes, important drawbacks of the CPS data are the smaller sample sizes and the absence of information about English proficiency.

The standard method for identifying Hispanics in CPS data is to use respondents' self-reported information about their ethnicity. In response to a question about their "origin or descent," individuals can report themselves to be non-Hispanic, or they can choose to identify as a member of one of the following Hispanic groups: Mexican (including Mexican American, Chicano, or Mexicano), Puerto Rican, Cuban, Central or South American, or the residual category of "other Hispanic." We employ this standard method for identifying Hispanics. An alternative method is to assign Hispanic ethnicity based on the countries of birth of the respondent and his or her parents, but this method cannot identify Hispanics beyond the second generation. Moreover, for the analyses reported below, using the alternative method to identify first- and second-generation Hispanics produces results similar to those obtained from the standard method.

In addition to reporting results for all three generational categories of Hispanics, we also present analogous statistics for non-Hispanic whites and

[29]We thank Rubén Rumbaut and Charles Morgan for making available their extract of the March 1998–2002 CPS data.

for non-Hispanic blacks. Here, the non-Hispanic samples include only individuals who are third and higher generation.

Figure 7-7 begins our intergenerational analysis of CPS data with a look at educational attainment.[30] We focus on differences between the second and third generations, because this is the information not available in the census data already discussed. Strikingly, average education levels are essentially the same for second and later generations of Hispanics. This finding seems surprising in light of the large schooling gains that occur between the first and second generations and the sizeable educational gap that remains between second-generation Hispanics and third-generation whites.

Mexicans and Puerto Ricans display the same general patterns as Hispanics overall, with substantial schooling growth between the first and second generations, little or no additional growth after the second generation, and a large educational deficit relative to whites that persists into at least the third generation. As before, Cubans stand out from the other groups with remarkably high levels of schooling. At over 14 years, the average education of second-generation Cubans is at least half a year above that of third-generation whites.

Figures 7-8 and 7-9 present a parallel analysis of annual earnings gaps. The graphs show the estimated percentage earnings deficits for each group relative to third-generation whites.[31] For Hispanic men (Figure 7-8), earnings gaps narrow across generations, with the biggest decline between the first and second generations and a smaller decline after that. The earnings deficit for Mexican men, for example, falls from 67 percent for immigrants to 38 percent for the second generation to 31 percent for later generations. For Puerto Rican men, the analogous earnings deficits are 48 percent for the first generation, 31 percent for the second generation, and 16 percent for later generations. Remarkably, the 39 percent earnings deficit among Cuban immigrants disappears by the second generation. For comparison purposes, note that the earnings gap for third-generation black men is 41 percent.

The bottom panel of Figure 7-8 shows what happens to these earnings gaps when we condition on schooling.[32] As before, all of the earnings

[30]Because our CPS samples include very few Cubans who are third generation, only statistics for the first and second generations are shown for this national-origin group. See Appendix Table A7-8 for the calculations underlying Figure 7-7, including standard errors and cell sample sizes. Appendix Table A7-8 also reports results for the two somewhat amorphous Hispanic subgroups identified by the CPS but not shown in Figure 7-1: Central/South Americans and "other Hispanics."

[31]See Appendix Table A7-9 for details of these estimates.

[32]Unlike the census, the March CPS does not collect information on English proficiency, so we cannot also adjust for this factor.

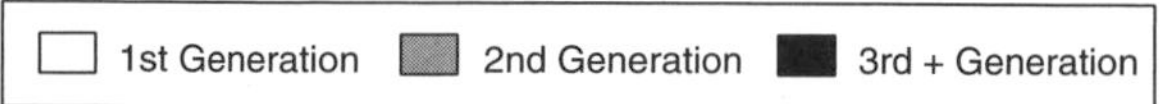

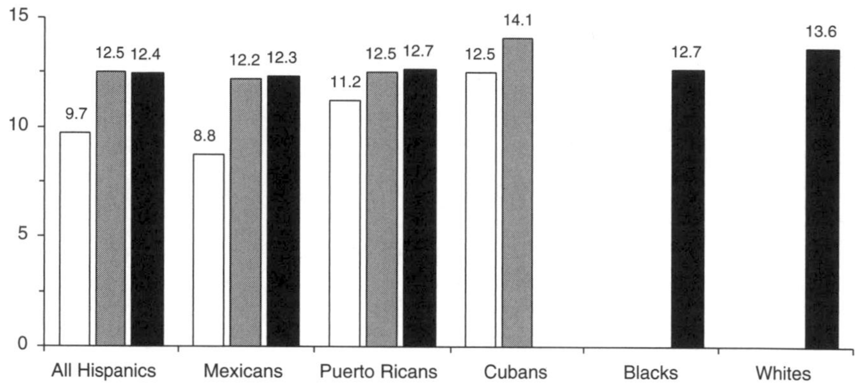

B. Women:

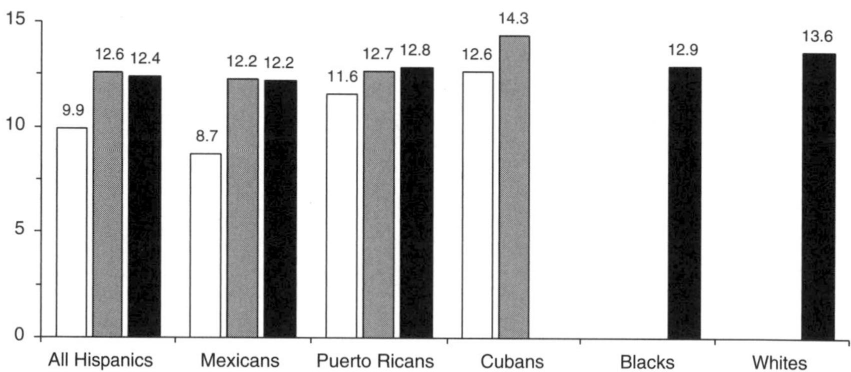

FIGURE 7-7 Average years of schooling, by gender, ethnicity, and generation.
NOTE: The samples include individuals ages 25 to 59. See Appendix Table A7-8 for further details.
SOURCE: March 1998–2002, CPS data.

deficits for Hispanic men shrink substantially after controlling for education, whereas this same adjustment produces a less dramatic decline in the earnings deficit of black men.

Figure 7-9 tells a similar story for Hispanic women. For Hispanics as a whole, the earnings gap is huge for immigrants (51 percent) and much smaller for the second and third generations (9–15 percent). Controlling

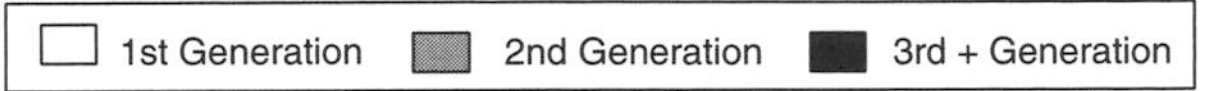

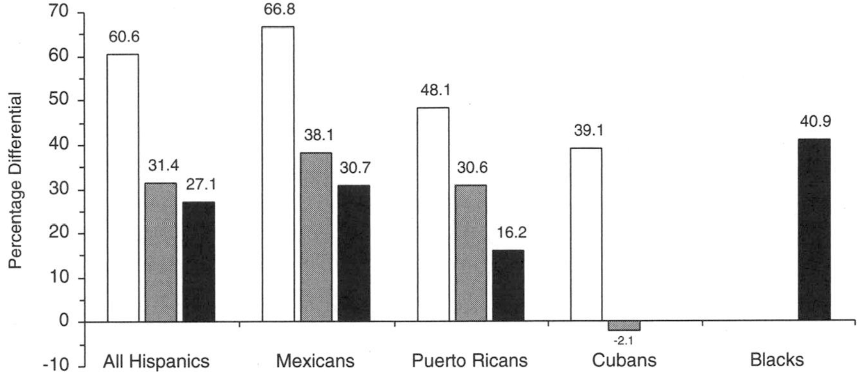

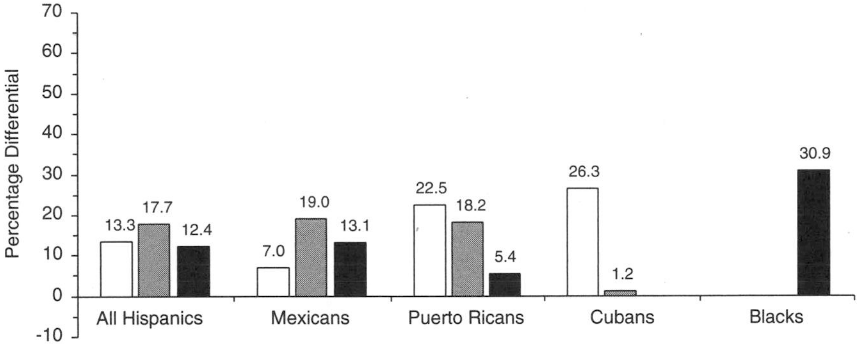

FIGURE 7-8 Male annual earnings deficits relative to 3rd+ generation whites, by ethnicity and generation.
NOTE: The samples include men ages 25 to 59 who worked during the calendar year preceding the survey. All of the reported differentials control for survey year, geographic location, and age. See Appendix Table A7-9 for further details.
SOURCE: March 1998–2002, CPS data.

for education dramatically lowers this gap for immigrants (to 5 percent) and eliminates it altogether for U.S. natives. The pattern is the same for each of the Hispanic subgroups. In fact, after adjusting for educational differences, U.S.-born women from every Hispanic national-origin group have average annual earnings as high as those of third-generation white women. As we saw earlier in the census data, black women possess a small

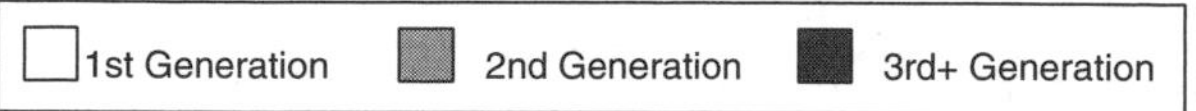

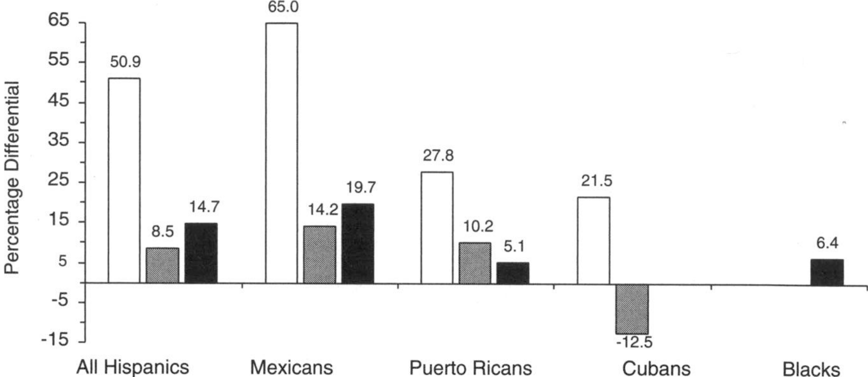

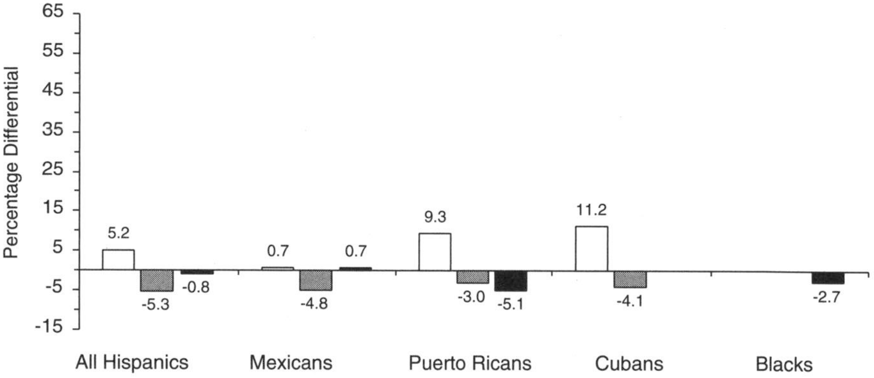

FIGURE 7-9 Female annual earnings deficits relative to 3rd+ generation whites, by ethnicity and generation.
NOTE: The samples include women ages 25 to 59 who worked during the calendar year preceding the survey. All of the reported differentials control for survey year, geographic location, and age. See Appendix Table A7-9 for further details.
SOURCE: March 1998–2002, CPS data.

earnings disadvantage relative to white women that disappears once we control for schooling.

The education data in Figure 7-7 and the earnings data in Figures 7-8 and 7-9 reveal substantial gains for Hispanics between immigrants and the second generation. In contrast, the same data show relatively minor differences between second-generation and later-generation Hispanics in terms of their labor market skills and success, despite the fact that in these dimensions U.S.-born Hispanics continue to trail whites by a considerable amount. Does this imply that intergenerational progress stalls for Hispanics after the second generation? Not necessarily. As noted by Borjas (1993) and Smith (2003), generational comparisons in a single cross-section of data do a poor job of matching immigrant parents and grandparents in the first generation with their actual descendants in later generations. Indeed, Smith (2003) found evidence of more substantial gains between second- and third-generation Hispanics when he combined cross-sectional data sets from successive time periods in order to compare second-generation Hispanics in some initial period with their third-generation descendants 25 years later. Yet even Smith's analysis shows some signs of intergenerational stagnation for Hispanics. In his Table 4, for example, five of the six most recent cohorts of Mexicans experience no wage gains between the second and third generations. Moreover, all studies conclude that large education and earnings deficits remain for third- and higher-generation Mexican Americans.[33]

If we assume that schooling is complete by the age of 25 and does not change thereafter, we can use our CPS samples to conduct an analysis of intergenerational changes in Hispanic educational attainment similar in spirit to that of Smith (2003). Table 7-8 presents average schooling levels like those displayed previously in Figure 7-7, except that now separate calculations have been done for two particular age groups: 25–34 and 50–59. By choosing age groups 25 years apart, we create a situation in which the older age group from a particular generation potentially represents the parental cohort for the younger age group in the next generation. For example, the cohort of immigrant men ages 50 to 59 is likely to include fathers of the second-generation cohort of sons ages 25 to 34. Following Smith (2003), we report calculations for Hispanics overall and also for Mexicans, the only Hispanic subgroup with adequate sample sizes for a separate analysis.

If we make comparisons within age groups by reading down the columns of Table 7-8, we tend to see the same story that emerged from Figure 7-7: huge educational improvement for Hispanics between the first and second generations but little progress after the second generation.[34] The story changes for the second and third generations, however, if we instead compare age/generation groups that could match parents with their children. Among Hispanic men, for example, average schooling rises from 12

[33]Borjas (1994) and Card, DiNardo, and Estes (2000) investigate patterns of intergenerational progress for many different national-origin groups (most of which are non-Hispanic).

[34]The older group of women is something of an exception, as they show schooling gains of about half a year between the second and third generations.

TABLE 7-8 Average Years of Schooling, by Gender, Ethnicity, Generation, and Age

	Men		Women	
Ethnicity/Generation	Ages 25–34	Ages 50–59	Ages 25–34	Ages 50–59
3rd+ generation whites	13.6 (0.01)	13.7 (0.02)	13.8 (0.01)	13.4 (0.01)
3rd+ generation blacks	12.8 (0.03)	12.4 (0.05)	13.0 (0.03)	12.6 (0.04)
All Hispanics				
1st generation	9.8 (0.05)	9.4 (0.10)	10.3 (0.05)	9.2 (0.09)
2nd generation	12.8 (0.05)	12.0 (0.16)	12.9 (0.05)	11.4 (0.16)
3rd+ generation	12.6 (0.04)	12.0 (0.10)	12.6 (0.05)	11.8 (0.09)
Mexicans				
1st generation	9.3 (0.05)	7.7 (0.14)	9.6 (0.06)	7.1 (0.13)
2nd generation	12.5 (0.07)	11.6 (0.19)	12.6 (0.06)	11.0 (0.18)
3rd+ generation	12.5 (0.05)	11.7 (0.12)	12.5 (0.05)	11.5 (0.11)

NOTE: Standard errors are shown in parentheses.
SOURCE: March 1998–2002, CPS data.

years for the older second generation to 12.6 years for the younger third generation. The analogous educational expansion between the second and third generations is even larger for Mexican men, from 11.6 to 12.5 years. Note that calculating progress between the first and second generations in this same way produces huge gains, even bigger than those we saw in Figure 7-7: 3.4 years for Hispanic men and 4.8 years for Mexican men.

Patterns are similar for women, with the implied intergenerational gains somewhat larger than those for men. For Hispanics overall, comparing older and younger women across generations yields schooling growth of 3.7 years between the first and second generations and 1.2 years between the second and third generations. For Mexican women, the corresponding gains are 5.5 years between the first and second generations and 1.5 years between the second and third generations. Despite this apparent progress, we should point out that young third-generation Hispanics still trail the average schooling of their white peers by a year or more.

Does this educational improvement between older second-generation Hispanics and younger third-generation Hispanics truly represent intergenerational progress, or could it be something else? One possibility is that it reflects secular trends that have raised average schooling levels for all young people relative to their elders. The data in Table 7-8 for third-generation whites suggest that this is not the case, however. For white men, the younger age group is not any more educated than the older age group. For white women, the younger age group has a schooling advantage of less than half a year, which accounts for at most a third of the estimated educational progress between the second and third generations of Hispanic women.

Another possibility is that the civil rights movement and related factors opened up educational opportunities for younger members of minority groups that were not available for their parents. For men there is some evidence consistent with this hypothesis, in that for blacks the younger age group averages almost half a year more schooling than the older age group, whereas for whites the younger age group actually has slightly less education than the older age group. If we believe that young Hispanics experienced a similar educational gain arising from increased educational opportunities for minorities, this could account for most of the estimated intergenerational progress between second- and third-generation Hispanic men, and for about half of the corresponding intergenerational progress for Mexican men. Note, however, that for women the educational advantage of the younger age group relative to the older age group is the same for blacks and whites, so this argument cannot account for any of the estimated intergenerational progress for Hispanic or Mexican women.

A different issue concerning the measurement of intergenerational progress for Hispanics arises because ethnic identification is to some extent endogenous, especially among people at least one or two generations removed from immigration to the United States (Alba, 1990; Waters, 1990). Consequently, the descendants of Hispanic immigrants who continue to identify themselves as Hispanic in the third and higher generations may be a select group.[35] In particular, if the most successful Hispanics are more likely to intermarry or for other reasons cease to identify themselves or their children as Hispanic, then available data may understate human capital and earnings gains between the second and third generations.

Duncan and Trejo (2005) have begun to investigate this issue with respect to Mexicans. Analyzing 2000 census data, they find that U.S.-born

[35]Bean, Swicegood, and Berg (2000) raise this possibility in their study of generational patterns of fertility for Mexican-origin women in the United States.

Mexican Americans who marry non-Mexicans are substantially more educated, on average, than are Mexican Americans who marry coethnics (whether they are Mexican Americans or Mexican immigrants). The educational selectivity of Mexican American intermarriage generates corresponding differences in the employment and earnings of Mexican Americans according to the ethnicity of their spouses. Moreover, the children of intermarried Mexican Americans are much less likely to be identified as Mexican than are the children of endogamous Mexican marriages. These forces combine to produce strong negative correlations among the education, employment, and earnings of Mexican American parents and the chances that their children retain a Mexican ethnicity. Several important steps remain to be done, however, before these correlations can be used to assess the magnitude of potential biases that might be obscuring the intergenerational progress of Mexican Americans.

CONCLUSION

This chapter has analyzed both the absolute and relative success that Hispanics have experienced in the U.S. labor market. Several conclusions emerge. First and foremost, the human capital disadvantages that characterize Hispanics as a group, especially those who are foreign-born, end up heavily shaping how they fare in the U.S. labor market. As we have documented above, Hispanics living in the United States today, especially Mexicans, have much lower levels of education than do whites or blacks. This schooling deficit is largely the result of an increasing share of Hispanics in the United States who are foreign-born and, in many cases, educated outside the United States. Not surprisingly, we also found that Hispanics in the United States have lower levels of English proficiency than their white or black counterparts. It is well documented that these forms of human capital, especially educational attainment, are important for success in the U.S. labor market, given the restructuring of the U.S. economy that has occurred over the past 25–30 years. As a result, we do find that Hispanics have tended to lag behind whites (although not blacks) in their rates of employment, presence in high-paying occupations, and overall levels of earnings.

A second major conclusion that emerges with respect to Hispanics concerns how their skills are valued, or rewarded, in the U.S. labor market. We consistently find that, after adjusting for the levels of human capital (e.g., schooling and English language proficiency), Hispanics do almost as well as whites with respect to both employment and labor market earnings. This fact is all the more notable, given that such adjustments for differences in these observable measures of human capital do not end up accounting for much of the gaps in labor market outcomes between blacks and whites. Finally, several more refined studies also indicate that there is difference in the returns in the earnings that Hispanics and whites receive for their schooling and accumulated work experiences. Taken together, this evidence clearly suggests that comparably skilled Hispanics are treated no differently from whites in the U.S. labor market.

The final issue concerns what one learns from generational and temporal changes with respect to what the future will bear for the success of Hispanics in the U.S. labor market. Here our findings are a bit less conclusive. In particular, we have found that there is clear progress in educational attainment and earnings between first- and second-generation Hispanics in the United States, both absolutely and relative to whites. With respect to progress between the second and higher generations, the evidence is less clear. As noted by Smith (2003), one does find evidence of progress between the second and higher generations in educational attainment once one appropriately aligns the data to reflect secular changes. At the same, the corresponding progress in earnings is less clear-cut, especially among younger cohorts of Mexicans. Moreover, forecasting what will happen to Hispanics with respect to their labor market success in the future hinges heavily on the rates and nature of Hispanic immigration to the United States and on how technological and institutional changes alter the requirements for success in the U.S. labor market.

ACKNOWLEDGMENTS

We wish to thank Jose Escarce, Charles Hirschman, Nancy Landale, Seth Sanders, Marta Tienda, and the anonymous reviewers for detailed comments on earlier drafts of this chapter. We also thank all of our colleagues on the National Research Council panel to study Hispanics in the United States, as well as the panel's staff, for invaluable support, encouragement, and inspiration. Any remaining errors are attributable to the authors.

REFERENCES

Ahituv, A., and Tienda, M. (2004). Employment motherhood, and school continuation decisions of young white, black, and Hispanic women. *Journal of Labor Economics*, *22*(1), 115–158.

Alba, R.D. (1990). *Ethnic identity: The transformation of white America.* New Haven, CT: Yale University Press.

Altonji, J.G., and Blank, R.M. (1999). Race and gender in the labor market. In O. Ashenfelter and D. Card (Eds.), *Handbook of labor economics* (vol. 3C, pp. 3143–3259). Amsterdam: North Holland Press.

Antecol, H., and Bedard, K. (2002). The relative earnings of young Mexican, black, and white women. *Industrial and Labor Relations Review*, *56*(1), 122–35.

Antecol, H., and Bedard, K. (2004, Spring). The racial wage gap. *Journal of Human Resources*, *39*(2), 564–583.

Bacolod, M., and Hotz, V.J. (2004, May). *Cohort changes in the transition from school to work: What changed and what consequences did it have for wages?* Unpublished manuscript, University of California, Los Angeles.

Bean, F.D., and Stevens, G. (2003). *America's newcomers and the dynamics of diversity.* New York: Russell Sage Foundation.

Bean, F.D., and Tienda, M. (1987). *The Hispanic population of the United States.* New York: Russell Sage Foundation.

Bean, F.D., Swicegood, C.G., and Berg, R. (2000, March). Mexican-origin fertility: New patterns and interpretations. *Social Science Quarterly, 81*(1), 404–420.

Bean, F.D., Trejo, S.J., Capps, R., and Tyler, M. (2001). *The Latino middle class: Myth, reality and potential.* Claremont, CA: Tomas Rivera Policy Institute.

Becker, G. (1975). *Human capital: A theoretical analysis with special reference to education* (2nd ed.). New York: Columbia University Press.

Bleakley, H., and Chin, A. (2004). Language skills and earnings: Evidence from childhood immigrants. *Review of Economics and Statistics, 86*(2), 481–496.

Borjas, G.J. (1993). The intergenerational mobility of immigrants. *Journal of Labor Economics, 11*(1), 113–135.

Borjas, G.J. (1994). Long-run convergence of ethnic skill differentials: The children and grandchildren of the great migration. *Industrial and Labor Relations Review, 47*(4), 553–573.

Borjas, G.J. (1995). Assimilation and changes in cohort quality revisited: What happened to immigrant earnings in the 1980s? *Journal of Labor Economics, 13*(2), 201–245.

Bound, J., and Johnson, G. (1992). Changes in the structure of wages in the 1980s: An evaluation of alternative explanations. *American Economic Review,* 82(3), 371–392.

Cameron, S., and Heckman, J. (1998). Life cycle schooling and dynamic selection bias: Models and evidence for five cohorts of American males. *Journal of Political Economy, 106*(2), 262–333.

Cameron, S., and Heckman, J. (2001). The dynamics of educational attainment for blacks, Hispanics, and whites. *Journal of Political Economy, 109*(3), 455–499.

Card, D. (2001). Estimating the return to schooling: Progress on some persistent econometric problems. *Econometrica, 69*(5), 1127–1160.

Card, D., DiNardo, J., and Estes, E. (2000). The more things change: Immigrants and the children of immigrants in the 1940s, the 1970s, and the 1990s. In G.J. Borjas (Ed.), *Issues in the economics of immigration* (pp. 227–269). Chicago, IL: University of Chicago Press.

Carlson, L.A., and Swartz, C. (1988, July). The earnings of women and ethnic minorities, 1959–1979. *Industrial and Labor Relations Review, 41*(4), 530–546.

Carnoy, M., Daley, H.M., and Hinojosa-Ojeda, R. (1993). The changing economic position of Latinos in the U.S. labor market since 1939. In R. Morales and F. Bonilla (Eds.), *Latinos in a changing U.S. economy: Comparative perspectives on growing inequality* (pp. 28–54). Newbury, CA: Sage.

Chiswick, B.R. (1977, February). Sons of immigrants: Are they at an earnings disadvantage? *American Economic Review, 67*(1), 376–380.

Chiswick, B.R. (1978, October). The effect of Americanization on the earnings of foreign-born men. *Journal of Political Economy, 86*(5), 897–921.

Cotton, J. (1985, December). More on the "cost" of being a black or Mexican-American male worker. *Social Science Quarterly, 66*(4), 867–885.

Darity, W., Jr., Guilkey, D., and Winfrey, W. (1995). Ethnicity, race, and earnings. *Economics Letters, 47*(3–4), 401–408.

DeFreitas, G. (1991). *Inequality at work: Hispanics in the U.S. labor force.* New York: Oxford University Press.

Donato, K.M., and Massey, D.S. (1993). Effect of the immigration reform and control act on the wages of Mexican migrants. *Social Science Quarterly*, *74*(3), 523–541.

Duncan, B., and Trejo, S. J. (2005). *Ethnic identification, intermarriage, and the hidden progress of Mexican Americans.* (Working Paper #04-05-02.) Austin: University of Texas Population Research Center.

Duncan, O.D., and Duncan, B. (1955, April). A methodological analysis of segregation indexes. *American Sociological Review*, *20*(2), 210–217.

Fairlie, R.W., and Meyer, B.D. (1996, Fall). Ethnic and racial self-employment differences and possible explanations. *Journal of Human Resources*, *31*(4), 757–793.

Grenier, G. (1984, Winter). The effects of language characteristics on the wages of Hispanic-American males. *Journal of Human Resources*, *19*(1), 35–52.

Griliches, Z. (1977). Estimating the returns to schooling: Some econometric problems. *Econometrica*, *45*(1), 1–22.

Grogger, J., and Trejo, S.J. (2002). *Falling behind or moving up? The intergenerational progress of Mexican-Americans.* San Francisco: Public Policy Institute of California.

Gwartney, J.D., and Long, J.E. (1978, April). The relative earnings of blacks and other minorities. *Industrial and Labor Relations Review*, *31*(3), 336–346.

Heckman, J. (1979). Sample selection bias as a specification error. *Econometrica*, *47*(1), 153-161.

Heckman, J., and Vytlacil, E. (1998). Instrumental variables methods for the correlated random coefficient model: Estimating the average rate of return to schooling when the return is correlated with schooling. *Journal of Human Resources*, *33*(4), 974–987.

Heckman, J., Lochner, L., and Todd, P. (2003). *Fifty years of Mincer earnings regressions.* (NBER Working Paper No. 9732.) Cambridge, MA: National Bureau of Economic Research.

Hotz, V.J., Xu, L. C., Tienda, M., and Ahituv, A. (2002). Are there returns to the wages of young men from working while in school? *Review of Economics and Statistics*, *84*(2), 221–236.

Katz, L., and Murphy, K. (1992). Changes in the relative wages, 1963–1987: Supply and demand factors. *Quarterly Journal of Economics*, *107*(1), 35–78.

Kilburn, R. (1993). *Minority representation in the U.S. military.* Unpublished Ph.D. dissertation, University of Chicago.

Kossoudji, S.A., and Cobb-Clark, D.A. (2002). Coming out of the shadows: Learning about legal status and wages from the legalized population. *Journal of Labor Economics*, *20*(3), 598–628.

Levy, F., and Murnane, R.J. (1992). U.S. earnings levels and earnings inequality: A review of recent trends and proposed explanations. *Journal of Economic Literature*, *30*(3), 1333–1381.

Massey, D.S. (1987, Summer). Do undocumented migrants earn lower wages than legal immigrants? New evidence from Mexico. *International Migration Review*, *21*(2), 236–274.

McManus, W., Gould, W., and Welch, F. (1983). Earnings of Hispanic men: The role of English language proficiency. *Journal of Labor Economics*, *1*(2), 101–130.

Mincer, J. (1958). Investment in human capital and personal income distribution. *Journal of Political Economy*, *66*(4), 281–302.

Mincer, J. (1974). *Schooling, experience, and earnings.* New York: National Bureau of Economic Research.

Mora, M.T. (1988, September). Did the English deficiency earnings penalty change for Hispanic men between 1979 and 1989? *Social Science Quarterly*, *79*(3), 581–594.

Murphy, K.M., and Welch, F. (1990). Empirical age-earnings profiles. *Journal of Labor Economics*, *8*(2), 202–229.

Neal, D.A., and Johnson, W.R. (1996). The role of premarket factors in black-white wage differences. *Journal of Political Economy, 104*(5), 869–895.

Neidert, L.J., and Farley, R. (1985, December). Assimilation in the United States: An analysis of ethnic and generation differences in status and achievement. *American Sociological Review, 50*(6), 840–850.

Passel, J.S. (2004). *Mexican immigration to the U.S.: The latest estimates.* Washington, DC: Migration Policy Institute.

Passel, J.S., Capps, R., and Fix, M. (2004). *Undocumented immigrants: Facts and figures.* Manuscript, Urban Institute, Washington, DC.

Perlmann, J., and Waldinger, R. (1997, Winter). Second generation decline? Children of immigrants past and present: A reconsideration. *International Migration Review, 31*(4), 893–922.

Portes, A., and Rumbaut, R.G. (1990). *Immigrant America: A portrait.* Berkeley: University of California Press.

Reimers, C.W. (1983, November). Labor market discrimination against Hispanic and black men. *Review of Economics and Statistics, 65*(4), 570–579.

Rivera-Batiz, F.L. (1999). Undocumented workers in the labor market: An analysis of the earnings of legal and illegal Mexican immigrants in the United States. *Journal of Population Economics, 12*(1), 91–116.

Rosen, S. (1977, Fall). Human capital: A survey of empirical research. In R. Ehrenberg (Ed.), *Research in labor economics* (vol. 1, pp. 3–40). Greenwich, CT: JAI Press.

Schoeni, R.F. (1997, Fall). New evidence on the economic progress of foreign-born men in the 1970s and 1980s. *Journal of Human Resources, 32*(4), 683–740.

Smith, J.P. (1991). *Hispanics and the American dream: An analysis of Hispanic male labor market wages, 1940–1980.* Santa Monica, CA: Rand Corporation.

Smith, J.P. (2001). Race and ethnicity in the labor market: Trends over the short and long term. In N.J. Smelser, W.J. Wilson, and F. Mitchell (Eds.), *America becoming: Racial trends and their consequences* (vol. II, pp. 52–97). Washington, DC: National Academy Press.

Smith, J.P. (2003, May). Assimilation across the Latino generations. *American Economic Review, 93*(2), 315–319.

Trejo, S.J. (1996, July). *Obstacles to the labor market progress of California's Mexican-origin workers.* (Working Paper, vol. 4, no. 1.) Berkeley: University of California, Chicano/Latino Policy Project.

Trejo, S.J. (1997). Why do Mexican-Americans earn low wages? *Journal of Political Economy, 105*(6), 1235–1268.

Trejo, S.J. (2003, Summer). Intergenerational progress of Mexican-origin workers in the U.S. labor market. *Journal of Human Resources, 38*(3), 467–489.

Waters, M.C. (1990). *Ethnic options: Choosing identities in America.* Berkeley: University of California Press.

Willis, R. (1986). Wage determinants: A survey and reinterpretation of human capital earnings functions. In O. Ashenfelter and R. Layard (Ed.), *Handbook of labor economics* (pp. 525–603). Amsterdam: North-Holland.

APPENDIX TABLE A7-1 Average Years of Schooling, by Gender, Detailed Ethnicity, and Nativity

	Men, by Nativity			Women, by Nativity		
Ethnicity	All	Foreign-Born	U.S.-Born	All	Foreign-Born	U.S.-Born
Whites			13.6 (0.005) [229,933]			13.6 (0.005) [234,958]
Blacks			12.4 (0.005) [301,402]			12.8 (0.004) [358,222]
All Hispanics	10.5 (0.01) [380,385]	9.5 (0.01) [247,079]	12.2 (0.01) [133,306]	10.8 (0.01) [362,044]	9.8 (0.01) [220,970]	12.4 (0.01) [141,074]
Mexicans	9.8 (0.01) [243,573]	8.5 (0.01) [154,878]	12.1 (0.01) [88,695]	10.1 (0.01) [216,338]	8.6 (0.01) [124,177]	12.2 (0.01) [92,161]
Puerto Ricans	11.7 (0.02) [33,927]	11.2 (0.03) [18,106]	12.4 (0.02) [15,821]	12.0 (0.02) [37,233]	11.4 (0.03) [19,847]	12.7 (0.02) [17,386]
Cubans	12.7 (0.03) [15,263]	12.4 (0.03) [12,104]	13.6 (0.05) [3,159]	12.9 (0.03) [14,328]	12.5 (0.03) [11,189]	14.2 (0.05) [3,139]
Dominicans	10.8 (0.04) [9,754]	10.7 (0.04) [8,932]	12.5 (0.11) [822]	11.0 (0.04) [12,008]	10.8 (0.04) [11,038]	13.2 (0.10) [970]
Salvadorans/ Guatemalans	9.0 (0.03) [21,988]	8.9 (0.03) [21,378]	12.1 (0.16) [610]	8.9 (0.03) [19,976]	8.8 (0.03) [19,330]	12.4 (0.15) [646]
Other Central Americans	11.2 (0.04) [9,830]	10.9 (0.04) [9,004]	13.4 (0.11) [826]	11.6 (0.04) [11,585]	11.4 (0.04) [10,664]	13.7 (0.10) [921]
Colombians	12.8 (0.04) [7,583]	12.7 (0.04) [6,851]	13.7 (0.11) [732]	12.6 (0.04) [9,236]	12.5 (0.04) [8,538]	14.2 (0.11) [698]
Peruvians/ Ecuadorans	12.3 (0.04) [9,126]	12.2 (0.04) [8,478]	13.8 (0.11) [648]	12.5 (0.03) [9,127]	12.3 (0.04) [8,394]	14.2 (0.10) [733]
Other South Americans	13.7 (0.04) [5,994]	13.6 (0.04) [5,363]	14.4 (0.10) [631]	13.7 (0.04) [6,214]	13.5 (0.04) [5,528]	14.7 (0.10) [686]
Other Hispanics	12.3 (0.02) [23,347]	13.3 (0.09) [1,985]	12.2 (0.02) [21,362]	12.5 (0.02) [25,999]	13.2 (0.08) [2,265]	12.4 (0.02) [23,734]

NOTE: Standard errors are shown in parentheses, and sample sizes are shown in brackets. The samples include individuals ages 25 to 59.
SOURCE: 2000 census, 5% PUMS.

APPENDIX TABLE A7-2 English Proficiency, by Gender, Detailed Ethnicity, and Nativity

	Men, by Nativity			Women, by Nativity		
Ethnicity	All	Foreign-Born	U.S.-Born	All	Foreign-Born	U.S.-Born
Whites						
Percent who speak English						
Only			96.9			96.8
Very well			2.5			2.6
Well			0.4			0.3
Not well			0.2			0.3
Not at all			0.007			0.008
Blacks						
Percent who speak English						
Only			96.6			97.2
Very well			2.5			2.0
Well			0.5			0.4
Not well			0.4			0.3
Not at all			0.008			0.008
All Hispanics						
Percent who speak English						
Only	17.4	5.9	38.6	18.1	6.2	37.1
Very well	34.4	26.3	49.2	36.1	26.3	51.7
Well	19.9	25.8	9.2	16.3	21.0	8.6
Not well	19.2	28.2	2.5	17.7	27.4	2.2
Not at all	9.1	13.9	0.4	11.8	18.9	0.4
Mexicans						
Percent who speak English						
Only	17.3	5.5	37.5	19.1	6.4	36.4
Very well	31.2	20.5	49.5	33.2	19.7	51.4
Well	19.6	25.4	9.8	14.6	18.5	9.4
Not well	21.0	31.7	2.7	18.5	30.4	2.4
Not at all	10.9	17.0	0.5	14.5	24.9	0.5
Puerto Ricans						
Percent who speak English						
Only	20.3	9.1	32.9	16.1	6.7	26.7
Very well	52.3	49.0	56.0	55.0	47.9	63.0
Well	17.0	24.4	8.7	16.5	23.5	8.5
Not well	8.3	13.7	2.2	9.4	16.3	1.7
Not at all	2.1	3.8	0.1	3.1	5.6	0.1
Cubans						
Percent who speak English						
Only	12.2	6.4	33.3	11.6	5.6	32.5
Very well	45.2	41.2	59.7	48.6	44.6	62.6
Well	16.1	19.1	5.3	14.2	17.3	3.4
Not well	16.8	21.0	1.4	14.7	18.5	1.3
Not at all	9.6	12.2	0.3	10.9	14.0	0.1

APPENDIX TABLE A7-2 Continued

Ethnicity	Men, by Nativity All	Men, Foreign-Born	Men, U.S.-Born	Women, by Nativity All	Women, Foreign-Born	Women, U.S.-Born
Dominicans						
Percent who speak English						
Only	6.7	5.6	17.7	6.2	5.5	13.5
Very well	29.1	25.5	67.8	26.7	22.5	74.6
Well	25.8	27.2	11.0	21.6	22.7	9.0
Not well	26.6	28.8	2.7	29.0	31.3	2.4
Not at all	11.8	12.8	0.9	16.5	18.0	0.5
Salvadorans/Guatemalans						
Percent who speak English						
Only	4.7	4.1	26.7	5.8	5.0	27.7
Very well	24.1	23.2	55.2	21.7	20.5	58.5
Well	28.8	29.3	11.6	24.7	25.2	8.7
Not well	30.2	30.9	5.5	31.5	32.4	3.3
Not at all	12.2	12.5	1.0	16.4	16.9	1.8
Other Central Americans						
Percent who speak English						
Only	9.8	6.5	44.1	9.7	6.6	45.1
Very well	34.6	33.6	45.7	35.1	34.2	45.7
Well	23.3	24.7	8.2	22.4	23.8	6.5
Not well	21.9	23.9	1.1	21.2	22.8	2.1
Not at all	10.4	11.3	0.9	11.6	12.6	0.7
Colombians						
Percent who speak English						
Only	7.3	4.9	30.0	6.3	4.5	27.1
Very well	36.4	34.0	57.7	31.6	28.9	63.8
Well	28.6	30.8	8.6	26.5	28.2	5.3
Not well	20.8	22.8	2.7	24.8	26.6	3.1
Not at all	6.8	7.5	1.0	10.9	11.7	0.6
Peruvians/Ecuadorans						
Percent who speak English						
Only	6.4	4.7	28.1	6.9	5.0	28.7
Very well	34.9	32.8	62.5	34.4	31.8	64.5
Well	29.1	30.9	6.2	25.7	27.5	5.6
Not well	23.4	25.0	2.5	24.3	26.3	1.0
Not at all	6.1	6.6	0.7	8.7	9.4	0.2
Other South Americans						
Percent who speak English						
Only	10.8	7.7	37.2	9.4	6.2	36.4
Very well	48.2	47.3	55.8	46.4	45.1	57.6
Well	25.7	28.0	5.9	25.7	28.3	4.8
Not well	12.1	13.5	0.9	14.2	15.8	1.2
Not at all	3.2	3.5	0.2	4.2	4.7	0

continues

APPENDIX TABLE A7-2 Continued

	Men, by Nativity			Women, by Nativity		
Ethnicity	All	Foreign-Born	U.S.-Born	All	Foreign-Born	U.S.-Born
Other Hispanics						
Percent who speak English						
Only	47.6	18.8	50.5	48.0	19.8	51.0
Very well	39.9	44.6	39.4	40.6	44.1	40.3
Well	9.3	24.4	7.8	8.4	23.9	6.8
Not well	2.9	10.5	2.1	2.5	10.2	1.7
Not at all	0.4	1.6	0.2	0.4	2.1	0.2

NOTE: The samples include individuals ages 25 to 59.
SOURCE: 2000 census, 5% PUMS.

APPENDIX TABLE A7-3 Annual Employment Rates, by Gender, Detailed Ethnicity, and Nativity

	Men, by Nativity			Women, by Nativity		
Ethnicity	All	Foreign-Born	U.S.-Born	All	Foreign-Born	U.S.-Born
Whites			0.918 (0.0006)			0.802 (0.0008)
Blacks			0.774 (0.0008)			0.777 (0.0007)
All Hispanics	0.868 (0.0005)	0.875 (0.0007)	0.856 (0.001)	0.670 (0.0008)	0.612 (0.001)	0.763 (0.001)
Mexicans	0.878 (0.0007)	0.885 (0.0008)	0.865 (0.001)	0.647 (0.001)	0.561 (0.001)	0.764 (0.001)
Puerto Ricans	0.800 (0.002)	0.766 (0.003)	0.838 (0.003)	0.677 (0.002)	0.608 (0.003)	0.755 (0.003)
Cubans	0.873 (0.003)	0.868 (0.003)	0.891 (0.006)	0.747 (0.004)	0.725 (0.004)	0.825 (0.007)
Dominicans	0.816 (0.004)	0.815 (0.004)	0.818 (0.013)	0.662 (0.004)	0.651 (0.005)	0.792 (0.013)
Salvadorans/ Guatemalans	0.900 (0.002)	0.901 (0.002)	0.859 (0.014)	0.679 (0.003)	0.675 (0.003)	0.776 (0.016)
Other Central Americans	0.890 (0.003)	0.891 (0.003)	0.879 (0.011)	0.718 (0.004)	0.708 (0.004)	0.831 (0.012)
Colombians	0.879 (0.004)	0.879 (0.004)	0.875 (0.012)	0.706 (0.005)	0.695 (0.005)	0.825 (0.014)
Peruvians/ Ecuadorans	0.905 (0.003)	0.903 (0.003)	0.935 (0.010)	0.721 (0.005)	0.710 (0.005)	0.843 (0.013)
Other South Americans	0.907 (0.004)	0.906 (0.004)	0.917 (0.011)	0.713 (0.006)	0.696 (0.006)	0.859 (0.013)
Other Hispanics	0.829 (0.002)	0.912 (0.006)	0.820 (0.003)	0.742 (0.003)	0.718 (0.009)	0.745 (0.003)

NOTE: Standard errors are shown in parentheses. The samples include individuals ages 25 to 59.
SOURCE: 2000 census, 5% PUMS.

APPENDIX TABLE A7-4 Employment Differentials, by Gender, Detailed Ethnicity, and Nativity

	Employment Differentials, Relative to U.S.-Born Whites					
	Men			Women		
Ethnicity/Nativity	(1)	(2)	(3)	(1)	(2)	(3)
U.S.-born blacks	–.147	–.125	–.125	–.023	–.001	–.002
	(.001)	(.001)	(.001)	(.001)	(.001)	(.001)
All Hispanics:						
All	–.058	.003	–.003	–.134	–.046	–.005
	(.001)	(.001)	(.001)	(.001)	(.001)	(.002)
Foreign-born	–.051	.031	.040	–.191	–.076	–.021
	(.001)	(.001)	(.002)	(.002)	(.002)	(.002)
U.S.-born	–.071	–.043	–.036	–.040	–.002	.006
	(.001)	(.001)	(.002)	(.002)	(.002)	(.002)
Mexicans:						
All	–.051	.027	.025	–.160	–.049	–.002
	(.001)	(.001)	(.002)	(.002)	(.002)	(.002)
Foreign-born	–.045	.062	.078	–.248	–.094	–.028
	(.001)	(.002)	(.002)	(.002)	(.002)	(.003)
U.S.-born	–.061	–.026	–.019	–.041	.005	.014
	(.002)	(.002)	(.002)	(.002)	(.002)	(.003)
Puerto Ricans:						
All	–.119	–.082	–.079	–.127	–.075	–.050
	(.003)	(.003)	(.003)	(.004)	(.003)	(.004)
Foreign-born	–.146	–.095	–.084	–.188	–.122	–.088
	(.004)	(.004)	(.004)	(.005)	(.005)	(.005)
U.S.-born	–.088	–.062	–.055	–.059	–.025	–.016
	(.004)	(.004)	(.004)	(.005)	(.005)	(.005)
Cubans:						
All	–.038	–.022	–.021	–.051	–.031	.011
	(.004)	(.004)	(.004)	(.006)	(.006)	(.006)
Foreign-born	–.039	–.016	–.001	–.069	–.040	.006
	(.005)	(.005)	(.005)	(.007)	(.006)	(.007)
U.S.-born	–.036	–.036	–.028	.006	–.005	.003
	(.009)	(.009)	(.009)	(.012)	(.012)	(.012)
Dominicans:						
All	–.096	–.041	–.044	–.135	–.050	.014
	(.005)	(.005)	(.005)	(.006)	(.006)	(.006)
Foreign-born	–.095	–.034	–.020	–.145	–.057	.004
	(.005)	(.005)	(.005)	(.006)	(.006)	(.006)
U.S.-born	–.104	–.080	–.071	–.025	–.003	.009
	(.017)	(.016)	(.016)	(.021)	(.021)	(.021)

continues

APPENDIX TABLE A7-4 Continued

Ethnicity/Nativity	Employment Differentials, Relative to U.S.-Born Whites					
	Men			Women		
	(1)	(2)	(3)	(1)	(2)	(3)
Salvadorians/Guatemalans:						
All	–.030	.064	.059	–.128	.018	.083
	(.003)	(.003)	(.004)	(.005)	(.005)	(.005)
Foreign-born	–.028	.071	.085	–.133	.013	.073
	(.003)	(.003)	(.004)	(.005)	(.005)	(.005)
U.S.-born	–.071	–.037	–.029	–.044	.001	.013
	(.021)	(.020)	(.020)	(.027)	(.026)	(.026)
Other Central Americans:						
All	–.035	.014	.012	–.087	–.021	.030
	(.005)	(.005)	(.005)	(.006)	(.006)	(.006)
Foreign-born	–.033	.023	.036	–.096	–.027	.021
	(.005)	(.005)	(.005)	(.006)	(.006)	(.007)
U.S.-born	–.051	–.043	–.037	.014	.018	.028
	(.017)	(.017)	(.017)	(.022)	(.021)	(.021)
Colombians:						
All	–.041	–.024	–.027	–.096	–.063	–.005
	(.006)	(.006)	(.006)	(.007)	(.007)	(.007)
Foreign-born	–.039	–.019	–.006	–.105	–.069	–.016
	(.006)	(.006)	(.006)	(.007)	(.007)	(.007)
U.S.-born	–.057	–.058	–.050	.002	–.005	.006
	(.018)	(.018)	(.018)	(.025)	(.024)	(.024)
Peruvians/Ecuadorans:						
All	–.013	.013	.010	–.080	–.040	.012
	(.005)	(.005)	(.005)	(.007)	(.007)	(.007)
Foreign-born	–.015	.016	.028	–.089	–.047	.003
	(.005)	(.005)	(.005)	(.007)	(.007)	(.007)
U.S.-born	.006	.005	.014	.019	.014	.023
	(.019)	(.019)	(.019)	(.025)	(.024)	(.024)
Other South Americans:						
All	–.014	–.014	–.015	–.092	–.089	–.050
	(.006)	(.006)	(.006)	(.008)	(.008)	(.008)
Foreign-born	–.014	–.012	–.001	–.109	–.102	–.065
	(.007)	(.007)	(.007)	(.009)	(.009)	(.009)
U.S.-born	–.016	–.028	–.021	.039	.016	.025
	(.020)	(.019)	(.019)	(.026)	(.025)	(.025)
Other Hispanics:						
All	–.094	–.065	–.063	–.062	–.021	–.011
	(.003)	(.003)	(.003)	(.004)	(.004)	(.004)
Foreign-born	–.009	.000	.009	–.089	–.071	–.046
	(.011)	(.011)	(.011)	(.014)	(.014)	(.014)
U.S.-born	–.103	–.072	–.067	–.056	–.015	–.009
	(.004)	(.003)	(.004)	(.005)	(.005)	(.005)

continues

APPENDIX TABLE A7-4 Continued

	Employment Differentials, Relative to U.S.-Born Whites					
	Men			Women		
Ethnicity/Nativity	(1)	(2)	(3)	(1)	(2)	(3)
Controls for:						
Geographic location	Yes	Yes	Yes	Yes	Yes	Yes
Age	Yes	Yes	Yes	Yes	Yes	Yes
Education	No	Yes	Yes	No	Yes	Yes
English proficiency	No	No	Yes	No	No	Yes

NOTE: The reported figures are estimated coefficients from least-squares regressions in which the dependent variable is a dummy variable indicating whether the respondent worked at all during the calendar year preceding the survey. Standard errors are shown in parentheses. The samples include individuals ages 25 to 59.
SOURCE: 2000 census, 5% PUMS.

APPENDIX TABLE A7-5 Self-Employment Rates, by Gender, Detailed Ethnicity, and Nativity

	Men, by Nativity			Women, by Nativity		
Ethnicity	All	Foreign-Born	U.S.-Born	All	Foreign-Born	U.S.-Born
Whites			0.139			0.081
			(0.0008)			(0.0007)
Blacks			0.058			0.034
			(0.0005)			(0.0004)
All Hispanics	0.082	0.084	0.079	0.066	0.080	0.050
	(0.0005)	(0.0007)	(0.001)	(0.0006)	(0.0008)	(0.001)
Mexicans	0.075	0.074	0.077	0.061	0.076	0.048
	(0.0006)	(0.0008)	(0.001)	(0.0007)	(0.0011)	(0.001)
Puerto Ricans	0.056	0.057	0.055	0.040	0.042	0.038
	(0.002)	(0.002)	(0.002)	(0.001)	(0.002)	(0.002)
Cubans	0.159	0.169	0.127	0.074	0.076	0.071
	(0.003)	(0.004)	(0.007)	(0.003)	(0.003)	(0.005)
Dominicans	0.102	0.105	0.073	0.061	0.066	0.024
	(0.004)	(0.004)	(0.011)	(0.003)	(0.003)	(0.006)
Salvadorans/ Guatemalans	0.076	0.076	0.068	0.106	0.109	0.029
	(0.002)	(0.002)	(0.012)	(0.003)	(0.003)	(0.008)
Other Central Americans	0.076	0.075	0.089	0.078	0.079	0.068
	(0.003)	(0.003)	(0.011)	(0.003)	(0.003)	(0.010)
Colombians	0.109	0.113	0.071	0.116	0.123	0.053
	(0.004)	(0.004)	(0.011)	(0.004)	(0.005)	(0.010)
Peruvians/ Ecuadorans	0.102	0.106	0.063	0.086	0.092	0.035
	(0.004)	(0.004)	(0.011)	(0.004)	(0.004)	(0.008)
Other South Americans	0.145	0.150	0.103	0.114	0.120	0.072
	(0.005)	(0.005)	(0.013)	(0.005)	(0.006)	(0.011)
Other Hispanics	0.103	0.140	0.099	0.065	0.104	0.061
	(0.002)	(0.009)	(0.002)	(0.002)	(0.008)	(0.002)

NOTE: Standard errors are shown in parentheses. The samples include individuals ages 25 to 59 who were employed during the census reference week.
SOURCE: 2000 census, 5% PUMS.

APPENDIX TABLE A7-6 Self-Employment Differentials, by Gender, Detailed Ethnicity, and Nativity

	Self-Employment Differentials, Relative to U.S.-Born Whites					
	Men			Women		
Ethnicity/Nativity	(1)	(2)	(3)	(1)	(2)	(3)
U.S.-born blacks	–.075	–.074	–.074	–.042	–.042	–.042
	(.001)	(.001)	(.001)	(.001)	(.001)	(.001)
All Hispanics:						
All	–.052	–.048	–.061	–.020	–.020	–.029
	(.001)	(.001)	(.002)	(.001)	(.001)	(.002)
Foreign-born	–.050	–.044	–.055	–.006	–.006	–.014
	(.002)	(.002)	(.002)	(.001)	(.002)	(.002)
U.S.-born	–.056	–.054	–.066	–.036	–.036	–.039
	(.002)	(.002)	(.002)	(.002)	(.002)	(.002)
Mexicans:						
All	–.059	–.055	–.066	–.029	–.029	–.037
	(.002)	(.002)	(.002)	(.002)	(.002)	(.002)
Foreign-born	–.057	–.051	–.060	–.015	–.015	–.024
	(.002)	(.002)	(.003)	(.002)	(.002)	(.003)
U.S.-born	–.061	–.060	–.071	–.041	–.041	–.044
	(.002)	(.002)	(.003)	(.002)	(.002)	(.002)
Puerto Ricans:						
All	–.073	–.072	–.087	–.033	–.033	–.039
	(.004)	(.004)	(.004)	(.003)	(.003)	(.003)
Foreign-born	–.082	–.080	–.097	–.034	–.034	–.041
	(.005)	(.005)	(.006)	(.005)	(.005)	(.005)
U.S.-born	–.065	–.063	–.076	–.031	–.031	–.034
	(.005)	(.005)	(.006)	(.004)	(.004)	(.004)
Cubans:						
All	.010	.011	–.003	–.011	–.011	–.018
	(.006)	(.006)	(.006)	(.005)	(.005)	(.005)
Foreign-born	.012	.013	.000	–.013	–.013	–.020
	(.006)	(.006)	(.007)	(.006)	(.006)	(.006)
U.S.-born	.005	.004	–.008	–.003	–.003	–.006
	(.011)	(.011)	(.011)	(.009)	(.009)	(.009)
Dominicans:						
All	–.029	–.026	–.039	–.009	–.010	–.022
	(.007)	(.007)	(.007)	(.006)	(.006)	(.006)
Foreign-born	–.028	–.025	–.036	–.006	–.006	–.016
	(.008)	(.008)	(.008)	(.006)	(.006)	(.006)
U.S.-born	–.029	–.028	–.044	–.036	–.036	–.039
	(.024)	(.024)	(.024)	(.017)	(.017)	(.017)

APPENDIX TABLE A7-6 Continued

	Self-Employment Differentials, Relative to U.S.-Born Whites					
	Men			Women		
Ethnicity/Nativity	(1)	(2)	(3)	(1)	(2)	(3)
Salvadorians/Guatemalans:						
All	–.054	–.049	–.062	.018	.017	.003
	(.005)	(.005)	(.005)	(.004)	(.005)	(.005)
Foreign-born	–.054	–.049	–.060	.021	.021	.011
	(.005)	(.005)	(.005)	(.005)	(.005)	(.005)
U.S.-born	–.050	–.049	–.062	–.049	–.049	–.052
	(.028)	(.028)	(.028)	(.022)	(.022)	(.022)
Other Central Americans:						
All	–.056	–.054	–.067	–.006	–.006	–.016
	(.007)	(.007)	(.007)	(.006)	(.006)	(.006)
Foreign-born	–.058	–.055	–.067	–.005	–.005	–.013
	(.007)	(.007)	(.007)	(.006)	(.006)	(.006)
U.S.-born	–.035	–.035	–.046	–.009	–.009	–.011
	(.022)	(.022)	(.022)	(.017)	(.017)	(.017)
Colombians:						
All	–.029	–.028	–.043	.037	.037	.025
	(.008)	(.008)	(.008)	(.006)	(.006)	(.006)
Foreign-born	–.028	–.027	–.041	.043	.043	.033
	(.008)	(.008)	(.008)	(.006)	(.006)	(.007)
U.S.-born	–.035	–.036	–.049	–.011	–.011	–.014
	(.024)	(.024)	(.024)	(.019)	(.019)	(.019)
Peruvians/Ecuadorans:						
All	–.031	–.030	–.045	.008	.008	–.004
	(.007)	(.007)	(.007)	(.006)	(.006)	(.006)
Foreign-born	–.030	–.029	–.042	.013	.013	.004
	(.007)	(.007)	(.007)	(.006)	(.006)	(.007)
U.S.-born	–.044	–.044	–.057	–.033	–.033	–.035
	(.024)	(.024)	(.024)	(.019)	(.019)	(.019)
Other South Americans:						
All	.006	.006	–.011	.032	.032	.023
	(.008)	(.008)	(.008)	(.007)	(.007)	(.007)
Foreign-born	.008	.008	–.008	.037	.037	.030
	(.009)	(.009)	(.009)	(.008)	(.008)	(.008)
U.S.-born	–.010	–.011	–.023	–.002	–.002	–.004
	(.025)	(.025)	(.025)	(.020)	(.020)	(.020)
Other Hispanics:						
All	–.038	–.037	–.046	–.027	–.027	–.030
	(.005)	(.005)	(.005)	(.004)	(.004)	(.004)
Foreign-born	.000	.000	–.014	.022	.022	.016
	(.014)	(.014)	(.015)	(.012)	(.012)	(.012)
U.S.-born	–.043	–.041	–.050	–.032	–.032	–.034
	(.005)	(.005)	(.005)	(.004)	(.004)	(.004)

continues

APPENDIX TABLE A7-6 Continued

	Self-Employment Differentials, Relative to U.S.-Born Whites					
	Men			Women		
Ethnicity/Nativity	(1)	(2)	(3)	(1)	(2)	(3)
Controls for:						
Geographic location	Yes	Yes	Yes	Yes	Yes	Yes
Age	Yes	Yes	Yes	Yes	Yes	Yes
Education	No	Yes	Yes	No	Yes	Yes
English proficiency	No	No	Yes	No	No	Yes

NOTE: The reported figures are estimated coefficients from least-squares regressions in which the dependent variable is a dummy variable indicating whether the respondent is self-employed. Standard errors are shown in parentheses. The samples include individuals ages 25 to 59 who were employed during the census reference week.
SOURCE: 2000 census, 5% PUMS.

APPENDIX TABLE A7-7 Annual Earnings Differentials, by Gender, Detailed Ethnicity, and Nativity

	Log Earnings Differentials, Relative to U.S.-Born Whites					
	Men			Women		
Ethnicity/Nativity	(1)	(2)	(3)	(1)	(2)	(3)
U.S.-born blacks	–.440	–.347	–.348	–.050	.026	.026
	(.004)	(.004)	(.004)	(.004)	(.004)	(.004)
All Hispanics:						
All	–.492	–.171	–.094	–.333	–.043	.016
	(.004)	(.004)	(.005)	(.005)	(.005)	(.006)
Foreign-born	–.588	–.169	–.045	–.492	–.083	.002
	(.004)	(.004)	(.007)	(.006)	(.006)	(.008)
U.S.-born	–.307	–.175	–.133	–.124	.004	.025
	(.006)	(.005)	(.006)	(.007)	(.006)	(.007)
Mexicans:						
All	–.542	–.141	–.057	–.397	–.027	.032
	(.004)	(.005)	(.006)	(.006)	(.006)	(.007)
Foreign-born	–.658	–.119	.024	–.633	–.053	.044
	(.005)	(.006)	(.008)	(.008)	(.008)	(.011)
U.S.-born	–.334	–.174	–.129	–.162	–.004	.019
	(.007)	(.007)	(.007)	(.008)	(.008)	(.009)
Puerto Ricans:						
All	–.380	–.218	–.162	–.172	–.028	.014
	(.011)	(.010)	(.011)	(.012)	(.012)	(.013)
Foreign-born	–.463	–.251	–.162	–.279	–.101	–.037
	(.015)	(.014)	(.015)	(.018)	(.017)	(.018)
U.S.-born	–.297	–.183	–.138	–.076	.036	.060
	(.015)	(.015)	(.015)	(.017)	(.017)	(.017)
Cubans:						
All	–.242	–.169	–.087	–.021	.025	.083
	(.016)	(.015)	(.016)	(.020)	(.019)	(.020)
Foreign-born	–.315	–.215	–.097	–.097	–.018	.053
	(.018)	(.017)	(.018)	(.022)	(.022)	(.022)
U.S.-born	.007	–.008	.036	.200	.150	.168
	(.033)	(.032)	(.032)	(.039)	(.038)	(.038)
Dominicans:						
All	–.637	–.363	–.263	–.475	–.178	–.085
	(.019)	(.019)	(.019)	(.022)	(.021)	(.022)
Foreign-born	–.672	–.379	–.246	–.532	–.212	–.112
	(.020)	(.020)	(.020)	(.023)	(.022)	(.023)
U.S.-born	–.267	–.175	–.115	.047	.122	.152
	(.065)	(.063)	(.063)	(.070)	(.068)	(.068)

continues

APPENDIX TABLE A7-7 Continued

	Log Earnings Differentials, Relative to U.S.-Born Whites					
	Men			Women		
Ethnicity/Nativity	(1)	(2)	(3)	(1)	(2)	(3)
Salvadorians/Guatemalans:						
All	–.599	–.112	–.008	–.500	.055	.153
	(.013)	(.012)	(.013)	(.017)	(.017)	(.018)
Foreign-born	–.610	–.111	.026	–.520	.051	.154
	(.013)	(.013)	(.014)	(.018)	(.017)	(.018)
U.S.-born	–.205	–.056	.001	–.048	.090	.119
	(.078)	(.076)	(.076)	(.089)	(.086)	(.086)
Other Central Americans:						
All	–.470	–.216	–.124	–.357	–.123	–.045
	(.019)	(.018)	(.019)	(.022)	(.021)	(.022)
Foreign-Born	–.502	–.224	–.100	–.405	–.148	–.064
	(.020)	(.019)	(.019)	(.023)	(.022)	(.023)
U.S.-born	–.143	–.121	–.080	.092	.101	.122
	(.063)	(.061)	(.061)	(.070)	(.068)	(.068)
Colombians:						
All	–.403	–.311	–.221	–.341	–.211	–.122
	(.021)	(.021)	(.021)	(.024)	(.024)	(.024)
Foreign-born	–.432	–.325	–.205	–.395	–.248	–.153
	(.022)	(.022)	(.022)	(.025)	(.025)	(.025)
U.S.-born	–.150	–.178	–.129	.176	.143	.167
	(.068)	(.066)	(.066)	(.080)	(.078)	(.078)
Peruvians/Ecuadorans:						
All	–.458	–.318	–.226	–.307	–.163	–.078
	(.019)	(.019)	(.019)	(.024)	(.024)	(.024)
Foreign-born	–.493	–.339	–.218	–.357	–.196	–.105
	(.020)	(.019)	(.020)	(.025)	(.025)	(.025)
U.S.-born	–.040	–.044	.006	.155	.142	.165
	(.070)	(.068)	(.068)	(.079)	(.077)	(.077)
Other South Americans:						
All	–.194	–.189	–.113	–.155	–.152	–.085
	(.024)	(.023)	(.023)	(.029)	(.028)	(.029)
Foreign-born	–.227	–.213	–.115	–.205	–.185	–.114
	(.025)	(.024)	(.024)	(.031)	(.030)	(.031)
U.S.-born	.069	.012	.055	.163	.075	.095
	(.072)	(.070)	(.070)	(.081)	(.079)	(.079)
Other Hispanics:						
All	–.319	–.184	–.152	–.168	–.033	–.013
	(.013)	(.013)	(.013)	(.015)	(.015)	(.015)
Foreign-born	–.165	–.116	–.035	–.114	–.085	–.033
	(.041)	(.039)	(.039)	(.048)	(.047)	(.047)
U.S.-born	–.331	–.192	–.160	–.168	–.027	–.011
	(.014)	(.013)	(.014)	(.016)	(.015)	(.016)

APPENDIX TABLE A7-7 Continued

	Log Earnings Differentials, Relative to U.S.-Born Whites					
	Men			Women		
Ethnicity/Nativity	(1)	(2)	(3)	(1)	(2)	(3)
Controls for:						
Geographic location	Yes	Yes	Yes	Yes	Yes	Yes
Age	Yes	Yes	Yes	Yes	Yes	Yes
Education	No	Yes	Yes	No	Yes	Yes
English proficiency	No	No	Yes	No	No	Yes

NOTE: The reported figures are estimated coefficients from least-squares regressions in which the dependent variable is the natural logarithm of annual earnings. Standard errors are shown in parentheses. The samples include individuals ages 25 to 59 who worked during the calendar year preceding the survey.
SOURCE: 2000 census, 5% PUMS.

APPENDIX TABLE A7-8 Average Years of Schooling, by Gender, Ethnicity, and Generation

	Men, by Generation				Women, by Generation			
Ethnicity	All	1st	2nd	3rd+	All	1st	2nd	3rd+
Whites				13.6				13.6
				(.007)				(.007)
				[110,226]				[115,031]
Blacks				12.7				12.9
				(.02)				(.02)
				[12,820]				[17,395]
All Hispanics	10.7	9.7	12.5	12.4	10.9	9.9	12.6	12.4
	(.02)	(.03)	(.04)	(.03)	(.02)	(.03)	(.04)	(.03)
	[26,190]	[16,772]	[3,539]	[5,879]	[27,489]	[16,627]	[4,150]	[6,712]
Mexicans	10.1	8.8	12.2	12.3	10.3	8.7	12.2	12.2
	(.03)	(.04)	(.06)	(.04)	(.03)	(.04)	(.05)	(.04)
	[16,316]	[10,051]	[2,009]	[4,256]	[16,064]	[8,852]	[2,344]	[4,868]
Puerto Ricans	11.9	11.2	12.5	12.7	12.1	11.6	12.7	12.8
	(.06)	(.10)	(.08)	(.15)	(.06)	(.09)	(.07)	(.14)
	[2,348]	[1,232]	[800]	[316]	[2,975]	[1,551]	[1,044]	[380]
Cubans	12.8	12.5	14.1	12.2	13.0	12.6	14.3	13.8
	(.09)	(.11)	(.15)	(.51)	(.09)	(.11)	(.17)	(.43)
	[1,116]	[853]	[229]	[34]	[1,116]	[868]	[208]	[40]
Central/South Americans	11.2	11.0	13.5	12.4	11.5	11.2	13.9	13.4
	(.06)	(.07)	(.15)	(.26)	(.06)	(.06)	(.14)	(.18)
	[4,352]	[3,935]	[277]	[140]	[4,931]	[4,428]	[324]	[179]
Other Hispanics	12.5	11.7	13.4	13.1	12.3	11.2	13.2	13.1
	(.07)	(.13)	(.17)	(.07)	(.06)	(.13)	(.14)	(.06)
	[2,058]	[701]	[224]	[1,133]	[2,403]	[928]	[230]	[1,245]

NOTE: Standard errors are shown in parentheses, and sample sizes are shown in brackets. The samples include individuals ages 25 to 59.
SOURCE: March 1998–2002, CPS data.

APPENDIX TABLE A7-9 Annual Earnings Differentials, by Gender, Ethnicity, and Generation

	Log Earnings Differentials, Relative to 3rd+ Generation Whites					
	Men			Women		
Ethnicity/Generation	(1)	(2)	(3)	(1)	(2)	(3)
3rd+ generation blacks	–.424	–.409	–.309	–.072	–.064	.027
	(.012)	(.012)	(.011)	(.012)	(.012)	(.011)
All Hispanics:						
All generations	–.539	–.499	–.138	–.356	–.340	–.016
	(.011)	(.011)	(.011)	(.013)	(.013)	(.013)
1st generation	–.644	–.606	–.133	–.521	–.509	–.052
	(.013)	(.013)	(.014)	(.017)	(.017)	(.017)
2nd generation	–.382	–.314	–.177	–.120	–.085	.053
	(.026)	(.026)	(.025)	(.029)	(.029)	(.028)
3rd+ generation	–.300	–.271	–.124	–.160	–.147	.008
	(.022)	(.022)	(.021)	(.024)	(.024)	(.023)
Mexicans:						
All generations	–.592	–.544	–.103	–.424	–.405	.003
	(.013)	(.013)	(.014)	(.017)	(.017)	(.017)
1st generation	–.719	–.668	–.070	–.668	–.650	–.007
	(.016)	(.016)	(.017)	(.023)	(.023)	(.024)
2nd generation	–.444	–.381	–.190	–.174	–.142	.048
	(.033)	(.033)	(.032)	(.037)	(.037)	(.036)
3rd+ generation	–.337	–.307	–.131	–.210	–.197	–.007
	(.024)	(.024)	(.024)	(.027)	(.027)	(.026)
Puerto Ricans:						
All generations	–.402	–.376	–.189	–.192	–.175	–.023
	(.035)	(.035)	(.034)	(.037)	(.037)	(.036)
1st generation	–.478	–.481	–.225	–.279	–.278	–.093
	(.048)	(.047)	(.046)	(.054)	(.054)	(.052)
2nd generation	–.357	–.306	–.182	–.135	–.102	.030
	(.059)	(.058)	(.057)	(.059)	(.059)	(.058)
3rd+ generation	–.236	–.162	–.054	–.081	–.051	.051
	(.095)	(.095)	(.092)	(.097)	(.097)	(.095)
Cubans:						
All generations	–.312	–.304	–.211	–.124	–.116	–.060
	(.046)	(.046)	(.045)	(.056)	(.056)	(.055)
1st generation	–.379	–.391	–.263	–.210	–.215	–.112
	(.053)	(.052)	(.051)	(.064)	(.064)	(.063)
2nd generation	–.061	.021	–.012	.073	.125	.041
	(.102)	(.102)	(.099)	(.122)	(.122)	(.119)
3rd+ generation	–.366	–.320	–.172	.365	.390	.355
	(.266)	(.264)	(.257)	(.271)	(.271)	(.264)

continues

APPENDIX TABLE A7-9 Continued

	Log Earnings Differentials, Relative to 3rd+ Generation Whites					
	Men			Women		
Ethnicity/Generation	(1)	(2)	(3)	(1)	(2)	(3)
Central/South Americans:						
All generations	–.545	–.509	–.200	–.365	–.353	–.049
	(.024)	(.024)	(.023)	(.028)	(.028)	(.027)
1st generation	–.576	–.546	–.207	–.423	–.414	–.073
	(.025)	(.025)	(.024)	(.030)	(.030)	(.029)
2nd generation	–.251	–.129	–.091	.072	.129	.148
	(.091)	(.091)	(.088)	(.100)	(.100)	(.097)
3rd+ generation	–.315	–.298	–.178	.055	.056	.107
	(.135)	(.134)	(.131)	(.142)	(.142)	(.138)
Other Hispanics:						
All generations	–.338	–.314	–.162	–.211	–.202	–.028
	(.039)	(.039)	(.038)	(.043)	(.043)	(.042)
1st generation	–.509	–.494	–.251	–.454	–.450	–.177
	(.059)	(.059)	(.058)	(.067)	(.067)	(.066)
2nd generation	–.394	–.309	–.265	–.026	.011	.102
	(.109)	(.108)	(.105)	(.119)	(.119)	(.116)
3rd+ generation	–.148	–.134	–.046	–.043	–.036	.066
	(.058)	(.058)	(.056)	(.063)	(.063)	(.061)
Controls for:						
Survey year	Yes	Yes	Yes	Yes	Yes	Yes
Geographic location	Yes	Yes	Yes	Yes	Yes	Yes
Age	No	Yes	Yes	No	Yes	Yes
Education	No	No	Yes	No	No	Yes

NOTE: The reported figures are estimated coefficients from least squares regressions in which the dependent variable is the natural logarithm of annual earnings. Standard errors are shown in parentheses. The samples include individuals ages 25 to 59 who worked during the calendar year preceding the survey.
SOURCE: March 1998–2002, CPS data.

8

Economic Well-Being

Cordelia Reimers

The social processes described in the preceding chapters—selective migration from the various countries of Latin America, family structure and household size, education, employment, and earnings—are important influences on the economic well-being of Hispanics in the United States. These processes vary considerably among Hispanic subgroups, leading to wide variation in their economic status. Building on those earlier chapters, this chapter examines the outcome of these processes as reflected in total household income, not just earnings, which were examined in Chapter 7. Household income is a more comprehensive measure of economic well-being than individual earnings because it includes the earnings of all household members, plus unearned income from public benefits and other sources. Thus, it gives a more complete picture of the economic resources available to Hispanics, which vitally affect their lives.[1]

As the earlier chapters have made clear, the Hispanic population is tremendously diverse, both across national-origin groups and across generations. Aggregate statistics for Hispanics as a group mainly reflect the

[1]The picture is still incomplete, however, because household income excludes fringe benefits (such as employer-provided health insurance), in-kind benefits (such as food stamps, Medicaid, and Medicare), capital gains on investments, and the services provided by assets (such as automobiles and owner-occupied houses). Some types of income are underreported, such as welfare benefits, business income, and dividends. Moreover, taxes and income diverted to other households (for example, remittances and child support) are not deducted. Finally, some households may not in fact pool income, as is implicitly assumed.

experience of Mexicans, who constitute about 60 percent of all Hispanics. The U.S. Census Bureau publishes data annually on individual, family, and household income and poverty rates for Hispanics overall and separately for Mexicans, Puerto Ricans, Cubans, Central and South Americans (combined), and other Hispanics (U.S. Bureau of the Census, 2003, Summary Table 1, Detailed Tables 12.1–15.2).[2] Scholars have produced a number of disaggregated analyses of family or household income based on the 1990 and earlier censuses and on Current Population Survey (CPS) data.[3] However, the available studies usually do not identify the smaller national-origin groups (such as Dominicans, Colombians, Salvadorans, and Guatemalans) beyond a catch-all category, Central and South Americans. Moreover, they could not distinguish among the generations born in the United States, because parents' birthplace is not in the decennial census and was not available in the CPS on a regular basis until 1994. This makes it difficult to trace the intergenerational changes in economic well-being for Latinos born in the United States in order to see how the course of assimilation is (or is not) proceeding. Nearly all of the earlier studies examined family income rather than household income, thus omitting nonrelatives' income and ignoring nonfamily households. In addition, the earlier studies are becoming somewhat dated.

Rather than simply review the findings of these older studies, this chapter takes advantage of the pooled 1998–2002 March CPS data that have been used in other chapters and are described in the appendix. This data set has detailed indicators of national origin and generation based on birthplace and parents' birthplace. As in other chapters, this more "objective" measure of national origin enables us to go beyond the self-identified groups

---

[2]The Census Bureau also published tables based on the 1990 census showing income and poverty rates for Hispanics by self-identified national origin for all the countries in Latin America, nativity, whether the foreign-born entered the United States in 1980 or later, and citizenship status (U.S. Bureau of the Census, 1993, Table 5). These tables have not yet been published for the 2000 census.

[3]For example, see the chapter on "Earnings and Economic Well-Being" in Bean and Tienda (1987). Amidst a wealth of information, it shows changes from 1970 to 1980 in family income and poverty rates and in sources of income for Mexicans, Puerto Ricans, Cubans, Central/South Americans, other Hispanics, and black and white non-Hispanics by nativity, type of headship, family size, and age of head. Other studies of the changing American income distribution, such as Karoly (1993) and Levy (1995, 1998), have compared family incomes for Hispanics in the aggregate with black and white non-Hispanics. Chiswick and Sullivan (1995) provide a more detailed picture of mean household income in 1989 of the foreign-born by date of arrival, separating Mexicans from other Latin Americans. A Bean et al. (1994) study is one of the rare earlier studies that disaggregates Mexicans by generation in the United States, but it focuses on social indicators, such as education and naturalization, rather than economic outcomes.

(Mexicans, Puerto Ricans, Cubans) in the CPS to distinguish Dominicans, Salvadorans and Guatemalans, Colombians, and Peruvians and Ecuadorians from other Central and South Americans. It also enables us to distinguish between immigrants who came to the United States as adults (the "1.0 generation") and their children who were born abroad but grew up in the United States (the "1.5 generation"), and between those in the second generation whose parents were both born abroad (the "2.0 generation") and those who have one parent born in the United States (the "2.5 generation"). Immigrants who came to the United States as children may resemble those who were born in the United States to two foreign-born parents more than they resemble immigrants who came as adults. Similarly, persons with one U.S.-born parent may resemble those with two U.S.-born parents (the "3+ generation") more than they resemble those with two immigrant parents. It is useful to examine whether the data support this conjecture.

Preliminary analysis of this data set revealed that the national-origin groups in Central America and in South America resemble each other enough in terms of economic status that they can be combined into these two groups, but that Central Americans and South Americans are quite different from each other and Dominicans differ from both. This chapter therefore treats these three groups separately, in addition to Mexicans, Puerto Ricans, and Cubans. To simplify the presentation, in this chapter I usually combine generations 1.0 and 1.5 (first-generation immigrants) and generations 2.0 and 2.5 (second-generation children of immigrants), while noting any significant differences within the first and second generations. The detailed tabulations are available in the appendix at the end of the chapter.

Using this data set, this chapter presents a detailed portrait of the household incomes of Latinos in the United States at the turn of the 21st century, by national origin and generation in the United States. It reveals the diversity behind the aggregate numbers for household income, its sources, and poverty rates for Hispanic subgroups classified by national origin and generation, compared with black and white non-Hispanics who were born in the United States of U.S.-born parents.[4] Such a portrait is not available anywhere in the existing literature. While giving a more nuanced picture of Hispanic well-being, it reveals more puzzles and raises more questions than can be answered here. The historical comparisons and mul-

[4]Throughout this chapter, for the sake of brevity I often refer to third (or higher) generation non-Hispanic whites and blacks simply as "whites" and "blacks." I use the terms "Hispanic" and "Latino" interchangeably. Although persons born in Puerto Rico are U.S. citizens by birth and thus are not immigrants, they are grouped with first-generation immigrants, and "U.S.-born" refers only to those born on the U.S. mainland.

tivariate analyses that would be necessary to explain all of the observed patterns are beyond the scope of this chapter and are not attempted here. I hope that the data presented in this chapter will stimulate further research to explain these patterns.

Annual household income and poverty rates are considered first, followed by sources of income in earnings, public benefits, and other unearned income, such as rent, interest, child support, scholarships, and gifts. I also investigate the extent to which Hispanics compensate for low earning capacity by doubling up in an extended household, so that several workers can contribute their earnings. Hispanic subgroups with larger households may have more total income, but less income per person. For each national-origin group, I note changes across generations. Which outcomes show progress from the first to the second generation, and which do not? Are there any changes from the second to the third generation? A separate section is devoted to the elderly, who are a small fraction of the Latino population in the United States today but who will become more important in the future.

I show that the economic status and sources of income of the various Hispanic subgroups are largely governed by their relative levels of education (which largely determine their earning capacity) and by family structure. The legal status of immigrants and phenotype also influence earning capacity. Thus, Mexican, Central American, Dominican, Puerto Rican, and recent Cuban immigrants are limited by lack of education, and in some cases by undocumented status and nonwhite appearance. Dominicans and Puerto Ricans are further limited by the prevalence of female-headed households. These underlying factors lead to striking similarities between Mexicans and Central Americans, between Puerto Ricans and Dominicans, and between Cubans and South Americans in their levels of household income and its sources. At the same time, they result in remarkable contrasts among these pairs of Hispanic-origin groups.

WORKING-AGE HISPANIC HOUSEHOLDS

Annual Income and Poverty Rates

The incomes of Mexican Americans—by far the largest group of Latinos—are very low. Their median annual household income ranges from \$30,000 (in 2002 dollars) for the immigrant generation to about \$40,000 for those who were born in the United States (see Table 8-1). In each generation they rank lower than the other Hispanic national-origin groups except for Dominicans and Puerto Ricans. However, Mexicans who were born in the United States have higher household incomes than blacks, whose median income is only \$32,000 per year. In contrast, the median

TABLE 8-1 Median Real Annual Income and Per Capita Income of Households, in 2002 Dollars, 1997–2001 Pooled

National Origin (Birthplace)	Households with Head Under Age 65: Generation — 1st: Foreign-Born	2nd: U.S.-Born, Foreign-Born Parent	3+: U.S.-Born, Both Parents U.S.-Born*
	Median Total Household Income (2002 $)		
Mexico	$29,799	$40,676	$39,306
Central America	33,626	49,138	
Puerto Rico	27,592	36,989	35,553
Dominican Republic	24,379	37,941	
Cuba	39,733	62,545	
South America	42,889	52,085	
All Hispanics (self-identity)*	31,470	40,505	39,903
Black non-Hispanics (self-identity)*			31,775
White non-Hispanics (self-identity)*			54,752
	Median Income Per Capita (2002 $)		
Mexico	$7,775	$12,994	$13,312
Central America	9,993	20,151	
Puerto Rico	10,308	13,059	13,053
Dominican Republic	7,726	13,739	
Cuba	14,581	22,678	
South America	14,729	20,316	
All Hispanics (self-identity)*	9,071	13,570	13,901
Black non-Hispanics (self-identity)*			13,388
White non-Hispanics (self-identity)*			22,480

*The samples for Hispanics overall and for 3+ generation Mexicans, Puerto Ricans, and black and white non-Hispanics are identified by the "subjective" Spanish-origin and race questions in the CPS.
SOURCE: Pooled March CPS files, 1998–2002, using household weights. Results for Hispanics are shown only for cells with at least 90 observations.

household headed by a third (or higher)-generation white non-Hispanic has an annual income of $55,000.

Dominicans and Puerto Ricans have even lower incomes than Mexicans. Immigrants from the Dominican Republic have the lowest median household incomes among first-generation Latinos ($24,000). Puerto Ricans born on the island are just a little higher ($28,000). By the second generation, these groups are better off than blacks, although their median household incomes are still lower than that of U.S.-born Mexicans.

In contrast, Cubans and South Americans are much better off than other Hispanic subgroups of the same generation. Among households headed by working-age Latino adults who were born abroad, South Americans have the highest median total income ($43,000), but among those who were born in the United States of foreign-born parents, Cubans take the lead with $63,000, which is even higher than white non-Hispanics' $55,000. Central Americans are an intermediate group, with incomes between those of Mexicans and Cubans and South Americans.

Income per person is a better measure of economic well-being, because a household's income must support everyone living there. By this measure, Mexicans are as low as or even lower than Dominicans and Puerto Ricans (see Table 8-1), because they have larger households. In the immigrant generation, for example, Mexicans' median per capita income ($7,800) is 25 percent less than Puerto Ricans, even though Mexicans' median total household income is 8 percent higher. Members of half the households headed by first-generation Mexicans and Dominicans are living on less than a third of the income available to half of third (or higher)-generation whites.[5]

Both total and per capita household incomes increase monotonically across generations for all nationalities, with the largest jumps occurring between the first and second generations.[6] Mexicans' income per person, for example, increases by two-thirds from the immigrant to the second generation.[7] When the first and second generations are disaggregated further, one finds that immigrants who arrived as children and grew up in the United States have higher incomes than those who arrived as adults, and the U.S.-born with one U.S.-born parent have higher incomes than those with two foreign-born parents (see Appendix Table A8-1). All U.S.-born Latino

[5]Foreign-born Salvadorans and Guatemalans are worse off than other Central Americans in terms of per capita income, although their total household incomes are similar, as shown in Appendix Table A8-1.

[6]The slight drops observed between the second and the third (and higher) generations of Mexicans and Puerto Ricans could result from the shift from parents' birthplace to self-identification. In the 2.5 generation, who have one mainland-born parent, income is slightly lower for those who identify themselves as Puerto Ricans than for those whose other parent was born in Puerto Rico (author's tabulation, not shown). This suggests that, when island-born Puerto Ricans intermarry with non–Puerto Ricans, the children who have higher incomes disproportionately identify with their non–Puerto Rican parent's national origin. This selective loss of the more successful in later generations could bias downward measures of intergenerational progress for those of Puerto Rican ancestry.

[7]These estimates of income by generation are defined by the generational status of the householder. On an individual level, the distinction among generations is blurred, as second-generation persons grow up in first-generation households and share their economic status.

subgroups have higher median total household incomes than blacks. However, because of their larger households, median per capita income of U.S.-born Mexicans and Puerto Ricans is at or slightly below that of blacks.

Cubans who came to the United States in childhood have the same high median household income ($65,000) as U.S.-born Cubans whose parents were both born in Cuba (see Appendix Table A8-1). This is considerably more than double the income of Cubans who were adults when they arrived. In that 1.0 generation, Cubans are no better off than Mexicans. The sharp contrast between Cubans of the 1.0 and 1.5 generations no doubt reflects differences between the early and later cohorts of immigrants. The Cuban exiles who came as adults in the 1960s brought more skills and capital with them than the later cohorts (Alba and Nee, 2003, pp. 189–191). Many of them are now too old to be in our sample of working-age Cuban households, but their advantages were passed on to their children (the 1.5 generation), whose incomes are well above those of whites. Today's working-age household heads of the 1.0 generation are mainly drawn from the less-skilled later cohorts.

Central Americans' median income jumps by almost 50 percent from the first to the second generation. This is also in part a cohort difference, as the Central American-born parents of second-generation household heads would have arrived in the United States even before the first wave of political exiles came from Nicaragua in the late 1970s and early 1980s. They are likely to have been idiosyncratic immigrants who were disproportionately drawn from their countries' elites. First-generation Central Americans, in contrast, have mostly come to the United States in the past 20 years, many as undocumented refugees from the civil wars and violence there. They are not highly skilled and did not receive official refugee status or U.S. government aid (Alba and Nee, 2003, pp. 196–197).

Lower median incomes are reflected in higher poverty rates and vice versa, with one exception: in the first generation, the Cubans' poverty rate is as high as that of Central Americans, despite the fact that the Cubans' median per capita income is much higher (Table 8-2). This indicates that there is greater inequality among the Cubans, as indicated by the contrast between the 1.0 and 1.5 generations discussed above. Within nationality and generation, poverty rates are higher among children than overall. Over half (54 percent) of Puerto Rican and nearly half (48 percent) of Dominican children who were born on those islands but are now on the mainland are being raised in poor families, as are 43 percent of Mexican-born children.[8]

[8]These poverty rates are only a rough indication of the proportion of each group that faces serious hardship, because they do not take account of in-kind benefits such as food stamps, Medicaid, school lunches, and housing subsidies; by the same token, the official poverty threshold is unrealistically low.

TABLE 8-2 Poverty Rates, 1997–2001 Pooled

National Origin (Birthplace)	Fraction of Persons with Family Income Below Poverty Threshold		
	Generation		
	1st: Foreign-Born	2nd: U.S.-Born, Foreign-Born Parent	3+: U.S.-Born, Both Parents U.S.-Born*
	All Ages		
Mexico	0.265	0.275	0.205
Central America	0.187	0.202	
Puerto Rico	0.285	0.257	0.301
Dominican Republic	0.305	0.372	
Cuba	0.179	0.126	0.052
South America	0.126	0.117	
All Hispanics (self-identity)*	0.238	0.266	0.204
Black non-Hispanics (self-identity)*			0.250
White non-Hispanics (self-identity)*			0.081
	Persons in Female-Headed Families		
Mexico	0.476	0.477	0.380
Central America	0.317	0.379	
Puerto Rico	0.519	0.441	0.471
Dominican Republic	0.471	0.584	
Cuba	0.374	0.343	
South America	0.246	0.252	
All Hispanics (self-identity)*	0.427	0.464	0.382
Black non-Hispanics (self-identity)*			0.394
White non-Hispanics (self-identity)*			0.211

*The samples for Hispanics overall and for 3+ generation Mexicans, Puerto Ricans, Cubans, and black and white non-Hispanics are identified by the "subjective" Spanish-origin and race questions in the CPS.

SOURCE: Pooled March CPS files, 1998–2002, using person weights. Results for Hispanics are shown only for cells with at least 90 observations.

Generation		
1st: Foreign-Born	2nd: U.S.-Born, Foreign-Born Parent	3+: U.S.-Born, Both Parents U.S.-Born*
Children Ages 0–17		
0.426	0.342	0.268
0.296	0.248	
0.536	0.363	0.356
0.481	0.422	
0.312	0.178	0.044
0.187	0.131	
0.399	0.331	0.269
		0.353
		0.106
Persons in Married-Couple Families		
0.228	0.210	0.117
0.138	0.135	
0.142	0.097	0.114
0.179	0.142	
0.115	0.055	0.013
0.087	0.070	
0.188	0.187	0.110
		0.080
		0.037

Not surprisingly, families headed by unmarried women are extremely likely to be poor, with poverty rates several times those of married-couple families of the same nationality and generation. This helps explain the very high poverty rates of Puerto Ricans and Dominicans. Controlling for headship status, one finds that Puerto Ricans have the highest poverty rate among the foreign-born female-headed families (52 percent), but Dominicans are highest among the U.S.-born (58 percent). Mexicans are second-poorest or a very close third among female-headed families. Among Latino married-couple families, Mexicans have the highest poverty rates regardless of generation.

Disaggregation of the second generation reveals that, unlike household incomes, which increase from each generation to the next, poverty rates do not improve for any group but Cubans until the 2.5 generation, who have at least one parent born on the U.S. mainland. The contrast between intergenerational growth of income and stagnation of poverty rates indicates that inequality increases across generations. Cuban poverty rates drop between the 1.0 and the 1.5 generation, mirroring the jump in income discussed above. By the third generation, the Cubans' poverty rate is even lower than that of white non-Hispanics' (5 versus 8 percent).

Public programs providing noncash benefits—Medicaid, Medicare, food stamps, school lunches, housing subsidies, and energy assistance—represent a significant addition to household resources for Hispanics. The valuation of Medicaid and Medicare coverage is problematic, however, because these values do not represent actual services received by the household, but are more like an imputed insurance premium. The groups with the lowest cash incomes tend to have the largest values of in-kind benefits. Excluding Medicaid and Medicare, the average value of the other noncash benefits (mainly food stamps) per household adds about 4 percent to the median Dominican immigrant household's economic resources—about twice as much as for blacks—and no more than 3 percent for other subgroups.[9]

In sum, whereas Chapter 7 reports that Mexicans have the lowest education and earnings among Latino subgroups, Mexicans do not have the lowest total household income or the highest poverty rate in each generation; Dominicans or Puerto Ricans do. This paradox can be explained by the characteristics reported in Chapters 3 and 5: Mexican households are less likely to be female-headed, are more likely to be extended, and are concentrated in different locations than Puerto Ricans and Domini-

[9]These percentages are derived by dividing the value in Appendix Table A8-7 by the value in Table 8-1.

cans. Mexicans do have the highest poverty rates among married-couple families, and they often share the bottom rung in per capita income.

Household incomes rise from generation to generation for all groups, but so does inequality, so that poverty rates generally do not drop until the 2.5 generation, who have one U.S.-born parent. By this generation, all Latino nationalities except Dominicans are less likely to be poor than blacks. At the other extreme, Cubans who were born or grew up in the United States have per capita incomes on a par with whites. However, these U.S.-born Hispanics' parents and grandparents who were born abroad were not necessarily comparable to today's immigrants from the same country. This is because, as described in Chapters 2 and 3, changing political and economic conditions in the countries of Latin America have sent waves of exiles and emigrants to the United States whose characteristics have varied over time.

These differences in economic well-being among Latino subgroups are broadly correlated with their earning capacities, as indicated by their education levels. The class backgrounds of the various cohorts of political refugees and economic migrants from each Latin American country affect the position they can achieve in the U.S. labor market and the advantages they can transmit to their children and grandchildren. Such advantages from education and class help explain the high incomes of South Americans and of Cubans whose parents came in the first wave of refugees. Legal status also affects the earnings of the first generation, as undocumented immigrants (who constitute a significant proportion of Mexicans, Central Americans, and Dominicans) are largely confined to marginal jobs and often cannot translate their skills into commensurate incomes. Phenotype may also play a role, as darker Hispanics are more likely to face racial discrimination in the United States than those who look like Europeans. In addition to education, legal status, and phenotype, which affect earning capacity, household structure also plays a major role, as the high female-headship rates of Puerto Ricans and Dominicans reduce their median household incomes.

Sources of Household Income

For a deeper understanding of why household incomes vary across nationalities and generations, it is useful to consider three sources of income: earnings, public benefits, and the incomes of extended household members (defined as persons of working age who are living in the household, other than the head and his or her spouse). The relative shares of income from these sources are influenced by three factors: first, the skills and earnings of the head and secondary earners, discussed in Chapter 7; second, household structure—that is, female headship and household extension beyond the head and spouse (including cohabitation, whether single young adults typically live with their parents until marriage, and whether elderly parents live with their children)—which was discussed in Chapter 5; and third, eligibility for and generosity of public benefit programs.

These three factors influence each other. For example, the share from a spouse's earnings depends on household structure—obviously, because female-headed families do not have a spouse, and less obviously, because grandparents or other extended-household members may provide child care, thus freeing the spouse to take a paid job. Similarly, the share from earnings will tend to be larger for groups that are more likely to have extended households containing multiple workers. Public benefit programs may affect earnings because welfare eligibility rules place ceilings on income.

Income from public benefits, in turn, depends on household structure, earnings, and other income (which in turn depend on household structure) as well as on legal status, time in the United States, and the state of residence. Single female family heads are more likely to be eligible for welfare benefits. Undocumented immigrants and temporary visitors are ineligible for benefits. Legal immigrants who entered the United States after August 1996 are barred from federally funded means-tested benefits for at least five years, but some states provide benefits for these recent immigrants from their own funds. The eligibility rules vary by state, as do the benefit levels.

Finally, household structure may be influenced by earning capacity and culture-based preferences, as discussed in Chapter 5. It has also been argued that the pre-1996 welfare program encouraged female headship among the poor because couples were not eligible for benefits in many states, but researchers have found little empirical evidence that welfare or welfare reform affected marriage rates.[10] Chapter 5 shows that female headship increases and structural/demographic familism declines across generations. It also shows the variation across Latino subgroups in the prevalence of extended households, which underlies the share of household income derived from members other than the head and spouse.

There are two reasons for household extension that have different implications for its impact on economic well-being: one is taking in others who need support, such as elderly relatives or fellow immigrants who have just arrived in the United States; the other is doubling up to save money by realizing economies of scale and to generate more income, either directly from extra earners or indirectly from help with child care, thus freeing a parent to work for pay. The first reason would reduce the per capita income of the household; the latter might increase it. The effect of education on

[10] Among the many studies of this topic, see Grogger, Karoly, and Klerman (2002) for a review of the literature on welfare reform and marriage.

household extension could go either way. More education leads to higher earnings, so that one can afford to take in others and support them; higher earnings also mean one can afford to indulge tastes for privacy. The correlation between income and household extension could also go either way, as more earners mean more income, but more income can "buy" more privacy.

This section examines strategies for generating income by having multiple earners in the household, by obtaining public benefits and other unearned income, and by pooling income from several generations or other relatives and nonrelatives living in the same household. It compares shares of income coming from earnings, from various public benefits (Social Security, Supplemental Security Income, and welfare), and from unearned income from private sources (such as rent, child support, and gifts). Finally, shares of income coming from the head's children and parents, from other relatives, from a cohabiting partner, and from other nonrelatives are compared.

Earnings

As one would expect, households headed by someone under age 65 get most of their income from earnings. One would expect the fraction of income derived from earnings to be greater for groups with more earners, higher skills, or less access to public benefits and asset income. Latino households headed by working-age adults have an unusually large number of workers. Except for Puerto Ricans and Dominicans, all Latino groups in all generations have more earners per household than third (or higher)-generation blacks (who average 1.4 earners, as shown in Appendix Table A8-8). The lowest skilled groups tend to have the most; households headed by Salvadoran and Guatemalan immigrants have 1.9 to 2.0 workers on average, and Mexican, Peruvian, and Ecuadorian immigrants have 1.8 to 1.9—even more than third (or higher)-generation working-age white non-Hispanics (1.7). This is surprising, since only half of Mexican women in this generation are employed. Mexican immigrant households must often include more than two potential workers, so that others can contribute earnings. By the second generation, however, Mexicans are on a par with whites, whereas Cubans and Central Americans still have 1.8 earners per household. The unusually low incomes of Puerto Ricans and Dominicans are due in part to the fact that they have fewer workers per household (1.3 to 1.6) than do other Latino groups, reflecting their high rates of female headship.

As one might expect of groups that include many undocumented labor migrants, in the foreign-born generation Mexicans and Central Americans derive over 90 percent of average household income from earnings, a larger share than other Latino groups, but this share declines across generations, as they gain access to public benefits and other income sources (Table 8-3). Reflecting their high earning capacity, South Americans and U.S.-born Cubans also get at least 88 percent of their household income from earnings, a considerably higher share than either blacks (78 percent) or whites (84 percent). In later generations, Mexicans and Central Americans are intermediate among Hispanics in this respect, with 86 percent of their household income coming from earnings. A smaller fraction of Puerto Rican and Dominican household income is derived from earnings than in other Latino groups—only 70 and 74 percent, respectively, among those who were born abroad, but this fraction increases across generations so that it eventually surpasses that of blacks.

In households headed by a working-age adult, earnings by the head's spouse contribute about one-fifth of the income, on average, for Hispanics and non-Hispanic whites (see Appendix Table A8-9). The one-fifth share is remarkably consistent across Hispanic national origins and generations, with the exceptions of Puerto Ricans and Dominicans. Reflecting the prevalence of single-mother families, a smaller fraction of their household income is derived from the earnings of a spouse (14 to 17 percent) than in other Latino groups. In this respect they are closer to blacks, only 12 percent of whose household income comes from the earnings of a spouse. Children's earnings contribute another 5 to 6 percent to the income of the average Hispanic adult-immigrant household, regardless of nationality. In subsequent generations, this fraction drops to 3 percent or less, similar to blacks and whites.

The parity of most Hispanic subgroups with whites in terms of spouse's earnings may seem inconsistent with the higher female headship rates among Hispanics shown in Chapter 5 and the lower labor force participation rates of Latinas than white married women. However, whites are more likely to live alone, so that the married-couple proportion of *all* households is similar for Hispanics and whites. Moreover, the gender gap in earnings is smaller for Hispanics than whites, partly offsetting the lower probability that married Latinas work outside the home.

Public Benefits and Other Unearned Income

Reflecting their high poverty rates, Dominicans and Puerto Ricans have the highest rates of public benefits receipt among Latinos. A total of 50 and 41 percent, respectively, of households headed by first-generation Dominicans and Puerto Ricans receive benefits from at least one of the major needs-tested programs: welfare, Supplemental Security Income (SSI), food stamps, or Medicaid (see Appendix Table A8-10). These rates are much higher than for blacks (30 percent) and whites (11 percent). They diminish

TABLE 8-3 Mean Shares of Household Income by Source: Earnings, Public Benefits, Other Unearned Income, 1997–2001 Pooled

National Origin (Birthplace)	Households with Head Under Age 65		
	Generation		
	1st: Foreign-Born	2nd: U.S.-Born, Foreign-Born Parent	3+: U.S.-Born, Both Parents U.S.-Born*
	Fraction of Household Income		
Mexico			
Earnings	0.909	0.857	0.856
Public benefits**	0.064	0.091	0.093
Other unearned income (including pensions)	0.027	0.052	0.051
Central America			
Earnings	0.908	0.861	
Public benefits**	0.056	0.065	
Other unearned income (including pensions)	0.036	0.073	
Puerto Rico			
Earnings	0.702	0.783	0.810
Public benefits**	0.235	0.161	0.139
Other unearned income (including pensions)	0.064	0.056	0.051
Dominican Republic			
Earnings	0.741	0.823	
Public benefits**	0.192	0.088	
Other unearned income (including pensions)	0.066	0.089	
Cuba			
Earnings	0.830	0.909	
Public benefits**	0.109	0.028	
Other unearned income (including pensions)	0.061	0.063	
South America			
Earnings	0.887	0.876	
Public benefits**	0.051	0.020	
Other unearned income (including pensions)	0.062	0.104	
All Hispanics (self-identity)*			
Earnings	0.876	0.848	0.851
Public benefits**	0.086	0.100	0.094
Other unearned income (including pensions)	0.038	0.052	0.056

continues

TABLE 8-3 Continued

National Origin (Birthplace)	1st: Foreign-Born	2nd: U.S.-Born, Foreign-Born Parent	3+: U.S.-Born, Both Parents U.S.-Born*
	Households with Head Under Age 65 — Generation — Fraction of Household Income		
Black non-Hispanics (self-identity)*			
Earnings			0.780
Public benefits**			0.150
Other unearned income (including pensions)			0.070
White non-Hispanics (self-identity)*			
Earnings			0.844
Public benefits**			0.067
Other unearned income (including pensions)			0.088

*The samples for Hispanics overall and for 3+ generation Mexicans, Puerto Ricans, and black and white non-Hispanics are identified by the "subjective" Spanish-origin and race questions in the CPS.

**Public benefits include Social Security, Supplemental Security Income, public assistance/welfare, unemployment insurance, veterans' benefits, and workers' compensation.

SOURCE: Pooled March CPS files, 1998–2002. Means are simple averages across households, using household weights. Households with zero or negative total income, or containing persons with negative income from any source, are excluded. Results for Hispanics are shown only for cells with at least 90 observations.

across generations, however, until Puerto Ricans with a mainland-born parent are somewhat less likely to receive any of these benefits than blacks.

Most of this aid is in the form of Medicaid and food stamps. Only 16 and 12 percent of first-generation Dominican and Puerto Rican households, respectively, receive welfare, and 11 and 14 percent, respectively, receive SSI. These are considerably higher than the rates for blacks (8 percent) or any other Hispanic nationality. Participation in each of these public cash benefit programs declines across generations of Dominicans, so that the rate for those born in the United States resembles that of blacks. In contrast, the fraction of Puerto Rican households that receive welfare is as high among those whose parents were born on the U.S. mainland as among those who were born on the island.

Not surprisingly given their high rates of benefit receipt, a larger fraction of Dominican and Puerto Rican household income comes from public cash benefits (specifically, Social Security, SSI, welfare, unemployment insurance, workers' compensation, and veterans' benefits) than in other Latino groups—19 and 24 percent, respectively, for Dominicans and Puerto Ricans who were born abroad (see Table 8-3). This share diminishes across generations so that Dominicans who were born in the United States and Puerto Ricans with mainland-born parents are less dependent on this source of income than are blacks (15 percent). Social Security and SSI are the most important public benefits for Puerto Ricans who came to the mainland as adults; whereas welfare is most important for Dominicans of all generations (see Appendix Table A8-11).

Because their poverty rates are similar to Puerto Ricans and Dominicans, one might expect Mexicans to receive public benefits at similar rates. However, this is not the case. Only 30 percent of households headed by Mexican immigrants receive benefits from welfare, SSI, food stamps, or Medicaid (see Appendix Table A8-10)—a rate 11 to 20 percentage points lower than that of the other two groups. The Mexicans' participation rate is the same as those of blacks and three times that of whites. Among U.S.-born Mexicans it is about 24 percent. Again, most of the aid is in the form of Medicaid and food stamps; only 4 to 6 percent of Mexican households in each generation receive welfare benefits (below blacks' 8 percent) and only 2 to 5 percent receive SSI, with a slight increase across generations. The share of Mexicans receiving Social Security (from disability or survivors' insurance or from elderly persons living in the household) doubles across generations from 5 to 10 percent, the same as whites but slightly below blacks.

As a result of these low rates of receipt of public cash benefits, Mexicans get a surprisingly small share of their household income from these benefits. The share for Mexican immigrants is similar to that for whites (just under 7 percent, as shown in Table 8-3). It is about 9 percent for Mexicans who were born in the United States. This is still much lower than for blacks, who rely on public income maintenance programs for 15 percent of their household income.

The contrast between Mexicans, on one hand, and Puerto Ricans and Dominicans, on the other, may reflect the greater prevalence of female-headed families among the latter groups. This makes them more likely to be eligible for public benefit programs. Moreover, programs are more generous in the Northeast, where Puerto Ricans and Dominicans are concentrated, than in Texas, where a large proportion of Mexicans live. In addition, Puerto Ricans, being U.S. citizens by birth, have greater access to public benefits than recent immigrants from Mexico and elsewhere.

Reflecting their relative income levels, Central Americans' rates of receipt of public benefits fall between those of Mexicans and South Americans (see Appendix Table A8-10). Like Mexicans, they derive only a small share of their household income from public benefits (see Table 8-3). In keeping with their high incomes, Cuban and South American households are even less dependent on public benefits than are whites. The exception is Cubans who came to the United States as adults, who get 8 percent of their household income from Social Security (see Appendix Table A8-11). More Cuban and South American households receive SSI than welfare, which may reflect the presence of elderly relatives who did not work enough in the United States to qualify for Social Security benefits.

Other sources of unearned income (such as rent, interest, child support, and gifts) constitute 7 percent of the average black household's income and 9 percent of that of whites (see Table 8-3). Among Latinos, only U.S.-born South Americans and Dominicans equal whites in this respect. The Dominican case is puzzling, but the South Americans are among the Hispanic subgroups with the highest incomes, a significant share of which may come from investments. Foreign-born Mexicans and Central Americans, in contrast, derive exceptionally low shares of household income (less than 4 percent) from these other sources.

Income of Extended-Household Members

Thus far I have examined the shares of household income from two sources, earnings and public benefits, across Hispanic subgroups. I now turn to the third major source: the income of extended-household members (defined here as persons of working age other than the head and spouse). As discussed in Chapter 5, household extension may be a response to economic need or an expression of cultural preferences (see Angel and Tienda, 1982a, 1982b, 1984; Feliciano, Bean, and Leach, 2006; Flippen and Tienda, 1998; Glick, Bean, and Van Hook, 1997; Ruggles, 1987). If the former, it could be one strategy for coping with low earning capacity; if the latter, it may reduce the per capita income of households. To determine which is the dominant reason is beyond the scope of this chapter, but I can describe the patterns of extension across Hispanic subgroups compared with blacks and whites, insofar as they are reflected in household income.[11]

Adapting the classification used by Glick et al. (1997) and Ruggles (1987), I distinguish two general types of household extension: "vertical"

[11]Share of household income is an imperfect measure of extendedness, because it omits extended members who have no income and it reflects the *relative* amounts of income from each source. By this measure household extendedness would decrease as the head's or spouse's income rises, without any change in household composition.

or multigenerational—including the head's adult children and parents; and "horizontal"—including other relatives and nonrelatives.[12] Depending on norms regarding marriage, a cohabiting partner may be another source of household income. According to Glick et al. (1997), horizontal extension is primarily a response to economic need, whereas vertical extension reflects cultural preferences as well as need. They find that horizontal extension occurs primarily among undocumented and other labor immigrants from Mexico and Central America and fades with time in the United States. In the immigrant generation, vertical extension is more common among refugees, who may migrate as multigenerational family units. Among labor immigrant groups, who typically migrate as single young adults, vertical extension may be more prevalent in the 1.5 and second than the 1.0 generation, because the former have parents living in the United States.

Reflecting typical living arrangements in the United States, Hispanic households get almost all of their income—80 percent or more—from the head and his or her spouse. Nevertheless, all groups of Hispanics except U.S.-born Cubans rely more on the income of extended-household members than do third (or higher)-generation non-Hispanic blacks and whites (see Table 8-4). This is especially true of first-generation Mexicans, Central Americans, and Dominicans. The average U.S.-born Cuban or white non-Hispanic household derives 9 percent of its income from members other than the head and spouse. For blacks, this share is 12 percent, whereas for Mexican, Central American, and Dominican immigrants it is 20 percent. For the other Latino subgroups and generations, it is 14 to 15 percent. Thus, among Latinos who were born abroad, Dominicans rely on extended-household members for income as much as Mexicans and Central Americans do. One way in which Puerto Ricans differ from Dominicans is that, in the first generation, Puerto Ricans (like Cubans and South Americans) rely less on extended-household income pooling.

In some ethnic groups, elderly parents typically live with their children, and single adults live with relatives rather than alone. Moreover, doubling up with others in the same household is one strategy for coping with poverty and child care.[13] I therefore next investigate whether the contribution of extended-household members to household income comes primarily from children and parents of the head, from doubling up with other rela-

[12]The data do not permit us to distinguish the spouse's parents (or the spouse's children who are not children of the head) from other relatives of the head. As a result the share from vertical extension is slightly understated, and the share from horizontal extension is correspondingly overstated.

[13]In this chapter "doubling up" refers to all types of household extension beyond the head and spouse.

TABLE 8-4 Mean Shares of Household Income by Source: Income of Extended-Household Members, 1997–2001 Pooled

	Households with Head Under Age 65		
	Generation		
National Origin (Birthplace)	1st: Foreign-Born	2nd: U.S.-Born, Foreign-Born Parent	3+: U.S.-Born, Both Parents U.S.-Born*
	Fraction of Household Income		
Mexico			
Head's children and parents**	0.077	0.075	0.061
Other relatives of head	0.066	0.034	0.021
Unmarried partner of head	0.016	0.028	0.030
Other nonrelatives	0.037	0.030	0.025
Central America			
Head's children and parents**	0.075	0.058	
Other relatives of head	0.062	0.016	
Unmarried partner of head	0.019	0.038	
Other nonrelatives	0.051	0.031	
Puerto Rico			
Head's children and parents**	0.088	0.054	0.061
Other relatives of head	0.020	0.021	0.021
Unmarried partner of head	0.022	0.030	0.031
Other nonrelatives	0.022	0.030	0.024
Dominican Republic			
Head's children and parents**	0.107	0.063	
Other relatives of head	0.048	0.028	
Unmarried partner of head	0.023	0.042	
Other nonrelatives	0.021	0.019	
Cuba			
Head's children and parents**	0.088	0.033	
Other relatives of head	0.027	0.013	
Unmarried partner of head	0.017	0.011	
Other nonrelatives	0.016	0.035	
South America			
Head's children and parents**	0.071	0.050	
Other relatives of head	0.036	0.024	
Unmarried partner of head	0.015	0.029	
Other nonrelatives	0.031	0.040	

TABLE 8-4 Continued

	Households with Head Under Age 65		
	Generation		
National Origin (Birthplace)	1st: Foreign-Born	2nd: U.S.-Born, Foreign-Born Parent	3+: U.S.-Born, Both Parents U.S.-Born*
	Fraction of Household Income		
All Hispanics (self-identity)*			
Head's children and parents**	0.079	0.067	0.059
Other relatives of head	0.055	0.031	0.019
Unmarried partner of head	0.018	0.027	0.029
Other nonrelatives	0.035	0.029	0.025
Black non-Hispanics (self-identity)*			
Head's children and parents**			0.063
Other relatives of head			0.020
Unmarried partner of head			0.020
Other nonrelatives			0.020
White non-Hispanics (self-identity)*			
Head's children and parents**			0.037
Other relatives of head			0.007
Unmarried partner of head			0.020
Other nonrelatives			0.025

*The samples for Hispanics overall and for 3+ generation Mexicans, Puerto Ricans, and black and white non-Hispanics are identified by the "subjective" Spanish-origin and race questions in the CPS.

**Includes grandchildren, who contribute 0.2 percent or less for each group.

SOURCE: Pooled March CPS files, 1998–2002. Means are simple averages across households, using household weights. Households with zero or negative total income, or containing persons with negative income from any source, are excluded. Results for Hispanics are shown only for cells with at least 90 observations.

tives, from a cohabiting partner of the head, or from other nonrelatives. The pattern varies by race/ethnicity and by generation in the United States for Hispanics, shedding some light on the question of "familism" and norms regarding cohabitation that were discussed at length in Chapter 5.

In general, for Hispanics who were born abroad, vertical and horizontal relatives are each more important than nonrelatives as a source of household income. Both types of relatives are generally more important sources of income for Hispanic immigrants than they are for blacks and whites. For blacks, too, relatives contribute more than nonrelatives. For the average non-Hispanic white household, income from nonrelatives and cohabiting partners is as important as income from relatives.

Among foreign-born Dominicans, 11 percent of household income comes from the head's children and parents (mostly children) living in the household. These vertical relatives contribute 7 to 9 percent of household income in the immigrant generation of other Latino national origins. For Mexicans, the share from the head's children and parents remains at 8 percent in the second generation, then drops to 6 percent in the third (and higher) generation. For the other Latino origin groups, however, the share from children and parents is smaller for the U.S.-born than the immigrant generation. Other (horizontal) relatives contribute 5 to 7 percent of household income for foreign-born Mexicans, Central Americans, and Dominicans, but less than 4 percent of household income for Puerto Ricans, Cubans, and South Americans. Except for Puerto Ricans, the share from horizontal relatives also drops sharply in the U.S.-born generation.

Thus, as expected, horizontal relatives are more important among less-skilled labor immigrants than in other groups. Nevertheless, in all groups, the head's children and parents contribute more to household income than horizontal relatives do. The decrease in the vertical relatives' share across generations (except for Mexicans), while not as dramatic as the decrease in horizontal relatives' share, suggests that having parents in the United States and the persistence of cultural preferences do not outweigh decreased need and the influence of U.S. norms regarding living arrangements. By this measure, U.S.-born Cubans are no more familistic than white non-Hispanics. It thus appears that structural/demographic familism may characterize the Hispanic immigrant generation, but it begins to fade by the second generation. (However, the patterns observed may reflect relative increases in other sources of income rather than changes in living arrangements.)

Among Latinos who were born abroad, Central Americans rely more on income from nonrelatives in the household (other than a cohabiting partner) than any other Hispanic group, deriving 5 percent of household income from this source. Central Americans have been coming to the United States in large numbers only in the past 20 years, so that new arrivals are a significant presence among them. Many young men and women arrive without family and share housing with compatriots. Established immigrants may take them in as boarders or live-in domestics (Alba and Nee, 2003, pp. 196–197; Mahler, 1995, pp. 202–203). For Central Americans and Mexicans, other nonrelatives contribute a smaller share in the second generation than the first, but for Puerto Ricans, Cubans, and South Americans this share increases across generations, and for Dominicans it remains stable. These patterns suggest that nonrelatives may play a similar role to horizontal relatives for the least-skilled immigrant groups. In the higher income Latino groups, in contrast, it may be more common for U.S.-born single young adults to move out of their parents' home and share an apartment with a roommate.

In part reflecting the prevalence of female headship, cohabiting partners contribute a larger share of income (4 percent) for Dominicans and Central Americans who were born in the United States than for other Latinos, blacks, or whites. For all groups except Cubans, the share from a cohabiting partner is larger in the second generation than the first.

To sum up, this section presents several distinct patterns of income sources among the Hispanic national-origin groups and generations, which are characterized by the shares of household income from earnings, public benefits, and extended-household members. Mexicans, Central Americans, South Americans, and U.S.-born Cubans depend on earnings for more of their household income than other groups. Dominicans and Puerto Ricans are much more dependent on public benefits than the others. Mexican, Central American, and Dominican immigrants get a larger share from extended-household members than other Hispanics, blacks, and whites. By the third (and higher) generation, Hispanics resemble blacks in this respect, but they rely more on earnings and less on public benefits than do blacks.

More research is needed on household extension, income pooling, and whether public benefits and household extension are alternative ways of coping with low earnings. For example, it is suggestive to observe that the low-skilled groups (Puerto Ricans and Dominicans) that have high female-headship rates and are concentrated in the Northeast, where benefits are relatively generous, tend to derive large shares of their income from public benefits; the low-skilled groups (foreign-born Mexicans and Central Americans) that have low female-headship rates and tend to live in the Southwest get a relatively small share from public benefits and an unusually large share from extended-household members. But we do not know the roles played by cultural preferences versus earning capacity in determining household structure, female headship, and therefore eligibility for public benefits.[14] And we do not know who primarily benefits from household extension—the head's nuclear family or the other members—or even whether there *is* a net benefit when the additional income is offset by the costs of added members. Angel and Tienda (1982a, 1982b, 1984) and Flippen and Tienda (1998) explore these questions using cross-sectional data without being able to reach firm conclusions; further investigation using longitudinal data would be useful.

[14]For an analysis of marital disruption across generations of Mexicans, see Bean, Berg, and Van Hook (1996). Also see Glick et al. (1997) and Feliciano et al. (2006) for analyses of the role of economic need in household extension.

ELDERLY HISPANICS

The numbers of elderly Latinos will grow rapidly in the future, although they are only a small proportion of the Hispanic population today, because immigration has surged in the past two decades and most immigrants come when they are young.[15] An examination of the situation of the Latino elderly today may give us some insights into how those currently of working age and their children are likely to fare in old age. Unlike the Latino households with heads under age 65 discussed in the previous section, who gain most of their income from working, households headed by someone over age 65 are heavily dependent on unearned income from public transfer programs. In this section I focus on poverty rates, Social Security and SSI receipt, and the contributions of extended-household members of elderly Latino immigrant households by country of origin and of elderly U.S.-born Mexicans by generation.[16]

Poverty Rates

Poverty among elderly Latino immigrants is a special concern because Latinos tend to work in jobs that do not provide pensions (or health insurance, for that matter) (Brown and Yu, 2002; Honig, 2000; Honig and Dushi, 2004). Moreover, they cannot get Social Security benefits unless they have worked for at least 10 years in covered jobs in the United States, and Social Security is responsible for keeping 39 percent of older Americans out of poverty (Social Security Administration, 2000, p. 133). Even if they qualify for Social Security, Latinos' low lifetime earnings translate into small benefit amounts. The alternative, SSI, has benefit levels that are below the poverty threshold. It is therefore not surprising to see (Table 8-5) that older Latino immigrants of all national origins are more likely to be poor than white non-Hispanics (8 percent of whom are poor), but it is somewhat surprising that in most cases Latinos' poverty rates do not exceed the rate

[15] According to the 1998–2002 CPS data used in this chapter, only about 5 percent of all Latinos and about 10 percent of Latino household heads are currently age 65 or older.

[16] The sample sizes of elderly in the pooled 1998–2002 March CPS are sufficient to examine elderly Mexicans of all generations, but the other national-origin groups have adequate samples only in the immigrant generation. Older Mexicans whose ancestors lived in the Southwest and California when they were part of Mexico or whose parents moved to the United States in the early 20th century are rather numerous, but few non-Mexican Latinos who were born in the United States have yet reached age 65. This is because large-scale migration to the United States from elsewhere in Latin America (outside Mexico) began only about 60 years ago, when Puerto Ricans began coming to New York in large numbers after World War II.

TABLE 8-5 Poverty Rates of Elderly Persons, 1997–2001 Pooled

National Origin (Birthplace)	Generation 1st: Foreign-Born	2nd: U.S.-Born, Foreign-Born Parent	3+: U.S.-Born, Both Parents U.S.-Born*
	Fraction of Persons Age 65+ with Family Income Below the Poverty Threshold		
Mexico	0.239	0.176	0.185
Central America	0.154	0.092	
Puerto Rico	0.271	0.049	
Dominican Republic	0.365		
Cuba	0.243		
South America	0.133		
All Hispanics (self-identity)*	0.232	0.176	0.178
Black non-Hispanics (self-identity)*			0.241
White non-Hispanics (self-identity)*			0.081

*The samples for Hispanics overall and for 3+ generation Mexicans and black and white non-Hispanics are identified by the "subjective" Spanish-origin and race questions in the CPS.

SOURCE: Pooled March CPS files, 1998–2002, using person weights. Results for Hispanics are shown only for cells with at least 90 observations.

for elderly blacks (24 percent). The exceptions are immigrants from the Dominican Republic and Puerto Rico, the poorest elderly Latinos, whose poverty rates are 37 and 27 percent, respectively. Elderly immigrants from Mexico and Cuba have poverty rates similar to elderly blacks, and elderly immigrants from Central and South America are less likely to be poor than the other groups. There is some improvement across generations of elderly Mexicans, as only 18 percent of those who were born in the United States are living in poverty.

This ranking of the nationalities in part reflects the living arrangements of the elderly and the ranking among younger immigrants with whom the elderly may be living. It also reflects the class backgrounds of those who came from the various countries in earlier decades, as discussed in Chapters 2 and 3. The relatively high poverty rates of elderly Cubans may seem surprising in light of the high skill level of the first wave of refugees. However, Cubans who are now 65 or older were already adults when the refugees began arriving in the United States in 1959. That a quarter of them are poor in old age points up the difficulty that many adult refugees had in adapting to life in the United States.

The extreme poverty of elderly island-born Dominicans and Puerto Ricans is no doubt related to the prevalence of female-headed families and lack of earnings in these groups when they were of working age and now among their children with whom they may be living. Perhaps the fact that older Latino immigrants of other national origins are no more likely to be poor than blacks, despite the fact that those who came to the United States in middle age or later are likely to get little or nothing from Social Security and pensions, is because they are more likely to live with their children who are not poor.[17]

Sources of Household Income

Retirement income for non-Hispanic whites in America rests on the proverbial three-legged stool, comprising Social Security, private pensions, and asset income from accumulated savings. Given Latinos' low rates of pension coverage noted above, it is not surprising that employer pensions are less important as a source of income for elderly households in all foreign-born Hispanic subgroups and for U.S.-born Mexicans than for whites or blacks (Table 8-6). Limited incomes during their working years make it difficult for most Latino groups to save for retirement (Cobb-Clark and Hildebrand, 2004; Smith, 1995; Wolff, in press). Social Security and other sources of income are therefore especially important for the Hispanic elderly. This section examines the shares of elderly household income from three of those sources: Social Security, SSI, and extended-household members.[18]

Households headed by elderly Latino immigrants and second-generation Mexicans whose parents were born in Mexico are less likely to get Social Security benefits than blacks (90 percent of whom receive Social

[17]Table 5-4 in Chapter 5 shows that elderly Hispanics of all nationalities are much less likely to live alone and more likely to live with other relatives, than blacks and whites. According to the 1998–2002 CPS data used in this chapter, 20 percent of Latinos, 13 percent of blacks, and 6 percent of whites age 65 or older were living in someone else's household who was not their spouse.

[18]The sources of income of households headed by elderly Latinos may give a distorted impression of the sources of income of all elderly Latinos, because it omits many of the elderly who live with their children in a household headed by someone under age 65, either by choice or because they cannot afford to live on their own. This chapter therefore does not discuss the sources of income for households headed by elderly Latinos in as much detail as it does for working-age adults. Detailed tables showing household income and its sources for households headed by elderly Latinos are available from the author upon request.

TABLE 8-6 Mean Shares of Household Income by Source: Social Security, SSI, Pensions, Income of Extended-Household Members, 1997–2001 Pooled

	Households with Head Age 65 or Older		
	Generation		
National Origin (Birthplace)	1st: Foreign-Born	2nd: U.S.-Born, Foreign-Born Parent	3+: U.S.-Born, Both Parents U.S.-Born*
	Fraction of Household Income		
Mexico			
Social Security	0.533	0.532	0.593
SSI	0.086	0.042	0.032
Private pensions	0.039	0.099	0.094
Extended-household members**	0.219	0.177	0.147
Central America			
Social Security	0.420		
SSI	0.095		
Private pensions	0.090		
Extended-household members**	0.199		
Puerto Rico			
Social Security	0.634		
SSI	0.125		
Private pensions	0.053		
Extended-household members**	0.113		
Dominican Republic			
Social Security	0.460	0.515	
SSI	0.247	0.016	
Private pensions	0.022	0.145	
Extended-household members**	0.185	0.097	
Cuba			
Social Security	0.563		
SSI	0.121		
Private pensions	0.049		
Extended-household members**	0.104		
South America			
Social Security	0.418		
SSI	0.041		
Private pensions	0.099		
Extended-household members**	0.166		
All Hispanics (self-identity)*			
Social Security	0.540	0.526	0.588
SSI	0.107	0.039	0.031
Private pensions	0.051	0.098	0.105
Extended-household members**	0.163	0.177	0.127

continues

TABLE 8-6 Continued

	Households with Head Age 65 or Older		
	Generation		
National Origin (Birthplace)	1st: Foreign-Born	2nd: U.S.-Born, Foreign-Born Parent	3+: U.S.-Born, Both Parents U.S.-Born*
	Fraction of Household Income		
Black non-Hispanics (self-identity)*			
Social Security			0.583
SSI			0.046
Private pensions			0.112
Extended-household members**			0.139
White non-Hispanics (self-identity)*			
Social Security			0.550
SSI			0.010
Private pensions			0.137
Extended-household members**			0.062

*The samples for Hispanics overall and for 3+ generation Mexicans, Puerto Ricans, and black and white non-Hispanics are identified by the "subjective" Spanish-origin and race questions in the CPS.

**Excluding only income of the head and spouse.

SOURCE: Pooled March CPS files, 1998–2002. Means are simple averages across households, using household weights. Households with zero or negative total income, or containing persons with negative income from any source, are excluded. Results for Hispanics are shown only for cells with at least 90 observations. Box indicates combined groups.

Security; see Appendix Table A8-12). Some Latino immigrants receive no Social Security benefits at all because they do not accumulate 10 years of covered earnings; others have low benefits because of a short earnings record. And 16 percent of Latino immigrant workers in the United States in 1997–2001 (almost 10 percent of all Latino workers) came after they were 30 years old.[19] Consequently, they will not have time to accumulate a full 35 years of covered earnings in the United States.

Moreover, Latinos are more likely to work in noncovered jobs or to have employers who do not report their earnings as domestics, agricultural

[19]Author's tabulations of March 1997–2001, CPS microdata.

workers, or in the informal economy. In 2000 7.4 percent of Hispanic workers were in farming, forestry, fishing, or private household service occupations, compared with only 2.6 percent of non-Hispanics (U.S. Census Bureau, 2001, Table 10.4). There is evidence that workers in these occupations are less likely than others to have had their earnings reported to Social Security (Kijakazi, 2002, p. 10). Furthermore, undocumented workers get no credit for their earnings while in that status. As a result of these characteristics, Latinos have shorter covered-earnings histories, lower average monthly earnings on record, and consequently, lower Social Security benefits than others with similar lifetime earnings. Besides, except for U.S.-born Cubans and South Americans, their earnings are lower than whites, as reported in Chapter 7. Consequently, only 77 percent of all elderly Hispanics received Social Security benefits in 1998, compared with 91 percent of older white non-Hispanics, and their median benefit was only 76.5 percent of whites (Social Security Administration, 2000, Tables I.9 and V.A.3).

The disaggregated data show that in the immigrant generation, rates of Social Security receipt range from 68 percent for Dominicans to 83 percent for Puerto Ricans. However, Mexicans with at least one U.S.-born parent are similar to blacks, but still below whites, in this respect (see Appendix Table A8-12). The lower rates of Social Security receipt for the foreign-born reflect their failure to accumulate an earnings record of 40 quarters in covered jobs. This may be due to the lack of coverage of jobs in agriculture and domestic service often held by low-skilled Hispanic immigrants, as well as the fact that immigrants who arrive in middle age may not work long enough in covered jobs to qualify for Social Security.[20]

Nevertheless, Social Security is the source of at least half of average household income for all groups except foreign-born Central Americans, South Americans, and Dominicans, who derive only 42 to 46 percent of the average household's income from this source (Table 8-6). Elderly island-born Puerto Ricans, third (and higher)-generation Mexicans, and blacks get similarly large shares of household income from Social Security on average (63, 59, and 58 percent, respectively) even though Puerto Ricans are less likely to receive it. This must be because they have less income from other sources than blacks, as their benefits are unlikely to be larger. Older foreign-born Cubans and first- and second-generation Mexicans get a smaller percentage of household income from Social Security, similar to whites (55 percent). These differences reflect current differences in other income, such as employer pensions, investment income, and earnings of

[20]Most of the whites, blacks, and U.S.-born Hispanics who do not receive Social Security benefits probably worked in government jobs, many of which are not covered by Social Security. This is unlikely to be an important factor for Hispanic immigrants.

younger household members, as well as differences in the elderly Latinos' eligibility for Social Security and their earlier earnings levels.

Low-income elderly individuals whose Social Security benefit is very low, or who do not qualify for Social Security at all, may qualify for SSI benefits. SSI beneficiaries are automatically covered by Medicaid as well. SSI is quite important for the Hispanic immigrant generation in old age, especially for Dominicans, who are the group least likely to receive Social Security benefits and who are most likely to be poor, so they qualify for SSI. Reflecting their degree of poverty, 45 percent of households headed by elderly Dominican immigrants receive SSI (see Appendix Table A8-12), which accounts for a quarter of their income, and 66 percent are covered by Medicaid. In addition, one-third of older island-born Puerto Rican households receive SSI and 53 percent receive Medicaid. These rates may reflect New York's relatively generous SSI and Medicaid program for the elderly as well as the poverty of these groups. They may continue in the future, given the low incomes of working-age Dominican and Puerto Rican household heads. For elderly Mexican, Cuban, and Central American immigrant households, the rates of SSI receipt are 21 to 24 percent, and the rates of Medicaid receipt are 37 to 39 percent, considerably higher than for blacks. South American immigrants and U.S.-born Mexicans, however, are no more likely than blacks to be on SSI (14 percent) or Medicaid (27 percent). By comparison, among elderly white households, only 4 percent get SSI and 10 percent are on the Medicaid rolls.

Another potential source of income for elderly Latinos is household extension.[21] The mean share of income from household members other than the head and spouse is 13 to 18 percent for older Hispanics in the aggregate (depending on generation), which is quite similar to working-age households (Table 8-6). It is 14 percent for blacks and 6 percent for whites. Most of this comes from vertical relatives, who contribute 19 percent of the income of older Mexican immigrants' households and 12 to 15 percent for U.S.-born Mexicans and foreign-born Central and South Americans and Dominicans (see Appendix Table A8-13). These are larger than the shares from vertical relatives in working-age Latino households. Older Cubans and Puerto Ricans get smaller shares of household income from vertical extension (6 and 9 percent, respectively) than the other first-generation Latinos. Horizontal relatives, however, provide a smaller share of income

[21]This implicitly assumes that household members actually pool their income and that the younger members are helping to support the elderly. Some intergenerational households may primarily benefit the younger generation, either through economic support or help with household tasks and child care (Flippen and Tienda, 1998).

(2 to 4 percent) for older than younger Latino households.[22] The differences among Latino national-origin groups and by age suggest differences in need and in familism, as older foreign-born Mexicans derive a larger share of their income from vertical relatives than do other groups.

SUMMARY AND CONCLUSIONS

This chapter has used the March CPS data for 1998–2002 to describe the levels of household income and its sources for Latinos classified by national origin and generation, compared with black and white non-Hispanics whose parents were born in the United States. It highlights the wide range of median household incomes and poverty rates across Hispanic groups. Aggregate statistics for all Hispanics combined mainly reflect the experience of Mexicans because they make up about 60 percent of the total Latino population. Currently, Hispanic immigrants in the aggregate have median household income that is virtually the same as blacks, although their per capita income is only two-thirds of blacks because their households are larger. Hispanics who were born in the United States of U.S.-born parents (about two-thirds of whom identify themselves as of Mexican origin) have median household income that is 25 percent above blacks, although still much below whites. However, the Hispanics' per capita income is only slightly above blacks. Their poverty rate is lower than blacks, but much higher than whites.

Disaggregation reveals that Puerto Ricans and Dominicans are at the bottom on most measures of economic well-being, with Mexicans near and sometimes at the bottom, too. Central Americans are somewhat better off than Mexicans. Furthermore, later generations of every Latino national origin are better off than earlier generations, with most of the improvement occurring between the first and second generations. Regardless of national origin, U.S.-born Hispanics have higher total household incomes than blacks. U.S.-born Mexicans and Puerto Ricans have slightly lower median per capita incomes than blacks, despite having higher household incomes, because the Hispanics have larger households. South Americans and Cubans who were born or grew up in the United States are at the top, and the

[22]These shares may understate the role of household extension in supporting the Latino elderly because they refer to households *headed by* older Latinos. The elderly who live in separate households may be those who can afford it, whereas lower income elderly are more likely to live with others. One-fifth of elderly Latinos live in someone else's household (not their spouse), and they have only half as much personal income on average as elderly household heads (author's tabulations). The member designated as "householder" is likely to be the one who owns or holds the lease on the home. Therefore, elderly persons who are not dependent on others' income may be more likely to be classified as "head of household."

U.S.-born among them are close to white non-Hispanics. However, one must use caution when attempting to use these cross-sectional differences among generations to predict the future. The (grand)parents of today's second- and third-generation Latinos were not necessarily comparable to today's immigrants from the same country, because changing political and economic conditions in sending countries have sent waves of exiles and emigrants with different characteristics to the United States at different times.

The differences in income among nationalities and generations reflect the variation in their education levels and household size and structure. For example, recent immigrants from Mexico, Central America, and the Dominican Republic have been predominantly low skilled, with consequently low household incomes. However, the reasons for a similar outcome may vary across nationalities, as in the case of Mexican, Dominican, and Puerto Rican poverty rates. As pointed out in Chapter 7, Mexicans are the least educated group in the immigrant generation, and—although subsequent generations have much more education than the first—Mexicans suffer from an educational deficit relative to blacks and whites even in the third (and higher) generation. This results in limited earning capacity. Dominicans in the United States today are largely recent immigrants with limited skills, and (as shown in Chapter 5) both they and Puerto Ricans are further handicapped by a high incidence of female-headed households. The double whammy of having only one potential earner and the gender wage gap depresses their potential household income. Cubans and South Americans are more educated than the other nationalities. As noted in Chapters 2 and 3, earlier waves of Cuban and Central American exiles were more skilled than recent refugees and economic migrants from those countries.

Examination of the sources of household income reveals that low-wage groups respond by adopting two general strategies for boosting household income: doubling up and obtaining public benefits. Extended-household members contribute larger shares of household income among most Hispanic subgroups than among black and white non-Hispanics. This may reflect Hispanic cultural values of familism as well as need, although there is little evidence that Hispanics are any more family-oriented than other migrants have been (Gambino, 1974). In the immigrant generation, Mexicans, Central Americans, and Dominicans are unusually reliant on extended-household members, but in the generations that have U.S.-born parents, Hispanics resemble blacks in this respect. The share of household income contributed by the head's children or parents (that is, vertical relatives) decreases less sharply across generations than the share due to other (horizontal) relatives.

The second strategy, reliance on public benefits, is the mirror image of household income, with the poorest groups deriving the largest shares of their income from this source. Thus, Puerto Ricans and Dominicans derive larger shares of their household income from public benefits than do other groups. This reflects their high female headship rates, their greater access to the more generous benefit programs in the Northeast, and the scarcity of jobs where they live. Female-headed families are more likely to be eligible for public benefits than married-couple families. Puerto Ricans, as U.S. citizens by birth, are eligible for public benefit programs, whereas new immigrants are not. Moreover, jobs are scarcer and benefit programs are more generous in New York and elsewhere in the Northeast, where Puerto Ricans and Dominicans are concentrated, than in Florida, California, and the Southwest, where the other Hispanic groups are concentrated. The high cost of living in New York further exacerbates the Puerto Ricans' and Dominicans' high levels of poverty.

Poverty rates of the elderly range widely across Hispanic subgroups, reflecting their income at younger ages. They are 36 percent for elderly foreign-born Dominicans and 27 percent for Puerto Ricans, even higher than the poverty rate for blacks (24 percent). Older foreign-born Mexicans and Cubans also have high poverty rates, similar to that of blacks. Reflecting the higher incomes of working-age members of the same national origin and generation, poverty rates are lower for elderly foreign-born Central and South Americans and the U.S.-born generations of Mexicans.

Latinos tend to work in jobs that do not offer pensions; other sources of income are therefore more important for elderly Hispanics than for blacks and whites. Gaining an adequate Social Security benefit is also a problem for Latinos who work at low wages, "off the books," or in sectors that until recently were not covered by Social Security, such as agriculture and household service. Elderly Hispanic households are heavily dependent on Social Security benefits, but—apart from Puerto Ricans and Cubans—foreign-born Hispanics do not rely on this source of income as much as whites or blacks. The share of their household income from Social Security ranges from 42 to 63 percent, being smallest for foreign-born Central and South Americans and largest for island-born Puerto Ricans, whose share from Social Security is even larger than blacks. These differences reflect the variation in income from other sources, including that provided by younger household members, as well as differences in the elderly Latinos' Social Security benefits.

Elderly immigrants who did not work long enough in covered jobs in the United States to qualify for Social Security and whose income is very low are likely to depend on SSI. Others may receive such a low Social Security benefit—due to a lifetime of low-wage work—that they also qualify for SSI. Elderly foreign-born Hispanic households (other than South Americans) get an even larger share of their income from SSI than do blacks, but SSI is a smaller share of income for U.S.-born Hispanics than for blacks.

Doubling up in an extended household contributes a similar share of the income of elderly households and of younger ones for most Hispanic groups and blacks, but more of it is from vertical relatives and less from horizontal relatives in the older group. Among older foreign-born Latinos, Mexicans and Central Americans have the largest shares of household income from children living with them, and Puerto Ricans and Cubans have the smallest.

The future economic well-being of Hispanics in the United States will depend on education and family structure—of new immigrants, their children, and their grandchildren who are born in the United States. There are grounds for both optimism and pessimism in the patterns revealed in this chapter. In future years the proportion of Hispanics who are first-generation immigrants will shrink due to the more rapid growth of the second and third generations, as shown in Chapter 3. Because the later generations have higher incomes than the first, this compositional effect alone would improve the overall economic well-being of each Hispanic nationality as time passes. Secularly declining fertility rates would also tend to raise per capita incomes and lower poverty rates over time. For Hispanics' incomes to converge with whites, however, their education levels must catch up. Otherwise the earnings gap will remain, and it may grow even wider as they remain trapped on the short end of the widening inequality in income between education levels.

The increase in female-headed households across generations of Hispanics, and their increase over time among Hispanics as well as blacks and whites, also act as a drag on household income. Because female-headed households have much lower incomes than married couples, overall economic well-being would decline over time due to this compositional effect alone. We already see its effect in the very low household incomes of Dominicans and Puerto Ricans, many of whose households are headed by single females. In the absence of a reversal of this trend, the future economic well-being of many Latinos will depend on improvements in women's wages and public benefit programs, as well as on removing the barriers to educational attainment that are described in Chapter 6.

It is too soon to tell what the long-term effects of welfare reform will be on the Latino groups that depend heavily on public benefits, particularly Dominicans and Puerto Ricans. It is also too soon to tell whether the dispersion of Mexicans, Puerto Ricans, and other Latinos from California and New York to new parts of the country, as described in Chapter 3, will enable their children to break out of the vicious cycle of poor schools–poor jobs–poverty. Much will depend on how the new destinations rise to the challenge of providing good schools for the newcomers.

DATA AND METHODS

The chapter is based on tabulations of the amounts and sources of income of the various Hispanic national-origin groups and immigrant generations, based on the pooled 1998–2002 March CPS files.[23] In the detailed appendix tables at the end of the chapter, a five-generation classification scheme is used (1.0: arrived as adult; 1.5: arrived as child; 2.0: U.S.-born, both parents foreign-born; 2.5: U.S.-born, one parent U.S.-born; 3.0+: U.S.-born, both parents U.S.-born). For the first four generations, an "objective" national-origin identification is used, based on the birthplace of the person and his or her parents. Third (or higher)-generation Mexicans, Puerto Ricans, and black and white non-Hispanics are identified by the "subjective" Spanish-origin and race questions in the CPS. In the tables presented in the text these five generations are reduced to three by combining generations 1.0 and 1.5 (the foreign-born) and generations 2.0 and 2.5 (the U.S.-born with at least one foreign-born parent).

Results are shown only for age/national-origin/generation groups that have at least 90 observations in the pooled CPS sample. To attain this sample size, countries or generations are sometimes combined. All results use the CPS March supplement weights in order to represent the U.S. population. All income amounts are adjusted for inflation using the consumer price index and are expressed in 2002 dollars. When computing shares of income by source, I compute the share of income derived from a particular source (Social Security, for instance) for each household, and then takes the average share across households in an origin-generation group. This answers the question, "What is the importance of Social Security benefits for the average household in the group?"

---

[23]Thanks to Rubén Rumbaut and Charles Morgan for providing the recoded data and tabulations of this data file.

REFERENCES

Alba, R., and Nee, V. (2003). *Remaking the American mainstream: Assimilation and contemporary immigration.* Cambridge, MA: Harvard University Press.

Angel, R., and Tienda, M. (1982a). Determinants of extended household structure: Cultural pattern or economic need? *American Journal of Sociology, 87*(6), 1360–1383.

Angel, R., and Tienda, M. (1982b). Headship and household composition among blacks, Hispanics, and other whites. *Social Forces, 61*(2), 508–530.

Angel, R., and Tienda, M. (1984). Household composition and income-generation strategies among non-Hispanic whites, blacks, and Hispanic-origin groups in the United States. In M.B. Brinkerhoff (Ed.), *Family and work: Comparative convergences* (pp. 141–169). Westport, CT: Greenwood Press.

Bean, F.D., and Tienda, M. (1987). *The Hispanic population of the United States.* New York: Russell Sage Foundation.

Bean, F.D., Chapa, J., Berg, R.R., and Sowards, K.A. (1994). Educational and sociodemographic incorporation among Hispanic immigrants to the United States. In B. Edmonston and J. S. Passel (Eds.), *Immigration and ethnicity: The integration of America's newest arrivals* (pp. 73–100). Washington, DC: Urban Institute Press.

Bean, F.D., Berg, R.R., and Van Hook, J.V.W. (1996). Socioeconomic and cultural incorporation and marital disruption among Mexican Americans. *Social Forces, 75*(2), 593–617.

Brown, E.R., and Yu, H. (2002). Latinos' access to employment-based health insurance. In M.M. Suarez-Orozco and M.A. Paez (Eds.), *Latinos: Remaking America* (pp. 236–253). Berkeley: University of California Press.

Chiswick, B.R., and Sullivan, T.A. (1995). The new immigrants. In R. Farley (Ed.), *State of the union: America in the 1990s* (vol. 2: Social Trends, pp. 211–270). New York: Russell Sage Foundation.

Cobb-Clark, D.A., and Hildebrand, V. (2004, April). *The wealth of Mexican Americans.* Unpublished paper, Social Policy Evaluation, Analysis, and Research Centre, Research School of the Social Sciences, Australian National University.

Feliciano, C., Bean, F.D., and Leach, M. (2006). *The strength of Latino families: Cultural myth or social capital asset?* In H.P. Pachon and R.O. de la Garza (Eds.), *Latinos: Past influence, future power.* Philadelphia: Temple University Press.

Flippen, C., and Tienda, M. (1998, September). *Family structure and economic well-being of black, Hispanic, and white pre-retirement adults.* Unpublished paper, Center for Demographic Studies, Duke University.

Gambino, R. (1974). *Blood of my blood: The dilemma of the Italian-Americans.* Garden City, NY: Doubleday.

Glick, J.E., Bean, F.D., and Van Hook, J.V.W. (1997). Immigration and changing patterns of extended family household structure in the United States: 1970–1990. *Journal of Marriage and the Family, 59*(1), 177–191.

Grogger, J., Karoly, L.A., and Klerman, J.A. (2002). *Consequences of welfare reform: A research synthesis.* (RAND Labor and Population Program. DRU-2676-DHHS.) Santa Monica, CA: RAND Corporation.

Honig, M. (2000). Minorities face retirement: Worklife disparities repeated? In O. S. Mitchell, P. Brett Hammond, and A. M. Rappaport (Eds.), *Forecasting retirement needs and retirement wealth* (pp. 234–252). Philadelphia: University of Pennsylvania Press.

Honig, M., and Dushi, I. (2004, June). *Worker demand for health insurance own-price and spousal options.* Report submitted to U.S. Department of Labor, Pension, and Welfare Benefits Administration, Washington, DC.

Karoly, L.A. (1993). The trend in inequality among families, individuals, and workers in the United States: A twenty-five year perspective. In S. Danziger and P. Gottschalk (Eds.), *Uneven tides: Rising inequality in America* (pp. 19–97). New York: Russell Sage Foundation.

Kijakazi, K. (2002). Impact of unreported Social Security earnings on people of color and women. National Academy on an Aging Society, Gerontological Society of America. *Public Policy and Aging Report, 12*(3), 9–12.

Levy, F. (1995). Incomes and income inequality. In R. Farley (Ed.), *State of the union: America in the 1990s* (vol. 1: Economic Trends, pp. 1–57). New York: Russell Sage Foundation.

Levy, F. (1998). *The new dollars and dreams: American incomes and economic change.* New York: Russell Sage Foundation.

Mahler, S.J. (1995). *American dreaming: Immigrant life on the margins.* Princeton, NJ: Princeton University Press.

Ruggles, S. (1987). *Prolonged connections: The rise of the extended family in nineteenth-century England and America.* Madison: University of Wisconsin Press.

Smith, J.P. (1995). Racial and ethnic difference in wealth in the Health and Retirement Study. *Journal of Human Resources, 30*, S158–S183.

Social Security Administration. (2000). *Income of the population 55 or older.* (SSA Publication No. 13-11871.) Office of Policy, Office of Research, Evaluation, and Statistics. Washington, DC: U.S. Government Printing Office.

U.S. Census Bureau. (1993). *Persons of Hispanic origin in the United States.* (1990 Census of Population, Report No. 1990 CP-3-3.) Washington, DC: U.S. Department of Commerce.

U.S. Census Bureau. (2001). *Current Population Survey: March 2000.* Ethnic and Hispanic Statistics Branch, Population Division. Available: http://www.census.gov/population/socdemo/hispanic/p20-535 [accessed March 6, 2001].

U.S. Census Bureau. (2003). *Current Population Survey: March 2002.* Ethnic and Hispanic Statistics Branch, Population Division. Available: http://www.census.gov/population/www/socdemo/hispanic/ho02.html [accessed June 18, 2003].

Wolff, E.N. (in press). Changes in household wealth in the 1980s and 1990s in the U.S. In E.N. Wolff (Ed.), *International perspectives on household wealth.* Northampton, MA: Elgar.

APPENDIX TABLE A8-1 Median Real Annual Income and Per Capita Income of Households, in 2002 Dollars, 1997–2001 Pooled

	Households with Head Under Age 65				
	Generation				
National Origin (Birthplace)	1.0: Arrived as Adult	1.5: Arrived as Child	2.0: U.S.-Born, Both Parents Foreign-Born	2.5: U.S.-Born, 1 Parent U.S.-Born	3+: U.S.-Born, Both Parents U.S.-Born*
	Median Total Household Income (2002 $)				
Mexico	$28,443	$31,565	$37,890	$44,147	$39,306
El Salvador, Guatemala	32,506	37,666	44,022 (El Salvador, Guatemala and Other Central America combined)	48,805	
Other Central America	32,460	39,699		62,358	
Puerto Rico	26,114	28,649	36,703	38,603	35,553
Dominican Republic	22,184	29,587	33,626		
Cuba	28,194	64,396	65,138	54,303	
Colombia	36,264	50,990			
Peru, Ecuador	37,840	44,750	50,791 (Colombia, Peru, Ecuador and Other South America combined)	52,085 (Colombia, Peru, Ecuador and Other South America combined)	
Other South America	49,997	53,277			
Hispanics (self-identity)*	30,297	33,626	38,863	43,375	39,903
Black non-Hispanics (self-identity)*					31,775
White non-Hispanics (self-identity)*					54,752
	Median Income Per Capita (2002 $)				
Mexico	$7,505	$8,289	$12,042	$14,038	$13,312
El Salvador, Guatemala	9,490	9,684	18,118 (El Salvador, Guatemala and Other Central America combined)	19,330	
Other Central America	10,447	13,244		27,896	
Puerto Rico	9,497	10,683	12,958	13,316	13,053
Dominican Republic	7,343	9,270	12,647		
Cuba	11,109	21,974	22,678	22,675	
Colombia	12,337	17,303			
Peru, Ecuador	12,190	14,221	19,483 (Colombia, Peru, Ecuador and Other South America combined)	23,068 (Colombia, Peru, Ecuador and Other South America combined)	
Other South America	17,721	25,562			
Hispanics (self-identity)*	8,721	9,718	13,041	14,560	13,901
Black non-Hispanics (self-identity)*					13,388
White non-Hispanics (self-identity)*					22,480

*The samples for Hispanics overall and for 3+ generation Mexicans, Puerto Ricans, and black and white non-Hispanics are identified by the "subjective" Spanish-origin and race questions in the CPS.

SOURCE: Pooled March CPS files, 1998–2002, using household weights. Results for Hispanics are shown only for cells with at least 90 observations. Boxes indicate combined groups.

APPENDIX TABLE A8-2 FOLLOWS

APPENDIX TABLE A8-2 Poverty Rates, 1997–2001 Pooled

	Fraction of Persons with Family Income Below Poverty Threshold				
	Generation				
National Origin (Birthplace)	1.0: Arrived as Adult	1.5: Arrived as Child	2.0: U.S.-Born, Both Parents Foreign-Born	2.5: U.S.-Born, 1 Parent U.S.-Born	3+: U.S.-Born, Both Parents U.S.-Born*
	All Ages				
Mexico	0.256	0.275	0.305	0.211	0.205
El Salvador, Guatemala	0.175	0.187	0.252	0.125	
Other Central America	0.195	0.205	0.258	0.132	
Puerto Rico	0.281	0.295	0.276	0.220	0.301
Dominican Republic	0.303	0.312	0.387	0.327	
Cuba	0.205	0.125	0.131	0.119	0.052
Colombia	0.154	0.132	0.155	0.073	
Peru, Ecuador	0.129	0.131	0.161	0.087	
Other South America	0.101	0.098	0.072	0.090	
Hispanics (self-identity)*	0.228	0.252	0.288	0.210	0.204
Black non-Hispanics (self-identity)*					0.250
White non-Hispanics (self-identity)*					0.081
	Persons in Female-Headed Families				
Mexico	0.480	0.475	0.525	0.392	0.380
El Salvador, Guatemala	0.310	0.321	0.474	0.286	
Other Central America	0.341	0.309	0.407	0.251	
Puerto Rico	0.525	0.531	0.450	0.423	0.471
Dominican Republic	0.455	0.497	0.587	0.569	
Cuba	0.420	0.281	0.366	0.315	
Colombia	0.289	0.283	0.347		
Peru, Ecuador	0.247	0.183	0.268	0.194	
Other South America	0.212	0.220			
Hispanics (self-identity)*	0.422	0.438	0.496	0.397	0.382
Black non-Hispanics (self-identity)*					0.394
White non-Hispanics (self-identity)*					0.211

*The samples for Hispanics overall and for 3+ generation Mexicans, Puerto Ricans, Cubans, and black and white non-Hispanics are identified by the "subjective" Spanish-origin and race questions in the CPS.

Generation				
1.0: Arrived as Adult	1.5: Arrived as Child	2.0: U.S.-Born, Both Parents Foreign-Born	2.5: U.S.-Born, 1 Parent U.S.-Born	3+: U.S.-Born, Both Parents U.S.-Born*
Children Ages 0–17				
	0.426	0.371	0.267	0.268
	0.291	0.272	0.165	
	0.302	0.300	0.173	
	0.536	0.443	0.278	0.356
	0.481	0.438	0.377	
	0.312	0.213	0.135	0.044
	0.205	0.177	0.079	
	0.191	0.167	0.102	
	0.165	0.092	0.096	
	0.399	0.354	0.265	0.269
				0.353
				0.106
Persons in Married-Couple Families				
0.217	0.240	0.243	0.133	0.117
0.135	0.124	0.168	0.069	
0.138	0.169	0.192	0.083	
0.160	0.129	0.113	0.071	0.114
0.186	0.171	0.151	0.117	
0.134	0.080	0.073	0.025	0.013
0.111	0.091	0.085	0.050	
0.083	0.097	0.122	0.058	
0.066	0.073	0.049	0.010	
0.179	0.201	0.211	0.120	0.110
				0.080
				0.037

SOURCE: Pooled March CPS files, 1998–2002, using person weights. Results for Hispanics are shown only for cells with at least 90 observations. Boxes indicate combined groups.

APPENDIX TABLE A8-3 Mean Shares of Household Income by Source: Earnings, Public Benefits, Other Unearned Income, 1997–2001 Pooled

	Households with Head Under Age 65				
	Generation				
National Origin (Birthplace)	1.0: Arrived as Adult	1.5: Arrived as Child	2.0: U.S.-Born, Both Parents Foreign-Born	2.5: U.S.-Born, 1 Parent U.S.-Born	3+: U.S.-Born, Both Parents U.S.-Born*
	Fraction of Household Income				
Mexico					
Earnings	0.908	0.911	0.865	0.849	0.856
Public benefits**	0.065	0.064	0.086	0.096	0.093
Other unearned income (incl pensions)	0.028	0.025	0.049	0.055	0.051
El Salvador, Guatemala					
Earnings	0.931	0.908		0.829	
Public benefits**	0.043	0.059		0.076	
Other unearned income (incl pensions)	0.026	0.033		0.095	
Other Central America					
Earnings	0.886	0.873	0.905	0.890	
Public benefits**	0.074	0.059	0.061	0.044	
Other unearned income (incl pensions)	0.040	0.068	0.034	0.066	
Puerto Rico					
Earnings	0.670	0.728	0.773	0.816	0.810
Public benefits**	0.272	0.205	0.172	0.122	0.139
Other unearned income (incl pensions)	0.058	0.068	0.055	0.062	0.051
Dominican Republic					
Earnings	0.721	0.785	0.813		
Public benefits**	0.211	0.154	0.107		
Other unearned income (incl pensions)	0.069	0.061	0.081		
Cuba					
Earnings	0.806	0.870	0.916	0.900	
Public benefits**	0.135	0.065	0.025	0.032	
Other unearned income (incl pensions)	0.059	0.066	0.059	0.068	

*The samples for Hispanics overall and for 3+ generation Mexicans, Puerto Ricans, and black and white non-Hispanics are identified by the "subjective" Spanish-origin and race questions in the CPS.

**Public benefits include Social Security, SSI, public assistance/welfare, unemployment insurance, veterans benefits, and workers' compensation.

APPENDIX TABLE A8-3 Continued

National Origin (Birthplace)	Households with Head Under Age 65: Generation: 1.0: Arrived as Adult	1.5: Arrived as Child	2.0: U.S.-Born, Both Parents Foreign-Born	2.5: U.S.-Born, 1 Parent U.S.-Born	3+: U.S.-Born, Both Parents U.S.-Born*
	Fraction of Household Income				
Colombia					
Earnings	0.880	0.913			
Public benefits**	0.076	0.027			
Other unearned income (incl pensions)	0.044	0.060			
Peru, Ecuador					
Earnings	0.876	0.898	0.885	0.862	
Public benefits**	0.069	0.042	0.026	0.012	
Other unearned income (incl pensions)	0.055	0.060	0.089	0.126	
Other South America					
Earnings	0.899	0.886			
Public benefits**	0.023	0.026			
Other unearned income (incl pensions)	0.078	0.087			
Hispanics (self-identity)*					
Earnings	0.875	0.878	0.847	0.851	0.851
Public benefits**	0.088	0.083	0.104	0.092	0.094
Other unearned income (incl pensions)	0.037	0.039	0.049	0.058	0.056
Black non-Hispanics (self-identity)*					
Earnings					0.780
Public benefits**					0.150
Other unearned income (incl pensions)					0.070
White non-Hispanics (self-identity)*					
Earnings					0.844
Public benefits**					0.067
Other unearned income (incl pensions)					0.088

SOURCE: Pooled March CPS files, 1998–2002. Means are simple averages across households, using household weights. Households with zero or negative total income, or containing persons with negative income from any source, are excluded. Results for Hispanics are shown only for cells with at least 90 observations. Boxes indicate combined groups.

APPENDIX TABLE A8-4 Mean Shares of Household Income by Source: Income of Extended-Household Members, 1997–2001 Pooled

	Households with Head Under Age 65				
	Generation				
National Origin (Birthplace)	1.0: Arrived as Adult	1.5: Arrived as Child	2.0: U.S.-Born, Both Parents Foreign-Born	2.5: U.S.-Born, 1 Parent U.S.-Born	3+: U.S.-Born, Both Parents U.S.-Born*
	Fraction of Household Income				
Mexico					
Head's children & parents**	0.090	0.057	0.085	0.065	0.061
Other relatives of head	0.065	0.067	0.046	0.022	0.021
Unmarried partner of head	0.013	0.021	0.025	0.031	0.030
Other nonrelatives	0.039	0.033	0.032	0.029	0.025
El Salvador, Guatemala					
Head's children & parents**	0.072	0.081		0.055	
Other relatives of head	0.066	0.072		0.007	
Unmarried partner of head	0.017	0.031		0.032	
Other nonrelatives	0.054	0.060		0.022	
Other Central America					
Head's children & parents**	0.078	0.067	0.072	0.051	
Other relatives of head	0.049	0.061	0.038	0.011	
Unmarried partner of head	0.015	0.020	0.050	0.036	
Other nonrelatives	0.042	0.042	0.056	0.022	
Puerto Rico					
Head's children & parents**	0.090	0.086	0.054	0.052	0.061
Other relatives of head	0.013	0.025	0.020	0.024	0.021
Unmarried partner of head	0.023	0.021	0.029	0.032	0.031
Other nonrelatives	0.031	0.015	0.025	0.044	0.024
Dominican Republic					
Head's children & parents**	0.124	0.071	0.059	0.074	
Other relatives of head	0.037	0.070	0.033	0.012	
Unmarried partner of head	0.017	0.035	0.041	0.044	
Other nonrelatives	0.023	0.018	0.019	0.019	

APPENDIX TABLE A8-4 Continued

	Households with Head Under Age 65				
	Generation				
National Origin (Birthplace)	1.0: Arrived as Adult	1.5: Arrived as Child	2.0: U.S.-Born, Both Parents Foreign-Born	2.5: U.S.-Born, 1 Parent U.S.-Born	3+: U.S.-Born, Both Parents U.S.-Born*
	Fraction of Household Income				
Cuba					
Head's children & parents**	0.096	0.075	0.038	0.026	
Other relatives of head	0.030	0.023	0.019	0.006	
Unmarried partner of head	0.017	0.017	0.013	0.008	
Other nonrelatives	0.015	0.018	0.022	0.053	
Colombia					
Head's children & parents**	0.078	0.050			
Other relatives of head	0.036	0.040			
Unmarried partner of head	0.016	0.024			
Other nonrelatives	0.030	0.034			
Peru, Ecuador					
Head's children & parents**	0.105	0.051	0.083	0.001	
Other relatives of head	0.047	0.059	0.037	0.003	
Unmarried partner of head	0.006	0.018	0.034	0.021	
Other nonrelatives	0.036	0.033	0.020	0.068	
Other South America					
Head's children & parents**	0.053	0.044			
Other relatives of head	0.022	0.008			
Unmarried partner of head	0.018	0.015			
Other nonrelatives	0.018	0.046			
All Hispanics (self-identity)*					
Head's children & parents**	0.088	0.065	0.072	0.058	0.059
Other relatives of head	0.054	0.058	0.036	0.022	0.019
Unmarried partner of head	0.015	0.022	0.028	0.027	0.029
Other nonrelatives	0.038	0.032	0.030	0.027	0.025

continues

APPENDIX TABLE A8-4 Continued

National Origin (Birthplace)	Households with Head Under Age 65				
	Generation				
	1.0: Arrived as Adult	1.5: Arrived as Child	2.0: U.S.-Born, Both Parents Foreign-Born	2.5: U.S.-Born, 1 Parent U.S.-Born	3+: U.S.-Born, Both Parents U.S.-Born*
	Fraction of Household Income				
Black non-Hispanics (self-identity)*					
Head's children & parents**					0.063
Other relatives of head					0.020
Unmarried partner of head					0.020
Other nonrelatives					0.020
White non-Hispanics (self-identity)*					
Head's children & parents**					0.037
Other relatives of head					0.007
Unmarried partner of head					0.020
Other nonrelatives					0.025

*The samples for Hispanics overall and for 3+ generation Mexicans, Puerto Ricans, and black and white non-Hispanics are identified by the "subjective" Spanish-origin and race questions in the CPS.

**Includes grandchildren, who contribute 0.2 percent or less for each group.

SOURCE: Pooled March CPS files, 1998–2002. Means are simple averages across households, using household weights. Households with zero or negative total income, or containing persons with negative income from any source, are excluded. Results for Hispanics are shown only for cells with at least 90 observations. Boxes indicate combined groups.

APPENDIX TABLE A8-5 Poverty Rates of Elderly Persons, 1997–2001 Pooled

National Origin (Birthplace)	Generation* 1.0: Arrived as Adult	2.0: U.S.-Born, Both Parents Foreign-Born	2.5: U.S.-Born, 1 Parent U.S.-Born	3.0+: U.S.-Born, Both Parents U.S.-Born**
	Fraction of Persons Age 65+ with Family Income Below the Poverty Threshold			
Mexico	0.231	0.184	0.157	0.185
El Salvador, Guatemala	0.208			
Other Central America	0.134			
Puerto Rico	0.311			
Dominican Republic	0.391	0.079	0.048	
Cuba	0.250			
Colombia	0.127			
Peru, Ecuador	0.198			
Other South America	0.092			
Hispanics (self-identity)**	0.236	0.176	0.175	0.178
Black non-Hispanics (self-identity)**				0.241
White non-Hispanics (self-identity)**				0.081

*Persons who entered the United States before 1950 are omitted because their age at arrival could not be determined if they were born before 1932, and the sample born 1932–1949 (i.e., generation 1.5) is too small for analysis.

**The samples for Hispanics overall and for 3+ generation Mexicans and black and white non-Hispanics are identified by the "subjective" Spanish-origin and race questions in the CPS.

SOURCE: Pooled March CPS files, 1998–2002, using person weights. Results for Hispanics are shown only for cells with at least 90 observations. Boxes indicate combined groups.

APPENDIX TABLE A8-6 Mean Shares of Household Income by Source: Social Security, SSI, Pensions, Income of Extended-Household Members, 1997–2001 Pooled

	Households with Head Age 65 or Older				
	Generation*				
National Origin (Birthplace)	1.0: Arrived as Adult	1.5: Arrived as Child	2.0: U.S.-Born, Both Parents Foreign-Born	2.5: U.S.-Born, 1 Parent U.S.-Born	3+: U.S.-Born, Both Parents U.S.-Born**
	Fraction of Household Income				
Mexico					
Social Security		0.501	0.527	0.543	0.593
SSI		0.092	0.047	0.031	0.032
Private pensions		0.029	0.107	0.082	0.094
Extended-household members***		0.233	0.186	0.152	0.147
Central America					
Social Security		0.351			
SSI		0.137			
Private pensions		0.060			
Extended-household members***		0.265			
Puerto Rico					
Social Security		0.618			
SSI		0.150			
Private pensions		0.044			
Extended-household members***		0.118			
Dominican Republic					
Social Security		0.450	0.580	0.468	
SSI		0.269	0.019	0.014	
Private pensions		0.023	0.126	0.159	
Extended-household members***		0.185	0.076	0.113	
Cuba					
Social Security		0.548			
SSI		0.128			
Private pensions		0.044			
Extended-household members***		0.110			
South America					
Social Security		0.419			
SSI		0.042			
Private pensions		0.100			
Extended-household members***		0.169			
Hispanics (self-identity)**					
Social Security		0.512	0.522	0.535	0.588
SSI		0.118	0.040	0.037	0.031
Private pensions		0.044	0.104	0.081	0.105
Extended-household members***		0.174	0.182	0.163	0.127

APPENDIX TABLE A8-6 Continued

	Households with Head Age 65 or Older				
	Generation*				
National Origin (Birthplace)	1.0: Arrived as Adult	1.5: Arrived as Child	2.0: U.S.-Born, Both Parents Foreign-Born	2.5: U.S.-Born, 1 Parent U.S.-Born	3+: U.S.-Born, Both Parents U.S.-Born**
	Fraction of Household Income				
Black non-Hispanics (self-identity)**					
Social Security					0.583
SSI					0.046
Private pensions					0.112
Extended-household members***					0.139
White non-Hispanics (self-identity)**					
Social Security					0.550
SSI					0.010
Private pensions					0.137
Extended-household members***					0.062

*Persons who entered the United States before 1950 are omitted because their age at arrival could not be determined if they were born before 1932, and the sample born 1932–1949 (i.e., generation 1.5) is too small for analysis.

**The samples for Hispanics overall and for 3+ generation Mexicans and black and white non-Hispanics are identified by the "subjective" Spanish-origin and race questions in the CPS.

***Excluding only income of the head and spouse.

SOURCE: Pooled March CPS files, 1998–2002. Means are simple averages across households, using household weights. Households with zero or negative total income, or containing persons with negative income from any source, are excluded. Results for Hispanics are shown only for cells with at least 90 observations. Boxes indicate combined groups.

APPENDIX TABLE A8-7 Mean Annual Value of In-Kind Public Benefits, Excluding Medicaid and Medicare, 1997–2001 Pooled

National Origin (Birthplace)	Households with Head Under Age 65				
	Generation				
	1.0: Arrived as Adult	1.5: Arrived as Child	2.0: U.S.-Born, Both Parents Foreign-Born	2.5: U.S.-Born, 1 Parent U.S.-Born	3+: U.S.-Born, Both Parents U.S.-Born*
	Value of In-Kind Public Benefits** in 2002 Dollars				
Mexico	$542	$530	$397	$366	$471
El Salvador, Guatemala	328	398	224	283	
Other Central America	400	236		151	
Puerto Rico	694	664	662	385	592
Dominican Republic	956	871	648		
Cuba	324	274	99	85	
Colombia	247	76			
Peru, Ecuador	178	207	174	52	
Other South America	90	133			
Hispanics (self-identity)**	485	500	449	344	446
Black non-Hispanics (self-identity)**					540
White non-Hispanics (self-identity)**					126

*The samples for Hispanics overall and for 3+ generation Mexicans, Puerto Ricans, and black and white non-Hispanics are identified by the "subjective" Spanish-origin and race questions in the CPS.

**Food stamps, school lunch, housing subsidies, energy assistance. All values except energy assistance are imputed by the Census Bureau.

SOURCE: Pooled March CPS files, 1998–2002, using household weights. Results for Hispanics are shown only for cells with at least 90 observations. Boxes indicate combined groups.

APPENDIX TABLE A8-8 Number of Earners Per Household, 1997–2001 Pooled

National Origin (Birthplace)	Households with Head Under Age 65				
	Generation				
	1.0: Arrived as Adult	1.5: Arrived as Child	2.0: U.S.-Born, Both Parents Foreign-Born	2.5: U.S.-Born, 1 Parent U.S.-Born	3+: U.S.-Born, Both Parents U.S.-Born**
	Mean Number with Nozero Annual Earnings				
Mexico	1.9	1.8	1.7	1.7	1.6
El Salvador, Guatemala	2.0	1.9	1.8	1.6	
Other Central America	1.8	1.7		1.8	
Puerto Rico	1.3	1.4	1.4	1.5	1.4
Dominican Republic	1.4	1.6	1.3		
Cuba	1.5	1.7	1.8	1.6	
Colombia	1.8	1.8			
Peru, Ecuador	1.9	1.8	1.6	1.6	
Other South America	1.7	1.7			
Hispanics (self-identity)*	1.8	1.7	1.6	1.7	1.6
Black non-Hispanics (self-identity)*					1.4
White non-Hispanics (self-identity)*					1.7

*The samples for Hispanics overall and for 3+ generation Mexicans, Puerto Ricans, and black and white non-Hispanics are identified by the "subjective" Spanish-origin and race questions in the CPS.

SOURCE: Pooled March CPS files, 1998–2002, using household weights. Results for Hispanics are shown only for cells with at least 90 observations. Boxes indicate combined groups.

APPENDIX TABLE A8-9 Mean Shares of Household Income by Source: Detailed Earnings of Head's Nuclear Family, 1997–2001 Pooled

	Households with Head Under Age 65				
	Generation				
National Origin (Birthplace)	1.0: Arrived as Adult	1.5: Arrived as Child	2.0: U.S.-Born, Both Parents Foreign-Born	2.5: U.S.-Born, 1 Parent U.S.-Born	3+: U.S.-Born, Both Parents U.S.-Born*
	Fraction of Household Income				
Mexico					
Earnings of head	0.517	0.557	0.522	0.546	0.554
Earnings of head's spouse	0.198	0.196	0.186	0.182	0.189
Earnings of head's children (excl subfam)	0.064	0.026	0.032	0.032	0.033
El Salvador, Guatemala					
Earnings of head	0.557	0.509		0.542	
Earnings of head's spouse	0.179	0.174		0.193	
Earnings of head's children (excl subfam)	0.056	0.023		0.031	
Other Central America					
Earnings of head	0.524	0.518	0.599	0.569	
Earnings of head's spouse	0.200	0.203	0.112	0.216	
Earnings of head's children (excl subfam)	0.053	0.004	0.019	0.033	
Puerto Rico					
Earnings of head	0.422	0.481	0.519	0.535	0.542
Earnings of head's spouse	0.135	0.135	0.161	0.155	0.150
Earnings of head's children (excl subfam)	0.051	0.045	0.015	0.021	0.022
Dominican Republic					
Earnings of head	0.411	0.494	0.523		
Earnings of head's spouse	0.156	0.141	0.171		
Earnings of head's children (excl subfam)	0.074	0.024	0.000		
Cuba					
Earnings of head	0.497	0.543	0.567	0.621	
Earnings of head's spouse	0.184	0.228	0.279	0.208	
Earnings of head's children (excl subfam)	0.063	0.037	0.007	0.007	

*The samples for Hispanics overall and for 3+ generation Mexicans, Puerto Ricans, and black and white non-Hispanics are identified by the "subjective" Spanish-origin and race questions in the CPS.

APPENDIX TABLE A8-9 Continued

National Origin (Birthplace)	Households with Head Under Age 65 — Generation: 1.0: Arrived as Adult	1.5: Arrived as Child	2.0: U.S.-Born, Both Parents Foreign-Born	2.5: U.S.-Born, 1 Parent U.S.-Born	3+: U.S.-Born, Both Parents U.S.-Born*
	Fraction of Household Income				
Colombia					
Earnings of head	0.538	0.576			
Earnings of head's spouse	0.205	0.214			
Earnings of head's children (excl subfam)	0.056	0.006			
Peru, Ecuador					
Earnings of head	0.525	0.531	0.563	0.545	
Earnings of head's spouse	0.184	0.224	0.166	0.238	
Earnings of head's children (excl subfam)	0.070	0.014	0.000	0.001	
Other South America					
Earnings of head	0.595	0.577			
Earnings of head's spouse	0.202	0.205			
Earnings of head's children (excl subfam)	0.038	0.016			
Hispanics (self-identity)*					
Earnings of head	0.513	0.538	0.534	0.554	0.553
Earnings of head's spouse	0.188	0.187	0.176	0.186	0.188
Earnings of head's children (excl subfam)	0.061	0.028	0.024	0.029	0.031
Black non-Hispanics (self-identity)*					
Earnings of head					0.568
Earnings of head's spouse					0.119
Earnings of head's children (excl subfam)					0.028
White non-Hispanics (self-identity)*					
Earnings of head					0.566
Earnings of head's spouse					0.204
Earnings of head's children (excl subfam)					0.023

SOURCE: Pooled March CPS files, 1998–2002. Means are simple averages across households, using household weights. Households with zero or negative total income, or containing persons with negative income from any source, are excluded. Results for Hispanics are shown only for cells with at least 90 observations. Boxes indicate combined groups.

APPENDIX TABLE A8-10 Public Benefits Receipt by Households, 1997–2001 Pooled

National Origin (Birthplace)	Households with Head Under Age 65 — Generation: 1.0: Arrived as Adult	1.5: Arrived as Child	2.0: U.S.-Born, Both Parents Foreign-Born	2.5: U.S.-Born, 1 Parent U.S.-Born	3+: U.S.-Born, Both Parents U.S.-Born*
	Fraction Receiving Public Assistance/Welfare				
Mexico	0.053	0.057	0.053	0.044	0.060
El Salvador, Guatemala	0.033	0.055	0.037 (El Salvador, Guatemala and Other Central America combined)	0.047	
Other Central America	0.043	0.024		0.030	
Puerto Rico	0.138	0.109	0.128	0.066	0.122
Dominican Republic	0.166	0.147	0.073		
Cuba	0.058	0.027	0.021	0.007	
Colombia	0.023	0.010			
Peru, Ecuador	0.019	0.006	0.005 (Colombia, Peru, Ecuador and Other South America combined)	0.000 (Colombia, Peru, Ecuador and Other South America combined)	
Other South America	0.005	0.012			
Hispanics (self-identity)*	0.056	0.062	0.071	0.047	0.060
Black non-Hispanics (self-identity)*					0.075
White non-Hispanics (self-identity)*					0.016
	Fraction Receiving Food Stamps				
Mexico	0.108	0.105	0.112	0.103	0.130
El Salvador, Guatemala	0.062	0.079	0.077 (El Salvador, Guatemala and Other Central America combined)	0.078	
Other Central America	0.100	0.062		0.022	
Puerto Rico	0.219	0.203	0.196	0.099	0.176
Dominican Republic	0.266	0.238	0.166		
Cuba	0.151	0.061	0.039	0.043	
Colombia	0.049	0.015			
Peru, Ecuador	0.042	0.033	0.053 (Colombia, Peru, Ecuador and Other South America combined)	0.000 (Colombia, Peru, Ecuador and Other South America combined)	
Other South America	0.008	0.038			
Hispanics (self-identity)*	0.111	0.111	0.127	0.098	0.126
Black non-Hispanics (self-identity)*					0.166
White non-Hispanics (self-identity)*					0.040

1.0: Arrived as Adult	1.5: Arrived as Child	2.0: U.S.-Born, Both Parents Foreign-Born	2.5: U.S.-Born, 1 Parent U.S.-Born	3+: U.S.-Born, Both Parents U.S.-Born*
Fraction Receiving SSI				
0.031	0.022	0.039	0.049	0.045
0.015	0.025	0.009	0.039	
0.043	0.038		0.010	
0.174	0.113	0.088	0.031	0.062
0.123	0.085	0.062		
0.087	0.039	0.021	0.000	
0.064	0.019	0.016	0.014	
0.050	0.025			
0.009	0.021			
0.049	0.039	0.050	0.042	0.045
				0.082
				0.028
Fraction Receiving Medicaid				
0.285	0.279	0.243	0.202	0.218
0.206	0.259	0.168	0.140	
0.241	0.189		0.065	
0.404	0.385	0.331	0.236	0.248
0.480	0.451	0.348		
0.273	0.132	0.078	0.058	
0.235	0.140	0.103	0.063	
0.220	0.183			
0.086	0.105			
0.277	0.277	0.251	0.195	0.209
				0.263
				0.098

continues

APPENDIX TABLE A8-10 Continued

National Origin (Birthplace)	Households with Head Under Age 65 Generation 1.0: Arrived as Adult	1.5: Arrived as Child	2.0: U.S.-Born, Both Parents Foreign-Born	2.5: U.S.-Born, 1 Parent U.S.-Born	3+: U.S.-Born, Both Parents U.S.-Born*
	Fraction Receiving Public Assistance/Welfare, SSI and/or Food Stamps				
Mexico	0.139	0.130	0.144	0.137	0.166
El Salvador, Guatemala	0.079	0.103	0.082	0.117	
Other Central America	0.132	0.093		0.044	
Puerto Rico	0.325	0.264	0.244	0.120	0.222
Dominican Republic	0.334	0.282	0.194		
Cuba	0.200	0.088	0.055	0.043	
Colombia	0.105	0.034			
Peru, Ecuador	0.085	0.054	0.069	0.014	
Other South America	0.015	0.068			
Hispanics (self-identity)*	0.150	0.143	0.162	0.129	0.160
Black non-Hispanics (self-identity)*					0.219
White non-Hispanics (self-identity)*					0.060
	Fraction Receiving Social Security				
Mexico	0.055	0.051	0.101	0.105	0.092
El Salvador, Guatemala	0.043	0.066	0.037	0.136	
Other Central America	0.062	0.087		0.102	
Puerto Rico	0.193	0.153	0.093	0.128	0.073
Dominican Republic	0.108	0.063	0.087		
Cuba	0.191	0.155	0.048	0.063	
Colombia	0.094	0.044			
Peru, Ecuador	0.090	0.055	0.023	0.018	
Other South America	0.048	0.069			
Hispanics (self-identity)*	0.078	0.074	0.086	0.101	0.091
Black non-Hispanics (self-identity)*					0.123
White non-Hispanics (self-identity)*					0.097

*The samples for Hispanics overall and for 3+ generation Mexicans, Puerto Ricans, and black and white non-Hispanics are identified by the "subjective" Spanish-origin and race questions in the CPS.

1.0: Arrived as Adult	1.5: Arrived as Child	2.0: U.S.-Born, Both Parents Foreign-Born	2.5: U.S.-Born, 1 Parent U.S.-Born	3+: U.S.-Born, Both Parents U.S.-Born*
Fraction Receiving Public Assistance/Welfare, SSI, Food Stamps and/or Medicaid				
0.304	0.295	0.259	0.214	0.241
0.226	0.265	0.187	0.146	
0.256	0.203		0.065	
0.423	0.401	0.344	0.252	0.279
0.505	0.478	0.360		
0.293	0.132	0.085	0.092	
0.235	0.140			
0.234	0.183	0.113	0.063	
0.090	0.113			
0.295	0.291	0.266	0.207	0.232
				0.299
				0.106
Fraction Receiving Medicare				
0.052	0.047	0.070	0.075	0.066
0.039	0.066	0.041	0.094	
0.055	0.072		0.065	
0.143	0.128	0.074	0.080	0.072
0.107	0.074	0.101		
0.180	0.134	0.060	0.055	
0.101	0.044			
0.083	0.078	0.075	0.027	
0.052	0.078			
0.072	0.067	0.065	0.073	0.066
				0.100
				0.065

SOURCE: Pooled March CPS files, 1998–2002, using household weights. Results for Hispanics are shown only for cells with at least 90 observations. Boxes indicate combined groups.

APPENDIX TABLE A8-11 Mean Shares of Household Income by Source: Detailed Public Benefits, 1997–2001 Pooled

	Households with Head Under Age 65				
	Generation				
National Origin (Birthplace)	1.0: Arrived as Adult	1.5: Arrived as Child	2.0: U.S.-Born, Both Parents Foreign-Born	2.5: U.S.-Born, 1 Parent U.S.-Born	3+: U.S.-Born, Both Parents U.S.-Born*
	Fraction of Household Income				
Mexico					
Social Security	0.021	0.020	0.033	0.039	0.039
SSI	0.009	0.007	0.014	0.021	0.018
Public assistance/welfare	0.022	0.023	0.024	0.018	0.023
El Salvador, Guatemala					
Social Security	0.016	0.013		0.038	
SSI	0.004	0.014		0.009	
Public assistance/welfare	0.011	0.024		0.019	
Other Central America					
Social Security	0.024	0.036	0.006	0.034	
SSI	0.021	0.009	0.022	0.001	
Public assistance/welfare	0.014	0.009	0.018	0.004	
Puerto Rico					
Social Security	0.099	0.076	0.036	0.071	0.029
SSI	0.097	0.059	0.047	0.012	0.030
Public assistance/welfare	0.066	0.055	0.076	0.027	0.068
Dominican Republic					
Social Security	0.052	0.020	0.019		
SSI	0.057	0.035	0.035		
Public assistance/welfare	0.089	0.082	0.046		
Cuba					
Social Security	0.081	0.039	0.011	0.017	
SSI	0.031	0.008	0.003	0.000	
Public assistance/welfare	0.013	0.012	0.005	0.002	
Colombia					
Social Security	0.033	0.011			
SSI	0.022	0.002			
Public assistance/welfare	0.006	0.005			
Peru, Ecuador					
Social Security	0.038	0.022	0.006	0.000	
SSI	0.013	0.007	0.006	0.003	
Public assistance/welfare	0.007	0.003	0.000	0.000	
Other South America					
Social Security	0.019	0.013			
SSI	0.001	0.001			
Public assistance/welfare	0.001	0.006			

continues

APPENDIX TABLE A8-11 Continued

	Households with Head Under Age 65				
	Generation				
National Origin (Birthplace)	1.0: Arrived as Adult	1.5: Arrived as Child	2.0: U.S.-Born, Both Parents Foreign-Born	2.5: U.S.-Born, 1 Parent U.S.-Born	3+: U.S.-Born, Both Parents U.S.-Born*
	Fraction of Household Income				
Hispanics (self-identity)*					
Social Security	0.032	0.028	0.031	0.040	0.038
SSI	0.019	0.016	0.023	0.017	0.018
Public assistance/welfare	0.023	0.027	0.038	0.018	0.024
Black non-Hispanics (self-identity)*					
Social Security					0.059
SSI					0.042
Public assistance/welfare					0.032
White non-Hispanics (self-identity)*					
Social Security					0.039
SSI					0.012
Public assistance/welfare					0.005

*The samples for Hispanics overall and for 3+ generation Mexicans, Puerto Ricans, and black and white non-Hispanics are identified by the "subjective" Spanish-origin and race questions in the CPS.

SOURCE: Pooled March CPS files, 1998–2002. Means are simple averages across households, using household weights. Households with zero or negative total income, or containing persons with negative income from any source, are excluded. Results for Hispanics are shown only for cells with at least 90 observations. Boxes indicate combined groups.

APPENDIX TABLE A8-12 Public Benefits Receipt by Households, 1997–2001 Pooled

	Households with Head Age 65 or Older			
	Generation*			
National Origin (Birthplace)	1.0: Arrived as Adult	2.0: U.S.-Born, Both Parents Foreign-Born	2.5: U.S.-Born, 1 Parent U.S.-Born	3+: U.S.-Born, Both Parents U.S.-Born**
	Fraction Receiving Social Security			
Mexico	0.810	0.868	0.910	0.902
Central America	0.742			
Puerto Rico	0.834			
Dominican Republic	0.684	0.919	0.878	
Cuba	0.794			
South America	0.798			
Hispanics (self-identity)**	0.795	0.866	0.916	0.894
Black non-Hispanics (self-identity)**				0.895
White non-Hispanics (self-identity)**				0.938
	Fraction Receiving Food Stamps			
Mexico	0.114	0.081	0.127	0.105
Central America	0.085			
Puerto Rico	0.228			
Dominican Republic	0.473	0.019	0.053	
Cuba	0.232			
South America	0.114			
Hispanics (self-identity)**	0.186	0.067	0.134	0.100
Black non-Hispanics (self-identity)**				0.124
White non-Hispanics (self-identity)**				0.028

*Persons who entered the United States before 1950 are omitted because their age at arrival could not be determined if they were born before 1932, and the sample born 1932–1949 (i.e., generation 1.5) is too small for analysis.

**The samples for Hispanics overall and for 3+ generation Mexicans and black and white non-Hispanics are identified by the "subjective" Spanish-origin and race questions in the CPS.

SOURCE: Pooled March CPS files, 1998–2002, using household weights. Results for Hispanics are shown only for cells with at least 90 observations. Boxes indicate combined groups.

Generation*			
1.0: Arrived as Adult	2.0: U.S.-Born, Both Parents Foreign-Born	2.5: U.S.-Born, 1 Parent U.S.-Born	3+: U.S.-Born, Both Parents U.S.-Born**
Fraction Receiving SSI			
0.240	0.153	0.126	0.120
0.226			
0.350			
0.453	0.074	0.048	
0.214			
0.130			
0.252	0.137	0.135	0.116
			0.139
			0.035
Fraction Receiving Medicaid			
0.392	0.279	0.269	0.247
0.385			
0.527			
0.656	0.100	0.120	
0.371			
0.282			
0.415	0.254	0.306	0.235
			0.273
			0.096

APPENDIX TABLE A8-13 Mean Shares of Household Income by Source: Income of Extended-Household Members, 1997–2001 Pooled

	Households with Head Age 65 Or Older		
	Generation		
National Origin (Birthplace)	1st: Foreign-Born	2nd: U.S.-Born, Foreign-Born Parent	3+: U.S.-Born, Both Parents U.S.-Born*
	Fraction of Household Income		
Mexico			
Head's children & grandchildren**	0.187	0.134	0.124
Other relatives of head	0.021	0.027	0.011
Unmarried partner of head	0.001	0.002	0.004
Other nonrelatives	0.009	0.014	0.008
Central America			
Head's children & grandchildren**	0.151		
Other relatives of head	0.034		
Unmarried partner of head	0.004		
Other nonrelatives	0.010		
Puerto Rico			
Head's children & grandchildren**	0.087		
Other relatives of head	0.015		
Unmarried partner of head	0.001		
Other nonrelatives	0.010		
Dominican Republic			
Head's children & grandchildren**	0.139	0.072	
Other relatives of head	0.024	0.011	
Unmarried partner of head	0.000	0.000	
Other nonrelatives	0.022	0.014	
Cuba			
Head's children & grandchildren**	0.057		
Other relatives of head	0.037		
Unmarried partner of head	0.006		
Other nonrelatives	0.004		
South America			
Head's children & grandchildren**	0.124		
Other relatives of head	0.021		
Unmarried partner of head	0.001		
Other nonrelatives	0.020		

APPENDIX TABLE A8-13 Continued

National Origin (Birthplace)	Households with Head Age 65 Or Older		
	Generation		
	1st: Foreign-Born	2nd: U.S.-Born, Foreign-Born Parent	3+: U.S.-Born, Both Parents U.S.-Born*
	Fraction of Household Income		
All Hispanics (self-identity)*			
Head's children & grandchildren**	0.125	0.131	0.108
Other relatives of head	0.026	0.030	0.009
Unmarried partner of head	0.002	0.002	0.003
Other nonrelatives	0.010	0.014	0.007
Black non-Hispanics (self-identity)*			
Head's children & grandchildren**			0.111
Other relatives of head			0.015
Unmarried partner of head			0.003
Other nonrelatives			0.010
White non-Hispanics (self-identity)*			
Head's children & grandchildren**			0.047
Other relatives of head			0.007
Unmarried partner of head			0.002
Other nonrelatives			0.006

*The samples for Hispanics overall and for 3+ generation Mexicans and black and white non-Hispanics are identified by the "subjective" Spanish-origin and race questions in the CPS.

**Includes parents, who contribute 0.6 percent or less for each group.

SOURCE: Pooled March CPS files, 1998–2002. Means are simple averages across households, using household weights. Households with zero or negative total income, or containing persons with negative income from any source, are excluded. Results for Hispanics are shown only for cells with at least 90 observations. Box indicates combined groups.

APPENDIX TABLE A8-14 Sample Sizes: Households

	Households with Head Under Age 65	
	Generation	
National Origin (Birthplace)	1st: Total Foreign-Born	1.0: Arrived as Adult
Mexico	9,837	6,002
El Salvador, Guatemala	1,618	1,143
Other Central America	933	666
Puerto Rico	1,941	878
Dominican Republic	947	648
Cuba	1,048	643
Colombia	616	477
Peru, Ecuador	700	506
Other South America	574	416
Hispanics (self-identity)*	18,440	11,523
Black non-Hispanics (self-identity)*		
White non-Hispanics (self-identity)*		

	Households with Head Age 65 or Older	
	Generation	
National Origin (Birthplace)	1st: Total Foreign-Born	1.0: Arrived as Adult**
Mexico	605	477
El Salvador, Guatemala	46	32
Other Central America	92	71
Puerto Rico	418	278
Dominican Republic	123	113
Cuba	520	485
Colombia	78	75
Peru, Ecuador	42	40
Other South America	81	77
Hispanics (self-identity)*	1,992	1,645
Black non-Hispanics (self-identity)*		
White non-Hispanics (self-identity)*		

*The samples for Hispanics overall and for 3+ generation Mexicans, Puerto Ricans, Cubans, and black and white non-Hispanics are identified by the "subjective" Spanish-origin and race questions in the CPS.

**Persons who were born before 1932 and entered the United States before 1950 are omitted because one cannot tell whether they belong to generation 1.0 or 1.5. They are included in the foreign-born total in column 1.

SOURCE: Pooled March CPS files, 1998–2002.

1.5: Arrived as Child	2.0: U.S.-Born, Both Parents Foreign-Born	2.5: U.S.-Born, 1 Parent U.S.-Born	3+: U.S.-Born, Both Parents U.S.-Born*
3,834	1,493	1,324	5,545
474	57	226	
267	77	105	
1,065	1,047	272	466
299	98	32	
405	180	115	49
139	53	21	
194	50	25	
158	58	48	
6,915	3,131	1,856	7,848
			21,628
			142,207

1.5: Arrived as Child**	2.0: U.S.-Born, Both Parents Foreign-Born	2.5: U.S.-Born, 1 Parent U.S.-Born	3+: U.S.-Born, Both Parents U.S.-Born*
15	492	186	487
0	7	57	
0	5	13	
17	52	7	20
1	0	3	
2	3	8	6
0	1	9	
1	1	0	
0	7	6	
36	573	203	815
			4,975
			33,760

APPENDIX TABLE A8-15 Sample Sizes: Households with Nonnegative Income (for Tables 8-3, 8-4, 8-6, Appendix Tables A8-3, A8-4, A8-6, A8-9, A8-11, and A8-13 on Shares of Income)

	Households with Head Under Age 65	
	Generation	
National Origin (Birthplace)	1st: Total Foreign-Born	1.0: Arrived as Adult
Mexico	9,624	5,877
El Salvador, Guatemala	1,579	1,118
Other Central America	917	655
Puerto Rico	1,882	850
Dominican Republic	905	622
Cuba	1,010	623
Colombia	593	460
Peru, Ecuador	684	496
Other South America	549	400
Hispanics (self-identity)*	17,959	11,237
Black non-Hispanics (self-identity)*		
White non-Hispanics (self-identity)*		

	Households with Head Age 65 or Older	
	Generation	
National Origin (Birthplace)	1st: Total Foreign-Born	1.0: Arrived as Adult**
Mexico	583	460
El Salvador, Guatemala	46	32
Other Central America	90	69
Puerto Rico	408	271
Dominican Republic	120	110
Cuba	498	463
Colombia	77	74
Peru, Ecuador	41	39
Other South America	80	76
Hispanics (self-identity)*	1,927	1,589
Black non-Hispanics (self-identity)*		
White non-Hispanics (self-identity)*		

*The samples for Hispanics overall and for 3+ generation Mexicans, Puerto Ricans, Cubans, and black and white non-Hispanics are identified by the "subjective" Spanish-origin and race questions in the CPS.

1.5: Arrived as Child	2.0: U.S.-Born, Both Parents Foreign-Born	2.5: U.S.-Born, 1 Parent U.S.-Born	3+: U.S.-Born, Both Parents U.S.-Born*
3,746	1,454	1,289	5,393
460	56	217	
262	73	99	
1032	1,022	265	452
283	94	32	
387	175	109	47
133	52	20	
188	47	25	
149	52	48	
6,720	3,040	1,812	7,615
			20,979
			136,630

1.5: Arrived as Child**	2.0: U.S.-Born, Both Parents Foreign-Born	2.5: U.S.-Born, 1 Parent U.S.-Born	3+: U.S.-Born, Both Parents U.S.-Born*
14	475	182	468
0	7	55	
0	5	13	
16	52	7	20
1	0	3	
2	3	8	5
0	0	9	
1	1	0	
0	5	6	
34	553	200	782
			4,868
			32,525

**Persons who were born before 1932 and entered the United States before 1950 are omitted because one cannot tell whether they belong to generation 1.0 or 1.5. They are included in the foreign-born total in column 1.

SOURCE: Pooled March CPS files, 1998–2002.

APPENDIX TABLE A8-16 Sample Sizes: Children and Elderly Persons

National Origin (Birthplace)	Persons Under Age 18 — Generation — 1st: Total Foreign-Born	1.0: Arrived as Adult**
Mexico	3,755	
El Salvador, Guatemala	378	
Other Central America	327	
Puerto Rico	623	
Dominican Republic	303	
Cuba	161	
Colombia	196	
Peru, Ecuador	193	
Other South America	194	
Hispanics (self-identity)*	6,212	
Black non-Hispanics (self-identity)*		
White non-Hispanics (self-identity)*		

National Origin (Birthplace)	Persons Age 65 or Older — Generation — 1st: Total Foreign-Born	1.0: Arrived as Adult***
Mexico	1,226	997
El Salvador, Guatemala	135	118
Other Central America	165	134
Puerto Rico	639	427
Dominican Republic	205	189
Cuba	920	859
Colombia	153	150
Peru, Ecuador	116	113
Other South America	146	139
Hispanics (self-identity)*	3,699	3,136
Black non-Hispanics (self-identity)*		
White non-Hispanics (self-identity)*		

*The samples for Hispanics overall and for 3+ generation Mexicans, Puerto Ricans, Cubans, and black and white non-Hispanics are identified by the "subjective" Spanish-origin and race questions in the CPS.

**By definition, there are no children under 18 in generation 1.0.

1.5: Arrived as Child	2.0: U.S.-Born, Both Parents Foreign-Born	2.5: U.S.-Born, 1 Parent U.S.-Born	3+: U.S.-Born, Both Parents U.S.-Born*
3,749	11,268	4,215	9,032
378	1,654	553	
327	722	342	
623	1,064	987	1,536
303	948	296	
161	438	369	165
196	396	195	
193	457	249	
194	203	237	
6,206	16,994	5,969	12,670
			21,987
			123,072

1.5: Arrived as Child***	2.0: U.S.-Born, Both Parents Foreign-Born	2.5: U.S.-Born, 1 Parent U.S.-Born	3+: U.S.-Born, Both Parents U.S.-Born*
36	765	281	761
0	12	81	
1	12	19	
29	79	19	39
2	0	3	
5	12	9	11
0	1	10	
1	1	0	
1	7	7	
71	908	302	1,287
			7,015
			50,006

***Persons who were born before 1932 and entered the United States before 1950 are omitted because one cannot tell whether they belong to generation 1.0 or 1.5. They are included in the foreign-born total in column 1.

SOURCE: Pooled March CPS files, 1998–2002.

APPENDIX TABLE A8-17 Sample Sizes: Persons, by Family Structure

	Persons in Single Female-Headed Families	
	Generation	
National Origin (Birthplace)	1st: Total Foreign-Born	1.0: Arrived as Adult**
Mexico	4,187	2,064
El Salvador, Guatemala	939	514
Other Central America	599	359
Puerto Rico	1,617	578
Dominican Republic	928	539
Cuba	628	421
Colombia	358	249
Peru, Ecuador	378	224
Other South America	230	157
Hispanics (self-identity)*	9,913	5,104
Black non-Hispanics (self-identity)*		
White non-Hispanics (self-identity)*		
	Persons in Married-Couple Families	
	Generation	
National Origin (Birthplace)	1st: Total Foreign-Born	1.0: Arrived as Adult**
Mexico	19,714	10,236
El Salvador, Guatemala	2,753	1,715
Other Central America	1,736	1,023
Puerto Rico	2,418	1,074
Dominican Republic	1,216	729
Cuba	2,221	1,465
Colombia	1,186	807
Peru, Ecuador	1,279	837
Other South America	1,100	692
Hispanics (self-identity)*	34,031	18,879
Black non-Hispanics (self-identity)*		
White non-Hispanics (self-identity)*		

*The samples for Hispanics overall and for 3+ generation Mexicans, Puerto Ricans, Cubans, and black and white non-Hispanics are identified by the "subjective" Spanish-origin and race questions in the CPS.

1.5: Arrived as Child**	2.0: U.S.-Born, Both Parents Foreign-Born	2.5: U.S.-Born, 1 Parent U.S.-Born	3+: U.S.-Born, Both Parents U.S.-Born*
2,052	3,411	1,832	5,983
414	446	268	
225	237	151	
984	1,317	619	1,125
383	661	132	
189	188	143	44
106	145	56	
153	146	62	
72	44	65	
4,635	6,543	2,927	8,736
			31,757
			83,583

1.5: Arrived as Child**	2.0: U.S.-Born, Both Parents Foreign-Born	2.5: U.S.-Born, 1 Parent U.S.-Born	3+: U.S.-Born, Both Parents U.S.-Born*
9,385	11,715	4,923	13,400
1,032	1,325	714	
699	638	373	
1,241	1,504	893	1,150
480	532	200	
725	689	410	210
379	398	201	
441	448	249	
403	284	251	
14,897	17,437	6,497	18,304
			27,357
			321,544

**Persons who were born before 1932 and entered the United States before 1950 are omitted because one cannot tell whether they belong to generation 1.0 or 1.5. They are included in the foreign-born total in column 1.

SOURCE: Pooled March CPS files, 1998–2002.

9

The Health Status and Health Behaviors of Hispanics

José J. Escarce, Leo S. Morales, and Rubén G. Rumbaut

The rapid growth in the Hispanic population, and especially in the number of Hispanic youth, represents one of the most dramatic and important demographic trends affecting the United States. Contemporary working-age Hispanic adults will age to become the first sizable wave of Hispanic seniors. More consequential, the large number of contemporary Hispanic children and adolescents will age to swell the ranks of Hispanic young and middle-aged adults within a decade or two. The health status and health behaviors of today's Hispanic youth will play a central role in shaping the long-term health and health care needs not only of Hispanics in the United States but also of all Americans.

Efforts to provide a detailed and comprehensive description of the health and health behaviors of Hispanics are complicated by a variety of factors. Hispanics living in the United States represent an increasing diversity of national-origin groups. Relatively new groups, including Dominicans, Salvadorans, Guatemalans, and Colombians, have grown rapidly, adding their numbers to well-established populations of Mexican, Puerto Rican, and Cuban origin. The available information suggests that health status differs across national-origin groups. In addition, the health of U.S. Hispanics differs by generational status. On numerous dimensions, foreign-born Hispanics—i.e., immigrants to the United States—have better health indicators than their U.S.-born counterparts. Among the foreign-born, moreover, health status and health behaviors may differ by degree of acculturation to American culture.

In this context, the gaps in the available data on the health and health behaviors of Hispanics impose serious limitations. One frequent and noteworthy problem is the lack of detailed data for subgroups of Hispanics defined by national origin and generation in the United States. Most studies group Hispanics into a single category or focus on Hispanics of Mexican origin, who are by far the most numerous. Another problem is the relative lack of detailed epidemiological data on the incidence and prevalence of common and important diseases, such as cardiovascular disease. Moreover, for many conditions, data are unavailable to assess incidence or prevalence according to immigrant status or, among the foreign-born, by length of residence in the United States and degree of acculturation.

Despite these limitations, researchers have learned a great deal about the health status and health behaviors of Hispanics over the past 25 years. The story that has emerged is a complex one, with some findings that warrant optimism and others that merit serious concern. The picture of both advantage and disadvantage that has surfaced must be appreciated and understood in order to develop interventions and design policies to improve Hispanic health.

In this chapter, we provide an overview of the health status and health behaviors of Hispanics in the United States. The chapter is divided into sections, as follows. The next section discusses mortality rates among Hispanics and compares them with rates for non-Hispanic whites and non-Hispanic blacks. This section also illustrates the variation in mortality across Hispanic national-origin groups. The three sections that follow cover, in order, the health status and health behaviors of Hispanic adults, the health status and health behaviors of Hispanic children and adolescents, and birth outcomes. The sixth section discusses the so-called epidemiological paradox, one of the most fascinating findings regarding the health of Hispanics and a source of controversy since it was first described. Finally, we conclude with a summary of our findings and what they mean for the health and health care needs of future generations of Hispanics in the United States.

Our objective is not to be comprehensive. Rather, our goal is to summarize research findings that have an especially strong bearing on future trends in Hispanic health. Accordingly, a major portion of the chapter is devoted to reviewing selected aspects of the health and health behaviors of Hispanic children and adolescents. We have chosen today's Hispanic youth as a major focus because their health has enormous implications for the future health and health care needs of all Americans.

MORTALITY

As Table 9-1 shows, Hispanics in the United States have lower age-adjusted mortality rates than both non-Hispanic whites and non-Hispanic

TABLE 9-1 Mortality Rates per 100,000 Persons for Non-Hispanic Whites, Non-Hispanic Blacks, and Hispanics, and for Hispanic National-Origin Groups, by Age and Gender, 2001

Males	Non-Hispanic Whites	Non-Hispanic Blacks	All Hispanics	Mexicans	Puerto Ricans	Cubans	Other Hispanics
All ages, age adjusted	1012.8	1393.7	802.5	779.0	1029.1	—	747.6
Under 1 year	611.6	1484.2	624.4	50.0	—	—	865.5
1–4 years	33.8	55.1	33.8	33.7	—	—	35.3
5–14 years	18.6	28.6	16.6	16.5	20.3	—	5.8
15–24 years	105.1	186.2	111.5	115.2	127.0	58.6	99.0
25–34 years	131.5	267.9	118.0	111.4	183.4	94.7	122.9
35–44 years	241.6	456.3	208.5	189.0	373.2	199.7	202.2
45–54 years	502.6	1014.6	443.9	396.6	767.3	428.0	440.4
55–64 years	1136.3	2055.4	923.9	882.1	1424.5	1010.4	763.4
65–74 years	2869.4	4218.9	2242.6	2228.9	2671.7	1849.0	2333.0
75–84 years	6851.5	8426.8	5258.0	5262.6	—	—	—
85 years and over	17055.3	16576.2	12888.3	—	—	—	—
Females							
All ages, age adjusted	713.5	925.5	544.2	536.2	667.6	450.6	649.6
Under 1 year	496.4	1217.8	518.9	490.5	—	—	584.0
1–4 years	26.3	43.6	27.2	27.6	—	—	27.6
5–14 years	13.9	19.3	12.7	13.4	12.4	—	10.6
15–24 years	41.9	56.8	33.7	32.2	40.7	—	36.1
25–34 years	60.9	122.4	45.2	39.0	80.7	—	49.9
35–44 years	134.9	285.7	97.0	88.9	170.0	100.3	87.2
45–54 years	291.0	591.5	226.7	214.2	317.0	08.7	216.2
55–64 years	723.5	1238.2	543.0	538.3	45.9	427.3	494.4
65–74 years	1864.1	2653.0	1408.0	1550.1	1345.2	1140.9	1274.3
75–84 years	4777.3	5645.1	3589.8	3759.9	—	3047.2	3112.5
85 years and over	14670.6	13951.4	11300.5	9989.8	—	—	—

SOURCE: Arias et al. (2003).

blacks (Arias, Anderson, Hsiang-Ching, Murphy, and Kochanek, 2003). In 2001, the age-adjusted death rate for Hispanic men was 802.5 per 100,000 persons, compared with 1012.8 for white men and 1393.7 for black men. The age-adjusted death rate for Hispanic women was 544.2 per 100,000, compared with 713.5 for white women and 925.5 for black women. The mortality advantage of Hispanics in comparison with whites is present throughout most of the age range, although the advantage grows at older ages. However, Hispanic infants and men ages 15 to 24 have slightly higher death rates than their white counterparts. It is worth noting that vital statistics data may understate mortality for Hispanics due to underidentification of Hispanic ethnicity on death certificates (Rosenberg et al., 1999). We discuss this in greater detail later in the chapter.

Mortality rates differ among Hispanic groups defined by national origin (Table 9-1). Men of Mexican origin and other Hispanic men have lower death rates than men of Puerto Rican origin. (An age-adjusted death rate was unavailable for Cuban men.) Women of Cuban origin have the lowest death rates, followed by Puerto Rican and other Hispanic women; women of Mexican origin have the highest death rates. Notably, all Hispanic groups except Puerto Rican men have lower age-adjusted death rates than non-Hispanic whites. For certain national-origin groups, death rates also differ by nativity, with the foreign-born having lower rates than the U.S.-born.

The two leading causes of death are heart disease and cancer among Hispanics, non-Hispanic whites, and non-Hispanic blacks (Table 9-2). Beyond the top two causes, however, the leading causes of death differ. In particular, homicide, chronic liver disease and cirrhosis, and conditions originating in the perinatal period are among the 10 leading causes of death for Hispanics, but not for whites. The age-adjusted death rate from homicide among Hispanic men was 11.8 per 100,000 persons in 2000, more than three times the rate of 3.6 for non-Hispanic white men (National Center for Health Statistics, 2003). In fact, homicide is responsible for the higher death rate among Hispanic men ages 15 to 24. Both alcohol use and chronic hepatitis infection contribute to the high death rates from chronic liver disease and cirrhosis among Hispanics (Caetano and Galvan, 2001; Vong and Bell, 2004).

The finding that age-adjusted mortality is lower for Hispanics than for non-Hispanic whites, despite the fact that Hispanics have lower socioeconomic status, is at the core of the "epidemiological paradox." This phenomenon, and its relationship to the finding of a mortality advantage for Hispanic immigrants from certain countries relative to their U.S.-born peers, is discussed in detail later in the chapter.

THE HEALTH AND HEALTH BEHAVIORS OF HISPANIC ADULTS

We begin with a discussion of the health status and health behaviors of Hispanic adults. We review data on common chronic conditions, including diabetes, hypertension, cardiovascular disease, and cancer; on activity limitations caused by chronic conditions; and on biological risk factors for chronic disease, including lipid levels and obesity. We also summarize the available information concerning mental health as well as relevant research

TABLE 9-2 Leading Causes of Death for Non-Hispanic Whites, Non-Hispanic Blacks, and Hispanics, by Sex, 2000

Racial or Ethnic Groups/Sex/Cause of Death	Number of Deaths
Non-Hispanic whites	
Men	
All causes	1,007,191
Diseases of heart	301,551
Malignant neoplasms	247,403
Cerebrovascular diseases	54,938
Chronic lower respiratory diseases	54,816
Unintentional injuries	53,329
Diabetes mellitus	26,009
Influenza and pneumonia	25,002
Suicide	21,293
Chronic liver disease and cirrhosis	15,002
Nephritis, nephrotic syndrome and nephrosis	14,385
Women	
All causes	1,064,096
Diseases of heart	320,168
Malignant neoplasms	232,608
Cerebrovascular diseases	89,642
Chronic lower respiratory diseases	58,024
Alzheimer's disease	32,936
Influenza and pneumonia	32,912
Diabetes mellitus	29,552
Unintentional injuries	29,263
Nephritis, nephrotic syndrome and nephrosis	15,213
Septicemia	14,088
Non-Hispanic blacks	
Men	
All causes	145,184
Diseases of heart	36,740
Malignant neoplasms	32,817
Unintentional injuries	8,531
Cerebrovascular diseases	8,026
Homicide	6,482
Human immunodeficiency virus (HIV) disease	5,400
Diabetes mellitus	4,771
Chronic lower respiratory diseases	4,238
Nephritis, nephrotic syndrome and nephrosis	3,074
Influenza and pneumonia	2,915
Women	
All causes	140,642
Diseases of heart	40,783
Malignant neoplasms	29,128
Cerebrovascular diseases	11,195
Diabetes mellitus	7,250

TABLE 9-2 Continued

Racial or Ethnic Groups/Sex/Cause of Death	Number of Deaths
Nephritis, nephrotic syndrome and nephrosis	3,837
Unintentional injuries	3,746
Chronic lower respiratory diseases	3,369
Septicemia	3,341
Influenza and pneumonia	3,075
HIV disease	2,448
Hispanics	
Men	
All causes	60,172
Diseases of heart	13,566
Malignant neoplasms	11,138
Unintentional injuries	6,696
Cerebrovascular diseases	2,865
Diabetes mellitus	2,507
Homicide	2,431
Chronic liver disease and cirrhosis	2,312
Suicide	1,525
HIV disease	1,493
Chronic lower respiratory diseases	1,451
Women	
All causes	47,082
Diseases of heart	12,253
Malignant neoplasms	10,022
Cerebrovascular diseases	3,322
Diabetes mellitus	2,821
Unintentional injuries	2,134
Influenza and pneumonia	1,322
Chronic lower respiratory diseases	1,238
Certain conditions originating in the perinatal period	951
Chronic liver disease and cirrhosis	875
Nephritis, nephrotic syndrome and nephrosis	841

SOURCE: National Center for Health Statistics (2003).

findings on health behaviors, including diet, cigarette smoking, alcohol consumption, and illicit drug use. Our focus on chronic conditions and biological and behavioral risk factors for chronic disease stems from our goal of assessing the dimensions of health status and health behaviors that have the greatest implications for the long-term health of Hispanics in the United States. For comparative purposes, the available data on Hispanics is contrasted principally with non-Hispanic whites and whenever possible among the major Hispanic national-origin groups and between foreign-born and U.S.-born Hispanics. We will also highlight the role of acculturation when the data allow.

Chronic Conditions

Diabetes Mellitus

The term "diabetes" refers to a group of diseases characterized by abnormal metabolism of glucose (sugar) and elevated blood glucose levels. Diabetes is one of the most common chronic conditions in the United States, and its prevalence is increasing (Harris, 1998). There are two types of diabetes. Type 1 diabetes is caused by an absolute deficiency of insulin and usually begins in childhood or early adulthood. Type 2 diabetes is caused by either reduced or increased insulin secretion coupled with insulin resistance and accounts for 90 to 95 percent of all cases of diabetes.

Compared with non-Hispanic whites, Hispanics have higher rates of Type 2 diabetes and other manifestations of abnormal glucose metabolism. For example, using data from the Hispanic Health and Nutrition Examination Survey (HHANES, 1982–1984), Flegal et al. (1991) found that 3.8 percent of Hispanics of Mexican origin who were 20 to 44 years old and 23.9 percent of Hispanics of Mexican origin who were 45 to 74 years old had diabetes, compared with 2.4 percent and 15.8 percent of Hispanics of Cuban origin and 4.1 percent and 26.1 percent of Puerto Ricans, respectively. The prevalence of diabetes for non-Hispanic whites was 1.6 percent for 20- to 44-year-olds and 12.0 percent for 45- to 74-year-olds.

Using more recent data from the Third National Health and Nutrition Examination Survey (NHANES III, 1988–1994), Harris et al. (1998a) found that the age-adjusted rate of diabetes was 13.8 percent for adults of Mexican origin and 7.3 percent for non-Hispanic white adults. Diabetes prevalence was higher for Mexicans than for non-Hispanic whites throughout the age range. Hispanics of Mexican origin also had higher rates than whites of impaired fasting glucose and impaired glucose tolerance, both of which indicate abnormal glucose metabolism and are frequent precursors of diabetes (Harris et al., 1998a).

Complications of diabetes include heart disease, blindness, kidney disease, and peripheral nervous system damage. Studies to assess the risk of developing diabetes complications among Hispanics have yielded conflicting results. For example, Harris et al. (1998b) found that people of Mexican origin with diabetes were more likely than non-Hispanic whites to develop diabetic retinopathy, which can lead to blindness, whereas other investigators have concluded that Hispanics are no different from other ethnic groups with regard to their risk of diabetic complications (Luchsinger, 2001). Notably, Harris et al. (1999) found worse glycemic control (i.e., control of blood sugar levels) among Hispanic adults with Type 2 diabetes compared with non-Hispanic whites.

Due to the higher prevalence of diabetes in Hispanics, the burden of complications attributable to diabetes is greater for Hispanics than for other groups. The health consequences of diabetes for Hispanics are also reflected in data on cause-specific mortality. Thus, in 2000 the age-adjusted rate of death from diabetes for Hispanics was 36.9 per 100,000 people, compared with 21.8 for non-Hispanic whites (National Center for Health Statistics, 2003). The number of years of potential life lost before age 75 per 100,000 people was 215.6 for Hispanics and 150.2 for non-Hispanic whites (National Center for Health Statistics, 2003). (The number of years of potential life lost is calculated by assuming that everyone would live to age 75.)

Hypertension

Hypertension, or chronic elevation of arterial blood pressure, is a major risk factor for heart disease and stroke. Previous reviews have concluded that the prevalence of hypertension in Hispanics is no greater than among non-Hispanic whites and may be lower (Pérez-Stable, Juarbe, and Moreno, 2001; Ramírez, 1996). However, data from the National Health and Nutrition Examination Surveys suggest that, while rates of hypertension were once lower among Hispanics than among non-Hispanic whites, these rates are now similar.

Using the HHANES (1982–1984) and NHANES II (1976–1980), Pappas, Gergen, and Carroll (1990) found lower age-adjusted rates of hypertension among Hispanic adults who were younger than 75 years old than among non-Hispanic whites. Specifically, age-adjusted rates of hypertension were 22.9 percent, 19.7 percent, and 20.5 percent for men of Mexican, Puerto Rican, and Cuban origin, respectively, compared with 32.6 percent for non-Hispanic white men. Similarly, age-adjusted rates of hypertension were 19.7 percent, 18.0 percent, and 13.8 percent for Mexican, Puerto Rican, and Cuban women compared with 25.3 percent for non-Hispanic white women. By contrast, NHANES III (1988–1994) and NHANES IV (1999–2000) found similar rates of hypertension among people of Mexican origin and non-Hispanic whites. The most recent data from NHANES IV found age-adjusted rates of hypertension of 30.6 percent and 25.0 percent, respectively, for adult men and women of Mexican origin who were less than 75 years old. The corresponding rates for non-Hispanic white men and women were 28.8 percent and 24.5 percent, respectively (National Center for Health Statistics, 2003). Hypertension is also common among elderly Hispanics. For example, analyses of the 1994 Hispanic Established Populations for the Epidemiologic Study of the Elderly investigation found that 61 percent seniors of Mexican origin had hypertension (Stroup-Benham, Markides, Espino, and Goodwin, 1999). The growing prevalence of hypertension in Hispanics—especially Hispanics of Mexican origin—could be due to the obesity epidemic that disproportionately affects this population, as we discuss later in the chapter.

Several studies have documented undertreatment of hypertension and poor blood pressure control in hypertensive Hispanics compared with non-Hispanic whites (Pappas et al., 1990; Satish, Stroup-Benham, Espino, Markides, Goodwin, 1998; Sudano and Baker, 2001). Adequate control of hypertension reduces the risk of stroke, coronary artery disease, congestive heart failure, and cardiovascular death.

Cardiovascular Disease

Cardiovascular disease, including ischemic heart disease and cerebrovascular disease, is the leading cause of death for all ethnic groups in the United States. The main risk factors include diabetes, hypertension, obesity, elevated low-density lipoprotein (LDL) cholesterol, low levels of high-density lipoprotein (HDL) cholesterol, and smoking. As discussed in earlier sections of this chapter, Hispanics have higher rates of diabetes and obesity than non-Hispanic whites. However, Hispanics have similar rates of hypertension and similar cholesterol profiles when compared with non-Hispanic whites, although Hispanics are less likely than whites to have their blood pressure controlled. Hispanics also have lower rates of smoking than non-Hispanic whites, as we discuss later on.

Few data are available on the epidemiology of ischemic heart disease among Hispanics. Studies have found both higher and lower prevalence and incidence of acute myocardial infarction among Hispanics of Mexican origin compared with non-Hispanic whites (Goff et al., 1997; Mitchell, Hazuda, Haffner, Patterson, and Stern, 1991; Rewers et al., 1993). Analyses of death certificate data suggest that mortality rates from heart disease are lower for Hispanics than for non-Hispanic whites (e.g., Liao et al., 1997; Sorlie, Backlund, Johnson, and Rogot, 1993). For example, vital statistics data for 2000 indicate that the age-adjusted death rate from heart disease among Hispanics was 196.0 per 100,000 people, compared with 255.5 per 100,000 people among non-Hispanic whites, while the age-adjusted death rate from ischemic heart disease among Hispanics was 153.2 per 100,000 people, compared with 186.6 per 100,000 people among non-Hispanic whites (National Center for Health Statistics, 2003). However, mortality rates based on vital statistics data have several limitations, including incomplete ascertainment of deaths and misclassification of cause of death or ethnicity (Pandey, Labarthe, Goff, Chan, and Nichaman, 2001). Studies that have validated the cause of death have yielded conflicting findings. Analyses of data from the Corpus Christi Heart Project found higher ischemic heart disease mortality in Hispanics of Mexican origin than in whites, especially among women (Pandy et al., 2001). A study based on data from the San Luis Valley Diabetics Study found similar ischemic heart disease mortality in both ethnic groups (Swenson et al., 2002). The controversy about how heart disease mortality in Hispanics compares with that in whites remains unsettled, and data from regional studies may not be generalizable.

Data on the incidence and prevalence of stroke in Hispanics also are scarce. In the Northern Manhattan Stroke Study, a population-based incidence study in the New York City area, the rates of stroke for Hispanics of all ages were twice as high as the rates for non-Hispanic whites (Jacobs, Boden-Albala, Lin, and Sacco, 2002; Sacco et al. 1998). (In this study, most of the Hispanics were presumably Puerto Ricans and Dominicans.) Several studies have found that Hispanics, including Hispanics in New York and in New Mexico, have a higher incidence than non-Hispanic whites of intracerebral hemorrhage (Bruno, Carter, Qualls, and Nolte, 1996; Frey, Jahnke, and Bulfinch, 1998; Sacco et al., 1998), suggesting an important role for uncontrolled hypertension. However, Hispanics and non-Hispanic whites have similar death rates after both ischemic and hemorrhagic stroke (Ayala et al., 2001).

In 2000, the age-adjusted death rates from strokes was 46.4 per 100,000 people for Hispanics and 59.0 per 100,000 people for non-Hispanic whites (National Center for Health Statistics, 2003). Interestingly, relative mortality rates from cerebrovascular disease vary by age. For people under age 65, Hispanics have higher mortality than non-Hispanic whites, whereas Hispanics older than age 65 have lower mortality than non-Hispanic whites in the same age group (Gillum, 1995; National Center for Health Statistics, 2003). Hispanics lost 207.8 potential years of life before age 75 from stroke, compared with 183.0 years for non-Hispanic whites.

Cancer

Cancer is a leading cause of death in all racial and ethnic groups. Registry data indicate that Hispanics experience overall lower cancer incidence rates than do non-Hispanic whites. Incidence rates are also lower among Hispanics for several major cancers, including cancer of the breast, lung, prostate, and colon and rectum. However, Hispanics have higher rates than non-Hispanic whites of certain cancers, including cervical and stomach cancer (Ramírez and Suárez, 2001).

Cancer mortality reflects differences in cancer incidence rates. In 2000, the age-adjusted death rate from cancer was 134.9 per 100,000 people among Hispanics, compared with 200.6 per 100,000 people among non-Hispanic whites. Hispanics also had lower mortality rates than non-Hispanic whites from cancers of the lung, breast, prostate, and colon and rectum. In addition, Hispanics lost fewer potential years of life before age

75 from cancer than non-Hispanic whites (1,098.2 versus 1,668.4 years of life lost per 100,000 people) (National Center for Health Statistics, 2003).

Activity Limitations from Chronic Conditions

Hispanics in general are less likely than non-Hispanic whites and non-Hispanic blacks to report activity limitations caused by chronic conditions. In 2001, the age-adjusted proportion of Hispanics reporting an activity limitation was 10.6 percent, compared with 12.1 percent for whites and 15.5 percent for blacks (National Center for Health Statistics, 2003). However, Hispanic seniors age 65 or older have higher rates of activity limitations and disability than their white counterparts (e.g., Markides and Rudkin, 1995).

Biological Risk Factors for Chronic Disease

Cholesterol Levels

Cholesterol levels are associated with the development of cardiovascular disease. Regional data from the 1980s indicate that Hispanics of Mexican origin had less favorable lipid profiles than non-Hispanic whites (e.g., Haffner, Stern, Hazuda, Rosenthal, and Knapp, 1986; Mitchell, Stern, Haffner, Hazuda, and Patterson, 1990). However, more recent data suggest that cholesterol levels for Hispanics are generally similar to those for non-Hispanic whites.

Pérez-Stable et al. (2001) summarized several studies based on the HHANES data. These studies found that total cholesterol levels were similar for men and women of Mexican, Puerto Rican, and Cuban origin, and that the levels for Hispanics compared favorably with those for non-Hispanic whites. More recent data from NHANES III and NHANES IV show similar or more favorable total cholesterol levels for men and women of Mexican origin compared with non-Hispanic whites. For instance, in NHANES IV the age-adjusted total cholesterol level for adult Mexican men less than 75 years old was 207 mg/dl, compared with 204 mg/dl for non-Hispanic white men. The age-adjusted total cholesterol level for Mexican women was 198 mg/dl, compared with 206 mg/dl for non-Hispanic white women (National Center for Health Statistics, 2003).

Lipoprotein fractions are generally similar for Hispanics of Mexican origin and non-Hispanic whites, although there are a few differences. Using NHANES III, Sundquist, Winkleby, and Pudaric (2001) found that the prevalence of high non-DL cholesterol (> 155 mg/dl) was 69 percent in Mexican-origin Hispanics age 65 or older, identical to the prevalence of 70 percent in whites. The prevalence of low-HDL cholesterol (< 40 mg/dl) was similar in Mexican-origin and white men of all ages. However, nearly one-half of Mexican-origin women between ages 20 and 64 had low HDL cholesterol levels, compared with less than 40 percent of white women (Park et al., 2003). Earlier data from HHANES found that Puerto Ricans were more likely than Mexicans or Cubans to have high-LDL and low-HDL cholesterol (Pérez-Stable et al., 2001).

Obesity

Overweight, defined as a body mass index (BMI) of 25 or more, and obesity, defined as a BMI of 30 or more, have reached epidemic proportions in the United States. The age-adjusted prevalence of obesity in the U.S. population rose from 22.9 percent in the early 1990s to 30.5 percent in 2000 (Flegal, Carroll, Ogden, and Johnson, 2002). Obesity increases the risk of diabetes, hypertension, cardiovascular disease, and premature mortality.

The rates of overweight and obesity have increased among Hispanics as well, and they remain higher in Hispanics than in non-Hispanic whites. For example, in NHANES III, 20.6 percent of adult men and 33.3 percent of adult women of Mexican origin were obese, compared with 19.9 percent and 22.7 percent of non-Hispanic white men and women, respectively. In the early waves of data from NHANES IV, 29.3 percent of men and 37.9 percent of women of Mexican origin were obese, compared with 27.2 percent and 30.3 percent of non-Hispanic white men and women (National Center for Health Statistics, 2003). Men and women of Mexican origin are also more likely than whites to be overweight.

Self-reported height and weight are less accurate than the actual measures obtained in NHANES. Nonetheless, self-reports from the 1997–2002 National Health Interview Survey (NHIS) allow us to compare rates of overweight and obesity across Hispanic national-origin groups. The data in Table 9-3 for Hispanics of Mexican origin and for non-Hispanic whites are consistent with the patterns observed in NHANES III and NHANES IV. The table also shows that rates of obesity are higher among Hispanics of Mexican or Puerto Rican origin than among Hispanics of Cuban origin and other Hispanics. In fact, the rates of obesity (BMI > 30) are similar for Cubans, other Hispanics, and whites, although the rates of overweight (BMI 25 to 30) are higher among Cubans and other Hispanics than among whites.

Table 9-4 reports data from 1997–2002 NHIS on rates of overweight and obesity among working-age Hispanics by sex, national origin, and nativity. For Hispanic men and women of Mexican origin and for other

TABLE 9-3 Body Mass Index by National Origin and Age

	Body Mass Index		
National Origin and Age (years)	< 25 (%)	25–30 (%)	> 30 (%)
All Hispanics			
18–44	41	38	21
45–64	28	44	29
> 64	36	44	20
Mexican			
18–44	37	40	23
45–64	23	45	33
> 64	33	45	22
Puerto Rican			
18–44	40	35	25
45–64	29	41	30
> 64	34	43	23
Cuban			
18–44	49	37	14
45–64	29	47	24
> 64	42	40	18
Other Hispanics			
18–44	47	37	16
45–64	35	43	22
> 64	40	44	16
Non-Hispanic whites			
18–44	51	32	16
45–64	37	40	24
> 64	44	38	18

SOURCE: 1997–2002 NHIS.

Hispanics, rates of obesity are higher for the U.S.-born than for the foreign-born. However, the findings for Hispanics of Cuban and Puerto Rican origin do not follow this pattern.

Recently, abdominal obesity, defined as a waist circumference of 102 centimeters (39.8 inches) or greater in men and 88 centimeters (34.3 inches) or greater in women, has been recognized as a risk factor for hypertension and abnormalities in glucose metabolism and lipid levels (Okosun, Liao, Rotimi, Prewitt, and Cooper, 2000; Okosun, Prewitt, and Cooper, 1999). In NHANES IV, men of Mexican origin had lower rates than non-Hispanic white men of abdominal obesity (35.5 versus 39.3 percent), whereas women of Mexican origin had higher rates of abdominal obesity than non-Hispanic white women (62.1 versus 53.6 percent). Nonetheless, temporal trends in abdominal obesity are ominous, especially for Mexican men. Between 1988 and 2000, the rate of abdominal obesity increased by 5.5 percentage points

TABLE 9-4 Body Mass Index for Hispanic Working-Age Adults By Sex, National Origin, and Nativity

	Body Mass Index					
	Men			Women		
National Origin and Nativity	< 25 (%)	25–30 (%)	± > 30 (%)	< 25 (%)	25–30 (%)	± > 30 (%)
All Hispanics						
Foreign-born	31	51	18	44	35	21
U.S.-born	29	46	26	44	31	26
Mexican						
Foreign-born	30	51	19	40	37	23
U.S.-born	26	46	28	39	32	29
Puerto Rican						
Foreign-born	29	44	27	39	35	27
U.S.-born	29	44	27	45	29	26
Cuban						
Foreign-born	29	50	21	41	41	18
U.S.-born	43	43	14	58	24	18
Other Hispanics						
Foreign-born	34	51	15	53	32	16
U.S.-born	32	47	21	51	30	19

SOURCE: 1997–2002 NHIS.

among men of Mexican origin, while it declined slightly among Mexican women (Okosun et al., 2003).

Abdominal obesity is also a component of the "metabolic syndrome," which is a strong risk factor for cardiovascular disease and includes impaired glucose tolerance, elevated blood pressure, elevated triglyceride levels, elevated levels of LDL cholesterol, and low levels of HDL cholesterol in addition to abdominal obesity. Using NHANES III, Ford, Giles, and Dietz (2002) found that Hispanics of Mexican origin had the highest age-adjusted prevalence of the metabolic syndrome (31.9 percent) of any racial or ethnic group. Mexican-origin women are more likely than non-Hispanic white or black women to have the metabolic syndrome, even after controlling for predisposing factors such as BMI, alcohol consumption, physical activity, and carbohydrate intake (Park et al., 2003).

Mental Health

Studies conducted since the 1980s have provided valuable information regarding the mental health of Hispanics in the United States. Early studies relied on standardized survey instruments to measure psychiatric symptoms and estimate "caseness" rates, defined as the proportion of persons with sufficient symptoms to indicate a need for treatment. The results of these studies were inconsistent (Vega and Alegría, 2001). However, a potential problem with these studies was that symptom scales measure transient or acute psychological distress rather than chronic psychiatric disorders using formal diagnostic criteria.

Later studies conducted in the 1980s were population studies that attempted to estimate the prevalence of psychiatric disorders, such as major depression, using diagnostic criteria derived from the Diagnostic and Statistical Manual of Mental Disorders (DSM). Three studies used the Diagnostic Interview Schedule: HHANES (Moscicki, Rae, Regier, and Locke, 1987), the Epidemiological Catchment Area study in Los Angeles (LAECA) (Burnam, Hough, Karno, Escobar, and Telles, 1987; Karno and Hough, 1987), and a study in Puerto Rico (Canino et al., 1987). These studies found that the rates of lifetime major depression among Mexicans in the Southwest (4.2 percent) and in Los Angeles (4.9 percent), Puerto Ricans on the island (4.6 percent), and Cubans in Miami (3.9 percent) were lower than those among non-Hispanic whites in Los Angeles (8.4 percent) or Puerto Ricans in the Northeast (8.9 percent). Moreover, in Los Angeles the rate for lifetime major depression among Mexican immigrants (3.3 percent) was about half the rate for the U.S.-born of Mexican origin (6.3 percent). Other psychiatric disorders were also more prevalent among U.S.-born Hispanics of Mexican origin and mainland-born Puerto Ricans than among Mexican immigrants and Puerto Ricans on the island.

Similarly, a 1995–1996 survey of adults of Mexican origin ages 18 to 59 in Fresno County, California, used the World Health Organization's Composite International Diagnostic Interview to estimate the rates of psychiatric disorders, permitting comparisons of rates of found in California with both the general U.S. population (as estimated by the National Comorbidity Study) and with survey results in Mexico City (Alderete, Vega, Kolody, and Aguilar-Gaxiola, 2000). The Fresno study reported lower rates of psychiatric disorders for immigrants than for U.S.-born Hispanics of Mexican origin; moreover, immigrants with fewer years in the United States had lower rates than those with longer duration of residence. In turn, the lower rates for recent immigrants were similar to those reported in Mexico City, whereas U.S.-born persons of Mexican origin had similar total lifetime rates as the general U.S. population.

The findings of these studies have raised intriguing questions about the role of acculturation in mental health among Hispanic adults in the United States. Vega and Alegría (2001) have interpreted the data to suggest that some Hispanics, such as Mexicans, Puerto Ricans, and Cubans, generally migrate to the United States with better mental health status than the U.S.

population as a whole. As they spend time in the United States, however, they develop an increased risk of mental health problems.

Health Behaviors

Diet

Studies of dietary intake patterns among non-Hispanic white and Hispanic adults have yielded a variety of interesting and sometimes conflicting findings. Data from NHANES III show that total energy intake was similar for non-Hispanic whites and Hispanics of Mexican origin. Total fat intake was higher among white men than among men of Mexican origin, but similar for white and Mexican-origin women. Dietary cholesterol intake was lower among white adults than among adults of Mexican origin (McDowell et al., 1994). In a community-based study of low-income adults and children, Winkleby, Albright, Howard-Pitney, Lin, and Fortmann (1994) found that, compared with non-Hispanic white adults, Hispanic adults consumed diets with less total fat, less saturated fat, more carbohydrates, and similar amounts of protein. By contrast, the San Antonio Heart Study found that men of Mexican origin consumed more saturated fat than white men. It is difficult to formulate valid generalizations regarding diet owing to the variety of complex, possibly regional influences on food preferences and on the ability to secure different types of food (e.g., Horowitz, Colson, Hebert, and Lancaster, 2004).

There is little research comparing dietary habits among Hispanic national-origin groups. In one study using HHANES data, Hispanics of Mexican origin had higher total fat and saturated fat intake than did Puerto Ricans or Cubans (Loria et al., 1995). Older Puerto Rican and Cuban adults met population guidelines for reducing chronic disease risk more often than any other group.

Multiple studies have shown that acculturation affects the dietary intake of Hispanics. Using data from the NHANES III, Dixon, Sundquist, and Winkleby (2000) found that Mexican immigrants met the recommended dietary guidelines or nutrient intakes more often than Hispanics of Mexican origin born in the United States. Winkleby et al. (1994) reported a graded relationship between acculturation and the intake of foods high in fat, including red meat, cheese, cured meats, and fried foods. In a study of Hispanics in rural Washington state, Neuhouser, Thompson, Coronado, and Solomon (2004) found that less acculturated Hispanics ate more fruits and vegetables and less fat than highly acculturated Hispanics and non-Hispanic whites.

Smoking

Hispanics have one of the lowest rates of cigarette smoking among racial and ethnic groups in the United States, and smoking prevalence has decreased during the past 10 to 15 years for most Hispanic subgroups (Marin, 2001). Moreover, the available data suggest that Hispanics smokers smoke fewer cigarettes per day than do non-Hispanic whites (Marin, 2001).

As shown in Table 9-5, data from the 1997–2002 NHIS are consistent with these patterns, although there are marked variations among Hispanic national-origin groups. The table shows that working-age Hispanics of Mexican origin and other Hispanics smoke at considerably lower rates than whites. Young adults (adults ages 18 to 44) of Cuban origin also have lower smoking rates than whites, whereas Puerto Ricans of all ages smoke at rates similar to those of whites. Consistent with these findings, Guendelman and

TABLE 9-5 Current Smoking by National Origin and Age

National Origin and Age (years)	% Current Smokers
All Hispanics	
18–44	20.2
45–64	20.2
> 64	9.9
Mexican	
18–44	18.5
45–64	19.4
> 64	9.9
Puerto Rican	
18–44	31.9
45–64	25.0
> 64	10.4
Cuban	
18–44	23.5
45–64	23.5
> 64	10.7
Other Hispanics	
18–44	18.6
45–64	18.4
> 64	9.2
Non-Hispanic whites	
18–44	30.8
45–64	25.1
> 64	10.6

SOURCE: 1997–2002 NHIS.

TABLE 9-6 Current Smoking by Hispanic Working-Age Adults, By Sex, National Origin, and Nativity

National Origin and Nativity	% Current Smokers	
	Men	Women
All Hispanics		
Foreign-born	24	10
U.S.-born	29	19
Mexican		
Foreign-born	23	8
U.S.-born	27	16
Puerto Rican		
Foreign-born	29	21
U.S.-born	39	28
Cuban		
Foreign-born	32	19
U.S.-born	26	17
Other Hispanics		
Foreign-born	21	9
U.S.-born	26	22

SOURCE: 1997–2002 NHIS.

Abrams (1994) reported that, among women of childbearing age, those of Mexican origin were less likely than white women to smoke.

Table 9-6 presents data on smoking by sex, national origin, and nativity from the 1997–2002 NHIS. The table shows that men and women born in Mexico, Puerto Rico, or other Hispanic countries are less likely than their U.S.-born counterparts to smoke. The difference in smoking rates between the foreign-born and the U.S.-born is especially marked among women of Mexican origin and other Hispanic women. In fact, smoking rates for foreign-born men of Mexican or other Hispanic origin are more than twice as high as the rates for their female counterparts, whereas the sex gap is much smaller for the U.S.-born in these national-origin groups. This pattern is not found among Hispanics of Cuban origin.

Other Health Behaviors

Hispanic men and women are less likely to drink alcohol than their non-Hispanic white counterparts. For example, in 2001, 61 percent of adult Hispanic men and 39 percent of Hispanic women reported being current drinkers, compared with 72 percent and 64 percent of white men and women, respectively (National Center for Health Statistics, 2003). Similar, Hispanics are slightly less likely than whites to use illicit drugs (National Center for Health Statistics, 2003).

Studies have shown a link between increasing acculturation and alcohol and drug use (e.g., Amaro, Whitaker, Coffman, and Heeren, 1990; Vega and Amaro, 1994). For example, in HHANES, marijuana use was five to eight times higher among highly acculturated Hispanics of Mexican origin and Puerto Ricans than among those who were not acculturated, controlling for other demographic factors. Other studies have documented adverse effects of acculturation among Hispanic groups with respect to cocaine use and alcohol consumption. The LAECA study in the 1980s found higher prevalence rates of drug abuse or dependence among U.S.-born Hispanics of Mexican origin than among Mexican immigrants, and among the latter, prevalence rates increased with longer residence in the United States (Burnam et al., 1987).

Studies have also reported adverse effects of acculturation among Hispanics of Mexican origin with respect to alcohol consumption (Gilbert, 1989; Markides, Krause, and Mendes de León, 1998), with the most pronounced effects found in women. Recently immigrated Mexican women have very low rates of alcohol abuse or dependence, but the prevalence of any alcohol abuse or dependence among U.S.-born women of Mexican origin is approximately five times greater than for immigrant women. Among men, the prevalence rate is approximately two times greater for the U.S.-born than for immigrants. Whereas in the general U.S. population heavy drinking and alcohol-related social problems tend to peak at ages 18 to 29 and to decline thereafter, these problems continue among Mexican-origin men in the United States at older ages.

Recent research has focused on the co-occurrence of alcohol, drug, and psychiatric disorders not related to substance use meeting DSM diagnostic criteria for mood disorder, anxiety disorder, or antisocial personality disorder. One study with a sample of Mexican-origin adults in central California (Vega, Sribney, and Achara-Abrahams, 2003) found that the prevalence of substance use disorders, consisting of alcohol or drug abuse or dependence, was highest among U.S.-born males (36 percent), followed by U.S.-born females (18 percent), immigrant males (17 percent), and immigrant females (2 percent). The prevalence of mood disorders ranged from a high of 22 percent among U.S.-born Mexican-origin women, to 15 percent for U.S.-born men, 9 percent for immigrant women, and a low of 7 percent for immigrant men. The study found co-occurring lifetime rates of alcohol or other drug disorder with nonsubstance-use psychiatric disorders of 12 percent for the U.S.-born and 3 percent for immigrants.

THE HEALTH AND HEALTH BEHAVIORS OF HISPANIC YOUTH

As discussed in the introduction to this chapter, Hispanic children and adolescents represent the largest and most rapidly growing minority group of youth in the United States. Youth of Mexican origin are by far the largest single national-origin group of Hispanic youth, numbering about 8 million and accounting for 62 percent of all Hispanic children and adolescents. Youth of Puerto Rican origin number nearly 1 million, accounting for 8 percent of Hispanic youth, while youth of Cuban origin number approximately 270,000 and account for 2 percent of Hispanic children and adolescents. Taken together, youth of Dominican, Central American, and South American origin number 1.5 million and account for 12 percent of Hispanic children and adolescents.

In this section, we review the data on the health status and health behaviors of Hispanic children and adolescents. We begin by summarizing the available information on two important chronic conditions—asthma and diabetes—and several other disorders that affect the well-being of Hispanic youth. We then discuss risk factors for chronic disease, including overweight, which is occurring in epidemic proportions among Hispanic youth and poses an enormous threat to the long-term health of Hispanics in the United States. Finally, we review the available data on the mental health of Hispanic youth.

Health Conditions

Diabetes

Type 1 diabetes accounts for the vast majority of cases of diabetes in childhood. The available information on the incidence of Type 1 diabetes among Hispanic youth is based on reports from individual cities. Puerto Rican children in Philadelphia have been reported to have higher incidence rates than non-Hispanic whites (Lipman, 1993; Lipman, Chang, and Murphy, 2003), whereas Hispanic children of Mexican origin in Southern California have been reported to have lower rates than whites (Gay et al., 1989; Lorenzi, Cagliero, and Schmidt, 1985). Hispanics in Chicago have been reported to have higher death rates from Type 1 diabetes than whites (Lipton, Good, Mikhailov, Freels, and Donoghue, 1999).

Historically, Type 2 diabetes has been exceedingly infrequent in childhood. However, although national data are lacking, several case reports point to the rising prevalence of Type 2 diabetes among Hispanic children. A research group in California reported that among low-income diabetic Hispanic children treated between 1990 and 1994, 31 percent had Type 2 diabetes (Neufeld, Raffel, Landon, Chen, and Vadheim, 1998). A pediatric research group in Florida reported that the proportion of patients with

Type 2 diabetes among all newly diagnosed cases of diabetes increased from 9.4 to 20 percent between 1994 and 1998. Hispanic ethnicity was an important risk factor for Type 2 diabetes in this cohort (Macaluso et al., 2002). Another study reported an annual average increase of 9 percent per year in the prevalence of early Type 2 diabetes among Hispanic and non-Hispanic black children between 1985 and 1994 (Keenan et al., 2000). The rising prevalence of Type 2 diabetes in minority children has been a topic of several recently published literature reviews (Dabelea, Pettitt, Lee Jones, and Arslanian, 1999; Fagot-Campagna, 2000; Rosenbloom, Joe, Young, and Winter, 1999). Lower levels of physical activity combined with unhealthy diets have been identified as important underlying causes for rising rates of overweight and diabetes in Hispanic children and adolescents (Gordon-Larsen, Adair, and Popkin, 2002; Gordon-Larsen, Harris, Ward, and Popkin, 2003).

Asthma

Asthma affects a disproportionate number of Hispanic children. In one large study of East Coast families, the percentage of families with at least one asthmatic child was 25 percent for Hispanics (mainly Puerto Rican), 18 percent for non-Hispanic blacks, and 10 percent for non-Hispanic whites (Beckett, Belanger, Gent, Holford, and Leaderer, 1996). Asthma affects different national-origin groups of Hispanic children unequally. Nearly two-thirds of the half million Hispanic children with asthma are Puerto Rican, and Puerto Rican children have the highest prevalence of asthma (11 percent) of any racial or ethnic group in the United States (Carter-Pokras and Gergen, 1993). By contrast, only 3 percent of children of Mexican origin and 5 percent of children of Cuban origin have asthma (Carter-Pokras and Gergen, 1993). In a study of asthma in New York City, Puerto Rican children had a significantly higher prevalence of asthma than Dominicans or other Hispanics living in the same buildings (Ledogar, Penchaszadeth, Iglesias Garden, and Garden Acosta, 2000). The reasons for such dramatic differences in asthma prevalence across national-origin groups remain unclear. On one hand, it has been suggested that Puerto Rican children may have a genetic predisposition to asthma not shared by other racial and ethnic groups in the United States (Flores and Zambrana, 2001); on the other hand, the social context of Puerto Ricans in the United States differs in multiple ways from that of other Hispanic groups.

Oral Health

Poor oral health is associated with a variety of adverse health outcomes in children and adolescents, including lower quality of life, poor nutritional status, and worse educational outcomes (Mouradian, Wehr, and Crall, 2000). In NHANES III, 34.9 percent of 2- to 5-year-olds and 37.2 percent of 6- to 17-year-old youth of Mexican origin had untreated caries, compared with 14.4 and 18.9 percent of non-Hispanic white youth, respectively (National Center for Health Statistics, 1999). Migrant and rural Hispanic children are at especially high risk for poor oral health and low rates of restored teeth. Among migrant Hispanic children ages 5 to 14, the mean proportion of teeth with carious surfaces is 65 percent compared with 17 percent for schoolchildren in the United States, and only 20 percent of Hispanic children in rural areas have restored dental surfaces compared with 76 percent of schoolchildren nationwide (National Institute of Dental Research, 1989). There is little information available about oral health in Hispanic children other than those of Mexican origin.

Lead Poisoning

Lead poisoning is the most common environmental health problem among children in the United States (Flores and Zambrana, 2001). High blood lead levels are associated with learning disabilities and impaired cognitive development. Lead exposure is a serious problem among Hispanic children living in the United States. Using NHANES III data, Morales, Gutierrez, and Escarce (2005) found that 6, 4, and 2 percent of youth of Mexican origin ages 1 to 4, 5 to 11, and 12 to 17, respectively, had blood lead levels exceeding 10 μg/dL, the current threshold for intervention. In addition, 29, 19, and 12 percent of these age groups, respectively, had blood lead levels exceeding 5 μg/dL, which is being considered by the Centers for Disease Control and Prevention as a new threshold based on recent data on the neuropsychiatric effects of low lead levels. A study using data from Florida found that the prevalence of elevated blood lead levels, defined as exceeding 10 μg/dL, was nearly three times higher among Hispanic than among non-Hispanic 2-year-olds (Hopkins, Quimbo, and Watkins, 1995). A potential source of lead exposure is traditional remedies used by immigrant parents (Flores and Zambrana, 2001).

Risk Factors for Chronic Disease

Risk of Overweight and Overweight

Risk of overweight and overweight have become major health problems for Hispanic youth in the United States. Data from three NHANES surveys since the mid-1970s indicate that the prevalence of overweight (defined as BMI > 95th percentile for age and sex) among youth of Mexican origin has grown dramatically over the last 25 years (Figure 9-1). Between

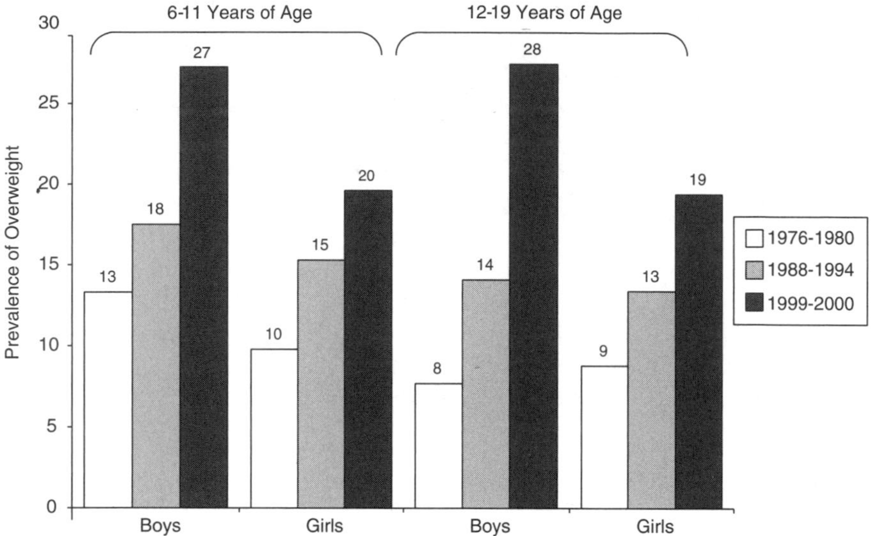

FIGURE 9-1 Time trends in overweight among children and adolescents of Mexican origin, 1976 to 2000.
SOURCE: National Center for Health Statistics (2003).

1976–1980 and 1999–2000 the prevalence of overweight in Mexican-origin youth rose from 13 to 27 percent for boys ages 6 to 11, from 10 to 20 percent for girls ages 6 to 11, from 8 to 28 percent for boys ages 12 to 19, and from 9 to 19 percent for girls ages 12 to 19 (National Center for Health Statistics, 2003). Current rates of overweight for girls of Mexican origin are nearly twice as high as rates for non-Hispanic white girls, and rates for Mexican-origin boys are more than twice as high as rates for white boys (National Center for Health Statistics, 2003). Strauss and Pollack (2001) confirmed the rapid rise in overweight among Hispanic youth using data from the National Longitudinal Survey of Youth. Using data from NHANES IV, Ogden, Flegal, Carroll, and Johnson (2002) found that 39 percent of boys and girls of Mexican origin ages 6 to 11 and 44 percent of boys and girls ages 12 to 19 were at risk of overweight (defined as BMI > 85th percentile). The same study found that only 26 percent of white boys and girls ages 6 to 11 and 27 percent of white boys and girls ages 12 to 19 were at risk of overweight.

Previous studies have found that nativity is associated with risk of overweight and overweight among Hispanic children and adolescents. For example, in an analysis of data from the National Longitudinal Study of Adolescent Health (Add-Health), which includes a nationally representa-

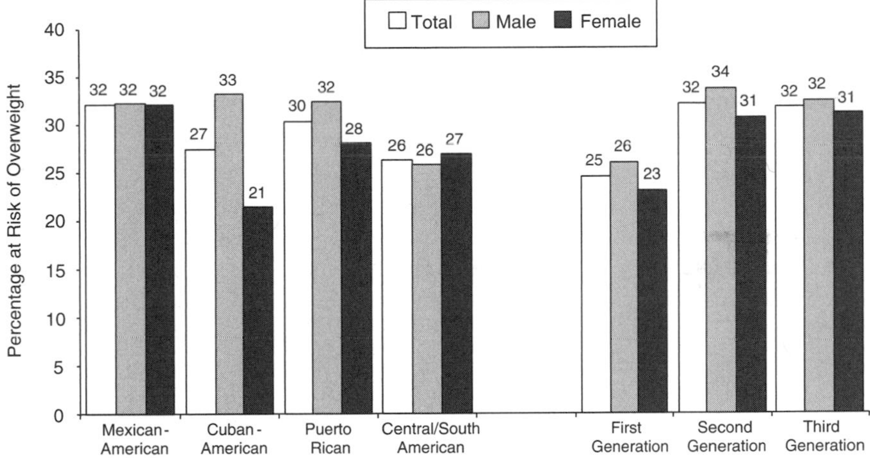

FIGURE 9-2 Risk of overweight among Hispanic adolescents by national-origin group and generational status.
SOURCE: Popkin and Udry (1998).

tive sample of adolescents in grades 7 to 12, Popkin and Udry (1998) found that second- and third-generation Hispanic adolescents were more likely to be at risk of overweight (defined as BMI > 85th percentile) than their first-generation counterparts. And 26 percent of first-generation adolescent boys and 23 percent of first-generation adolescent girls were at risk of overweight, compared with 33 percent of second- and third-generation boys and 31 percent of second- and third-generation girls (Figure 9-2). They also found significant differences across Hispanic national-origin groups. Thus adolescents of Mexican and Puerto Rican origin were the most likely to be at risk of overweight, while Cuban girls and boys and girls of Central American or South American origin had lower rates (Figure 9-2).

Gordon-Larsen et al. (2003) used the Add-Health data to analyze the association between measures of acculturation, such as language spoken at home, duration of residence in the United States, and the proportion of foreign-born neighbors, on one hand, and overweight and overweight-related behaviors, on the other. They found that acculturation was associated with rates of overweight among first-generation adolescents of Mexican, Puerto Rican, and Cuban origin. However, acculturation was unassociated with rates of overweight in second-generation Hispanic adolescents. Gordon-Larsen et al. (2003) also found rapid acculturation of overweight-related behaviors, such as diet and physical inactivity. Taken together, the studies by Popkin and Udry (1998) and Gordon-Larsen et al. (2003) suggest that measures of acculturation, such as language spoken at home and length of residence in the United States, capture the critical dimensions of acculturation that affect weight among first-generation Hispanic youth. Among second- and third-generation youth, however, generation per se is a better indicator than other acculturation measures of the behaviors that influence weight.

Childhood obesity has important health consequences in childhood and adulthood. Several studies have found that of childhood obesity persists into adulthood (Rolland-Cachera et al., 1987; Serdula et al., 1993; Siervogel, Roche, Guo, Mukherjee, and Chumlea, 1991), and that the likelihood of obesity in adulthood is greater for obese adolescents (Guo, Roche, Chumlea, Gardner, and Siervogel, 1994). Childhood obesity in Hispanic children is also associated with abnormal glucose metabolism, as manifested by resistance to the glucose-lowering effects of insulin and impaired glucose tolerance (Cruz et al., 2004; Sinha et al., 2002). Insulin resistance and impaired glucose tolerance are intermediate stages in the natural history of Type 2 diabetes (Polonsky, Sturis, and Bell, 1996) and predict the risk of developing diabetes (Edelstein et al., 1997) and cardiovascular disease (Haffner, Stern, Hazuda, Mitchell, and Patterson, 1990). In one study, 28 percent of overweight Hispanic children with a family history of diabetes were found to have impaired glucose tolerance (Goran et al., 2004). Obesity is also associated with other risk factors for atherosclerosis.

Risk Factors for Atherosclerosis

A number of recent studies have documented high levels of risk factors for atherosclerosis and cardiovascular disease among Hispanic youth, and especially among youth of Mexican origin. The risk factors that have been studied include blood pressure, fasting insulin levels, insulin resistance, and lipid levels.

Studies comparing blood pressure in Hispanic and non-Hispanic white children and adolescents have yielded conflicting results. However, several recent reports have found higher average blood pressure in youth of Mexican origin than in white youth. Using NHANES IV, Muntner, He, Cutler, Wildman, and Whelton (2004) found that mean age-adjusted systolic blood pressure was 2.7 mm Hg higher among Mexican-origin boys ages 8 to 17 than among their white peers. Other studies based on small regional samples have similarly found higher blood pressures in children and adolescents of Mexican origin than in white youth (Menard, Park, and Yuan, 1999; Sorof, Lai, Turner, Poffenbarger, and Portman, 2004; Tortolero et al., 1997). Muntner et al. (2004) also found that blood pressure in children and adolescents had increased over the last decade, and that the increase was partially attributable to the rising prevalence of overweight.

Recent studies have documented higher fasting insulin levels and more frequent indicators of insulin resistance and glucose intolerance among Hispanic than white children and adolescents (Reaven, Nader, Berry, and Hoy, 1998; Shea et al., 2003; Tortolero et al., 1997; Winkleby, Robinson, Sundquist, and Kraemer, 1999). In addition, several researchers have reported that Hispanic youth have higher triglyceride levels and lower levels of HDL cholesterol than white youth (e.g., Reaven et al., 1998; Tortolero et al., 1997). Reaven et al. (1998) found that multiple risk factors for atherosclerosis are more likely to occur together in children of Mexican origin than in white children. The available evidence suggests that the differences between Hispanic and white youth in the prevalence of these risk factors for atherosclerosis are at least partly explained by differences in BMI.

Health Behaviors

Physical Activity

Lower levels of physical activity combined with unhealthy diets have been identified as important underlying causes for rising rates of obesity and diabetes in Hispanic children and adolescents (Gordon-Larsen et al., 2002, 2003). In Add-Health, Hispanic adolescent boys were less likely than white boys to engage in low-intensity bouts of physical activity, and Hispanic adolescent girls were less likely than white girls to engage in both low-intensity and high-intensity physical activity. Hispanic adolescent girls also spent more time than white girls engaged in sedentary activities, such as television watching (Gordon-Larsen et al., 2002).

National health surveys have also found differences between Hispanic and non-Hispanic white children and adolescents in levels of physical activity. Based on data from the 1992 National Health Interview Survey-Youth Risk Behavior Survey, 49 percent of Hispanics ages 12 to 21, compared with 55 percent of non-Hispanic whites, reported vigorous or moderate physical activity lasting at least 20 minutes on at least 3 of 7 days during the preceding week (Surgeon General's Report on Physical Activity and Health, 1996). Similarly, results from a national school-based survey of students in grades 9 to 12 indicate that 57 percent of Hispanic youth, compared with 67 percent of non-Hispanic white youth, participated in vigorous or moderate physical activity on 3 of 7 days in the preceding week (Surgeon General's Report on Physical Activity and Health, 1996).

Diet

The existing research suggests that acculturation is associated with worse dietary habits among Hispanics of all ages (Dixon et al., 2000; Guendelman and Abrams, 1995; Schaffer, Velie, Shaw, and Todoroff, 1998;

Siega-Riz and Popkin, 2001). Although few studies have focused on the dietary habits of Hispanic children and adolescents, they tend to show that immigrant children have better dietary habits that their U.S.-born counterparts. For example, in Add-Health, foreign-born adolescents of Mexican origin reported higher intake of rice, beans, fruits, and vegetables and lower intake of fast foods and cheese than their U.S.-born counterparts (Gordon-Larsen et al., 2003). Gordon-Larsen et al. (2003) also found that island-born Puerto Rican adolescents had higher intake of fruits and milk than their mainland-born counterparts, while foreign-born Cuban adolescents had higher fruit intake than their U.S.-born peers.

In a study based on older HHANES data, there were no significant differences in daily intake between foreign-born and U.S.-born Hispanic children ages 2 to 5 (Mendoza and Dixon, 1999). However, among 6- to 11-year-olds, foreign-born children of Mexican origin consumed more bread, vegetables, and fruits and fewer servings of added fat than their U.S.-born peers; no differences were seen between mainland- and island-born Puerto Rican school-age children or between U.S.-born and foreign-born Cuban children (Mendoza and Dixon, 1999). Among adolescents, foreign-born Mexicans consumed more bread, vegetables, and fruits and less added fat than their U.S.-born counterparts; island-born Puerto Rican adolescents consumed less milk and added fat than their U.S.-born counterparts; and foreign-born Cuban adolescents consumed more fruits and vegetables than their U.S.-born peers (Mendoza and Dixon, 1999).

Smoking, Alcohol, and Drugs

Multiple studies have shown high rates of tobacco use, alcohol consumption, and illicit drug among Hispanic adolescents. For example, the Monitoring the Future study found that, in 2002, 39 percent of Hispanic adolescents in twelfth grade reported use of any illicit drug in the past 12 months, 48 percent reported consumption of alcohol in the past 30 days, and 21 percent reported smoking at least one cigarette in the past 30 days (Johnston, O'Malley, and Bachman, 2003). Rates of drug use and alcohol consumption for Hispanics were comparable to those for non-Hispanic whites but higher than for non-Hispanic blacks; smoking rates for Hispanics were lower than for whites but higher than for blacks (Figure 9-3). In an earlier analysis, 25 percent of Hispanic tenth-graders reported heavy drinking and drug use in the last 30 days, a proportion comparable to whites (Johnston, O'Malley, and Bachman, 1998).

In analyses of data for a nationally representative sample of high school seniors, youth of Cuban origin and whites were found to have the highest levels of tobacco, alcohol, and illicit drug use, followed by youth of Mexican origin and youth of Puerto Rican origin. Hispanic youth from

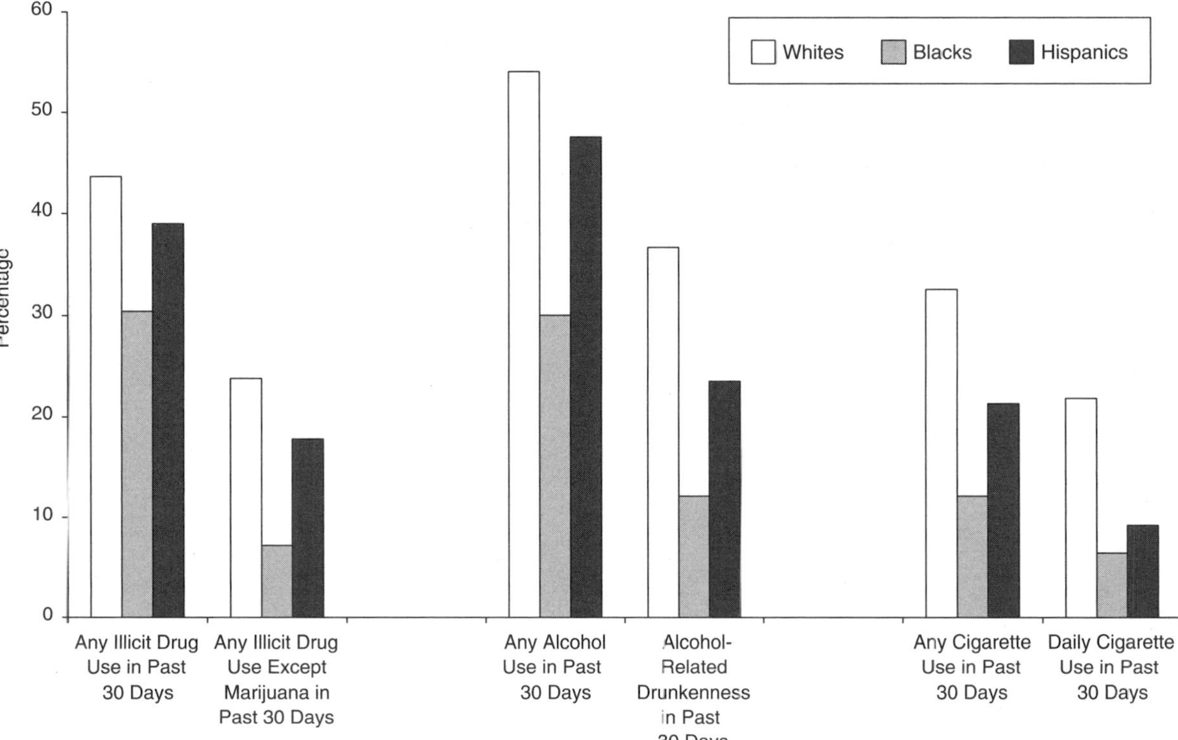

FIGURE 9-3 Illicit drug use, alcohol consumption, and tobacco use among twelfth graders, by race and ethnicity, 2002.
SOURCE: Johnston et al. (2003).

other Latin American countries had low levels of drug use (Wallace et al., 2002). Specifically, 33 percent of Cuban-origin youth reported any illicit drug use in the past 30 days, compared with 26 percent of youth of Mexican or Puerto Rican origin and 19 percent of other Hispanics. And 57 percent of Cuban-origin youth reported smoking in the past 30 days, compared with 51 percent of Mexican-origin youth, 45 percent of Puerto Ricans, and 48 percent of other Hispanics. And 30 percent of Cuban-origin youth reported having a drink in the past 30 days, compared with 26 percent of Mexican-origin youth, 30 percent of Puerto Ricans, and 25 percent of other Hispanics.

Acculturation is associated with higher rates of cigarette smoking, particularly among Hispanic girls (e.g., Casas et al., 1998; Epstein, Botvin, and Díaz, 1998; Gordon-Larsen et al., 2003; Landrine, Richardson, Klonoff, and Flay, 1994), and greater drug use among Hispanic boys and girls (e.g., Blake, Ledsky, Goodenow, and O'Donnell, 2001; Epstein, Botvin, and Díaz, 2001; Gfroerer and Tan, 2003; Kulis, Marsiglia, and Hurdle, 2003). However, the handful of studies that address acculturation and alcohol consumption among Hispanic adolescents have not found a consistent relationship. In some studies acculturation was unassociated with alcohol consumption (Elder et al., 2000), in others more acculturated adolescents were more likely to drink (Brindis, Wolfe, McCarter, Ball, and Starbuck-Morales, 1995; Polednak, 1997), and in still others more acculturated adolescents were less likely to drink (Nielsen and Ford, 2001).

Teenage Childbearing

Hispanic girls have higher rates of teenage childbearing than non-Hispanic white girls. In 2001, 5.8 percent of live births to Hispanic women were to girls younger than age 18, compared with 2.3 percent of births to white women (Martin et al., 2002). Puerto Ricans had the highest proportion of births to girls younger than age 18 (7.4 percent), followed by Mexicans (6.2 percent), Central and South Americans (3.1 percent), and Cubans (2.7 percent). Foreign-born Hispanic mothers from all national-origin groups are much less likely to be teenagers than their U.S.-born peers (Martin et al., 2002).

Mental Health

Studies suggest that Hispanic youth, and especially youth of Mexican origin, have the highest prevalence of depression of any ethnic group (Doi, Roberts, Takeuchi, and Suzuki, 2001; Knight, Virdin, Ocampo, and Roosa, 1994; Roberts and Chen, 1995). A study in Texas found that 31 percent of adolescent girls of Mexican origin had depressive symptoms, compared with 16 percent of non-Hispanic white girls (Emslie, Weinberg, Rush, Adams, and Rintelmann, 1990). In 1999, 26 percent of Hispanic adolescent girls reported considering suicide, compared with 23 percent of non-Hispanic white adolescent girls (National Center for Health Statistics, 2000), and 20 percent of Hispanic adolescent girls attempted suicide, compared with 9 percent of white adolescent girls (National Center for Health Statistics, 2000). Although injurious suicide attempts were also higher among Hispanic adolescent girls (5 percent) than non-Hispanic whites (2 percent) (National Center for Health Statistics, 2000), Hispanic adolescents complete suicide at lower rates than youth of other ethnic groups (Canino and Roberts, 2000).

Among Hispanics, foreign-born youth experience lower self-esteem and higher levels of suicidal thoughts than U.S.-born youth (e.g., Portes and Rumbaut, 2001). However, U.S.-born Hispanic youth exhibit more serious health risk behaviors and conduct problems than foreign-born youth.

BIRTH OUTCOMES

Hispanic women have higher fertility rates than non-Hispanic white and non-Hispanic black women (Giachello, 2001). For example, in 2001 Hispanics had 96.0 births per 1,000 women ages 15 to 44, compared with 57.7 births for white women and 69.1 births for black women (National Center for Health Statistics, 2003). However, there is enormous variation in fertility across Hispanic national-origin groups. Thus women of Mexican origin have the highest fertility rates of all ethnic groups in the United States, whereas women of Cuban origin have the lowest rates (Giachello, 2001).

Hispanics generally have excellent birth outcomes. In 2001, 6.47 percent of live births to Hispanic mothers were low birthweight (< 2,500 grams) and 1.14 percent were very low birthweight (< 1,500 grams), compared with 6.76 and 1.17 percent, respectively, of live births to non-Hispanic white mothers and 13.07 and 3.08 percent, respectively, of live births to non-Hispanic black mothers. Of the Hispanic national-origin groups, mothers of Mexican origin have the lowest rates of low-birthweight and very-low-birthweight infants and Puerto Rican mothers have the highest rates.

Infant mortality rates are also lower for Hispanic women than for non-Hispanic whites and non-Hispanic blacks (Table 9-7). As with fertility rates and low birthweight births, there is considerable variation in infant mortality rates across Hispanic national-origin groups. Hispanics of Cuban origin have among the lowest infant mortality rates in the United States, and Hispanics of Mexican and Central American or South American origin have low rates as well. By contrast, infants of Puerto Rican mothers have

TABLE 9-7 Infant, Neonatal, and Postneonatal Mortality Rates for Non-Hispanic White, Non-Hispanic Black, and Hispanic Mothers, 2000

Race and Hispanic Origin of Mother	Infant Deaths per 1,000 Live Births	Neonatal Deaths per 1,000 Live Births	Postneonatal Deaths per 1,000 Live Births
Non-Hispanic white	5.7	3.8	1.9
Non-Hispanic blacks	13.6	9.2	4.4
Hispanic	5.6	3.8	1.8
Mexican	5.4	3.6	1.8
Puerto Rican	8.2	5.8	2.4
Cuban	4.5	3.2	n.a.
Central and South American	4.6	3.3	1.4
Other and unknown Hispanic or Latino	6.9	4.6	2.3

NOTE: n.a. = not available.
SOURCE: National Center for Health Statistics (2003).

relatively high death rates (Table 9-7). The low infant mortality rates for Mexican and Central American women, and especially for immigrant women from these countries, have attracted a great deal of attention because they are unexpected in the context of these women's low socioeconomic status. These findings are discussed in greater detail in the next section.

THE EPIDEMIOLOGICAL PARADOX

The term "epidemiological paradox" refers to a consistent finding in the research literature that, on certain measures of health, Hispanics in the United States have more favorable indicators than non-Hispanic whites. This finding is considered paradoxical because, as discussed earlier in this volume, Hispanics in the United States have much less favorable socioeconomic profiles than whites. A large body of research has demonstrated a positive, graded relationship between socioeconomic status and health (Adler and Ostrove, 1999; Feinstein, 1993).

There have been numerous studies to confirm and attempt to understand the causes of the epidemiological paradox since it was first described. In this section, we review the evidence for the epidemiological paradox in two main indicators of health: adult mortality and birth outcomes. We also discuss proposed explanations for the epidemiological paradox and how they might apply to adult mortality and birth outcomes.

Adult Mortality

Studies that have compared the mortality experience of Hispanic adults, in the aggregate, and non-Hispanic white adults have consistently found that Hispanics have similar or lower mortality rates after adjusting for age and sex differences in the populations (e.g., Elo and Preston, 1997; Liao et al., 1998; Singh and Siahpush, 2001; Sorlie et al., 1993). These studies also indicate that the Hispanic mortality advantage widens with age. For example, using data from the National Longitudinal Mortality Study (NLMS), Sorlie et al. (1993) found that age-adjusted mortality rates for Hispanic men and women age 45 or older were 18 to 28 percent lower than the rates for their white counterparts; mortality rates were similar for Hispanics and whites ages 25 to 44. Using NLMS data, Elo and Preston (1997) also documented that Hispanic mortality advantage widens after controlling for socioeconomic status. This is unsurprising given the established inverse relationship between socioeconomic status and mortality.

Several studies have attempted to further understanding of the epidemiological paradox by examining mortality differences between Hispanics and non-Hispanic whites by national-origin group or nativity or both (e.g., Abraido-Lanza, Dohrenwend, Ng-Mak, and Turner, 1999; Hummer, Rogers, Amir, Forbes, and Frisbie, 2000; Palloni and Arias, 2004; Singh and Siahpush, 2001; Sorlie et al., 1993). Although the precise findings of these studies differ, in general they suggest that the evidence of an epidemiological paradox in mortality is much stronger for some groups of Hispanics than for others. For instance, Hummer et al. (2000) used the National Health Interview Survey-Multiple Cause of Death (NHIS-MCD) linked data file to examine mortality differences between non-Hispanic whites, on one hand, and Hispanics of Mexican, Puerto Rican, Cuban, Central American or South American, and other Hispanic origin, on the other. They found a sizable mortality advantage for Hispanics of Mexican, Central American or South American, and other Hispanic origin in analyses that controlled for age, sex, and socioeconomic status, but not for Puerto Ricans or Cubans. In addition, they found lower mortality among foreign-born compared with U.S.-born Hispanics. Using the NLMS, Abraido-Lanza et al. (1999) found that Hispanics of Mexican, Puerto Rican, Cuban, and other Hispanic origin all had lower mortality than whites after controlling for age, sex, and socioeconomic status. Among Hispanics of Mexican or other Hispanic origin, moreover, the mortality advantage extended to both the foreign-born and the U.S.-born.

Palloni and Arias (2004) recently published the most detailed analysis to date of mortality differences between Hispanic and non-Hispanic white adults. Using the NHIS-MCD linked data file, these investigators examined mortality over a nine-year period for adults age 35 and older. They found that, controlling for demographic characteristics and socioeconomic status, only foreign-born men and women of Mexican and other Hispanic origin experienced a mortality advantage when compared with non-Hispanic whites. There were no significant differences in mortality between non-Hispanic whites, on one hand, and either U.S.-born Mexicans, U.S.-born other Hispanics, foreign-born or U.S.-born Puerto Ricans, or foreign-born or U.S.-born Cubans, on the other.

Three explanations have been proposed for the epidemiological paradox in adult mortality. The first explanation attributes the findings to data artifacts. Vital statistics data, in particular, may understate mortality for Hispanics. Mortality rates based on vital statistics data are drawn from two distinct sources. The denominator for the rates is drawn from census data in which individuals self-identify their race and ethnicity; the numerator, by contrast, is drawn from death certificates on which proxy respondents identify the race and ethnicity of decedents. Previous research has shown that Hispanics are underidentified on death certificates, resulting in underreporting of Hispanic deaths (Rosenberg et al., 1999). Of note, this explanation may apply to both foreign-born and U.S.-born Hispanics. However, it does not affect the NMLS or NHIS-MCD data, in which individuals self-identified their race and ethnicity at baseline and this information was subsequently linked with death certificates.

The second explanation attributes the epidemiological paradox to selective migration in and out of the United States. Proponents of the selective migration explanation have termed selective in- and out-migration the "healthy-migrant effect" and the "salmon-bias effect," respectively (Abraido-Lanza et al., 1999). The healthy-migrant effect posits that Hispanic migrants are selected from their native populations based on certain traits, including better physical and mental health (Abraido-Lanza et al., 1999; Palloni and Morenoff, 2001). The salmon-bias effect posits that some foreign-born Hispanic subgroups may have a propensity to return to their country of origin following periods of unemployment or poor health (Abraido-Lanza et al., 1999). The net impact of the healthy-migrant and salmon-bias effects is to produce a foreign-born Hispanic population in the United States with a more favorable health profile than non-Hispanic whites. The healthy-migrant and salmon-bias effects may apply to foreign-born Hispanics but not to the U.S.-born. Moreover, the salmon-bias effect is expected to be a factor mainly for immigrants from countries of origin to which return migration is feasible and easy, especially Mexico (Palloni and Arias, 2004).

The third explanation attributes the epidemiological paradox to social and cultural characteristics that differentiate Hispanics from whites, rather than to selection. According to this explanation, Hispanics benefit from protective social and cultural characteristics that operate by positively influencing individual health and lifestyle behaviors, family structure, and social networks (e.g., Abraido-Lanza et al., 1999; Sorlie et al., 1993). Drawing on this perspective, acculturation research has sought to examine the effects of cultural assimilation on the health of Hispanics as the behavioral and social norms typical of their home culture are replaced by those more typical of the United States. In general, the literature suggests that the effects of acculturation on health behaviors are negative, although these effects depend on the specific behavior and study population under investigation. Protective social and cultural characteristics are expected to exert a stronger effect on the health of foreign-born than U.S.-born Hispanics, since these characteristics are lost with acculturation.

To date, a definitive explanation for the epidemiological paradox in adult mortality remains elusive. In their recent study, Palloni and Arias (2004) claimed to find indirect evidence of a salmon-bias effect to account for the mortality advantage of Mexican immigrants relative to whites, but they could not account for the mortality advantage experienced by the foreign-born of other Hispanic origin. Furthermore, using a variety of indirect tests, they found no evidence of healthy-migrant or acculturation effects. By contrast, Abraido-Lanza et al. (1999) interpreted the results of their mortality analyses as providing no evidence of either a healthy-migrant effect or a salmon-bias effect. Instead, they emphasized the possibility that their findings were due to protective effects of cultural factors. Finally, Jasso, Massey, Rosenzweig, and Smith (2004) interpreted data on health status and life expectancy from a variety of sources as offering strong evidence of a healthy-migrant effect among Hispanic immigrants to the United States.

Birth Outcomes

The epidemiological paradox is also manifested in birth outcomes, including rates of low birthweight and infant mortality. Overall, birth outcomes for Hispanic women are much better than expected given their socioeconomic status. For instance, in 2001 the infant mortality rate (IMR) for Hispanics was 5.4 per 1,000 live births, compared with 5.7 for non-Hispanic whites and 13.5 for non-Hispanic blacks (Mathews, Menacker, and MacDorman, 2003). Among Hispanic national-origin groups, Cubans (4.2) and Central/South Americans (5.0) had the lowest IMRs followed by Mexicans (5.2) and Puerto Ricans (8.5), who were the only group with an IMR above that for whites. Previous studies using regional and national data have consistently found similar results (e.g., Landale, Oropesa, and Gorman, 1999; Williams, Binkin, and Clingman, 1986).

Notably, Hispanic immigrant women have lower IMRs than their U.S.-born peers, despite having lower incomes and educational attainment (Mathews et al., 2003). For example, in 2001, the IMRs for foreign-born and U.S.-born women of Mexican origin were 4.7 and 5.9, respectively.

The IMRs for island-born and mainland-born Puerto Rican women were 7.8 and 8.8, respectively; the IMRs for foreign-born and U.S.-born women of Cuban origin were 3.8 and 4.7, respectively; and the IMRs foreign-born and U.S.-born women of Central American or South American origin were 4.9 and 5.3, respectively.

As with the findings for adult mortality, the main explanations that have been posited for the favorable birth outcomes among Hispanic women include selective migration and protective effects of cultural and social characteristics. To assess the role of selective migration, Weeks, Rumbaut, and Ojeda (1999) compared the pregnancy outcomes of Mexican immigrant women who delivered in San Diego; Mexican women who delivered just across the border in Tijuana, Mexico; U.S.-born women of Mexican origin who delivered in San Diego; and non-Hispanic whites. They found that Mexican women who delivered in Tijuana had the lowest rate of low-birthweight births, and they interpreted this finding as evidence against selective migration to the United States by healthier women or return migration to Mexico by women with poor outcomes.

Evidence for the protective effects of cultural characteristics comes from studies suggesting that acculturation has negative effects on birth outcomes and on behaviors associated with favorable birth outcomes. For example, Guendelman and Abrams (1995) found that immigrant Mexican women of childbearing age had a lower risk of eating a poor diet than U.S.-born women of Mexican origin, whose nutrient intake resembled that of non-Hispanic whites. Using data from the Fragile Families and Child Well-being Study, Kimbro, Lynch, and McLanahan (2004) found that nearly 90 percent of immigrant Mexican mothers breastfed their infants, compared with two-thirds of second-generation and just over half of third-generation women of Mexican origin. Additional analyses found that as acculturation (measured using a 7-item scale) increased, the probability of breastfeeding declined. Other studies have found that, compared with Mexican-born women, U.S.-born women are significantly more likely to have diets lower in fruits and cereals and higher in fats and milk products, to smoke, and to abuse drugs and alcohol (Rumbaut and Weeks, 1996, 1998).

CONCLUSIONS

This review of the health and health behaviors of Hispanics in the United States has uncovered several major themes. To begin, the Hispanic population is far from monolithic with respect to these outcomes. Research has documented important differences in health and health behaviors by national origin, nativity and generation, and measures of acculturation. Hispanics of Puerto Rican origin tend to have worse health status indicators than other national-origin groups, including higher mortality and less favorable birth outcomes. Conversely, Hispanics of Mexican and Central American or South American origin often exhibit favorable health indicators despite low socioeconomic status. Studies have found lower mortality, better birth outcomes, healthier diets, lower rates of overweight and obesity, and other favorable outcomes among foreign-born compared with U.S.-born Hispanics from most national-origin groups.

Within this variation, our review has documented a number of optimistic findings regarding the health and health behaviors of Hispanics. With the exception of Puerto Ricans, Hispanics have lower age-adjusted mortality than non-Hispanic whites. In the context of Hispanics' low socioeconomic status, this finding is considered so remarkable that it has been called the epidemiological paradox. Research on the epidemiological paradox suggests that the mortality advantage of Hispanics is concentrated among foreign-born Mexicans, Central Americans, and South Americans, and that at least part of the advantage is due to selective migration. Nonetheless, these studies have also found that mortality rates for most U.S.-born Hispanics, in whom selective migration is much less likely to play a role, are at least as favorable as those for non-Hispanic whites.

The other main manifestation of the epidemiological paradox is in birth outcomes. Hispanic women have similar or more favorable birth outcomes, including lower rates of low birthweight and infant mortality, than non-Hispanic white women, again with the exception of Puerto Ricans. As with mortality, the Hispanic advantage in birth outcomes is greater among the foreign-born, but even U.S.-born Hispanic women experience birth outcomes that rival those of whites. Protective cultural and social characteristics of Hispanic immigrants have been invoked to explain the excellent birth outcomes of foreign-born women, but relatively favorable outcomes persist even as these characteristics are lost in the second generation. Although recent studies have furthered our understanding of patterns of mortality and birth outcomes among Hispanics, a full and widely accepted explanation for the epidemiological paradox remains elusive.

Other optimistic findings regarding the health and health behaviors of Hispanic adults include lower incidence rates than whites for several major cancers, relatively low rates of activity limitations (except for seniors), mental health profiles that resemble those of whites, and lower smoking rates than whites. Hispanic adolescents also smoke at lower rates than white adolescents. And with the exception of Puerto Ricans, Hispanic children have low rates of asthma, the major chronic disease of childhood.

Our review has also uncovered a number of worrisome findings regarding the health and health behaviors of Hispanics. Several of these concern Hispanic adults. By far the most ominous findings, however, pertain to Hispanic children and adolescents. In fact, our findings regarding trends in overweight among Hispanic youth raise the possibility of a marked deterioration in the health of the Hispanic population of the United States over the next several decades.

The epidemic of overweight and obesity in the United States has affected all racial and ethnic groups, but Hispanics have been especially hard hit. According to the most recent NHANES data, nearly one-third of adult men and two-fifths of adult women of Mexican origin in the United States are obese. These rates easily surpass the rates for non-Hispanic whites, especially in the case of women, and adult Hispanics are also more likely than whites to be overweight. The rising prevalence of overweight and obesity among Hispanic adults are likely to lead to higher rates of diabetes, hypertension, and cardiovascular disease. Diabetes is nearly twice as frequent among Hispanics of Mexican origin as among whites, and Hispanics bear a higher burden than whites of diabetic complications. The available data suggest that Hispanics of Mexican origin and whites have a similar prevalence of hypertension, but even this is a change from the pattern 25 years ago, when hypertension was considerably less common among Hispanics. Current trends in overweight and obesity raise the likelihood of an aging Hispanic population burdened by much higher rates of cardiovascular disease, stroke, kidney disease, blindness, and other complications of obesity, diabetes, and hypertension. These developments would have major implications for rates of disability and mortality among Hispanics.

Recent changes in the distribution of BMI among Hispanic youth pose an even greater threat to the future health of the Hispanic population of the United States. Hispanic children and adolescents are much more likely than non-Hispanic white children and adolescents to be at risk of overweight or overweight. Moreover, the rate of overweight has been increasing much more rapidly for Hispanic youth than for whites. The most recent data indicate that two-fifths of children of Mexican origin ages 6 to 11 and nearly half of adolescents ages 12 to 19 are at risk of overweight, while more than one-fourth of Mexican-origin boys of all ages and one-fifth of girls are overweight. Although foreign-born Hispanic children and adolescents have lower rates than their U.S.-born peers of risk of overweight and overweight, the rates for foreign-born youth are nonetheless very high.

The health consequences of current trends in BMI for Hispanic youth are already evident. The rising prevalence of Type 2 diabetes among Hispanic children is unprecedented, and portends the future development of diabetic complications in Hispanic adults in much larger numbers and at much younger ages than historical norms. Other consequences of the epidemic in risk of overweight and overweight among Hispanic youth include increasing blood pressure and high rates of insulin resistance, glucose intolerance, and lipid abnormalities. It seems inevitable that the Hispanic population of the United States will experience much higher rates of cardiovascular disease and other manifestations of atherosclerosis as today's Hispanic youth moves into adulthood.

Unhealthy diets combined with low levels of physical activity are important underlying causes of the rising rates of overweight in Hispanic children and adolescents. In this context, our review has raised serious concerns about the future dietary habits of Hispanics. The available evidence suggests that acculturation is associated with less healthy diets among Hispanics of all ages, and that second-generation Hispanic youth have worse dietary habits than immigrant youth. The process of acculturation is likely to lead today's immigrant youth to adopt less healthy diets that put them at higher risk of overweight. The second-generation offspring of today's immigrant adults are likely to be at high risk for unhealthy diets and excessive weight as well.

The other data we have reviewed on the health and health behaviors of Hispanic youth are less worrisome than the data on obesity and its complications. Nonetheless, we uncovered several findings of concern with regard to the well-being of Hispanic youth and especially to their educational performance. Health conditions and behaviors that affect educational performance are noteworthy, because the educational outcomes and attainment of today's Hispanic youth have important implications for the future economic trajectory of Hispanics in the United States.

Hispanic children and adolescents have considerably worse oral health than their non-Hispanic white peers. Poor oral health is associated with a variety of adverse outcomes among youth, including lower quality of life and worse educational outcomes. Hispanic children also have higher blood lead levels than white children and, consequently, are at much higher risk for the adverse effects of lead poisoning on cognitive development. The Centers for Disease Control and Prevention are currently considering lowering the threshold blood lead level for intervention from 10 μg/dL to 5 μg/dL. More than one-fourth of preschool-age children and one-fifth of elementary schoolchildren of Mexican origin have blood lead levels that would meet the revised threshold. Other threats to the well-being and educational performance of Hispanic youth, and in particular, of adolescent girls, include relatively high rates of depression and teenage childbearing. Finally, the available evidence suggests that the process of acculturation is associated with higher rates of smoking and illicit drug use among Hispanic youth, implying that these may become more salient problems among the second-generation offspring of today's immigrant adults.

Our review suggests that addressing the rising prevalence of overweight and obesity among Hispanics must be a priority for public health. Hispanic youth, in particular, should be targeted by public health and community-based efforts to prevent overweight before it has a chance to develop. The available data on the relationship between acculturation and both overweight and diet suggest that interventions to help Hispanic families preserve the dietary habits that they bring with them from their countries of origin could have an important role to play. However, although Hispanics have been disproportionately affected by the epidemic of overweight and obesity in the United States, no racial or ethnic group is unscathed. Hispanics must be included in broader societal initiatives to address this epidemic.

Other health problems that disproportionately affect Hispanic youth and that may be amenable to public health and community-based interventions include poor oral health, high blood lead levels, and teenage childbearing. Interventions designed to preserve and build on salutary elements of Hispanic culture may be helpful in dealing with smoking, drug use, and teenage childbearing among Hispanic youth and in promoting favorable birth outcomes among Hispanic women. More research is needed on how acculturation to American culture affects the health and health behaviors of Hispanics and on how interventions that exploit the beneficial elements of Hispanic culture can be designed.

Finally, if present trends continue, the U.S. health care system of the future will be faced with much larger numbers of Hispanic patients suffering from such chronic conditions as diabetes, hypertension, and cardiovascular disease as well as from the consequences of these conditions. Hispanics currently face numerous barriers to receiving timely, appropriate, and high quality health care. These barriers, and what must be done to address them, are discussed in detail in the next chapter.

REFERENCES

Abraido-Lanza, A.F., Dohrenwend, B.P., Ng-Mak, D.S., and Turner, J.B. (1999). The Latino mortality paradox: A test of the "salmon bias" and healthy migrant hypotheses. *American Journal of Public Health*, *89*(10), 1748–1751.

Adler, N.E., and Ostrove, J.M. (1999). Socioeconomic status and health: What we know and what we don't. In N.E. Adler, M. Marmot, B.S. McEwen, and J. Stewart (Eds.), *Socioeconomic status and health in industrial nations: Social, psychological and biological pathways* (pp. 3–16). New York: New York Academy of Sciences.

Alderete, E., Vega, W.A., Kolody, B., and Aguilar-Gaxiola, S. (2000). Lifetime prevalence of and risk factors for psychiatric disorders among Mexican farm workers in California. *American Journal of Public Health*, *90*(4), 608–614.

Amaro, H., Whitaker, R., Coffman, J., and Heeren, T. (1990). Acculturation and marijuana and cocaine use: Findings from HHANES 1982–84. *American Journal of Public Health*, *80*(suppl.), 54–60.

Arias, E., Anderson, R.N., Hsiang-Ching, K., Murphy, S.L., and Kochanek, K.D. (2003). *Deaths: Final data for 2001*. (National Vital Statistics Reports; Vol. 52, No. 3.) Hyattsville, MD: National Center for Health Statistics.

Ayala, C., Greenlund, K., Croft, J.B., Keenan, N.L., Donehoo, R.S., Giles, W.H., Kittner, S.J., and Marks, J.S. (2001). Racial/ethnic disparities in mortality by stroke subtype in the United States, 1995–1998. *American Journal of Epidemiology*, *154*(11), 1057–1063.

Beckett, W.S., Belanger, K., Gent, J.F., Holford, T.R., and Leaderer, B.P. (1996). Asthma among Puerto Rican Hispanics: A multiethnic comparison study of risk factors. *American Journal of Respiratory and Critical Care Medicine*, *154*(4 Pt 1), 894–899.

Blake, S., Ledsky, R., Goodenow, C., and O'Donnell, L. (2001). Recency of immigration, substance use, and sexual behavior among Massachusetts adolescents. *American Journal of Public Health*, *91*, 794–798.

Brindis, C., Wolfe, A.L., McCarter, V., Ball, S., and Starbuck-Morales, S. (1995). The associations between immigrant status and risk-behavior patterns in Latino adolescents. *Journal of Adolescent Health*, *17*(2), 99–105.

Bruno, A., Carter, S., Qualls, C., and Nolte, K.B. (1996). Incidence of spontaneous intracerebral hemorrhage among Hispanics and non-Hispanic whites in New Mexico. *Neurology*, *47*(2), 405–408.

Burnam, M.A., Hough, R.L., Karno, M., Escobar, J.I., and Telles, C.A. (1987). Acculturation and lifetime prevalence of psychiatric disorders among Mexican Americans in Los Angeles. *Journal of Health and Social Behavior*, *28*(March), 89–102.

Caetano, R., and Galvan, F.H. (2001). Alcohol use and alcohol-related problems among Latinos in the United States. In M. Aguirre-Molina, C.W. Molina, and R.E. Zambrana (Eds.), *Health issues in the Latino community* (pp. 383–412). San Francisco, CA: Jossey-Bass.

Canino, G., and Roberts, R.E. (2000). Suicidal behavior among Latino youth. In L. Davidson and U. Loso (Eds.), *Suicide prevention now: Linking research to practice* (pp. 66–78). Atlanta: Centers for Disease Control.

Canino, G.J., Bird, H.R., Shrout, P.E., Rubio-Stipec, M., Bravo, M., Martinez, R., Sesman, M., and Guevara, L.M. (1987). The prevalence of specific psychiatric disorders in Puerto Rico. *Archives of General Psychiatry*, *44*(8), 727–735.

Carter-Pokras, O.D., and Gergen, P.J. (1993). Reported asthma among Puerto Rican, Mexican-American, and Cuban children, 1982 through 1984. *American Journal of Public Health*, *83*(4), 580–582.

Casas, J.M., Bimbela, A., Corral, C.V., Yanez, I., Swaim, R.C., Wayman, J.C., and Bates, S. (1998). Cigarette and smokeless tobacco use among migrant and nonmigrant Mexican American youth. *Hispanic Journal of Behavioral Science*, *20*(1), 102–121.

Cruz, M.L., Weigensberg, M.J., Huang, T.T., Ball, G., Shaibi, G.Q., and Goran, M.I. (2004). The metabolic syndrome in overweight Hispanic youth and the role of insulin sensitivity. *Journal of Clinical Endocrinology and Metabolism*, *89*(1), 108–113.

Dabelea, D., Pettitt, D.J., Lee Jones, K., and Arslanian, S.A. (1999). Type 2 diabetes mellitus in minority children and adolescents: An emerging problem. *Journal of Clinical Endocrinology and Metabolism*, *28*(4), 709–729.

Dixon, L.B., Sundquist, J., and Winkleby, M. (2000). Differences in energy, nutrient, and food intakes in a U.S. sample of Mexican-American women and men: Findings from the third National Health and Nutrition Examination Survey, 1988–1994. *American Journal of Epidemiology*, *152*(6), 548–557.

Doi, Y., Roberts, R.E., Takeuchi, K., and Suzuki, S. (2001). Multiethnic comparison of adolescent major depression based on the DSM-IV criteria in a U.S.-Japan study. *Journal of the American Academy of Child and Adolescent Psychiatry*, *40*(11), 1308–1315.

Edelstein, S.L., Knowler, W.C., Bain, R.P., Andres, R., Barrett-Connor, E.L., Dowse, G.K., Haffner, S.M., Pettitt, D.J., Sorkin, J.D., Muller, D.C., Collins, V.R., and Hamman, R.F. (1997). Predictors of progression from impaired glucose tolerance to NIDDM: An analysis of six prospective studies. *Diabetes*, *46*(4), 701–710.

Elder, J.P., Campbell, N.R., Litrownik, A.J., Ayala, G.X., Slymen, D.J., Parra-Medina, D., and Lovato, C.Y. (2000). Predictors of cigarette and alcohol susceptibility and use among Hispanic migrant adolescents. *Preventive Medicine*, *31*(2 Pt 1), 115–123.

Elo, I.T., and Preston, S.H. (1997). Racial and ethnic differences in mortality at older ages. In National Research Council, *Racial and ethnic differences in the health of older Americans* (pp. 10–42). Committee on Population, L. G. Martin and B. J. Soldo (Eds.). Washington, DC: National Academy Press.

Emslie, G.J., Weinberg, W.A., Rush, A.J., Adams, R.M., and Rintelmann, J.W. (1990). Depressive symptoms by self-report in adolescence: Phase I of the development of a questionnaire for depression by self-report. *Journal of Child Neurology*, *5*(2), 114–121.

Epstein, J.A., Botvin, G.J., and Díaz, T. (1998). Linguistic acculturation and gender effects on smoking among Hispanic youth. *Preventive Medicine*, *27*, 583–589.

Epstein, J.A., Botvin, G.J., and Díaz, T. (2001). Linguistic acculturation associated with higher marijuana and polydrug use among Hispanic adolescents. *Substance Use and Misuse*, *36*(4), 477–499.

Fagot-Campagna, A. (2000), Emergence of type 2 diabetes mellitus in children: Epidemiological evidence. *Journal of Pediatric Endocrinology and Metabolism*, *13*(Suppl. 6), 1395–1402.

Feinstein, J.S. (1993). The relationship between socioeconomic status and health: A review of the literature. *Milbank Quarterly*, *71*(2), 279–322.

Flegal, K.M., Carroll, M.D., Ogden, C.L., and Johnson, C.L. (2002). Prevalence and trends in obesity among U.S. adults, 1999–2000. *Journal of the American Medical Association*, *288*(14), 1772–1773.

Flegal, K.M., Ezzati, T.M., Harris, M.I., Haynes, S.G., Juarez, R.Z., Knowler, W.C., Pérez-Stable, E.J., and Stern, M.P. (1991). Prevalence of diabetes in Mexican Americans, Cubans, and Puerto Ricans from the Hispanic Health and Nutrition Examination Survey, 1982–1984. *Diabetes Care*, *14*(7), 628–638.

Flores, G., and Zambrana, R.E. (2001). The early years: The health of children and youth. In C.W. Molina, M. Aguirre-Molina, and R.E. Zambrana (Eds.), *Health issues in the Latino community* (pp. 77–106). San Francisco, CA: Jossey-Bass.

Ford, E.S., Giles, W.H., and Dietz, W.H. (2002). Prevalence of the metabolic syndrome among U.S. adults: Findings from the third National Health and Nutrition Examination Survey. *Journal of the American Medical Association*, *287*(3), 356–359.

Frey, J.L., Jahnke, H.K., and Bulfinch, E.W. (1998). Differences in stroke between white, Hispanic, and Native American patients: The Barrow Neurological Institute stroke database. *Stroke*, *29*(1), 29–33.

Gay, E.C., Hamman, R.F., Carosone-Link, P.J., Lezotte, D.C., Cook, M., Stroheker, R., Klingensmith, G., and Chase, H.P. (1989). Colorado IDDM Registry: Lower incidence of IDDM in Hispanics. Comparison of disease characteristics and care patterns in biethnic populations. *Diabetes Care*, *12*(10), 701–708.

Giachello, A.L. (2001). The reproductive years: The health of Latinas. In M. Aguirre-Molina, C.W. Molina, and R.E. Zambrana (Eds.), *Health issues in the Latino community* (pp. 107–156). San Francisco, CA: Jossey-Bass.

Gilbert, M. (1989). Alcohol consumption patterns in immigrant and later generation Mexican American women. *Hispanic Journal of Behavioral Science*, *9*, 299–313.

Gillum, R.F. (1995). Epidemiology of stroke in Hispanic Americans. *Stroke*, *26*(9), 1707–1712.

Gfroerer, J.C., and Tan, L.L. (2003). Substance use among foreign-born youths in the United States: Does the length of residence matter? *American Journal of Public Health*, *93*(11), 1892–1895.

Goff, D.C., Nichaman, M.Z., Chan, W., Ramsey, D.J., Labarthe, D.R., and Ortiz, C. (1997). Greater incidence of hospitalized myocardial infarction among Mexican Americans than non-Hispanic whites. The Corpus Christi Heart Project, 1988–1992. *Circulation*, *95*(6), 1433–1440.

Goran, M.I., Bergman, R.N., Avila, Q., Watkins, M., Ball, G.D., Shaibi, G.Q., Weigensberg, M.J., and Cruz, M.L. (2004). Impaired glucose tolerance and reduced beta-cell function in overweight Latino children with a positive family history for type 2 diabetes. *Journal of Clinical Endocrinology and Metabolism, 89*(1), 207–212.

Gordon-Larsen, P., Adair, L.S., and Popkin, B.M. (2002). Ethnic differences in physical activity and inactivity patterns and overweight status. *Obesity Research, 10*(3), 141–149.

Gordon-Larsen, P., Harris, K.M., Ward, D.S., and Popkin, B.M. (2003). Acculturation and overweight-related behaviors among Hispanic immigrants to the U.S.: The National Longitudinal Study of Adolescent Health. *Social Science and Medicine, 57*, 2023–2034.

Guendelman, S., and Abrams, B. (1994). Dietary, alcohol, and tobacco intake among Mexican-American women of childbearing age: Results from HANES data. *American Journal of Health Promotion, 8*(5), 363–372.

Guendelman, S., and Abrams, B. (1995). Dietary intake among Mexican American women: Generational differences and a comparison with white non-Hispanic women. *American Journal of Public Health, 85*(1), 20–25.

Guo, S.S., Roche, A.F., Chumlea, W.C., Gardner, J.D., and Siervogel, R.M. (1994). The predictive value of childhood body mass index values for overweight at age 35. *American Journal of Clinical Nutrition, 59*(4), 810–819.

Haffner, S.M., Stern, M.P., Hazuda, H.P., Rosenthal, M., and Knapp, J.A. (1986, May). The role of behavioral variables and fat patterning in explaining ethnic differences in serum lipids and lipoproteins. *American Journal of Epidemiology, 123*(5), 830–839.

Haffner, S.M., Stern, M.P., Hazuda, H.P., Mitchell, B.D., and Patterson, J.K. (1990). Cardiovascular risk factors in confirmed prediabetic individuals: Does the clock for coronary heart disease start ticking before the onset of clinical diabetes? *Journal of the American Medical Association, 263*(21), 2893–2898.

Harris, M.I. (1998). Diabetes in America: Epidemiology and scope of the problem. *Diabetes Care, 21*(Suppl 3), C11–C14.

Harris, M.I., Flegal, K.M., Cowie, C.C., Eberhardt, M.S., Goldstein, D.E., Little, R.R., Wiedmeyer, H.M., and Byrd-Holt, D.D. (1998a). Prevalence of diabetes, impaired fasting glucose, and impaired glucose tolerance in U.S. adults. The Third National Health and Nutrition Examination Survey, 1988–1994. *Diabetes Care, 21*(4), 518–524.

Harris, M.I., Klein, R., Cowie, C.C., Rowland, M., and Byrd-Holt, D.D. (1998b). Is the risk of diabetic retinopathy greater in non-Hispanic blacks and Mexican Americans than in non-Hispanic whites with type 2 diabetes? A U.S. population study. *Diabetes Care, 21*(8), 1230–1235.

Harris, M.I., Eastman, R.C., Cowie, C.C., Flegal, K.M., and Eberhardt, M.S. (1999). Racial and ethnic differences in glycemic control of adults with type 2 diabetes. *Diabetes Care, 22*(3), 403–408.

Hopkins, R.S., Quimbo, R., and Watkins, S.M. (1995). Elevated blood lead prevalence in Florida two-year-olds. *Journal of Florida Medical Association, 82*, 193–197.

Horowitz, C.R., Colson, K.A., Hebert, P.L., and Lancaster, K. (2004). Barriers to buying healthy foods for people with diabetes: Evidence of environmental disparities. *American Journal of Public Health, 94*(9), 1549–1554.

Hummer, R.A., Rogers, R.G., Amir, S.H., Forbes, D., and Frisbie, W.P. (2000). Adult mortality differentials among Hispanic subgroups and non-Hispanic whites. *Social Science Quarterly, 81*(1), 459–476.

Jacobs, B.S., Boden-Albala, B., Lin, I.F., and Sacco, R.L. (2002). Stroke in the young in the Northern Manhattan Stroke Study. *Stroke, 33*, 2789–2790.

Jasso, G., Massey, D.S., Rosenzweig, M.R., and Smith, J.P. (2004). Immigrant health: Selectivity and acculturation. In National Research Council, *Critical perspectives on racial and ethnic differences in health in late life* (pp. 227–266). Committee on Population,

N.B. Anderson, R.A. Bulatao, and B. Cohen (Eds.). Washington, DC: The National Academies Press.

Johnston, L.D., O'Malley, P.M., and Bachman, J.G. (1998). *National survey results on drug use from the Monitoring the Future study, 1975–1997.* (NIH Publication No. 98-4345.) Bethesda, MD: National Institute on Drug Abuse.

Johnston, L.D., O'Malley, P.M., and Bachman, J.G. (2003). *Monitoring the Future national survey results on adolescent drug use: Overview of key findings, 2002.* (NIH Publication No. 03-537). Bethesda, MD: National Institute on Drug Abuse.

Karno, M., and Hough, R.L. (1987). Lifetime prevalence of specific psychiatric disorders among Mexican Americans and non-Hispanic whites in Los Angeles. *Archives of General Psychiatry, 44*(August), 695–701.

Keenan, H., el Deirawi, K., Walsh, M., Grover, V.V., Alva, E., Onyemere, K., and Lipton, R. (2000). Are trends in diabetes incidence changing for minority children? *Annuals of Epidemiology, 10*(7), 459.

Kimbro, R.T., Lynch, S.M., and McLanahan, S. (2004). *The Hispanic paradox and breastfeeding: Does acculturation matter? Evidence from the fragile families study.* (Center for Research on Child Wellbeing Working Paper #04-01.) Princeton, NJ: Princeton University.

Knight, G.P., Virdin, L.M., Ocampo, K.A., and Roosa, M. (1994). An examination of the cross-ethnic equivalence of measures of negative life events and mental health among Hispanic and Anglo-American children. *American Journal of Community Psychology, 22*(6), 767–783.

Kulis, S., Marsiglia, F.F., and Hurdle, D. (2003). Gender identity, ethnicity, acculturation, and drug use: Exploring differences among adolescents in the Southwest. *Journal of Community Psychology, 31*(2), 167–188.

Landale, N.S., Oropesa, R.S., and Gorman, B.K. (1999). Immigration and infant health: Birth outcomes of immigrant and native women. In National Research Council and Institute of Medicine, *Children of immigrants: Health, adjustment, and public assistance* (pp. 244–285). Board on Children, Youth, and Families, D.J. Hernández (Ed.). Washington, DC: National Academy Press.

Landrine, H., Richardson, J.L., Klonoff, E.A., and Flay, B. (1994). Cultural diversity in the predictors of adolescent cigarette smoking: The relative influence of peers. *Journal of Behavioral Medicine, 17*(3), 331–346.

Ledogar, R.J., Penchaszadeth, A., Iglesias Garden, C.C., and Garden Acosta, L. (2000). Asthma and Latino cultures: Different prevalence reported among groups sharing the same environment. *American Journal of Public Health, 90*(6), 929–935.

Liao, Y., Cooper, R.S., Cao, G., Kaufman, J.S., Long, A.E., and McGee, D.L. (1997). Mortality from coronary heart disease and cardiovascular disease among adult U.S. Hispanics: Findings from the National Health Interview Survey (1986 to 1994). *Journal of the American College of Cardiology, 30*(5), 1200–1205.

Liao, Y., Cooper, R.S., Cao, G., Durazo-Arvizu, R., Kaufman, J.S., Luke, A., and McGee, D.L. (1998). Mortality patterns among adult Hispanics: Findings from the NHIS 1986 to 1990. *American Journal of Public Health, 88*(2), 227–232.

Lipman, T.H. (1993). The epidemiology of type I diabetes in children 0–14 year of age in Philadelphia. *Diabetes Care, 16*(6), 922–925.

Lipman, T.H., Chang, Y., and Murphy, K.M. (2003). The epidemiology of type 1 diabetes in children in Philadelphia 1990–1994: Evidence of an epidemic. *Diabetes Care, 26*(1), 260.

Lipton, R., Good, G., Mikhailov, T., Freels, S., and Donoghue, E. (1999). Ethnic differences in mortality from insulin-dependent diabetes mellitus among people less than 25 years of age. *Pediatrics, 103*(5 Pt 1), 952–956.

Lorenzi, M., Cagliero, E., and Schmidt, N.J. (1985). Racial differences in incidence of juvenile-onset type 1 diabetes: Epidemiologic studies in southern California. *Diabetologia, 28*(10), 734–738.

Loria, C.M., Bush, T.L., Carroll, M.D., Looker, A.C., McDowell, M.A., Johnson, C.L., and Sempos, C.T. (1995). Macronutrient intakes among adult Hispanics: A comparison of Mexican Americans, Cuban Americans, and mainland Puerto Ricans. *American Journal of Public Health, 85*(5), 684–689.

Luchsinger, J.A. (2001). Diabetes. In M. Aguirre-Molina, C.W. Molina, and R.E. Zambrana (Eds.), *Health issues in the Latino community* (pp. 277–300). San Francisco, CA: Jossey-Bass.

Maculuso, C.J., Bauer, U.E., Deeb, L.C., Malone, L.C., Chaudhari, M., Silverstein, J., Eidson, M., Goldberg, R.B., Gaughan-Bailey, B., Brooks, R.G., and Rosenbloom, A.L. (2002). Type 2 diabetes mellitus among Florida children and adolescents, 1994 through 1998. *Public Health Reports, 117*(4), 373–379.

Marin, G. (2001). Tobacco use among Latinos. In M. Aguirre-Molina, C.W. Molina, and R.E. Zambrana (Eds.), *Health issues in the Latino community* (pp. 413–434). San Francisco, CA: Jossey-Bass.

Markides, K.S., and Rudkin, I. (1995). *Health status of Hispanic elderly in the United States.* Galveston: University of Texas Medical Branch.

Markides, K.S., Krause, N., and Mendes de León, C.F. (1998). Acculturation and alcohol consumption among Mexican Americans. *American Journal of Public Health, 78*, 1178–1181.

Martin, J.A., Hamilton, B.E., Ventura, S.J., Menacker, F., Park, M.M., and Sutton, P.D. (2002). Births: Final data for 2001. *National Vital Statistics Report, 51*(2).

Mathews, T.J., Menacker, F., and MacDorman, M.F. (2003). Infant mortality statistics from the 2001 period linked birth/infant death data set. *National Vital Statistics Report, 52*(2), 1–28.

McDowell, M.A., Briefel, R.R., Alaimo, K., Bischof, A.M., Caughman, C.R., Carroll, M.D., Loria, C.M., and Johnson, C.L. (1994). Energy and macronutrient intakes of persons ages 2 months and over in the United States: Third National Health and Nutrition Examination Survey, Phase 1, 1988–91. *Advance Data* (255), 1–24.

Menard, S.W., Park, M.K., and Yuan, C.H. (1999). The San Antonio Biethnic Children's Blood Pressure Study: Auscultatory findings. *Journal of Pediatric Health Care, 13*(5), 237–244.

Mendoza, F.S., and Dixon, L.B. (1999). The health and nutritional status of immigrant Hispanic children: Analyses of the Hispanic Health and Nutrition Examination Survey. In National Research Council and Institute of Medicine, *Children of immigrants: Health, adjustment, and public assistance* (pp. 187–243). Board on Children, Youth, and Families, D.J. Hernández (Ed.). Washington, DC: National Academy Press.

Mitchell, B.D., Stern, M.P., Haffner, S.M., Hazuda, H.P., and Patterson, J.K. (1990). Risk factors for cardiovascular mortality in Mexican Americans and non-Hispanic whites. San Antonio Heart Study. *American Journal of Epidemiology, 131*(3), 423–433.

Mitchell, B.D., Hazuda, H.P., Haffner, S.M., Patterson, J.K., and Stern, M.P. (1991). Myocardial infarction in Mexican-Americans and non-Hispanic whites. The San Antonio Heart Study. *Circulation, 83*(1), 45–51.

Morales, L.S., Gutierrez, P., and Escarce, J.J. (2005). Demographic and socioeconomic factors associated with blood lead levels among Mexican-American children and adolescents in the United States. *Public Health Reports, 120*(4), 448-454.

Moscicki, E.K., Rae, D., Regier, D.A., and Locke, B. (1987). The Hispanic health and nutrition examination survey: Depression among Mexican-Americans, Cuban-Americans, and Puerto Ricans. In M. Gavitia and J.D. Arana (Eds.), *Health and behavior: Research agenda for Hispanics* (pp. 145–159). Simon Bolívar Research Monograph Series 1. Chicago: University of Illinois Press.

Mouradian, W.E., Wehr, E., and Crall, J.J. (2000). Disparities in children's oral health and access to dental care. *Journal of the American Medical Association, 284*(20), 2625–2631.

Muntner, P., He, J., Cutler, J.A., Wildman, R.P., and Whelton, P.K. (2004). Trends in blood pressure among children and adolescents. *Journal of the American Medical Association, 291*(17), 2107–2113.

National Center for Health Statistics (NCHS). (1999). *Health, United States, 1999, with Health and Aging Chartbook.* (Department of Health and Human Services, DHHS Publication No. 1999–1232.) Hyattsville, MD: U.S. Department of Health and Human Services, Centers for Disease Control and Prevention.

National Center for Health Statistics (NCHS). (2000). *Health, United States, 2000, with Adolescent Health Chartbook.* (Department of Health and Human Services, DHHS Publication No. 2000-1232-1.) Hyattsville, MD: U.S. Department of Health and Human Services, Centers for Disease Control and Prevention.

National Center for Health Statistics (NCHS). (2003). *Health, United States, 2003.* (Department of Health and Human Services, DHHS Publication No. 2003-1232.) Hyattsville, MD: U.S. Department of Health and Human Services, Centers for Disease Control and Prevention.

National Institute of Dental Research. (1989). *Oral health of United States children, the national survey of dental caries in U.S. school children, 1986–87: National and regional findings.* (DHHS Publication No. (NIH) 89-2247.) Bethesda, MD: U.S. Department of Health and Human Services, Public Health Service, National Institutes of Health.

Neufeld, N.D., Raffel, L.J., Landon, C., Chen, Y.D., and Vadheim, C.M. (1998). Early presentation of type 2 diabetes in Mexican-American youth. *Diabetes Care, 21*(1), 80–86.

Neuhouser, M.L., Thompson, B., Coronado, G.D., and Solomon, C.C. (2004). Higher fat intake and lower fruit and vegetables intakes are associated with greater acculturation among Mexicans living in Washington state. *Journal of the American Diet Association, 104*(1), 51–57.

Nielsen, A.L., and Ford, J.A. (2001). Drinking patterns among Hispanic adolescents: Results from a national household survey. *Journal of Studies on Alcohol, 62*(4), 448–456.

Ogden, C.L., Flegal, K.M., Carroll, M.D., and Johnson, C.L. (2002). Prevalence and trends in overweight among US children and adolescents, 1999–2000. *Journal of the American Medical Association, 288*(14), 1728–1732.

Okosun, I.S., Prewitt, T.E., and Cooper, R.S. (1999). Abdominal obesity in the United States: Prevalence and attributable risk of hypertension. *Journal of Human Hypertension, 13*(7), 425–430.

Okosun, I.S., Liao, Y., Rotimi, C.N., Prewitt, T.E., and Cooper, R.S. (2000). Abdominal adiposity and clustering of multiple metabolic syndrome in white, black, and Hispanic Americans. *Annuals of Epidemiology, 10*(5), 263–270.

Okosun, I.S., Choi, S.T., Boltri, J.M., Parish, D.C., Chandra, K.M., Dever, G.E., and Lucas, A. (2003). Trends of abdominal adiposity in white, black, and Mexican-American adults, 1988 to 2000. *Obesity Research, 11*(8), 1010–1017.

Palloni, A., and Arias, E. (2004). Paradox lost: Explaining the Hispanic adult mortality advantage. *Demography, 41*(3), 385–415.

Palloni, A., and Morenoff, J. (2001). Interpreting the paradoxical in the Hispanic paradox: Demographic and epidemiological approaches. *Annals of the New York Academy of Sciences, 954*, 140–174.

Pandey, D.K., Labarthe, D.R., Goff, D.C., Chan, W., and Nichaman, M.Z. (2001). Community-wide coronary heart disease mortality in Mexican Americans equals or exceeds that in non-Hispanic whites: The Corpus Christi Heart Project. *American Journal of Medicine*, *110*(2), 81–87.

Pappas, G., Gergen, P.J., and Carroll, M. (1990). Hypertension prevalence and the status of awareness, treatment, and control in the Hispanic Health and Nutrition Examination Survey (HHANES), 1982–84. *American Journal of Public Health*, *80*(12), 1431–1436.

Park, Y.W., Zhu, S., Palaniappan, L., Heshka, S., Carnethon, M.R., and Heymsfield, S.B. (2003). The metabolic syndrome: Prevalence and associated risk factor findings in the U.S. population from the Third National Health and Nutrition Examination Survey, 1988–1994. *Archives of Internal Medicine*, *163*(4), 427–436.

Pérez-Stable, E., Juarbe, T., and Moreno-John, G. (2001). Cardiovascular disease. In M. Aguirre-Molina, C.W. Molina, and R.E. Zambrana (Eds.), *Heath issues in the Latino community* (pp. 245–276). San Francisco, CA: Jossey-Bass.

Polednak, A.P. (1997). Gender and acculturation in relation to alcohol use among Hispanic (Latino) adults in two areas of the northeastern United States. *Substance Use and Misuse*, *32*(11), 1513–1524.

Polonsky, K.S., Sturis, J., and Bell, G.I. (1996). Seminars in medicine of the Beth Israel Hospital, Boston. Non-insulin-dependent diabetes mellitus: A genetically programmed failure of the beta cell to compensate for insulin resistance. *New England Journal of Medicine*, *334*(12), 777–783.

Popkin, B.M., and Udry, J.R. (1998). Adolescent obesity increases significantly in second and third generation U.S. immigrants. *Journal of Nutrition*, *128*(4), 701–706.

Portes, A., and Rumbaut, R.G. (2001). *Legacies: The story of the immigrant second generation.* Berkeley and New York: University of California Press and Russell Sage Foundation.

Ramírez, A.G. (1996). Hypertension in Hispanic Americans: Overview of the population. *Public Health Reports*, *3*(Suppl 2), 25–26.

Ramírez, A.G., and Suárez, L. (2001). The impact of cancer on Latino populations. In M. Aguirre-Molina, C.W. Molina, and R.E. Zambrana (Eds.), *Health issues in the Latino community* (pp. 211–224). San Francisco: Jossey-Boss.

Reaven, P., Nader, P.R., Berry, C., and Hoy, T. (1998). Cardiovascular disease insulin risk in Mexican-American and Anglo-American children and mothers. *Pediatrics*, *101*(4), 12–18.

Rewers, M., Shetterly, S.M., Hoag, S., Baxter, J., Marshall, J., and Hamman, R.F. (1993). Is the risk of coronary heart disease lower in Hispanics than in non-Hispanic whites? The San Luis Valley Diabetes Study. *Ethnic Disparities*, *3*(1), 44–54.

Roberts, R.E., and Chen, Y.W. (1995). Depressive symptoms and suicidal ideation among Mexican-origin and Anglo adolescents. *Journal of the American Academy of Child and Adolescent Psychiatry*, *34*(1), 81–90.

Rolland-Cachera, M.F., Deheeger, M., Guilloud-Bataille, M., Avons, P., Patois, E., and Sempe, M. (1987). Tracking the development of adiposity from one month of age to adulthood. *Annals of Human Biology*, *14*(3), 219–229.

Rosenberg, H.M., Maurer, J.D., Sorlie, P.D., Johnson, N.J., MacDorman, M.F., Hoyert, D.L., Spitler, J.F., and Scott, C. (1999). Quality of death rates by race and Hispanic origin: A summary of current research, 1999. *Vital Health Statistics, Series*, *2*(128). Hyattsville, MD: National Center for Health Statistics.

Rosenbloom, A.L., Joe, J.R., Young, R.S., and Winter, W.E. (1999). Emerging epidemic of type 2 diabetes in youth. *Diabetes Care*, *22*(2), 345–354.

Rumbaut, R.G., and Weeks, J.R. (1996). Unraveling a public health enigma: Why do immigrants experience superior perinatal health outcomes? *Research in the Sociology of Health Care*, *13*, 335–388.

Rumbaut, R.G., and Weeks, J.R. (1998). Children of immigrants: Is Americanization hazardous to infant health? In H.E. Fitzgerald, B.M. Lester, and B. Zuckerman (Eds.), *Children of color: Research, health, and public policy issues* (pp. 159–183). New York: Garland.

Sacco, R.L., Boden-Albala, B., Gan, R., Chen, X., Kargman, D.E., Shea, S., Paik, M.C., and Hauser, W.A. (1998). Stroke incidence among white, black, and Hispanic residents of an urban community: The Northern Manhattan Stroke Study. *American Journal of Epidemiology, 147*(3), 259–268.

Satish, S., Stroup-Benham, C.A., Espino, D.V., Markides, K.S., and Goodwin, J.S. (1998). Undertreatment of hypertension in older Mexican Americans. *Journal of the American Geriatric Society, 46*(4), 405–410.

Schaffer, D.M., Velie, E.M., Shaw, G.M., and Todoroff, K.P. (1998). Energy and nutrient intakes and health practices of Latinas and white non-Latinas in the 3 months before pregnancy. *Journal of the American Dietary Association, 98*(8), 876–884.

Serdula, M.K., Ivery, D., Coates, R.J., Freedman, D.S., Williamson, D.F., and Byers, T. (1993). Do obese children become obese adults? A review of the literature. *Preventive Medicine, 22*(2), 167–177.

Shea, S., Aymong, E., Zybert, P., Shamoon, H., Tracy, R.P., Deckelbaum, R.J., and Basch, C.E. (2003). Obesity, fasting plasma insulin, and c-reactive protein levels in healthy children. *Obesity Research, 11*, 95–103.

Siega-Riz, A.M., and Popkin, B.M. (2001). Dietary trends among low socioeconomic status women of childbearing age in the United States from 1977 to 1996: A comparison among ethnic groups. *Journal of American Medical Women's Association, 56*(2), 44–48, 72.

Siervogel, R.M., Roche, A.F., Guo, S.M., Mukherjee, D., and Chumlea, W.C. (1991). Patterns of change in weight/stature from 2 to 18 years: Findings from long-term serial data for children in the Fels longitudinal growth study. *International Journal of Obesity, 15*(7), 479–485.

Singh, G.K., and Siahpush, M. (2001). All-cause and cause-specific mortality of immigrants and native born in the United States. *American Journal of Public Health, 91*(3), 392–399.

Sinha, R., Fisch, G., Teague, B., Tamborlane, W.V., Banyas, B., Allen, K., Savoye, M., Rieger, V., Taksali, S., Barbetta, G., Sherwin, R.S., and Caprio, S. (2002). Prevalence of impaired glucose tolerance among children and adolescents with marked obesity. *New England Journal of Medicine, 346*(11), 802–810.

Sorlie, P.D., Backlund, E., Johnson, N.J., and Rogot, E. (1993). Mortality by Hispanic status in the United States. *Journal of American Medical Association, 270*(20), 2464–2468.

Sorof, J.M., Lai, D., Turner, J., Poffenbarger, T., and Portman, R.J. (2004). Overweight, ethnicity, and the prevalence of hypertension in school-aged children. *Pediatrics, 113*(3 Pt 1), 475–482.

Strauss, R.S., and Pollack, H.A. (2001). Epidemic increase in childhood overweight, 1986–1998. *Journal of American Medical Association, 286*(22), 2845–2848.

Stroup-Benham, C.A., Markides, K.S., Espino, D.V., and Goodwin, J.S. (1999). Changes in blood pressure and risk factors for cardiovascular disease among older Mexican-Americans from 1982–1984 to 1993–1994. *Journal of American Geriatric Society, 47*(7), 804–810.

Sudano, J.J., Jr., and Baker, D.W. (2001). Antihypertensive medication use in Hispanic adults: A comparison with black adults and white adults. *Medical Care, 39*(6), 575–587.

Sundquist, J., Winkleby, M.A., and Pudaric, S. (2001). Cardiovascular disease risk factors among older black, Mexican-American, and white women and men: An analysis of NHANES III, 1988–1994. Third National Health and Nutrition Examination Survey. *Journal of American Geriatric Society, 49*(2), 109–116.

Surgeon General's Report on Physical Activity and Health. (1996). Available: http://www.cdc.gov/nccdphp/sgr/sgr.htm [accessed March 29, 2004].

Swenson, C.J., Trepka, M.J., Rewers, M.J., Scarbro, S., Hiatt, W.R., and Hamman, R.F. (2002). Cardiovascular disease mortality in Hispanics and non-Hispanic whites. *American Journal of Epidemiology*, *156*(10), 919–928.

Tortolero, S.R., Goff, D.C., Nichaman, M.Z., Labarthe, D.R., Grunbaum, J.A., and Hanis, C.L. (1997). Cardiovascular risk factors in Mexican-American and non-Hispanic white children. *Circulation*, *96*, 418–423.

Vega, W.A., and Alegría, M. (2001). Latino mental health and treatment in the United States. In M. Aguirre-Molina, C.W. Molina, and R.E. Zambrana (Eds.), *Health issues in the Latino community* (pp. 179–208). San Francisco, CA: Jossey-Bass.

Vega, W.A., and Amaro, H. (1994). Latino outlook: Good health, uncertain prognosis. *Annual Review of Public Health*, *15*, 39–67.

Vega, W.A., Sribney, W., and Achara-Abrahams, I. (2003). Co-occurring alcohol, drug, and other psychiatric disorders among Mexican-origin people in the United States. *American Journal of Public Health*, *93*(7), 1057–1064.

Vong, S., and Bell, B.P. (2004). Chronic liver disease mortality in the United States, 1990–1998. *Hepatology*, *39*(2), 476–483.

Wallace, J.M., Jr., Bachman, J.G., O'Malley, P.M., Johnston, L.D., Schulenberg, J.E., and Cooper, S.M. (2002). Tobacco, alcohol, and illicit drug use: Racial and ethnic differences among U.S. high school seniors, 1976–2000. *Public Health Reports*, *117*(Suppl 1), S67–S75.

Weeks, J.R., Rumbaut, R.G., and Ojeda, N. (1999). Reproductive outcomes among Mexican-origin women in San Diego and Tijuana: Testing the migration selectivity hypothesis. *Journal of Immigrant Health*, *1*(2), 77–90.

Williams, R.L., Binkin, N.J., and Clingman, E.J. (1986). Pregnancy outcomes among Spanish-surname women in California. *American Journal of Public Health*, *76*, 387–391.

Winkleby, M.A., Albright, C.L., Howard-Pitney, B., Lin, J., and Fortmann, S.P. (1994). Hispanic/white differences in dietary fat intake among low educated adults and children. *Preventive Medicine*, *23*(4), 465–473.

10

Access to and Quality of Health Care

José J. Escarce and Kanika Kapur

The health of a population is influenced by both its social and its economic circumstances and the health care services it receives. As discussed in other chapters of this report, on average the socioeconomic status of Hispanics in the United States is considerably lower than that of non-Hispanic whites. Hispanics also face a variety of barriers to receiving health care services of high quality. Some of these barriers result from their low socioeconomic status; others are due to several specific features of the Hispanic population.

The low average socioeconomic status of Hispanics, compared with non-Hispanic whites, is reflected in their family income, educational attainment, occupational characteristics, and asset accumulation. In 1999, for example, 23 percent of Hispanics lived in poverty, compared with 8 percent of non-Hispanic whites, and 56 percent of Hispanic adults age 25 or older had a high school diploma, compared with 88 percent of non-Hispanic white adults. Hispanics are much more likely than whites to work in agriculture, construction, domestic and food services, and other low-wage occupations. Conversely, they are less likely than whites to work in managerial, professional, technical, sales, or administrative support positions.

The low average income and educational attainment of Hispanics are obstacles to receiving timely and appropriate health care. Low-income people are less able to afford the out-of-pocket costs of care, even if they have health insurance coverage. Low education may impair people's ability to navigate the complex health care delivery system, communicate with health care providers, and understand providers' instructions. In addition,

Hispanics' low incomes and occupational characteristics are associated with low rates of health insurance coverage. Lacking health insurance makes the costs of health care services prohibitive for many people and is the most important barrier to adequate health care access.

Specific features of the Hispanic population that affect their access to health care include degree of acculturation, language, and immigration status. More than two-fifths of Hispanics in the United States are foreign-born, and many are recent immigrants who retain their cultural beliefs and behaviors regarding health and health care. Most foreign-born Hispanics primarily speak Spanish, and fewer than one-fourth report speaking English very well. In 2000, only 28 percent of foreign-born Hispanics were naturalized citizens, a rate lower than the rates of naturalization for other immigrant groups. Among Hispanics who are not citizens, a sizable number are undocumented immigrants.

These features of the Hispanic population have both direct effects on reducing access to health care and indirect effects through their association with lower rates of health insurance coverage. The jobs available to recent and undocumented immigrants who lack proficiency in English are unlikely to provide health insurance as a benefit of employment. Furthermore, under recent legislation, recent immigrants and noncitizens may receive fewer benefits than earlier immigrants and citizens from public health insurance programs.

In this chapter, we review the evidence on access to health care for Hispanics and on the quality of health care that they receive. We provide a summary of the existing research and also present new data from recent national surveys. To provide a context for interpreting the data, our tabulations compare Hispanics with non-Hispanic whites and non-Hispanic blacks. We also focus on specific features that are of particular importance to Hispanics, including national origin, length of time in the United States, language, and citizenship, and we assess how these features are associated with access to and quality of health care. Our analyses of national-origin groups are constrained by data availability. Thus, of necessity, most of the analyses focus on Hispanics of Mexican, Puerto Rican, and Cuban origin, in addition to a residual category of "other" Hispanics.

ACCESS TO HEALTH CARE

Access to health care refers to the degree to which people are able to obtain appropriate care from the health care system in a timely manner. Researchers who study access to care often distinguish between "potential access," which refers to the presence or absence of financial and nonfinancial barriers to obtaining appropriate and timely care, and "realized access," which refers to the quantity of health care actually received.

Barriers to Access

Hispanics face a variety of financial and nonfinancial barriers to obtaining appropriate and timely health care. Degree of acculturation, language, and immigration status all directly affect access to care. Recent arrivals to the United States are more likely to be isolated from mainstream U.S. society and to be unfamiliar with the U.S. health care system, a situation that may interfere with obtaining appropriate and timely care (Wells, Golding, Hough, Burnam, and Karno, 1989).

Limited proficiency in English affects Hispanics' ability to seek and obtain health care and reduces access to health information in the media (Ruiz, Marks, and Richardson, 1992). In addition, communication is central to the process of health care delivery and has profound effects on patient–provider relationships and on the health care people receive. Studies have found that language barriers between providers and patients may result in excessive ordering of medical tests, lack of understanding of medication side effects and provider instructions, decreased use of primary care, increased use of the emergency department, and inadequate follow-up (David and Rhee, 1998; Morales, Cunningham, Brown, Liu, and Hays, 1999; Timmins, 2002). The unique sociopolitical status of undocumented immigrants poses considerable barriers to health care access as well.

Two key barriers to health care access are not having health insurance coverage and not having a usual source of care. Health insurance reduces the out-of-pocket costs of health care and has been shown to be the single most important predictor of utilization. Without health insurance coverage, many people find health care unaffordable and forgo care even when they think they need it. Having a usual source of care reduces nonfinancial barriers to obtaining care, facilitates access to health care services, and increases the frequency of contacts with health care providers. In particular, having a usual source of care provides a locus of entry into the complex health care delivery system when care is needed and serves as the link to more specialized types of care (Lewin-Epstein, 1991). Compared with people who lack a usual source of care, people with a usual source are less likely to have difficulty obtaining care or to go without needed care.

Hispanics rank poorly on both barriers to access, as we review below.

Health Insurance

Historically, lack of health insurance coverage has been a major problem for Hispanics, who are substantially more likely to be uninsured than non-Hispanic whites. For example, in 2004, 36 percent of Hispanics under age 65 lacked health insurance coverage, compared with 15 percent of whites (Rhoades, 2005). Rates of being uninsured vary across Hispanic subgroups defined by national origin; for instance, Mexicans and Central and South Americans have higher uninsured rates than Puerto Ricans or Cubans (Carrasquillo, Orav, Brennan, and Burstin, 2000; Hoffman and Pohl, 2000). Other studies have found that uninsured rates are higher for foreign-born compared with U.S.-born Hispanics and for noncitizens compared with citizens (e.g., Carrasquillo et al., 2000). Uninsured rates are especially high among undocumented immigrants; Berk, Schur, Chavez, and Frankel (2000) estimated that between 68 and 84 percent of undocumented immigrants in southern California are uninsured. The causes of low health insurance coverage among Hispanics are multiple and complex.

Hispanics are much less likely than non-Hispanic whites to receive health insurance as a benefit from an employer, which is the most common source of health insurance coverage for working-age adults and their children in the United States. Using the 1996 Medical Expenditure Panel Survey (MEPS), Monheit and Vistnes (2000) found that 42 percent of nonelderly Hispanics had employer-provided insurance, compared with 71 percent of nonelderly whites. Among workers, rates of employer-provided insurance coverage were 48 and 77 percent for Hispanic and white males, respectively, and 61 and 80 percent for Hispanic and white women. Hispanic male and female workers were less likely than their white counterparts to be offered health insurance by their employers (56 versus 81 percent or males and 62 versus 75 percent for females). This is consistent with other data showing that Hispanics are less likely than whites to work for an employer that offers health insurance to some employees, and they are less likely than whites to be eligible to participate if they work for such an employer (Quinn, 2000). Moreover, only 76 percent of Hispanic males who were offered insurance took it up, compared with 85 percent of white males. Take-up rates were about three-fourths for both Hispanic and white women.

Monheit and Vistnes (2000) also used multivariate regression analysis and decomposition techniques to examine the causes of low rates of employer-provided insurance among Hispanics. About three-fifths of the 29 percentage-point gap in insurance coverage between Hispanic and white male workers was explained by differences in the characteristics of workers and their employers, including poverty status, wages, education, and firm size. The remaining two-fifths of the coverage gap was explained by differences between Hispanics and whites in the relationship between worker and employer characteristics and insurance coverage. Thus, Hispanic males in poor, low-income, or middle-income households; those earning low wages; and those in firms with fewer than 25 workers were less likely than their white peers to have employer-provided insurance. Interestingly, nearly all the insurance coverage gap which Hispanic female workers experienced was explained by worker and employer characteristics.

Other analyses of employer-provided insurance have emphasized differences between Hispanics and whites in job characteristics (e.g., Schur and Feldman, 2001). Hispanics are more likely than whites to be employed in agriculture, construction, domestic and food services, and retail trade. Moreover, in these industries Hispanics are much less likely than whites to be in executive, administrative, or managerial occupations or in professional specialties. The industries and occupations in which Hispanics commonly work are less likely than others to offer health insurance as a benefit of employment. Hispanics also are more likely than whites to work in small firms, in seasonal occupations, and part-time, all of which are associated with a lower probability of being offered health insurance as a benefit of employment. Notably, Monheit and Vistnes (2000) found little effect of industry and occupation on employer-provided insurance in their multivariate analyses, although firm size remained an important factor. It is likely that the effects of industry and occupation were captured by such worker characteristics as wages, income, and education.

A focus group study conducted by the Commonwealth Fund investigated the barriers to employer-provided insurance for Hispanic workers (Perry, Kannel, and Castillo, 2000). This study found that, for many Hispanics seeking a job, getting the job is the primary concern, and the second concern is salary. Most uninsured participants in the focus groups admitted not asking about health insurance when they applied for their jobs and reported that health insurance takes a back seat to basic needs such as food and rent. A few participants noted that Hispanic workers, especially those recently arrived in the United States, are unfamiliar with the system of employer-based health insurance and may not sign up for coverage. Other participants cited language barriers to obtaining information about health insurance options.

Given the complex array of factors that affect employer-provided health insurance coverage, the considerable variation in rates of this coverage across subgroups of Hispanics is unsurprising. Differences in rates of employer-provided coverage have been documented by national origin, nativity, length of residence in the United States, and language (Schur and Feldman, 2001).

Public health insurance programs for low-income people, such as Medicaid and the State Children's Health Insurance Program (SCHIP), provide health insurance coverage to many low-income Hispanics. Nonetheless, these programs are not sufficient to close the health insurance gap between Hispanics and non-Hispanic whites. Many Hispanics—especially Mexicans and Cubans—live in states with restrictive eligibility rules for Medicaid and SCHIP, including Arizona, Florida, New Mexico, and Texas. By contrast, Puerto Ricans tend to live in New York and New Jersey, where Medicaid and SCHIP eligibility rules are less restrictive (Dubay, Haley, and

Kenney, 2002; Morales, Lara, Kington, Valdez, and Escarce, 2002). Also, the 1996 Personal Responsibility and Work Opportunity Reconciliation Act (PRWORA, the federal welfare reform law) barred legal immigrants who entered the United States after August 1996 from receiving federal Medicaid or SCHIP benefits for the first five years in the country, leaving it to the states to decide whether to cover the costs of these benefits without a federal contribution (Zimmerman and Tumlin, 1999). Only 15 states use state funds to cover new immigrants during their initial five-year period in the United States, and only 9 states provide full benefits to undocumented immigrants. Finally, several factors have recently conspired to inhibit Hispanics' enrollment in public health insurance programs, even when they are eligible for benefits. This is especially the case for immigrants who are not naturalized citizens.

The limits on new immigrants' eligibility for Medicaid and the time limits on welfare benefits under PRWORA led to general confusion about Medicaid eligibility and affected Medicaid participation by many immigrants who entered the United States long before 1996. Under federal immigration law, people may be barred from entering the United States or moving from temporary to permanent resident status if the government determines that they may become "public charges." In the mid-1990s, the Immigration and Naturalization Service (INS) and the California Medicaid program interpreted the public charge requirements of federal law as meaning that immigrants had to repay the value of Medicaid benefits received or place their residency status in jeopardy (Ku and Matani, 2001). Although in 1999 the INS clarified that Medicaid participation would not affect the determination of public charge status, the earlier interpretation led to a widespread belief that immigrants should avoid enrolling in Medicaid, even if they were eligible (Schlosberg and Wiley, 1998). Ku and Matani (2001) reported that Medicaid participation among low-income noncitizens fell and rates of uninsurance rose from 1995 to 1998. Similarly, Kaushal and Kaestner (2005) found a sizable increase in the proportion of uninsured among foreign-born, unmarried women and their children after PRWORA was implemented. Since PRWORA changed eligibility only for immigrants who entered the United States after 1996, observers attribute this decline in Medicaid participation to effects on immigrants who arrived before 1996 and were still eligible. Enrollment in SCHIP of U.S.-born children of immigrants appears to have been affected as well (Ku and Matani, 2001). Of note, PRWORA is unlikely to have affected Puerto Ricans, since they are U.S. citizens from birth whether they live on the island or the mainland.

Uncertainty about Medicaid (and SCHIP) eligibility and the risks of enrolling in Medicaid were added to other long-standing barriers to participation in public health insurance programs, such as lack of information and language. Studies suggest that lack of awareness of eligibility for Medicaid and SCHIP is widespread among Hispanics. For example, fewer than half of the participants in the focus group study described earlier had heard of the SCHIP program in their state (Perry et al., 2000). Language barriers also hamper both initial and continuous enrollment in public insurance programs. Knowledge gaps and difficulties with the enrollment process have been identified as important causes of incomplete SCHIP uptake among all children (Kenney and Haley, 2001); these factors are likely to be even more important for Hispanic children.

To complement our literature review, we used the 1997–2001 National Health Interview Surveys (NHIS) to examine recent patterns of health insurance coverage for Hispanics, non-Hispanic whites, and non-Hispanic blacks. As Table 10-1 shows, Hispanics in all age groups are much more likely than whites and blacks to be uninsured. Hispanics of Mexican origin have the highest uninsured rates, whereas the rates for Puerto Ricans and Cubans are only about half the rates for Mexicans. However, Puerto Ricans are much more likely than Cubans to rely on Medicaid or SCHIP as sources of health insurance coverage.

As anticipated, nativity, time since arrival in the United States, and citizenship are associated with health insurance coverage (Table 10-2). Nearly one-half of foreign-born, working-age Hispanic adults are uninsured, compared with 27 percent of working-age Hispanic adults born in the United States. Furthermore, among the foreign-born the uninsured rate is much higher for those who have been in the United States less than five years and for noncitizens than for those who have been in the United States longer than five years and for naturalized citizens, respectively. Notably, the uninsured rate does not vary by nativity for Hispanics of Puerto Rican origin, a pattern that differs from that of the other national-origin groups and probably reflects the unique circumstances of Puerto Ricans regarding U.S. citizenship. Nativity is associated with health insurance coverage among Hispanic seniors, although the differences in uninsured rates by nativity are much smaller for seniors than for working-age adults, presumably as a result of the Medicare program. Overall, 9 percent of foreign-born Hispanic seniors are uninsured, compared with 2 percent of U.S.-born seniors.

Table 10-3 shows the relationship between language preference, as assessed by the language of the survey, and health insurance coverage among Hispanic working-age adults. Overall, Hispanics who prefer Spanish are twice as likely as those who prefer English to be uninsured (57 versus 29 percent). This is due to much higher rates of employer-sponsored coverage for working-age adults who prefer English, combined with a minimal difference in Medicaid coverage by language preference. However, the pattern for Puerto Ricans again differs from that of the other national-origin groups. Puerto Rican working-age adults who prefer Spanish have a much higher

TABLE 10-1 Health Insurance Coverage, by Age Category and National Origin

	Coverage					
Age and National Origin	Employer (%)	Medicaid (%)	Medicare (%)	Other (%)	Uninsured (%)	Number
All Hispanics						
Children	43	27	1	3	28	40,483
Working-age adults	48	8	2	3	40	62,170
Seniors	18	26	81	9	6	5,726
Mexican						
Children	41	26	1	2	32	26,677
Working-age adults	45	7	1	2	46	38,203
Seniors	17	24	80	10	7	3,047
Puerto Rican						
Children	43	41	1	4	12	3,474
Working-age adults	53	19	4	4	23	5,438
Seniors	18	30	85	8	3	562
Cuban						
Children	61	16	1	10	14	1,026
Working-age adults	59	5	3	11	24	2,957
Seniors	14	30	88	8	2	903
Other Hispanics						
Children	47	26	7	4	24	9,306
Working-age adults	50	7	2	4	38	15,572
Seniors	22	27	77	10	8	1,214
Non-Hispanic white						
Children	76	10	0	6	9	72,101
Working-age adults	75	3	3	7	14	185,580
Seniors	39	5	93	33	1	43,243
Non-Hispanic wlack						
Children	48	35	1	4	14	23,602
Working-age adults	58	12	4	5	24	40,667
Seniors	29	18	85	13	3	6,037

SOURCE: 1997–2001 NHIS.

rate of Medicaid coverage than those who prefer English; as a result, the difference in uninsured rates by language preference is much smaller for Puerto Ricans than for the other groups.

Usual Source of Care

Not having a usual source of health care is another key barrier to health care access. A usual source of care is a health care provider where people usually go when they are sick or need advice about their health. Having a

TABLE 10-2 Health Insurance Coverage for Working-Age Adults, by Nativity, Years in United States, and Citizenship

Nativity, Years in U.S., and Citizenship	Coverage					
	Employer (%)	Medicaid/ SCHIP (%)	Medicare (%)	Other (%)	Uninsured (%)	Number
All Hispanics						
U.S.-born	60	9	2	4	27	24,625
Foreign-born	40	8	2	3	49	37,236
< 5 years in U.S.	19	5	0	2	74	4,611
> 5 years in U.S.	45	8	2	3	43	21,584
Noncitizen	31	6	1	2	61	19,591
Citizen	58	10	3	5	26	9,585
Mexican						
U.S.-born	60	8	2	4	28	16,041
Foreign-born	34	6	1	1	58	22,016
< 5 years in U.S.	16	3	0	1	80	2,933
> 5 years in U.S.	40	7	1	1	52	12,418
Noncitizen	28	6	1	1	65	13,412
Citizen	55	6	2	3	35	3,984
Puerto Rican						
U.S.-born	55	17	3	5	23	2,691
Foreign-born	51	21	6	4	22	2,708
< 5 years in U.S.	37	28	2	8	25	187
> 5 years in U.S.	54	21	6	4	20	1,736
Cuban						
U.S.-born	69	4	1	9	17	687
Foreign-born	55	6	3	12	26	2,248
< 5 years in U.S.	30	10	1	2	57	251
> 5 years in U.S.	58	5	4	13	22	1,404
Noncitizen	37	8	2	8	47	719
Citizen	67	4	5	14	13	989
Other Hispanics						
U.S.-born	62	8	2	4	25	5,206
Foreign-born	44	7	1	4	45	10,264
< 5 years in U.S.	21	3	0	5	71	1,240
> 5 years in U.S.	50	8	1	4	38	6,026
Noncitizen	35	7	1	3	55	5,399
Citizen	63	7	2	5	24	2,540

SOURCE: 1997–2001 NHIS.

usual source of care reduces barriers to care that may arise from the difficulty and cost of searching for a health care provider. Familiarity with a particular provider may also make people more comfortable in seeking care, make it easier to make appointments at convenient times, and reduce

TABLE 10-3 Health Insurance Coverage for Working-Age Adults, by Language Preference

Language Preference	Coverage					
	Employer (%)	Medicaid/ SCHIP (%)	Medicare (%)	Other (%)	Uninsured (%)	Number
All Hispanics						
English	59	8	2	4	29	30,320
Spanish	31	10	2	2	57	23,660
Mexican						
English	59	6	2	3	31	17,382
Spanish	28	8	1	1	63	15,537
Puerto Rican						
English	57	16	4	5	21	3,770
Spanish	34	34	6	2	27	1,035
Cuban						
English	71	4	3	7	17	851
Spanish	49	6	3	14	29	1,726
Other Hispanics						
English	60	6	2	5	28	8,317
Spanish	32	10	1	2	55	5,362

SOURCE: 1997–2001 NHIS.

uncertainty about the costs or other inconveniences involved in obtaining care. A usual source of care enhances continuity and provides the connection with more specialized forms of care. Not surprisingly, people with a usual source of care are more likely than those without a usual source to get care and less likely to have difficulty obtaining care or to go without receiving needed services.

However, not all types of usual source of care are the same. Private physicians' offices and health maintenance organizations are believed to represent the most appropriate settings for primary care, as they foster continuity of care and facilitate preventive care. By contrast, public clinics, hospital outpatient departments, and emergency departments are characterized by long waiting times, less satisfactory patient–physician relationships, and less continuity of care (Lewin-Epstein, 1991; Petchers and Milligan, 1988).

Studies show that Hispanics are less likely than non-Hispanic whites to have a usual source of care (Hargraves, Cunningham, and Hughes, 2001), and more than one-third of immigrants lack a usual source. Furthermore, among Hispanics, Spanish speakers are less likely than English speakers to have a usual source (Schur and Albers, 1996; Weinick and Krauss, 2000). Hispanics also are more likely than whites to rely on community or public clinics or hospital outpatient departments rather than physicians' offices or health maintenance organizations as their usual source of care (Doty, 2003a; Lewin-Epstein, 1991).

However, U.S.-born Hispanics are more likely than immigrants to have a physician's office or a health maintenance organization as their usual source of care, and naturalized immigrants are nearly twice as likely as noncitizens to have these types of usual source (Ku and Matani, 2001).

Table 10-4 presents data on usual source of care for Hispanics, non-Hispanic whites, and non-Hispanic blacks, obtained from the 1997–2001 NHIS. Overall, Hispanics in all age groups are more likely than whites and blacks to lack a usual source of care, and they are less likely to have a physician's office as their usual source. As with health insurance coverage, the differences between Hispanics and whites are most pronounced for Hispanics of Mexican origin: 14 percent of Mexican children and 33 percent of Mexican working-age adults lack a usual source of care. By contrast, the proportions of Puerto Ricans and Cubans lacking a usual source of care are similar to or only slightly higher than the proportions of whites and blacks. The main difference between Puerto Ricans and Cubans is the type of usual source: Puerto Ricans are less likely than Cubans to use a physician's office as their usual source of care, but more likely to use a clinic.

Nativity, time since arrival in the United States, and citizenship are associated with having a usual source of care (Table 10-5). Foreign-born, working-age Hispanic adults are more likely than Hispanic adults born in the United States to lack a usual source of care. This pattern is also observed for every national-origin group except Puerto Ricans, for whom having a usual source of care is unrelated to nativity. Moreover, among foreign-born Hispanics those who arrived in the United States less than five years ago and those who are not citizens are twice as likely to lack a usual source as those who have been in the United States longer than five years and naturalized citizens, respectively. Nativity, time since arrival, and citizenship are also associated with having a physician's office as the usual source of care. Only 20 percent of recent immigrants have a physician's office as their usual source of care. Nativity is unassociated with having a usual source of care among Hispanic seniors.

Finally, Table 10-6 shows the relationship between language preference and having a usual source of care. Overall, Hispanic working-age adults who prefer Spanish are nearly twice as likely to lack a usual source of care than those who prefer English. This pattern also holds for Mexicans, Cubans, and other Hispanics. For Puerto Ricans, by contrast, language preference is unassociated with having a usual source of care, although Puerto

TABLE 10-4 Usual Source of Care, by Age Category and National Origin

Age and National Origin	Source of Care: No Usual Source of Care (%)	Physician's Office (%)	Clinic or Hospital Output Department (%)	ER (%)	Other (%)	Number
All Hispanics						
Children	12	59	27	1	1	17,848
Working-age adults	28	49	20	1	1	23,770
Seniors	6	72	20	1	1	2,731
Mexican						
Children	14	56	28	1	1	11,157
Working-age adults	33	44	20	1	1	13,736
Seniors	7	74	18	0	1	1,411
Puerto Rican						
Children	6	63	29	1	0	1,677
Working-age adults	15	56	25	2	1	2,510
Seniors	5	62	31	1	1	313
Cuban						
Children	7	79	12	1	1	568
Working-age adults	18	68	11	2	1	1,166
Seniors	2	80	16	1	0	427
Other Hispanics						
Children	10	62	27	1	0	4,446
Working-age adults	26	51	21	2	1	6,358
Seniors	7	69	21	1	1	580
Non-Hispanic white						
Children	4	80	16	0	1	36,119
Working-age adults	15	67	16	1	1	84,493
Seniors	4	82	12	0	1	24,670
Non-Hispanic black						
Children	7	65	26	1	0	10,822
Working-age adults	16	58	23	2	1	19,151
Seniors	5	71	22	1	1	3,490

SOURCE: 1997–2001 NHIS.

Ricans who prefer English are more likely than those who prefer Spanish to have a physician's office as their usual source.

Other Barriers

An important structural barrier to health care access faced by many Hispanic patients is distance to medical care providers, in general, coupled

TABLE 10-5 Usual Source of Care for Working-Age Adults, by Nativity, Years in United States, and Citizenship

Nativity, Years in U.S., and Citizenship	Source of Care					
	No Usual Source of Care (%)	Physician's Office (%)	Clinic or Hospital Output Department (%)	ER (%)	Other (%)	Number
All Hispanics						
U.S.-born	21	59	18	1	1	9,857
Foreign-born	34	41	22	2	1	13,892
< 5 years in U.S.	56	20	20	2	2	1,755
> 5 years in U.S.	28	45	23	2	1	8,529
Noncitizen	43	31	23	2	2	7,030
Citizen	18	58	21	1	1	3,782
Mexican						
U.S.-born	23	58	17	1	1	6,060
Foreign-born	42	33	22	1	1	7,671
< 5 years in U.S.	62	14	20	1	3	1,051
> 5 years in U.S.	36	38	24	1	1	4,614
Noncitizen	47	27	23	1	2	4,594
Citizen	26	51	20	1	2	1,412
Puerto Rican						
U.S.-born	17	57	23	2	1	1,261
Foreign-born	14	56	27	2	1	1,244
< 5 years in U.S.	22	50	27	1	0	102
> 5 years in U.S.	13	55	29	2	1	812
Cuban						
U.S.-born	14	71	11	2	2	267
Foreign-born	20	67	11	2	1	896
< 5 years in U.S.	n.a.	n.a.	n.a.	n.a.	n.a.	96
> 5 years in U.S.	18	69	11	2	1	607
Noncitizen	37	46	15	1	1	308
Citizen	10	79	9	2	0	406
Other Hispanics						
U.S.-born	18	61	18	1	1	2,269
Foreign-born	29	45	22	2	1	4,081
< 5 years in U.S.	53	23	19	3	2	506
> 5 years in U.S.	24	50	23	2	2	2,496
Noncitizen	36	36	24	2	2	2,109
Citizen	16	61	20	1	1	1,028

NOTE: n.a. = not available. Percentages not reported if fewer than 100 observations.
SOURCE: 1997–2001 NHIS.

TABLE 10-6 Usual Source of Care for Working-Age Adults, by Language Preference

Language Preference	Source of Care					
	No Usual Source of Care (%)	Physician's Office (%)	Clinic or Hospital Output Department (%)	ER (%)	Other (%)	Number
All Hispanics						
English	21	57	19	1	1	13,587
Spanish	39	35	23	1	1	9,409
Mexican						
English	25	55	18	1	1	7,380
Spanish	45	30	23	1	1	5,903
Puerto Rican						
English	15	59	23	2	1	1,953
Spanish	15	48	34	2	0	500
Cuban						
English	14	72	11	2	2	390
Spanish	22	66	11	1	1	744
Other Hispanics						
English	20	59	18	1	1	3,864
Spanish	36	35	25	3	1	2,262

SOURCE: 1997–2001 NHIS.

with low availability of Hispanic health care professionals, in particular. In California, communities with a high proportion of Hispanic residents are four times more likely than communities with a high proportion of non-Hispanic whites to have a shortage of physicians, irrespective of income level (Komaromy et al., 1996). The low number of Hispanic physicians undoubtedly contributes to these geographic patterns, as Hispanic physicians are much more likely than other physicians to locate in Hispanic communities.

The low number of Hispanic physicians also exacerbates the effects on patients of geographic physician shortages. Hispanic physicians are more likely than other physicians to care for Hispanic patients, even after accounting for the demographic composition of the community (Komaromy et al., 1996). Hispanics perceive that Hispanic physicians provide care of higher quality than do other physicians (Saha, Komaromy, Koepsell, and Bindman, 1999), and they tend to seek care from Hispanic physicians because of personal preference and language, irrespective of location and socioeconomic factors (Gray and Stoddard, 1997; Saha, Taggart, Komarony, and Bindman, 2000). For example, Saha et al. (2000) found that more than two-fifths of Hispanic patients considered the physician's ability to speak Spanish when choosing a physician.

Cultural differences between patients and health care providers may create barriers to access as well. According to Betancourt, Green, and Carrillo (2002), cultural differences encompass patients' ability to recognize symptoms of diseases, thresholds for seeking care, expectations of care, and the ability to understand prescribed treatments, all of which are likely to affect Hispanic patients' patterns of seeking care as well as providers' responses to their Hispanic patients.

Barriers to obtaining appropriate and timely health care may arise from the behavior of providers. There is considerable evidence that many well-meaning people who are not overtly biased hold unconscious negative racial attitudes and stereotypes (e.g., Dovidio, Brigham, Johnson, and Gaertner, 1996). There is also evidence that health care providers are influenced in their clinical decisions by patients' race and ethnicity. Although most of this research pertains to blacks, studies based on patient reports suggest that these provider attitudes and behaviors may influence the care that Hispanics receive as well.

Lillie-Blanton and colleagues (2000) analyzed data from interviews with a nationally representative sample of U.S. adults. They found that 30 percent of Hispanics believe racism, defined as people being treated worse than others because of their race or ethnicity, is a "major problem" in health care, compared with 16 percent of non-Hispanic whites. In addition, more than one-half of Hispanics thought the health care system treats people unfairly based on their race or ethnicity, and nearly three-fourths thought it treats people unfairly based on how well they speak English. More than one-half of Hispanics thought Hispanics received lower quality of care than whites. Perhaps most significant, 36 percent of Hispanics, compared with 15 percent of whites, reported that they, a family member, or a friend had been treated unfairly by the medical care system because of their race or ethnicity. And 13 percent of Hispanics, compared with 1 percent of whites, reported personally experiencing unfair treatment.

These barriers to health care access may have profound effects on Hispanic patients' decisions to seek care. For example, parents of low-income Hispanic children report that low affordability, language problems, transportation problems, long waiting times in the office, poor communication with providers, and lack of cultural understanding by clinic staff are obstacles to access that occasionally caused them not to bring their children in for care (Flores, Abreu, Olivar, and Kastner, 1998). Language barriers, in particular, may cause Spanish speakers not to seek needed care.

Health Care Utilization

In this section, we review the status of Hispanics with regard to their utilization of health care services. We discuss the use of prenatal care and preventive health care services, rates of ambulatory visits and hospitalizations, and medical care expenditures.

Prenatal Care

Early and continuous prenatal care is thought to promote good health outcomes for both mothers and infants. Although the effects of prenatal care are difficult to measure, it is widely believed that early prenatal care fosters healthier pregnancies by enabling health care providers to identify and treat maternal conditions and behaviors that can adversely affect the initial stages of fetal development, provide medical advice, and assess the risk of a poor pregnancy outcome (Giachello, 2001). Prenatal care may also provide an entry point to the health care system, especially for women who do not have a usual source of care. Women who begin prenatal care after the first trimester of pregnancy or who have no prenatal care receive less preventive care and education and have a higher risk of undetected complications.

Historically, Hispanic women have been less likely than non-Hispanic white women to receive early prenatal care. For example, in both 1980 and 1990, 60 percent of Hispanic women received prenatal care beginning in the first trimester, compared with more than 80 percent of white women (National Center for Health Statistics, 2003). However, the gap between Hispanic and white women has been shrinking in recent years. In 1995, 71 percent of Hispanic women began prenatal care in their first trimester, compared with 87 percent of white women; in 2001, the proportions who began prenatal care in the first trimester were 76 percent and 89 percent, respectively. As shown in Table 10-7, Hispanic women and non-Hispanic black women have similar rates of receiving early prenatal care.

As with most other access indicators, aggregate data mask important differences in prenatal care across Hispanic groups defined by national origin. Hispanics of Mexican origin have long had the lowest rate of prenatal care, whereas the rate for Cubans has often exceeded that for non-Hispanic whites. Puerto Rican and Hispanics of other Central or South American origin fare better than Mexicans but worse than whites.

Other studies have found that Hispanic mothers born in the United States are more likely than foreign-born Hispanic mothers to receive prenatal care in the first trimester (Giachello, 2001). However, the difference—76 versus 73 percent in 1999—is very small, especially when compared

TABLE 10-7 Receipt of Prenatal Care for Live Births, By National Origin

	Prenatal Care		
National Origin	First Trimester (%)	Second Trimester (%)	Third Trimester or None (%)
All Hispanics	76	18	6
Mexicans	75	19	6
Puerto Ricans	79	16	5
Cubans	92	7	1
Central/South Americans	77	17	6
Other/unknown	77	17	5
Non-Hispanic whites	89	9	2
Non-Hispanic blacks	75	19	7

SOURCE: National Center for Health Statistics (2003). Data set for 2001.

with the effect of nativity on health insurance coverage and usual source of care.

Lack of health insurance coverage may make prenatal care unaffordable for many Hispanic women. Additional barriers are likely to include language and cultural incompatibility between women and their prenatal care providers, lack of understanding or knowledge of prenatal care, and fear of the effect of seeking care on immigrant status.

Thus the narrowing of disparities in prenatal care between Hispanics and whites during the 1990s is noteworthy, especially in light of the high proportion of Hispanics who lack health insurance. Many analysts believe that recent expansions in Medicaid eligibility have enabled more low-income women, including Hispanic women, to access prenatal care (e.g., Morbidity and Mortality Weekly Report, 2000; Ray, Mitchell, and Piper, 1997). Others, however, underscore a persistent gap in prenatal care between women with private and with public insurance coverage (Braveman, Bennettt, Lewis, Egerter, and Showstack, 1993).

Preventive Services

The goal of preventive health care services is to reduce morbidity and mortality through the prevention or detection of disease. For the last decade and a half, the United States Preventive Services Task Force has assessed the available evidence on the effectiveness of preventive health care services and issued recommendations regarding their use. Recommended preventive services for children include immunizations against a wide and growing array of infectious diseases. Recommended preventive services for adults vary by age, but generally include screening tests for certain cancers as well as selected immunizations.

Hispanics are less likely than non-Hispanic whites to receive recommended preventive services, although, as with prenatal care, the gap between Hispanics and whites has narrowed in recent years. By contrast, Hispanics are more likely than non-Hispanic blacks to receive certain preventive services. For example, in 1995, 68 percent of Hispanic children 19 to 35 months of age had received the recommended doses of diphtheria and tetanus toxoids and pertussis vaccine, oral poliovirus vaccine, measles vaccine and haemophilus influenzae Type B vaccine, compared with 76 percent of white children and 70 percent of black children (National Center for Health Statistics, 2003). By 2001, the proportions were 77, 79, and 71 percent, respectively. In 2001, Hispanic and white children had similar rates of hepatitis B and varicella vaccines (National Center for Health Statistics, 2003), whereas Hispanics had higher rates than blacks. A likely explanation for the shrinking gap in childhood vaccination rates is the Vaccines for Children program, which was created in 1994 and provides vaccines free of charge to eligible children, including uninsured children (Centers for Disease Control and Prevention, 2004).

In contrast to children, Hispanic seniors continue to lag non-Hispanic white seniors in the receipt of age-appropriate vaccinations (National Center for Health Statistics, 2003). For example, in 1999–2001, only 31 percent of Hispanic adults age 65 and older reported ever receiving a pneumococcal vaccine, compared with 56 percent of white seniors and 32 percent of black seniors. And 55 percent of Hispanic seniors reported receiving a flu shot during the preceding 12 months, compared with 67 percent of whites and 47 percent of blacks.

Working-age Hispanic women lag both non-Hispanic white and non-Hispanic black women in the rates of mammography and pap smears (National Center for Health Statistics, 2003). In 2000, only 54 percent of Hispanic women 40 to 49 years old and 66 percent of Hispanic women 50 to 64 years old reported receiving a mammogram within the previous two years, compared with 67 and 81 percent of white women in these age groups, respectively, and 61 percent and 78 percent of black women. Mexican women had the lowest mammography rates (61 percent for women 40 to 64 years old), while Cubans had the highest rates (80 percent). In addition, 79 percent of Hispanic women 18 to 49 years old and 76 percent of Hispanic women 50 to 64 years old reported receiving a pap smear within the previous three years, compared with 87 and 85 percent of white women in these age groups, respectively, and 89 and 84 percent of black women. Sambamoorthi and McAlpine (2003) found that socioeconomic status and health insurance coverage explain the disparities between working-age Hispanic and white women in their rates of pap smears and mammograms. Interestingly, Hispanic, white, and black women who were 65 years and older reported similar rates of mammography and pap smears, suggesting an important role for Medicare coverage.

Recent data show that only 18 percent of Hispanics 50 years old and older receive colon cancer screening, compared with 28 percent of whites. Only 58 percent of Hispanic smokers receive smoking cessation counseling, compared with 82 percent of white smokers. Using MEPS, Stewart and Silverstein (2002) found that Hispanics were less likely than whites and blacks to have a blood pressure or cholesterol screening, although the differences in rates were explained by differences in health insurance coverage and socioeconomic status.

Visits and Hospitalizations

The available evidence suggests that the barriers to access faced by Hispanics result in lower use of health care. Most studies have found fewer ambulatory visits among Hispanics than among non-Hispanic whites, even controlling for demographic and socioeconomic factors, health status, and type of health insurance (e.g., Fiscella, Franks, Doescher, and Saver, 2002; Guendelman and Wagner, 2000; Weinick, Jacobs, Stone, Ortega, and Burstin, 2004). These studies have also documented differences across Hispanic subgroups defined by national origin. For example, Weinick et al. (2004) found that Hispanics of Puerto Rican or Cuban origin were more likely than those of Mexican or Central American origin to have had a visit during the preceding year. Other studies have found lower utilization among Hispanics who speak Spanish, compared with English speakers, and among those who are less acculturated (e.g., Fiscella et al., 2002; Solis, Marks, Garcia, and Shelton, 1990; Weinick et al., 2004). In fact, using data from the Community Tracking Survey, Fiscella et al. (2002) found a sizable difference between Spanish-speaking Hispanics and whites in physician visits and mental health visits, but no difference between English-speaking Hispanics and whites. However, using MEPS data, Weinick et al. (2004) found differences in ambulatory visit rates between Hispanics and whites regardless of language. The difference in findings between these two studies may reflect their use of different data sources; although both surveys are national in scope, MEPS is the only one that is nationally representative. Physician visit rates are much lower for undocumented Hispanic immigrants than for their legal counterparts (Berk et al., 2000). Studies of hospitalization rates have yielded mixed results, with some studies finding similar rates for Hispanics and whites and others finding lower rates for Hispanics (e.g., Berk et al., 2000; Freiman, 1998; Weinick et al., 2004).

We used data from the 1996–2000 MEPS to assess current patterns of utilization for Hispanics, non-Hispanic whites, and non-Hispanic blacks. Table 10-8 presents descriptive data on ambulatory visits to physicians and to nonphysician providers. Hispanic children are much less likely than white children to have a physician visit during the year, and they have fewer visits on average. Similarly, working-age Hispanics are less likely than whites to have a physician visit and have fewer visits. However, Hispanic children have more physician visits than black children, and working-age Hispanics have similar physician visit rates as their black counterparts.

TABLE 10-8 Visit and Hospitalization Rates, by Age Category and National Origin

	Visit and Hospitalization Rates					
Age and National Origin	Had Physician Visit (%)	Mean Number of Visits	Had Non-Physician Visit (%)	Mean Number of Visits	Had Inpatient Stay (%)	Number
All Hispanics						
Children	56	1.5	11	0.4	2	9,932
Working-age adults	52	2.6	16	0.8	7	15,270
Seniors	86	7.0	30	1.9	18	1,536
Mexican						
Children	53	1.4	10	0.3	2	7,350
Working-age adults	50	2.2	14	0.7	6	10,690
Seniors	84	6.7	25	1.7	19	875
Puerto Rican						
Children	63	1.9	12	0.5	2	1,011
Working-age adults	59	3.8	21	1.6	9	1,358
Seniors	87	n.a.	26	n.a.	21	137
Cuban						
Children	64	2.6	13	0.9	5	315
Working-age adults	55	3.5	15	0.7	7	640
Seniors	91	n.a.	28	n.a.	13	197
Non-Hispanic white						
Children	71	2.4	22	0.9	2	15,403
Working-age adults	69	3.5	35	2.0	7	42,360
Seniors	89	7.0	51	2.7	17	10,837
Non-Hispanic black						
Children	51	1.2	9	0.3	2	5,610
Working-age adults	57	2.7	17	1.0	8	9,675
Seniors	85	5.7	29	1.7	18	1,857

NOTE: n.a. = not available. Mean number of visits not reported if fewer than 250 observations.
SOURCE: 1996–2000 MEPS.

There is no difference between Hispanic and white seniors in their rates of physician visits.

In contrast to the findings for physician visits, Hispanics in all age groups have fewer visits than whites to nonphysician providers, and the rates of visits to nonphysician providers for Hispanic children and working-age adults are less than half the rates for whites. Rates of visits to nonphysician providers are similar for Hispanics and blacks. Use of inpatient hospital care is similar for Hispanics, whites, and blacks.

Table 10-8 also demonstrates important differences in utilization across Hispanic groups defined by national origin. Puerto Rican children and working-age adults and Cuban working-age adults have higher rates of ambulatory visits than Mexicans do. In fact, the average number of physician visits by Puerto Rican and Cuban working-age adults equals or exceeds the corresponding figures for non-Hispanic whites, although fewer Puerto Ricans and Cubans than whites have a visit to a physician during the year.

Additional tabulations found that nativity, time since arrival in the United States, and citizenship are all associated with the rate of ambulatory visits among working-age Hispanic adults. Thus, 48 percent of foreign-born Hispanics have a physician visit during the year, compared with 57 percent of the U.S.-born, and 12 percent of foreign-born Hispanics have a visit to a nonphysician provider, compared with 21 percent of the U.S.-born. Foreign-born Hispanics average 2.4 physician visits annually, compared with 2.7 visits for the U.S.-born. Among the foreign-born, Hispanics who have been in the United States less than five years and noncitizens have much lower rates of ambulatory visits, respectively, than Hispanics who have been in the United States longer than five years and naturalized citizens. These patterns are also found in Hispanic groups defined by national origin, with the exception of Puerto Ricans.

Working-age Hispanic adults who prefer English have more ambulatory visits to physicians and to nonphysician providers than those who prefer Spanish. Specifically, 58 percent of English speakers had a physician visit during the year, compared with 46 percent of Spanish speakers. The average numbers of annual visits were 2.8 and 2.4, respectively.

Finally, we used multivariate logistic regression analysis to examine differences in the probability of having a physician visit, having a nonphysician visit, and having an inpatient stay between working-age Hispanics and non-Hispanic whites by national origin, by nativity, and by language preference, controlling for age, sex, income, education, marital status, health insurance coverage, and health status (measured using self-rated general health and chronic conditions). We found that, other things being equal, Hispanics in all national-origin groups are significantly less likely than whites to have a physician or nonphysician visit ($P < .001$). Hispanics of Mexican origin are less likely than whites to use inpatient hospital care ($P < .001$), but the other national-origin groups are hospitalized at rates similar to whites. We also found that foreign-born Hispanics are significantly less likely than their U.S.-born peers to have a physician visit ($P < .05$) or nonphysician visit ($P < .001$), and that Spanish-speaking Hispanics are less likely than English speakers to have a nonphysician visit ($P < .001$). Interestingly, both U.S.-born Hispanics and English-speaking Hispanics are less likely than whites to have a physician or nonphysician visit ($P < .001$), indicating that even the most advantaged Hispanics have lower use than whites, other things being equal.

Medical Care Expenditures

Analyses of medical care expenditures are useful because expenditures capture both quantitative and qualitative aspects of health care utilization. There are few studies of differences in medical care expenditures between Hispanics and non-Hispanic whites. Using data from the 1987 National Medical Expenditure Survey, Freiman (1998) found lower expenditures for Hispanics than whites even controlling for demographic and socioeconomic factors, health status, and health insurance coverage. By contrast, using data from MEPS, Escarce and Kapur (2003) found that Hispanic and white seniors had similar total expenditures for medical care. However, public sources of payment accounted for a much larger share of total expenditures for Hispanic seniors than for white seniors. Specifically, 82 percent of total medical care expenditures for Hispanic seniors were from Medicare or Medicaid, compared with 65 percent for white seniors. The differences in the distribution of payment sources between Hispanics and whites were nearly fully explained by differences in socioeconomic status and dual eligibility for Medicaid.

Table 10-9 presents descriptive data for Hispanics, non-Hispanic whites, and non-Hispanic blacks on total medical expenditures and expenditures for prescription drugs, obtained from the 1996–2000 MEPS. Hispanic children and working-age adults are less likely than whites to incur medical expenditures during the year, and their average expenditures are considerably lower. By contrast, Hispanic children are slightly more likely than black children to incur medical expenditures, and their average expenditures are higher. Hispanic children and working-age adults also have much lower expenditures than whites for prescription drugs, whereas Hispanic children have higher prescription drug expenditures than black children. Notably, Hispanic, white, and black seniors have similar total medical care expenditures and prescription drug expenditures.

As in previous comparisons, there are differences in medical care expenditures across Hispanic groups defined by national origin. In particular,

TABLE 10-9 Total Medical Care Expenditures and Prescription Drug Expenditures, by Age Category, and National Origin

Age and National Origin	Expenditures				
	Had Medical Care Expenditure (%)	Mean Total Expenditures (%)	Had Drug Expenditure ($)	Mean Drug Expenditures ($)	Number
All Hispanics					
Children	64	460	45	57	9,932
Working-age adults	62	1,164	50	181	15,267
Seniors	93	5,131	86	799	1,536
Mexican					
Children	62	459	44	55	7,350
Working-age adults	59	1,013	48	157	10,688
Seniors	92	5,335	86	794	874
Puerto Rican					
Children	72	498	48	74	1,010
Working-age adults	71	1,980	59	302	1,357
Seniors	93	n.a.	90	n.a.	137
Cuban					
Children	67	n.a.	48	n.a.	315
Working-age adults	66	1,419	53	255	640
Seniors	96	n.a.	83	n.a.	197
Non-Hispanic white					
Children	80	611	57	90	15,403
Working-age adults	80	1,853	67	343	42,360
Seniors	95	5,380	88	844	10,837
Non-Hispanic black					
Children	61	362	40	43	5,610
Working-age adults	69	1,682	55	246	9,675
Seniors	92	5,319	86	790	1,857

NOTE: n.a. = not available. Mean expenditures not reported if fewer than 500 observations.
SOURCE: 1996–2000 MEPS.

working-age adults of Puerto Rican origin have much higher average total expenditures and expenditures for prescription drugs than Mexicans do.

Additional analyses found that nativity, time since arrival in the United States, and citizenship are associated with the level of medical care expenditures. As anticipated, foreign-born, working-age Hispanics have lower total expenditures and lower expenditures for prescription drugs than Hispanics born in the United States. In addition, among the foreign-born, those who arrived in the United States less than five years ago have much lower expenditures than those who have been in the United States longer than five years. Expenditures for noncitizens, on average, are less than half as large as expenditures for naturalized citizens.

Working-age Hispanics who prefer Spanish have lower total expenditures and expenditures for prescription drugs than do Hispanics who prefer English. Only 57 percent of working-age Hispanics who prefer Spanish incur medical care expenditures during the year, and only 44 percent have expenditures on prescription drugs. By comparison, 69 percent of working-age Hispanics who prefer English incur medical care expenditures, and 53 percent spend on prescription drugs.

As in the preceding section, we used multivariate logistic regression analysis to assess differences in the probability of incurring medical expenditures and incurring prescription drug expenditures between working-age Hispanics and non-Hispanic whites by national origin, by nativity, and by language preference, controlling for other factors than can affect the use of health care. We found that, other things being equal, Hispanics in all national-origin groups are significantly less likely than whites to incur medical or prescription drug expenditures ($P < .001$). In addition, foreign-born Hispanics are significantly less likely than U.S.-born Hispanics to incur expenditures ($P < .001$), and Spanish speakers are less likely than English speakers to do so ($P < .001$). Notably, both U.S.-born Hispanics and English-speaking Hispanics are less likely than whites to incur medical or prescription drug expenditures ($P < .001$), other things being equal.

QUALITY OF HEALTH CARE

According to the Institute of Medicine (1990), quality of health care consists of the "degree to which health services for individuals and populations increase the likelihood of desired health outcomes and are consistent with current professional knowledge." Receiving high quality of care is an important component of maintaining the health of any population.

Quality of health care can be evaluated on the basis of structure, process, or outcome (Donabedian, 1980). Structure refers to the characteristics and attributes of health care providers. Process refers to the components of the encounters between providers and patients, although the emphasis is usually on technical components of care, such as the appropriateness of the services provided and the technical skill with which the services are performed. Outcome refers to the effects of care on patients' health, such as amelioration of symptoms or reduction in morbidity or in the probability of death (Blumenthal, 1996; Brook, McGlynn, and Cleary, 1996).

In practice, many researchers on the quality of health care agree that the measurement of technical quality should depend much more on process data than on health outcomes (Brook et al., 1996). Process data are more sensitive indicators of quality than outcomes, because poor outcomes do not necessarily follow errors in processes of care. Moreover, some poor outcomes are very rare, or they may lag poor process by many years. The development of process measures of quality of care has improved dramatically in recent years (Brook et al., 1996).

Over the last decade and a half, there has been growing recognition that patients' opinions about their health care are also important indicators of quality (Blumenthal, 1996; Cleary and McNeil, 1988). Patients are in the best position to judge the nontechnical dimensions of their encounters with providers, including the quality of their interpersonal interactions and communication with providers, providers' ability to gain their trust, and the timeliness and responsiveness of the care they receive. Consequently, assessments of health care quality have increasingly incorporated patient reports of their experiences with health care and measures of their satisfaction with that care.

It is worth underscoring that the quality of interpersonal interactions between patients and providers and patient satisfaction with their care can affect the technical quality of care and health outcomes. For example, studies have found that satisfaction is associated with health care utilization, patient compliance with provider recommendations, and willingness to initiate malpractice litigation (Sherbourne, Hays, Ordway, DiMatteo, and Kravitz, 1992; Vaccarino, 1977; Zastowny, Roghmann, and Cafferata, 1989). In addition, dissatisfaction with care has been linked with switching providers and disenrollment from health plans, which can affect continuity of care (Marquis, Davies, and Ware, 1983; Newcomer, Preston, and Harrington, 1996).

Process of Care

Few studies have assessed process quality of care for Hispanic patients. Studies of quality of care for ischemic heart disease have generally suggested that Hispanics and non-Hispanic whites receive similar quality. For example, using data from the National Registry of Myocardial Infarction, Canto et al. (1998) found that Hispanics with a heart attack were as likely as whites to receive thrombolytic therapy, coronary angiography, and revascularization procedures. Similarly, Leape, Hilborne, Bell, Kamberg, and Brook (1999) analyzed data from 13 hospitals in New York City and found that, among patients in whom revascularization was clinically necessary, Hispanics were as likely as whites to receive revascularization procedures. In contrast, Hannan et al. (1999) found that Hispanics in New York state were less likely than whites to receive appropriate revascularization procedures even controlling for type of health insurance. Most likely, the divergent findings of these studies reflect geographic differences in patterns of care as well as variations in methods across the studies. Controlling for severity of disease and insurance status, Shapiro et al. (1999) found that Hispanics were less likely than whites to receive appropriate drug therapy for human immunodeficiency virus infection.

Several recent studies have compared process quality of care for Hispanic and white Medicare beneficiaries enrolled in Medicare managed care plans (e.g., McBean, Huang, Virnig, Lurie, and Musgrave, 2003; Virnig et al., 2002, 2004). These studies found worse quality for Hispanics on certain important indicators, such as cholesterol management after a cardiovascular event, control of blood sugar in diabetes, and rates of follow-up after a hospitalization for mental illness. Quality was similar for other indicators, however, including administration of beta blockers after a heart attack, preventive care for diabetics, and control of high blood pressure.

Satisfaction with Care

Several studies have assessed Hispanics' experiences and satisfaction with health care. An early review of the literature on the relationship between patient characteristics and satisfaction with care found no relationship between race or ethnicity and satisfaction (Hall and Dornan, 1990). More recent studies, however, have found differences in both experiences of care and satisfaction by race and ethnicity. Morales et al. (1999) found that Hispanics are less satisfied than whites with communication with health care providers in medical group practices. Phillips, Mayer, and Aday (2000) found that Hispanics were twice as likely as whites to perceive that clinicians fail to provide needed information. Doty (2003b) found that one-third of Hispanics, compared with 16 percent of whites, reported having a problem understanding or communicating with their physicians. Furthermore, only 56 percent of Hispanics were very satisfied with their health care, compared with 65 percent of whites. In contrast, Morales and colleagues (2001) found no differences in global ratings of care between Hispanic and white adults enrolled in 53 commercial and 31 Medicaid managed care plans across the United States.

Not surprisingly, language seems to matter enormously in Hispanics' reports of their experiences with health care as well as in their global ratings of care. Weech-Maldonado and colleagues (2001) used the Consumer Assessment of Health Plans Survey (CAHPS) to evaluate parents' assessments of their children's care in 33 Medicaid managed care plans in 6 states. Hispanics who spoke Spanish reported worse experiences than whites with regard to timeliness of care, provider communication, staff helpfulness, and health plan service, whereas Hispanics who spoke English reported experiences similar to those of whites. In striking contrast to their reports of care, however, Hispanics who spoke Spanish gave higher global ratings to their physicians and to their health plans than both whites and English-speaking Hispanics.

Weech-Maldonado and colleagues (2003) also used the CAHPS to evaluate adults' assessments of their care in 156 Medicaid managed care plans in 14 states. They found a gradient in patients' reports of their experiences with care according to English fluency. Thus Hispanics who spoke English reported slightly worse experiences than whites with regard to timeliness of care and staff helpfulness; Spanish-speaking Hispanics reported substantially worse experiences than whites with regard to timeliness of care, provider communication, and staff helpfulness; and the reports of bilingual Hispanics were intermediate. Similar to the earlier study of children, however, Hispanics—and especially those who spoke Spanish—gave higher global ratings to their physicians and health plans than whites did.

Other smaller studies support a role for language as well. In a study of patients treated in medical group practices, Morales et al. (1999) found lower satisfaction with communication among Spanish-speaking Hispanics compared with English speakers. In a recent survey (Doty, 2003b), nearly half of Spanish speakers reported problems communicating with or understanding their physician. Carrasquillo et al. (1999) found that non-English-speaking patients were less satisfied than patients who spoke English with the care they received during visits to the emergency room.

The importance of language is further underscored by the findings of recent studies of the effect of interpreters. Morales et al. (2003) used CAHPS to assess the impact of interpreters on parents' experiences with their children's care in the California SCHIP program. They found that Hispanics who needed interpreters but never or only sometimes had one reported worse experiences than patients who did not need interpreters with regard to provider and staff communication, access to care, and health plan service. However, Hispanics who needed interpreters and always had one reported as good or better experiences than patients who did not need interpreters.

Other studies also show benefits of interpreters, although they are not nearly as favorable as the analysis of children in the California SCHIP program. For example, Baker, Hayes, and Fortier (1998) studied Hispanic adults seen in a public hospital emergency department. They found that patients who communicated adequately with their provider without an interpreter gave higher ratings to interpersonal aspects of their care than patients who communicated through an interpreter. The latter patients, in turn, gave higher ratings than patients who communicated directly with the provider but said an interpreter should have been called. Using data from a primary care clinic, Rivadeneyra and colleagues (2000) found that providers more often ignored comments from Spanish-speaking patients who used an interpreter than from English speakers. In a study of Spanish-speaking patients seen in a primary care clinic at a public hospital, Fernandez et al. (2004) found that physicians' fluency in Spanish was associated with more favorable patient ratings of interpersonal aspects of their care despite the availability of interpreter services.

Taken together, the findings summarized in the preceding paragraphs confirm the primacy of language in patients' experiences with health care. The studies suggest that Hispanics who speak Spanish report much worse experiences with care than whites do, whereas English-speaking Hispanics report similar or only slightly worse experiences than whites. Furthermore, access to interpreters improves the care experiences of Spanish speakers, although they still lag the experiences of patients who speak English well. An important caveat is that the major studies of the role of language—i.e., those based on the CAHPS—included only low-income patients eligible for Medicaid or SCHIP (Morales et al., 2003; Weech-Maldonado et al., 2001, 2003). The only large study that included commercially insured patients did not assess language preference or proficiency (Morales et al., 2001). Similarly, most of the studies of interpreters have used data from individual institutions and consequently may not be generalizable.

The finding in several studies that Spanish-speaking Hispanics give higher global ratings than English speakers to their physicians and health plans despite reporting worse care experiences is counterintuitive. Researchers have suggested that reports of care experiences are less subjective than global ratings, and that the high global ratings given by Spanish speakers reflect their low expectations regarding their interactions with the health care system (e.g., Weech-Maldonado et al., 2001). This may be especially true for low-income Medicaid recipients and for recent immigrants whose prior experiences in their countries of origin are likely to have been in health care systems that provide markedly inferior care to the less privileged. An alternative explanation is that the high global ratings given to their physicians reflect a cultural disposition among Hispanics to be deferential to those who are presumed to be of higher status. This explanation is consistent with the particularly high global ratings given to physicians by Spanish speakers. Additional research on this issue is needed.

The important role of interpreters in improving Hispanics' experiences with health care is noteworthy. According to a directive from the U.S. Department of Health and Human Services issued in August 2000, any entity receiving federal funds must offer and provide language assistance services to all patients with limited English proficiency at no cost, at all points of contact, and in a timely manner during all hours of operation. Interpretation by telephone is available throughout the United States via the AT&T language line, in which patient, provider, and interpreter communicate through a conference call. Interpreters are costly, however, and many providers are not in compliance with the directive. In fact, only about half of Hispanic patients who need an interpreter usually get one, and in most cases the interpreter is a staff person in the health care facility, a relative, or a friend and not a trained medical interpreter (Doty, 2003b). Studies have found that the type of interpreter affects patient satisfaction: patients generally prefer professional medical interpreters, including telephone interpreters, over ad hoc interpreters such as clinic staff, relatives, or friends (Hornberger et al., 1996; Lee, Batal, Maselli, and Kutner, 2002). Errors in interpretation may have clinical consequences (Flores et al., 2003).

Most of the available evidence suggests that interpreters do not make the experiences of Spanish speakers equivalent to those of English speakers. Interpreters appear to facilitate technical aspects of care, but they may not fully compensate for the effect of language differences between patients and providers on interpersonal aspects of care. As discussed earlier, the quality of interpersonal interactions between patients and providers can affect the technical quality of care and health outcomes.

CONCLUSION

Our summary of the existing research and our analysis of recent data are consistent with the notion that Hispanics have lower access to health care than do non-Hispanic whites. Hispanics in all age groups are much less likely than whites to have health insurance coverage or a usual source of health care, and they face numerous other barriers to access as well. Unsurprisingly, Hispanics have lower rates of use of prenatal care and preventive services than whites, although for certain of these services the gap between Hispanics and whites has narrowed in recent years. Hispanic children and working-age adults also have fewer physician visits than their white counterparts, and Hispanics of all ages have fewer visits to nonphysician providers than whites. Hispanics and whites have similar hospitalization rates. However, Hispanic children and working-age adults have much lower total medical care expenditures and expenditures for prescription drugs than whites do. Notably, Hispanic and white seniors have similar rates of physician visits and similar medical care expenditures, probably as a consequence of the availability of Medicare coverage to most seniors and the generosity of federal thresholds for dual Medicaid eligibility.

Aggregate data for all Hispanics mask large and important differences across Hispanic groups defined by national origin. In general, Hispanics of Mexican origin fare worse on indicators of access to health care than Puerto Ricans or Cubans, although Mexicans' indicators often resemble those of other Hispanics (i.e., Hispanics from other countries in Central or South America). Thus, compared with Mexicans, Puerto Ricans and Cubans are more likely to have health insurance coverage and a usual source of health care, have more physician visits, and have higher expenditures for medical care. Nonetheless, there are noteworthy differences in access indicators between Puerto Ricans and Cubans. For instance, Puerto Rican children and working-age adults are much more likely than their Cuban counterparts to obtain health insurance through public insurance programs like Medicaid or SCHIP, and they are less likely than Cubans to have a physician's office as their usual source of care.

Nativity, time since arrival in the United States, immigration status, and language also play crucial roles in determining indicators of health care access. Foreign-born Hispanics consistently have much worse access indicators than Hispanics born in the United States, except in the case of Puerto Ricans, for whom nativity makes little difference. Among the foreign-born, moreover, Hispanics who arrived in the United States less than five years ago and noncitizens have worse access indicators than those who arrived more than five years ago and naturalized citizens, respectively. Similarly, Hispanics who speak only Spanish or who prefer Spanish generally have worse access indicators than those who speak English. Puerto Ricans are again the exception, as their indicators of health care access do not differ by language preference.

Notably, socioeconomic status and health insurance coverage explain disparities between working-age Hispanic and white women in their rates of pap smears and mammograms. By contrast, our multivariate analyses suggest that differences in the probability of having a physician visit, having a nonphysician visit, and incurring medical expenditures between Hispanics and non-Hispanic whites, between foreign- and U.S.-born Hispanics, and between English- and Spanish-speaking Hispanics are not fully explained by socioeconomic status, health insurance, and health status. Thus, the effect of social class on access to care accounts for some, but not all, of the differences we reported by national origin, by nativity, and by language preference. Other barriers to access reviewed in this chapter, which are harder to measure and capture in quantitative analyses, are likely to affect the utilization of care by Hispanics.

Much less information is available regarding the quality of health care for Hispanics than regarding access to care. The available evidence indicates that process quality of care is similar or slightly worse for Hispanics, although the number of studies is very limited. Moreover, these studies have not assessed the role of national origin, language, or other factors that are associated with access to care. More information is available regarding Hispanics' experiences and satisfaction with care. These studies have found that Hispanics who speak only Spanish have worse experiences with health care than both whites and Hispanics who speak English. In fact, English speakers appear to have care experiences that are very similar to those of non-Hispanic whites. Furthermore, the use of interpreters improves the care experiences of Hispanics who speak Spanish, but even with interpreters the experiences of Spanish speakers lag those of English speakers. An intriguing finding of the research to date is that Spanish-speaking Hispanics give higher global ratings to their physicians and health plans than whites do, despite reporting worse experiences. This may be a manifestation of Spanish speakers' low expectations of the health care delivery system, or it may reflect a cultural disposition to be deferential to health care professionals.

The data summarized in this chapter raise a number of critical issues for public and private policy makers concerned about the well being of Hispanics in the United States, for health care providers, and for the health care system more generally. Continued immigration of Hispanics from Mexico and other countries in Central and South America, coupled with diffusion of these immigrants to new areas of the United States, will challenge our current approaches for providing health insurance coverage and health care to populations with low socioeconomic status. Given current trends in employer-sponsored health insurance, it seems inevitable that the number and proportion of uninsured Hispanics will grow rapidly in the next few years. The apparent success of Medicaid eligibility expansions in increasing low-income women's use of prenatal care and of the Vaccines for Children program in reducing disparities in childhood vaccination rates demonstrates the potential of public programs and public–private partnerships to enhance uninsured people's access to essential health care services. However, further large-scale expansions of federally subsidized programs, such as Medicaid and SCHIP, seem unlikely in this age of welfare reform and federal budget deficits. Progress in insuring more of the uninsured is likely to depend on state initiatives.

Growth in the number of uninsured Hispanics, in turn, will place increasing stress on the so-called health care safety net. This loosely organized system for making health care available to uninsured people includes public clinics and hospitals, many teaching hospitals, and free and reduced-price care provided by community physicians and hospitals. Many observers believe that the safety net has already been stretched thin by the growth of managed care and the increasing role of market forces in health care, and there is evidence that many health care providers have curtailed their provision of charity care. In a recent study, Marquis et al. (2004) found that the capacity of the safety net in different communities is strongly influenced by local economic conditions. Thus access to health care for uninsured Hispanics who must rely on safety net providers is likely to depend in large part on the strength of the economy in the communities where they live. This observation is especially salient for recent immigrants choosing new destinations in the United States.

Finally, the growth and geographic dispersion of the Hispanic population will challenge health care delivery systems and providers unaccustomed to caring for diverse groups of patients. In recent years, the concept of cultural competence has been proposed as a key factor in reducing racial and ethnic disparities in access to and quality of health care. According to Betancourt et al. (2002), "cultural competence describes the ability of systems to provide care to patients with diverse values, beliefs, and behaviors, including tailoring delivery to meet patients' social, cultural, and linguistic needs." Despite the lack of empirical evidence linking cultural competence to improvements in care, experts in both the public and private sectors consider cultural competence a crucial element of strategies to reduce disparities in care. Interestingly, a recent study found that physicians' self-rating of their cultural competence in caring for Spanish-speaking Hispanics with diabetes was associated with more favorable patient ratings of interpersonal aspects of care (Fernandez et al., 2004).

The data presented in this chapter indicate that finding ways to overcome the barriers posed by language must be a key component of providing culturally competent care to Hispanics. In most studies, lack of English fluency emerges as an important access barrier even controlling for other demographic and socioeconomic factors. Language clearly exerts a powerful influence on patients' experiences with care as well. In 2001, the Department of Health and Human Services issued a set of national standards for culturally and linguistically appropriate services in health care. Not surprisingly, the provision of information and services in patients' preferred language, including patient access to qualified, professional interpreters, assumes a central role in several of the standards (U.S. Department of Health and Human Services, 2001). Policy makers must also develop effective approaches for increasing the number of Spanish-speaking health care providers.

REFERENCES

Baker, D.W., Hayes, R., and Fortier, J.P. (1998). Interpreter use and satisfaction with interpersonal aspects of care for Spanish-speaking patients. *Medical Care, 36*(10), 1461–1470.

Berk, M.L., Schur, C.L., Chavez, L.R., and Frankel, M. (2000, July–August). Health care use among undocumented Latino immigrants. *Health Affairs, 19*(4), 51–64.

Betancourt, J.R., Green, A.R., and Carrillo, J.E. (2002, October). *Cultural competence in health care: Emerging frameworks and practical approaches.* New York: Commonwealth Fund. Available: http://www.cmwf.org [accessed May, 16 2004].

Blumenthal, D. (1996). Part 1: Quality of care—what is it? *New England Journal of Medicine, 335*, 891–894.

Braveman, P., Bennett, T., Lewis, C., Egerter, S., and Showstack, J. (1993, March). Access to prenatal care following major Medicaid eligibility expansions. *Journal of the American Medical Association, 269*(10), 1285–1289.

Brook, R.H., McGlynn, E.A., and Cleary, P.D. (1996). Part 2: Measuring quality of care. *New England Journal of Medicine, 335*, 966–970.

Canto, J.G., Taylor, H.A., Jr., Rogers, W.J., Sanderson, B., Hilbe, J., and Barron, H.V. (1998). Presenting characteristics, treatment patterns, and clinical outcomes of non-black minorities in the National Registry of Myocardial Infarction 2. *American Journal of Cardiology, 82*(9), 1013–1018.

Carrasquillo, O., Carrasquillo, A.I., and Shea, S. (2000). Health insurance coverage of immigrants living in the United States: Differences by citizenship status and country of origin. *American Journal of Public Health, 90*, 917–923.

Carrasquillo, O., Orav, E.J., Brennan, T.A., and Burstin, H. (1999). Impact of language barriers on patient satisfaction in an emergency department. *Journal of General Internal Medicine, 14*, 82–87.

Centers for Disease Control and Prevention. (2004). National immunization program, vaccines for children program. Available: http://www.cdc.gov/nip/vfc/Default.htm [accessed May 22, 2004].

Cleary, P.D., and McNeil, B.J. (1988). Patient satisfaction as an indicator of quality care. *Inquiry, 25*, 25–36.

David, R.A., and Rhee, M. (1998). The impact of language as a barrier to effective health care in an underserved urban Hispanic community. *Mount Sinai Journal of Medicine, 65*(5–6), 393–397.

Donabedian, A. (1980). *Explorations in quality assessment and monitoring: Vol. 1.* The definition of quality and approaches to its assessment. Ann Arbor, MI: Health Administration Press.

Doty, M. (2003a, October). *Insurance, access, and quality of care among Hispanic populations: 2003 chartpack.* New York: Commonwealth Fund. Available: http://www.cmwf.org/publications/publications_show.htm?doc_id=221241 [accessed May 04, 2004].

Doty, M. (2003b, February). *Hispanic patients' double burden: Lack of health insurance and limited English.* New York: Commonwealth Fund.

Dovidio, J.F., Brigham, J.C., Johnson, B.T., and Gaertner, S.L. (1996). Stereotyping, prejudice, and discrimination: Another look. In N. Macrae, C. Stangor, and M. Hewstone (Eds.), *Stereotypes and stereotyping* (pp. 276–319). New York: Guilford.

Dubay, L., Haley, J., and Kenney, G. (2002). *Children's eligibility for Medicaid and SCHIP: A view from 2000.* (Assessing the New Federalism, Policy Brief No. B-41.) Washington, DC: Urban Institute.

Escarce, J.J., and Kapur, K. (2003). Racial and ethnic differences in public and private medical care expenditures among aged Medicare beneficiaries. *Milbank Quarterly, 81*, 249–275.

Fernandez, A., Schillinger, D., Grumbach, K., Rosenthal, A., Stewart, A.I., Wang, F., and Perez-Stable, E.J. (2004). Physician language ability and cultural competence: An exploratory study of communication with Spanish-speaking patients. *Journal of General Internal Medicine*, *19*(2), 167–174.

Fiscella, K., Franks, P., Doescher, M.P., and Saver, B.G. (2002). Disparities in health care by race, ethnicity, and language among the insured: Findings from a national sample. *Medical Care*, *40*, 52–59.

Flores, G., Abreu, M., Olivar, M.A., and Kastner, B. (1998). Access barriers to health care for Latino children. *Archives of Pediatric and Adolescent Medicine*, *152*(11), 1119–1125.

Flores, G., Laws, M.B., Mayo, S.J., Zuckerman, B., Abreu, M., Medina, L., and Hardt, E.J. (2003). Errors in medical interpretation and their potential clinical consequences in pediatric encounters. *Pediatrics*, *111*, 6–14.

Frieman, M.P. (1998, October). The demand for health care among racial/ethnic subpopulations. *Health Services Research*, *33*(4 Pt 1), 867–890.

Giachello, A.L. (2001). The reproductive years: The health of Latinas. In M. Aguirre-Molina, C.W. Molina, and R.E. Zambrana (Eds.), *Health issues in the Latino community* (pp. 107–156). San Francisco: Jossey-Bass.

Gray, B., and Stoddard, J.J. (1997, August). Patient-physician pairing: Does racial and ethnic congruity influence selection of a regular physician? *Journal of Community Health*, *22*(4), 247–259.

Guendelman, S., and Wagner, T.H. (May, 2000). Health services utilization among Latinos and white non-Latinos: Results from a national survey. *Journal of Health Care for the Poor and Underserved*, *11*(2), 179–194.

Hall, J.A., and Dornan, M.C. (1990). Patient sociodemographic characteristics as predictors of satisfaction with medical care: A meta-analysis. *Social Science Medicine*, *30*(7), 811–818.

Hannan, E.L., van Ryn, M., Burke, L., Stone, D., Kumar, D., Arani, D., Pierce, W., Rafii, S., Sanborn, T.A., Sharma, S., Slater, J., and DeBuono, B.A. (1999). Access to coronary artery bypass surgery by race/ethnicity and gender among patients who are appropriate for surgery. *Medical Care*, *37*(1), 68–77.

Hargraves, J.L., Cunningham, P.J., and Hughes, R.G. (2001). Racial and ethnic differences in access to medical care in managed care plans. *Health Services Research*, *36*(5), 853–868.

Hornberger, J.C., Gibson, C.D., Wood, W., Dequeldre, C., Corso, I., Palla, B., and Bloch, D. A. (1996). Eliminating language barriers for non-English-speaking patients. *Medical Care*, *34*, 845–856.

Institute of Medicine. (1990). *Medicare: a strategy for quality assurance*. Committee to Design a Strategy for Quality Review and Assurance in Medicare, K.N. Lohr (Ed.). Washington, DC: National Academy Press.

Kaushal, N., and Kaestner, R. (2005). Welfare reform and health insurance of immigrants. *Health Services Research*, *40*(3), 697–721.

Kenney, G., and Haley, J. (2001). Why aren't more uninsured children enrolled in Medicaid or SCHIP? (Assessing the New Federalism, Policy Brief No. B-35.) Washington, DC: Urban Institute.

Komaromy, M., Grumbach, K., Drake, M., Vranizan, K., Lurie, N., Keane, D., and Bindman, A.B. (1996). The role of black and Hispanic physicians in providing health care for underserved populations. *New England Journal of Medicine*, *334*(20), 1305–1310.

Ku, L., and Matani, S. (2001, January/February). Left out: immigrants' access to health care and insurance. *Health Affairs*, *20*(1), 247–256.

Leape L.L., Hilborne, L.H., Bell, R., Kamberg, C., and Brook, R.H. (1999). Underuse of cardiac procedures: do women, ethnic minorities, and the uninsured fail to receive needed revascularization? *Annals of Internal Medicine*, *130*(3), 183–192.

Lee, L.J., Batal, H.A., Maselli, J.H., and Kutner, J.S. (2002). Effect of Spanish interpretation method on patient satisfaction in an urban walk-in clinic. *Journal of General Internal Medicine*, *17*, 641–645.

Lewin-Epstein, N. (1991). Determinants of regular source of health care in black, Mexican, Puerto Rican, and non-Hispanic white populations. *Medical Care*, *29*(6), 543–557.

Lillie-Blanton, M., Brodie, M., Rowland, D., Altman, D., and McIntosh, M. (2000). Race, ethnicity, and the health care system: Public perceptions and experiences. *Medical Care Research and Review*, *57*(Suppl 1), 218–235.

Marquis, M.S., Davies, A.R., and Ware, J.E. (1983). Patient satisfaction and change in medical care provider: A longitudinal study. *Medical Care*, *21*, 821–829.

Marquis, M.S., Rogowski, J.A., and Escarce, J.J. (2004). Recent trends and geographic variation in the safety net. *Medical Care*, *42*(5), 403–405.

McBean, A.M., Huang, Z., Virnig, B.A., Lurie, N., and Musgrave, D. (2003). Racial variation in the control of diabetes among elderly Medicare managed care beneficiaries. *Diabetes Care*, *26*, 3250–3256.

Monheit, A.C., and Vistnes, J.P. (2000). Race/ethnicity and health insurance status: 1987 and 1996. *Medical Care Research and Review*, *57*(Suppl 1), 11–35.

Morales, L.S., Lara, M., Kington, R.S., Valdez, R.O., and Escarce, J.J. (2002). Socioeconomic, cultural and behavioral factors effecting Hispanic health outcomes. *Journal of Health Care for the Poor and Underserved*, *13*(4), 477–503.

Morales, L.S., Elliott, M.N., Weech-Maldonado, R., and Hays, R.D. (2003). *The impact of interpreters on parents' experiences with ambulatory care for their children.* RAND working paper. Santa Monica, CA: RAND.

Morales, L.S., Elliott, M.N., Weech-Maldonado, R., Spritzer, K.L., and Hays, R.D. (2001). Differences in CAHPS adult survey reports and ratings by race and ethnicity: An analysis of the national CAHPS benchmarking data 1.0. *Health Services Research*, *36*, 595–617.

Morales, L.S., Cunningham, W.E., Brown, J.A., Liu, H., and Hays, R.D. (1999). Are Latinos less satisfied with communication by health care providers? *Journal of General Internal Medicine*, *14*, 409–417.

Morbidity and Mortality Weekly Report. (2000). Entry into prenatal care—United States, 1989–1997. *Morbidity and Mortality Weekly Report*, *49*(18), 393–398.

National Center for Health Statistics. (2003, September). *Health, United States, 2003.* (DHHS Publication No. 2003-1232.) Washington, DC: U.S. Department of Health and Human Services.

Newcomer, R., Preston, S., and Harrington, C. (1996). Health plan satisfaction and risk of disenrollment among social/HMO and fee-for-service recipients. *Inquiry*, *33*, 144–154.

Perry, M., Kannel, S., and Castillo, E. (2000, December). *Barriers to health coverage for Hispanic workers: Focus group findings.* (Publication no. 425.) New York: Commonwealth Fund.

Petchers, M.K., and Milligan, S.E. (1988). Access to health care in a black urban elderly population. *The Gerontologist*, *28*(2), 213–217.

Phillips, K.A., Mayer, M.L., and Aday, L.A. (2000). Barriers to care among racial/ethnic groups under managed care. *Health Affairs (Millwood)*, *19*(4), 65–75.

Quinn, K. (2000, March). *Working without benefits: The health insurance crisis confronting Hispanic Americans.* New York: Commonwealth Fund.

Ray, W.A., Mitchel, E.F., Jr., and Piper, J.M. (1997). Effect of Medicaid expansions on preterm birth. *American Journal of Preventive Medicine*, *13*(4), 292–297.

Rhoades, J.A. (2005). The uninsured in America, 2004: *Estimates for the U.S. civilian noninstitutionalized population under age 65.* (Statistical Brief #83.) Rockville, MD: Agency for Healthcare Research and Quality. Available: http://www.meps.ahrq.gov/papers/st83/stat83.pdf [accessed January 2006].

Rivadeneyra, R., Elderkin-Thompson, V., Silver, R.C., and Waitzkin, H. (2000). Patient centeredness in medical encounters requiring an interpreter. *American Journal of Medicine, 108*(6), 470–474.

Ruiz, M.S., Marks, G., and Richardson, J.L. (1992). Language acculturation and screening practices of elderly Hispanic women: The role of exposure to health-related information from the media. *Journal of Aging and Health, 4*(2), 268–281.

Saha, S., Komaromy, M., Koepsell, T.D., and Bindman, A.B. (1999). Patient-physician racial concordance and the perceived quality and use of health care. *Archives of Internal Medicine, 159*, 997–1004.

Saha, S., Taggart, S.H., Komaromy, M., and Bindman, A.B. (2000). Do patients choose physicians of their own race? *Health Affairs (Millwood), 19*(4), 76–83.

Sambamoorthi, U., and McAlpine, D.D. (2003). Racial, ethnic, socioeconomic, and access disparities in the use of preventive services among women. *Preventive Medicine, 37*(5), 475–484.

Schlosberg, C., and Wiley, B. (May 1998). *The impact of INS public charge determinations on immigrant access to health care.* Washington, DC: National Health Law Program and National Immigration Law Center. Available: http://www.healthlaw.org/pubs/19980522publiccharge.html.

Schur, C.L., and Albers, L.A. (1996). Language, sociodemographics, and health care use of Hispanic adults. *Journal of Health Care for the Poor and Underserved, 7*(2), 140–158.

Schur, C.L., and Feldman, J. (2001, May). *Running in place: How job characteristics, immigrant status, and family structure keep Hispanics uninsured.* Millwood, VA: Project HOPE Center for Health Affairs.

Shapiro M.F., Morton, S.C., McCaffrey, D.F., Senterfitt, J.W., Fleishman, J.A., Perlman, J.F., Athey, L.A., Keesey, J.W., Goldman, D.P., Berry, S.H., and Bozzette, S.A. (1999). Variations in the care of HIV-infected adults in the United States: Results from the HIV Cost and Services Utilization Study. *Journal of American Medical Association, 281*(24), 2305–2315.

Sherbourne, C.D., Hays, R.D., Ordway, L., DiMatteo, M.R., and Kravitz, R. (1992). Antecedents of adherence to medical recommendations: Results from the Medical Outcomes Study. *Journal of Behavioral Medicine, 15*, 447–468.

Solis, J.M., Marks, G., Garcia, M., and Shelton, D. (December 1990). Acculturation, access to care, and use of preventive services by Hispanics: Findings from HHANES 1982–84. *American Journal of Public Health, 80*(Suppl 1), 1–9.

Stewart, S.H., and Silverstein, M.D. (2002). Racial and ethnic disparity in blood pressure and cholesterol measurement. *Journal of General Internal Medicine, 17*(6), 405–411.

Timmins, C.L. (2002). The impact of language barriers on the health care of Latinos in the United States: A review of the literature and guidelines for practice. *Journal of Midwifery and Women's Health, 47*, 80–96.

U.S. Department of Health and Human Services, Office of Minority Health. (2001, March). *National standards for culturally and linguistically appropriate services in health care.* Final report. Washington, DC: Author.

Vaccarino, J.M. (1977). Malpractice: The problem in perspective. *Journal of the American Medical Association, 238*, 861–863.

Virnig, B., Huang, Z., Lurie, N., Musgrave, D., McBean, A., and Dowd, B. (2004). Does Medicare managed care provide equal treatment for mental illness across races? *Archives of General Psychiatry, 61*, 2001–2005.

Virnig, B.A., Lurie, N., Huang, Z., Musgrave, D., McBean, A. and Dowd, B. (2002). Racial variation in quality of care among Medicare+Choice enrollees. *Health Affairs, 21*(6), 224–230.

Weech-Maldonado, R., Morales, L.S., Spritzer, K., Elliott, M.N., and Hays, R.D. (2001). Racial and ethnic differences in parents' assessments of pediatric care in Medicaid managed care. *Health Services Research*, *36*, 575–594.

Weech-Maldonado, R., Morales, L.S., Elliott, M., Spritzer, K., Marshall, G., and Hays, R.D. (2003). Race/ethnicity, language, and patients' assessments of care in Medicaid managed care. *Health Services Research*, *38*, 789–808.

Weinick, R.M., and Krauss, N.A. (2000). Racial/ethnic differences in children's access to care. *American Journal of Public Health*, *90*(11), 1771–1774.

Weinick, R.M., Jacobs, E.A., Stone, L.C., Ortega, A.N., and Burstin, H. (2004). Hispanic health care disparities: Challenging the myth of a monolithic Hispanic population. *Medical Care*, *42*, 313–320.

Wells, K.B., Golding, J.M., Hough, R.L., Burnam, M.A., and Karno, M. (1989). Acculturation and the probability of use of health services by Mexican Americans. *Health Services Research*, *24*(2), 237–257.

Zastowny, T.R., Roghmann, K.J., and Cafferata, G.L. (1989). Patient satisfactions and the use of health services. *Medical Care*, *27*, 705–723.

Zimmermann, W., and Tumlin, K.C. (1999). *Patchwork policies: State assistance for immigrants under welfare reform.* (Assessing the New Federalism, Occasional Paper No. 24.) Washington, DC: Urban Institute.

11

Latino Civic and Political Participation

Louis DeSipio

With each passing election, claims of potential Latino[1] political influence increase and efforts to harness that influence grow. In the 2000 presidential race, for example, both parties made substantive and symbolic outreach to Latinos; each built their potentially winning set of states in the Electoral College on expectations for Latino turnout in specific states. The presumption of these activities is the existence of a "Latino vote" or, more generally a "Latino politics" that can be organized to express a Latino voice in political outcomes. This chapter analyzes the phenomenon of Latino politics with three guiding questions. First, I consider the validity of a Latino politics in the singular that has greater predictive value than the politics of the specific Latino national-origin groups. Here, I define politics broadly to include community-based civic activities, both in the United States and abroad; electoral politics; agenda setting and influence; and representation, with the recognition that the existing scholarship disproportionately focuses on electoral politics. Second, I examine electoral and nonelectoral politics to assess how Latino politics manifests itself and the

[1]In this chapter, I use the terms "Latino" and "Hispanic" interchangeably to refer to individuals who trace their origin or ancestry to the Spanish-speaking countries of Latin America or the Caribbean. I should note that the outset that most Latino politics (like politics in general) is local. At the local level, a single national-origin group usually dominates the local Latino population, so there is a great possibility of Latino politics being framed in national-origin terms. Increasingly, even at the local level, however, the ethnic dimension of this politics is discussed as Latino or Hispanic.

institutional and demographic barriers that prevent Latinos from meeting the sometimes unrealistic levels of influence expected of them. Finally, I assess possible trajectories for the Latino politics of the next two decades, arguing that this future Latino politics is highly uncertain and is itself under construction.

As a prelude to this analysis, I identify a cleavage that appears throughout this discussion. In all politics and certainly in Latino politics as well, mass and elite interests can diverge. Around the questions of the reality of a Latino politics, Latino mass and elite interests diverge considerably, though arguably this division is narrowing.

Over the past 20 years, Hispanic elites, particularly non-Cuban Hispanic elites, have organized primarily as Hispanics and not around their national-origin identities. While recognizing differences based on national origins and regions, these Hispanic elites have seen instrumental advantages in organizing to speak primarily with a pan-ethnic voice. Although there has been little scholarly analysis of Latino elite ethnic identification (Farkas et al., 1998; Márquez, 2003, particularly Chapter 6; O'Connor and Epstein, 1988), the organizational structure of the major Latino policy research organizations demonstrates this trend clearly. Each of the major Hispanic organizations—the Mexican American Legal Defense and Education Fund, the League of United Latin American Citizens, the National Council of La Raza, the National Association of Latino Elected and Appointed Officials (NALEO), the Tomás Rivera Policy Institute (TRPI),[2] and the Congressional Hispanic Caucus, as examples—has a board of directors that reflects the diversity of the Latino community and focuses their energies on issues that unite Latino communities. The exception to this pattern of elite organizing around a pan-ethnic frame is the Cuban American National Foundation (CANF), which has focused its energies entirely on Cuba and the needs of Cuban Americans and has not sought to build bridges to other Latino groups.

At the mass level, the primary ethnic identities of Hispanics remain focused on their national origins (see Chapter 1; de la Garza, DeSipio, García, García, and Falcón, 1992; Oboler, 1995; Suro, 2002). While these patterns diminish somewhat among immigrants with longer periods of U.S. residence and over successive generations, national origin remains the primary personal identity for the majority of Latinos. This pattern is even more remarkable considering the elite efforts to frame a Latino/Hispanic identity and a national Latino politics over the past 25 years. Certainly,

[2]In the interests of academic disclosure, I should note that I worked as a staff member at NALEO for three years and as a consultant for an additional seven years. I am currently a research scholar at TRPI.

most Latinos include the pan-ethnic identities among their package of identities, but when asked to focus on the one that first comes to mind, nation of origin or ancestry is most often mentioned by the majority.

Recognizing this ambivalence about pan-ethnicity at the mass level establishes an important first step to the discussion of Latino politics. While the majority population and Latino elites may speak of a Latino political community or a Latino vote, its existence may in fact be more of a wish than a reality, at least to the degree that it is recognized by those who provide that vote or make up that community.

THE FOUNDATIONS OF A U.S. LATINO POLITICS: SHARED EXPERIENCE AND COMMON INTERESTS

Scholarly study of Latino civic and electoral participation, Latino political attitudes, and the political dimensions of naturalization is a relatively new phenomenon. Although there are a few political studies from as early as the 1920s and 1930s, most of the available scholarship postdates the extension of the Voting Rights Act (VRA) to Hispanic communities in 1975. This early period in Latino political history is nevertheless important for understanding their contemporary political experience. Although largely unrecognized at the time, several formative political experiences laid the foundation for the extension of VRA coverage to Latinos. In many ways, the 1975 extension of the VRA defines the beginning of the era of a national recognition of and expectations for Hispanic politics rather than the politics of Mexican Americans, Puerto Ricans, or Cuban Americans. Federal legislation alone, however, does not guarantee the existence of a meaningful Latino politics. Instead, I argue that changes in immigration law in the mid-1960s and the dramatic changes in the composition of the Latino population that followed created the foundation for a set of shared interests among Latinos of different origins and ancestries, giving rise to a Latino politics that can be distinguished from the politics of other demographic groups. Both of these phenomena—the shared experiences that underpin national expectations of a singular voice in Latino politics and incentives for Hispanic leaders to organize to link with a seemingly unified voice to express the needs of Mexican Americans, Cuban Americans, Puerto Ricans, and other Latinos—must be understood as the twin foundations of today's Latino politics.

Shared Experiences and the Roots of Contemporary Latino Politics

The roots of contemporary Hispanic politics can be traced to the 19th century incorporation of Latin American and Caribbean populations into the expanding American empire (González, 2000) and to the initial state efforts to incorporate and exclude Latino populations. Characterizing Mexican Americans in the Southwest in the 19th and early 20th centuries or Puerto Ricans from the 1880s to the 1950s as "Hispanics" is a contemporary reading of history to be sure; acknowledging that they experienced similar forms of political exclusion and neglect that distinguished them from other immigrant and native populations in this same period is both historically accurate and key to identifying the foundations of shared experiences.

The extensive historical scholarship on the legal status, citizenship rights, land rights, elite political activities, and social relations of the former Mexican and Caribbean nationals offer insights into early forms of Latino politics. Space limitations preclude a detailed chronicle of the early Hispanic politics (Arellano, 2000; Gonzalez, 2000; Gutierrez, 1995; Jennings and Rivera, 1984; Sánchez Korrol, 1994). Instead, I highlight three elements of the pre-1975 formative period that conflict somewhat with common understandings of the Hispanic political past. This gap between the popular and scholarly understandings of the early Latino political reality explain the extension of the VRA to Latinos in 1975, and the bill's less dramatic impact on Latino voting than on black voting. Most significant is that, despite some superficial similarities, Latino political history is distinct from that of blacks with whom Latinos are sometimes, inaccurately, conflated. This point is particularly important because Congress's 1975 extension of the VRA to Hispanics and other language minorities, largely as a remedy for low political participation, erroneously assumed that Latino and black political needs were similar. As a result, the VRA has been less successful in remedying low rates of Hispanic participation.

Three historical circumstances and geographic realities undermined the ability of Latinos to express a cohesive voice to federal policy makers as Congress began to consider how best to remedy low Latino voting rates.

The first distinction between the Latino, in this case Mexican American, and black experiences involves the original mode of incorporation into U.S. society. Neither blacks nor Mexican Americans entered the United States voluntarily, but Mexican Americans joined the United States as citizens with treaty-based guarantees of land rights and the right of repatriation to Mexico. Although these treaty guarantees were quickly violated, Mexican Americans began their large-scale presence in the United States with representation and an elected leadership that never entirely disappeared, as occurred for blacks elected to office during Reconstruction. The territorial and state governments of New Mexico have always retained a significant plurality of Mexican American officeholders. And 20th-century Texas legislatures have included at least one Mexican American representative. At the local level, many Texas and New Mexico counties had continual Mexican American representation; California differed in this respect.

Uninterrupted Mexican American representation in parts of the Southwest reflects a second difference of the black and Latino political experiences, yet it constitutes a shared political foundational experience of Mexican Americans and Puerto Ricans in this era. Whereas blacks in the South faced intimidation and violence if they sought to participate in electoral politics, the modal experience for Latinos was one of manipulation—through political machines—and neglect (de la Garza and DeSipio, 1993; Montejano, 1987). Southwestern machine politics should not be confused with the machine experiences of many European immigrants in cities in the Northeast and Midwest because the Mexican American machines controlled votes for generations. Most of the European immigrant machines lost their hold on their clientele after a generation or two, and machines survived only by recruiting newer immigrants. Although Mexican American machines tended to serve the interests of local economic elites, often controlled by non-Hispanic whites, they encouraged Mexican American electoral participation and ensured the election of Mexican American officeholders. Thus, manipulation was the norm. Examples of violence against Mexican Americans seeking to exercise the franchise notwithstanding (Arellano, 2000; Montejano, 1987), the far bigger problem was the passivity that results from long-term machine politics and the commensurate sense of political incapacity they spurred among Mexican Americans.

U.S.-resident Puerto Ricans of this era also faced periods of political exclusion and periods of neglect (Jennings and Rivera, 1984; Sánchez Korrol, 1994). New York machine politics was in decay by the mid-20th century, effectively squelching active outreach (the Socialists did a bit more in the 1930s). Fearing Puerto Rican influence in close elections, some political leaders sought to disenfranchise them through language and literacy tests. Chicago's machine did not incorporate Puerto Rican voters in this era, nor did it actively exclude them.

A third political foundational experience is the relatively slow emergence of a civic infrastructure among Latinos compared with blacks of this era. Despite some notable exceptions, Mexican Americans and Puerto Ricans had poorer civic networks than did blacks in the middle of the 20th century. Among the reasons for this difference are the geographic dispersion of Mexican American populations in the Southwest, the predominantly rural nature of the population until the 1950s, circular migration flows among Puerto Ricans after the 1940s, and continued immigration. Also important in the weak development of Latino civic infrastructure are the electoral and partisan opportunities to shape policy outcomes enjoyed by Latino community elites that were denied to blacks (Pycior, 1997). This combination of opportunities for some Latino elites (particularly in Texas and New Mexico) to hold office combined with the rural and dispersed population bases to reduce the incentives for Latino community leaders to build community-based civic infrastructure prior to the 1950s. By contrast and despite the legal barriers, the denial of black political rights after Reconstruction created strong incentives at all class levels to organize to gain a political voice. With electoral politics precluded, civic organizing was a priority for all blacks.

Although Mexican Americans, Puerto Ricans, and other Latino populations had some local civic and political organizations prior to 1975, these were, for the most part, not integrated nationally. Rather, they reflected the reality of the Mexican American and Puerto Rican populations in this period—regional populations with little intergroup contact. Consequently, they were not able to present a cohesive voice to Congress when it began to consider how best to address low Latino voting rates.

The VRA is nevertheless the first pillar of contemporary Latino politics: a statutory recognition of a political community united by shared exclusion, particularly linguistic exclusion. As is discussed below, this federal recognition alone was insufficient for the emergence of a pan-ethnic politics. Moreover, when Congress extended the VRA to Latinos in 1975, there was little sense of a shared Latino political agenda at the mass level. During the 30 years that have since elapsed, this shared agenda has begun to emerge.

A Contemporary Latino Politics of Shared Interests

Despite the fact that many Latinos do not identify pan-ethnically or understand what they share in common with Latinos of other national origins, the majority share a set of issue preferences that distinguish them from other U.S. political constituencies. The emergence of this shared issue preference is sped by the high levels of mass migration from Latin America and the Caribbean over the past 40 years, which is the final pillar of contemporary Latino politics. The need to incorporate new Hispanic migrants into community politics has been a continuing community pressure, especially since the 1960s. Continuing new migration adds to difficulties in civic organizing (Gutiérrez, 1995). Throughout the 20th century, Latino political elites, and particularly Mexican American political elites, have had to overcome the legacies of past neglect while simultaneously dedicating community resources to the incorporation of new immigrants.[3] With the surge in Latino migration since the 1970s, and particularly since the 1980s

[3]Certainly, some of the responsibilities for political socialization could have been shouldered by public education, as they were for the European immigrants of this era. The public education provided to Latinos in this era, particularly Latino immigrants, was quite poor and did not include resources for social or political incorporation (San Miguel, 1987).

(see Chapters 2 and 3), civic integration pressures increased dramatically. Immigration has also increased the likelihood that Latinos of different national origins will come in contact with each other (see Chapter 4).

Opinion polls conducted over the past decade consistently demonstrate that Hispanics are focused on issues that create opportunities for their economic and social advance, what I have dubbed an "immigrant-settlement agenda" (DeSipio and de la Garza, 1999).[4] Driving this immigrant-settlement agenda is the large share of the Latino population comprised of immigrants and their children who recognize that their advance in U.S. society depends on civil rights protections and publicly funded social services, particularly education. Asked about the most important issue facing the United States or the communities in which they reside, education almost always tops the list (de la Garza et al., 1992; Henry J. Kaiser Family Foundation, 2000; San Jose Mercury News, 2000; Suro, 2002; Tomás Rivera Policy Institute, 2000). Other top issues include the delivery of social services, public safety, public transportation, and reducing discrimination. These same issues appear, for the most part, when results are disaggregated by national origin. Cuban Americans are somewhat more likely than other national-origin groups to mention assistance for the elderly, but this too broadly fits in a social policy agenda.

It is noteworthy that Cuban Americans, who are often presented as the outliers in discussions of Latino political pan-ethnic unity, also prioritize these issues on their agendas (de la Garza et al., 1992, Tables 7.1, 7.2, 9.16, 10.38, 10.39, and 10.81). Depending on the poll and when it is conducted, Cubans are somewhat more likely than other Hispanics to mention a foreign policy issue, specifically Castro and Cuba. It is easy to focus on strong Cuban American attitudes on foreign policy to identify differences in political priorities among Latinos of different origins, but on domestic issues Cuban Americans are quite moderate and often ally with Democrats in Florida to ensure funding for social service programs, particularly programs for the elderly. As a practical example, neither Cuban American member of Congress signed the Republican Contract with America in 1994 because it cut federal social welfare benefits for immigrants. Although public opinion data are sparse on Latino national-origin groups that have begun to immigrate in large numbers in the past 25 years, available evidence indicates that Dominicans, Salvadorans, Guatemalans, and Salvador-

[4]In this model, we contrast the immigrant-settlement agenda with an earlier Latino political agenda focused on civil rights demands. We argue that increased immigration has undercut Latino support for demand making based on claims of past exclusion and remedial politics (the "civil rights agenda") as this notion of past exclusion is not relevant to an increasing share of the Latino population.

ans share this immigrant-settlement policy agenda (DeSipio, Pachon, Gold, and Vargas, 1998).

A domestic agenda that emphasizes social issues partially distinguishes Latinos from non-Latinos. By comparison, non-Latinos are much more likely to name economic issues as policy priorities. Moreover, on shared priorities such as education, they often express different emphases. The Anglo discussion of education, as exemplified in the 2000 presidential race, focused on teacher and student testing and quality measures. When probed about what they mean by education, Latinos emphasize the process of education, mentioning such issues as expanding the number of schools, reducing class sizes, and adding to the cultural sensitivity of teachers and curricula. Other educational concerns expressed by Latinos include ensuring that children are able to advance to the next educational level.

A second way the Latino policy agenda differs from that of the majority has to do with taxation and the size of government. In contrast to the direction of national and state policy since at least since 1980, Latinos of all national origins report a willingness to pay additional taxes for an expansion in government programs. Cuban Americans are as likely as other Hispanic-origin groups to take positions advocating higher taxes and expanded government on such issues as crime control and drug prevention, child care services, environmental protection, science and technology, defense, and programs for refugees and immigrants (de la Garza et al., 1992, Tables 7.2, 7.4, and 10.40). A willingness to pay higher taxes for expanded government services reflects higher levels of trust in the U.S. government among Hispanics relative to non-Hispanics (de la Garza et al., 1992, Tables 6.3 and 10.32; Suro, 2002). Of all Hispanic national-origin groups, Cuban Americans reported the highest levels of trust in the U.S. government.

Equally worthy of note are the issues that do not dominate this Latino agenda. Only a small share of Latinos identify ethnic-specific issues, such as U.S. relations with Latin America or bilingual education, as the top issue facing their nation or their communities of residence. These issues do not appear even when surveys probe on the most important issue facing Latinos. Immigration is somewhat more commonly mentioned, but Latino positions are very different from those of non-Hispanics in that both express concern about the volume of contemporary migration. Compared to non-Hispanics, however, Latinos are more concerned that immigrants, regardless of status, be treated fairly. Finally, the issues of the conservative agenda—abortion, family values, the death penalty—are rarely mentioned as *important* issues, a theme elaborated further in the discussion of partisanship below.

Latino leaders are working to build on this issue-based foundation for a pan-ethnic Latino politics. National Latino civic and civil rights organizations, such as the National Council of La Raza and the Mexican American Legal Defense and Education Fund, focus their organizational energies around the issues that unite Latinos regardless of national origin. These elite and organizational efforts to forge a pan-ethnic political agenda is assisted by a second consequence of large-scale immigration in Latino communities. Increasingly, Latinos are coming into regular contact with Latinos of different national origins. When the VRA was extended to Latinos in 1975, most areas of Hispanic concentration were relatively homogeneous by national origin. Today, most major cities have multiple Latino national-origin groups among their populations. Although one dominates, most urban Latinos live in multiethnic settings and consequently experience their shared political goals.

The extension of the VRA to Latinos in 1975 recognized a shared history of political exclusion and manipulation, often based on language. Hence, Congress characterized the newly covered population as the "Spanish language minority." It would have been presumptuous in 1975 to assume that the language minority shared a political agenda. Thirty years hence, however, changes in the composition of the Latino population, elite efforts at political unity, and changed residential patterns have laid the foundation for the creation of a modestly cohesive Latino issue agenda that differs in important ways from that of non-Latinos. A shared issue agenda, however, neither ensures partisan unity nor guarantees routine political influence. It nevertheless provides a basis for references to and analyses of "Latino politics," with the caveat that their political agenda(s) and it/their eventual direction remains in formation.

Latino Civic Engagement and Political Influence

What is the nature, extent, and consequence of Latino political engagement? To answer this question, I analyze three dimensions of Latino civic engagement and political influence. First I offer a brief overview of comparative civic and electoral participation rates for Latinos and non-Latinos. Second, I analyze the institutional structures and demographic characteristics that explain much of this gap. Finally, I assess Hispanic influence on the shape of contemporary political outcomes.

Latinos participate politically at lower rates than non-Hispanic whites and blacks.[5] The magnitude of the gap varies depending on the type of

[5]Despite the steady increase in scholarly interest in Latino politics over the past 25 years, the data available for analysis of Latino political values, attitudes, and behaviors remain sparse. Governmental data sources available to scholars interested in nonpolitical questions about the status of Hispanic communities in the United States are of limited utility to scholars of politics because, for the most part, they do not ask questions about political values, attitudes, and behaviors. Scholars of Latino politics are also disadvantaged in that the major data sources on U.S. political behaviors, most notably the University of Michigan's American

participation, but the pattern is consistent. Population composition differences between Latino and non-Latino populations explain much of this gap and can be measured reliably. The remainder is the result of institutional arrangements and the legacies of past exclusion, but these factors cannot be measured as accurately with available survey and turnout data.

Most scholarship on Latino politics focuses on electoral politics (de la Garza, 2004), but their below-average participation also obtains for activities in which non-U.S. citizen Latinos can engage. Although reliable comparative data for other immigrant populations are lacking, available evidence indicates that immigrant Latinos are not substituting political activity in their countries of origin for U.S. political engagement.

Latino Civic Engagement

The most common forms of civic engagement in Latino communities, as in the population as a whole, are voting, organizational activity, charitable activities, and school-based activities. The share of Latinos who participate in each of these activities varies, but rarely exceeds half of adults. In recent presidential elections, for example, approximately 45 percent of Latino U.S. citizen adults voted (de la Garza and DeSipio, 2005); the percentage increased slightly to 47 percent in 2004. Turnout is much higher in Puerto Rican elections (a theme I return to later); more than 82 percent of Puerto Ricans on the island voted in the 2000 elections. Among parents, surveys find that 30 to 40 percent are involved with activities in their children's schools on a regular basis (de la Garza et al., 1992, Tables 8.12 and 10.73). Approximately 40 percent of Latinos report making charitable contributions in a prior year. If church membership is excluded, approximately one-third of Latinos are members of community-based organizations (de la Garza and Lu, 1998). Churches see higher participation rates, in the range of 70 percent, but it is not clear that these activities are civic in nature (DeSipio, forthcoming).

These levels of participation vary somewhat across Latino national-origin groups, but the intra-Latino differences disappear when socioeco-

---

National Election Study, do not have a sufficient subsample of Latino citizens for separate analysis and often exclude Latino noncitizens entirely from their samples. As a result, empirical Latino political research must often rely on national surveys of Latinos that may not allow for direct comparison to non-Latino populations or on local or regional survey or polling data with relatively small samples that make it hard to compare across Latino national-origin groups or across regions. National data, for the most part, allow comparisons of the largest Latino national-origin groups (Mexican Americans, Puerto Ricans, and Cuban Americans). They are weaker, however, on other cleavages in Latino communities, most notably immigrant generation.

nomic differences are accounted for. In general, Latinos participate in these common civic activities at lower rates than non-Hispanic whites or blacks (de la Garza et al., 1992, Table 8.11; Verba, Schlozman, and Brady, 1995: Chapter 8). The one exception to this pattern is self-reported involvement in school-based activities among parents, in which Latino and non-Latino participation rates are similar.

Other forms of civic engagement, such as protest, lobbying, making contributions to or working for political campaigns, and seeking to influence the policy-making process, involve smaller shares of Hispanics. No more than 10 percent of Latinos report having been involved in these activities. These patterns are broadly similar to those of other racial and ethnic groups. Few consistent differences appear among Latino national-origin groups in these less common activities (de la Garza et al., 1992, Table 8.11; DeSipio et al., 1998).

Immigrant Latinos have the opportunity to participate in a form of politics available to few non-Hispanic whites and blacks—involvement in the politics of their home countries or home communities. Similar patterns appear in Latino immigrant transnational behaviors that appear in U.S. political activities (see Table 11-1). Across a range of electoral, civic, and organizational activities, relatively few participate (DeSipio, Pachon, de la Gaza, and Lee, 2003). Approximately one-third of Latino immigrants reported that they attended a cultural or educational event related to their home country in the past year, but less than 1 in 10 attended a rally for home-country political candidates, attended a meeting to discuss home-country political affairs, or sought assistance from the home-country embassy or consulate. The exception to this pattern is a passive activity, following home-country politics in the news. Dominican immigrants and Puerto Rican migrants are more likely to have been engaged in transnational political activities than Mexican or Salvadoran immigrants (a result that persists in multivariate tests).

This pattern of lower Latino participation extends to voting as well. Approximately 57.9 percent of U.S. citizen adult Latinos were registered to vote at the time of the 2004 election, and 47.2 percent turned out to vote (see Table 11-2).[6] The registration and turnout rates are approximately 10 percent lower than those of non-Hispanic blacks and 18 percent lower than those of non-Hispanic whites. During the period for which there are reli-

[6]The source of these data is the Current Population Survey (CPS) voter supplement. These data are based on self-reporting and consistently overestimate actual turnout. Hispanics overreport at a higher rate than non-Hispanics (Shaw, de la Garza, and Lee, 2000). Citizenship status is also self-reported. As a result, the denominator in calculations of voter turnout, citizen voting age adults, is also likely to be an overestimate.

TABLE 11-1 Latino Immigrant/Migrant Home National Participation

Participation	% Mexican Immigrant	% Puerto Rican Migrant	% Salvadoran Immigrant	% Dominican Immigrant
	Country of Origin-focused Political Activities in Period Since Migration			
Followed HC politics in the Spanish-language media	63.6	66.5	48.0	67.1
Voted in HC elections	9.5	14.6	8.5	15.0
Contributed money to candidate running for office or political party in HC	2.0	5.3	2.8	6.3
Attended U.S. rally of HC candidate or political party	2.7	11.6	2.3	17.3
Contact by HC representative to solicit involvement in HC political or cultural affairs	3.0	8.1	1.8	11.5
	Country of Origin-focused Political Activities in Year Prior to the Survey			
Attended a meeting to discuss HC politics	6.2	14.6	5.8	21.8
Attended a cultural or educational event related to HC	26.6	42.7	23.1	43.9
Membership in organization promoting cultural ties between U.S. and HC	6.7	15.2	5.6	12.8
Membership hometown organization	8.5	12.1	7.8	22.6
Sought assistance from embassy/consulate/Puerto Rican government	6.0	4.5	5.0	3.0

NOTE: HC = home country.
SOURCE: DeSipio (2003a, Table 2).

able data on Latino turnout, they have voted at lower rates than blacks and whites. While these gaps have narrowed slightly, Latino turnout has not increased, despite the considerable growth in outreach to Latino voters over the past 20 years.

Although there is relatively little research on the effect of immigrant generation on political behavior, available evidence suggests that immi-

TABLE 11-2 Registration and Turnout Among U.S. Citizen Adults, by Race/Ethnic Group, 2000

Race/Ethnicity	Adult U.S. Citizen Population (000s)	% Registered	Number Registered (000s)	% Voted	Number Voted (000s)
Non-Hispanic white	148,159	75.1	111,318	67.2	99,567
Non-Hispanic black	23,346	68.7	16,035	60.0	14,016
Latino	16,088	57.9	9,308	47.2	7,587
Asian/Pacific Islander	6,270	51.8	3,247	44.1	2,768

SOURCE: Author's calculations based on U.S. Census Bureau (2005, Table 4a).

grants are less likely to be involved in civic and nonelectoral political activities than are U.S. citizen Latinos (DeSipio, 2003b). Participation among immigrants generally increases with longer residence in the United States (DeSipio, 1996a). Once naturalized, Latino immigrants participate at lower rate than do U.S.-born Latinos (DeSipio, 1996b; Levitt and Olson, 1996; Minnite, Holdaway, and Hayduk, 1999; Mollenkopf, Olson, and Ross, 2001). Small sample sizes in surveys require some caution in generalization, but at least in terms of voting, the available evidence indicates that the third generation votes at higher rates than the second generation, controlling for demographic predictors of participation (DeSipio, 2003b).

In sum, Latino engagement in the civic and political life of the United States has been extensively measured, and the patterns found are relatively consistent. Latino engagement looks like that of other populations except that the rates are lower. Latinos have high levels of political efficacy (the sense that they can have individual influence over government) and generally trust government and civic institutions, so that lower levels of participation should not be interpreted as dissatisfaction with U.S. politics. Instead, as I discuss in the next section, the Latino-non-Latino participation gap results from institutional structures that lead to differential levels of mobilization and compositional differences between Latino and non-Latino populations.

Institutional Structures and Demographic Barriers

The reasons for Latino civic and electoral participation and nonparticipation are for the most part not unique to Latino communities. Rather, many of the factors that shape Latino participation affect all U.S. populations, but the impact is more pronounced for Latinos, owing to compositional differences between Latino and non-Latino populations. These compositional characteristics, however, do not explain all participation differences. Institutional differences also play a role. One such institutional factor already mentioned is distinct—the VRA. After analyzing its influence on Latino participation, I turn to some more general institutional factors that shape the political behaviors of all contemporary electorates.

Institutional Structures Shaping Latino Political Engagement

In 1975, Congress extended VRA coverage to four language-minority communities—Hispanics, Asian Americans, American Indians, and Alaskan Natives. Congress targeted these populations, and not all ethnic or linguistic minorities, on grounds that they had experienced multigenerational exclusion based on linguistic difference. Congress extended to these populations the same coverage that blacks had received in 1965—federal oversight of voter registration, voting procedures, and electoral rule changes—in areas with high concentrations of blacks and lower than average black voter turnout. The 1975 VRA extension added one specific protection for language minorities, bilingual election materials. Congress added to these targeted protections in 1982 when it mandated that jurisdictions had a responsibility to draw districts that would elect the candidate of a covered minority group's choice in areas where the size and concentration of the minority population allowed for drawing such a district. This "majority-minority" districting provision shifted the focus of the act from eliminating barriers to participation to encouraging minority officeholding.

The overall effect of VRA on Latino empowerment has been positive (but perhaps not as positive as many think), yet these benefits have come at a cost. First, Congress failed to use the opportunity of the 1975 extension to examine why Latinos voted at lower rates than non-Hispanic whites.[7] Instead, it simply assumed that the reasons were the same as those for blacks (de la Garza and DeSipio, 1993). In other words, neither in 1975 nor in subsequent debates over VRA extension did Congress assess the unique features of Latino political history that shape Latino political behavior today, most notably the multiple generations of voter manipulation among eligible Hispanic voters. The "one size fits all" solution does not address the core reasons for low Latino electoral participation.

Second, by creating opportunities for Latino officeholding, in some

---

[7]The VRA, particularly the 1965 act, is often portrayed as an act to remove barriers. While this was certainly the primary focus of the legislation, a close reading of testimony in 1965, 1970, and 1975 shows that many in Congress also saw the act as having a related goal: to increase electoral participation among the covered minority populations (de la Garza and DeSipio, 1993).

cases ahead of the community mobilization traditionally necessary to elect people to office, the VRA shifted the focus of weak community and civic organizations away from mass organization and toward electing Latinos to office. This is an important goal. It may have, however, short-circuited the process of organizational development in Latino communities just as group numbers were reaching levels of critical mass sufficient for political mobilization.

Finally, because the VRA linked the needs of all Latinos in a blanket extension to the Spanish-heritage population, it may have eventually undercut legislative or judicial support for continued Latino VRA coverage (the VRA is next up for renewal in 2007). To the extent that Congress examined political history to justify VRA extension to Latinos, it looked primarily to the Mexican American experience and to a lesser degree to that of Puerto Ricans. Other Latinos, including those yet to establish a critical mass through immigration, were brought into coverage, despite an explicit decision by Congress not to extend VRA coverage to all ethnic or linguistic minorities. Congress or the courts may eliminate VRA coverage for all Latinos in the future, including coverage of descendants of Mexican Americans and Puerto Ricans who faced sustained electoral manipulation and exclusion, if the perception arises that the primary beneficiaries are post-1965 immigrants and their children.

The extension of VRA coverage to Latinos in 1975 jumpstarted a new incentive structure for new institutions in American politics to reach out to Latinos. Prior to 1975, Hispanic political participation was characterized by the absence of institutional incentives to participate and the failure to adapt institutions that have successfully spurred mobilization among other populations. The Latino population includes a disproportionate share of individuals who need incentives to vote and to participate in other forms of civic activity, such as new immigrants, Hispanics who were socialized politically during periods when their participation was discouraged by law or practice, and descendants of those never socialized into U.S. politics.

The experience of Latinos is not unique in U.S. immigrant history. What differs today is that political and civic institutions that mobilized new participants in the past have lost their ability to fill this role in American democracy. Most notable among these are political parties which, from the 1830s on, served as the engine of mass political participation in the United States. This role steadily declined throughout the 20th century as parties shifted their focus to fundraising, candidate recruitment, and technical support for candidates. Contemporary parties do little to mobilize new voters (Wattenberg, 2002). Instead, they have become increasingly skilled at identifying voters who turn out regularly. Prior to an election, they inform regular voters, but reach out to less regular voters only in the most competitive of races. Party skill at drawing electoral districts, single-member plurality electoral systems, and relatively low turnout among new voters reduces the number of these competitive races. The Latino community is disadvantaged by such strategies because it has a higher share of registered voters who do not go to the polls and a higher share of adult citizens who are not registered.

This selective outreach is reinforced by candidates and campaigns. Increasingly, candidates rely on expensive "air wars" (advertising campaigns) that provide information and encouragement to people who are likely to vote but do little to educate or mobilize people who are more distant from electoral politics. To pay for these air wars, candidates spend a higher share of their time fundraising and less time meeting citizens. Personal outreach, whether by candidates or their supporters, has been shown to spur Latino turnout, even when controlling for the effects of age, education, and income (Shaw et al., 2000).

Parties are certainly not the only civic institution that could take a role in mobilization. Unions have traditionally filled this role for many immigrants, as have ethnic civic organizations. But like parties, unions have also declined as mass organizations. Their decline, however, slowed somewhat in the 1990s. Several unions in New York and Los Angeles can attribute their revitalization to outreach to Latinos and other immigrants. Examples include New York's Health and Hospital Workers (Local 1199) and Los Angeles's Hotel Workers and Restaurant Employees. Based on their experiences, the American Federation of Labor has begun to invest in a campaign to reach out to Latinos and other immigrants and to recast trade unionism's traditional animosity toward expansive immigration policies.

Civic organizations can also fill gaps left by the decline in party-based mobilization. The NALEO has experimented over the past four years with targeted mobilization in high- and medium-concentration Latino areas and among the newly naturalized. Although they demonstrate a positive impact on turnout, their efforts are very expensive and are difficult to fund with philanthropic support because of risks that their efforts can be perceived as partisan. Electoral mobilization methodologies are poorly developed, hence their effectiveness is often limited (Green and Gerber, 2004).

State and local electoral laws also shape the opportunity for Latino electoral engagement. Latinos, and particularly Mexican Americans, are overwhelmingly concentrated in "reform" states, such as California. Reform states structured their electoral laws to reduce the power of organized interests and political parties. In California, for example, campaigns for all but state-level and national races are nonpartisan (Segura and Woods, 2002). So, there is no "D" or "R" cue for voters. The absence of this cue makes voting more confusing and difficult, dampening participation among adult citizens with low levels of political socialization. These reform states also practice various forms of direct democracy, such as the initiative, referendum, and recall. These direct democracy tools were passed with the notion that they would decentralize the democracy, but they confuse new participants, increase the information cost of participating, and also create the opportunity for majorities to limit the political gains of electoral minorities. Again, they serve to dampen Latino participation relative to Anglo participation.

More recently, many reform states have implemented term limits. Initially, term limits served as a boon to Latino officeholding, as they sped the transition from Anglo to Latino officeholders in districts where Latino population concentration rose. After the initial positive impact on Latino electability, however, term limits slowed the development of Latino electoral leadership. Newly elected Latinos did not have the opportunity to develop legislative and leadership skills that many of their Anglo and black predecessors had. Almost as soon as they are elected, these officeholders have to begin to plan their move to the next level of elective office. One reason that there are so few Latinos competing for statewide or national office is that legislatures that traditionally served as training grounds for executive office cannot fill this role when legislators are termed out after six or eight years.

The impact of the institutional factors on Latino turnout appears in a clear natural experiment examining electoral turnout among Puerto Ricans living on the island and on the mainland (Cámara Fuertes, 2004). Unlike other Latino migrants, Puerto Ricans become immediately eligible to register to vote in the United States upon migration and to vote within one month of arrival. Despite these relatively equal opportunities to participate politically in the United States or in Puerto Rico, turnout in Puerto Rican elections is approximately twice as high as Puerto Rican participation in mainland elections. The explanation for this difference is not entirely institutional; Puerto Rican elections involve contests between parties that are organized around the central question in island politics—status. But the structure of elections also differs, most notably in the near universal voter registration in Puerto Rico, the close competition between the two leading parties, the relative infrequency of elections and smaller number of races being contested, and the clear focus on party affiliation and party loyalty among all candidates. Each of these characteristics makes voting easier in Puerto Rico and increases turnout. At over 80 percent, Puerto Rico boasts a very high turnout among democracies.

Latino Demographics and Their Consequences for Civic and Electoral Participation

A second part of the explanation for the gaps between Latinos and non-Hispanic whites is demographic and is not contested among scholars of

Latino politics (de la Garza, 2004). Because the best data focus on voting, I use them to elaborate this point, but similar patterns exist for other forms of participation.

Table 11-3 presents CPS estimates of voter turnout in the 2000 election. Two things are evident from these tabulations. First, similar patterns appear for Latinos, non-Hispanic whites, and non-Hispanic blacks. Younger people vote at lower rates than do older people. Individuals with lower incomes vote at lower rates than people with higher incomes. And people with lower levels of formal education vote at lower rates than people with higher levels of education. The gap in turnout between the youngest, lowest

TABLE 11-3 Turnout Rates and Share of Adult Citizen Population for Age, Education, and Income Cohorts of Latinos, Non-Hispanic Whites, and Non-Hispanic Blacks, 2000

	Latino Adult		Non-Hispanic White Adult		Non-Hispanic Black Adult	
Age, Education, and Income	Turnout %	Citizen % of Category	Turnout %	Citizen % of Category	Turnout %	Citizen % of Category
Age						
18–24	25.6	19.1	38.1	11.7	36.2	16.1
25–44	43.2	43.4	57.8	37.7	56.5	43.8
45–64	55.8	25.9	69.7	32.1	65.5	27.9
65–74	61.1	7.0	73.7	9.8	69.2	7.7
75+	58.9	4.5	70.8	8.8	60.3	4.5
Education						
Less than 9 years	38.5	14.6	38.5	3.7	47.0	5.8
9–12 years, no diploma	30.4	17.1	38.2	8.3	43.1	14.8
High school graduate	41.8	32.8	54.0	33.3	51.7	35.0
Some college	52.3	24.1	65.0	28.6	63.0	29.4
B.A. or equivalent	67.5	7.6	76.9	17.5	74.4	10.5
Advanced degree	73.8	3.7	83.4	8.5	78.6	4.5
Family Income (per year)						
Less than $5,000	27.7	2.9	36.8	0.8	35.6	3.9
$5,000–$9,999	38.7	5.1	39.7	1.6	43.2	7.6
$10,000–$14,999	34.6	9.1	44.8	3.3	51.1	8.7
$15,000–$24,999	38.8	15.3	53.8	7.5	54.0	13.3
$25,000–$34,999	44.3	14.8	60.0	10.6	60.4	12.7
$35,000–$49,000	48.9	15.3	63.7	15.0	63.2	13.8
$50,000–$74,999	51.9	15.6	70.9	20.1	67.3	15.2
$75,000+	67.1	13.6	76.4	26.5	75.9	11.3
Refused	40.3	8.3	52.5	14.6	48.2	13.4

SOURCE: de la Garza and DeSipio (2005, Table 1.2) (based on U.S. Census Bureau, 2005, Tables 2, 6, and 9).

education, and lowest family income categories and the highest is wider than the gap between Latinos and non-Latinos. Latinos do vote at lower rates than whites in most categories, but these gaps are narrower than across the age, education, and income categories. Second, the adult citizen Latino population includes higher shares of young individuals, those with lower incomes, and those with less formal education. More than 30 percent of Hispanic adult citizens, for example, have less than a high school education. Just 12 percent of non-Hispanic white adult citizens have less than a high school education. These differences in composition are largely responsible for Hispanic–non-Hispanic participation gaps.

A final demographic factor that dampens Latino participation relative to Anglo participation is high rates of non-U.S. citizenship. Since the passage of the VRA, the Latino electorate increased by 183 percentage points (see Table 11-4). Eligible noncitizens who do not vote increased slightly less (176 percent). The number of adult non-U.S. citizens rose from 1.9 million in 1976 to more than 8.4 million in 2000, a 350 percent increase. Stated differently, each new Latino voter was matched by one nonvoter in this same period and nearly two adult non-U.S. citizen Latinos. Thus, the share of Latino nonparticipants in electoral politics or in other forms of civic engagement is much higher than for either blacks or whites, and these nonparticipants are overwhelmingly non-U.S. citizens. These nonparticipants not only mute the political voice of Latinos, but also they make predictions about the future (the final task of this chapter) more uncertain.

Institutions, Demographics, and Participation: An Overview

When these demographic factors are accounted for in multivariate analyses, a gap remains between Latino and non-Hispanic white participation (Bass and Casper, 2001; Calvo and Rosenstone, 1989; DeSipio, 1996a; Wolfinger and Rosenstone, 1980). Several hypotheses have been offered to explain the remaining gap and generally focus on institutional structures, but empirical data are insufficient to fully test them. The most actively debated among these is a hypothesis that the concentration of Latino adults in areas of very low electoral competition reduces mobilization incentives for candidates and other political institutions (Barreto, Segura, and Woods, 2002; de la Garza and DeSipio, 1993; de la Garza, Menchaca, and DeSipio, 1994; Leighley, 2001). Other explanations relate to the dampening effect on Latino participation of a high share of naturalized citizens in the adult citizen population, because of evidence of lower participation among the naturalized than the U.S.-born (DeSipio, 1996b; Pantoja, Ramirez, and Segura, 2001); the disproportionate effects of electoral laws on Latino turnout, because of Latino concentration in reform states (Alvarez and Ansolabehere 2002); and a residual tie to home-country politics among immigrant Latinos (Jones-Correa, 1998).

TABLE 11-4 Latino Adult Voters, Adult Citizen Nonvoters, and Adult Non-U.S. Citizens, 1976–2000

Year	Latino Voters (,000)	Citizen Nonvoters (,000)	Non-U.S. Citizens (,000)	Ratio: Noncitizens to Voters
1976	2,098	2,620	1,876	0.89:1
1980	2,453	3,112	2,645	1.08:1
% change 1976–1980	+16.9	+18.8	+41.0	
1984	3,092	3,622	3,027	0.98:1
% change 1980–1984	+26.0	+16.4	+14.4	
1988	3,710	4,368	4,815	1.30:1
% change 1984–1988	+20.0	+20.6	+59.1	
1992	4,238	4,540	5,910	1.39:1
% change 1988–1992	+14.2	+3.9	+22.7	
1996	4,928	6,281	7,217	1.46:1
% change 1992–1996	+16.3	+38.3	+22.1	
2000	5,934	7,224	8,440	1.42:1
% change 1996–2000	+20.4	+15.0	+16.9	
% change 1976–2000	+182.8	+175.7	+349.9	

NOTE: CPS voting data likely overreport turnout and the U.S. citizen population. Despite this overreporting, they are the only source that allows comparison of Latino turnout and nonparticipation across elections.
SOURCE: de la Garza and DeSipio (2005, Table 1.1).

Latinos and the Shape of American Politics

Despite their muted political voice, Latinos do influence American politics. This impact will increase as the Latino population grows and the population meets the threshold for influence in district-based elections and municipal politics that reward population concentration. I examine three expressions of Latino political influence. First, partisanship and ideology measure individual attitudes and indicate potential for both unity and division among Latinos. The second, representation, assesses how Latinos have used institutional guarantees in the VRA combined with the power of their growing numbers to increase their formal representation in American politics. Finally, I assess naturalization, which I maintain is both the most important yet most unpredictable resource at the disposal of the community that will determine its future political voice.

Latino Partisanship and Ideology

Latinos are strong partisans (see Table 11-5). Mexican Americans and Puerto Ricans are strong Democrats; Florida Cuban Americans are strong Republicans, while their New Jersey coethnics vote reliably Democratic.

TABLE 11-5 Latino U.S. Citizen Partisanship and Ideology (%)

Partisanship and Ideology	Mexican Americans	Puerto Ricans	Cuban Americans	Central/South Americans
Partisanship				
Democrats	49	57	37	57
Republicans	25	19	41	18
Independent	11	10	12	11
Something else	11	8	5	9
Don't know	4	6	5	5
Ideology				
Liberal	24	29	41	26
Moderate	36	21	28	34
Conservative	35	37	24	30
Don't know	5	12	6	9

NOTE: Partisanship includes partisans and partisan leaners, respondents who initially identify as independents.
SOURCE: Henry J. Kaiser Family Foundation (2000).

This strong partisanship distinguishes Latinos from non-Hispanic whites, who are divided in their loyalties to the two parties. This strong Latino partisanship does not mean that Latinos are as partisan as blacks, who routinely offer the Democrats an eight-to-one advantage nationally.

These levels of Latino partisanship have been relatively stable over the past 25 years. Republicans made some small gains in Latino partisanship during the 1980s, but not in the period since. Rather, the interesting shift has been among some Cuban Americans who have moved more toward the Democrats, or at least used their votes tactically in specific elections. It is quite possible, for example, that Bill Clinton beat Bob Dole among Cuban Americans.

These partisan loyalties are tied to the issue base of each party. Republicans, for example, often focus on Mexican American opposition to abortion, support for the death penalty, and support for traditional gender roles, to predict that Mexican Americans will become Republican. As I indicated in the discussion of Latino issue preference, these issues rarely drive Mexican American political engagement. Instead, concern with education and social service delivery cements Mexican American and Puerto Rican loyalty to the Democrats. Yet Democrats have not predicted a Florida Cuban conversion. Arguably, however, when Fidel Castro leaves office and foreign policy assumes lower priority on the Cuban American agenda, the same issues that link Mexican Americans and Puerto Ricans to the Democrats will spur a shift among Cuban Americans to the Democrats. I do not expect that this will happen quickly, but I also do not see the foundation for non-Cuban Latinos to shift to the Republicans, as some pundits predict.

Latino ideology is less understood and needs further study. Beginning with the Latino National Political Survey, there has been a relatively consistent but surprising finding that Latinos identify themselves ideologically as moderates and conservatives (see Table 11-5). This ideological self-identification conflicts somewhat with the policy concerns of the community, which generally seek an expanded role for government (and a willingness to pay more taxes to fund these government activities). They also contradict the partisan loyalties of most Latinos to the Democrats. While I do not resolve this conflict here, I suspect that ideological self-identification reflects a different understanding of the meanings of "liberal" and "conservative" in Latino communities. This difference in meaning is particularly evident among immigrants who do not associate liberal and conservative with the same policies that majority populations do. Instead, conservatism reflects a desire to protect what has been achieved. If Latinos see government as an ally in achieving success in U.S. society, both moderates and conservatives can advocate expanded government and increased taxation.

Representation and Elective Office

In the period since the extension of the VRA to Latinos, the number of Latino officeholders has increased dramatically. The only pre-1975 count of Latino officeholders found that, in 1973, there were 1,280 in the 6 states with the largest Latino populations (Lemus, 1973). By 2003, these same states had 4,130 Latino office holders, an increase of 228 percent (see Table 11-6). Nationally, there were 4,623 Latino office holders in 2003.

Clearly, Latinos have been gaining access to elective office, but the surge in Latino officeholding has barely kept pace with demographic growth. Because neither immigrants nor new births—the components of growth—can immediately vote, maintaining parity with population growth represents an achievement. That said, Latinos are as underrepresented as they were at the beginning of the modern era of Latino politics. Being a much larger population, however, this has more serious implications for governance and policy making. Less than 1 percent of officeholders nationwide are Latino.

The vast majority of Latino officeholders are elected for local offices, such as school board members and city council members. Approximately 200 can be found in state legislative offices, in statewide offices, or in the U.S. Congress. One Latino holds a governorship—New Mexico's Bill Richardson—and three Latinos serve in the U.S. Senate. Traditionally, local offices serve as the steppingstones for election to more senior positions, so

TABLE 11-6 Latino Elected Officials 1973–2003, Selected Years

Year	Six States	Nationally
1973	1,280	—
1984	2,793	3,128
1996	3,447	3,622
2003	4,130	4,623
Change		
1973–2003	+228.0%	—
1984–2003	+47.9%	+47.8%

NOTES: The first effort to collect data on Latino officeholders, conducted in 1973, focused only on six states—Arizona, California, Florida, New Mexico, New York, and Texas. The first national list was compiled in 1984. These data exclude officials elected to local school councils in Chicago who are elected by parents in local school jurisdictions and not by all registered voters.
SOURCES: Author's compilations based on Lemus (1973); National Association of Latino Elected and Appointed Officials Educational Fund Roster of Hispanic Elected Officials various years.

in some sense the growth in the pool of Latino officeholders bodes well for the future.

Several recent elections, however, have cast some doubt on the likelihood of the quick rise of a new pool of Latinos in national and statewide office. Over the past few years, serious Latino candidates have lost races for governor in California and Texas and for the mayoralties of Los Angeles, Houston, and New York. After an initial defeat in 2001, Antonio Villaraigosa was elected mayor of Los Angeles in 2005. All Latinos in the U.S. Congress represent districts at least 40 percent Latino, as do most Latinos in state legislatures. Only one Latino in Congress gained office by beating an Anglo incumbent. There are a few more such seats that are not represented by Latinos, but future gains in officeholding will have to come from victories in districts with lower densities of Hispanics. Should legal challenges to the majority-minority districting provisions of the VRA succeed, such as the Supreme Court's ruling in *Shaw v. Reno*, steady growth in the number of Latino elected officials could end and underrepresentation will increase.

When asked, Latinos indicate that they want to be represented by the best person, not necessarily the best Latino candidate. While I have been dubious of these responses in the past (they appear on multiple surveys), I am increasingly convinced. In several recent elections, and most notably in California's recall replacement election, a large share of Latino voters did not vote for the leading Latino candidate. In the California case, the Latino candidate—Lieutenant Governor Bustamante—ran a poor campaign that did little to reach out to Latino voters. He paid a price for this neglect (DeSipio and Masuoka, 2006). In other recent cases, Latinos in Democratic areas have rejected Latino Republican candidates in favor of white Latino Democrats (Michelson and Leon, 2001).

The consequences of Latino representation for Latino community empowerment have been less well studied than the individual dimensions of Latino participation and policy preferences (de la Garza, 2004). Studies of this question are considerably more difficult because they require analysis of the political cultures and local political coalitions of individual jurisdictions, but they will take on increasing importance in coming years. The VRA has ensured that the number of Latino officeholders and the share of the Latino population represented by Latino officeholders have steadily increased. As the VRA itself is challenged and new gains have to come at the expense of black populations in some areas, coalitional politics will take on added importance for Latino empowerment.

Naturalization

Future growth in Latino electoral participation will depend on spurring naturalization trends. A recent estimate indicates that 4.2 million Latino legal permanent residents are eligible for naturalization (as are 3.5 million non-Latino legal permanent residents) (NALEO Educational Fund, 2004). Available survey evidence indicates that the vast majority of Latinos eligible for U.S. citizenship want, someday, to become citizens. Approximately 85 percent of Latino immigrants intend to become U.S. citizens, two thirds of citizenship-eligible Latino immigrants have done something concrete to naturalize, and slightly more than 40 percent have naturalized (DeSipio, 1996a). While achieving this goal will require considerable effort on the part of ethnic and national leaders, alone it will not be sufficient to ensure higher Latino electoral participation.

The number of Latinos naturalizing is growing (see Table 11-7). In the early 1990s, the average number of Latinos naturalizing each year rose from 36,000 to 90,000. By 1996, the number had grown to as many as 422,000 and now averages in the high 100,000s. Although Mexican immigrants make up the majority of these new U.S. citizens (as they do of Latino legal immigrants to the United States), the numbers of Dominican, Salvadoran, and Colombian naturalized immigrants have also grown rapidly.

TABLE 11-7 Naturalization Trends by Country of Origin, 1991–2002

Year	All Countries (000s)	Spanish-Speaking Latin American/ Caribbean (000s)	Latin America/ Caribbean Share of Total (%)	Mexico	Cuba	Dominican Republic	El Salvador	Columbia
1991	308	50	16.2	23	10	6	4	6
1992	240	36	15.1	13	8	8	2	6
1993	315	61	19.4	24	15	12	3	10
1994	434	90	20.8	46	16	11	6	12
1995	488	138	28.2	82	18	10	14	13
1996	1,045	422	40.4	255	62	29	35	27
1997	598	215	36.0	143	13	21	18	12
1998	463	166	36.0	112	15	12	12	7
1999	840	307	36.6	208	25	23	23	13
2000	889	282	31.7	190	16	25	24	14
2001	608	159	26.2	103	11	15	14	11
2002	574	170	29.6	77	11	16	11	11

NOTE: Naturalization levels rounded to the nearest thousand.
SOURCE: U.S. Department of Homeland Security (2003, Table 35).

The surge of naturalization in the late 1990s—resulting from a combination of a national challenge to the status and rights of U.S. immigrants, Immigration and Naturalization Service policy changes, and active promotion of naturalization rights in immigrant communities—reduced the number of immigrants eligible to naturalize. The number of citizenship-eligible immigrant Latinos remains large, however, and is growing again.

The formal rules for naturalization as a U.S. citizen are modest relative to most other immigrant-receiving countries. Immigrants must have resided legally in the United States for five years (three if married to a U.S. citizen). They must also demonstrate the ability to speak, write, and read English and demonstrate knowledge of basic U.S. history and civics. They must submit an application to the Bureau of Citizenship and Immigration Services (formerly the naturalization branch of the Immigration and Naturalization Service) and pay a fee of $320, plus a separate $70 fee for fingerprinting. As part of the application, they must demonstrate that they are of "good moral character," generally interpreted to mean that applicants have not committed serious crimes in the United States; are not a public charge (that they have not received needs-based social welfare benefits for more than half of the previous five years); and are willing to take an oath to defend the Constitution that requires that they abjure loyalty to their former sovereign. Applications filed take approximately 15 months for review.

Of these requirements, the most innocuous—the application form—proves to be the most burdensome. Approximately twice as many Latinos eligible for naturalization request but do not complete the application as complete the naturalization process (Pachon and DeSipio, 1994). The current application is 10 pages and includes questions on hereditary titles to nobility and service in Nazi concentration camps.

This finding partially explains the gap between immigrants who naturalize and immigrants who do not. As with voting, naturalization is more likely to occur among older immigrants with higher incomes and more formal education. Longer residence in the United States and the higher share of life spent in the United States also increase the likelihood of naturalization (DeSipio, 1996a). Among Asian immigrants, there also appears to be a relationship between naturalization and the desire to immigrate relatives, but this relationship is less clear among immigrants from the Americas.

As was evident during the surge of naturalization in the late 1990s, increased community resources to support naturalization raise the likelihood that interested immigrants will complete the naturalization process. Community-based resources are not a constant. In the past, immigrant service agencies and political parties have promoted naturalization, but today those resources are rare (DeSipio, 1996a). Latino immigrants report that the most important reason for naturalizing is to achieve political voice and to vote, so this elite neglect has an impact on Latino political power.

One change in the structure of naturalization deserves note and may change the current dynamic. Many immigrant-sending countries, including many Latin American nations, are expanding opportunities for naturalized citizens to maintain the citizenship of their country of origin. While immigrants formally renounce their former citizenship at the time of naturalization, the United States does not prevent its newest citizens from reestablishing their former citizenship. To the extent that concerns about loss of nationality prevented some immigrants from pursuing U.S. citizenship, this new tolerance for and promotion of dual nationality may expand the pool of immigrants pursuing naturalization.

THE LATINO POLITICAL FUTURE

The discussion so far establishes that the Latino political agenda, to the extent that it exists, is driven by a set of issues that bridge Latino national-origin groups and immigrant generations. While these issues are neither outside the American mainstream nor particularly controversial (contrary to what Huntington [2004] might fear), they do have the potential to shift debates in American politics by matters of degree. A Latino-influenced American political order would focus to a much greater degree on public education, social services, and health issues. It would not seek continued reductions in the size and scope of government, as has been the focus of national politics for the last 25 years, and would instead seek to enhance government capacity in domestic politics.

The extent to which Latinos have been able to organize around this shared political agenda is somewhat limited by institutional and demographic barriers that are not unique to the Latino community, but have a disproportionate impact because of the composition of the population and its geographic locations. For these reasons, the Latino politics of the period since the VRA has rarely lived up to the hype that surrounds it. Outcomes that disappoint naïve observers—such as the mayoral losses in Los Angeles, New York, and Houston in 2001 and the gubernatorial losses in Texas and California in 2002 and 2003—far exceed the unexpected victories—such as Loretta Sánchez's congressional victory over Republican Robert Dornan in California in 1996.

Politics, however, is not simply a numbers game (though, ultimately, votes must be counted). Well-placed individuals and the serendipity of calculations of winning coalitions can propel individuals to unexpected levels of prominence and with them the electoral group they are perceived to represent. Many unmet expectations of the Latino politics since the passage of the VRA would be diminished in the popular mind if, for example, Henry Cisneros had been selected as Walter Mondale's running mate in 1984 and that ticket had won, or if New Mexico Governor Bill Richardson had been selected as John Kerry's running mate and that ticket had won in 2004. The latter scenario has been enhanced by the win in the Florida U.S. Senate race by former Secretary of Housing and Urban Development Mel Martinez, the win in the Colorado U.S. Senate race by Attorney General Ken Salazar, and the appointment of Representative Robert Menendez to the U.S. Senate from New Jersey. Clearly, a handful of victories, no matter how important, would not change the bigger picture of unmet expectations and lower than average levels of electoral participation and other forms of civic engagement, but they would move Latino politics to a new level of national prominence and, arguably, policy influence.

Ultimately, though, for Latinos to effectively use politics to routinely achieve their public policy needs, democratic institutions must be more responsive to their demands. To show possible directions for the future, I propose three models (these are adapted from the discussion of 20th-century new electorates in DeSipio [1996a]). The most optimistic assumes some national trigger that moves into the electorate many in the large pool of Latino adults who either do not vote or are ineligible to vote due to noncitizenship. Conceivably, such a trigger could dramatically increase the Latino electorate over a few elections and strengthen their political influence. The converse of this has the Latino electorate following the pattern of non-Latino electorates, with even less successful recruitment of new voters and the ongoing reinforcement of the passivity that results from the legacy of past exclusion. Under this scenario, Latino votes decline between some elections and the strong partisanship that Latinos display declines to such a degree that parties and candidates reduce their already limited mobilization efforts. Finally, the most likely scenario is that Latinos will continue to see incremental growth over successive election cycles based on the gradual growth of the Latino electorate. Over time, however, even slow incremental growth increases the chances that Latinos will be the critical deciding factor in electoral outcomes.

The American electorate has seen the rapid mobilization of previously small electorates. Most recently, blacks moved from an infinitesimal share of the national electorate to between 5 and 10 percent as soon as the VRA was passed. Much community organization preceded black political mobilization, but a scenario can be envisioned in which Latino nonvoters (who numbered 20 million in 2004) feel a comparable urgency to become participants and act on their growing numbers. When California voters had to decide on Proposition 187, which excluded illegal immigrants from social services, health care, and public education, Latino registration and voting surged. This surge also included a surge in naturalization. While this momentum was localized and dissipated somewhat, particularly when the Immigration and Naturalization Service slowed the pace of naturalization reviews, a comparable trigger on the national level could boost Latino electoral participation dramatically. Presumably, the pool of nonvoters required for this scenario to be effective are noncitizens, so naturalization would have to precede political participation. Naturalization backlogs—eventually involving waits of years—might well dampen whatever urgency fueled the potential surge.

A second possible trajectory for Latino politics is that it will become indistinguishable from majority politics. European ethnics—who were critical to the Roosevelt coalition but now are defined not by their ethnicity but by class, state, and, perhaps, children's sporting practices—illustrate this scenario. Women joined the electorate with much fanfare in the 1920s, as did 18- to 20-year-olds in 1972, but they quickly disappeared as potentially cohesive electorates. A decline or disappearance of a salient Latino politics could result from repeated defeats in high-profile races building on the passivity that results from the legacies of past exclusion. In a sense, in this scenario, the energy would be taken out of the Latino political movement. The continual inflow of newly naturalized Latino citizens as well as second-generation Latinos coming of political age, however, renders this scenario unlikely for the foreseeable future.

What is left, then, is a continuation and perhaps acceleration of the Latino politics that has emerged since the extension of the VRA in 1975: incremental growth in the electorate accompanied by an increase in the mass recognition of a shared Latino policy agenda (encouraged by continued elite efforts to form a Latino political community).

Incrementalism in this scenario does not imply political unimportance. Assuming naturalizations at the rates of the early 2000s and the political maturity of the second generation when it moves into its late 30s and 40s, current growth levels would ensure that the Latino share of the national vote would increase from the 6.0 percent of 2004 to 7.4 percent in 2012 and 9.5 in 2024 (see Table 11-8). The Latino vote in some of the larger states would be even more sizeable: 21.7 percent of California's vote in 2012 compared with 16.2 percent in 2004; 18.2 percent of Florida's 2012 vote compared with 11.2 percent in 2004; 8.2 percent of New York's 2012 vote compared with 8.0 percent in 2004; and 21.7 percent of Texas's 2012 vote compared with 19.3 percent in 2004.

Do these numbers necessarily mean that Latinos will be more influential (or that Latinos will be more involved in other forms of politics)? Not necessarily, but even with gradually increasing numbers, the odds of serendipitous opportunities, such as a Richardson selection or a few more Senate victories, grow. More importantly, larger numbers increase the incentive for non-Latinos to vote with Latinos in close elections. As the nation—and

TABLE 11-8 Estimates of Future Latino Votes, 2012 and 2024, National and Selected States

				Latino Share of Statewide Vote			
Year	Latino Vote (,000)	Total Vote (,000)	Latino (%)	California (%)	Florida (%)	New York (%)	Texas (%)
1976	2,098	86,698	2.4				
1980	2,453	93,066	2.6				
1984	3,092	101,878	3.0				
1988	3,710	102,224	3.6	7.9	7.0	5.7	13.8
1992	4,238	113,866	3.7	9.6	7.1	5.0	13.6
1996	4,928	105,017	4.7	11.7	9.2	7.5	17.1
2000	5,934	110,826	5.3	13.9	11.2	7.2	18.6
2004	7,587	125,736	6.0	16.2	11.2	8.0	19.3
2012 (estimated)	8,791	118,583	7.4	21.7	18.2	8.2	21.7
2024 (estimated)	12,023	126,883	9.5				

NOTE: Estimates for 2012 and 2024 assume continued incremental increase in Latino voting and a slower (and somewhat more erratic) increase in the total vote. The state-level Current Population Survey estimates have too much sampling error to develop reliable estimates for Latino and total votes or for 2024.
SOURCE: Author's estimates based on U.S. Census Bureau, Voting and Election in the November Elections, various years.

particularly its largest states—becomes increasingly multiethnic, coalition politics will become more the norm. This middle trajectory of incremental growth relies on the continuing reality of a shared Latino issue agenda and ethnic leaders who seek to organize across national origin and generation lines. Ultimately, then, the Latino politics of the near future rests on the questions that underpin my analysis. The tensions between the low levels of political affect across Latino populations and the reality of a marginally distinct issue agenda will remain. As more elected national Hispanic leaders emerge, however, Latinos will have a clearer image of what Latino politics is and leaders who can shape that agenda in the public eye. That should speed the process of building a Latino politics that has unfolded over the past 30 years.

REFERENCES

Alvarez, R.M., and Ansolabehere, S. (2002). *California votes: The promise of election day registration.* New York: Demos. Available: http://www.demos-usa.org/demos/Pubs/california_votes.pdf, [accessed August 21, 2003].

Arellano, A. (2000). The people's movement: Las gorras blancas. In E. Gonzalez-Berry and D.R. Maciel (Eds.), *The contested homeland: A Chicano history of New Mexico* (pp. 59–82). Albuquerque: University of New Mexico Press.

Barreto, M.A., Segura, G.M., and Woods, N.D. (2002, April). *Rest assured? Estimating the potential mobilizing or demobilizing effects of overlapping majority-minority districts.* Paper prepared for presentation the annual meetings of the Midwest Political Science Association, Chicago.

Bass, L.E., and Casper, L.M. (2001). Differences in registering and voting between native-born and naturalized Americans. *Population Research and Policy Review*, *20*, 483–511.

Cámara Fuertes, L.R. (2004). *The phenomenon of Puerto Rican voting.* Gainesville: University Press of Florida.

Calvo, M.A., and Rosenstone, S.J. (1989). *Hispanic political participation.* San Antonio, TX: Southwest Voter Research Institute.

de la Garza, R.O. (2004). Latino politics. *Annual Review of Political Science*, *7*, 91–123.

de la Garza, R.O., and DeSipio, L. (1993). Save the baby, change the bathwater, and scrub the tub: Latino electoral participation after seventeen years of Voting Rights Act coverage. *Texas Law Review*, *71*(7), 1479–1539.

de la Garza, R.O., and DeSipio, L. (2005). *Muted voices: Latino politics in the 2000 elections.* Lanham, MD: Rowman and Littlefield.

de la Garza, R.O., and Lu, F. (1998). Explorations into Latino voluntarism. In D. Campoamor, W.A. Díaz, and H.A.J. Ramos (Eds.), *Nuevos senderos: Reflections on Hispanics and philanthropy* (pp. 55–78). Houston, TX: Arte Público Press.

de la Garza, R.O., Menchaca, M., and DeSipio, L. (Eds.). (1994). *Barrio ballots: Latino politics in the 1990 election.* Boulder, CO: Westview Press.

de la Garza, R.O., DeSipio, L., García, F.C., García, J.A., and Falcón, A. (1992). *Latino voices: Mexican, Puerto Rican, and Cuban perspectives on American politics.* Boulder, CO: Westview Press.

DeSipio, L. (1996a). *Counting on the Latino vote: Latinos as a new electorate.* Charlottesville: University Press of Virginia.

DeSipio, L. (1996b). Making citizens or good citizens? Naturalization as a predictor of organizational and electoral behavior among Latino immigrants. *Hispanic Journal of Behavioral Sciences*, *18*(2), 194–213.

DeSipio, L. (2003a). *Transnational politics and U.S. citizenship: Do home country political ties limit Latino immigrant pursuit of U.S. civic engagement and citizenship?* Paper presented at conference, A Nation of Immigrants: Ethnic Identity and Political Incorporation, Berkeley, CA, May 2–3.

DeSipio, L. (2003b). *The second generation: Political behaviors of adult children of immigrants in the United States.* Paper presented at the Summer Institute on International Migration, University of California, San Diego, June.

DeSipio, L. (Forthcoming). Power in the pews? Religious diversity and Latino political attitudes and behaviors. In J.M. Wilson (Ed.), *Faith and politics in the American religious mosaic: Trends and prospects for a new millennium.* Manuscript, Southern Methodist University.

DeSipio, L., and de la Garza, R.O. (1999). Beyond civil rights? Immigration and the shifting foundation of Latino politics. Paper presented at *Geographies of Latinidad: Mapping Latina/o studies for the twenty-first century*, University of Illinois at Urbana-Champaign.

DeSipio, L., and Masuoka, N. (2006. Opportunities lost? Latinos, Cruz Bustamante, and California's recall. In S. Bowler and B. Cain (Eds.), *Clicker politics: Essays on the California recall* (pp. 112-127). Upper Saddle River, NJ: Pearson.

DeSipio, L., Pachon, H., de la Garza, R.O., and Lee, J. (2003). *Immigrant politics at home and abroad: How Latino immigrants engage the politics of their home communities in the United States.* Claremont, CA: Tomás Rivera Policy Institute.

DeSipio, L., Pachon, H., Gold, R., and Vargas, A. (1998). *America's newest voices: Colombians, Dominicans, Guatemalans, and Salvadorans in the United States examine their public policy needs.* Los Angeles and Claremont, CA: National Association of Latino Elected and Appointed Officials Educational Fund and the Tomás Rivera Policy Institute.

Farkas, S., Duffett, A., Immerwahr, S., Johnson, J., McHugh, J., de la Garza, R.O., Baraona, M., Orozco, M., Pachon, H., and Pantoja, A. (1998). *Here to stay: The domestic and international priorities of Latino leaders.* New York and Claremont, CA: Public Agenda and the Tomás Rivera Policy Institute.

González, J. (2000). *Harvest of empire: A history of Latinos in America.* New York: Viking.

Green, D.P., and Gerber, A.S. (2004). *Get out the vote! How to increase voter turnout.* Washington, DC: Brookings Institution Press.

Gutiérrez, D.G. (1995). *Walls and mirrors: Mexican Americans, Mexican immigrants, and the politics of ethnicity.* Berkeley: University of California Press.

Henry J. Kaiser Family Foundation. (2000). *National survey of Latinos in America.* The Washington Post/Kaiser Family Foundation/Harvard University Survey Project. Menlo Park, CA: Henry J. Kaiser Family Foundation.

Huntington, S. (2004). *Who are we? Challenges to America's national identity.* New York: Simon and Schuster.

Jennings, J., and Rivera, M. (Eds.). (1984). *Puerto Rican politics in urban America.* Westport, CT: Greenwood Press.

Jones-Correa, M. (1998). *Between two nations: The political predicament of Latinos in New York City.* Ithaca, NY: Cornell University Press.

Leighley, J.E. (2001). *Strength in numbers? The political mobilization of racial and ethnic minorities.* Princeton, NJ: Princeton University Press.

Lemus, F. (1973). *National roster of Spanish surnamed officials.* Los Angeles: Aztlán Publications.

Levitt, M., and Olson, D. (1996). *Immigration and political incorporation: But do they vote?* Paper prepared for presentation at the 1996 Northeastern Political Science Association Meeting, Boston, November.

Márquez, B. (2003). *Constructing identities in Mexican American political organizations: Choosing issues, taking sides.* Austin: University of Texas Press.

Michelson, M., and Leon, E. (2001). *Does ethnicity trump party? Latino voting behavior in California's 20th District.* Paper prepared for presentation at the Western Political Science Association Meetings, Las Vegas, March.

Minnite, L.C., Holdaway, J., and Hayduk, R. (1999, September). *Political incorporation of immigrants in New York.* Paper prepared for the 1999 annual meeting of the American Political Science Association, Atlanta, GA.

Mollenkopf, J., Olson, D., and Ross, T. (2001). Immigrant political participation in New York and Los Angeles. In M. Jones-Correa (Ed.), *Governing American cities: Interethnic coalitions, competition, and conflict* (pp. 17–70). New York: Russell Sage Foundation Press.

Montejano, D. (1987). *Anglos and Mexicans in the making of Texas, 1836–1986.* Austin: University of Texas Press.

National Association of Latino Elected and Appointed Officials Educational Fund. (Various Years, 1984–2003). *National directory of Latino elected officials* and *National roster of Hispanic elected officials.* Los Angeles: Author.

National Association of Latino Elected and Appointed Officials Educational Fund. (2004, April 30). *Four million Latino legal permanent residents eligible for U.S. citizenship as exorbitant fee hike takes effect.* Press Release. Los Angeles: Author.

Oboler, S. (1995). *Ethnic labels, Latino lives: Identity and the politics of (re)presentation in the United States.* Minneapolis: University of Minnesota Press.

O'Connor, K., and Epstein, L. (1988). A legal voice for the Chicano community: The activities of the Mexican-American Legal Defense and Education Fund, 1968–1982. In F.C. García (Ed.), *Latinos and the political system* (pp. 255–268). South Bend, IN: University of Notre Dame Press.

Pachon, H., and DeSipio, L. (1994). *New citizens by choice: Political perspectives of Latino immigrants.* Boulder, CO: Westview Press.

Pantoja, A., Ramírez, R., and Segura, G.M. (2001). Citizens by choice, voters by necessity: Patterns in political mobilization by naturalized Latinos. *Political Research Quarterly, 54*(4), 729–750.

Pycior, J.L. (1997). *LBJ and Mexican Americans: The paradox of power.* Austin: University of Texas Press.

Sánchez Korrol, V.E. (1994). *From colonia to community: The history of Puerto Ricans in New York City.* Berkeley: University of California Press.

San Jose Mercury News. (2000). *Special report: A Mercury News poll of Latinos.* Available: http://www.mercurycenter.com/local/center/polldata.htm [accessed June 18, 2005].

San Miguel, G., Jr. (1987). *"Let all of them take heed": Mexican Americans and the campaign for educational equality in Texas, 1910–1981.* Austin: University of Texas Press.

Segura, G., and Woods, N. (2002). Targets of opportunity: California's blanket primary and the political representation of Latinos. In B.E. Cain and E.R. Gerber (Eds.), *Voting at the political fault line: California's experiment with the blanket primary* (pp. 248–269). Berkeley: University of California Press.

Shaw, D., de la Garza, R.O., and Lee, J. (2000). Examining Latino turnout in 1996: A three states, validated survey approach. *American Journal of Political Science, 44*(2), 338–346.

Suro, R. (2002). *2002 National survey of Latinos.* Menlo Park, CA and Washington, DC: Kaiser Family Foundation and Pew Hispanic Center.

Tomás Rivera Policy Institute. (2000). *TRPI pre-election survey of Latino registered voters, October 2000.* Unpublished data. Claremont, CA: Tomás Rivera Policy Institute.

U.S. Census Bureau. (2002). *Voting and registration in the election of November 2000.* Detailed Tables. Series P-20 #542. Washington, DC: Author. Available: http://www.census.gov/population/www/socdemo/voting/p20-542.html [accessed February 15, 2003].

U.S. Census Bureau. (2005). *Voting and registration in the election of November 2004. Detailed tables.* Available: http://www.census.gov/population/www/socdemo/voting/cps2004.html [accessed July 2005].

U.S. Department of Homeland Security, Office of Immigration Statistics. (2003). *2002 yearbook of immigration statistics.* Washington, DC: Author.

Verba, S., Schlozman, K.L., and Brady, H.E. (1995). *Voice and equality: Civic voluntarism in American politics.* Cambridge, MA: Harvard University Press.

Wattenberg, M.P. (2002). *Where have all the voters gone?* Cambridge, MA: Harvard University Press.

Wolfinger, R.E., and Rosenstone, S. (1980). *Who votes?* New Haven, CT: Yale University Press.

A

Contents

Multiple Origins, Uncertain Destinies: Hispanics and the American Future

REFERENCES

APPENDIXES

A Methods
B Biographical Sketches of Panel Members and Staff
C Contents: *Hispanics and the Future of America*

INDEX

B
Biographical Sketches of Contributors

CRISTINA BRADATAN is assistant professor of sociology at the University of Central Florida. She serves as a book review editor for the Balkan Academic News network. Her publications focus on family and fertility, immigration, population policies, cuisine, and cultural identity in European countries. She has a Ph.D. in sociology and demography from the Pennsylvania State University and an M.S. in statistics from the University of Bucharest.

LOUIS DeSIPIO is an associate professor in the Department of Political Science and the Chicano/Latino Studies Program at the University of California, Irvine (UCI). His research focuses on Latino politics, the process of political incorporation of new and formerly excluded populations into U.S. politics, and public policies such as immigration, immigrant settlement, naturalization, and voting rights. He is the author of *Counting on the Latino Vote: Latinos as a New Electorate* (1996) and the coauthor of *Making Americans/Remaking America: Immigration and Immigrant Policy* (1998). He is also the author and editor of a seven-volume series on Latino political values, attitudes, and behaviors. He served as interim director of the University of Illinois at Urbana-Champaign Latina/Latino Studies Program from 1999 to 2002 and the acting director of the UCI Chicano/Latino Studies Program in 2004. He serves as graduate director in the UCI Department of Political Science and undergraduate advisor in the Chicano/Latino Studies Program.

BRIAN DUNCAN is assistant professor of economics at the University of Colorado at Denver. He also taught economics at the University of California at Santa Barbara. His research focuses on public finance, labor, and econometrics. He has served as a referee for the *Journal of Public Health* and *Economic Inquiry* and in 2001 was awarded the Lancaster prize in social sciences. He has authored numerous published articles, including *Modeling Charitable Contributions of Time and Money* (1999) and *Pumpkin Pies and Public Goods: The Raffle Fundraising Strategy* (2002). He has a Ph.D. in economics from the University of California, Santa Barbara.

JORGE DURAND is professor of anthropology at the University of Guadalajara, México, and codirector of the Mexican Migration Project and the Latin American Migration Project sponsored by Princeton University and the University of Guadalajara. He is a member of the Mexican Academy of Sciences and a foreign associate of the National Academy of Sciences. He has studied and written about Mexican migration to the United States for the past 20 years. His publications in this field include *Return to Aztlán* (1987), *Más allá de la línea* (1984), *Miracles on the Border* (1995), *Migrations Mexicaines aux Etats-Unis* (1995), *La experiencia migrante* (2000), *Beyond Smoke and Mirrors* (2002), and *Clandestinos: Migración mexicana en los albores del siglo XXI* (2003).

JOSÉ J. ESCARCE is professor of medicine at the David Geffen School of Medicine at the University of California, Los Angeles and senior natural scientist at the RAND Corporation. His research interests include racial and ethnic disparities in health and health care, immigrant health, provider and patient behavior under economic incentives, technological change in medicine, and the impact of health care market structure on costs and quality. He has served on the National Advisory Council for Health Care Policy, Research, and Evaluation of the U.S. Department of Health and Human Services; was a member of the Institute of Medicine's Committee on Understanding and Eliminating Racial and Ethnic Disparities in Health Care; and is senior associate editor of the journal *Health Services Research*. He serves on the board of education of the public school district in Santa Monica, California, a small urban district where one-third of the students are Hispanic. He is a graduate of Princeton University and has an M.S. in physics from Harvard University and M.D. and Ph.D. degrees, the latter in health economics, from the University of Pennsylvania.

MARY J. FISCHER is assistant professor of sociology at the University of Connecticut. Previously she served as the project manager for the National Longitudinal Survey of Freshmen at Princeton University and the University of Pennsylvania. She is a coauthor of *The Source of the River* (2004) and the author or coauthor of numerous articles appearing in *City and Community*, the *Dubois Review*, *Ethnic and Racial Studies*, *EurAmerica*, the *International Migration Review*, *Social Problems*, *Social Science Research*, *Sociological Perspectives*, and the *Urban Affairs Review*. She has a Ph.D. in sociology and demography from the University of Pennsylvania.

JENNIFER FLASHMAN is a doctoral student in sociology at the University of California, Los Angeles. Her research interests include social demography, social stratification, education, and quantitative methods. She recently completed a master's paper entitled "Delayed Selection: Changes in the Process of College Choice for Men and Women." She is currently extending that work and preparing it for publication.

V. JOSEPH HOTZ is professor of economics at the University of California, Los Angeles (UCLA), and research associate at the California Center for Population Research and the National Bureau of Economic Research. He also serves as chair of the oversight board of the California Census Research Data Center and received a fellow award from the Econometric Society. Previously he was chair of the Department of Economics at UCLA and a member of the social science and population peer review panel of the National Institutes of Health. His research interests include labor economics, economic demography, and applied economics. He is currently co-principal investigator on numerous projects, including ones on tax policy and low-wage labor markets and designing new models for explaining family change and variation. He has written and published many articles on such topics as family change, teenage childbearing, and income tax. He has M.S. and Ph.D. degrees in economics from the University of Wisconsin–Madison.

KANIKA KAPUR is a lecturer in the School of Economics at University College in Dublin. She is also an adjunct economist at the RAND Corporation. Her research has dealt with health insurance, health utilization, and socioeconomic and racial differences in health care. She has published in *Health Services Research*, *Health Affairs*, and the *Industrial and Labor Relations Review*. She has a B.A. from Dartmouth College and a Ph.D. in economics from Northwestern University.

NANCY S. LANDALE is professor of sociology and demography at the Pennsylvania State University. Her research focuses on family patterns and health outcomes of racial and ethnic minorities in the United States, especially Hispanic populations. She has written extensively about the roles of migration and assimilation in the family patterns and infant health outcomes of Puerto Ricans. She was the principal investigator for the Puerto

Rican Maternal and Infant Health Study, a study of infant health among mainland and island Puerto Ricans. Articles from the study have focused on the role of selective migration in infant mortality; the role of assimilation in health behaviors and stress; the financial and nonfinancial contributions of nonresident, cohabiting, and married fathers; and the influence of skin color on low birthweight. She was a member of the National Research Council's Committee on the Health and Adjustment of Immigrant Families and Children.

SYLVIA MARTINEZ is a Ph.D. candidate at the University of Chicago. She is a research assistant for the Alfred P. Sloan Center on Parents, Children, and Work. Her research interests include education, working families, and Latino/Latina studies. Her paper titled "Women's Intrinsic and Extrinsic Motivations for Working" was published in the volume *Being Together Working Apart: Dual-Career Families and the Work-Life Balance*.

FAITH MITCHELL is a senior program officer at the National Academies, where she has been on the staff since 1995. Her professional experience includes ethnographic field research, academic appointments, philanthropy, and government service. She is coeditor of several National Research Council reports, including *Terrorism: Perspectives from the Behavioral and Social Sciences*; *Discouraging Terrorism: Some Implications of 9/11*; *America Becoming: Racial Trends and Their Consequences*; *Governance and Opportunity in Metropolitan America*; and *Premature Death in the New Independent States*. Her doctorate is in medical anthropology.

LEO S. MORALES is associate professor of medicine and public health at the University of California, Los Angeles, and a health policy analyst at the RAND Corporation. His areas of research include Latino and immigrant health, health care disparities, patient satisfaction with health care, and cross-cultural survey research methods. He is currently principal investigator for an evaluation study of a multiple-site intervention to improve interpreter services for Spanish-speaking Latino patients and director of the measurement cores for two health disparities centers at UCLA: the Project Export Center on Disparities and the UCLA Center for Health Improvement for Minority Elders. He is a board-certified general internist at UCLA Medical Center, where he sees patients and supervises medical residents.

R. SALVADOR OROPESA is professor of sociology and demography at the Pennsylvania State University and research associate at the Population Research Institute. He currently serves as associate editor of the *Journal of Family Issues* and previously served on the editorial board of the *American*

Sociological Review. His research interests include families, immigration, health, and Latin America and the Caribbean. His most recent published work covers such topics as income distribution, infant health, marriage, and poverty. He has a Ph.D. from the University of Washington.

ANN OWENS is a graduate student in the sociology and social policy program at Harvard University. Previously she served as the project director at the Sloan Center on Parents, Children, and Work at the University of Chicago, contributing to many projects, including an advanced placement sociology course pilot program, a random educational intervention designed to encourage minority students' participation in the health industry, a national conference focused on the work–family balance of dual-career families, and the production of two edited volumes, one on working families and one on the sociology of education. She has written on such topics as the educational consequences of adolescents' experiences of stereotyping in the classroom, how working families spend time at home, how family structure affects child outcomes, and the transition from adolescence to adulthood. She has a B.A. in sociology with honors from the University of Chicago.

CORDELIA REIMERS is professor emerita of economics at Hunter College and the Graduate School of the City University of New York (CUNY), where she taught from 1982 to 2003. In recent years she has also been a senior economist at the Council of Economic Advisers in Washington and a visiting scholar at the Russell Sage Foundation. Prior to joining the faculty of CUNY, she was an assistant professor of economics and public affairs at Princeton University. Her research has focused on racial and ethnic differences in labor market outcomes and on Social Security and retirement behavior. Recent papers concern the effects of welfare reform on low-skilled New Yorkers and the effects of 9/11 on low-skilled minority and immigrant workers in New York City. She has a B.S. in history from the University of Wisconsin–Madison and a Ph.D. in economics from Columbia University.

RUBÉN G. RUMBAUT is professor of sociology at the University of California, Irvine, and co-director of its Center for Research on Immigration, Population and Public Policy. He is the founding chair of the section on international migration of the American Sociological Association and a member of the National Research Council's Committee on Population. He codirects the Children of Immigrants Longitudinal Study, begun in 1991, as well as a new large-scale study of Immigration and Intergenerational Mobility in Metropolitan Los Angeles. He coauthored *Immigrant America: A*

Portrait; *Origins and Destinies: Immigration, Race and Ethnicity in America*; *California's Immigrant Children: Theory, Research, and Implications for Educational Policy*; *Immigration Research for a New Century: Multidisciplinary Perspectives*; and *On the Frontier of Adulthood: Theory, Research, and Public Policy*. The book he coauthored with Alejandro Portes, *Legacies: The Story of the Immigrant Second Generation*, won the distinguished scholarship award of the American Sociological Association and the W.I. Thomas and Florian Znaniecki award for best book in the immigration field. A native of Havana, Cuba, he has a Ph.D. in sociology from Brandeis University.

BARBARA SCHNEIDER is professor of sociology and human development at the University of Chicago and will join the faculty at Michigan State University as the John A. Hannah chair in the School of Education in fall 2005. She currently directs the Data Research and Development Center, and codirects the Alfred P. Sloan Center on Parents, Children, and Work. Interested in the lives of adolescents and their families and schools, she has written widely on these topics. She is the coauthor of *The Ambitious Generation: America's Teenagers, Motivated But Directionless*; *Becoming Adult: How Teenagers Prepare for the World of Work*; and *Trust in Schools, A Core Resource for Improvement*. She and Linda Waite have recently completed a book based on findings from the Sloan 500 Family Study exploring the lives of working families. She is currently conducting a new random assignment project, TEACH Research, designed to improve adolescents' transition to college. She serves on a number of advisory boards including the American Educational Research Association grants board. Recently, she was selected by the American Sociological Association as the new editor of *Sociology of Education*.

EDWARD TELLES is professor of sociology at the University of California, Los Angeles. He has published widely in the area of immigration, race and ethnic relations, social demography, and urban sociology. In 2004–2005, as a visiting scholar at the Russell Sage Foundation, he wrote a large part of a book on intergenerational change among Mexican Americans, based on random sample surveys of Los Angeles and San Antonio in 1965 and 2000. He was program officer in human rights for the Ford Foundation in Rio de Janeiro from 1997 to 2000. He has received awards from the National Institute of Child and Human Development, the National Science Foundation, and the Fulbright Commission. He will be the 2006 recipient of the distinguished scholarly publication award from the American Sociological Association for his book *Race in Another America: The Significance of Skin Color in Brazil*. In 2005, he received the Otis Dudley Duncan award from the population section from the same association. He has a B.A. in anthropology from Stanford University and a Ph.D. in sociology from the University of Texas at Austin.

MARTA TIENDA is Maurice P. During '22 professor in demographic studies and professor of sociology and public affairs at Princeton University and former director of the Office of Population Research. She has held appointments at the University of Chicago, where she served as chair of sociology, and the University of Wisconsin. She is a fellow of the American Academy of Arts and Sciences, the American Academy of Political and Social Sciences, and the American Association for the Advancement of Science, as well as past president of the Population Association of America. She serves as board member of the Federal Reserve Bank of New York, the Princeton Medical Center, the Sloan Foundation, the Jacobs Foundation of Switzerland, and the Corporation of Brown University. Her coauthored and coedited publications include *The Hispanic Population of the United States* (1987), *Divided Opportunities* (1988), *The Color of Opportunity* (2001), *Youth in Cities* (2002), and *Ethnicity and Causal Mechanisms* (2005). She has a Ph.D. in sociology from the University of Texas at Austin.

STEPHEN TREJO is an associate professor of economics at the University of Texas at Austin. Previously he was a member of the economics faculty at the University of California, Santa Barbara. His research focuses on public policy issues involving labor markets, including overtime pay regulation, the experiences of immigrants, and obstacles to the economic progress of minority groups. He has a Ph.D. in economics from the University of Chicago.